Customized Media Access Required for This Course

PEARSON ALWAYS LEARNING

Fundamentals of Speech Communication

Taken from:

Public Speaking: Strategies for Success, Seventh Edition
by David Zarefsky

Human Communication: the Basic Course, Eleventh Edition
by Joseph A. DeVito

Human Communication: the Basic Course, Twelfth Edition
by Joseph A. DeVito

Persuasion, Social Influence, and Compliance Gaining, Fifth Edition
by Robert H. Gass and John S. Seiter

The Development of Language, Eighth Edition
by Jean Berko Gleason and Nan Bernstein Ratner

Interpersonal Communication: Relating to Others, Seventh Edition
by Steven A. Beebe, Susan J. Beebe, and Mark V. Redmond

News: The Politics of Illusion, Ninth Edition
by W. Lance Bennett

Argumentation and Critical Decision Making, Eighth Edition
by Richard D. Rieke, Malcolm O. Sillars, and Tarla Rai Peterson

Intercultural Competence: Interpersonal Communication Across Cultures, Seventh Edition
by Myron W. Lustig and Jolene Koester

Modern Rhetorical Criticism, Third Edition
by Roderick P. Hart and Suzanne Daughton

Cover Art: Courtesy of Stockbyte, Digital Vision, and EyeWire/Getty Images

Taken from:

Public Speaking: Strategies for Success, Seventh Edition
by David Zarefsky
Copyright © 2014, 2011, 2008, 2005 by Pearson Education, Inc.
Published by Allyn and Bacon
Boston, Massachusetts 02116

Human Communication: the Basic Course, Eleventh Edition
by Joseph A. DeVito
Copyright © 2009, 2006 by Pearson Education, Inc.
Published by Allyn and Bacon
Boston, Massachusetts 02116

Human Communication: the Basic Course, Twelfth Edition
by Joseph A. DeVito
Copyright © 2012, 2009, 2006 by Pearson Education, Inc.
Published by Allyn and Bacon

Persuasion, Social Influence, and Compliance Gaining, Fifth Edition
by Robert H. Gass and John S. Seiter
Copyright © 2014, 2011, 2008, 2005, 2002 by Pearson Education, Inc.
Published by Allyn and Bacon

The Development of Language, Eighth Edition
by Jean Berko Gleason and Nan Bernstein Ratner
Copyright © 2013, 2009, 2005, 2001, 1997 by Pearson Education, Inc.
Published by Allyn and Bacon

Interpersonal Communication: Relating to Others, Seventh Edition
by Steven A. Beebe, Susan J. Beebe, and Mark V. Redmond
Copyright © 2014, 2011, 2008, 2005 by Pearson Education, Inc.
Published by Allyn and Bacon

News: The Politics of Illusion, Ninth Edition
by W. Lance Bennett
Copyright © 2012, 2009, 2007 by Pearson Education, Inc.
Published by Longman
New York, New York 10010

Argumentation and Critical Decision Making, Eighth Edition
by Richard D. Rieke, Malcolm O. Sillars, and Tarla Rai Peterson
Copyright © 2013, 2009, 2006 by Pearson Education, Inc.
Published by Allyn and Bacon

Intercultural Competence: Interpersonal Communication Across Cultures, Seventh Edition
by Myron W. Lustig and Jolene Koester
Copyright © 2013, 2010, 2006 by Pearson Education, Inc.
Published by Allyn and Bacon

Modern Rhetorical Criticism, Third Edition
by Roderick P. Hart and Suzanne Daughton
Copyright © 2013, 2009, 2005, 2001, 1997 by Pearson Education, Inc.
Published by Allyn and Bacon

This special edition published in cooperation with Pearson Learning Solutions.

Pearson Learning Solutions, 501 Boylston Street, Suite 900, Boston, MA 02116
A Pearson Education Company
www.pearsoned.com

Printed in the United States of America

10 11 12 13 14 VOUD 19 18 17 16 15

000200010271800048

TS

ISBN 10: 1-269-45629-6
ISBN 13: 978-1-269-45629-6

Brief Contents

Contents

CHAPTER

1

Human Communication

Taken from *Human Communication: The Basic Course*, Eleventh Edition, by Joseph A. DeVito.

Of all the knowledge and skills you have, those concerning communication will prove the most useful. Your ability to communicate will always influence and play a crucial part in how effectively you live your personal and professional lives. It's vital to your success to learn how communication works and to master its most essential skills.

In this chapter you'll learn about:

- the benefits, forms, and purposes of human communication.
- the major elements in the human communication process.
- the essential principles that explain how communication works.

You'll learn to:

- communicate with a clear understanding of the essential elements and how they relate to one another.
- use the essential principles of human communication to increase your own effectiveness in interpersonal, small group, and public speaking.

Let's begin this chapter with a clear explanation of what you'll get out of this text and course and what forms of communication you'll study.

The Benefits, Forms, and Purposes of Human Communication

You'll benefit greatly from studying the forms of communication covered in this course. So let's begin our exploration with an introduction of these benefits. Next we'll preview the forms of human communication you'll cover and look at some of the purposes served when you communicate.

The Benefits of Human Communication

A perfectly legitimate question to ask before beginning your study of any subject is "why?" You may ask yourself, "Why should I learn about human communication? What will it do for me? What will I be able to do after taking this course that I wasn't able to do before? In short, how will I benefit from the study of human communication presented in this course and in this text?"

Actually, you'll benefit in lots of ways. Your knowledge of human communication and your mastery of many of its skills will enable you to better:

- **Present yourself as a confident, likable, approachable, and credible person.** Your effectiveness in just about any endeavor depends heavily on your *self-presentation*—your ability to present yourself in a positive light, through your verbal and nonverbal messages. Incidentally, it is also largely through your skills of self-presentation (or lack of them) that you display negative qualities as well.
- **Build friendships, enter into love relationships, work with colleagues, and interact with family members.** These are the *interpersonal and relationship skills* for initiating, maintaining, repairing, and sometimes dissolving relationships of all kinds. And unless you're going to be living totally alone, these are skills you'll use every day, in every encounter. These are the skills that businesses of all kinds have on their lists of most important competencies for organizational success; they are an essential part of business competence (Bassellier & Benbasat, 2004).
- **Interview to gain information, to successfully present yourself to get the job you want, and to participate effectively in a wide variety of other interview types.** *Interviewing skills* will help get you the job you want and ultimately the career you're preparing for in college.
- **Participate effectively in relationship and task groups—informative, problem-solving, and brainstorming groups, at home or at work.** These *group interaction and leadership skills* will help you both as a group member and as a leader. In a workplace world that operates largely on group interaction, these skills are increasingly essential if you are to be an effective organizational member and will help you rise in the organization. After all, people in power will often come to know you best through your group (that is, communication) performance.
- **Communicate information to and influence the attitudes and behaviors of small and large audiences.** These *presentation* or *public speaking skills* will enable you to manage your fear and make it work for you rather than against you. Effective public speaking is essential in leadership positions of all kinds; whether in politics, business, education, or medicine, leaders speak publicly.
- **Use the media critically and with awareness of the techniques media use to influence you.** *Media literacy skills* will make you a more

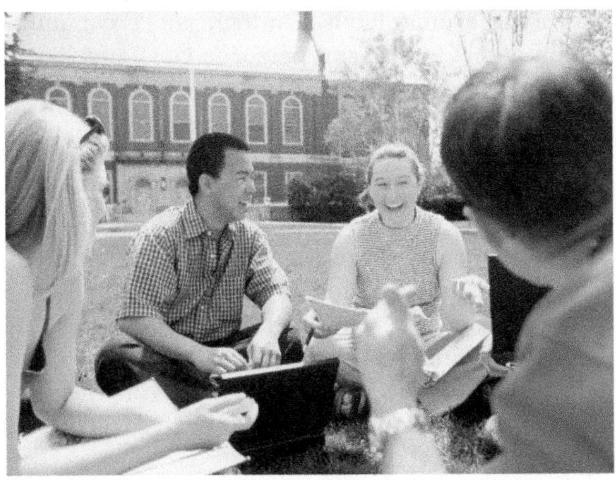

Communication Choice Points

Throughout this chapter you'll find marginal items, labeled What Do You Say? that identify a communication choice point, a point at which you need to make a decision and say something (or, of course, decide to remain silent). These What do you say? items are designed to encourage you to apply the skills discussed in the text to a wide variety of communication situations.

informed and empowered user of the many media that you encounter on a daily basis. Without such skills, you risk being used by the media for their ends alone. Much as a lack of media literacy will disempower you, competence in media literacy—the aim of the discussions of media literacy throughout this text—will empower you and put you in charge. The first of these Media Watch boxes appears on page 6 and explains in more detail what media literacy is.

You'll learn these skills and reap the benefits as you learn the various areas or forms of communication, to which we now turn.

The Forms of Human Communication

The forms of human communication vary from one-person communication (in which you talk to yourself) to communication with millions (as in public speaking, mass communication, and computer-mediated communication). Here we look briefly at each of these forms.

Intrapersonal Communication

Intrapersonal communication is communication you have with yourself. Through intrapersonal communication you talk with, learn about, and judge yourself. You persuade yourself of this or that, reason about possible decisions to make, and rehearse messages that you plan to send to others. In intrapersonal communication you might, for example, wonder how you did in an interview and what you could have done differently. You might conclude you did a pretty good job but that you need to be more assertive when discussing salary. Increasing your self-awareness, your mindfulness, and your ability to think critically about all types of messages will aid you greatly in improving your own intrapersonal communication. And this information—on the self, perception, listening, and verbal and nonverbal messages—will provide a foundation for learning about the various forms of human communication.

Interpersonal Communication

Interpersonal communication is communication between two persons or among a small group of persons. Most often, the communication emphasized in the study of interpersonal communication is communication of a continuing personal (rather than temporary and impersonal) nature; it's communication between or among intimates or those involved in close relationships—friends, romantic partners, family, and coworkers, for example. These relationships are interdependent, meaning that the actions of one person have some impact on the other person; whatever one person does influences the other person. Sometimes interpersonal communication is pleasant, but sometimes it erupts into conflict, making each person's communication especially significant for the other.

Interpersonal communication can take place face-to-face as well as through electronic channels (as in e-mail, instant messaging, or chat rooms, for example) or even via traditional letter-writing. Whether you e-mail your friends or family about your plans for the weekend, ask someone in class for a date, or confront a colleague's racist remarks at the water cooler, you're communicating interpersonally.

Interviewing

Interviewing is communication that proceeds by question and answer. Through interviewing you learn about others and what they know; you counsel or get counseling from others; or you get or don't get the job you want. Today much interviewing (especially initial interviews) takes place through e-mail and (video) phone conferencing.

Small Group Communication

Small group communication is communication among members of groups of about 5 to 10 people. Small group communication serves both *relationship* *needs* such as those for companionship, affection, or support and *task needs* such as balancing the family budget, electing a new chairperson, or designing a new ad campaign. Through small group communication you interact with others, solve problems, develop new ideas, and share knowledge and experiences. You live your work and social life largely in groups, from school orientation meetings to executive board meetings, from informal social groups to formal meetings discussing issues of local or international concern. You also may live a good part of your life in online chat rooms, where you may interact with people from different cultures living thousands of miles away, and in social network chat (for example, MyFace, MySpace, Facebook, Xanga) where you learn about and chat with others.

Organizational Communication

Organizational communication is communication that takes place within an organization among members of the organization. Conferencing with colleagues, working in teams, talking with a supervisor, or giving employees directions are just a few examples of organizational communication. The study of organizational communication offers you guidelines for improving your own formal and informal communication in an organizational setting.

Public Speaking

Public speaking, also termed *public communication* or *presentational speaking*, is communication between a speaker and an audience. Audiences range in size from several people to hundreds, thousands, and even millions. Through public communication others inform and persuade you. And you, in turn, inform and persuade others—to act, to buy, or to think in a particular way.

Much as you can address large audiences face-to-face, you also can address such audiences electronically and through the mass media. Through newsgroups, blogs, or social networks, for example, you can post a "speech" for anyone to read and then read their reactions to your message. And with the help of the more traditional mass media of radio and television, you can address audiences in the hundreds of millions as they sit alone or in small groups scattered throughout the world.

Computer-Mediated Communication

The term **computer-mediated communication** refers to communication between people that takes place through some computer connection. E-mail, chat room, newsgroup, instant messaging, website, and blog communication are all examples of computer-mediated communication, often abbreviated CMC. In large part, the principles of face-to-face and computer-mediated communication are similar; if you're effective in one mode, you're likely to be effective in others. The principles and skills we'll discuss will prove applicable to all forms of communication. Table 1.1 presents a summary of some of the ways in which computer-mediated communication differs from face-to-face communication.As you continue reading about these elements in this chapter, you may want to return to this table and add your own ideas to those presented here.

Table 1.1
Face-to-Face and Computer-Mediated Communication

Here is a brief summary of some communication concepts and some of the ways in which face-to-face and computer-mediated communication are similar and different.

Human Communication Element	Face-to-Face Communication	Computer-Mediated Communication
Sender [presentation of self, impression management, speaking turn]	• Visual appearance communicates who you are; personal characteristics (sex, approximate age, race, etc.) are overt and open to visual inspection; receiver controls the order of what is attended to; disguise is difficult. • You compete for the speaker's turn and time with the other person(s); you can be interrupted.	• You present the self you want others to see; personal characteristics are covert and are revealed when you want to reveal them; speaker controls the order of revelation; disguise or anonymity is easy. • It's always your turn; speaker time is unlimited; you can't be interrupted.

Human Communication Element	Face-to-Face Communication	Computer-Mediated Communication
Receiver [number, interests, third party, impression formation]	• One or a few who are in your visual field. • Limited to those you have the opportunity to meet; often difficult to find people who have the same interests you do especially in isolated communities with little mobility. • Your messages can be overheard by or repeated to third parties, but not verbatim and not with the same accuracy as online. • Impressions are based on the verbal and nonverbal cues receiver perceives.	• One, a few, or as many as you find in a chat room, have on your e-mail list, or who read your bulletin board posts. • Virtually unlimited; you can more easily and quickly find people who match your interests. • Your messages can be retrieved by others or forwarded verbatim to a third party or to hundreds of third parties (with or without your knowledge). • Impressions are based on text messages (usually) receiver reads.
Context [physical, temporal]	• Where you both are; together in essentially the same physical space. • As it happens; you have little control over the context once you're in a communication situation. • Communication is *synchronous*—messages are exchanged at the same time.	• Where you and receiver each want to be, separated in space. • You can more easily choose the timing—when you want to respond. • Communication may be synchronous, as in chat rooms and instant messaging, or *asynchronous*—messages are exchanged at different times, as in e-mail and bulletin board postings.
Channel	• Auditory plus visual plus tactile plus proxemic (related to distance) • Two-way channel enabling immediate interactivity.	• Visual for text (though auditory and visual for graphics and video are available). • Two-way channels, some enabling immediate and some delayed interactivity.
Messages [verbal, nonverbal, permanence]	• Spoken words along with gestures, eye contact, accent, paralinguistic (vocal but nonverbal) cues, space, touch, clothing, hair, and all the other nonverbal cues. • Temporary unless recorded; speech signals fade rapidly. • Rarely are abbreviations verbally expressed.	• Written words in purely text-based CMC, though that's changing. • Messages are permanent unless erased. • Limited nonverbal cues; some can be created with emoticons or words, and some (like smells and touch) cannot. • Use lots of abbreviations.
Feedforward	• Conveyed nonverbally and verbally early in the interaction.	• In e-mail it's given in the headings and subject line, as well as in the opening sentences.
Ethics and Deception	• Presentation of false physical self is more difficult, though not impossible; presenting false psychological and social selves is easier. • Nonverbal leakage cues often give you away when you're lying.	• Presentation of false physical self as well as false psychological and social selves is relatively easy. • Can probably lie more easily.

Mass Communication

Mass communication is communication from one source to many receivers, who may be scattered throughout the world. Mass communication takes place via at least the following media outlets:

- *newspapers*
- *television*
- *radio*
- *film and video*
- *music*
- *the Internet, the Web, and blogs*

The coverage of mass communication in this book focuses on media literacy and aims to help you to become a wiser, more critical user of the media (see the first Media Watch box).

As you can see if you glance through your college catalogue, each of these forms of communication is likely to be covered in separate and more detailed courses in public speaking, small group communication, interpersonal communication, mass communication, and so on. In this course and in this text, the essentials of these communication forms are introduced, giving you the knowledge and skills to become a more effective communicator, and at the same time the background to move on to more detailed study, whether in more in-depth courses or in your own reading. Table 1.2, on page 7, gives you an overview of these varied forms of human communication.

Through these varied forms of communication, you'll accomplish a number of different purposes. Let's take a look at several of these purposes.

The Purposes of Human Communication

The purposes of human communication may be conscious or unconscious, recognizable or unrecognizable. And although communication technologies are changing rapidly and drastically—we send e-mail, work at computer terminals, and telecommute, for example—the purposes of communication

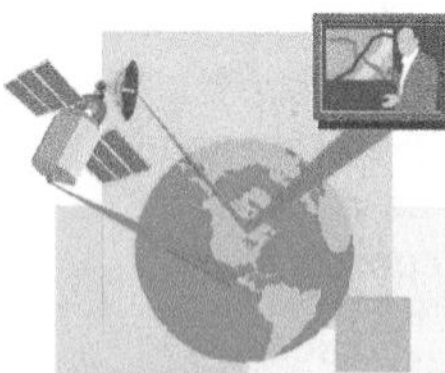

MEDIA WATCH

What Is Media Literacy?

[I]t is precisely because they [the mass media] are so familiar that we need to study them. Familiarity, for example, may blind us to the distinct kind of communication that takes place through the mass media, and especially to the processes by which they influence us.

—*Kathleen Hall Jamieson and Karlyn Kohrs Campbell*

Media literacy—as you'll discover in this Media Watch box—covers a range of skills that are vital to dealing with the mass media. Because these skills are so important, Media Watch boxes are presented throughout the text, reminding you that the media are influencing you in ways you need to be aware of.

Media literacy may be defined as your ability to understand, analyze, evaluate, and produce mass communication messages (television, film, music, radio, billboards, advertising, public relations, newspapers and magazines, books, websites and blogs, newsgroups and chat rooms).

Because the media influence you in numerous ways (only some of which you may be conscious of), it's crucial that you learn how this influence is exerted so that you, rather than the media, can determine what influences you and what doesn't. Looked at in this way, media literacy is a form of empowerment. It can help you to use the media more intelligently; to understand, analyze, and evaluate media messages more effectively; to influence the messages that the media send out; and to create your own mediated messages.

Increasing Media Literacy

Increase your sensitivity to media by examining your own use of media. If possible, keep a record or log of all the time you spend on media in one day, the media you use most often, the purposes you use the media for, the rewards you get from the media, and especially the ways in which the media might be influencing you. Also, increase your sensitivity by supplementing these Media Literacy boxes with visits to some interesting websites; try, for example, Citizens for Media Literacy at www.main.nc.us/cml *and the Media Education Foundation at* www.mediaed.org.

Table 1.2
Forms of Human Communication

This table identifies and arranges the forms of communication in terms of the number of persons involved, from one (in intrapersonal communication) to thousands and millions (in mass communication). It also previews (in general) the progression of topics in this book.

Forms of Human Communication	Some Common Purposes	Some Theory-Related Concerns	Some Skills-Related Concerns
Intrapersonal: communication with the self 	To think, reason, analyze, reflect	How does a person's self-concept develop? How does the self-concept influence communication? How can problem-solving and analyzing abilities be improved and taught? What is the relationship between personality and communication?	Enhancing self-esteem, increasing self-awareness, improving problem-solving and analyzing abilities, increasing self-control, reducing stress, managing intrapersonal conflict
Interpersonal: communication between two persons 	To discover, relate, influence, play, help	What is interpersonal effectiveness? Why do people develop relationships? What holds friends, lovers, and families together? What tears them apart? How can relationships be repaired?	Increasing effectiveness in one-to-one communication, developing and maintaining effective relationships (friendship, love, family), improving conflict resolution abilities
Interviewing: communication that proceeds through questions and answers 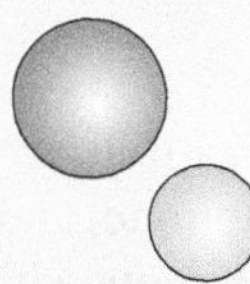	To learn, evaluate, influence	What makes a leader? What type of leadership works best? What roles do members play in groups? What do groups do well, and what do they fail to do well? How can groups be made more effective?	Increasing effectiveness as a group member, improving leadership abilities, using groups to achieve specific purposes (for example, solving problems, generating ideas)
Small group: communication within a small group of persons 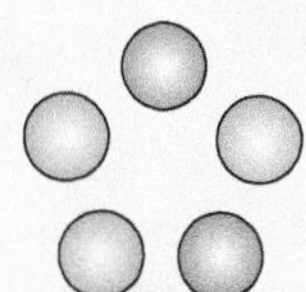	To share information, generate ideas, solve problems, help	What makes a leader? What type of leadership works best? What roles do members play in groups? What do groups do well, and what do they fail to do well? How can groups be made more effective?	Increasing effectiveness as a group member, improving leadership abilities, using groups to achieve specific purposes (for example, solving problems, generating ideas)
Organizational: communication within an organization 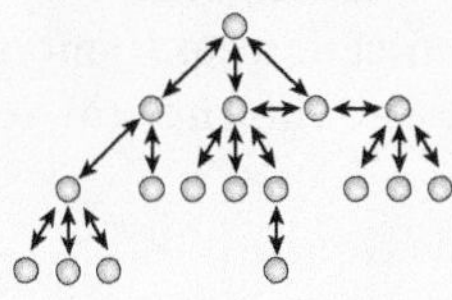	To inform, persuade, relate	What leadership styles work best in organizations? How and why do organizations grow and deteriorate? What role does culture play in the organization?	Transmitting information, motivating workers, dealing with feedback, dealing with the grapevine, increasing satisfaction

Forms of Human Communication	Some Common Purposes	Some Theory-Related Concerns	Some Skills-Related Concerns
Public: communication of speaker with audience 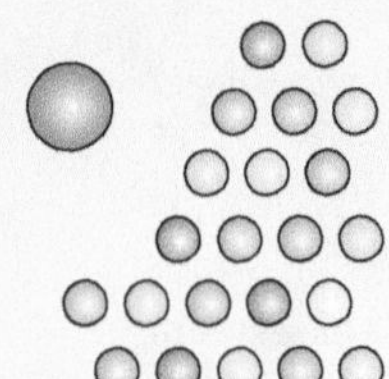	To inform, persuade, entertain	What kinds of organizational structure work best in informative and persuasive speaking? How can audiences be most effectively analyzed and adapted to? How can ideas be best developed for communication to an audience?	Communicating information more effectively; increasing persuasive abilities; developing, organizing, styling, and delivering messages with greater effectiveness
Computer-mediated: communication between people through computers 	To discover, relate, influence, play, help	Are there gender differences? In what ways is CMC more efficient? How can modalities be combined?	Increasing security in e-communications, combining CMC with face-to-face communication
Mass: communication addressed to an extremely large audience, mediated by audio and/or visual means 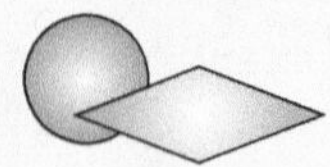	To entertain, persuade, and inform	What functions do the media serve? How do the media influence us? How can we influence the media? In what ways is information censored by the media for the public? How does advertising work?	Improving our ability to use the media to greater effectiveness, increasing our ability to control the media, avoiding being taken in by advertisements and tabloid journalism

have remained essentially the same throughout the computer revolution and are likely to continue through whatever revolutions follow. Five general purposes of communication can be identified: To discover, to relate, to help, to persuade, and to play (see Figure 1.1 on page 9).

To Discover

One of the major purposes of communication concerns personal discovery. When you communicate with another person, you learn about yourself as well as about the other person. In fact, your self-perceptions result largely from what you've learned about yourself from others during communications, especially your interpersonal encounters. Communication also helps you discover the external world—the world of objects, events, and other people. Communication enables you to reduce your uncertainty about people and about the world, and reducing uncertainty in turn enables you to communicate more effectively.

To Relate

You probably spend much of your communication time and energy establishing and maintaining social relationships. You communicate with your close friends in school, at work, on the phone, and over the Internet. You talk with your parents, children, and brothers and sisters. You interact with your relational partner. All told, this takes a great deal of your time and attests to the importance of the relational purpose of communication.

To Help

You fulfill the helping purpose when you constructively criticize, express empathy, work with a group to solve a problem, or listen attentively and supportively to a public speaker. Not surprisingly, obtaining and giving help are among the major functions of Internet communication and among the major reasons people use the Internet (Meier, 2000, 2002).

To Persuade

In your everyday interpersonal and group encounters, you often try to persuade—to change the attitudes and behaviors of others. You try to get people to vote a particular way, try a new diet, buy a particular item, see a movie, visit a website, take a

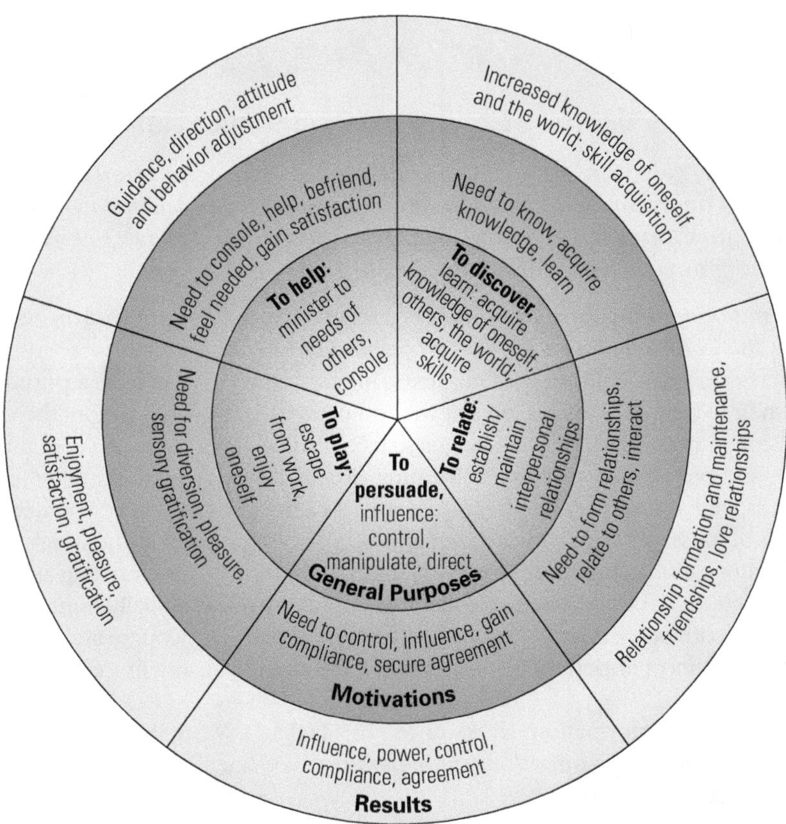

Figure 1.1

The Purposes of Human Communication

Shown here are the five general purposes of communication—but the aims of communication also can be looked at from at least two other perspectives. First, purposes may be seen as motives for engaging in communication. That is, you engage in communication to satisfy your need for knowledge or to form relationships. Second, these purposes may be viewed in terms of the results you want to achieve. That is, you engage in interpersonal communication to increase your knowledge of yourself and others or to exert influence or power over others. Any communication act serves a unique combination of purposes, is prompted by a unique combination of motives, and can produce a unique combination of results. A similar typology of purposes comes from research on motives for communicating. In a series of studies, Rubin and her colleagues (Rubin & Martin, 1998; Rubin, Fernandez-Collado, & Hernandez-Sampieri, 1992; Rubin & Martin, 1994; Rubin, Perse, & Barbato, 1988; Rubin & Rubin, 1992; Graham, 1994; Graham, Barbato, & Perse, 1993) have identified six primary motives for communication: pleasure, affection, inclusion, escape, relaxation, and control. How do these compare to the five purposes discussed here?

specific course, believe that something is true or false, value or devalue some idea, and so on. In interviews, you may try to persuade a company to hire you; in public speaking, you may try to persuade your audience that you should be elected to hold a certain office or position. Some researchers, in fact, argue that all communication is persuasive and that all our communications seek some persuasive goal (Canary, Cody, & Manusov, 2000).

To Play

Communication as play includes motives of pleasure, escape, and relaxation (Barbato & Perse, 1992; Rubin, Perse, & Barbato, 1988). You tell jokes, say clever things, and relate interesting stories largely for the pleasure it gives to you and your listeners. Similarly, you may communicate because it relaxes you, allowing you to get away from pressures and responsibilities.

These five purposes are the reasons you communicate. The next section will help explain how you communicate by exploring the elements involved in the communication act.

The Elements of Human Communication

Before examining the definition of the term *communication* and its various elements, take a moment to think about your beliefs about communication by taking the self-test on page 10.

ASK THE RESEARCHER

Values of a Human Communication Course

These brief Q&As are designed to illustrate the close connection between theory and research on the one hand and practical skills on the other. In each Ask the Researcher box, a question is posed to a national or international expert, who responds as if speaking directly with a student.

I'm taking this course in human communication. I am not certain what practical uses this course will have for me. Why should I be taking this course? You interact with others every day in a variety of contexts. In most contexts, you have a purpose in mind: To learn or to persuade. In job interviews, you need to know what factors the employers are seeking in nonverbal behavior, language use, attitude, level of knowledge, amount of enthusiasm, and personal motivation. In learning situations, you need to know when to ask a question as well as how to frame your question. As a manager of others, you need to know what kinds of messages will motivate your subordinates to perform at their highest levels. Human communication is significant for every aspect of your life from learning at school to obtaining positions in corporations to soliciting a salary increase. Socially, human communication is at the core of what makes relationships work or fail. This course and this book may be among the most important instruments in developing you as a more sensitive and effective person.

For further information: Hickson, M., III, Stacks, D. W., & Padgett-Greely, M. (1998). *Organizational communication in the personal context: From interview to retirement.* Boston: Allyn & Bacon.

Mark Hickson III (Ph.D., Southern Illinois University) is a professor of communication studies at the University of Alabama at Birmingham. He teaches courses in communication theory, nonverbal communication, and organizational communication.

TEST YOURSELF

What Do You Believe about Communication?

Respond to each of the following statements with T (true) if you believe the statement is usually true or F (false) if you believe the statement is usually false.

____ **1.** Good communicators are born, not made.

____ **2.** The more a couple communicates, the better their relationship will be.

____ **3.** When two people are in a close relationship for a long period of time, one person should not have to communicate his or her needs and wants; the other person should know what these are.

____ **4.** Complete openness should be the goal of any meaningful interpersonal relationship.

____ **5.** Interpersonal or group conflict is a reliable sign that the relationship or group is in trouble.

____ **6.** Like good communicators, leaders are born, not made.

____ **7.** Fear of speaking in public is detrimental and must be eliminated.

HOW DID YOU DO? As you may have figured out, all seven statements are generally false. As you read this text, you'll discover not only why these beliefs are false but also the trouble you can get into when you assume they're true. Briefly, here are some of the reasons why each of the statements is generally false:

1. Effective communication is a learned skill; although some people are born brighter or more extroverted than others, all can improve their abilities and become more effective communicators.
2. If you practice bad communication habits, you're more likely to grow less effective than to become more effective; consequently, it's important to learn and follow the principles of effectiveness.

3. This assumption is at the heart of many interpersonal difficulties: People aren't mind readers, and to assume that they are merely sets up barriers to open and honest communication (see Chapter 4).
4. Although you may feel ethically obligated to be totally honest, this is generally not an effective strategy. In fact, "complete" anything is probably a bad idea.
5. Interpersonal conflict does not have to involve a winner and a loser; both people can win.
6. Leadership, like communication and listening, is a learned skill that you'll develop as you learn the principles of human communication in general and of group leadership in particular.
7. Most speakers are nervous; managing, not eliminating, the fear will enable you to become effective regardless of your current level of fear.

WHAT WILL YOU DO? Consider how these beliefs about communication influence the way you communicate. Then, as you read this book and participate in class discussions and activities, reexamine your beliefs about communication and consider how new beliefs would influence the way you communicate. The theories and research discussed in this text will help you reconsider your own beliefs about communication, and the skill-building activities will help you practice new ways of communicating. Three excellent websites containing a variety of self-tests on emotional intelligence, personality, knowledge, relationships, careers, and more are www.allthetests.com, www.queendom.com/tests, and www.psychologytoday.com.

Defining Communication

Communication occurs when one person (or more) sends and receives messages that are distorted by noise, occur within a context, have some effect, and provide some opportunity for feedback. Figure 1.2 illustrates the elements present in all communication acts, whether intrapersonal, interpersonal, small group, public speaking, or mass communication—or whether face-to-face, by telephone, or over the Internet: (1) context, (2) sources-receivers, (3) messages, (4) channels, (5) noise, and (6) effects. In addition, we'll examine the role of ethics in communication.

Communication Context

All communication takes place in a **context** that has at least four dimensions: (1) physical, (2) social-psychological, (3) temporal, and (4) cultural (Figure 1.3 on page 12). The *physical context* is the tangible or concrete environment in which communication takes place—the room or hallway or park. This physical context exerts some influence on the content of your messages (what you say) as well as on the form (how you say it).

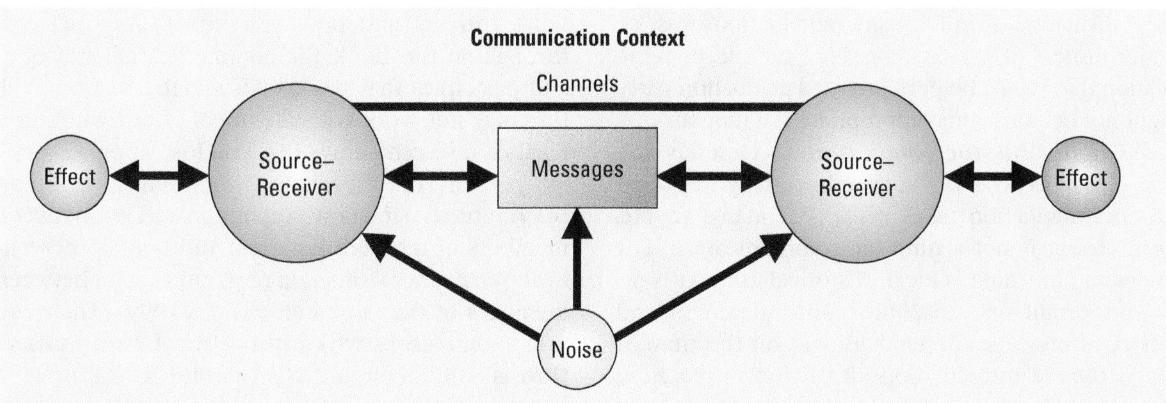

Figure 1.2

The Elements of Human Communication

This is a simplified view of the elements of human communication and their relationship to one another. Messages (including feedforward and feedback) are sent simultaneously through a variety of channels from one source–receiver to another. The communication process takes place in a context (physical, cultural, social-psychological, and temporal) and is subjected to interference by noise (physical, psychological, and semantic). The interaction of messages with each source–receiver leads to some effect.

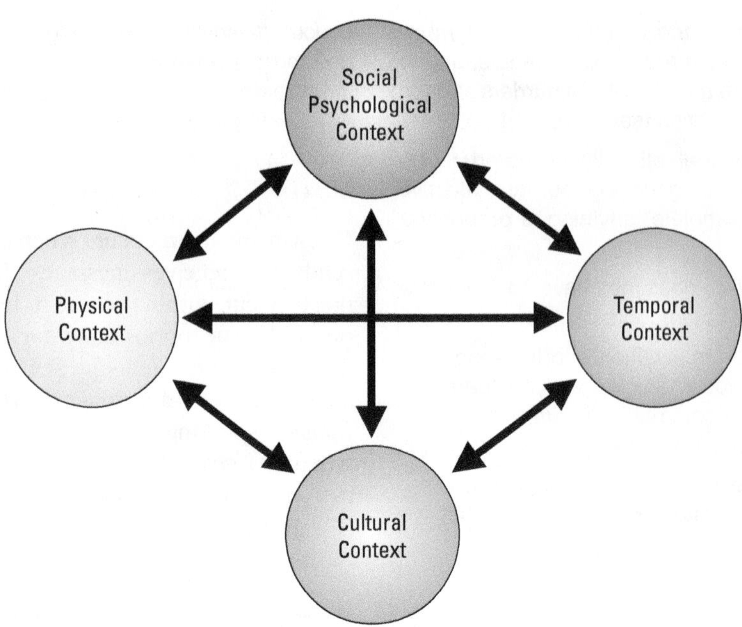

Figure 1.3
The Communication Context
This figure is intended to illustrate that the communication context is not a single entity but consists of a variety of contexts that affect communication—and, perhaps most important, to remind you that each dimension of context influences each other dimension.

The *social-psychological context* includes, for example, the status relationships among the participants, the roles and the games that people play, and the cultural rules of the society in which people are communicating. It also includes the friendliness or unfriendliness, formality or informality, and seriousness or humorousness of the situation. For example, communication that would be permitted at a graduation party might not be considered appropriate at a funeral.

The *temporal (or time) context* includes the time of day as well as the time in history in which the communication takes place. For many people, the morning is not a time for communication. For others, the morning is ideal. Historical context is no less important—because the appropriateness and impact of messages depend, in part, on the time in which they're uttered. Consider, for example, how messages on racial, sexual, or religious attitudes and values would be differently framed and responded to in different times in history. Still another aspect of time is how a message fits into the sequence of communication events. For example, consider the varied meanings a "simple" compliment paid to a friend would have depending on whether you said it immediately after your friend paid you a compliment, immediately before you asked your friend for a favor, or during an argument.

The *cultural context* has to do with your (and others') **culture**: the beliefs, values, and ways of behaving that are shared by a group of people and passed down from one generation to the next. Cultural factors affect every interaction and influence what you say and how you say it. As you'll see throughout this book, the communication strategies and principles that work with members of one culture may not work with members of other cultures. Further, research shows that you lose approximately 50 percent of information communicated in an *inter*cultural situation (communication between members of different cultures) and only 25 percent in an *intra*cultural situation (communication between members of the same culture) (Li, 1999). These are just some reasons why **intercultural communication** is so difficult and why culture is so crucial to communication.

These four dimensions of context interact with one another. For example, arriving late for an appointment (temporal context) might violate a cultural rule, which might lead to changes in the social-psychological context, perhaps creating tension and unfriendliness, which in turn might lead to changes in the physical context—for example, choosing a less intimate restaurant for your lunch meeting.

Sources-Receivers

The compound term *sources-receivers* emphasizes that each person involved in communication is both a **source** (or speaker) and a **receiver** (or listener). You send messages when you speak, write, gesture, or smile. You receive messages in listening, reading, smelling, and so on. As you send messages, however, you're also receiving messages. You're receiving your own messages (you hear yourself, you feel your own movements, you see many of your own gestures), and you're receiving the messages of the other person—visually, aurally, or even through touch or smell. As you assign meaning to these verbal and nonverbal signals, you're performing receiving functions.

Source-Receiver Encoding-Decoding

The act of producing messages—for example, speaking or writing—is called **encoding**. By putting your ideas into sound waves or into a computer program you're putting these ideas into a **code**, hence encoding. The act of receiving messages—for example, listening or reading—is called **decoding**. By translating sound waves or words on a screen into ideas you take them out of code, which is decoding. Thus, speakers or writers are called **encoders**, and listeners or readers, **decoders**.

As with sources-receivers, the compound term *encoding-decoding* emphasizes that you perform these functions simultaneously, at least in face-to-face communication. As you speak (encoding), you're also deciphering the responses of the listener (decoding). In computer communication this simultaneous exchange of messages occurs only sometimes. In e-mail (as well as snail mail) and newsgroup communication, for example, the sending and receiving may be separated by several days or much longer. In chat groups and instant messaging, on the other hand, communication takes place in real time; the sending and receiving take place (almost) simultaneously.

Source-Receiver Competence

The term **communication competence** refers to your knowledge of the social aspects of communication (Rubin, 1982, 1985; Spitzberg & Cupach, 1989). Communication competence includes knowledge of such factors as the role of context in influencing the content and form of communication messages—for example, the knowledge that in certain contexts and with certain listeners one topic is appropriate and another is not. Knowledge about the rules of nonverbal behavior—for example, the appropriateness of touching, vocal volume, and physical closeness—is also part of communication competence.

Communication competence also includes your ability to apply this knowledge in communicating. So when you read about communication competence, realize that it includes both an understanding of how communication works, *and* the ability to use this understanding in communicating effectively. Keep in mind, however, that communication competence is culture specific; the way communication works and the elements that make it effective differ from one culture to another.

Messages

Communication **messages** take many forms. You send and receive messages through any one or any combination of sensory organs. Although you may customarily think of messages as being verbal (oral or written), you also communicate nonverbally. Everything about you communicates. For example, the clothes you wear and the way you walk, shake hands, tilt your head, comb your hair, sit, and smile all communicate messages.

In face-to-face communication the actual message signals (the movements in the air) are evanescent; they fade almost as they're uttered. Some written messages, especially computer-mediated messages such as those sent via e-mail, are unerasable. E-mails that are sent among employees in a large corporation, for example, are often stored on disk or tape.

Two special types of messages include *feedback* (the messages you send that are reactions to other messages) and *feedforward* (the messages you send as preface to your "main" messages). Both feedback and feedforward are **metamessages**—messages that communicate about other messages. Such communication about communication, or **metacommunication**, may be verbal ("I agree with you" or "Wait until you hear this one") or nonverbal (a smile or a prolonged pause). Or, as is most often the case, it's some combination of verbal and nonverbal signals.

Feedback Messages

Throughout the listening process, a listener gives a speaker **feedback**—messages sent back to the speaker reacting to what is said. Feedback tells the speaker what effect he or she is having on the listener(s). This can take many forms: A frown or a smile, a yea or a nay, a pat on the back or a punch in the mouth are all types of feedback. Sometimes feedback is easy to identify, but sometimes it isn't (Skinner, 2002).

Part of the art of effective communication is the ability to discern feedback and to adjust messages on the basis of that feedback. For example, on the basis of feedback, a speaker may adjust messages by

Negative Communication Effects

An e-mail that you wrote to a close friend in anger (but never intended to send) was sent. You want to reduce the negative effects of such an e-mail.

WHAT DO YOU SAY?

strengthening, deemphasizing, or changing the content or form of the messages. These adjustments then serve as feedback to the receiver—who, in response, readjusts his or her feedback messages. The process is circular, with one person's feedback serving as the stimulus for the other person's feedback, just as any message serves as the stimulus for another person's message.

Another type of feedback is the feedback you get from listening to yourself: You hear what you say, you feel the way you move, you see what you write. On the basis of this self-feedback you adjust your messages; for example, you may correct a mispronunciation, shorten your story, or increase your volume.

You can view feedback in terms of five important dimensions: positive-negative, person-focused-message-focused, immediate-delayed, low-monitored-high-monitored, and supportive-critical.

- *Positive-negative.* **Positive feedback** (smiles, applause, and head nods signifying approval) tells the speaker that the message is being well received and that he or she should continue speaking in the same general mode. **Negative feedback** (frowns, boos, puzzled looks, gestures signifying disapproval) tells the speaker that something is wrong and that some adjustment needs to be made.
- *Person-focused-message-focused.* Feedback may center on the person ("You're sweet," "You've got a great smile") or on the message ("Can you repeat that phone number?" "Your argument is a good one").
- *Immediate-delayed.* In interpersonal situations feedback is most often conveyed immediately after the message is received. In other communication situations, however, the feedback may be delayed; for example, feedback from an interview may come weeks after the interview took place. In media situations some feedback comes immediately—for example, through Nielsen ratings; other feedback comes much later, through consumers' viewing and buying patterns.
- *Low-monitored-high-monitored.* Feedback varies from the spontaneous and totally honest reaction (low-monitored feedback) to the carefully constructed response designed to serve a specific purpose (high-monitored feedback). In most interpersonal situations you probably give feedback spontaneously; you allow your responses to show without any monitoring. At other times, however, you may be more guarded, as when your boss asks you how you like your job or when your grandmother asks what you think of her holiday fruitcake.
- *Supportive-critical.* Supportive feedback confirms the worth of a person and of what that person says; it occurs when, for example, you console another or when you encourage the other to talk; it often involves **affirmation** of the person's self-definition. Critical feedback, on the other hand, is evaluative. When you give critical feedback you judge another's performance—as in, for example, evaluating a speech or coaching someone learning a new skill.

Each feedback opportunity, then, presents you with choices along at least these five dimensions. To use feedback effectively, you need to make educated choices along these dimensions. Realize that these categories are not exclusive. Feedback does not have to be either critical or supportive; it can be both. For example, in teaching someone how to become a more effective interviewer, you might critically evaluate a practice interview but you might also express support for the effort. Similarly, you might respond to a friend's question immediately and then after a day or two elaborate on your response.

Feedforward Messages

Feedforward is information you provide before sending your primary messages; it reveals something about the messages to come (Richards, 1951). Feedforward includes such diverse examples as the preface or the table of contents in a book, the opening paragraph of a chapter, movie previews, magazine covers, and introductions in public speeches. Feedforward has four major functions: (1) to open the channels of communication, (2) to preview the message, (3) to altercast, and (4) to disclaim.

- **To open the channels of communication**. Often we preface our messages with comments whose only function is to open the channels of communication (Malinowski, 1923; Lu, 1998). The infamous "opening line" ("Do you come here often?" or "Haven't we met before?") is a clear example of this type of feedforward. Another type of feedforward serving this function of opening the channels is **phatic communication** or "small talk." It's the "how are you" and "nice weather" greetings that are designed to maintain rapport and friendly relationships (Placencia, 2004; Burnard, 2003). Similarly, listeners' short comments that are unrelated to the content of the conversation but that indicate interest and attention may also be considered phatic communication in that they keep the channels of communication open (McCarthy, 2003).
- **To preview future messages**. Feedforward messages frequently preview other messages. Feedforward may, for example, preview the content ("I have news for you"), the importance ("Listen to this before you make a move"), the form or style ("I'll be brief"), or the positive or negative quality of subsequent messages ("You're not going to like this, but here's what I heard").
- **To altercast**. The type of feedforward known as **altercasting** asks the receiver to approach your message in a particular role or even as someone else (McLaughlin, 1984; Weinstein & Deutschberger, 1963; Johnson, 1993; Pratkanis, 2000). For example, you might ask a friend, "As a single mother, what do you think of the new child care proposals?" This question casts your friend into the role of single mother (rather than that of teacher, Democrat, or Baptist, for example). It asks your friend to assume a particular perspective.
- **To disclaim**. A **disclaimer** is a statement that aims to ensure that your message will not reflect negatively on you. Disclaimers entice the listener to hear your message as you wish it to be heard rather than through some assumption that might reflect negatively on you (Hewitt & Stokes, 1975). For example, to ensure that people listen to you fairly, you might disclaim any thought that you're biased against one gender: "I'm no sexist, but. . . ."

Channels

The communication **channel** is the medium through which the message passes. Communication rarely takes place over only one channel; you may use two, three, or four different channels simultaneously. For example, in face-to-face interactions you speak and listen (vocal channel), but you also gesture and receive signals visually (visual channel). In chat groups, you type and read words and use various symbols and abbreviations to communicate the emotional tone of the message. If your computer system is especially sophisticated, you may communicate via the Internet through audio and visual means as well. In addition, in face-to-face communication you emit and detect odors (olfactory channel). Often you touch another person, and this too communicates (tactile channel).

At times, one or more channels may be damaged. For example, in individuals with visual difficulties, the visual channel is impaired, and so adjustments have to be made. Table 1.3 gives you an idea of how such adjustments between those with and without visual impairments can make communication more effective.

Noise

Noise is anything that interferes with your receiving a message. At one extreme, noise may prevent a message from getting from source to receiver. A roaring noise or line static can easily prevent entire messages from getting through to your receiver. At the other extreme, with virtually no noise interference, the message of the source and the message received are almost identical. Most often, however, noise distorts some portion of the message a source sends as it travels to a receiver. Like messages that may be auditory or visual, noise comes in both auditory and visual forms. Four types of noise are especially relevant:

- *Physical noise* is interference that is external to both speaker and listener; it interferes with the physical transmission of the signal or message. Examples include the screeching of passing cars, the hum of a computer, sunglasses, extraneous messages, illegible handwriting, blurred type or fonts that are too small or difficult to read, misspellings and poor grammar, and popup ads.
- *Physiological noise* is created by barriers within the sender or receiver such as visual impairments, hearing loss, articulation problems, and memory loss.

Table 1.3

Interpersonal Communication Tips

Between People with and People without Visual Impairments

People vary greatly in their visual abilities; some people are totally blind, some are partially sighted, and some have unimpaired vision. Ninety percent of individuals who are "legally blind" have some vision. All of us, however, have the same need for communication and information. Here are some tips for making communication between blind and sighted people more effective.

If you're the sighted person and are talking with a blind person:

1. *Identify yourself.* Don't assume the blind person will recognize your voice.
2. *Face your listener; you'll be easier to hear.* At the same time, don't shout. People who are visually impaired are not hearing impaired. Speak at your normal volume.
3. Because your gestures, eye movements, and facial expressions cannot be seen by the visually impaired listener, *encode into speech all the meanings—both verbal and nonverbal—that you wish to communicate.*
4. *Use audible turn-taking cues.* When you pass the role of speaker to a person who is visually impaired, don't rely on nonverbal cues; instead, say something like "Do you agree with that, Joe?"
5. *Use normal vocabulary, and discuss the same kinds of topics you would discuss with sighted people.* Don't avoid terms like "see" or "look" or even "blind." Don't avoid discussing a television show, or a painting, or the way your new car looks; these are normal conversational topics for all people.

If you are a visually impaired person and are interacting with a sighted person:

1. *Help the sighted person meet your special communication needs.* If you want your surroundings described, ask. If you want the person to read the road signs, ask.
2. *Be patient with the sighted person.* Many people are nervous talking with people who are visually impaired for fear of offending. Put them at ease in a way that also makes you more comfortable.

These suggestions were drawn from www.cincyblind.org/what_do_you_do_.htm and www.rnib.org/uk/ (both accessed October 23, 2004).

- *Psychological noise* is mental interference in speaker or listener and includes preconceived ideas, wandering thoughts, biases and prejudices, closed-mindedness, and extreme emotionalism. You're likely to run into psychological noise when you talk with someone who is closed-minded or who refuses to listen to anything he or she doesn't already believe.
- *Semantic noise* is created when the speaker and listener have different meaning systems; it includes language or dialectical differences, the use of jargon or overly complex terms, and ambiguous or overly abstract terms whose meanings can be easily misinterpreted. You see this type of noise regularly—for example, in the medical doctor who uses "medicalese" without explanation or in the insurance salesperson who speaks in the jargon of the insurance industry.

As you can see from these examples, all communications contain noise. Noise cannot be totally eliminated, but its effects can be reduced. Making your language more precise, sharpening your skills for sending and receiving nonverbal messages, and improving your listening and feedback skills are some ways to combat the influence of noise.

Communication Effects

Communication always has some **effect** on one or more persons involved in the communication act. For every communication act, there is some consequence. Generally three types of effects are distinguished.

- **Intellectual (or cognitive) effects** are changes in your thinking. When you acquire information from a class lecture, for example, the effect is largely intellectual.
- **Affective effects** are changes in your attitudes, values, beliefs, and emotions. Thus, when you become frightened when watching the latest horror movie, its effect is largely affective. Similarly, after a great experience with, say, a person of another culture, your feelings about that culture may change. Again, the effect is largely affective (but perhaps also intellectual).

- **Psychomotor effects** are changes in overt behaviors such as, for example, learning new bodily movements such as how to throw a curve ball or how to paint a room or learning to use different verbal and nonverbal behaviors.

These effects are not as separate as they might at first seem. In many cases, a single message—say a public speech on homelessness—may inform you (intellectual effect), move you to feel differently (affective effect), and lead you to be more generous when you come upon a homeless person (psychomotor effect).

Ethics

Because communication has consequences, it also involves questions of **ethics**, of right and wrong (Bok, 1978; Jaksa & Pritchard, 1994). For example, while it might be (temporarily) effective to exaggerate or even lie in order to sell a product or get elected, it would not be ethical to do so.

The ethical dimension of communication is complicated because ethics is so interwoven with our personal philosophy of life and with the culture in which we have been raised that it's difficult to propose general guidelines for specific individuals. Nevertheless, ethical responsibilities need to be considered as integral to any communication act. The decisions you make concerning communication must be guided by what you consider right as well as by what you consider effective.

In thinking about the ethics of communication, you can take the position that ethics is objective or that it's subjective. In an *objective view* you'd claim that the morality of an act—say, a communication message—is absolute and exists apart from the values or beliefs of any individual or culture. This objective view holds that there are standards that apply to all people in all situations at all times. In this way of thinking, if lying, advertising falsely, using illegally obtained evidence, and revealing secrets, for example, are considered unethical, then they'll be considered unethical regardless of the circumstances surrounding them or of the values and beliefs of the culture in which they occur.

In a *subjective view* you'd claim that the morality of an act depends on the culture's values and beliefs as well as on the particular circumstances. Thus, from a subjective position you would claim that the end might justify the means—a good result can justify the use of unethical means to achieve that result. You would further argue that lying is wrong to win votes or sell cigarettes, but that lying can be ethical if the end result is positive (such as trying to make someone who is unattractive feel better by telling them they look great, or telling a critically ill person that they'll feel better soon).

To emphasize the central role of ethics in all aspects of communication, this text includes Reflections on Ethics boxes. The first such discussion continues explaining the nature of ethics and discusses the three major areas of ethics (below).

REFLECTIONS ON ETHICS

The Areas of Ethics

According to the Internet Encyclopedia of Philosophy (www.iep.utm.edu/e/ethics.htm), the field of ethics consists of three areas:

- *Metaethics* concerns itself with the origins of ethical principles (where they come from—God? Social conventions? Cultural norms?) and with the meanings of various ethical concepts (What is responsibility? What is right? What is wrong?).
- *Normative ethics* concerns itself with articulating the standards of right and wrong; this is the area that proposes specific ethical principles (for example, Don't lie; Don't willfully hurt another person). It is from normative ethics that we learn the principles governing what is ethical and what is unethical.
- *Applied ethics* concerns itself with the ethical implications of controversial issues (Is capital punishment ethical? Is preventing marriage by same-sex couples ethical? Is it ethical to engage in war?).

These three areas often intersect. For example, the ethics of capital punishment is clearly *applied ethics,* as it focuses on a controversial issue. But this topic also draws on the insights of *metaethics* (Where do the rights to kill another person come from? Who has the right to kill another human being?) and on *normative ethics* (By what standard does one person claim the right to kill another person? Under what conditions might it be justifiable to kill another person?).

Ethical Choice Point

In a class discussion of ethics, your instructor presents the following possible ethical guidelines: (1) Behavior is ethical when you feel in your heart that you're doing the right thing; (2) Behavior is ethical when it is consistent with your religious beliefs; (3) Behavior is ethical when it's legal within the society; (4) Behavior is ethical when the majority of people would consider it ethical; and (5) Behavior is ethical when the end result is in the interest of the majority. How would you respond to these guidelines? Would you accept any as an accurate statement of what constitutes ethical behavior? Would you reject any? Why?

The Elements in Transaction

Communication is **transactional**, which means that the elements in communication are interdependent. Each person in the communication act is both speaker and listener; each person is simultaneously sending and receiving messages (see Figure 1.4) (Barnlund, 1970; Watzlawick, 1977, 1978; Watzlawick, Beavin, & Jackson, 1967; Wilmot, 1987).

There are several implications and ramifications of this transactional view.

- First, "transactional" means that *communication is an-ever changing process.* It's an ongoing activity; all the elements of communication are in a state of constant change. You're constantly changing, the people with whom you're communicating are changing, and your environment is changing. Nothing in communication ever remains static.

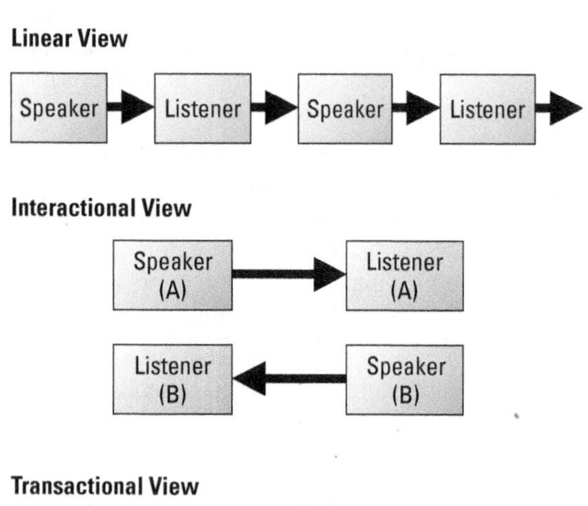

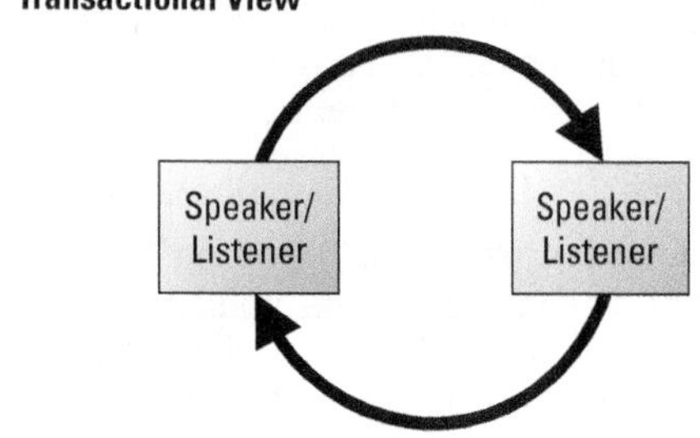

Figure 1.4

Three Views of Communication

The top diagram represents a linear view of communication, in which the speaker speaks and the listener listens. The middle diagram represents an interactional view, in which speaker and listener take turns speaking and listening; A speaks while B listens, then B speaks while A listens. The bottom diagram represents a transactional view. This is the view that most communication theorists hold. In the transactional view, each person serves simultaneously as speaker and listener; at the same time that you send messages, you're also receiving messages from your own communications and also from the messages of the other person(s).

- Second, in any transactional process, *each element relates integrally to every other element*; each exists in relation to the others. For example, there can be no source without a receiver. There can be no message without a source. There can be no feedback without a receiver. Because of this interdependence, a change in any one element of the process produces changes in the other elements. For example, you're talking with a group of your friends when your mother enters the group. This change in "audience" will lead to other changes. Perhaps you or your friends will adjust what you're saying or how you say it. The new situation may also influence how often certain people talk, and so on. Regardless of what change is introduced, other changes will be produced as a result.
- Third, *each person in a communication transaction acts and reacts on the basis of a multitude of factors.* For example, the way you act in a communication situation will naturally depend on the immediate context, which in turn is influenced by your history, past experiences, attitudes, cultural beliefs, self-image, future expectations, emotions, and a host of related issues. One implication of this is that actions and reactions in communication are determined not only by what is said, but also by the way each person interprets what is said. Your responses to a movie, for example, don't depend solely on the words and pictures in the film but also on your previous experiences, present emotions, knowledge, physical well-being, and other factors. Similarly, two people listening to the same message will often derive two very different meanings. Although the words and symbols are the same, each person interprets them differently because each is influenced differently by their history, present emotions, and so on.

The Principles of Human Communication

Here we'll explore several important principles that govern how communication works and that have important implications for your own communication effectiveness: (1) Communication is a package of signals; (2) communication is a process of adjustment; (3) communication involves content and relationship dimensions; (4) communication is ambiguous; (5) communication sequences are punctuated; (6) communication involves symmetrical and complementary transactions; and (7) communication is inevitable, irreversible, and unrepeatable. Before reading these principles, take a look at the Understanding Theory and Research box on "Communication Theories" on page 20.

Communication Is a Package of Signals

Communication behaviors, whether they involve verbal messages, gestures, or some combination thereof, usually occur in "packages" (Pittenger, Hockett, & Danehy, 1960). Usually, that is, verbal and nonverbal behaviors reinforce or support each other. All parts of a message system normally work together to communicate a particular meaning. You don't express fear with words while the rest of your body is relaxed. You don't express anger through your posture while your face smiles. Your entire body works together—verbally and nonverbally—to express your thoughts and feelings.

In any form of communication, whether interpersonal, small group, public speaking, or mass media, you probably pay little attention to this "packaging." It goes unnoticed. But when there's an incongruity—when the weak handshake belies the confident verbal greeting, when the nervous posture belies the focused stare, when the constant preening belies the verbal expressions of being comfortable and at ease—you take notice. Invariably you begin to question the credibility, the sincerity, and the honesty of the individual.

Often, contradictory messages are sent over a period of time. Note, for example, that in the following interaction the employee is being given two directives—use initiative and don't use initiative. These **mixed messages** place the employee in a "double bind"—regardless of what he or she does, rejection will follow.

EMPLOYER: You've got to learn to take more initiative. You never seem to take charge, to take control.

EMPLOYEE: [Takes the initiative, makes decisions.]

EMPLOYER: You've got to learn to follow the chain of command and not do things just because you want to.

EMPLOYEE: [Goes back to old ways, not taking any initiative.]

EMPLOYER: Well, I told you. We expect more initiative from you.

Contradictory messages may be the result of the desire to communicate two different emotions or feelings. For example, you may like a person and want to communicate a positive feeling, but you may also feel resentment toward this person and want to communicate a negative feeling as well. The result is that you communicate both feelings; for example, you say that you're happy to see the person but your facial expression and body posture communicate your negative feelings (Beier, 1974). In this example, and in many similar cases, the socially acceptable message is usually communicated verbally while the less socially acceptable message is communicated nonverbally.

Communication Is a Process of Adjustment

Communication can take place only to the extent that the communicators use the same system of signals (Pittenger, Hockett, & Danehy, 1960). You will not be able to communicate with another person to the extent that your language systems differ. In reality, however, no two persons use identical signal systems, so a process of **adjustment** is relevant to all forms of communication. Parents and children, for example, not only have largely different vocabularies but also have different meanings for the terms they do share. Different cultures, even when they use a common language, often have greatly different nonverbal communication systems. To the extent that these systems differ, meaningful and effective communication will not take place.

Part of the art of communication is identifying the other person's signals, learning how they're used, and understanding what they mean. Those in close relationships will realize that learning the other person's signals takes a great deal of time and often a great deal of patience. If you want to understand what another person means (by smiling, by saying "I love you," by arguing about trivia, by making self-deprecating comments), rather than simply acknowledging what the other person says or does, you have to learn that person's system of signals.

This principle of adjustment is especially important in intercultural communication, largely because people from different cultures use different signals—and sometimes also use the same signals to signify quite different things. Focused eye contact means honesty and openness in much of the United States. But in Japan and in many Hispanic cultures, that same behavior may signify arrogance or disrespect if, say, engaged in by a youngster with someone significantly older.

Communication Accommodation

Generally, you're likely to view someone who is similar to you more positively and to see that person as more attractive than someone who is dissimilar. For example, in one study roommates who had similar communication attitudes (both were high in their

UNDERSTANDING THEORY AND RESEARCH

Communication Theories

In addition to the theory and research discussed throughout the text, Understanding Theory and Research boxes highlight a particular theory or hypothesis about communication and focus attention on the nature and function of theory and research in the study of human communication.

A **theory** is a generalization that explains how something works—for example, gravity, blood clotting, interpersonal attraction, or communication. In academic writing, the term *theory* is usually reserved for a well-established system of knowledge about how things work or how things are related. A theory is still fundamentally a generalization, but it's often supported by research findings and other well-accepted theories.

The theories you'll encounter in this book try to explain how communication works—for example, how you accommodate your speaking style to your listeners, how communication works when relationships deteriorate, how friends self-disclose, how problem-solving groups communicate, how speakers influence audiences, and how the media affect people. As you can see from even these few examples, theories provide general principles that help you understand an enormous number of specific events.

One great value of communication theories is that they help you predict future events. Because theories summarize what's been found, they can offer reasonable predictions for events that you've never encountered. For example, theories of persuasion will help you predict what kinds of emotional appeals will be most effective in persuading a specific audience. Or theories of conflict resolution will enable you to predict what strategies would be effective or ineffective in resolving differences.

Despite their many values, theories don't reveal truth in any absolute sense. Rather, theories reveal some degree of accuracy, some degree of truth. In the natural sciences (such as physics and chemistry), theories are extremely high in accuracy. If you mix two parts of hydrogen to one part of oxygen, you'll get water—every time you do it. In social and behavioral sciences such as communication, sociology, and psychology, the theories are far less accurate in describing the way things work and in predicting how things will work.

This failure to reveal truth, however, does not mean that theories are useless. In increasing your understanding and your ability to predict, theories are extremely helpful. Theories often have practical implications as you work on developing your own communication skills. For example, theories of interpersonal attraction offer practical insights into how to make yourself more attractive to others; theories of leadership offer practical advice on how you can more effectively exert your own leadership. This interrelationship between theories and skills is a theme you'll find throughout this book. The more you know about how communication works (that is, the theories and research), the more likely you'll be able to use it effectively (that is, build your communication skills).

Working with Theories and Research

- *Log on to one of the academic databases to which you have access and browse through issues of* Quarterly Journal of Speech, Communication Monographs, *or* Communication Theory *(or scan similar journals in your own field of study); you'll be amazed at the breadth and depth of academic research and theory.*

Relationship Ambiguity

You've been dating someone on and off for a year or so and you'd like to invite your date to meet your parents (you're anxious to see what they think about your partner) but aren't sure how your date will perceive this invitation.

WHAT DO YOU SAY?
In what context?

willingness to communicate and low in their verbal aggressiveness) liked each other better and were more satisfied with their status as roommates than those with dissimilar attitudes (Martin & Anderson, 1995). Similarly, you're likely to judge a speaker as more believable when his or her language intensity is similar to your own (Aune & Kikuchi, 1993). And you're likely to see those whose speech rate is similar to yours as more sociable and intimate than those who speak much more slowly or more rapidly than you do (Buller, LePoire, Aune, & Eloy, 1992). In interethnic interactions, people who saw themselves as similar in communication styles were attracted to each other more than to those they perceived as having different communication styles (Lee & Gudykunst, 2001). These findings, and many more like them, support **communication accommodation theory**, the theory that you adjust to or accommodate to the speaking style of your listeners in order to gain a variety of benefits—not only believability and likeability, as already noted, but also general social approval and even communication efficiency (Giles, Mulac, Bradac, & Johnson, 1987).

Communication Involves Content and Relationship Dimensions

Communications, to a certain extent at least, refer to the real world, to something external to both speaker and listener. At the same time, however, communications also refer to the relationships between the parties (Watzlawick, Beavin, & Jackson, 1967). In other words, communication has both **content and relationship dimensions**.

For example, an employer may say to a worker, "See me after the meeting." This simple message has a content aspect and a relational aspect. The **content message** refers to the behavioral response expected—namely, that the worker see the employer after the meeting. The **relationship message** tells how the communication is to be dealt with. For example, the use of the simple command says that there's a status difference between the two parties: The employer can command the worker. This aspect is perhaps seen most clearly if you imagine the worker giving this command to the employer; to do so would be awkward and out of place, because it would violate the expected relationship between employer and worker.

In any communication situation, the content dimension may stay the same but the relationship aspect may vary. For example, the employer could say to the worker either "You had better see me after the meeting" or "May I please see you after the meeting?" In each case, the content is essentially the same; that is, the message being communicated about the behaviors expected is the same. But the relationship dimension is very different. The first example signifies a definite superior–inferior relationship and even a put-down of the worker. In the second, the employer signals a more equal relationship and shows respect for the worker.

Similarly, at times the content may be different but the relationship essentially the same. For example, a teenager might say to his or her parents, "May I go away this weekend?" or "May I use the car tonight?" The content of the two messages is clearly very different. The relationship dimension, however, is

UNDERSTANDING THEORY AND RESEARCH

Communication Research

Research is usually conducted on the basis of some theory and its predictions—although sometimes the motivation to conduct research comes from a simple desire to answer a question. Communication research is a systematic search for information about communication, the very information that is discussed throughout this text; for example, information about perception and listening, verbal and nonverbal messages, interpersonal interactions, small group encounters, and public speaking situations.

Some research is designed to explore what exists; for example, *What do people say after getting caught in a lie?* Other research is designed to describe the properties of some communication behavior; for example, *What are the various types of excuses?* Still other research aims to predict what will happen in different situations; for example, *What types of excuses will work best in a business relationship?* Research findings bearing on these questions help explain how communication works and suggest ways to use communication more effectively.

In evaluating communication research (or any kind of research), ask yourself three questions:

- **Are the results reliable?** In establishing reliability, a measure of the extent to which research findings are consistent, you ask if another researcher, using the same essential tools, would find the same results. Would the same people respond in the same way at other times? If the answer to such questions is yes, then the results are reliable. If the answer is no, then the results may be unreliable.
- **Are the results valid?** Validity is a measure of the extent to which a measuring instrument measures what it claims to measure. For example, does your score on an intelligence test really measure what we think of as intelligence? Does your score on a test of communication apprehension measure what most people think of as constituting apprehension?
- **Do the results justify the conclusion?** Results and conclusions are two different things. Results are objective findings such as "men scored higher than women on this test of romanticism." Conclusions are the researcher's (or reader's) interpretation of the results and might include, for example, "Men are more romantic than women."

Working with Theories and Research

- *What question about communication would you like answered? Research the question and find out if the question has already been answered. If not, how might you go about conducting your own research to secure the answer?*

essentially the same. It clearly denotes a superior-inferior relationship in which permission to do certain things must be secured.

Ignoring Relationship Dimensions

Problems may arise when the distinction between the content and relationship levels of communication is ignored. Consider a couple arguing over the fact that Pat made plans to study with friends during the weekend without first asking Chris if that would be all right. Probably both would have agreed that to study over the weekend was the right choice to make. Thus the argument is not at all related to the content level. The argument centers on the relationship level. Chris expected to be consulted about plans for the weekend. Pat, in not doing so, rejected this definition of the relationship.

Let me give you a personal example. My mother came to stay for a week at a summer place I had. On the first day she swept the kitchen floor six times, though I had repeatedly told her that it did not need sweeping: I would be tracking in dirt and mud from outside, so all her effort would be wasted. But she persisted in sweeping, saying that the floor was dirty and should be swept. On the content level we were talking about the value of sweeping the kitchen floor.

Content and Relationship Messages

An older relative frequently belittles you, though always in a playful way. But it's uncomfortable and probably not very good for your self-esteem. You're determined to stop the behavior but not lose the relationship.

WHAT DO YOU SAY?
Through what channel?

But on the relationship level we were talking about something quite different. We were each saying, "This is my house." When we realized this (though only after considerable argument), I stopped complaining about the relative usefulness of sweeping a floor that did not need sweeping, and she stopped sweeping it.

For another insight consider the following interchange:

Thom: I'm going bowling tomorrow. The guys at the plant are starting a team. [He focuses on the content and ignores any relational implications of the message.]

Sofia: Why can't we ever do anything together? [She responds primarily on a relational level, ignoring the content implications of the message and expressing her displeasure at being ignored in his decision.]

Thom: We can do something together anytime; tomorrow's the day they're organizing the team. [Again, he focuses almost exclusively on the content.]

This example reflects research findings that show that men tend to focus more on content messages, whereas women focus more on relationship messages (Pearson, West, & Turner, 1995). Once we recognize this gender difference, we may be able to develop increased sensitivity to the opposite sex.

Recognizing Relationship Dimensions

Here's essentially the same situation but with added sensitivity to relationship messages:

Thom: The guys at the plant are organizing a bowling team. I'd sure like to be on the team. Do you mind if I go to the organizational meeting tomorrow? [Although he focuses on content, he shows awareness of the relational dimensions by asking if this would be a problem. He also shows this in expressing his desire rather than his decision to attend this meeting.]

Sofia: That sounds great, but I'd really like to do something together tomorrow. [She focuses on the relational dimension but also acknowledges his content message. Note too that she does not respond as if she has to defend herself or her emphasis on relational aspects.]

Thom: How about you meet me at Luigi's for dinner after the organizational meeting? [He responds to the relational aspect without abandoning his desire to join the bowling team—and seeks to incorporate it into his communications. He attempts to negotiate a solution that will meet both Sofia's and his needs and desires.]

Sofia: Perfect. I'm dying for spaghetti and meatballs. [She responds to both messages, approving of both his joining the team and their dinner date.]

Arguments over content are relatively easy to resolve. You can look something up in a book or ask someone what actually took place. Arguments on the relationship level, however, are much more difficult to resolve, in part because you (like me in the example with my mother) may not recognize

BUILDING COMMUNICATION SKILLS

Distinguishing Content from Relationship Messages

Deborah Tannen, in *You're Wearing That?* (2006), gives examples of content and relationship communication and the problems that can result from different interpretations. For example, the mother who says, "Are you going to wear those earrings?" may think she's communicating solely a content message. To the daughter, however, the message is largely relational and is a criticism of the way she intends to dress. (Of course, the mother may have intended criticism.) Often, questions that may appear to be objective and focused on content are perceived as attacks, as in the title of Tannen's book. Identify the possible content and relational messages that a receiver might get in being asked the following questions:

- *You're* calling me?
- Did you say, *you're* applying to *medical* school?
- You're in *love*?
- You paid a *hundred dollars* for that?
- And that's *all* you did?

Content and relationship messages serve different communication functions. Being able to distinguish between these functions is a prerequisite for using and responding to messages effectively.

that the argument is in fact about your relationship. The accompanying Building Communication Skills box, Distinguishing Content and Relationship Messages, provides additional insight into this important distinction.

Communication Is Ambiguous

Ambiguous messages are messages with more than one potential meaning. Sometimes this **ambiguity** occurs because we use words that can be interpreted differently. Informal time terms offer good examples; *soon, right away, in a minute, early, late,* and similar terms often mean different things to different people. The terms are ambiguous. A more interesting type of ambiguity is grammatical ambiguity. You can get a feel for this type of ambiguity by trying to paraphrase—rephrase in your own words—the following sentences:

1. What has the cat in its paws?
2. Visiting relatives can be boring.
3. They are flying planes.

You can interpret and paraphrase each of these in at least two different ways:

1. What monster has the cat in its paws? What does the cat have in its paws?
2. To visit relatives can be boring. Relatives who visit can be boring.
3. Those people are flying planes. Those planes are for flying.

Although these examples are particularly striking—and are the work of linguists, or specialists who analyze language—some degree of ambiguity exists in all communication; all messages are ambiguous to some degree. In other words, when you express an idea, you never communicate your meaning exactly and totally; rather, you communicate your meaning with some reasonable accuracy—enough to give the other person a reasonably clear sense of what you mean. Sometimes, of course, you're less accurate than you anticipated: Your listener "gets the wrong idea," or "gets offended" when you only meant to be humorous, or "misunderstands your emotional meaning." Because of this inevitable uncertainty, you may qualify what you're saying, give an example, or ask, "Do you know what I mean?" These tactics help the other person understand your meaning and reduce uncertainty (to some degree).

Similarly, all relationships contain uncertainty. Consider a close relationship of your own and ask yourself the following questions. Answer on a scale ranging from 1 (completely or almost completely uncertain) to 6 (completely or almost completely certain). How certain are you about:

- what you can or cannot say to each other in this relationship? Do you know what the sore spots are or what topics are best avoided?

- whether or not you and your partner feel the same way about each other? Would you each describe your relationship similarly?
- the future of the relationship? Do you each see your future and the relationship's future in the same way?

Very likely you were not able to respond to all three questions with 6s, and it's equally likely that your relationship partner would be unable to respond with all 6s. These questions from a relationship uncertainty scale (Knobloch & Solomon, 1999)—and other similar tests—illustrate that you probably experience some degree of uncertainty about the norms that govern your relationship communication (question 1), the degree to which each of you defines the relationship in similar ways (question 2), and the relationship's future (question 3).

Any communication situation can be ambiguous. In small group or organizational situations, you may be unsure of how you or your ideas are being evaluated. You may be unsure of the hierarchy in the organization. You may be unsure of what style of leadership will prove effective and what style will cause resentment. In public speaking you probably face the greatest ambiguity; namely, how your audience will respond to your speech. Will they be in favor of what you're advocating or against it? Will they understand certain technical terms, or will you have to define them? Will they be willing to pay attention?

By developing the skills of communication presented in this text, you'll be able to reduce ambiguity and make your meanings as unambiguous as possible. In this connection take a look at the accompanying Building Communication Skills box, Resolving Ambiguity (page 27).

Communication Is Punctuated

Communication events are continuous transactions. There's no clear-cut beginning or ending. As a participant in or an observer of the communication act, you engage in punctuation: You divide up this continuous, circular process into causes and effects, or **stimuli** and **responses**. That is, you segment this continuous stream of communication into smaller pieces. You label some of these pieces causes or stimuli and others effects or responses.

Consider an example: The students are apathetic; the teacher does not prepare for classes. Figure 1.5 (a) illustrates the sequence of events, in which there's no absolute beginning and no absolute end. Each action (the students' apathy and the teacher's lack of preparation) stimulates the other. But there's no initial stimulus. Each of the events may be regarded as a stimulus and each as a response, but there's no way to determine which is which.

Consider how the teacher might divide up this continuous transaction. Figure 1.5 (b) illustrates the teacher's perception of the situation. From this point of view, the teacher sees the students' apathy as the stimulus for his or her lack of preparation, and the lack of preparation as the response to the students' apathy. In Figure 1.5 (c) we see how the students might divide up the transaction. The students might see this "same" sequence of events as beginning with the teacher's lack of preparation as the stimulus (or cause) and their own apathy as the response (or effect).

Take another example: Pat cooks; Chris criticizes the cooking. Pat begins to exert less effort, Chris criticizes more, Pat exerts still less effort, Chris continues to criticize, and so on. Pat may see the argument as beginning with Chris's negative comments—the criticism is the cause and exerting less effort is the effect. Chris may see the argument as beginning with Pat's lousy cooking—lack of effort is the cause and justifiable criticism is the effect.

This tendency to divide up the various communication transactions in sequences of stimuli and responses is referred to as **punctuation of communication** (Watzlawick, Beavin, & Jackson, 1967). People punctuate the continuous sequences of events into stimuli and responses for ease of understanding and remembering. And, as both the preceding examples illustrate, people punctuate communication in ways that allow them to look good and that are consistent with their own self-image.

If communication is to be effective, if you're to understand what another person means from his or her point of view, then you have to see the sequence of events as punctuated by the other person. Further, you have to recognize that your punctuation does not reflect what exists in reality. Rather, it reflects your own unique but fallible perception.

Communication Involves Symmetrical and Complementary Transactions

Relationships can be described as either symmetrical or complementary (Watzlawick, Beavin, & Jackson, 1967). In a **symmetrical relationship** the two individuals mirror each other's behavior. The behavior of one person is reflected in the behavior of the other. If one member nags, the other member responds in kind. If one member expresses jealousy, the other member expresses jealousy. If one member is passive, the other member is passive. The relationship is one of equality, with

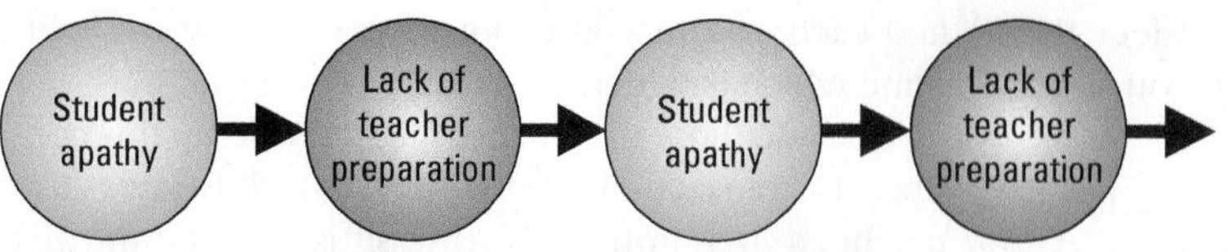

(a) The sequence of events punctuated by the teacher

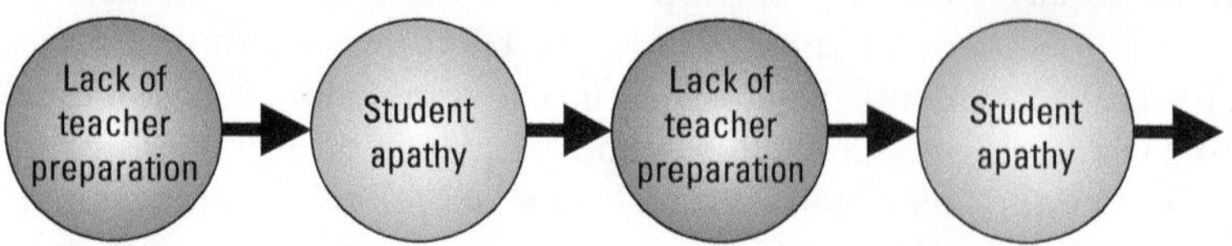

(b) The sequence of events punctuated by the students

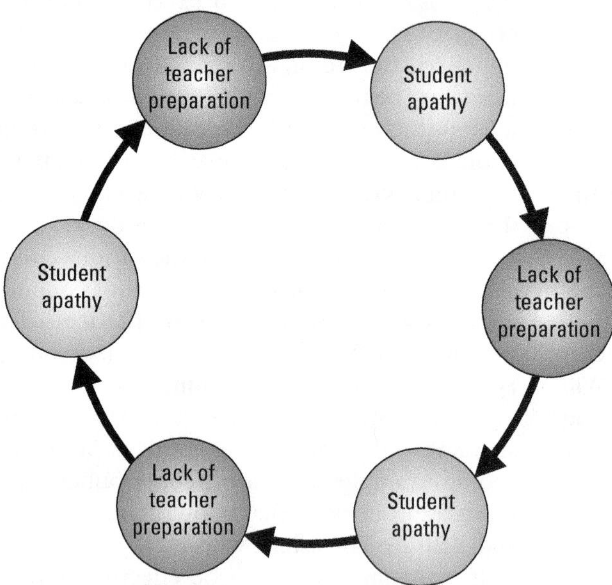

(c) The sequence of events as it exists in reality

Figure 1.5
The Sequence of Events
Try using this three-part figure, discussed in the text, to explain what might go on when Pat complains about Chris's nagging and Chris complains about Pat's avoidance and silence.

the emphasis on minimizing the differences between the two individuals.

Note, however, the problems that can arise in this type of relationship. Consider the situation of a husband and wife, both of whom are aggressive. The aggressiveness of the husband fosters aggressiveness in the wife; the anger of the wife arouses anger in the husband. As this escalates, the aggressiveness can no longer be contained, and the relationship is consumed by aggression.

In a **complementary relationship**, in contrast, the two individuals engage in different behaviors. The behavior of one serves as the stimulus for the complementary behavior of the other. In complementary relationships the differences between the parties are maximized. One partner acts as the superior and the other as the inferior, one is passive and the other active, one strong and the other weak. At times cultures establish such relationships—as, for example, the complementary relationship between teacher and student or between employer and employee. Early marriages are likely to be complementary relationships in which each person tries to complete himself or herself. When these couples separate and form new partnerships, the new relationships are likely to be symmetrical and to involve a kind of reconfirmation of each partner's own identity (Prosky, 1992). Generally, research finds that complementary couples have a lower marital adjustment level than do symmetrical couples (Main & Oliver, 1988; Holden, 1991; McCall & Green, 1991).

A problem in complementary relationships—familiar to many college students—is the situation created by extreme rigidity. Whereas the complementary relationship between a nurturing and pro-

BUILDING COMMUNICATION SKILLS

Resolving Ambiguity

These exercises, presented in Building Communication Skills boxes throughout the text, are designed to stimulate you to think more actively about the concepts and skills covered in the chapter and to help you practice your developing communication skills.

Here are a few ambiguous situations; for each, indicate what you would say to resolve the ambiguity. If possible, try to share your responses with others in a small group and perhaps combine responses to come up with the ideal way to reduce the ambiguity. Or responses from a larger group can be written on index cards (anonymously), collected, and read aloud for the entire group to evaluate.

1. You've been dating Pat on and off for the past six months. Today, Pat asks you to come to dinner and meet the parents. You're not sure if this means that Pat wants to get more serious (which you do not want) or if it's a simple dinner invitation with no additional motives. How might you disambiguate this dinner invitation message?
2. At an appraisal interview, your supervisor says that your work over the last six months has improved considerably—then smiles and says, "But there's always more that we need to do," and then nonverbally indicates that the interview is over and you can return to work. Since you're considering other job offers, you want to know in more detail how your current employer sees you and your prospects for advancement. How might you disambiguate this job appraisal?
3. You receive a written invitation to address the eighth-grade class of your local middle school on careers in communication. The invitation said little more than that a conference on careers is planned and that they are hoping you'll be one of the speakers. This is too ambiguous for you; you need to know in more detail what will be expected of you. How might you disambiguate this invitation to speak?
4. You've been invited to a colleague's house for dinner. Around two hours before you're scheduled to leave for the dinner, it begins to snow, and your colleague calls to say that you shouldn't feel you have to come to dinner in the snow; the roads may get dangerous. The snow is only a light dusting, and your SUV would have no trouble getting there. You wonder what your colleague was really saying—whether it's "I'd like to cancel the dinner and I'm using the snow as an excuse" or "I'm concerned about your safety and I don't want you to travel in potentially dangerous weather just because of this dinner." What do you say?

Messages and relationships are often ambiguous; instead of assuming one interpretation is right and another wrong, it may be useful to try to disambiguate the message and find out exactly what the speaker means.

tective mother and a dependent child is at one stage vital and essential to the life of the child, a **rigid complementarity** when the child is older can become a handicap to further development, if the change so essential to growth is not allowed to occur.

Communication Is Inevitable, Irreversible, and Unrepeatable

Communication is a process that is inevitable, irreversible, and unrepeatable. Communication messages are always being sent (or almost always), can't be reversed or uncommunicated, and are always unique and one-time occurrences. Let's look at these qualities in more detail.

Inevitability

In many instances communication takes place even though one of the individuals does not think he or she is communicating or does not want to communicate. Consider, for example, the student sitting in the back of the classroom with an expressionless face, perhaps staring out the window. Although the student might claim not to be communicating with the

Irreversibility

Without thinking you make some culturally insensitive remarks and even though everyone laughs politely, you want to explain that you're really not the kind of person who normally talks this way.

WHAT DO YOU SAY?

teacher, the teacher may derive any of a variety of messages from this behavior; for example, that the student lacks interest, is bored, or is worried about something. In any event, the teacher is receiving messages even though the student may not intend to communicate. In an interactional situation, you can't avoid communicating (Watzlawick, Beavin, & Jackson, 1967); communication is inevitable. This principle of **inevitability** does not mean, of course, that all behavior is communication. For example, if the student looked out the window and the teacher failed to notice this, no communication would have taken place.

Further, when you're in an interactional situation you can't avoid responding to the messages of others. For example, if you notice someone winking at you, you must respond in some way. Even if you don't respond actively or openly, that lack of response is itself a response, and it communicates. Again, if you don't notice the winking, then obviously communication has not occurred.

Irreversibility

Notice that you can reverse the processes of only some systems. For example, you can turn water into ice and then the ice back into water. And you can repeat this reversal process as many times as you wish. Other systems, however, are irreversible. You can turn grapes into wine, but you can't turn the wine back into grapes—the process can go in only one direction. Communication is such an irreversible process. Once you say something, once you press the send key on your e-mail, you can't uncommunicate it. You can of course try to reduce the effects of your message by saying, for example, "I really didn't mean what I said" or "I was so angry I couldn't think straight." But regardless of how you try to negate or reduce the effects of a message, the message itself, once it has been sent and received, can't be reversed.

Because of **irreversibility** (and unerasability), be careful not to say things you may be sorry for later. Especially in conflict situations, when tempers run high, avoid saying things you may later wish to withdraw. Commitment messages—"I love you" messages and their variants—also need to be monitored. And in group and public communication situations, when messages are received by many people, it's crucial to recognize their irreversibility. Similarly, online messages that could be interpreted as sexist, racist, homophobic, or ageist, which you thought were private or erased from your computer, may later be recalled and retrieved by others, creating all sorts of problems for you and your organization.

As a result of the differences between the permanency of electronic communication and the evanescence of face-to-face communication, you may wish to be cautious in your electronic messages. E-mail is probably your most common form of computer communication, though these cautions also apply to all other forms of electronic communication, including newsgroup postings, instant messages, and website messages. In an organizational context, it's important to find out what the e-mail policy of the company is. One survey found that 75 percent of companies had written e-mail policies but that less than half of all companies surveyed trained their workers in e-mail policies (Coombes, 2003).

- E-mails are difficult to destroy. Often e-mails you think you deleted will remain on servers and workstations and may be retrieved by a clever hacker.
- E-mails can readily be made public; the ease of forwarding e-mails to others or of posting your comments on websites makes it especially important that you consider carefully what you write. The message that you intend for one person may actually be received by many others, too.
- E-mails are not privileged communication and can easily be used against you, especially in the workplace. Criticizing a colleague may one day leave you open to accusations of discrimination. Passing along sexist, racist, homophobic, or ageist "jokes" to a friend may one day fuel accusations of a hostile working environment and cost your employer millions, as such "jokes" cost Chevron a few years ago.
- E-mails provide permanent records: They make it impossible for you to say, for example, "That's not exactly what I said," because exactly what you said will be there in black and white.
- E-mail files may be accessed by others, such as a nosy colleague at the next desk or a visiting neighbor, and can then be sent to additional outsiders.

Unrepeatability

The reason for the **unrepeatability** of communication is simple: Everyone and everything is constantly changing. As a result, you can never recapture the exact same situation, frame of mind, or relationship dynamics that defined a previous communication act. For example, you can never repeat meeting someone for the first time, making a first impression in an interview, or resolving a specific group problem.

You can, of course, try again, as when you say, "I'm sorry I came off so forward, can we try again?" But even after you say this, you have not erased the initial impression. Instead you try to counteract this initial and perhaps negative impression by going through the motions again.

Summary: Human Communication

This unit explained the benefits, forms, and purposes of human communication; the major elements of human communication, and several functional principles that explain how human communication works.

1. Communication is the act, by one or more persons, of sending and receiving messages that occur within a context, are distorted by noise, have some effect (and some ethical dimension), and provide some opportunity for feedback.
2. The major skills to be learned here include self-presentation, relationship, interviewing, group interaction and leadership, and presentation.
3. The major types of human communication are intrapersonal, interpersonal, small group, organizational, public, computer-mediated, and mass communication.
4. Communication is multipurposeful; we use communication to discover, to relate, to help, to persuade, and to play.
5. The universals of communication—the elements present in every communication act—are the context, including culture; source–receiver sending or encoding processes and receiving or decoding processes; messages; channels; noise; feedback and feedforward; effects; and ethics.
6. The communication context has at least four dimensions: physical, social–psychological, temporal, and cultural.
7. Culture consists of the collection of beliefs, attitudes, values, and ways of behavior shared by a group of people and passed down from one generation to the next through communication rather than genes.
8. Communication competence is knowledge of the elements and rules of communication, which vary from one culture to another.
9. Communication is a transactional process in which each person simultaneously sends and receives messages.
10. Noise is anything that distorts a message; it's present to some degree in every communication transaction and may be physical, physiological, psychological, or semantic in origin.
11. Feedback is information or messages that are sent back to the source. It may come from the source itself or from the receiver, and may be characterized along such dimensions as positive and negative, person-focused and message-focused, immediate and delayed, low-monitored and high-monitored, and supportive and critical.
12. Feedforward messages preface other messages and may be used to open the channels of communication, to preview future messages, to disclaim, and to altercast.
13. Communication messages may be of varied forms and may be sent and received through any combination

of sensory organs. The communication channel is the medium through which the messages are sent.

14. Communication always has an effect. Effects may be cognitive, affective, or psychomotor.
15. Ethics in communication consists of the rightness or wrongness—the morality—of a communication transaction. Ethics is integral to every communication transaction.
16. Communication is normally a package of signals, each reinforcing the other. Opposing communication signals from the same source result in contradictory messages.
17. The double bind, a special kind of contradictory message, may be created when contradictory messages are sent simultaneously.
18. Communication is a process of adjustment and takes place only to the extent that the communicators use the same system of signals.
19. Communication involves both content dimensions and relationship dimensions.
20. Communication is ambiguous and often can be interpreted in different ways.
21. Communication sequences are punctuated for processing. Different people divide up the communication sequence into stimuli and responses differently.
22. Communication involves symmetrical and complementary transactions.
23. In any interaction situation, communication is inevitable; you can't avoid communication, nor can you not respond to communication.
24. Communication is irreversible. You can't uncommunicate.
25. Communication is unrepeatable. You can't duplicate a previous communication act.

Key Terms in Human Communication

Here are the essential terms used in this chapter. In addition, flash cards are available online at MyCommunicationLab (www.mycommunicationlab.com) to help you further master the vocabulary of human communication.

adjustment
affirmation
altercasting
ambiguity
channel
code
communication
communication accommodation theory
communication competence
complementary relationship
computer-mediated communication
content and relationship dimensions
content messages
context
culture
decoder
decoding
disclaimer
effect
encoder
encoding
ethics
feedback
feedforward
inevitability
intercultural communication
interpersonal communication
interviewing
intrapersonal communication
irreversibility
mass communication
messages
metacommunication
metamessages
mixed messages
negative feedback
noise
organizational communication
phatic communication
positive feedback
public speaking
punctuation of communication
receiver
relationship messages
responses
rigid complementarity
small group communication
source
stimuli
symmetrical relationship
theory
transactional
unrepeatability

Thinking Critically about Human Communication

1. **Reading Feedback.** Based on your own experiences, do you find that instructors who accurately read and respond to student feedback are better liked than instructors who can't read feedback as accurately? Is there a relationship between the ability to read feedback and the ability to communicate information or to motivate or persuade an audience? In what ways might the ability to give effective feedback influence the growth or deterioration of a relationship?
2. **Feedforward.** In this book there are several examples of feedforward; for example (1) the cover, (2) the "Welcome" section, (3) the tables of contents, (4) each chapter's opening page, (5) each chapter's opening paragraph, and (6) the section headings within units. What more specific purposes do each of these serve?
3. **Online and Off-line Activities.** A report dated August 11, 2004, by the Pew Internet and American Life Project (The Internet and Daily Life, www.pewinternet.org/PPF/r/131/report_display.asp, accessed February 10, 2005) noted that people are more likely to "get news, play games, pay bills, send cards, look up phone numbers and addresses, buy tickets, check sports scores, listen to music, schedule appointments, and communicate with friends" off-line than online. Why do you think this is the case? Do you think the items on this list will change over the next 5 years? Over the next 20 years?
4. **Synchronous and Asynchronous Messaging.** In face-to-face and chat room communication, messages are exchanged with virtually no delay; communication is synchronous. In other forms of communication—for example, snail or e-mail and blog posts—the messages may be exchanged with considerable delay; communication here is asynchronous. What differences in communication style can you attribute to synchronicity and asynchronicity?
5. **Inevitability, Irreversibility, and Unrepeatability.** Identify one or two or three rules or guidelines that the concepts of inevitability, irreversibility, and unrepeatability would suggest for each of the following situations: (a) the first day at a new job, (b) asking for a date, (c) a face-to-face job interview, (d) chatting in an online group, (e) meeting with a dying friend, (f) popping the question, (g) introducing yourself in class, (h) arguing with your romantic partner, (i) seeing an old friend after many years, (j) giving a speech to regain the goodwill of the people, and (k) leading a group of colleagues in a brainstorming session.

Log On! My Communication Lab

WWW.MYCOMMUNICATIONLAB.COM

MyCommunicationLab will provide you with a broad collection of materials that will help you master the theory and skills of this course and this text; it will also make your experience in this course more enjoyable and more varied. There are practice tests, crossword puzzles, videos, and figures and tables from a variety of books; all of these will prove useful supplements for each unit in the text. At the end of each unit you'll find a brief note of just some of the materials available on MCL that are relevant to the unit.

For Unit 1, visit MCL for such exercises as the following: Using Communication Channels, Modeling Human Communication, Responding to Contradictory Messages, Symmetrical and Complementary Relationships, Applying the Principles, Analyzing an Interaction, Principles of Communication, and Communication Competence.

While in MCL click on the Research Navigator tab and you'll find a wealth of research materials that you can use throughout this course and especially in the public speaking section.

CHAPTER

2

Language Development

Taken from *Development of Language*, Eighth Edition, by Jean Berko Gleason and Nan Bernstein Ratner.

By the time they are 3 or 4 years old, children everywhere in the world have acquired the major elements of the languages spoken around them, regardless of how complex they may be. The development of language is an amazing, yet basically universal, human achievement. It poses some of the most challenging theoretical and practical questions of our times: Does an infant, or even the developing fetus, process language? If so, what aspects of speech and language can they perceive? What if no one spoke to them—would children invent language by themselves? How do young children acquire complex grammar? Are humans unique, or do other animals have language as we define it? What if we raised a chimp as if it were our own child—would it learn to use language in the same way that a human child does? Do parrots who talk know what they are saying? Are there theories that can adequately account for language development? Is language a separate capacity, or is it simply one facet of our general cognitive ability? What is it that individuals actually must know in order to have full adult competence in language, and to what extent is the development of those skills representative of universal processes? What about individual differences? What happens when language develops atypically, and is there anything we can do about it? What happens to language skills as one grows older: What do we lose, and what, if anything, gets better as we age? These are some of the questions that intrigue researchers in language development, and they have led to the plan of this book.

Once children begin to acquire language, they make rapid progress. By the time they are of school age and even before they can read, they can vary their speech to suit the social and communicative nature of a situation; they know the meaning and pronunciation of literally thousands of words, and they use the major sentence types and grammatical forms—subjects, objects, verbs, plurals, and tenses—of their language quite correctly. Language development, however, does not cease when people reach school age, nor, for that matter, adolescence or maturity; language development continues throughout our lives. The reorganization and reintegration of mental processes that are typical of other intellectual functions can also be seen in language, as the changes that accompany maturity lead to modification of linguistic capacity. This book, therefore, is written from a developmental perspective that covers the entire life span. Although most studies of language development have centered on children, the questions we ask require the study of mature and aging individuals as well.

This chapter is divided into four major sections. The first section provides a brief overview of *the course of language development* from early infancy to old age. It serves as a preview of the chapters that follow.

The second section notes some of the unique *biological foundations* for language that make its development possible in humans. Our biological endowment is necessary but not sufficient to ensure language development, which does not occur without social interaction.

The third section describes the major *linguistic systems* that individuals must acquire. Rather than endorsing any particular linguistic theory, we present descriptive information that has provided the framework for much basic research in language acquisition. More technical linguistic material is presented in the chapters devoted to particular topics such as the acquisition of syntax or of the sound system. If there is a unifying perspective that the authors of this book share, it is the view that individuals acquire during their lives an **internalized representation** of language that is systematic in nature and amenable to study.

The fourth and final section of this chapter focuses on the background and methods of the *study of language development*.

An Overview of the Course of Language Development

Communication Development in Infancy

Even before babies are born, they are listening to the language spoken around them: Research shows that newborns prefer to hear the language or languages they heard while *in utero*. During their first months, infants have communicative abilities that underlie language, long before they say their first words. Babies are intensely social beings: They gaze into the eyes of their caregivers and are sensitive to the emotional tone of the voices around them. They pay attention to the language spoken to them; they take their turn in conversation, even if that turn is only a burble. If they want something, they learn to make their intentions known. In addition to possessing the social motivations that are evidenced so early in life, infants are also physiologically equipped to process incoming speech signals; they are even capable of making fine distinctions among speech sounds. By the age of 6 months, babies have already begun to categorize the sounds of their own language, much as adult speakers do. By the age of about 11 months, many babies understand 50 or more common words, and point happily at the right person when someone asks, "Where's Daddy?"

At approximately the same age that they take their first steps, many infants produce their first words. Like walking, early language appears at around the same age and in much the same way all over the world, regardless of their society or culture or the characteristics of the language that is being acquired.

Phonological Development: Learning Sounds and Sound Patterns

Midway through their first year, infants begin to babble, playing with sound much as they play with their fingers and toes. Early in their second year, for most children, the babbling of the prelinguistic infant gives way to words. There has been considerable controversy over the relation between babbling and talking, but most researchers now agree that babbling blends into early speech and may continue even after the appearance of recognizable words. Once infants have begun to speak, the course of language development appears to have some universal characteristics. Typically, toddlers' early utterances contain only one word, usually a word that is simple to pronounce and concrete in meaning. It is important to recognize that different constraints act upon the child's **comprehension** and **production** of a particular form and that children may comprehend things more sophisticated than what they are able to say. Some sounds are more difficult to pronounce than others, and combinations of consonants may prove particularly problematic. Within a given language, or when acquiring more than one language, children solve the phonological problems they encounter in varying ways.

Semantic Development: Learning the Meanings of Words

The ways in which speakers relate words to their referents and their meanings are the subject matter of **semantic development.** Just as there are constraints on the phonological shapes of children's early words, there appear to be limits on the kinds of meanings of those early words; for instance, very young children's vocabularies are more likely to contain words that refer to objects that move *(bus)* than objects that are immobile *(bench)*. Their vocabularies reflect their daily lives and are unlikely to refer to events that are distant in time or space or to anything of an abstract nature. Early words like *hi, doggie, Mommy,* and *juice* refer to the objects, events, and people in the child's immediate surroundings. As they enter the school years, children's words become increasingly complex and interconnected, and children also gain a new kind of knowledge: **metalinguistic awareness.** This new ability makes it possible for them to think about their language, understand what words are, and even define them.

Putting Words Together: Morphology and Syntax in the Preschool Years

Sometime during their second year, after they know about fifty words, most children progress to a stage of two-word combinations. Words that they said in the one-word stage are now combined into these brief utterances, without articles, prepositions, inflections, or any of the other grammatical modifications that adult language requires. The child can now say such things as "That doggie," meaning "That is a doggie," and "Mommy juice," meaning "Mommy's juice," or "Mommy, give me my juice," or "Mommy is drinking her juice."

An examination of children's two-word utterances in many different language communities has shown that everywhere in the world children at this age are expressing the same kinds of thoughts and intentions in the same kinds of utterances. They ask for more of something; they say no to something; they notice something, or they notice that it has disappeared. This leads them to produce utterances like "More milk!" "No bed!" "Hi, kitty!" and "All-gone cookie!"

A little later in the two-word stage, another dozen or so kinds of meanings appear. For instance, children may name an actor and a verb: "Daddy eat." They may modify a noun: "Bad doggie." They may specify a location: "Kitty table." They may name a verb and an object, leaving out the subject: "Eat lunch." At this stage children are expressing these basic meanings, but they cannot use the language forms that indicate number, gender, and tense. Toddler language is in the here and now; there is no tomorrow and no yesterday in language at the two-word stage. What children can say is closely related to their level of cognitive and social development, and a child who cannot conceive of the past is unlikely to speak of it. As the child's utterances grow longer, grammatical forms begin to appear. In English, articles, prepositions, and inflections representing number, person, and tense begin to be heard. Although the two-word stage has some universal characteristics across all languages, what is acquired next depends on the features of the language being learned. English-speaking children learn the articles *a* and *the,* but in a language such as Russian, there are no articles. Russian grammar, on the other hand, has features that English grammar does not. One remarkable finding has been that children acquiring a given language do so in essentially the same order. In English, for instance, children learn *in* and *on* before other prepositions such as *under.* After they learn regular plurals and pasts, like *juices* and *heated,* they create some **overregularized** forms of their own, like *gooses* and *eated.*

Researchers account for children's early utterances in varying ways. Research in the field that was originally inspired by the linguistic theories that began to emerge in the 1960s interpreted early word combinations as evidence that the child was a young cryptographer, endowed with a cognitive impetus to develop syntax and a grammatical system. In more recent times, the child's intentions and need to communicate them to others have been offered as explanations of grammatical development. However, children's unique ability to acquire complex grammar, regardless of the motivation behind it, remains at the heart of linguistic inquiry.

Language in Social Contexts: Development of Communicative Competence

Language development includes acquiring the ability to use language appropriately in a multiplicity of social situations. This complex ability is often referred to as **communicative competence**. The system of rules that dictates the way language is used to accomplish social ends is often called **pragmatics**. An individual who acquires the phonology, morphology, syntax, and semantics of a language has acquired **linguistic competence**. A sentence such as "Pardon me, sir, but might I borrow your pencil for a moment?" certainly shows that the speaker has linguistic competence, since it is perfectly grammatical. If, however, this sentence is addressed to your grandmother, it is just as certainly inappropriate. Linguistic competence is not sufficient; speakers must also acquire communicative competence, which goes beyond linguistic competence to include the ability to use language appropriately in many different situations. In other words, it requires knowledge of the social rules for language use, or pragmatics. During the preschool years, young children learn to respond to social situations by making polite requests or clarifying their own utterances. Their parents are typically eager that they learn to be polite. Parents' intuitions about the importance of using language in socially appropriate ways are borne out by research that shows that inappropriate children are often unpopular or disliked. Speakers ultimately learn important variations in language that serve to mark their gender, regional origin, social class, and occupation. Other necessary variations are associated with such things as the social setting, topic of discourse, and characteristics of the person being addressed.

Theoretical Approaches to Language Acquisition

In general, explaining what it is that children acquire during the course of language development is easier than explaining how they do it. Do parents shape their children's early babbling into speech through reinforcement and teaching strategies? Or is language perhaps an independent and **innate** faculty, built into the human biobehavioral system? Learning theorists and linguistic theorists do not agree on these basic principles. Between the theoretical poles represented by learning theorists on the one hand and linguistic theorists on the other lie three different interactionist perspectives.

1. *Cognitive interactionists* who rely primarily on the theories of Piaget believe that language is just one facet of human cognition and that children in acquiring language are basically learning to pair words with concepts they have already acquired. Other, more recent, cognitive interactionists study language from the perspective of the neural architecture that supports it. They see children as processors of information, and they use computers to model the ways neural connections supporting language are strengthened through exposure to adult speech.
2. *Social interactionists* emphasize the child's motivation to communicate with others. They emphasize the role that the special features of **child-directed speech (CDS)** may play in facilitating children's language acquisition.
3. *Gestural and usage-based theorists* are more concerned with the roots of language that are demonstrated when even very young children

begin to communicate through gestures, pointing, shared attention, and other nonverbal but goal-directed and social behaviors.

Variation in Language Development: Implications for Research and Theory

Even though this brief overview has emphasized the regularities and continuities that have been observed in the development of language, it is important to know that individual differences have been found in almost every aspect of the process, even during the earliest period of development. In the acquisition of phonology, for instance, some children are quite conservative and avoid words they have difficulty pronouncing; others are willing to take a chance. Early words and early word combinations reveal different strategies in acquiring language. Although much research has been devoted to finding commonalities in language acquisition across children, it is important to remember that there is also variation in the onset of speech, the rate at which language develops, and the style of language used by the child. This should not surprise us; we know that babies differ in temperament, cognitive style, and in many other ways. In addition, children's early language may reflect their social class, their gender, whether they are growing up mono- or bilingual, and preferences of adults in their society; for instance, American parents stress the names of things, but nouns are not so important in all societies. Any comprehensive theory of language development must account for individual differences; those who work with children must be aware of them.

Atypical Language Development

Language has been a human endowment for so many millennia that it is exceptionally robust. There are conditions, however, that may lead to atypical language development—for instance, sensory problems such as deafness. In this case the capacity for language is intact, but lack of accessible auditory input makes the acquisition of oral language difficult. In some cases, technology can provide access to the auditory signal using hearing aids or cochlear implants; in other cases, children with hearing impairment who learn a manual language such as **American Sign Language (ASL)** are able to communicate in a complete and sophisticated language.

Children who are diagnosed with intellectual disability, such as most children with **Down syndrome**, may show rather standard patterns of language development, but at a slower rate than typically developing children. On the other hand, children with **autism spectrum disorder** and those with **pervasive developmental disorder** frequently exhibit patterns of language development that are atypical in multiple ways; they may have particular problems, for instance, in understanding what other people know and in adjusting their language accordingly. Occasionally children suffer from **specific language impairment**, problems in language development accompanied by no other obvious physical, sensory, or emotional difficulties. Still other children have particular problems producing speech, even though their internal representation of language is intact: They may stutter or have motor or physical impairments.

Language and Literacy in the School Years

By the time they get to kindergarten, children have amassed a vocabulary of about 8,000 words, and they can handle questions, negative statements, dependent clauses, compound sentences, and a great variety of other constructions. They have also learned much more than vocabulary and grammar—they have learned to use language in many different social situations. They can, for instance, talk baby talk to babies, tell jokes to their friends, and speak politely to strangers. Their communicative competence is growing.

During the school years, children are increasingly called upon to interact with peers; peer speech is quite different from speech to parents, and it is often both humorous and inventive. Jokes, riddles, and play with language constitute a substantial portion of schoolchildren's spontaneous speech. Faced with many new models, school-age children also learn from television and films, and their speech may be marked by expressions from their favorite entertainments.

New cognitive attainments in the school years make it possible for children to talk in ways that they could not as preschoolers, and they develop **metalinguistic awareness**, the ability to think about language itself. They become increasingly adept at producing connected, multi-utterance speech and can create narratives that describe their past experiences. To succeed in school, children must also learn to use **decontextualized language**: language that is not tied to the here and now. They develop the ability to provide explanations and descriptions using decontextualized language.

The attainment of literacy marks a major milestone in children's development, and it calls upon both their metalinguistic abilities (for instance, they must understand what a word is) and their new abilities to use decontextualized language. Study of the cognitive processes involved in reading and the development of adequate models that represent the acquisition of this skill are two topics that actively involve researchers in developmental psycholinguistics.

Children who come from literate households know a great deal about reading and writing before formal instruction begins and thus are at an advantage in school. Children who are bilingual may have some advantages in the acquisition of the metalinguistic knowledge that develops in the school years. Once children have acquired the ability to read and write, these new skills, in turn, have profound effects upon their spoken language. Learning to read is not an easy task for all children; this extremely complex activity requires intricate coordination of a number of separate abilities. Humans have been speaking since the earliest days of our prehistory, but reading has been a common requirement only in very modern times; we should not be surprised, therefore, that reading skills vary greatly in the population. Reading problems, such as **dyslexia**, pose serious theoretical and practical problems for the psycholinguistic researcher.

Developments in the Adult Years

In the normal course of events, language development, like cognitive development, moral development, or psychological development, continues beyond the point where the individual has assumed the outward appearance of an adult. During the teen years, young people acquire their own special style, and part of being a successful teenager rests in knowing how to talk like one. Then, in adulthood, there are new linguistic attainments.

Language is involved in psychological development, and one of the major life tasks facing young people is the formation of an identity—a sense of who they are. A distinct personal linguistic style is part of one's special identity. Further psychological goals of early adulthood that call for new or expanded linguistic skills include both entering the world of work and establishing intimate adult relations with others. Language development during the adult years varies greatly among individuals, depending on such things as their education and social and occupational roles. Actors, for instance, must learn not only to be heard by large audiences but to speak the words of others using varying voices and regional dialects. Working people learn the special tones of voice and terminology associated with their own occupational register or code.

With advancing age, numerous linguistic changes take place. For instance, some word-finding difficulty is inevitable; the inability to produce a name that is "on the tip of the tongue" is a phenomenon that becomes increasingly familiar as one gets older. Hearing loss and memory impairment can affect an older person's ability to communicate. However, not all changes are for the worse: Vocabulary increases, as does narrative skill. In preliterate societies, for instance, the official storytellers are typically older members of the community. Although most individuals remain linguistically vigorous in their later years, language deterioration becomes severe for some, and they may lose both comprehension and voluntary speech. The **aphasias** and **dementias** exact their linguistic toll on affected individuals, whose speech may become as limited as that of young children.

The Biological Bases of Language

Animal Communication Systems

Human language has special properties that have led many researchers to conclude that it is both **species specific** and **species uniform**; that is, it is unique (specific) in the human species and essentially similar, or uniform in all of members of our human species (Lenneberg, 1967; Pääbo, 2003). The characteristics that distinguish human language are illuminated when they are compared with those of nonhuman animal communication systems. Other animals are clearly able to communicate at some level with one another as well as with humans. Cats and dogs meow and bark in varied ways and are able to convey a variety of messages to us by methods such as scratching at the door or looking expectantly at their dishes. These signals are limited in scope and clearly not language, although one enterprising Japanese inventor has devised an electronic collar intended to translate your dog's different barks (Gregory, 2009). (It is not clear how well this device, called BowLingual, works, but in 2002 its inventors received an Ig Nobel Prize for "promoting peace and harmony between the species.")

Bee Communication

Bees have been shown to have an elaborate communication system. The ethologist Karl von Frisch (1950) began to study bees in the 1920s and won a Nobel Prize in 1973 for his studies of bee communication.

Unlike the expressive meowing of a hungry cat, in many senses the communication system of the bee is referential—it tells other bees about, or refers to, something in the outside world. A bee returning to the hive after finding nectar-filled flowers collects an audience and then performs a dance that indicates the direction and the approximate distance of the nectar from the hive. Other bees watch, join the dance, and then head for the flowers. The bee's dance is actually a miniature form of the trip to the flowers rather than a symbolic statement. There is nothing symbolic or arbitrary about dancing toward the north to indicate that other bees should fly in that direction. Moreover, although the movements of the dance have structure and meaning, there is only one possible conversational topic: where to find nectar. Even this repertoire is seriously limited; bees cannot, for instance, tell one another that the flowers are pretty or that they are bored with their job.

Nonprimate Mammals and Birds

Many animals have ways of communicating with other members of their species. Dolphins, who are intelligent and social mammals, employ elaborate systems of whistles that can be heard at a distance by other dolphins under water. This vocal communication reflects highly developed skills on which dolphins rely in surroundings that would make visual interactions difficult. During the first year of its life, each baby bottlenose dolphin learns a "signature whistle" by which it can be recognized (Tyack, 2000). Later on, bottlenose dolphins display vocal learning behaviors that are seen in birds but not in other nonhuman mammals. They are able to imitate the whistles of other dolphins and use this "whistle matching" when they address one another (Janik, 2000).

African elephants communicate with one another in many ways, including seismically. They have as many as twenty-five different vocal calls and a number of "rumbles" that are below the threshold of human hearing. These subsonic communications are carried through the ground and can be sensed and understood by other elephants as much as a dozen miles away. In one study, Namibian elephants reacted to long-distance predator warnings given by members of their own group, but were unimpressed by similar warnings issued by unfamiliar Kenyan elephants (O'Connell, 2007).

Some birds use a variety of meaningful calls to court one another, to warn of danger, or to indicate that it is time to fly home. The eerie cry of the loon is just one of a number of distinct and meaningful calls made by these inhabitants of northern lakes. Recent research reveals that male loons convey information about their size to potential rivals through the auditory frequency of their yodels (Piper, Mager, & Walcott, 2011).

All of these communication systems are useful for the creatures that use them, and each one resembles human language in some respect, but they are all tied to the stimulus situation, limited to the "here and now" and to a restricted set of messages. Human language has characteristics not found in their entirety in these other systems.

Not all researchers agree on the list of criteria that should be used in describing true *language.* However, most would agree on at least these three, cited by Roger Brown (1973):

1. True language is marked by *productivity* in the sense that speakers can make many new utterances and can recombine or expand the forms they already know to say things they have never heard before. This feature is also called *recombination, recursion,* or *generativity,* depending on the author and emphasis.
2. It also has *semanticity* (or *symbolism*); that is, language represents ideas, events, and objects symbolically. A word is a symbol that stands for something else.
3. Language offers the possibility of *displacement*—messages need not be tied to the immediate context.

Human language is unique because it enables its users to comment on any aspect of their experience and to consider the past and the future, as well as referents that may be continents away or only in the imagination. The natural communication systems of nonhumans do not meet these criteria of language.

Alex could tell you what color the blocks are, and he could count them as well.

Attempts to teach human language to talking birds, however, have produced some extremely provocative results. For instance, an African grey parrot named Alex knew the word *yummy* and he knew the word *bread.* When someone brought in a birthday cake, something he had never seen before, he tasted his portion and exclaimed, "Yummy bread!" The ability to combine communicative concepts as shown in this example has long been thought to be exclusive to humans. Alex could recognize the colors, shapes, and numbers of objects and answer novel questions about them in English. Faced with an array of blocks, he was asked, "How many blue blocks?" Alex correctly answered, "six." He was right about 80 percent of the time (Pepperberg & Gordon, 2005).

Experiments with a number of young grey parrots have shown that they can learn to label common objects if they have human tutors who provide interactive lessons; they do not learn from passive listening to lessons on audio recordings or from watching videos, but do best when the words are presented in context by a friendly and informative person. Interacting with a parrot can be an unnerving experience—one that makes us marvel that a bird whose brain is the size of a walnut can speak to us in clear and appropriate human language. Do African grey parrots have the same sort of linguistic skill human children do? One view is that they do not and that the birds are responding to complex learned cues. Another interpretation of the evidence is that language is not a unitary set of features, but a continuum on which grey parrots have clearly alighted. Although Alex died unexpectedly at the relatively young age of 31 in 2007, further research with African grey parrots continues.

Dogs have recently made their entrance into the comprehension side of the human language arena. Dogs are not able to produce human words, except, after much coaxing, some very limited approximations to expressions such as "I love you." A version of this modified yowling by a husky named Mishka has been viewed approximately 48 million times on YouTube (www.youtube.com/watch?v=qXo3NFqkaRM). There is, however some recent intriguing research on language comprehension by a breed often viewed as the smartest of all pups, the border collie. In one set of studies, a border collie named Chaser acquired the names of 1,022 objects during a three-year training period and could very accurately select a toy with the right name from a large array. Even more impressive, Chaser was able to infer that a name she had never heard before belonged to a new, unnamed object among the ones she already knew. For instance, an unfamiliar doll was included among her toys. When asked to bring "Darwin," a name she had not heard before, she correctly inferred that the unfamiliar name belonged to the unfamiliar object and promptly delivered the doll (Pilley & Reid, 2011). By inferring that a new name must belong to a novel object, Chaser was demonstrating a principle of vocabulary acquisition commonly ascribed to human children.

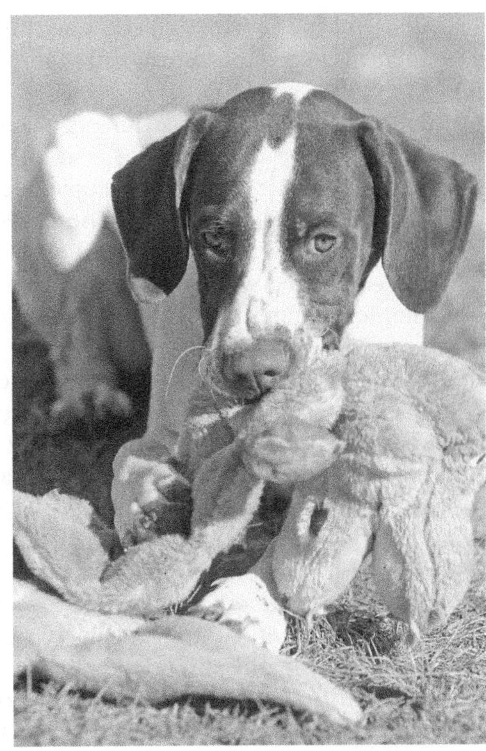

Dominic knows the names of his toys and will bring you the right one if you ask him for the alligator.

Primate Language

Researchers have long wondered if primates are capable of learning human language. Chimpanzees, in particular, have been the subject of much research. Chimpanzees are intelligent, social, and communicative animals. They use a variety of vocal cries in the wild, including a food bark and a danger cry. There have been numerous attempts to teach language to chimpanzees, who possess genetic structures very similar to our own and are our closest relatives in the animal world, and at least one major gorilla language project is still ongoing (Tanner, Patterson, & Byrne, 2006). Koko the gorilla is now more than 40 years old and knows thousands of signs and words. Her trainer, Francine Patterson, has also reported that Koko is able to express very human-like feelings, such as her sadness at the death of a kitten. Koko is featured in books and films and on her own web site. The chimpanzee studies have provided us with much useful and controversial data on the ability of nonhumans to acquire human language.

Gua and Viki. In 1931 Indiana University professor Winthrop Kellogg and his wife, Luella, became the first American family to raise a chimpanzee and a child together (Kellogg, 1980). The Kelloggs brought an infant chimpanzee named Gua into their home; she stayed with them and their infant son, Donald, for 9 months. No special effort was made to teach Gua to talk, and although she was ahead of Donald in her motor development, she did not babble and did not learn to say any words. Some wonderful old films comparing Donald and Gua are available on the Internet. See, for instance, www.archive.org/details/comparative_tests_on_human_chimp_infants.

In the 1940s psychologists Catherine and Keith Hayes (Hayes, 1951) set out to raise a baby chimpanzee named Viki as if she were their own child. This included outfitting her in little dresses and introducing her to strangers as their daughter. (One horrified motel owner actually believed that Catherine Hayes had given birth to Viki.) The Hayeses tried to teach language to Viki. They assumed that chimpanzees were rather like children with developmental delays and that with love and patient instruction Viki would learn to talk. After six years of training, Viki understood a great deal, but she was able to produce, with great difficulty, only four words: *mama, papa, cup,* and *up.* She was never able to say more, and in order to pronounce a /p/, she had to hold her lips together with her fingers. The Hayeses' research with Viki showed that chimpanzees do not have the specialized articulatory and physiological abilities that make spoken language possible.

After these failed experiments, other researchers began to realize that true language need not be spoken. The Deaf community in the United States, for instance, uses a gestural rather than a spoken language, American Sign Language (ASL). ASL is a complete language, with its own grammar and a rich vocabulary, all of which can be conveyed by facial expression, movements of the upper torso, and the shape and movement of the hands in front of the body; it is the equal of vocal language in its capacity to communicate complex human thought (Klima & Bellugi, 1979; Hoza, 2008). A new appreciation of the richness of ASL led to innovative experiments with chimpanzees.

Washoe. The first attempt to capitalize on the ability to comprehend language and the natural gestural ability of a chimpanzee by teaching her signed human language was made by Beatrice and Allen Gardner at the University of Nevada in 1966 (Gardner & Gardner, 1969). The Gardners moved a 10-month-old chimpanzee named Washoe into a trailer behind their house and began to teach her ASL. Washoe became a chimp celebrity. During the time she was involved in this project, she learned over 130 ASL signs, as well as how to combine them into utterances of several signs (Gardner & Gardner, 1994). On seeing her trainer, she was able to sign "Please tickle hug hurry," "Gimme food drink," and similar requests.

Washoe was able to sign many of the same things that are said by children in the early stages of language acquisition before they learn the grammatical refinements of their own language (Brown, 1970; Van Cantfort & Rimpau, 1982). Unlike English-speaking children, she did not pay attention to word order, and at the time her training ceased in the fifty-first month, it was not clear whether her sign language was actually grammatically structured in the sense that even a young child's is (Brown, 1970; Klima & Bellugi, 1972). However, through vocabulary tests of Washoe, as well as of several other chimpanzees they worked with, the Gardners were able to demonstrate that children's and chimpanzees' first 50 words are very similar.

The chimpanzees studied by the Gardners also extended, or generalized, their words in much the same way that humans do—for instance, calling a hat they had never seen before *hat.* The question of whether a chimpanzee is capable of syntax remained open. This is an important theoretical question, because syntax makes *productivity*—one of the hallmarks of human language—possible. On the practical side, the remarkable successes attained with chimps led to innovative programs that teach sign language to children with communication disorders (Toth, 2009).

Nim Chimpsky. An attempt to answer the question of whether chimpanzees can make grammatical sentences was made by a professor at Columbia University, Herbert S. Terrace (1980). Terrace adopted a young male chimp, whom he named Nim Chimpsky (a play on the name of Noam Chomsky, the well-known linguist who emphasizes the uniquely human ability to use language). The plan was to raise Nim in a rich human environment, teach him ASL, and then analyze the chimp's emerging ability to combine signs into utterances, paying special attention to any evidence that he could indeed produce grammatical signed sentences. Nim began to sign early: He produced his first sign, "drink," when he was only 4 months old. However, his later utterances never progressed much beyond the two- or three-sign stage.

He signed "Eat Nim" and "Banana me eat," but when he made four-sign utterances, he added no new information, and unlike even young children, he used no particular word order. He signed "Banana me eat banana," in which the additional word is merely repetitive. Analyzing the extensive data collected in this project, Terrace concluded that there was no evidence that the chimp could produce anything that might be called a sentence.

An even more serious question regarding the chimpanzee's linguistic capability was raised after Terrace and his associates studied the videotaped interactions of young Nim and his many teachers. They found that Nim understood little about conversational turn taking, often interrupting his teachers, and that very little of what Nim signed actually originated with the chimp. Most of what he signed was prompted by the teacher and contained major constituents of the teacher's prior signed utterance to him.

Terrace carried his study further by analyzing films made available to him by other ape-language projects and arrived at the same conclusion: Much of what the chimps signed had just been signed to them. The signing chimps appeared to be responding at least in part to subtle cues from their trainers. Armed with this information, some critics went so far as to suggest that the chimps were modern equivalents of Clever Hans. Clever Hans was a horse who was famous for his mental powers in early twentieth-century Germany, until it was discovered that, rather than doing arithmetic, he was sensitive to minute physical cues in the people around him who knew the answers to the questions he was being asked. The question of the apes' potential was not completely settled by this study, since, as other researchers pointed out, children also interrupt and repeat parts of what adults say. Also, as Terrace himself was aware, the project had various shortcomings; for instance, Nim may have had too many trainers, and not all of them were equally proficient in ASL. Nim Chimpsky died in 2000 at the age of 26. The story of the project was recently chronicled by Hess (2008), and a major Hollywood film about this experiment, called *Project Nim,* came out in 2011.

Kanzi. Although it may be true that apes are not capable of adult language as we know it, the chimpanzee studies have indicated that there are substantial similarities between very young children's and chimpanzees' abilities to engage in symbolic communication. Early chimpanzee studies used the common chimp (*Pan troglodytes*) and had the same self-limiting characteristic: The common chimp can become difficult, even dangerous, to work with once sexual maturity is attained.

Research by D. M. Rumbaugh and E. S. Savage-Rumbaugh with a pygmy chimp, or bonobo (*P. paniscus*) named Kanzi, who was born in 1980 and now lives at the Great Ape Trust of Iowa in Des Moines (Rumbaugh, Savage-Rumbaugh, King, & Taglialatela , 2011), led to new speculation about primate cultural and linguistic abilities. The bonobo was virtually unheard of until the mid-1970s, when they were found in the remote rain forests of the Democratic Republic of Congo. Bonobos are smaller, less aggressive, more social, more intelligent, and more communicative than the common chimp. Kanzi surprised his trainers when he acquired some manual signs merely by observing his mother's lessons. He has been the subject of an intensive longitudinal study, and he understands complex language and at least 500 spoken words. Studies of his understanding of spoken English show that he comprehends word order and basic syntax. For instance, if asked to "Put the milk in the jelly" or to "Put the jelly in the milk," Kanzi obligingly does so, proving that he is attending to language word order and not simply carrying out activities that are evident from the nonverbal situation. He became a father in 2010 with the birth of his son, Teco. Kanzi now has a complex social life; he makes tools and engages in artistic and musical activities, and his accomplishments have gone far beyond those of any of the earlier chimps. Kanzi's linguistic abilities remain at the level of a 2- or 3-year-old child. It is not clear whether his (or any nonhuman's) linguistic skills are on the same continuum as our own, or if they are qualitatively different (Trachsel, 2010). You can read about Kanzi and his companions online at www.greatapetrust.org.

The Biological Base: Humans

Language in humans is clearly dependent on their having a society in which to learn it, other humans to speak to, and the emotional motivation and intelligence to make it possible; humans have also evolved with specialized capacities for speech and neural mechanisms related to language. Recent work in genetics has pointed to a specific gene, *FOXP2,* that is related to speech and language and that may have been the result of a mutation that occurred in our ancestors about 120,000 years ago (Pääbo, 2003). It is clear, however, that no single gene could account for the complexity and robustness of human language. Other genes have also been implicated in language development, such as those referred to as ASPM and MCPH1, and current thinking in the molecular genetics world is that these genes are regulatory in nature and that they are part of a complex signaling system that affects many different traits (Misyak & Christiansen, 2011).

Children who are physiologically and psychologically intact will acquire the language of those around them if they grow up among people who speak to them. This human social interaction is necessary; there is no evidence that infants can acquire language from watching television, for instance. There are some strong arguments for the case that language is biologically determined—that it owes its existence to specialized structures in the brain and in the neurological systems of humans. Some of these biological specifications underlie the social and affective characteristics of infants that tie them to the adults around them and serve as precursors to language development. For instance, infants are intensely interested in human faces, and there is evidence that the infant brain contains neurons that are specialized for the identification of human faces and for the recognition of emotions in faces (Locke, 1993). As they interact with the people around them, infants build a social brain that helps direct them to the information that is important to process—speech sounds, for instance, and not a variety of environmental noises.

Researchers are currently intrigued by the discovery of **mirror neurons** and their possible role in cognitive, linguistic, and social development (Fogassi & Ferarri, 2007). Mirror neurons are a class of neurons that activate when an individual either engages in an activity or observes another engage in that activity, or hears associated sounds (Kohler, Keysers, Umiltà, Fogassi, Gallese, & Rizzolatti, 2002). Mirror neurons may be an integral part of what we recognize as empathy and imitation—the explanation, for instance, for why it is that when you stick your tongue out at a newborn baby, she then sticks her tongue out at you! One of the many implications for language development is the likelihood that when adults speak to babies, they are actually activating the infants' neural patterns for language.

Language-Sensitive Areas in the Brain

Unlike our relatives the apes, humans have areas in the cerebral cortex that are known to be associated with language. Language, however, is not *in* those areas of the brain. The contemporary view is very much that language localization patterns result from the dynamic activity of neural networks that are constantly optimizing the storage and retrieval of information (Ross, 2010). The two hemispheres of the brain are not symmetrical (Geschwind, 1982). Most individuals, about 85 percent of the population, are right-handed, and almost all right-handers have their language functions represented in their left hemisphere. Of the left-handed population, perhaps half also have their language sensitive areas in the left hemisphere; therefore, the vast majority of the populace is **lateralized** for language in the left hemisphere. The right hemisphere, however, also participates in some aspects of language processing. For instance, recognition of the emotional tone of speech appears to be a right-hemisphere function.

Imaging techniques such as functional magnetic resonance imaging (fMRI) have made it possible to study the normal brain in action. Before imaging techniques were developed, most of our information about specialized areas came from the study of what happens when the brain is injured, through an accident, for instance, or as a result of a stroke. Damage to the language-sensitive areas of the brain results in **aphasia**, a generalized communication disorder with varying characteristics depending on the site of the lesion (Goodglass, 1993). There are at least three well-established major language-related areas in the left hemisphere (see Figure 2.1).

- **Broca's area** in the left frontal region (inferior frontal gyrus) is very near to that part of the motor strip that controls the tongue and lips, and damage to Broca's area results in a typical aphasic syndrome, called *Broca's aphasia,* in which the patient has good comprehension but much difficulty with pronunciation and producing the little words of the language, such as articles and prepositions. For instance, when one patient seen in Boston was asked how he planned to spend the weekend at home, he replied, with labored articulation, "Boston College. Football. Saturday."
- **Wernicke's area** is located in the posterior left temporal lobe, near the auditory association areas of the brain. Damage to Wernicke's area produces an aphasia that is characterized by fluent speech with many **neologisms** (nonsense words) and poor comprehension. One patient with Wernicke's aphasia, when asked to name an ashtray, said, "That's a fremser." When he was later asked to point to the fremser, however, he had no idea what the examiner meant.
- The **arcuate fasciculus** is a band of subcortical fibers that connects Wernicke's area with Broca's area (see Figure 2.1). If you ask someone to repeat what you say, the incoming message is processed in Wernicke's area and then sent out over the arcuate fasciculus to Broca's area, where it is programmed for production. Patients with lesions in the arcuate fasciculus are unable to repeat; their disorder is called **conduction aphasia**. There are also areas of the brain known to be associated with written

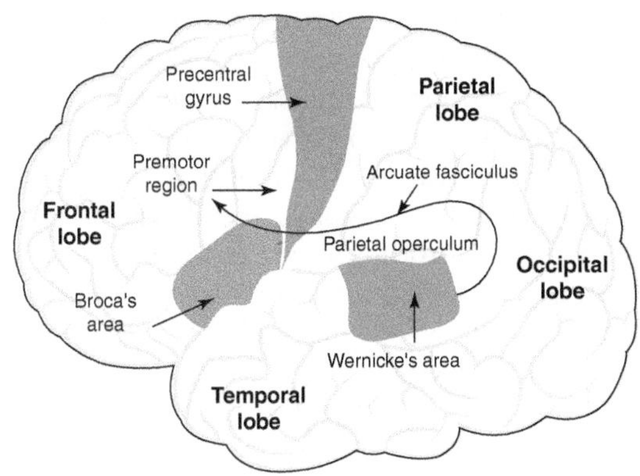

Figure 2.1

Language Areas in the Left Hemisphere

Broca's area, at the foot of the motor strip, is involved in the programming of speech for production. Wernicke's area, adjacent to the auditory cortex, is involved in the comprehension of language we hear. The arcuate fasciculus is a bundle of subcortical fibers that connects Broca's and Wernicke's areas. In order to repeat a word we hear (e.g., *cat*), we process it first in Wernicke's area, and then send a representation of it via the arcuate fasciculus to Broca's area, where its spoken form is organized. Damage to the arcuate fasciculus results in conduction aphasia, characterized by an inability to repeat words.

language; damage to the angular gyrus, for instance, impairs the ability to read.

A child aged 5 or 6 who suffers left-brain damage will in all likelihood recover complete use and comprehension of language. However, adults who become aphasic are liable to remain so if they do not recover in the first half-year after their injury. Specialized language areas of the brain are found in adults, but there is evidence that in young children, the neural circuits are not yet so firmly committed, and the nonlanguage hemisphere can take over in the event of damage to the dominant hemisphere.

The brains of infants are not fully formed and organized at birth. The brains of newborns have many fewer synapses (connections) than those of adults. By the age of about 2 years, the number of synapses reaches adult levels, and then increases rapidly between the ages of 4 and 10, far exceeding adult levels. During this period of synaptic growth, there is a concurrent pruning process as connections that are not used die off. This process may help to explain the neurological bases of sensitive or critical periods in development. If, for instance, an infant does not hear language or does not establish an emotional bond with an adult, the neural networks that underlie language and emotion may be weakened. By the age of 15 or 16, the number of synapses has returned to adult levels.

Special Characteristics

In examining the attempts to teach language to apes, we saw that language is probably unique to our species; the specialized areas of the brain contribute to that uniqueness. Human beings, of course, also have unique cognitive abilities and unique social settings in which to acquire language. These are discussed in later chapters—the intent here is to describe briefly the neuroanatomical foundations that make language acquisition possible. As Eric Lenneberg (1967) pointed out, language development in humans is associated with other maturational events. The appearance of language is a developmental milestone, roughly correlated with the onset of walking.

In addition to possessing specialized brain structures, humans, unlike other creatures, have a long list of adaptations in such things as the development of their heads, faces, vocal cords, and larynxes, and the ability to coordinate making speech sounds with breathing and swallowing. Humans perform a remarkably complex (and dangerous) set of actions when they engage in everyday activities such as having a talk over lunch. As noted earlier, our ape relatives do not have the capacity for speech; vocal tract reconstructions have also shown that even Neanderthal men and women had quite limited vocalizing capacity and would have been incapable of the rapidly articulated speech common to all modern humans, who typically produce about 140 words a minute in ordinary conversation. With the evolution of *Homo sapiens,* the position of the larynx was lowered, and rapid, clear speech became a physical possibility (Lieberman, 2011).

Lenneberg (1967) listed a number of additional features as evidence that language is specific to humans and uniform across our species in its major characteristics:

1. **The onset of speech is regular.** The order of appearance of developmental milestones, including speech, is regular in the species—it is not affected by culture or the language to be learned.
2. **Speech is not suppressible.** Typically developing children learn to talk if they are in contact with older speakers. The wide variations that exist within and across cultures have all provided suitable environments for children to learn language.
3. **Language cannot be taught to other species.** Lenneberg made this claim in the 1960s, before

there were results from the bonobo and parrot studies, and time may have proven him right. However, it is also clear that chimpanzees can be taught sign language comparable to the language of young children and parrots can do more than ask for crackers; thus this claim's validity hinges on a particular definition of language.

4. **Languages everywhere have certain universals.** They are structured in accordance with principles of human cognition, and a human infant can learn any language. At the same time, there are universal constraints on the kinds of rules that children can learn. The universals that are found in all languages include phonology, grammar, and semantics. These systematic aspects of language, along with another universal, the existence of social rules for language use, provide the research arena for developmental psycholinguistics.

The Structure of Language: Learning the System

Competence and Performance

A speaker who knows the syntactic rules of a language is said to have *linguistic competence.* Competence in this case refers to the inner, largely unconscious, knowledge of the rules, not to the way the person speaks on any particular occasion. The expression of the rules in everyday speech is *performance.* In the normal course of events, speakers produce utterances that include false starts, slips of the tongue, and various other errors. These are performance errors and are not thought to reflect the speakers' underlying competence. There is also a general assumption among linguists that, within a given linguistic community, all adults who are native speakers of the language and not neurologically impaired in some way share linguistic competence; this claim, however, has never been substantiated and there is increasing evidence that, though all typically developing children acquire language, they do not all do so in the same way, nor do they all arrive at the same level of competence (Arnon & Clark, 2011) It is possible to find out a great deal about adults' syntax by asking them to judge the grammatical acceptability of a sentence. However, in studying children, researchers must either rely on performance for clues to competence or design clever experiments to probe inner knowledge, since young children do not have the metalinguistic ability required to discuss questions of "grammaticality."

When children learn language, what is it that they must learn? Language has many subsystems having to do with sound, grammar, meaning, vocabulary, and knowing the right way to say something on a particular occasion in order to accomplish a specific purpose. Knowing the language entails knowing its **phonology**, **morphology**, **syntax**, and **semantics**, as well as its social rules, or **pragmatics**. The speaker who knows all this has acquired communicative competence.

Phonology

What are the sounds of English? Although we all speak the language, without specific training it is difficult to describe the sounds we make when we speak, and even harder to explain the rules for their combination. Phonology includes all of the important sounds, the rules for combining them to make words, and such things as the stress and intonation patterns that accompany them. Each language has its own set of important sounds, which are actually categories of sounds that include a number of variations. For instance, in English we pronounce the sound /t/ many different ways: At the beginning of a word like *top* it is pronounced with a strong aspiration, or puff of air (you can check this by holding the back of your hand near your mouth and saying *top* vigorously). We pronounce a word like *stop* without the puff of air, unaspirated. Some speakers produce a different, unreleased /t/ when they say a word like *hat* at the end of a sentence: They leave their tongues in place at the point of articulation. Many speakers pronounce yet another kind of /t/ in a word like *Manhattan* by releasing the air through their noses at the end. A phonetician would hear these /t/ sounds as four different sounds: aspirated, unaspirated, unreleased, and nasally released. For ordinary English speakers, however, these are all just one sound. A group of similar sounds that are regarded as all the same by the speakers of a language are called **phonemes**. The different /t/ sounds just described are all part of one /t/ phoneme in English. Children have to learn to recognize and produce the phonemes of their own language and to combine those phonemes into words and sentences with the right sorts of intonational patterns. Some parts of the system, such as consonant-vowel combinations, are acquired early on. Others are not acquired until well into the elementary school years: for instance, the ability to distinguish between the stress patterns of *HOT dog* (frankfurter, at the picnic) and *hot DOG* (Ruby, at the beach) when the words are presented without a context (Vogel & Raimy, 2002).

English has some sounds that are rarely found in other languages of the world, such as the *th* sound in *this*. Many African languages contain phonemic clicks rather similar to the sounds we make in English when we say what is written as "tsk tsk" or when we encourage a horse to go faster. In some languages, tone is a phoneme: In Chinese, a rising or falling tone on a word can change its meaning entirely. When the tones are produced correctly, the sentence "Mama ma ma ma?" means "Did mother chide the horse?"

Morphology

When a new word like *abdominoplasty* comes into the English language, adult speakers can immediately tell what its plural is; they do not have to look it up in a dictionary or consult with an expert. They are able to pluralize a word that they have never heard before because they know the English inflectional morphological system. A **morpheme** is the smallest unit of meaning in a language; it cannot be broken into any smaller parts that have meaning. Words can consist of one or more morphemes. The words *cat* and *danger* each consist of one morpheme, which is called a **free morpheme** because it can stand alone. **Bound morphemes**, on the other hand, cannot stand alone and are always found attached to free morphemes; they appear affixed to free morphemes as prefixes, suffixes, or within the word as infixes. *Happiness, unclear,* and *singing* contain the bound morphemes *-ness, un-,* and *-ing*. Bound morphemes can be used to change one word into another word that may be a different part of speech; for instance, *-ness* turns the adjective *happy* into the noun *happiness*. In this case, they are called **derivational morphemes** because they can be used to derive new words.

Other bound morphemes do not change the basic word's meaning so much as they modify it to indicate such things as tense, person, number, case, and gender. These variations on a basic word are *inflections,* and the morphemes that signal these changes are *inflectional morphemes*. Languages like Latin, Russian, and Hungarian are highly inflected. The verb to *love (amare)* in Latin has six separate forms in the present tense: the singular forms *amo, amas,* and *amat* (I love, you love, he/she loves) and the plural forms *amamus, amatis,* and *amant* (we love, you love, they love).

Compared with Latin, English has few verb inflections in the present tense: an added *-s* for the third person (he *loves*) and no inflection for other persons (I, we, you, they *love*). Latin indicates the subject and object of its sentences using case inflections—*agricola amat puellam* and *puellam amat agricola* both mean "The farmer loves the girl." The endings of the words mark the subject and the object. English does not have case endings on its nouns: Whether the girl loves the farmer or the farmer loves the girl is indicated entirely by word order. Grammar teachers, perhaps influenced by their knowledge of Latin, have tended to confuse the issue in English by referring to nouns as being in the subjective or objective case when, in fact, there are no separate noun case forms in English. Pronouns, on the other hand, have subjective, objective, and possessive forms: *I, me,* and *my*.

English inflectional morphology includes the progressive of the verb (e.g., *singing*); the past, pronounced with /d/, /t/, or /ə d/ *(played, hopped, landed);* and the third-person singular verb and the noun plural and possessive, all of which use /z/, /s/, or /ə z/ in spoken language *(dogs, cats, watches)*. Whether one says, "He dogs my steps" (verb), "It's the dog's dish" (possessive), or "I have ten dogs" (plural), the inflected form is pronounced in exactly the same way. The forms of the inflections vary depending on the last sound of the word being inflected, and there is a complex set of rules that adult speakers know (at some level) that enables them to make a plural or past tense of a word that they have never heard before.

One task for the student of language development is to determine whether children have knowledge of morphology and, if so, how it is acquired and to what extent it resembles the rule system that adults follow.

Syntax

The syntactic system includes the rules for how to combine words into acceptable phrases and sentences and how to transform sentences into other sentences. A competent speaker can take a basic sentence like "The cat bites the dog" and make a number of transformations of it: "The cat bit the dog," "The cat didn't bite the dog," "Did the cat bite the dog?," and "Wasn't the dog bitten by the cat?" Knowledge of syntax allows the speaker to generate an almost endless number of new sentences and to recognize those that are not grammatically acceptable. If you heard a nonsense sentence like "The daksy wug wasn't miggled by the mimsy zibber," you could not know what happened because the vocabulary is unfamiliar. On the other hand, the morphology and syntax of the sentence convey a great deal of information, and with this information you could make a number of new, perfectly grammatical sentences: "The wug is daksy," "The zibber did not miggle the wug," and "The zibber is mimsy."

There is a great deal of controversy among researchers as to whether young children just learning language are acquiring syntactic structures, that is, grammatical rules, or whether it is more reasonable to characterize their early utterances in terms of the semantic relations they are trying to express. The child who says, "Mommy eat lunch," can be said to have learned to produce subject-verb-object constructions and to be following English syntactic rules specifying that the subject comes first in active sentences. (Even very young children do not say, "Lunch eat Mommy.") To describe the language of young children, however, it is probably more useful to note the kinds of semantic relations the children are using. In this case the child is expressing knowledge that an action (eat) is taking place and that there is an agent (Mom) and an object (lunch).

Once children begin to produce longer sentences, however, they add the grammatical words of the language and begin to build sentences according to syntactic rules. They learn how to make negatives, questions, compound sentences, passives, and imperatives. Later, they add very complex structures, including embedded forms. The child who early on was limited to sentences like "Mommy eat lunch" can eventually comprehend and produce "The lunch that Grandpa cooked the baby sitter was eaten by Mommy" in full confidence that the caregiver was neither cooked by Grandpa nor eaten by Mom.

Semantics

The semantic system includes our mental dictionary, or lexicon. Word meanings are complicated to learn; words are related to one another in complex networks, and awareness of words—for example, the ability to think about words, comes later than does word use. A very young child may use a word that occurs in adult language, but that word does not mean exactly the same thing, nor does it have the same internal status for the child as it does for the adult. Two-year-olds who say "doggie," for instance, may call sheep, cows, cats, and horses "doggie," or they may use the word in reference to a particular dog, without knowing that it refers to a whole class of animals. Vocabulary is structured hierarchically, and words are attached to one another in semantic networks. Dogs are a class of animals, and the adult who knows the meaning of *dog* also knows, for instance, that it belongs to a group known as domestic animals, it is a pet, it is related to wolves, it is animate, and so on. Studying semantic development in children involves examining how they acquire the semantic system, beginning with simple vocabulary. Ultimately, it includes studying their metalinguistic knowledge, which enables them to notice the words in their language and comment on them.

The Social Rules for Language Use

Linguistic competence involves knowing how to construct grammatically acceptable sentences. Language, however, must be used in a social setting to accomplish various ends. Speakers who know how to use language *appropriately* have more than linguistic competence; they have communicative competence, a term first used by Dell Hymes (1972). Pragmatics, another term for the social uses of language, refers to the use of language to express one's intentions and get things done in the world. Adult pragmatics may include many interpersonal or social functions such as denying, refusing, blaming, offering condolences, and flattering, and even very young children use pragmatic functions such as labeling and demanding.

Communicative competence includes being able to express one's intent appropriately in varying social situations. The importance of knowing the right forms becomes obvious when social rules are violated. Consider the use of directives. If you are seated in an aisle seat of a bus, next to a stranger, and you are cold because the window is open, you can express your intent in a syntactically correct sentence: "Shut that window." This could lead to an angry reaction or, at the very least, to the impression that you are a rude person. If, instead, you say, "I wonder if you would mind shutting the window?" compliance and the beginning of a pleasant conversation will probably follow. Knowing the politeness rules of language is part of communicative competence.

Communicative competence includes important topics such as the ability to make conversation. Making conversation requires various skills, including, for instance, knowing something about what your listener already knows. Some conversational principles we follow include the following (Grice, 1975):

1. **Say as much as you need to, but not too much.** For instance, if a mother asks a child where her notebook is, and the child answers, "Julie has it," this is fine if her mother knows who Julie is. If the child says "Julie has it. She's my sister and also your daughter," she is being sarcastic or humorous.
2. **Be truthful.** Participants in a conversation expect one another not to lie or embellish the facts.
3. **Be relevant.** Contributions to the conversation are expected to be relevant. If a child responds to the question, "What do you like for

lunch?" by saying, "I like my kitty," she is violating the relevance principle (or exhibiting serious antisocial tendencies).

4. **Present information in a logical order.** To say, "We put on our pajamas and took a bath," violates this principle of logical order, since presumably bathing precedes putting on pajamas.

Adults, of course, violate these conversational rules in order to achieve certain very human ends: to be ironic, for instance, or to make a joke, or perhaps to be deceptive or insulting. Every type of interaction between individuals requires observance of social conventions, and adults do not leave children's development of these rules to chance: Whereas they may not correct syntactic violations except in the most superficial cases (see Chapter 5), they are active participants in their children's use of the appropriate (often polite) forms (Ely & Gleason, 2006). Just as there are phonological and grammatical rules, there are also rules for the use of language in social context. Mature language users know how to speak like men or women, to conduct discourse, and to speak in appropriate ways to different people. They can talk baby talk to babies and be formal and deferential when appearing in court. All of these are part of communicative competence, which is the goal of language development.

The Study of Language Development

The Ancient Roots of Child Language Study

Probably the first recorded account of a language acquisition study is found in the work of the Greek historian Herodotus. Herodotus, sometimes called the father of history, lived from about 484 to 425 B.C.E. In Book 2 of his *History,* he relates the story of the ancient Egyptian king Psamtik I (664–610 B.C.E.), also called Psammetichus, who wanted to prove that the Egyptians were the original human race.

In order to do this, Psamtik ordered a shepherd to raise two children, caring for their needs but not speaking to them. "His object herein was to know, after the indistinct babblings of infancy were over, what word they would first articulate." The king believed that the children would begin to speak in the language of the oldest group of humans, without ever hearing any language. This is perhaps the strongest version of a nativist theory of language development that one could have: Babies arrive in the world with a specific language already in their brains.

When the children were about 2 years old, the shepherd went to their quarters one day. They ran up to him with their hands outstretched, saying "Becos." *Becos* was not a word that anyone recognized. The king, according to Herodotus, asked around the kingdom and eventually was told that *becos* meant "bread" in the Phrygian language, whereupon the Egyptians gave up their claim to being the oldest race of humans and decided that they were in *second* place, behind the Phrygians.

Even though interest in language development has ancient roots, the systematic study of children's language is fairly recent, in part because the science of linguistics, with its special analytic techniques, came of age in the twentieth century. In earlier times the structural nature of language was not well understood, and research tended to concentrate on the kinds of things that children said rather than on their acquisition of productive linguistic subsystems.

Studies in the Nineteenth and Twentieth Centuries

Many studies of children, including notes on their language, were published in Germany, France, and England during the latter half of the nineteenth century and the early years of the twentieth century. One of the main early figures in the United States in the field of developmental psychology, G. Stanley Hall, taught at Clark University in Worcester, Massachusetts. Hall (1907) was interested in "the content of children's minds." Hall inspired a school of American students of child language.

The kinds of questions that child language researchers asked during this period were related primarily to philosophical inquiries into human nature. This was true of Charles Darwin (1877), who kept careful diaries on the language development of one of his sons. Many of these early investigations included valuable insights into language. The early studies were typically in the form of diaries with observations of the authors' own children. Notable exceptions were studies of "wild children" and isolated children who had failed to acquire language. Just as in antiquity, there was philosophical interest in the effects of isolation on language development; that interest has been sustained to the present day. *The Wild Boy of Aveyron,* a landmark study of a feral child, Victor, was written in the eighteenth century (and retold by Lane, 1979), and the study of Genie, an American girl who was kept isolated from other humans, was published not too long ago (Curtiss, 1977; Lapointe, 2005).

During the first half of the twentieth century, many psychologists still kept diary records of their

One of the first child language research subjects, "Adam" grew up to be an author and public speaker.

children. In the field of education, children's language was studied in order to arrive at norms, to describe gender and social class differences, and to search for the causes and cures of developmental difficulties. Educational psychologists frequently used group tests with large numbers of children, and there was a great interest in such things as the average sentence length used by children at different grade levels, or the kinds of errors they made in grammar or pronunciation (McCarthy, 1954).

Research from the 1950s to the Present

The mid-1950s saw a revolution in child language studies. Work on descriptive linguistics (Gleason, 1955) and the early work of Noam Chomsky (1957) provided new models of language for researchers to explore. At the same time, a behaviorist theory of language put forth by B. F. Skinner (1957) inspired other groups of investigators to design studies aimed at testing this learning theory.

Psycholinguistics came into being as a field when linguists and psychologists combined the techniques of their disciplines to investigate whether the systems described by the linguist had psychological reality in the minds of speakers. The linguistic description of English might, for instance, point out that the plural of words ending in /s/ or /z/ is formed by adding /ə z/, as, for example, in *kiss* and *kisses.* A task for the psycholinguist was to demonstrate that the linguistic description matched what speakers actually do, that speakers have a "rule" for the formation of the plural that is isomorphic (i.e., identical in form) with the linguist's descriptive rule. Some of the earliest questions in cognitive science dealt with the mental representation of the units of language.

In the decade of the 1960s, after the powerful grammatical model advanced by Chomsky became widely known, there was an explosion of research into children's acquisition of syntax. The 1960s were characterized by studies of grammar; many projects studied a small number of children over a period of time, writing grammars of the children's developing language. At Harvard University, for instance, a group of researchers, many of whom were to become prominent individually, worked with Roger Brown (1973) on a project that studied the language development of three children called Adam, Eve, and Sarah (not their real names). Members of Brown's research group visited the children once a month in their homes and made tape recordings of each child with his or her parents, engaged in everyday activities. The recordings were brought back to the laboratory and transcribed, and the resulting transcriptions were studied by a team of faculty and graduate students that met in a weekly seminar. Adam, Eve, and Sarah became very famous in the linguistics community. Although the ethics of research require us to maintain the anonymity of participants unless they agree otherwise, we were recently in touch with grownup Adam, who gave us permission to provide an update about him. Adam grew up to be a prolific author, public speaker, CEO, and philanthropist, who himself has offered a unique framework on effective human interaction called Intelligent Influence.

As the 1960s drew to a close, the dominance of syntax in research gave way to a broadening interest that included the context in which children's language emerges and an emphasis on the kinds of semantic relations children are trying to express in their early utterances. The early 1970s saw a spate of studies on the language addressed to children; many of these were conducted to shed light on the innateness controversy. Researchers wanted to know whether children were innately programmed to discover the rules of language all by themselves, or whether adults provided them with help or even with language learning lessons.

Studies of the 1980s and 1990s included all of the traditional linguistic topics: phonology, morphology, syntax, semantics, and pragmatics. Now, in the second decade of the twenty-first century, there is growing interest in cross-cultural research in language development and in understanding how language development interfaces with other aspects of children's social and psychological development; in acquiring a language, children become members of a society, with all of its unique cultural practices and belief systems.

Cross-cultural studies and studies of children in nontypical developmental situations are also vital to our ultimate understanding of the process of language acquisition. What happens, for instance, if a child spends her first year in one language community and then, just as she is about to begin speaking, she finds herself in a new family that speaks a new and totally unrelated language? This is the case with international adoptions. In the past few years, thousands of young children have come to the United States from a variety of countries. These children are of great interest to the linguistics community. A recent meta-analysis of a number of studies of internationally adopted children points out that these children are essentially learning a first language for the second time; there is great variability in their language outcomes, with adoption before the age of one year one of the best predictors that their language will be comparable to that of their non-adopted peers (Scott, Roberts & Glennon, 2011.)

In addition to basic linguistic studies, social class and gender differences in language, bilingualism, stylistic variation in acquisition and use, and the language addressed to children are examples of topics found in current journals and on the programs of professional meetings. While historically, research with typical and atypical language learners often was conducted and reported in different settings and journals, researchers are increasingly integrating work across populations to gain better insights into the bases of normal and disordered language development.

The study of language acquisition has obviously changed in major ways in the twenty-first century. It has become more international and interdisciplinary, and researchers now make use of sophisticated contemporary technology. Early studies were typically of monolingual, middle-class, English-speaking children. There is now a community of scholars from all over the world, many of whom are members of the International Association for the Study of Child Language (IASCL). Study of many different languages and cultures is changing our ideas about what might be universal in acquisition. The inclusion of atypical populations and dual language learners is helping build theory. At the same time this research provides information that has real-world applications in the development of both remedial programs for children at risk and educational programs for children who, for example, speak different languages at home and at school. Language development researchers now acknowledge that most children in the world are not monolingual.

Research Methods

Modern technology has made it possible to collect accurate data on language development and for researchers around the world to share data and data analysis programs. In collecting new data, researchers must obtain informed consent from the participants (or their parents) and follow the strict ethical guidelines set down by their institutions and by government funding agencies. Psamtik's study could never be conducted under current scientific research guidelines.

Equipment

Increasingly sophisticated audio and video equipment has greatly simplified data collection. Powerful computers with immense memory capacity make it possible to conduct research that was unimaginable just a few years ago. For instance, in a remarkable recent project, Deb Roy, a researcher at MIT with an engineering background, has recorded 230,000 hours of the home life of his son over the first three years of his life, including everything that was said to the child as well as every child utterance, making it possible to follow the evolution, in context, of every word that the child acquired. Deb Roy's data are not yet fully analyzed, but you can hear him talk about the study and see some striking computer landscapes of the child's early words online at www.ted.com/talks/deb_roy_the_birth_of_a_word.html. The Internet includes many video clips of typical child language, as well as samples from people who have impaired or exceptional language skills. These illustrate a variety of the concepts that we will cover in this text. In addition, several other excellent TED talks on language development, including one by Patricia Kuhl, can be seen online. TED is an acronym for Technology, Entertainment, Design, and the name of a nonprofit organization devoted to promoting "Ideas Worth Spreading."

Studies of prelinguistic infants or of cortical reactions to linguistic stimuli at any age require especially sensitive recording equipment and may use sophisticated imaging technology. Imaging is a way of observing mental activity related to language. It can show if a very young infant is able to distinguish among speech sounds, because if the infant notices a difference, there will be some kind of reaction in the brain that can be measured (Kuhl, 2010). Imaging devices are able to do this in various noninvasive ways:

They can measure *electrical changes* in the brain, because brain activity produces electrical current; **event-related potentials (ERPs)** measure changes in current. **Magnetoencephalography (MEG)** measures the tiny magnetic changes that accompany changes in electrical activity.

They can measure *blood flow*, because increased brain activity is accompanied by increased blood flow to the area that is activated; **functional magnetic resonance imaging (fMRI)** measures changes in oxygen; increased blood flow to an activated area carries more oxygen with it.

Near-Infrared Spectroscopy (NIRS) also measures blood changes, but in this case the machine records the changes in hemoglobin that accompany increased blood flow.

With the exception of event-related potential equipment, imaging is expensive and not easily accessible. Imaging studies also require rather restricted and careful experimental tasks, rather than observation of natural language use in context. Many language development studies, however, use standard laboratory equipment, and others are conducted with easily acquired video and audio recorders. This makes it possible to film in the laboratory or in participants' homes with a minimum of intrusion. Regardless of the method of recording, it is necessary to make a transcription of the data for analysis. This involves writing down as exactly as possible everything that is said on the recording, preferably following a standard format that makes computer analysis possible (see Figure 2.2). The major program that researchers use to analyze language samples is called CLAN (Computerized Language Analysis), a tool developed by the CHILDES (Child Language Data Exchange System) project (you can visit the project and its open-access databases and freely distributed software at http://childes.psy.cmu.edu/).

Research Design

Language development studies can be either *cross-sectional* or *longitudinal* in their design. Cross-sectional studies use two or more groups of participants. If, for instance, you wanted to study the development of the negative between the ages of 2 and 4, you could study a group of 2-year-olds and a group of 4-year-olds and then describe the differences in the two groups' use of negation. Longitudinal studies follow individual participants over time; one might study the same children's use of negatives at specified periods between the ages of 2 and 4.

Cross-sectional studies make it possible to obtain a great deal of data about a large number of participants in a short time; one doesn't have to wait two years to get results. Longitudinal designs are used to study individuals over time when questions such as the persistence of traits or the effects of early experience are relevant. If, for instance, you wanted to know whether children who are late talkers have problems learning to read, you would have to use a longitudinal design.

Both cross-sectional and longitudinal studies can be either *observational* or *experimental*. Observational studies involve a minimum of intrusion by the researcher. Naturalistic observational studies attempt to capture behavior as it occurs in real life; for instance, one might record and analyze family speech at the dinner table. Controlled observational studies can be carried out in various settings, including the laboratory, where the researcher provides certain constants for all participants. Fathers might come to the laboratory with their daughters and be observed reading them a book provided by the researcher. Observational research can indicate what kinds of behaviors correlate with one another, but it cannot reveal which behavior might cause another.

@Begin
@Participants: CHI Charlie Child, MOT Mother, FAT Father
@Date: 7-JUL-1996
@Filename: CHARLIE.CHA
@Situation: Home Dinner Conversation.
*MOT: did you tell Dad what we did today?
*MOT: who'd we see?
*CHI: who?
*MOT: remember?
*CHI: Judy and my friend.
*MOT: did we see Michael?
*CHI: yes.
*FAT: was Mike at the beach?
*CHI: no.
*FAT: that's because he had work to do.
*FAT: do you remember the name of the beach you went to?
*CHI: not this time.
*FAT: you don't remember it this time?
*FAT: it was Winger-: what?
*FAT: Winger-Beach?
*CHI: yes.
*FAT: Winger Sheek Beach.
*CHI: Winger Sheek Beach.
*FAT: that's the one.
*CHI: Winger Beach.
*MOT: did you go swimming, Charlie?
*CHI: I went swimming, Dad.
*FAT: you did?
*FAT: did you wear water wings?
*CHI: no.
*FAT: no?
@End

Figure 2.2
Sample Transcript
This excerpt from CHILDES can be analyzed by a number of CLAN programs that can automatically compute MLU, list all vocabulary by speaker, and derive many standardized measures.

In experimental research, the researcher has some control and can manipulate variables. Typical experimental research includes:

- Hypotheses about what will happen
- An experimental group of participants that receives the treatment (training, for instance) and a control group that receives no special treatment
- Independent variables, manipulated by the experimenter (training, exposure to a TV program, etc.)
- Dependent variables: the behaviors that are measured (for instance, the participants' use of a particular grammatical form)
- Randomization: assignment of participants at random to control or experimental conditions
- Standardization of procedures (all participants receive the same instructions, etc.)

If you wanted to see whether training makes a difference in the acquisition of the passive voice, for instance, you might take a group of thirty 3-year-olds and randomly assign them to two groups, a control group and an experimental group of fifteen children each. The experimental group would receive training in the passive; the control group, no special treatment. Finally, both groups could be asked to describe some pictures they had never seen before, and differential use of the passive would be recorded. If the trained group used passives and the control group did not, there would be evidence that training causes accelerated acquisition of one aspect of grammar. Experimental research can easily be replicated in the laboratory, but it may not be easily generalized to the outside world.

In addition to clear-cut observational and experimental methods, language development researchers use a variety of research techniques. These include *standard assessment measures,* in which participants can be compared or evaluated on the basis of their responses to published standardized language tests. These are useful for indicating whether a participant's language is developing at a typical rate or whether some facet of development is out of line with the others.

Imitation is a technique used by many researchers: You simply ask the child to say what you say. Imitation reveals a great deal about children's language, since they typically cannot imitate sentences that are beyond their stage of development. This is true of adults as well—try imitating a few sentences in Bulgarian the next time you meet someone from Sofia who is willing to say them to you.

Elicitation is a technique that works well when a particular language form is the target and you want to give your participants all the help they need (short of the answer itself). In investigating the plural through elicitation, you might show your participants a picture, first of one and then of two bird-like creatures, and say, "This is a wug. Now there is another one. There are two of them. There are two?" The participant obligingly fills in "wugs." This technique works well with aphasic patients, especially severe Broca's aphasics who have very little voluntary speech.

The *interview* is an old technique, but one that can be very effective if the researcher has the time to do more than ask a list of questions and fill in a form. Researchers of the Piagetian school frequently use an interview type called the *clinical method.* This is an open-ended interview in which the sequence of questions depends on the answers the participant has given. In studying metalinguistic awareness, the investigator might ask a series of questions, such as "Is *horse* a word? Why? (Or why not?) What is a word? How do you know? What is your favorite word? Why?" The choice of method depends very much on the theoretical inclination of the investigator. Since without some sort of intervention on the part of the researcher it might take a very long time before participants say the kinds of things that interest us, many ingenious methods for studying language production have been designed (Menn & Bernstein Ratner, 2000).

CHILDES

As noted earlier, one of the most significant events in language development research has been the creation of the Child Language Data Exchange System **CHILDES**. CHILDES was launched in 1984 at Carnegie Mellon University under the direction of Brian MacWhinney and Catherine Snow (Berko Gleason & Thompson, 2002; MacWhinney, 2000). The system is made up of three main parts:

1. Transcription rules for transcribing spoken language in a standardized way that makes computer analysis possible. The rules are called **CHAT** (acronym for Codes for the Human Analysis of Transcripts). Figure 2.2 shows a sample transcript.
2. Computer programs that can run on the CHAT files to do such things as instantly list every word used by a child. The programs are called **CLAN** (acronym for Computerized Language Analysis programs). They can also search for groups of words, compute linguistic attributes of utterances, and analyze discourse patterns between participants in conversations.

3. The database: Digital files in 25 different languages, containing language data that have been contributed from over one hundred research projects around the world.

CHILDES is web-based and available without cost to researchers everywhere. A visit to its main website at http://childes.psy.cmu.edu is recommended. There you will find the programs and data, as well as much useful information. Many powerful computer programs are included in CLAN (MacWhinney, 2000). Some of the advantages of CHILDES are that it allows (1) data sharing among researchers, who can test their hypotheses on many more participants, (2) increased precision and standardization in coding, and (3) automation of many coding procedures. CLAN programs can operate on any or all speakers' output and can automatically derive the mean length of utterance, a total list of words used as well as their frequency, and other data of immense value to the language researcher. Data from many studies in English and other languages are available; even older studies, such as Brown's famous work on Adam, Eve, and Sarah from the 1960s, have been scanned and entered, thus making these data available to anyone who wants them.

One of the most recent developments in CHILDES is an interactive Internet resource that links transcripts with digitized video and audio data: It is possible to read the transcript online, view the participants, and hear the actual speech, all at the same time (MacWhinney, 2001).

SUMMARY

Babies seek the love and attention of their caregivers. Before they are even 1 year old, they are able to make fine discriminations among the speech sounds they hear, and they begin to communicate nonverbally with those around them. Young children acquire the basic components of their native language in just a few years: *phonology, morphology, semantics, syntax,* and the social rules for language use, often called *pragmatics.* By the time they are of school age, children control all of the major grammatical and semantic features. Language development, however, proceeds throughout the life cycle; as individuals grow older, they acquire new skills at every stage of their lives, and in the declining years they are vulnerable to a specific set of language disabilities. To elucidate both the scope and the nature of language development, this book is written from a lifespan perspective.

Babies begin to acquire language during their first months, long before they say their first words; language is built upon an earlier affective communicative base. Midway through the first year, infants begin to babble, an event seen by many researchers as evidence of linguistic capacity. Near their first birthdays, infants say their first words. Early words, word meanings, and word combinations have universal characteristics, since toddlers' language is similar across cultures. Children's progress toward learning the particular grammatical structure of their own language follows a predictable order that is common to all children learning that language.

Although there are universal characteristics, there are also patterns of individual variation in language development. Different theories of language development emphasize *innate mechanisms, learning principles, cognitive characteristics, social interaction,* and the *gestural-usage* bases of language.

During the school years, children perfect their knowledge of complex grammar, and they learn to use language in many different social situations. They develop *metalinguistic awareness,* the ability to consider language as an object. At the same time, they learn another major linguistic system: the written language. The demands of literacy remove a child's language from the here and now and emphasize *decontextualized language.* Not all children learn to read with ease.

Teenagers develop a distinct personal linguistic style, and young adults must acquire the linguistic register common to their occupations. With advancing age, numerous linguistic changes take place; there is some inevitable loss of word-finding ability, but vocabulary and narrative skill may improve.

Human language has special properties that have led many researchers to conclude that it is *species specific* and *species uniform.* Humans can talk about any part of their experience. Sea mammals employ communicative systems of whistles and grunts, and many birds have been shown to have a variety of meaningful calls. None of these systems equals human language, however, which is *productive,* has *semanticity,* and offers the possibility of *displacement.*

During the past seventy-five years, many researchers have attempted to discover whether language is really unique to humans or if it can be learned by other species. Recent studies have shown that African grey parrots and dogs have some sophisticated linguistic abilities. Early studies that tried to teach spoken language to chimpanzees showed conclusively that primates cannot speak as humans do. More recent studies have taught American Sign Language (ASL) to chimpanzees and have met with mixed results. The signing chimps may be responding at least in part to subtle cues from their trainers, but the question of the apes' potential is not completely settled. These studies have shown that there are substantial similarities between very young children's and chimpanzees' abilities to engage in symbolic communication.

Language development requires social interaction, but spoken language in humans is possible only because we have evolved with specialized neural mechanisms that subserve language. These include special areas in the brain, such as *Broca's area, Wernicke's area,* and the *arcuate fasciculus.* Other evidence of humans' biological disposition for language includes the regular onset of speech and the facts that speech is not suppressible, language cannot be taught to other species, and languages everywhere have universals.

The study of language development includes research into major linguistic subsystems. The *phonological system* is composed of the significant sounds of the language and the rules for their combination; the *morphological system* includes the minimal units that carry meaning; *syntax* refers to the rules by which sentences are constructed in a given language; and the *semantic systems* contain the meanings of words and the relationships between them. Finally, to function in society, speakers must know the social or *pragmatic rules* for language use. Individuals must be able to comprehend and produce all of these systems in order to attain *communicative competence.*

Although interest in language development has ancient roots, the scientific study of this subject began in the 1950s, with the appearance of new linguistic and psychological theories of language that gave birth to the combined discipline now known as *developmental psycholinguistics.* Developmental psycholinguists use all of the research techniques, designs, and resources employed by psychologists and linguists, as well as a few that are unique, such as CHILDES, a shared computerized bank of language data, as well as specialized transcription formats and computer programs for analyzing language.

Suggested Projects

1. Choose three related articles on language development from the *Journal of Child Language,* or from another journal, such as *Applied Psycholinguistics.* Write an introduction, explaining what the major questions of the research are, and then, for each article, describe the methods used by the authors, the participants, any special equipment that was needed, and the nature of the results. In a separate discussion section, compare the results of the studies.
2. List some stereotypic notions people have about language development. For instance: Girls talk more than boys. Babies say "goo goo, ga ga." Children call rabbits "wabbits." Children can learn a language watching television, and so on. Pick one of these beliefs and design a study to find out if it is true. Since this is a thought experiment, you don't have to worry about how long it would take or how much it would cost, but be explicit in describing exactly how you would proceed, what data you would need to collect, and how you would analyze it in order to answer your question.
3. Read papers on studies with the border collie Chaser, the gorilla Koko, the chimp Kanzi, and the parrot Alex. Summarize the language claims that are made for each of these animals and draw some conclusions of your own about which of them you think comes closest to having language.

Suggested Readings

Berko Gleason, J., & Thompson, R. B. (2002). Out of the baby book and into the computer: Child language research comes of age. *Contemporary Psychology, APA Review of Books, 47,* 4, 391–394.

Brown, R. W. (1970). The first sentences of child and chimpanzee. In R. W. Brown (Ed.), *Psycholinguistics.* New York: Macmillan.

Pilley, J. W., & Reid, A. K. (2011). Border collie comprehends object names as verbal referents. *Behavioural Processes, 86*(2), 184–195.

Key Terms in Language Development

American Sign Language (ASL)
aphasia
arcuate fasciculus
autism spectrum disorder
bound morpheme
Broca's area
CHAT
child-directed speech (CDS)
CHILDES

CLAN
communicative competence
comprehension
conduction aphasia
decontextualized language
dementia
derivational morpheme
Down syndrome
dyslexia
event-related potentials (ERPs)
free morpheme
functional magnetic resonance imaging (fMRI)
innate
internalized representation
lateralized
linguistic competence
magnetoencephalography (MEG)
metalinguistic awareness
mirror neurons
morpheme
morphology
Near-Infrared Spectroscopy (NIRS)
neologisms
overregularized
pervasive developmental disorder
phoneme
phonology
pragmatics
production
semantic development
semantics
species specific
species uniform
specific language impairment
speech acts
syntax
Wernicke's area

REFERENCES

Arnon, I., & Clark, E. (Eds.). (2011). *Experience, variation and generalization: Learning a first language.* Amsterdam: Benjamins.

Berko Gleason, J., & Thompson, R. B. (2002). Out of the baby book and into the computer: Child language research comes of age. *Contemporary Psychology, APA Review of Books, 47,* 4, 391–394.

Brown, R. W. (1970). The first sentences of child and chimpanzee. In R. W. Brown (Ed.), *Psycholinguistics.* New York: Macmillan.

Brown, R. W. (1973). *A first language.* Cambridge, MA: Harvard University Press.

Chomsky, N. (1957). *Syntactic structures.* The Hague: Mouton.

Curtiss, S. (1977). *Genie: A psycholinguistic study of a modern day "wild" child.* New York: Academic Press.

Darwin, C. (1877). A biographical sketch of an infant. *Mind, 2,* 285–294.

Ely, R., & Berko Gleason, J. (2006). I'm sorry I said that: Apologies in young children's discourse. *Journal of Child Language, 33,* 599–620.

Fogassi, L., & Ferrari, P. F. (2007). Mirror neurons and the evolution of embodied language. *Current Directions in Psychological Science, 16,* 3, 136–141.

Gardner, R. A., & Gardner, B. T. (1969). Teaching sign language to a chimpanzee. *Science,* 165, 664–672.

Gardner, R. A., & Gardner, B. T. (1994). Development of phrases in the utterances of children and cross-fostered chimpanzees. In R. A. Gardner, B. T. Gardner, B. Chiarelli, & F. X. Plooij (Eds.), *The ethological roots of culture.* NATO ASI series D: Behavioural and Social Sciences (Vol. 78, pp. 223–255). Dordrecht, The Netherlands: Kluwer Academic.

Geschwind, N. (1982). Specializations of the brain. In W. S.-Y. Wang (Ed.), *Human communication: Language and its psychobiological bases.* San Francisco: W. H. Freeman.

Gleason, H. A. (1955). *An introduction to descriptive linguistics.* New York: Henry Holt.

Goodglass, H. (1993). *Understanding aphasia.* San Diego, CA: Academic Press.

Gregory, L. (2009). *Stupid science: Weird experiments, mad scientists, and idiots in the lab.* Riverside, NJ: McMeel.

Grice, H. P. (1975). Logic and conversation. In P. Cole & J. Morgan (Eds.), *Syntax and semantics* (Vol. 3). New York: Academic Press.

Hall, G. S. (1907). *Aspects of child life and education.* New York: Appleton.

Hayes, C. (1951). *The ape in our house.* New York: Harper.

Hess, E. (2008). *Nim Chimpsky: The chimp who would be human.* New York: Bantam Books.

Hoza, J. (2008). Five nonmanual modifiers that mitigate requests and rejections in American sign language. *Sign Language Studies,* 8(3), 264–288.

Hymes, D. (1972). On communicative competence. In J. Pride & J. Holmes (Eds.), *Sociolinguistics.* Hammondsworth, UK: Penguin.

Janik, V. M. (2000). Whistle matching in wild bottlenose dolphins *(Tursiops truncatus).* Science, 289, 1355–1357.

Kellogg, W. N. (1980). Communication and language in the home raised chimpanzee. In T. Sebeok & J. Umiker Sebeok (Eds.), *Speaking of apes.* New York: Plenum Press.

Klima, E. S., & Bellugi, U. (1972). The signs of language in child and chimpanzee. In R. Alloway, L. Krames, & P. Pliner (Eds.), *Communication and affect: A comparative approach.* New York: Academic Press.

Klima, E. S., & Bellugi, U. (1979). *The signs of language.* Cambridge, MA: Harvard University Press.

Kohler, E., Keysers, C., Umiltà, M. A., Fogassi, L., Gallese, V., & Rizzolatti, G. (2002). Hearing sounds, understanding actions: Action representation in mirror neurons. *Science, 297,* 846–848.

Kuhl, P. K. (2010). Brain mechanisms in early language acquisition. *Neuron, 67,* 713.

Lane, H. (1979). *The wild boy of Aveyron.* Cambridge, MA: Harvard University Press.

LaPointe, L. (2005). Feral children. *Journal of Medical Speech-Language Pathology, 13*(1), vii–ix.

Lenneberg, E. (1967). *The biological foundations of language.* New York: Wiley.

Lieberman, D. E. (2011). *The evolution of the human head.* Cambridge, MA: Harvard University Press.

Locke, J. L. (1993). *The child's path to spoken language.* Cambridge, MA: Harvard University Press.

MacWhinney, B. (2000). *The CHILDES Project: Tools for analyzing talk: Transcription format and programs, Vol. I* (3rd ed.) and *The CHILDES Project: Tools for analyzing talk: The database, Vol. II* (3rd ed.). Mahwah, NJ: Erlbaum.

MacWhinney, B. (2001). From CHILDES to TalkBank: New systems for studying human communication. In M. Almgren, A. Barreña, M. Ezeizaberrena, I. Idiazabal, and B. MacWhinney (Eds.), *Research on child language acquisition* (pp. 17–34). Somerville, MA: Cascadilla.

McCarthy, D. (1954). Language development in children. In P. Mussen (Ed.), *Carmichael's manual of child psychology.* New York: Wiley.

Menn, L., & Bernstein Ratner, N. (Eds.). (2000). *Methods for studying language production.* Mahwah, NJ: Erlbaum.

Misyak, J. & Christiansen, M. (2011). Genetic variation and individual differences in language. In I. Arnon and E. Clark (Eds.), *Experience, variation and generalization: Learning a first language* (pp. 223–238). Amsterdam: Benjamins.

O'Connell, C. (2007). *The elephant's secret sense: The hidden life of the wild herds of Africa.* New York: Free Press.

Pääbo, S. (2003). The mosaic that is our genome. *Nature, 421,* 409–412.

Pepperberg, I. M., & Gordon, J. D. (2005). Number comprehension by a grey parrot *(Psittacus erithacus),* including a zero-like concept. *Journal of Comparative Psychology, 119,* 2, 197–209.

Pilley, J. W., & Reid, A. K. (2011). Border collie comprehends object names as verbal referents. *Behavioural Processes,* 86(2), 184–195.

Piper, W., Mager, J., & Walcott, C. (2011). Marking loons, making progress. *American Scientist,* 99(3), 220–227.

Ross, E. D. (2010). Cerebral localization of functions and the neurology of language: Fact versus fiction or is it something else? *Neuroscientist,* 16(3), 222–243.

Rumbaugh, D. E., Savage-Rumbaugh, S. E., King, J. E. & Taglialatela, J. P. (2011). The foundations of primate intelligence and language skills. In *The Human Brain Evolving: Paleoneurological Studies in Honor of Ralph L. Holloway.* Bloomington, IN: Stone Age Institute Press.

Scott, K. A., Roberts, J. A. & Glennen, S. (2011). How well do children who are internationally adopted acquire language? A meta-analysis. *Journal of Speech, Language and Hearing Research, 54,* 1153–1169.

Skinner, B. F. (1957). *Verbal behavior.* Englewood, NJ: Prentice-Hall.

Tanner, J. E., Patterson, F.G. & Byrne, R.W. (2006) . The development of spontaneous gestures in zoo-living gorillas and sign-taught gorillas: From action and location to object representation. *Journal of Developmental Processes, 1,* 69–102.

Terrace, H. S. (1980). *Nim: A chimpanzee who learned sign language.* New York: Knopf.

Toth, A. (2009). Bridge of signs: Can sign language empower non-deaf children to triumph over their communication disabilities? *American Annals of the Deaf, 154*(2), 85–95.

Trachsel, M. (2010). Human uniqueness in the age of ape language research. *Society & Animals,* 18(4), 397–412.

Tyack, P. L. (2000). Dolphins whistle a signature tune. *Science, 289,* 1310–1311.

Van Cantfort, T. E., & Rimpau, J. G. (1982). Sign language studies with children and chimpanzees. *Sign Language Studies, 34,* 15–72.

Vogel, I., & Raimy, E. (2002). The acquisition of compound vs. phrasal stress in English. *Journal of Child Language, 29,* 225–250.

von Frisch, K. (1950). *Bees, their vision, chemical senses, and language.* Ithaca, NY: Cornell University Press.

CHAPTER

3

Nonverbal Messages

Taken from *Human Communication: The Basic Course*, Eleventh Edition, by Joseph A. DeVito.

When you smile, nod your head in agreement, or wave your hand to someone, you're communicating nonverbally. In fact, some researchers argue that you actually communicate more information nonverbally than you do with words.

In this chapter you'll learn about:

- the functions nonverbal communication serves and how nonverbal communication interacts with your verbal messages.
- the channels of nonverbal communication.
- the role of culture and gender in nonverbal communication.

You'll learn to:

- communicate more effectively with nonverbal messages.
- respond appropriately to the nonverbal messages of others.
- communicate with an awareness of cultural and gender influences and differences in nonverbal communication.

Nonverbal communication is communication without words. You communicate nonverbally when you gesture, smile or frown, widen your eyes, move your chair closer to someone, wear jewelry, touch someone, raise your vocal volume, or even say nothing. The crucial aspect of nonverbal communication is that the message you send is in some way received by one or more other people. If you gesture while alone in your room and no one is there to see you, then, most theorists would argue, communication has not taken place. The same, of course, is true of verbal messages; if you recite a speech and no one hears it, then communication has not taken place.

Using nonverbal communication effectively can yield two major benefits (Burgoon & Hoobler, 2002). First, the greater your ability to send and receive nonverbal signals, the higher your attractiveness, popularity, and psychosocial well-being are likely to be. Second, the greater your nonverbal skills, the more successful you're likely to be at influencing (or deceiving) others. Skilled nonverbal communicators are highly persuasive, and this persuasive power can be used to help or support another or it can be used to deceive and fool.

Research shows that of the two genders, women are the better senders and receivers of nonverbal messages in most contexts (Hall, 1998; Burgoon & Hoobler, 2002). For example, in a review of 21 research studies, 71 percent of the findings showed women to be superior nonverbal senders. And in a review of 61 studies on decoding, 84 percent showed women to be superior receivers (Hall, 1998).

The Functions of Nonverbal Communication

Let's consider the functions of nonverbal communication by looking at (1) the ways in which nonverbal messages are integrated with verbal messages, and (2) the functions that researchers have focused on most extensively.

Integrating Nonverbal and Verbal Messages

In face-to-face communication you blend verbal and nonverbal messages to best convey your meanings. While speaking, you also smile, frown, or gesture, for example. It's this combination of verbal and nonverbal signals that communicates your meanings. Here are six ways in which nonverbal messages interact with verbal messages: (1) accenting, (2) complementing, (3) contradicting, (4) regulating, (5) repeating, and (6) substituting (Knapp & Hall, 2005):

- Nonverbal communication often serves to *accent* or emphasize some part of the verbal message. You might, for example, raise your voice to underscore a particular word or phrase; bang your fist on the desk to stress your commitment; or look longingly into someone's eyes when saying, "I love you."
- Nonverbal communication may *complement* or add nuances of meaning not communicated by your verbal message. Thus, you might smile when telling a story (to suggest that you find it humorous), or frown and shake your head when recounting someone's deceit (to suggest your disapproval).
- You may deliberately *contradict* your verbal messages with nonverbal movements—for example, by crossing your fingers or winking to indicate that you're lying.
- Movements may be used to *regulate*—to control or indicate your desire to control—the flow of verbal messages, as when you purse your lips, lean forward, or make hand gestures to indicate that you want to speak. You might also put up your hand or vocalize your pauses (for example, with "um" or "ah") to indicate that you have not finished and are not ready to relinquish the floor to the next speaker.

- You can *repeat* or restate the verbal message nonverbally. You can, for example, follow your verbal "Is that all right?" with raised eyebrows and a questioning look, or motion with your head or hand to repeat your verbal "Let's go."
- You may also use nonverbal communication to *substitute for* or take the place of verbal messages. For instance, you can signal "OK" with a hand gesture. You can nod your head to indicate yes or shake your head to indicate no.

Serving Varied Communication Functions

Although nonverbal communication serves the same functions as verbal communication, nonverbal researchers have singled out several specific functions as especially significant (Burgoon, Buller, & Woodall, 1996; Burgoon & Hoobler, 2002).

To Manage Self-Impression

It is largely through the nonverbal communications of others that you form impressions of them. Based on a person's body size, skin color, and dress as well as on the way the person smiles, maintains eye contact, and expresses himself or herself facially, you form impressions—you judge who the person is and what the person is like. Nonverbal researchers group these impressions into five categories (Leathers, 1997; Mehrabian, 1971).

- credibility, or how competent and believable you find the person
- likability, or how much you like or dislike the person
- attractiveness, or how attractive you find the person
- dominance, or how powerful the individual is
- status, or relative rank or standing of the person; a relaxed rather than a tense posture and large gestures contribute to an impression of higher status

And, of course, you reveal yourself largely through the same nonverbal signals you use to size up others. But not only do you communicate your true self nonverbally; you also strive to manage the impression that you give to others. For example,

ASK THE RESEARCHER

Cues for Success

I'm running for office in a class election, and I want to know what I can do nonverbally to make myself more likable and more credible and hence more likely to be elected. Any suggestions?

In a campaign speech, enhance your physical appearance (if female, moderate makeup; if male, shave) and dress slightly better than expected at your school. You should engage in pleasant facial expressions, use a slightly faster speech rate with a good range of inflection, and speak from your diaphragm. Engage in a moderate amount of gestures, but keep them between your neck and waist and spread them away from your body. Engage your audience with a slight forward lean to show interest in them.

In interpersonal contexts where you have already enhanced your physical appearance, close your distance slightly if your listener agrees with you, but increase your distance slightly if s/he disagrees with you. If you have not enhanced your appearance, maintain your initial distance. Allow your natural emotions to flow (provide positive feedback, unless you totally disagree with the point), reduce your range of gestures, and speak with a confident, slightly faster than normal rate, but at a conversational volume.

For further information: Hickson, M. L., Stacks, D. W., & Moore, N. J. (2003). *Nonverbal communication: Studies and applications*. Los Angeles: Roxbury. And Richmond, V. P., & McCroskey, J. C. (2003). *Nonverbal behavior in interpersonal relations*. Boston: Allyn & Bacon.

Don W. Stacks (Ph.D., University of Florida) is a professor of advertising and public relations at the University of Miami. He teaches courses in public relations, research methods, nonverbal communication, persuasion, and communication theory and directs the undergraduate and graduate programs in advertising and public relations.

you may do your best to appear brave when you're really scared, or to appear happy when you're really sad.

To Define Relationships

Much of your relationship life is lived nonverbally: Largely through nonverbal signals, you communicate your relationship to another person and that person communicates to you. Holding hands, gazing into each other's eyes, and even dressing alike are ways in which you communicate closeness in your interpersonal relationships.

You also use nonverbal signals to communicate your relationship dominance and status (Knapp & Hall, 1997). The large corner office with the huge desk communicates high status, just as the basement cubicle communicates low status.

To Structure Interaction

When you're in conversation, you give and receive cues—to speak, to listen, to comment on what the speaker just said. Turn-taking cues regulate and structure the interaction. These turn-taking cues may be verbal (as when you say, "What do you think?"), but most often they're nonverbal—a nod of the head in the direction of someone else, for example, signals that you're ready to give up your speaking turn and want this other person to say something.

You also show that you're listening and that you want the conversation to continue (or that you're not listening and want the conversation to end) largely through nonverbal signals.

To Influence

Much as you influence others by what you say, you also influence others by your nonverbal signals. A focused glance that says you're committed, gestures that further explain what you're saying, and appropriate dress signaling that "I'll easily fit in with this company" are a few examples of how you influence others with nonverbal signals.

And, of course, with the ability to influence comes the ability to deceive—to lie, to mislead another person into thinking something is true when it's false or that something is false when it's true. Using your eyes and facial expressions to communicate a liking for other people when you're really just interested in gaining their support for your promotion is an often-seen example of nonverbal deception.

Not surprisingly, you also may try to use nonverbal signals to detect deception in others. For example, you may suspect a person of lying if he or she avoids eye contact, fidgets, or sends verbal and nonverbal messages that are inconsistent. But be careful. Research shows that it is much more difficult to tell when someone is lying than you probably think it is. Using nonverbal cues in an effort to detect lying is likely to get you into trouble by leading you to formulate incorrect conclusions (Burgoon & Hoobler, 2002; Burgoon & Bacue, 2003; Knapp & Hall, 2005; Park, Levine, McCornack, Morrison, & Ferrara, 2002). For example, you may judge a person who avoids eye contact as lying when the eye avoidance may really be due to shyness or to a cultural rule that discourages eye contact, as does Japanese culture (Axtell, 1993).

To Communicate Emotion

Although people often explain and reveal emotions verbally, nonverbal expressions communicate a great part of emotional experience. It is largely through facial expressions that you reveal your level of happiness or sadness or confusion, for example. Of course, you also reveal your feelings by posture (for example, whether tense or relaxed), gestures, and eye movements and even by the extent to which your pupils dilate.

Nonverbal messages often serve to communicate unpleasant messages—messages you might feel uncomfortable saying in words (Infante, Rancer, & Womack, 2002). For example, you might avoid eye contact and maintain large distances between yourself and someone with whom you don't want to interact, or with whom you want to decrease the intensity of your relationship.

The Channels of Nonverbal Communication

Nonverbal communication is probably most easily explained in terms of the various channels through which messages pass. Here we'll survey 10 channels: (1) body, (2) face, (3) eye, (4) space, (5) artifactual, (6) touch, (7) paralanguage, (8) silence, (9) time, and (10) smell.

The Body

Two areas of the body are especially important in communicating messages. First, the movements you make with your body communicate; second, the general appearance of your body communicates.

Body Movements

Researchers in **kinesics**, or the study of nonverbal communication through face and body movements, identify five major types of movements: emblems, illustrators, affect displays, regulators, and adaptors (Ekman & Friesen, 1969; Knapp & Hall, 1997).

Emblems. **Emblems** are body gestures that directly translate into words or phrases; for example, the OK sign, the thumbs-up for "good job," and the V for victory. You use these consciously and purposely to communicate the same meaning as the words. But emblems are culture specific, so be careful when using your culture's emblems in other cultures. For example, when President Nixon visited Latin America and gestured with the OK sign, intending to communicate something positive, he was quickly informed that this gesture was not universal. In Latin America the gesture has a far more negative meaning. Here are a few cultural differences in the emblems you may commonly use (Axtell, 1993):

- In the United States, to say "hello" you wave with your whole hand moving from side to side, but in a large part of Europe that same signal means "no." In Greece such a gesture would be considered insulting.
- The V for victory is common throughout much of the world; but if you make this gesture in England with the palm facing your face, it's as insulting as the raised middle finger is in the United States.
- In Texas the raised fist with little finger and index finger held upright is a positive expression of support, because it represents the Texas longhorn steer. But in Italy it's an insult that means "Your spouse is having an affair with someone else." In parts of South America it's a gesture to ward off evil, and in parts of Africa it's a curse: "May you experience bad times."
- In the United States and in much of Asia, hugs are rarely exchanged among acquaintances; but among Latins and southern Europeans, hugging is a common greeting gesture, and failing to hug someone may communicate unfriendliness.

Illustrators. **Illustrators** enhance (literally "illustrate") the verbal messages they accompany. For example, when referring to something to the left, you might gesture toward the left. Most often you illustrate with your hands, but you can also illustrate with head and general body movements. You might, for example, turn your head or your entire body toward the left. You might also use illustrators to communicate the shape or size of objects you're talking about. Research points to an interesting advantage of illustrators: They increase your ability to remember. In one study people who illustrated their verbal messages with gestures remembered some 20 percent more than those who didn't gesture (Goldin-Meadow, Nusbaum, Kelly, & Wagner, 2001).

Affect Displays. **Affect displays** are movements of the face (smiling or frowning, for example) but also of the hands and general body (body tension or relaxation, for example) that communicate emotional meaning. Often affect displays are unconscious; you smile or frown, for example, without awareness. At other times, however, you may smile consciously, trying to convey your pleasure or satisfaction. Not surprisingly, people who smile spontaneously are judged to be more likable and more approachable than people who don't smile or people who pretend to smile (Gladstone & Parker, 2002).

Regulators. **Regulators** are behaviors that monitor, control, coordinate, or maintain the speaking of another individual. When you nod your head, for example, you tell the speaker to keep on speaking; when you lean forward and open your mouth, you tell the speaker that you would like to say something.

Adaptors. **Adaptors** are gestures that satisfy some personal need, such as scratching to relieve an itch or moving your hair out of your eyes. **Self-adaptors** are self-touching movements (for example, rubbing your nose). **Alter-adaptors** are movements directed at the person with whom you're speaking, such as removing lint from someone's jacket or straightening a person's tie or folding your arms in front of you to keep others a comfortable distance from you. **Object-adaptors** are gestures focused on objects, such as doodling on or shredding a Styrofoam coffee cup.

Body Appearance

Your general body appearance also communicates. Height, for example, has been shown to be significant in a wide variety of situations. Tall presidential candidates have a much better record of winning the election than do their shorter opponents. Tall people seem to be paid more and are favored by interviewers over shorter job applicants (Keyes, 1980; Guerrero, DeVito, & Hecht, 1999; Knapp & Hall, 2005). Taller people also have higher self-esteem and greater career success than do shorter people (Judge & Cable, 2004).

Your body also reveals your ethnicity (through skin color and tone) and may also give clues as to your more specific nationality. Your weight in proportion to your height will also communicate messages to others, as will the length, color, and style of your hair.

Your general **attractiveness** is also a part of body communication. Attractive people have the advantage in just about every activity you can name. They get better grades in school, are more valued as friends and lovers, and are preferred as coworkers (Burgoon, Buller, & Woodall, 1996). Although we normally think that attractiveness is culturally determined—and to some degree it is—research seems to indicate that definitions of attractiveness are universal (Brody, 1994). A person rated as attractive in one culture is likely to be rated as attractive in other cultures—even in cultures whose people are widely different in appearance.

Facial Communication

Throughout your interactions, your face communicates various messages, especially your emotions. Facial movements alone seem to communicate the degree of pleasantness, agreement, and sympathy felt; the rest of the body doesn't provide any additional information. But for other emotional messages—for example, the intensity with which an emotion is felt—both facial and bodily cues send messages (Graham, Bitti, & Argyle, 1975; Graham & Argyle, 1975).

So important are these cues in communicating your full meaning that graphic representations are commonly used in Internet communication. In graphic user interface chat groups, buttons are available to help you encode your emotions graphically. Table 3.1 identifies some of the more common "emoticons," icons that communicate emotions.

Some researchers in nonverbal communication claim that facial movements may express at least the following eight emotions: happiness, surprise, fear, anger, sadness, disgust, contempt, and interest (Ekman, Friesen, & Ellsworth, 1972). Facial expressions of these emotions are generally called primary affect displays: They indicate relatively pure, single emotions. Other emotional states and other facial displays are combinations of these various primary emotions and are called affect blends. You communicate these blended feelings with different parts of your face. Thus, for example, you may experience both fear and disgust at the same time. Your eyes and eyelids may signal fear, and movements of your nose, cheek, and mouth area may signal disgust.

Facial Management

As you learned your culture's nonverbal system of communication, you also learned certain **facial management techniques** that enable you to communicate your feelings to achieve the effect you want—for example, ways to hide certain emotions and to emphasize others. Consider your own use of such techniques. As you do so, think about the types of interpersonal situations in which you would use each of the following facial management techniques (Malandro, Barker, & Barker, 1989; Metts & Planalp, 2002). Would you

- *Intensify?* For example, would you exaggerate surprise when friends throw you a party to make your friends feel better?
- *Deintensify?* Would you cover up your own joy about a successful outcome in the presence of a friend who didn't receive such good news?

Table 3.1
Some Popular Emoticons

Here are a few of the many popular emoticons used in computer communication. The first six are popular in the United States; the last three are popular in Japan and illustrate how culture influences such symbols. That is, because Japanese culture considers it impolite for women to show their teeth when smiling, the emoticon for a woman's smile shows a dot signifying a closed mouth. Two excellent websites that contain extensive examples of smileys, emoticons, acronyms, and shorthand abbreviations are www.netlingo.com/smiley.cfm and www.netlingo.com/emailsh.cfm.

Emoticon	Meaning	Emoticon	Meaning
:-)	Smile; I'm kidding	*This is important*	Substitutes for underlining or italics
:-(	Frown; I'm feeling down	<G>	Grin; I'm kidding
*	Kiss	<grin>	Grin; I'm kidding
{}	Hug	^.^	Woman's smile
{*****}	Hugs and kisses	^_^	Man's smile
This is important	Gives emphasis, calls special attention to	^ o ^	Happy

Smiling

Sam smiles almost all the time. Even when he criticizes or reprimands a subordinate, he ends with a smile and this dilutes the strength of his message. As Sam's supervisor, you need him to realize what he's doing and to change his nonverbals.

WHAT DO YOU SAY?
Through what channel?
In what context?

- *Neutralize?* Would you cover up your sadness to keep from depressing others?
- *Mask?* Would you express happiness in order to cover up your disappointment at not receiving the gift you expected?
- *Simulate?* Would you express an emotion you don't feel?

These tactics of facial management help you display emotions in socially acceptable ways. For example, when someone gets bad news in which you may secretly take pleasure, the cultural display rule dictates that you frown and otherwise nonverbally signal your displeasure. If you place first in a race and your best friend barely finishes, the display rule requires that you minimize your expression of pleasure in winning and avoid any signs of gloating. If you violate these display rules, you'll seem insensitive. So although facial management techniques may be deceptive, they're also expected—in fact required—by the rules of polite interaction.

Encoding-Decoding Accuracy

One popular question concerns the accuracy with which people can encode and decode emotions through facial expressions. It can be difficult to separate the ability of the encoder from the ability of the decoder, however. Thus, a person may be quite adept at communicating emotions nonverbally, but the receiver may prove insensitive. On the other hand, the receiver may be good at deciphering emotions, but the sender may be inept. For example, introverts are not as accurate at decoding nonverbal cues as are extroverts (Akert & Panter, 1986).

Despite this difficulty, research in 11 different countries shows that women are better than men at both encoding and decoding nonverbal cues (Rosenthal & DePaulo, 1979). It may be argued that because men and women play different roles in society, they've learned different adaptive techniques and skills to help them perform these roles. Thus, in most societies women are expected to be more friendly, nurturing, and supportive and so learn these skills (Eagly & Crowley, 1986).

Accuracy in decoding also varies with the emotions themselves. Some emotions are easier to encode and decode than others. In one study, for example, people judged facial expressions of happiness with an accuracy ranging from 55 to 100 percent, surprise from 38 to 86 percent, and sadness from 19 to 88 percent (Ekman, Friesen, & Ellsworth, 1972).

Eye Communication

Research on the messages communicated by the eyes (a study known technically as oculesis) shows that these messages vary depending on the duration, direction, and quality of the eye behavior. For example, in every culture there are strict, though unstated, rules for the proper duration for eye contact. In U.S. culture the average length of a gaze is 2.95 seconds. The average length of mutual gaze (two persons gazing at each other) is 1.18 seconds (Argyle & Ingham, 1972; Argyle, 1988). When eye contact falls short of this amount, you may think the person is uninterested, shy, or preoccupied. When the appropriate amount of time is exceeded, you may perceive the person as showing unusually high interest.

The direction of the eye also communicates. In much of the United States, you're expected to glance alternately at the other person's face, then away, then again at the face, and so on. The rule for the public speaker is to scan the entire audience, not focusing for too long on or ignoring any one area of the audience. When you break these directional rules, you communicate different meanings—abnormally high or low interest, self-consciousness, nervousness over the interaction, and so on. The quality of eye behavior—how wide or how narrow your eyes get during interaction—also communicates meaning, especially interest level and such emotions as surprise, fear, and disgust. Some researchers note that eye contact serves to enable gay men and

UNDERSTANDING THEORY AND RESEARCH

The Facial Feedback Hypothesis

The **facial feedback hypothesis** holds that your facial expressions influence physiological arousal (Lanzetta, Cartwright-Smith, & Kleck, 1976; Zuckerman, Klorman, Larrance, & Spiegel, 1981). In one study, for example, participants held a pen in their teeth to simulate a sad expression and then rated a series of photographs. Results showed that mimicking sad expressions actually increased the degree of sadness the subjects reported feeling when viewing the photographs (Larsen, Kasimatis, & Frey, 1992). Further support for this hypothesis comes from a study that compared (1) participants who felt emotions such as happiness and anger with (2) participants who both felt and expressed these emotions. In support of the facial feedback hypothesis, people who felt and expressed the emotions became emotionally aroused faster than did those who only felt the emotion (Hess, Kappas, McHugo, & Lanzetta, 1992).

Generally, research finds that facial expressions can produce or heighten feelings of sadness, fear, disgust, and anger. But this effect does not occur with all emotions; smiling, for example, doesn't seem to make us feel happier (Burgoon & Bacue, 2003). Further, it has not been demonstrated that facial expressions can eliminate one feeling and replace it with another. So if you're feeling sad, smiling will not eliminate the sadness and replace it with gladness. A reasonable conclusion seems to be that your facial expressions can influence some feelings, but not all (Burgoon & Bacue, 2003).

Working with Theories and Research

- *What effect do you observe when you express your emotions? Do your feelings get stronger? Weaker?*

lesbians to signal their homosexuality and perhaps their interest in the other person—an ability referred to as "gaydar" (Nicholas, 2004).

Eye Contact and Eye Avoidance

Eye contact can serve a variety of functions. One such function is to seek feedback. In talking with someone, we look at her or him intently, as if to say, "Well, what do you think?" As you might predict, listeners gaze at speakers more than speakers gaze at listeners. In public speaking, you may scan hundreds of people to secure this feedback.

A second function is to inform the other person that the channel of communication is open and that he or she should now speak. You see this regularly in conversation, when one person asks a question or finishes a thought and then looks to you for a response. And one study found that eye contact was the most frequently noted nonverbal behavior used to tell library users that the librarian was approachable (Radford, 1998).

Eye movements may also signal the nature of a relationship, whether positive (an attentive glance) or negative (eye avoidance). You can also signal your power through **visual dominance** behavior (Exline, Ellyson, & Long, 1975). The average person, for example, maintains a high level of eye contact while listening and a lower level while speaking. When people want to signal dominance, they may reverse this pattern—maintaining a high level of eye contact while talking but a much lower level while listening.

By making eye contact you psychologically lessen the physical distance between yourself and another person. When you catch someone's eye at a party, for example, you become psychologically close though physically far apart.

Eye avoidance, too, can serve several different functions. When you avoid eye contact or avert your glance, you may help others maintain their privacy. For example, you may do this when you see a couple arguing in public. You turn your eyes away (though your eyes may be wide open) as if to say, "I don't mean to intrude; I respect your privacy," a behavior referred to as **civil inattention** (Goffman, 1971).

Eye avoidance can also signal lack of interest—in a person, a conversation, or some visual stimulus. At times, too, you may hide your eyes to block out unpleasant stimuli (a particularly gory or violent scene in a movie, for example) or close your eyes to block out visual stimuli and thus heighten other senses. For

BUILDING COMMUNICATION SKILLS

Choosing a Seat

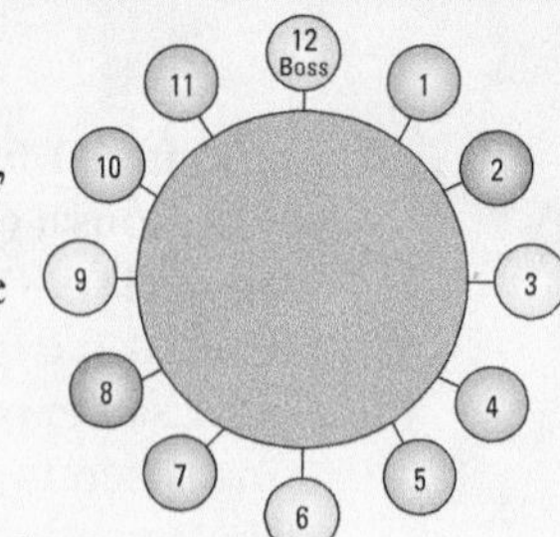

Look at the diagram here, which represents a table with 12 chairs, one of which is already occupied by the "boss." Below are listed five messages you might want to communicate. For each of these messages, indicate (a) where you would sit to communicate the desired message, and (b) any other messages that your seating position will make it easier for you to communicate.

1. You want to polish the apple and ingratiate yourself with your boss.
2. You aren't prepared and want to be ignored.
3. You want to challenge your boss on a certain policy that will come up for a vote.
4. You want to be accepted as a new (but important) member of the company.
5. You want to get to know the person already seated at position number 5.

Every nonverbal (and verbal) message that you send has an impact, even the seat you select at a meeting. Your messages always reveal (to some extent) who you are and what others will think of you.

example, you may listen to music with your eyes closed. Lovers often close their eyes while kissing, and many prefer to make love in a dark or dimly lit room.

Pupil Dilation

In the fifteenth and sixteenth centuries, Italian women put drops of belladonna (which literally means "beautiful woman") into their eyes to enlarge the pupils so that they would look more attractive. Contemporary **pupillometrics** research supports the intuitive logic of these women; dilated pupils are judged more attractive than constricted ones (Hess, 1975; Marshall, 1983). In one study, researchers retouched photographs of women; in half they enlarged the pupils, and in the other half they made them smaller (Hess, 1975). Men were then asked to judge the women's personalities from the photographs. The photos of women with small pupils drew responses such as "cold," "hard," and "selfish"; those with dilated pupils drew responses such as "feminine" and "soft." Interestingly, the male observers could not verbalize the reasons for their different perceptions. Pupil dilation and our reactions to changes in the pupil size of others may function below the level of conscious awareness.

Pupil size also reveals your interest and level of emotional arousal. Your pupils enlarge when you're interested in something or when you are emotionally aroused. When homosexuals and heterosexuals were shown pictures of nude bodies, the homosexuals' pupils dilated more when they viewed same-sex bodies, whereas the heterosexuals' pupils dilated more when they viewed opposite-sex bodies (Hess, Seltzer, & Schlien, 1965). These pupillary responses are also observed in persons with profound mental retardation (Chaney, Givens, Aoki, & Gombiner, 1989). Perhaps we judge dilated pupils as more attractive because we respond to them as indicative of a person's interest in us. And that may be the reason why both models and fuzzy beanbag toys have exceptionally large pupils.

Space Communication

Space is an especially important factor in interpersonal communication, although we seldom think about it. Edward T. Hall (1959, 1963, 1976) pioneered the study of spatial communication and called this research area **proxemics**. We can examine this broad area by looking at (1) proxemic distances and (2) territoriality.

Proxemic Distances

Edward Hall (1959, 1963, 1976) distinguishes four **proxemic distances**, or **spatial distances**: the physical distances that define the types of relationships between people and the types of communication in which they are likely to engage (see Table 3.2).

Table 3.2
Relationships and Proxemic Distances

Note that these four distances can be further divided into close and far phases and that the far phase of one level (say, personal) blends into the close phase of the next level (social). Do your relationships also blend into one another? Or are, say, your personal relationships totally separate from your social relationships?

Relationship	Distance
Intimate relationship	Intimate distance 0 ——— 18 inches close phase — far phase
Personal relationship	Personal distance 1 ——— 4 feet close phase — far phase
Social relationship	Social distance 4 ——— 12 feet close phase — far phase
Public relationship	Public distance 12 ——— 25+ feet close phase — far phase

Intimate Distance. In **intimate distance**, ranging from actual touching to 18 inches, the presence of the other individual is unmistakable. Each person experiences the sound, smell, and feel of the other's breath. You use intimate distance for lovemaking, comforting, and protecting. This distance is so short that most people don't consider it proper in public.

Personal Distance. Personal distance refers to the protective "bubble" that defines your personal space, ranging from 18 inches to 4 feet. This imaginary bubble keeps you protected and untouched by others. You can still hold or grasp another person at this distance, but only by extending your arms; this allows you to take certain individuals such as loved ones into your protective bubble. At the outer limit of personal distance, you can touch another person only if both of you extend your arms. This is the distance at which you conduct most of your interpersonal interactions; for example, talking with friends and family.

Social Distance. At **social distance**, ranging from 4 to 12 feet, you lose the visual detail you have at personal distance. You conduct impersonal business and interact at a social gathering at this social distance. The more distance you maintain in your interactions, the more formal they appear. In offices of high officials, the desks are positioned so the official is assured of at least this distance from clients.

Public Distance. Public distance, from 12 to more than 25 feet, protects you. At this distance you could take defensive action if threatened. On a public bus or train, for example, you might keep at least this distance from a drunken passenger. Although at this distance you lose fine details of the face and eyes, you're still close enough to see what is happening.

The specific distances that we maintain between ourselves and other people depend on a wide variety of factors (Burgoon, Buller, & Woodall, 1996; Burgoon & Bacue, 2003). Among the most significant are *gender* (in same-sex dyads women sit and stand closer to each other than do men, and people approach women more closely than they approach men); *age* (people maintain closer distances with similarly aged others than they do with those much older or much

Proxemics

Like the close-talker in an episode of Seinfeld, one of your team members at work maintains an extremely close distance when talking. Coupled with the fact that this person is a heavy smoker and reeks of smoke, you need to say something.

WHAT DO YOU SAY?
Through what channel?

younger); and *personality* (introverts and highly anxious people maintain greater distances than do extroverts). Not surprisingly, we maintain shorter distances with people we're familiar with than with strangers and with people we like than with those we don't like. One theoretical explanation of the dynamics of spatial distances is discussed in the accompanying Understanding Theory and Research box (on page 67).

Territoriality

One of the most interesting concepts in ethology (the study of animals in their natural surroundings) is **territoriality**, a possessive or ownership reaction to an area of space or to particular objects. Two interesting dimensions of territoriality are territory types and territorial markers.

Territory Types. Three types of territory are often distinguished: primary, secondary, and public (Altman, 1975). **Primary territories** are your exclusive preserve: your desk, room, house, or backyard, for example. In these areas you're in control. The effect is similar to the **home field advantage** that a sports team has when playing in its own ballpark. When you're in these home territories, you generally have greater influence over others than you would in someone else's territory. For example, in their own home or office, people generally take on a kind of leadership role; they initiate conversations, fill in silences, assume relaxed and comfortable postures, and maintain their positions with greater conviction. Because the territorial owner is dominant, you stand a better chance of getting your raise approved, your point accepted, or a contract resolved in your favor if you're in your own primary territory (home, office) rather than in someone else's (Marsh, 1988).

Secondary territories, although they don't belong to you, are associated with you—perhaps because you've occupied them for a long time or they were assigned to you. For example, your desk in a classroom may become a secondary territory if it is assigned to you or if you regularly occupy it and others treat it as yours. Your neighborhood turf, a cafeteria table where you usually sit, or a favorite corner of a local coffee shop may be secondary territories. You feel a certain "ownership-like" attachment to the place, even though it's really not yours in any legal sense.

Public territories are areas that are open to all people, such as a park, movie house, restaurant, or beach. European cafés, food courts in suburban malls, and the open areas in large city office buildings are public spaces that bring people together and stimulate communication.

The electronic revolution, however, may well change the role of public space in stimulating communication (Drucker & Gumpert, 1991; Gumpert & Drucker, 1995). For example, home shopping clubs make it less necessary for people to go downtown or to the mall, and shoppers consequently have less opportunity to run into other people and to talk and exchange news. Similarly, electronic mail permits us to communicate without talking and without leaving the house to mail a letter. Perhaps the greatest change is telecommuting (Giordano, 1989), in which workers can go to work without leaving their homes. The face-to-face communication that normally takes place in an office is replaced by communication via computer.

Territoriality is closely linked to **status**. Generally, the size and location of your territories signal your status within your social group. For example, male animals will stake out a particular territory and con-

UNDERSTANDING *THEORY* AND *RESEARCH*

Space Violations

Expectancy violations theory, developed by Judee Burgoon, explains what happens when you increase or decrease the distance between yourself and another person in an interpersonal interaction (Burgoon, 1978; Burgoon & Bacue, 2003). Each culture has certain expectancies for the distance that people are expected to maintain in their conversations. And, of course, each person has certain idiosyncrasies. Together, these determine expected distance. If you violate the expected distance to a great extent (small violations most often go unnoticed), the relationship itself comes into focus; the other person begins to turn attention away from the topic of conversation to you and to your relationship with him or her.

If this other person perceives you positively—for example, if you're a high-status person or you're particularly attractive—then you'll be perceived even more positively if you violate the expected distance. If, on the other hand, you're perceived negatively and you violate the norm, you'll be perceived even more negatively.

Working with Theories and Research

- *Do your own experiences support this theory of space expectancy violations? What do you see happening when space expectations are violated?*

sider it their own. They will allow prospective mates to enter but will defend the territory against entrance by others, especially by other males of the same species. The larger the animal's territory, the higher the status of animal within the herd. The size and location of human territories also say something about status (Mehrabian, 1976; Sommer, 1969). An apartment or office in midtown Manhattan or downtown Tokyo, for example, is extremely high-status territory. The cost of the territory restricts it to those who have lots of money.

Territory Markers. Much as animals mark their territory, humans mark theirs with three types of **markers**: central markers, boundary markers, and earmarkers (Hickson, Stacks, & Moore, 2003). **Central markers** are items you place in a territory to reserve it. For example, you place a drink at the bar, books on your desk, or a sweater over the chair to let others know that these territories belong to you.

Boundary markers set boundaries that divide your territory from "theirs." In the supermarket checkout line, the bar placed between your groceries and those of the person behind you is a boundary marker. Similarly, the armrests separating your seat from those of the people on either side at a movie theater and the molded plastic seats on a bus or train are boundary markers.

Earmarkers—a term taken from the practice of branding animals on their ears—are those identifying marks that indicate your possession of a territory or object. Trademarks, nameplates, and initials on a shirt or attaché case are all examples of earmarkers. Some teenagers, for example, perhaps because they can't yet own territories, often use markers to indicate a kind of pseudo-ownership or appropriation of someone else's or a public territory for their own use (Childress, 2004). Examples of graffiti and the markings of gang boundaries come quickly to mind.

Artifactual Communication

Artifactual communication is communication via objects made by human hands. Thus, color, clothing, jewelry, and the decoration of space would be considered artifactual. Let's look at each of these briefly.

Color Communication

There is some evidence that colors affect us physiologically. For example, respiratory movements increase with red light and decrease with blue light. Similarly, eye blinks increase in frequency when eyes are exposed to red light and decrease when exposed to blue. These responses seem consistent with our intuitive feelings about blue being more soothing and red more arousing. When a school changed the color of its walls from orange and white to blue, the blood pressure of the students decreased and their academic performance increased (Ketcham, 1958; Malandro, Barker, & Barker, 1989).

Color communication also influences perceptions and behaviors (Kanner, 1989). People's acceptance of a product, for example, is largely determined by its packaging, especially its color. In one study the very same coffee taken from a yellow can was described as weak, from a dark brown can as too strong, from a red can as rich, and from a blue can as mild. Even your acceptance of a person may depend on the colors he or she wears. Consider, for example, the comments of one color expert (Kanner, 1989): "If you have to pick the wardrobe for your defense lawyer heading into court and choose anything but blue, you deserve to lose the case." Black is so powerful it could work against the lawyer with the jury. Brown lacks sufficient authority. Green would probably elicit a negative response.

Clothing and Body Adornment

People make inferences about who you are, at least in part, from the way you dress. Whether these inferences are accurate or not, they will influence what people think of you and how they react to you. Your socioeconomic class, your seriousness, your attitudes (for example, whether you're conservative or liberal), your concern for convention, your sense of style, and perhaps even your creativity will all be judged in part by the way you dress (Molloy, 1975, 1977, 1981; Burgoon, Buller, & Woodall, 1996; Knapp & Hall, 2005). In the business world, your clothing may communicate your position within the hierarchy and your willingness and desire to conform to the norms of the organization. It also may communicate your professionalism, which seems to be the reason why some organizations favor dress codes (Smith, M. H., 2003). On campus, college students will perceive an instructor dressed informally as friendly, fair, enthusiastic, and flexible; they will see the same instructor dressed formally as prepared, knowledgeable, and organized (Malandro, Barker, & Barker, 1989).

Try personalizing this brief discussion by considering, for example, how you'd dress in each of such situations as these:

- to interview for a job at a prestigious and conservative law firm
- to appear friendly but serious as you teach your first college class
- to appear as the trendiest partygoer at the trendiest spot in town
- to make your romantic partner's parents (you've been dating about six months), about whom you know very little, think you're absolutely wonderful
- to attend a parent–teacher conference (you're the parent) at your child's preschool and appear very concerned and involved, though in truth you've not participated in any of the school's activities

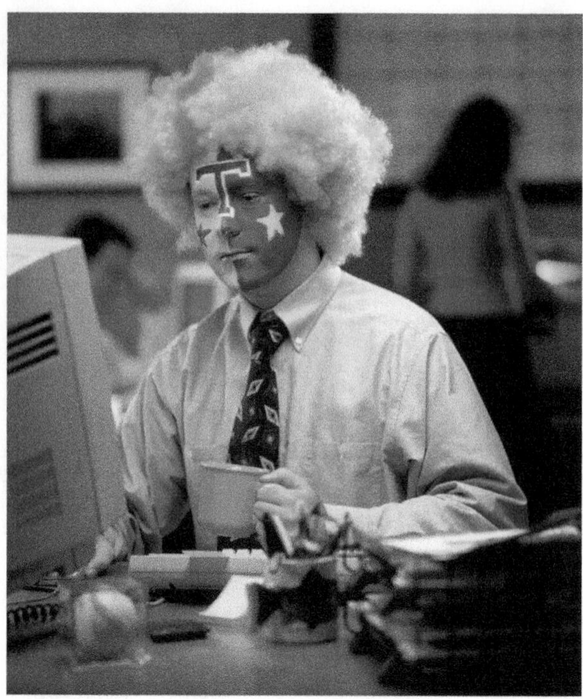

Clothing Communication

One of your friends has been passed over for promotion several times and you think you know the reason: Your friend dresses inappropriately, though generally not as bad as the guy in the photo. You want to help your friend.

WHAT DO YOU SAY?
Through what channel? In what context?

Very likely you'd dress very differently in each of these situations, attesting to the importance of clothing in impression formation.

The way you wear your hair says something about your attitudes—from a concern about being up-to-date, to a desire to shock, to perhaps a lack of interest in appearances. Men with long hair will generally be judged as less conservative than those with shorter hair. Your jewelry also communicates about you. Wedding and engagement rings are obvious examples that communicate specific messages. College rings and political buttons likewise communicate specific messages. If you wear a Rolex watch or large precious stones, others are likely to infer that you're rich. Men who wear earrings will be judged differently from men who don't. What judgments are made will depend on who the receiver is, the communication context, and all the factors identified throughout this text.

Body piercings are now common, especially among the young. Nose, nipple, tongue, and belly button jewelry (among other piercings) send a variety of messages. Although people wearing such jewelry may wish to communicate positive meanings, research indicates that those interpreting these messages seem to infer that the wearer is communicating an unwillingness to conform to social norms and a willingness to take greater risks than people without such piercings (Forbes, 2001). It's worth noting that in a study of employers' perceptions, applicants with eyebrow piercings were rated and ranked significantly lower than those without such piercings (Acor, 2001). In another study, nose-pierced job candidates were scored lower on measures of credibility such as character and trust as well as sociability and hirability (Seiter & Sandry, 2003). And in health care situations, tattoos and piercings may communicate such undesirable traits as impulsiveness, unpredictability, and a tendency toward being reckless or violent (Rapsa & Cusack, 1990; Smith, M. H., 2003).

Tattoos, whether temporary or permanent, likewise communicate a variety of messages—often the name of a loved one or some symbol of allegiance or affiliation. Tattoos also communicate to the wearers themselves. For example, tattooed students see themselves (and perhaps others do as well) as more adventurous, creative, individualistic, and risk-prone than those without tattoos (Drews, Allison, & Probst, 2000).

The accompanying Media Watch box continues this discussion of clothing by looking at clothing with specific verbal messages.

Space Decoration

The way you decorate your private spaces also communicates about you. The office with a mahogany

MEDIA WATCH

Legible Clothing

Legible clothing is anything that you wear that displays some verbal message; it's clothing that literally can be read. In some instances the message proclaims status; it tells others that you are, for example, rich or stylish or youthful. The Gucci or Louis Vuitton logos on your luggage communicate your financial status. In a similar way your sweatshirt with the word "Bulls" or "Pirates" emblazoned across it communicates your interest in sports and your favorite team.

Legible clothing is being bought and worn in record numbers. Many designers and manufacturers have their names integrated into the design of the clothing: DKNY, Calvin Klein, Armani, L. L. Bean, the Gap, and Old Navy are just a few examples. At the same time that you're paying extra to buy the brand name, you're also providing free advertising for the designer.

T-shirts and sweatshirts are especially popular as message senders. One study surveyed 600 male and female students as to the types of T-shirt messages they preferred (Sayre, 1992). Four messages were cited most often:

- Affiliation messages, such as a club or school name, communicate that you're a part of a larger group.
- Trophy names, such as those of a high-status concert or perhaps a ski lodge, say that you were in the right place at the right time.
- Metaphorical expressions, such as pictures of rock groups or famous athletes, reveal that you're part of a current trend.
- Personal messages, such as statements of beliefs or philosophies, tell others that you're willing to express your beliefs publicly.

Increasing Media Literacy

Affiliation messages may create problems when they identify the wearer as a member of a gang, because wearing gang colors can contribute to violence, especially in schools (Burke, 1993; Zimmerman, 2000). How do you feel about these and other provocative types of clothing messages? Do you feel that some clothing messages should be prohibited? If so, which ones? Or do you feel that such messages should be protected by the First Amendment to the Constitution, which guarantees freedom of speech?

desk and bookcases and oriental rugs communicates your importance and status within an organization, just as a metal desk and bare floor indicate a worker much farther down in the hierarchy.

Similarly, people will make inferences about you based on the way you decorate your home. The expensiveness of the furnishings may communicate your status and wealth; their coordination may convey your sense of style. The magazines may reflect your interests, and the arrangement of chairs around a television set may reveal how important watching television is to you. The contents of bookcases lining the walls reveal the importance of reading in your life. In fact, there's probably little in your home that will not send messages from which others will draw inferences about you. Computers, wide-screen televisions, well-equipped kitchens, and oil paintings of great-grandparents, for example, all say something about the people who live in the home.

Similarly, the absence of certain items will communicate something about you. Consider what messages you'd get from a home where no television, phone, or books could be seen.

People will also make judgments as to your personality on the basis of room decorations. Research finds, for example, that people will make judgments about your openness to new experiences (distinctive decorating usually communicates this, as would different types of books and magazines and travel souvenirs) and even about your conscientiousness, emotional stability, degree of extroversion, and agreeableness. Not surprisingly, bedrooms prove more revealing of personality than offices (Gosling, Ko, Mannarelli, & Morris, 2002).

Touch Communication

The study of **touch communication**, technically referred to as **haptics**, suggests that touch is perhaps the most primitive form of communication (Montagu, 1971). Developmentally, touch is probably the first sense to be used. Even in the womb the child is stimulated by touch. Soon after birth the child is fondled, caressed, patted, and stroked. In turn, the child explores its world through touch. In a short time the child learns to communicate many different meanings through touch.

The Meanings of Touch

Touch communicates a wide range of messages (Jones & Yarbrough, 1985). Here are five major types of messages that will illustrate this great variety.

- Touch communicates positive feelings; for example, support, appreciation, inclusion, sexual interest or intent, composure, immediacy, affection, trust, similarity and quality, and informality (Jones & Yarbrough, 1985; Burgoon, 1991). Touch also stimulates self-disclosure (Rabinowitz, 1991).
- Touch often communicates your intention to play, either affectionately or aggressively.
- Touch may control the behaviors, attitudes, or feelings of other people. To obtain compliance, for example, you touch a person to communicate "move over," "hurry," "stay here," or "do it." You might also touch a person to gain his or her attention, as if to say "look at me" or "look over here." In some situations touching can even amount to a kind of **nonverbal dominance** behavior. Touch even seems to increase a waitperson's tips. Researchers found that people who were touched by a female waitperson on the hand or shoulder tipped more than those who weren't touched (Crusco & Wetzel, 1984; Stephen & Zweigenhaft, 1986).
- Ritualistic touching centers on greetings and departures; examples are shaking hands to say "hello" or "good-bye," hugging, kissing, or putting your arm around another's shoulder when greeting or saying farewell.
- Task-related touching is associated with the performance of some function, as when you remove a speck of dust from another person's coat, help someone out of a car, or check someone's forehead for fever.

Touch Avoidance

Much as you have a need and desire to touch and be touched, you also have a tendency to avoid touch from certain people or in certain circumstances (Andersen & Leibowitz, 1978). You may wish to examine your own **touch avoidance** tendency by taking the following self-test.

TEST YOURSELF

Do You Avoid Touch?

This test is composed of 18 statements concerning how you feel about touching other people and being touched. Please indicate the degree to which each statement applies to you according to the following scale: 1 = strongly agree; 2 = agree; 3 = undecided; 4 = disagree; and 5 = strongly disagree.

____ **1.** A hug from a same-sex friend is a true sign of friendship.

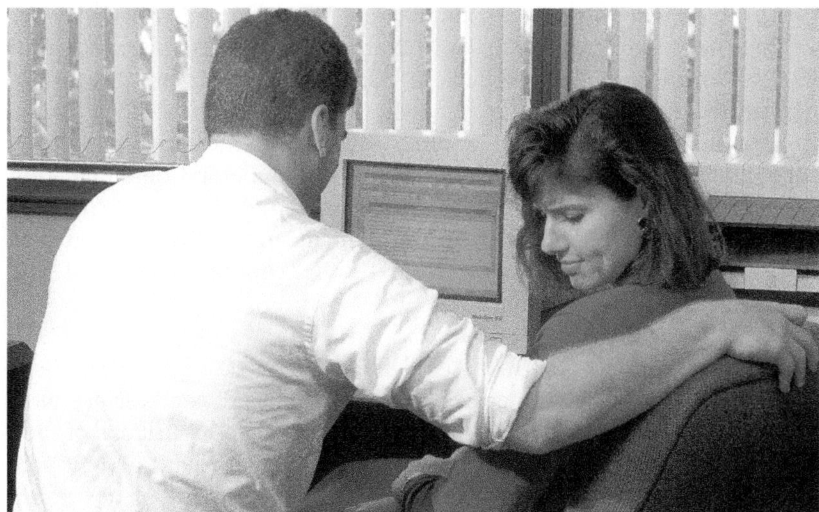

Touch Boundaries

A colleague at work continually touches you in passing—your arm, your shoulder, your waist. These touches are becoming more frequent and more intimate. You want this touching to stop.

WHAT DO YOU SAY?

To whom? Through what channel?

____ **2.** Opposite-sex friends enjoy it when I touch them.

____ **3.** I often put my arm around friends of the same sex.

____ **4.** When I see two friends of the same sex hugging, it revolts me.

____ **5.** I like it when members of the opposite sex touch me.

____ **6.** People shouldn't be so uptight about touching persons of the same sex.

____ **7.** I think it is vulgar when members of the opposite sex touch me.

____ **8.** When a member of the opposite sex touches me, I find it unpleasant.

____ **9.** I wish I were free to show emotions by touching members of the same sex.

____ **10.** I'd enjoy giving a massage to an opposite-sex friend.

____ **11.** I enjoy kissing a person of the same sex.

____ **12.** I like to touch friends that are the same sex as I am.

____ **13.** Touching a friend of the same sex does not make me uncomfortable.

____ **14.** I find it enjoyable when my date and I embrace.

____ **15.** I enjoy getting a back rub from a member of the opposite sex.

____ **16.** I dislike kissing relatives of the same sex.

____ **17.** Intimate touching with members of the opposite sex is pleasurable.

____ **18.** I find it difficult to be touched by a member of my own sex.

HOW DID YOU DO? To score your touch avoidance questionnaire:

1. Reverse your scores for items 4, 7, 8, 16, and 18. Use these reversed scores in all future calculations.
2. To obtain your same-sex touch avoidance score (the extent to which you avoid touching members of your sex), total the scores for items 1, 3, 4, 6, 9, 11, 12, 13, 16, and 18.
3. To obtain your opposite-sex touch avoidance score (the extent to which you avoid touching members of the opposite sex), total the scores for items 2, 5, 7, 8, 10, 14, 15, and 17.
4. To obtain your total touch avoidance score, add the subtotals from steps 2 and 3.

The higher the score, the higher the touch avoidance—that is, the greater your tendency to avoid touch. In studies by Andersen and Leibowitz (1978), who constructed this test, average opposite-sex touch avoidance scores were 12.9 for males and 14.85 for females. Average same-sex touch avoidance scores were 26.43 for males and 21.70 for females. How do your scores compare with those of the college students in Andersen and Leibowitz's study? Is your touch avoidance likely to be higher when you are interacting with persons who are culturally different from you? Can you identify types of people and types of situations in which your touch avoidance would be especially high? Especially low?

WHAT WILL YOU DO? Are you satisfied with your score? Would you like to change your touch avoidance tendencies? What might you do about them?

Source: From "The Development and Nature of the Construct Touch Avoidance" by Andersen et al., *Journal of Nonverbal Behavior*, 3(2) 89–106. With kind permission from Springer Science and Business Media.

Researchers using the self-test presented here have found several interesting connections between touch avoidance and other factors (Andersen & Liebowitz, 1978). For example, touch avoidance is positively related to communication apprehension. If you have a strong fear of oral communication, then you probably also have strong touch avoidance tendencies. Touch avoidance is also high in those who self-disclose less.

Both touch and self-disclosure are intimate forms of communication. People who are reluctant to get close to another person by self-disclosing also seem reluctant to get close by touching.

Older people avoid touch with opposite-sex persons more than younger people do. As people get older they're touched less by members of the opposite sex; this decreased frequency of touching may lead them to avoid touching.

Not surprisingly, touch also varies with your relationship stage. In the early stages of a relationship, you touch little; in intermediate stages (involvement and intimacy), you touch a great deal; and at stable or deteriorating stages, you again touch little (Guerrero & Andersen, 1991, 1994).

Paralanguage: The Vocal Channel

Paralanguage is the vocal but nonverbal dimension of speech. It has to do not with what you say but with how you say it. A traditional exercise students use to increase their ability to express different emotions, feelings, and attitudes is to repeat a sentence while accenting or stressing different words. One popular sentence is, "Is this the face that launched a thousand ships?" Significant differences in meaning are easily communicated depending on where the speaker places the stress. Consider the following variations:

- Is *this* the face that launched a thousand ships?
- Is this the *face* that launched a thousand ships?
- Is this the face that *launched* a thousand ships?
- Is this the face that launched a *thousand ships*?

Each sentence communicates something different; in fact, each asks a different question, even though the words are exactly the same. All that distinguishes the sentences is stress, one aspect of paralanguage. In addition to stress and **pitch** (highness or lowness), paralanguage includes such **voice qualities** as **rate** (speed), **volume** (loudness), rhythm, and pauses or hesitations as well as the vocalizations you make in crying, whispering, moaning, belching, yawning, and yelling (Trager, 1958, 1961; Argyle, 1988). A variation in any of these features communicates. When you speak quickly, for example, you communicate something different from when you speak slowly. Even though the words may be the same, if the speed (or volume, rhythm, or pitch) differs, the meanings people receive will also differ. The Building Communication Skills exercise, "Expressing Praise and Criticism," explores the different meanings that variations in paralanguage (and other nonverbal signals) can communicate.

Judgments about People

Paralanguage cues are often used as a basis for judgments about people; for example, evaluations of their emotional state or even their personality. A listener can accurately judge the emotional state of a speaker from vocal expression alone if both speaker and listener speak the same language. Paralanguage cues are not so accurate when used to communicate emotions to those who speak a different language (Albas, McCluskey, & Albas, 1976). Also, some emotions are easier to identify than others; it's easy to distinguish between hate and sympathy but more difficult to distinguish between fear and anxiety. And, of course, listeners vary in their ability to decode, and speakers in their ability to encode emotions (Scherer, 1986).

Judgments about Communication Effectiveness

In one-way communication (when one person is doing all or most of the speaking and the other person is doing all or most of the listening), those who talk fast (about 50 percent faster than normal) are more persuasive (MacLachlan, 1979). People agree more with a fast speaker than with a slow speaker and find the fast speaker more intelligent and objective.

When we look at comprehension, rapid speech shows an interesting effect. When the speaking rate is increased by 50 percent, the comprehension level drops by only 5 percent. When the rate is doubled, the comprehension level drops only 10 percent. These 5 and 10 percent losses are more than offset by the increased speed; thus, the faster rates are much more efficient in communicating information. If speeds are more than twice the rate of normal speech, however, comprehension begins to fall dramatically.

Do exercise caution in applying this research to all forms of communication (MacLachlan, 1979). For example, if you increase your rate to increase efficiency, you may create an impression so unnatural that others will focus on your speed instead of your meaning.

BUILDING COMMUNICATION SKILLS

Expressing Praise and Criticism

Consider how nonverbal messages can communicate praise and criticism by reading each of the following statements, first to communicate praise and second, criticism. In the second and third columns, record the nonverbal signals you used to help you communicate these differences in meaning between praise and criticism.

Message	Nonverbal cues to communicate praise	Nonverbal cues to communicate criticism
You lost weight.		
You look happy.		
You're an expert.		
Your parents are something else.		

You cannot speak a sentence without using nonverbal signals, and these signals influence the meaning the receiver gets. Acquiring the skills of nonverbal communication will help you communicate your meanings more effectively whether in interpersonal, small group, or public speaking.

Silence

Like words and gestures, **silence**, too, communicates important meanings and serves important functions (Johannesen, 1974; Jaworski, 1993). Silence allows the speaker *time to think*, time to formulate and organize his or her verbal communications. Before messages of intense conflict, as well as before those confessing undying love, there's often silence. Again, silence seems to prepare the receiver for the importance of these future messages.

Some people use silence as a *weapon* to hurt others. We often speak of giving someone "the silent treatment." After a conflict, for example, one or both individuals may remain silent as a kind of punishment. Silence used to hurt others may also take the form of refusing to acknowledge the presence of another person, as in disconfirmation; here silence is a dramatic demonstration of the total indifference one person feels toward the other.

Sometimes silence is used as a *"response to personal anxiety,"* shyness, or threats. You may feel anxious or shy among new people and prefer to remain silent. By remaining silent you preclude the chance of rejection. Only when you break your silence and make an attempt to communicate with another person do you risk rejection.

Silence may be used to *prevent communication* of certain messages. In conflict situations silence is sometimes used to prevent certain topics from surfacing and to prevent one or both parties from saying things they may later regret. In such situations silence often allows us time to cool off before expressing hatred, severe criticism, or personal attacks—which, as we know, are irreversible.

Like the eyes, face, and hands, silence can also be used to *communicate emotional responses* (Ehrenhaus, 1988). Sometimes silence communicates a determination to be uncooperative or defiant; by refusing to engage in verbal communication, you defy the authority or the legitimacy of the other person's position. Silence is often used to communicate annoyance, particularly when accompanied by a pouting expression, arms crossed in front of the chest, and nostrils flared. Silence may express affection or love, especially when coupled with long and longing gazes into each other's eyes.

Of course, you may also use silence when you simply have *nothing to say*, when nothing occurs to you, or when you don't want to say anything. James Russell Lowell expressed this best: "Blessed are they who have nothing to say, and who cannot be persuaded to say it." Silence may also be used to avoid responsibility for any wrongdoing (Beach, 1990–91).

REFLECTIONS ON ETHICS

Silence

Remaining silent is at times your right. For example, you have the right to remain silent so as not to incriminate yourself. You have a right to protect your privacy—to withhold information that has no bearing on the matter at hand. And thus, your previous relationship history, affectional orientation, or religion is usually irrelevant to your ability to function in a job, and thus may be kept private in most job-related situations. On the other hand, these issues may be relevant when, for example, you're about to enter a more intimate phase of a relationship—then there may be an obligation to reveal information about yourself that could have been kept hidden at earlier relationship stages.

At other times, however, you have an obligation *not* to remain silent; and in fact in some cases it may be unlawful to say nothing. For example, you do not have the right to remain silent and to refuse to reveal information about crimes you've seen others commit. You have a legal obligation to report such crimes and in some cases even suspicions of crime. Psychiatrists, clergy, and lawyers—fortunately or unfortunately—are often exempt from this requirement to reveal information about criminal activities when the information had been gained through privileged communication with clients.

Ethical Choice Point

On your way to work, you witness a father verbally abusing his three-year-old child. You worry that he might psychologically harm the child, and your first impulse is to speak up and tell this man that verbal abuse can have lasting effects on the child and often leads to physical abuse. At the same time, you don't want to interfere with his right to speak to his child, and you certainly don't want to make him angrier. What is your ethical obligation in this case? What would you do in this situation?

Time Communication

The study of **temporal communication**, known technically as **chronemics**, concerns the use of time—how you organize it, react to it, and communicate messages through it (Bruneau, 1985, 1990). Consider, for example, your **psychological time** orientation; the emphasis you place on the past, present, and future. In a past orientation, you have special reverence for the past. You relive old times and regard old methods as the best. You see events as circular and recurring, so the wisdom of yesterday is applicable also to today and tomorrow. In a present orientation, however, you live in the present: for now, not tomorrow. In a future orientation, you look toward and live for the future. You save today, work hard in college, and deny yourself luxuries because you're preparing for the future. Before reading more about time, take the following self-test.

TEST YOURSELF

What Time Do You Have?

For each statement, indicate whether the statement is true (T) or false (F) in relation to your general attitude and behavior. (A few statements are purposely repeated to facilitate scoring and analysis of your responses.)

____ **1.** Meeting tomorrow's deadlines and doing other necessary work comes before tonight's partying.

____ **2.** I meet my obligations to friends and authorities on time.

____ **3.** I complete projects on time by making steady progress.

____ **4.** I am able to resist temptations when I know there is work to be done.

____ **5.** I keep working at a difficult, uninteresting task if it will help me get ahead.

____ **6.** If things don't get done on time, I don't worry about it.

____ **7.** I think that it's useless to plan too far ahead, because things hardly ever come out the way you planned anyway.

____ **8.** I try to live one day at a time.

____ **9.** I live to make better what is rather than to be concerned about what will be.

____ **10.** It seems to me that it doesn't make sense to worry about the future, since fate determines that whatever will be, will be.

____ **11.** I believe that getting together with friends to party is one of life's important pleasures.

____ **12.** I do things impulsively, making decisions on the spur of the moment.

____ **13.** I take risks to put excitement in my life.

____ **14.** I get drunk at parties.

____ **15.** It's fun to gamble.

____ **16.** Thinking about the future is pleasant to me.

____ **17.** When I want to achieve something, I set subgoals and consider specific means for reaching those goals.

____ **18.** It seems to me that my career path is pretty well laid out.

____ **19.** It upsets me to be late for appointments.

____ **20.** I meet my obligations to friends and authorities on time.

____ **21.** I get irritated at people who keep me waiting when we've agreed to meet at a given time.

____ **22.** It makes sense to invest a substantial part of my income in insurance premiums.

____ **23.** I believe that "A stitch in time saves nine."

____ **24.** I believe that "A bird in the hand is worth two in the bush."

____ **25.** I believe it is important to save for a rainy day.

____ **26.** I believe a person's day should be planned each morning.

____ **27.** I make lists of things I must do.

____ **28.** When I want to achieve something, I set subgoals and consider specific means for reaching those goals.

____ **29.** I believe that "A stitch in time saves nine."

HOW DID YOU DO? This time test measures seven different factors. If you selected true (T) for all or most of the statements within any given factor, you are probably high on that factor. If you selected false (F) for all or most of the statements within any given factor, you are probably low on that factor.

The first factor, measured by items 1–5, is a future, work motivation, perseverance orientation. These people have a strong work ethic and are committed to completing a task despite difficulties and temptations. The second factor (items 6–10) is a present, fatalistic, worry-free orientation. High scorers on this factor live one day at a time, not necessarily to enjoy the day but to avoid planning for the next day or anxiety about the future.

The third factor (items 11–15) is a present, pleasure-seeking, partying orientation. These people enjoy the present, take risks, and engage in a variety of impulsive actions. The fourth factor (items 16–18) is a future, goal-seeking, planning orientation. These people derive special pleasure from planning and achieving a variety of goals.

The fifth factor (items 19–21) is a time-sensitivity orientation. People who score high are especially sensitive to time and its role in social obligations. The sixth factor (items 22–25) is a future, practical action orientation. These people do what they have to do—take practical actions—to achieve the future they want.

The seventh factor (items 26–29) is a future, somewhat obsessive daily planning orientation. High scorers on this factor make daily "to do" lists and devote great attention to specific details.

WHAT WILL YOU DO? Now that you have some idea of how you treat time, consider how these attitudes and behaviors work for you. For example, will your time orientations help you achieve your social and professional goals? If not, what might you do about changing these attitudes and behaviors?

Source: From "Time in Perspective" by Alexander Gonzalez and Philip G. Zimbardo in *Psychology Today*, V. 19, pp. 20–26. Reprinted with permission of *Psychology Today* magazine, Copyright © 1985.

The time orientation you develop depends largely on your socioeconomic class and your personal experiences (Gonzalez & Zimbardo, 1985). For example, parents with unskilled and semiskilled occupations are likely to teach their children a present-orientated fatalism and a belief that enjoying yourself is more important than planning for the future. Parents who are teachers, managers, and in other professions, teach their children the importance of planning and preparing for the future, along with strategies for success.

Different **cultural time** perspectives also account for much intercultural misunderstanding, as different cultures often teach their members drastically different time orientations. For example, members of some Latin cultures would rather be late for an appointment than end a conversation abruptly or before it has come to a natural end. So the Latin may see lateness as a result of politeness. But others may see this as impolite to the person with whom he or she had the appointment (Hall & Hall, 1987).

Smell Communication

Smell communication, or **olfactory communication**, is extremely important in a wide variety of situations and is now big business. For example, there's some evidence (though clearly not very conclusive evidence) that the smell of lemon contributes to a perception of health, the smells of lavender and eucalyptus increase alertness, and the smell of rose oil reduces blood pressure. Findings such as these have contributed to the growth of aromatherapy and to a new profession of aromatherapists (Furlow, 1996). Because humans possess "denser skin concentrations of scent glands than almost any other mammal," it has been argued that it only remains for us to discover how we use scent to communicate a wide variety of messages (Furlow, 1996, p. 41). Research also finds that smells can influence your body's chemistry, which in turn influences your emotional state. For example, the smell of chocolate results in the reduction of theta brain waves, which produces a sense of relaxation and a reduced level of attention (Martin, 1998).

Here are some of the most important messages scent seems to communicate.

- *Attraction messages.* Humans use perfumes, colognes, after-shave lotions, powders, and the like to enhance their attractiveness to others and to themselves. After all, you also smell yourself. When the smells are pleasant, you feel better about yourself. Women, research finds, prefer the scent of men who bear a close genetic similarity to themselves; this finding may account in part for our attraction to people much like ourselves (Ober, Weitkamp, Cox, Dytch, Kostyu, & Elias, 1997; Wade, 2002). And although we often think of women as the primary users of perfumes and scents, increasingly men are using them as well—not only the cologne and aftershave lotions they have long used but also, more recently, body sprays, which have become big business with a market estimated at $180 million (Dell, 2005).
- *Taste messages.* Without smell, taste would be severely impaired. For example, without smell it would be extremely difficult to taste the difference between a raw potato and an apple. Street vendors selling hot dogs, sausages, and similar foods are aided greatly by the smells, which stimulate the appetites of passersby.
- *Memory messages.* Smell is a powerful memory aid; you often recall situations from months and even years ago when you encounter a similar smell.
- *Identification messages.* Smell is often used to create an image or an identity for a product. Advertisers and manufacturers spend millions of dollars each year creating scents for cleaning products and toothpastes, for example, which have nothing to do with their cleaning power. There's also evidence that we can identify specific significant others by smell. For example, young children were able to identify the T-shirts of their brothers and sisters solely on the basis of smell (Porter & Moore, 1981).

Culture and Nonverbal Communication

This chapter has already noted a few cultural and gender differences in nonverbal communication. The importance of culture in certain areas of nonverbal communication, however, has become the focus of sustained research. Here we consider just a sampling of research on gesture, facial expression, eye communication, colors, touch, silence, and time.

Culture and Gesture

There is much variation in gestures and their meanings among different cultures (Axtell, 1993). Consider a few common gestures that you might use even without thinking, but that could easily get you into trouble if you used them in another culture (also, take a look at Figure 3.1):

- Folding your arms over your chest would be considered defiant and disrespectful in Fiji.
- Waving your hand would be insulting in Nigeria and Greece.
- Gesturing with the thumb up would be rude in Australia.
- Tapping your two index fingers together would be considered an invitation to sleep together in Egypt.
- Pointing with your index finger would be impolite in many Middle Eastern countries.
- Bowing to a lesser degree than your host would be considered a statement of your superiority in Japan.
- Inserting your thumb between your index and middle finger in a clenched fist would be viewed as a wish that evil fall on the person in some African countries.
- Resting your feet on a table or chair would be insulting and disrespectful in some Middle Eastern cultures.

Culture and Facial Expression

The wide variations in facial communication that we observe in different cultures seem to reflect different attitudes about what reactions are permissible in public rather than differences in the way humans show emotions. For example, Japanese and American students watched a film of a surgical operation (Ekman, 1985). The students were videotaped both in an interview situation about the film and alone while watching the film. When alone the students showed very similar reactions; in the interview, however, the American students displayed facial expressions indicating displeasure, whereas the Japanese students did not show any great emotion. Similarly, it's considered "forward" or inappropriate for Japanese women to reveal broad smiles, and so

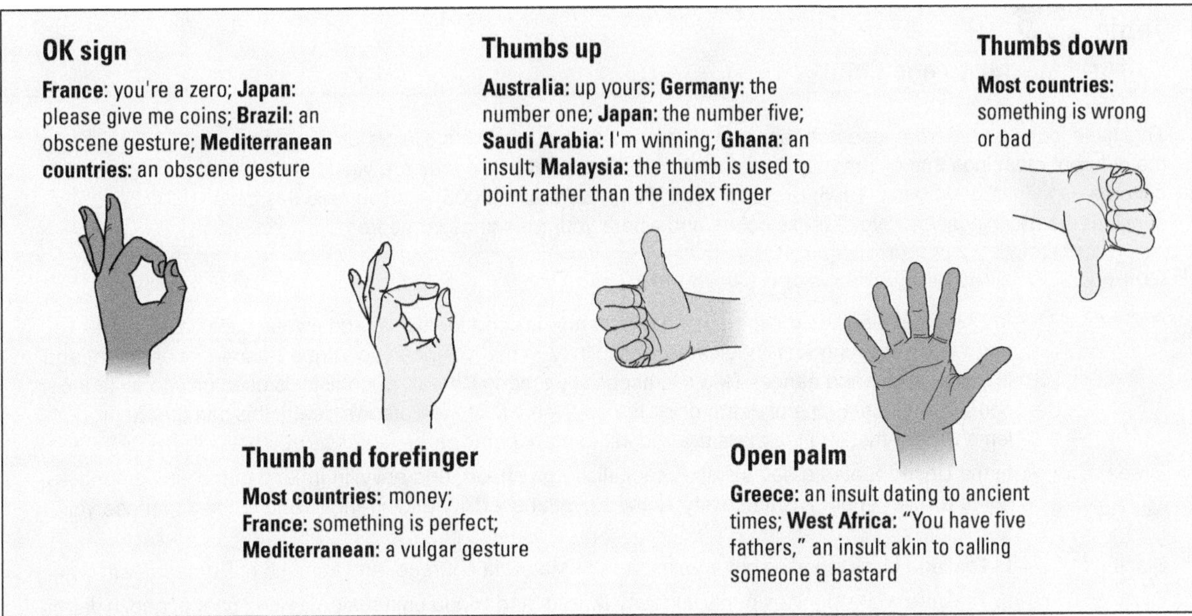

OK sign
France: you're a zero; Japan: please give me coins; Brazil: an obscene gesture; Mediterranean countries: an obscene gesture
Thumbs up
Australia: up yours; Germany: the number one; Japan: the number five; Saudi Arabia: I'm winning; Ghana: an insult; Malaysia: the thumb is used to point rather than the index finger
Thumbs down
Most countries: something is wrong or bad
Thumb and forefinger
Most countries: money; France: something is perfect; Mediterranean: a vulgar gesture
Open palm
Greece: an insult dating to ancient times; West Africa: "You have five fathers," an insult akin to calling someone a bastard

Figure 3.1
Some Cultural Meanings of Gestures
Cultural differences in the meanings of nonverbal gestures are often significant. The over-the-head clasped hands that signify victory to an American may signify friendship to a Russian. To an American, holding up two fingers to make a V signifies victory or peace. To certain South Americans, however, it is an obscene gesture that corresponds to the American's extended middle finger. This figure highlights some additional nonverbal differences. Can you identify others?

many Japanese women will hide their smile, sometimes with their hands (Ma, 1996). Women in the United States, on the other hand, have no such restrictions and so are more likely to smile openly. Thus, the difference may not be in the way people in different cultures express emotions but rather in the cultural rules for displaying emotions in public (Matsumoto, 1991).

Similarly, people in different cultures may decode the meanings of facial expression differently. For example, American and Japanese students judged the meaning of a smiling and a neutral facial expression. The Americans rated the smiling face as more attractive, more intelligent, and more sociable than the neutral face. In contrast, the Japanese rated the smiling face as more sociable but not as more attractive—and they rated the neutral face as more intelligent (Matsumoto & Kudoh, 1993).

Culture and Eye Communication

Not surprisingly, eye messages vary with both culture and gender. Americans, for example, consider direct eye contact an expression of honesty and forthrightness, but the Japanese often view this as a lack of respect. A Japanese person will glance at the other person's face rarely, and then only for very short periods (Axtell, 1990). Interpreting another's eye contact messages with your own cultural rules is a risky undertaking; eye movements that you may interpret as insulting may have been intended to show respect.

Women make eye contact more and maintain it longer (both in speaking and in listening) than men. This holds true whether women are interacting with other women or with men. This difference in eye behavior may result from women's greater tendency

Table 3.3
Cultural Meanings and Color

This table, constructed from research reported by various culture watchers, illustrates only some of the different meanings that colors may communicate and especially how they are viewed in different cultures (Dreyfuss, 1971; Hoft, 1995; Dresser, 1996; Singh & Pereira, 2005). As you read this table consider the meanings you give to these colors and where your meanings came from.

Color	Cultural Meanings and Comments
Red	In China red signifies prosperity and rebirth and is used for festive and joyous occasions; in France and the United Kingdom it indicates masculinity, in many African countries blasphemy or death, and in Japan anger and danger. Red ink, especially among Korean Buddhists, is used only to write a person's name at the time of death or on the anniversary of the person's death; this can create problems when American teachers use red ink to mark homework.
Green	In the United States green signifies capitalism, go ahead, and envy; in Ireland patriotism; among some Native Americans femininity; to the Egyptians fertility and strength; and to the Japanese youth and energy.
Black	In Thailand black signifies old age, in parts of Malaysia courage, and in much of Europe death.
White	In Thailand white signifies purity, in many Muslim and Hindu cultures purity and peace, and in Japan and other Asian countries death and mourning.
Blue	In Iran blue signifies something negative, in Ghana joy; among the Cherokee it signifies defeat, for the Egyptian virtue and truth, and for the Greek national pride.
Yellow	In China yellow signifies wealth and authority; in the United States caution, cowardice, and support for troops; in Egypt happiness and prosperity; and in many countries throughout the world femininity.
Purple	In Latin America purple signifies death, in Europe royalty, in Egypt virtue and faith, in Japan grace and nobility, in China barbarism, and in the United States nobility and bravery.

to display their emotions (Wood, 1994). When women interact with other women, they display affiliative and supportive eye contact, whereas when men interact with other men, they avert their gaze (Gamble & Gamble, 2003).

Culture and Colors

Colors vary greatly in their meanings from one culture to another. Some of these cultural differences are summed up in Table 3.3; but before looking at the table, think about the meanings given to such colors as red, green, black, white, blue, yellow, and purple in your own culture or cultures.

Culture and Touch

The several functions and examples of touching discussed so far have been based on studies in North America; in other cultures these functions are not served in the same way. In some cultures, for example, some task-related touching is viewed negatively and is to be avoided. Among Koreans, it is considered disrespectful for a store owner to touch a customer in, say, handing back change; it is considered too intimate a gesture. Members of other cultures that are used to such touching may consider the Korean's behavior cold and aloof. Muslim children are socialized not to touch members of the opposite sex, a practice which can easily be interpreted as unfriendly by American children who are used to touching each other (Dresser, 1996).

For example, in one study on touch, college students in Japan and in the United States were surveyed (Barnlund, 1989). Students from the United States reported being touched twice as much as did the Japanese students. In Japan there is a strong taboo against touching between strangers, and the Japanese are therefore especially careful to maintain sufficient distance.

Some cultures—including many in southern Europe and the Middle East—are contact cultures; others are noncontact cultures, such as those of northern Europe and Japan. Members of contact cultures maintain close distances, touch one another in conversation, face one another more directly, and maintain longer and more focused eye contact. Members of noncontact cultures maintain greater distance in their interactions, touch one another rarely (if at all), avoid facing one another directly, and maintain much less direct eye contact. As a result, southern Europeans may perceive northern Europeans and Japanese as cold, distant, and uninvolved. Southern Europeans may in turn be perceived as pushy, aggressive, and inappropriately intimate.

Culture, Paralanguage, and Silence

Cultural differences also need to be taken into consideration in evaluating the results of the studies on speech rate, as different cultures view speech rate differently. For example, in one study Korean male speakers who spoke rapidly were given unfavorable credibility ratings, as opposed to the results obtained by Americans who spoke rapidly (Lee & Boster, 1992). Researchers have suggested that in individualistic societies a rapid-rate speaker is seen as more competent than a slow-rate speaker, whereas in collectivist cultures a speaker who uses a slower rate is judged as more competent.

Similarly, all cultures do not view silence as functioning in the same way (Vainiomaki, 2004). In the United States, for example, silence is often interpreted negatively. At a business meeting or even in an informal social group, the silent member may be seen as not listening, having nothing interesting to add, not understanding the issues, being insensitive, or being too self-absorbed to focus on the messages of others. Other cultures, however, view silence more positively. In many situations in Japan, for example, silence is a response that is considered more appropriate than speech (Haga, 1988).

The traditional Apache, to take another example, regard silence very differently than do European Americans (Basso, 1972). Among the Apache, mutual friends do not feel the need to introduce strangers who may be working in the same area or on the same project. The strangers may remain silent for several days. This period enables them to observe and to form judgments about each other. Once this assessment is made, the individuals talk. When courting, especially during the initial stages, the Apache remain silent for hours; if they do talk, they generally talk very little. Only after a couple has been dating for several months will they have lengthy conversations. These periods of silence are generally attributed to shyness or self-consciousness; but the use of silence is explicitly taught to Apache women, who are especially discouraged from engaging in long discussions with their dates. Silence during courtship is a sign of modesty to many Apache.

Culture and Time

People in different cultures view time very differently. Here are three aspects of time and some cultural differences: the social clock, formal and informal time, and monochronism versus polychronism.

The Social Clock

Your culture maintains an implicit "schedule" for the right time to do a variety of important things; for example, the right time to start dating, to finish college, to buy your own home, or to have a child. This unspoken timetable provides you with a **social clock**, a schedule that tells you if you're keeping pace with your peers, are ahead of them, or are falling behind (Neugarten, 1979). On the basis of this social clock, which you learned as you grew up, you evaluate your own social and professional development. If you're in synch with the rest of your peers—for example, if you started dating at the "appropriate" age or if you're finishing college at the "appropriate" age—then you'll feel well adjusted, competent, and a part of the group. If you're late, you'll probably experience feelings of dissatisfaction. And although in some cultures the social clock is becoming more flexible and more tolerant of deviations from the conventional timetable, it still exerts pressure to keep pace with your peers (Peterson, 1996).

Formal and Informal Time

Days are astronomically determined by the earth's rotation on its axis, months by the moon's movement around the earth, and years by the earth's rotation around the sun. But the rest of our time divisions are cultural (largely religious) in origin.

In the United States and in most of the world, formal time divisions include seconds, minutes, hours, days, weeks, months, and years. Some cultures, however, may use phases of the moon or the seasons to delineate their most important time periods. Other formal time units exist, too. For example, in the United States, if your college is on the semester system, your courses are divided

Table 3.4
Monochronic and Polychronic Time

As you read down this table, based on Hall and Hall (1987), note the potential for miscommunication that these differences might create when M-time and P-time people interact. Have any of these differences ever created interpersonal misunderstandings for you?

The Monochronic-Time Person	The Polychronic-Time Person
does one thing at a time	does several things at once
treats time schedules and plans very seriously; feels they may be broken only for the most serious of reasons	treats time schedules and plans as useful (not sacred); feels they may be broken for a variety of causes
considers the job the most important part of life, ahead of even family	considers the family and interpersonal relationships more important than the job
considers privacy extremely important; seldom borrows or lends to others; works independently	is actively involved with others; works in the presence of and with lots of people at the same time

into 50- or 75-minute periods that meet two or three times a week for 14-week periods. Eight semesters of 15 or 16 periods per week equal a college education. As these examples illustrate, formal time units are arbitrary. The culture establishes them for convenience.

Informal time terms are more hazy and subject to interpretation—terms such as "forever," "immediately," "soon," "right away," or "as soon as possible." This type of time creates the most communication problems, because the terms have different meanings for different people.

Attitudes toward both formal and informal time vary from one culture to another. One study, for example, measured the accuracy of clocks in six cultures—those of Japan, Indonesia, Italy, England, Taiwan, and the United States. Japan had the most accurate and Indonesia had the least accurate clocks. The researchers also measured the speed at which people in these six cultures walked, and results showed that the Japanese walked the fastest, the Indonesians the slowest (LeVine & Bartlett, 1984).

Monochronism and Polychronism

Another important distinction is that between **monochronic** and **polychronic time orientations** (Hall, 1959, 1976, 1987). Monochronic people or cultures—such as those of the United States, Germany, Scandinavia, and Switzerland—generally schedule one thing at a time. In these cultures time is compartmentalized and there is a time for everything. Polychronic people or cultures, on the other hand—groups such as Latin Americans, Mediterranean people, and Arabs—tend to schedule more than one thing at the same time. Eating, conducting business with several different people, and taking care of family matters may all be conducted simultaneously. No culture is entirely monochronic or polychronic; rather, these are general tendencies that are found across a large part of the culture. Some cultures combine both time orientations; in Japan and in some American groups, for example, both orientations are found. Table 3.4 identifies some of the distinctions between these two time orientations.

Summary: Nonverbal Messages

In this unit we explored nonverbal communication—communication without words. We considered body movements, facial and eye movements, spatial and territorial communication, artifactual communication, touch communication, paralanguage, silence, time communication, and smell communication. Finally, we looked at cultural variations in many types of nonverbal communication.

1. Nonverbal messages may accent or emphasize a part of a verbal message; complement or add nuances of meaning not communicated by a verbal message; contradict verbal messages (for example, when you cross your fingers or wink to indicate that you're lying); regulate, control, or show a wish to control the flow of verbal messages; repeat or restate a verbal message; or substitute for or take the place of verbal messages.
2. Nonverbal messages serve important communications functions: They help us form and manage impressions, form and define relationships, structure conversation and social interaction, influence others, and express emotions.
3. The five categories of body movements are emblems (nonverbal behaviors that directly translate words or phrases); illustrators (nonverbal behaviors that accompany and literally "illustrate" verbal messages); affect displays (nonverbal movements that communicate emotional meaning); regulators (nonverbal movements that coordinate, monitor, maintain, or control the speaking of another individual); and adaptors (nonverbal behaviors that are emitted without conscious awareness and that usually serve some kind of need, as in scratching an itch).
4. Facial movements may communicate a variety of emotions. The most frequently studied are happiness, surprise, fear, anger, sadness, disgust, and contempt. Facial management techniques enable you to control the extent to which you reveal the emotions you feel.
5. The facial feedback hypothesis claims that facial display of an emotion can lead to physiological and psychological changes.
6. Through eye contact you may seek feedback, signal others to speak, indicate the nature of a relationship, or compensate for increased physical distance. Eye avoidance may help you avoid prying or may signal a lack of interest.
7. Pupil enlargement shows a person's level of interest and positive emotional arousal.
8. Proxemics is the study of the communicative functions of space and spatial relationships. Four major proxemic distances are (1) intimate distance, ranging from actual touching to 18 inches; (2) personal distance, ranging from 18 inches to 4 feet; (3) social distance, ranging from 4 to 12 feet; and (4) public distance, ranging from 12 to more than 25 feet.
9. Your treatment of space is influenced by such factors as status, culture, context, subject matter, gender, age, and positive or negative evaluation of the other person.
10. Territoriality has to do with your possessive reaction to an area of space or to particular objects.
11. Artifactual communication consists of messages conveyed through human-made articles; for example, communication through color, clothing and body adornment, and space decoration.
12. The study of haptics indicates that touch may convey a variety of meanings, the most important being positive affect, playfulness, control, ritual, and task-relatedness. Touch avoidance is the desire to avoid touching and being touched by others.
13. Paralanguage involves the vocal but nonverbal dimensions of speech. It includes rate, pitch, volume, rhythm, and vocal quality as well as pauses and hesitations. Paralanguage helps us make judgments about people, their emotions, and their believability.
14. Silence may communicate a variety of meanings, from messages aimed at hurting another (the silent treatment) to deep emotional responses.
15. The study of time communication (chronemics) explores the messages communicated by our treatment of time.
16. Smell can communicate messages of attraction, taste, memory, and identification.
17. Among the cultural differences that researchers have focused on are facial expressions and displays, eye communication, the meanings of color, the appropriateness and uses of touch, the uses of silence, and the ways in which different cultures treat time.

KEY TERMS IN NONVERBAL MESSAGES

adaptors
affect displays
alter-adaptors
artifactual communication
attractiveness
boundary marker
central marker
chronemics
civil inattention
color communication
cultural time
earmarker
emblems
expectancy violations theory
facial feedback hypothesis
facial management techniques
haptics
home field advantage
illustrators
informal time
intimate distance
kinesics
markers
monochronic time orientation
nonverbal communication
nonverbal dominance
object-adaptors
olfactory communication
paralanguage
personal distance
pitch
polychronic time orientation
primary territories
proxemic distances
proxemics
psychological time
public distance
public territories
pupillometrics
rate
regulators
secondary territories
self-adaptors
silence
social clock
social distance
spatial distance
status
temporal communication
territoriality
touch avoidance
touch communication
visual dominance
voice qualities
volume

THINKING CRITICALLY ABOUT NONVERBAL MESSAGES

1. **Physical Appearance.** On a 10-point scale, with 1 indicating "not at all important" and 10 indicating "extremely important," how important is body appearance to your own romantic interest in another person? Do the men and women you know conform to the stereotypes of males being more concerned with physical appearance and females more concerned with personality?
2. **Status and Invasion.** One signal of status is an unwritten "law" granting the right of invasion. Higher-status individuals have more of a right to invade the territory of others than vice versa. The boss, for example, can invade the territory of junior executives by barging into their offices, but the reverse would be unacceptable. In what ways do you notice this "right" of territorial invasion in your workplace?
3. **Blaming the Victim.** A popular defense tactic in criminal trials for sex crimes against women, gay men, and lesbians is to blame the victim by implying that the way the victim was dressed provoked the attack. Currently, New York and Florida are the only states that prohibit defense attorneys from referring to the way a sex-crime victim was dressed at the time of the attack (*New York Times*, July 30, 1994, p. 22). What do you think of this? If you don't live in New York or Florida, have there been proposals in your state to similarly limit this popular defense tactic?
4. **Gender and Nonverbal Communication.** Here is a brief summary of findings from research on gender differences in nonverbal expression (Burgoon, Buller, & Woodall, 1996; Eakins & Eakins, 1978; Pearson, West, & Turner, 1995; Arliss, 1991; Shannon, 1987): (1) Women smile more than men; (2) women stand closer to one another than do men and are generally approached more closely than men; (3) both men and women, when speaking, look at men more than at women; (4) women both touch and are touched more than men; (5) men extend their bodies, taking up greater areas of space, more than women. What problems might these differences create when men and women communicate with each other?
5. **Liking Cues.** What nonverbal cues should you look for in judging whether someone likes you? List cues in the order of their importance, beginning with 1 for the cue that is of most value in making your judgment. Do you really need two lists? One for judging a woman's liking and one for a man's?

Log On! My Communication Lab

WWW.MYCOMMUNICATIONLAB.COM

Several exercises and self-tests will help you better understand how nonverbal communication works and will give you opportunities to practice the skills of nonverbal communication: Facial Expressions, Eye Contact, Interpersonal Interactions and Space, Artifacts and Culture: The Case of Gifts, Communicating Vocally but Nonverbally, Communicating Emotions Nonverbally, Recognizing Verbal and Nonverbal Message Functions, Coloring Meanings, Deciphering Paralanguage Cues, Do You Avoid Touch? Also take the monochronic and polychronic time test and explore the activities on the human face, the human voice, and spatial communication. Recognizing Facial Expressions of Emotions is an interesting and instructive simulation.

An interesting blog dealing with nonverbal communication is available at www.geocities.com/marvin_hecht/nonverbal.html (accessed June 3, 2006).

CHAPTER

Interpersonal Communication

Taken from *Human Communication: The Basic Course*, Eleventh Edition, by Joseph A. DeVito.

Much of your life focuses on relationships: friends, lovers, and family relations probably occupy an enormous part of your day-to-day thoughts and experiences.

In this chapter you'll learn about:

- the ways in which relationships develop, the stages they go through.
- the theories that attempt to account for our relationship decisions and choices.

You'll learn to:

- communicate in ways appropriate to your relationship stage.
- assess your own relationship behavior and make adjustments as needed.

A good way to begin the study of interpersonal relationships is to examine your own relationships (past, present, or those you look forward to) by taking the following self-test, "What Do Your Relationships Do for You?" It highlights the advantages and the disadvantages that relationships serve.

TEST YOURSELF

What Do Your Relationships Do for You?

Focus on your own relationships in general (friendship, romantic, family, and work); or focus on one particular relationship (say, your life partner or your child or your best friend); or focus on one type of relationship (say, friendships), and respond to the following by indicating the extent to which your relationship(s) serve each of these functions. Use a 10-point scale on which 1 indicates that your relationship(s) never serves this function, 10 indicates that your relationship(s) always serves this function, and the numbers in between indicate levels between these extremes.

____ **1.** My relationships help to lessen my loneliness.

____ **2.** My relationships put uncomfortable pressure on me to expose my vulnerabilities.

____ **3.** My relationships help me to secure stimulation (intellectual, physical, and emotional).

____ **4.** My relationships increase my obligations.

____ **5.** My relationships help me gain in self-knowledge and in self-esteem.

____ **6.** My relationships prevent me from developing other relationships.

____ **7.** My relationships help enhance my physical and emotional health.

____ **8.** My relationships scare me because they may be difficult to dissolve.

____ **9.** My relationships maximize my pleasures and minimize my pains.

____ **10.** My relationships hurt me.

HOW DID YOU DO? The numbers from 1 to 10 that you used to respond to each statement should give you some idea of how strongly your relationships serve these advantages. The odd-numbered statements (1, 3, 5, 7, and 9) express what most people would consider advantages of interpersonal relationships:

(1) One of the major benefits of relationships is that they help to lessen loneliness (Rokach, 1998; Rokach & Brock, 1995). They make you feel that someone cares, that someone likes you, that someone will protect you, that someone ultimately will love you. (3) As plants are heliotropic and orient themselves to light, humans are stimulotropic and orient themselves to sources of stimulation (Davis, 1973). Human contact is one of the best ways to secure this stimulation—intellectual, physical, and emotional. Even an imagined relationship seems better than none, one type of which is covered in the Media Watch box on "Parasocial Relationships" on page 88.

(5) Through contact with others you learn about yourself and see yourself from different perspectives and in different roles, as a child or parent, as a coworker, as a manager, as a best friend. Healthy interpersonal relationships help enhance self-esteem and self-worth. Simply having a friend or romantic partner (at least most of the time) makes you feel desirable and worthy.

(7) Research consistently shows that interpersonal relationships contribute significantly to physical and emotional health (Rosen, 1998; Goleman, 1995; Rosengren, 1993; Pennebacker, 1991) and to personal happiness (Berscheid & Reis, 1998). Without close interpersonal relationships you're more likely to become depressed, and this depression, in turn, contributes significantly to physical illness. Isolation, in fact, contributes as much to mortality as high blood pressure, high cholesterol, obesity, smoking, or lack of physical exercise (Goleman 1995).

(9) The most general function served by interpersonal relationships, and the function that encompasses all the others, is that of maximizing pleasure and minimizing pain. Your good friends, for example, will make you feel even better about your good fortune and less hurt when you're confronted with hardships.

The even-numbered statements (2, 4, 6, 8, and 10) express what most people consider disadvantages of interpersonal relationships:

(2) Close relationships put pressure on you to reveal yourself and to expose your vulnerabilities. While this is generally worthwhile in the context of a supporting and caring relationship, it may backfire if the

relationship deteriorates and these weaknesses are used against you.

(4) Close relationships increase your obligations to other people, sometimes to a great extent. Your time is no longer entirely your own. And although you enter relationships to spend more time with these special people, you also incur time (and perhaps financial) obligations with which you may not be happy.

(6) Close relationships can lead you to abandon other relationships. Sometimes the other relationship involves someone you like but your partner can't stand. More often, however, it's simply a matter of time and energy; relationships take a lot of both and you have less to give to these other and less intimate relationships.

(8) The closer your relationship, the more emotionally difficult it is to dissolve, a feeling which may be uncomfortable for some people. If the relationship is deteriorating, you may feel distress or depression. In some cultures, for example, religious pressures may prevent married couples from separating. And if lots of money is involved, dissolving a relationship can often mean giving up the fortune you've spent your life accumulating.

(10) And, of course, your partner may break your heart. Your partner may leave you—against all your pleading and promises. Your hurt will be in proportion to how much you care and need your partner. If you care a great deal, you're likely to experience great hurt; if you care less, the hurt will be less—it's one of life's little ironies.

WHAT WILL YOU DO? One way to use this self-test is to consider how you might lessen the disadvantages of your interpersonal relationships; at least those disadvantages that you find are always or almost always present in your relationships. Consider, for example, if your own behaviors are contributing to the disadvantages. Do you bury yourself in one or two relationships and discourage the development of others? At the same time, consider how you can maximize the advantages that your relationships currently serve.

Relationship Stages

It's useful to look at interpersonal relationships as created and constructed by the individuals involved. That is, in any interpersonal relationship—say between Pat and Chris—there are actually several relationships: (1) the relationship that Pat sees, (2) the relationship as Chris sees it, (3) the relationship that Pat wants and is striving for, (4) the relationship that Chris wants. And of course there are the many relationships that friends and relatives see and that they reflect back in their communications; for example, the relationship that Pat's mother (who dislikes Chris) sees and reflects in her communication with Pat and Chris is very likely to influence Pat and Chris in some ways. And then there's the relationship that a dispassionate researcher/observer would see. Looked at in this way, there are many interpersonal relationships in any interpersonal relationship.

This is not to say that there is no *real* relationship; it's just to say that there are many real relationships. And because there are these differently constructed relationships, people often disagree about a wide variety of issues and evaluate the relationship very differently. Regularly on *The Jerry Springer Show* and *Maury*, you see couples who see their relationship very differently. The first guest thinks all is going well until the second guest comes on and explodes—often identifying long-held dissatisfactions and behaviors that shock the partner.

The quality that makes a relationship interpersonal is **interdependency**; that is, the actions of one person have an impact on the other; one person's actions have consequences for the other person. The actions of a stranger (for example, actions such as working overtime or flirting with a coworker) will have no impact on you; you and the proverbial stranger are independent—your actions have no effect on each other. If, however, you were in an interpersonal relationship and your partner worked overtime or flirted with a coworker, it would affect you and the relationship in some way.

The six-stage model shown in Figure 4.1 on page 87 describes the significant stages you may go through as you try to achieve your relationship goals. As a general description of relationship development (and sometimes dissolution), the stages seem standard: They apply to all relationships, whether friendship or love, whether face-to-face or computer-mediated. The six stages are contact, involvement, intimacy, deterioration, repair, and dissolution. Each stage can be divided into an initial and a final phase.

As important as the stages themselves is the movement from stage to stage, depicted in Figure 4.1 by the different types of arrows. The exit arrows show that each stage offers the opportunity to exit the relationship: After saying hello, you can say good-bye and exit. The vertical or movement arrows going to the next stage and back again represent the fact that you can move either to a more intense stage (say, from involvement to intimacy) or to a less intense stage (say, from intimacy to deterioration). The self-reflexive arrows—the arrows that return to the beginning of

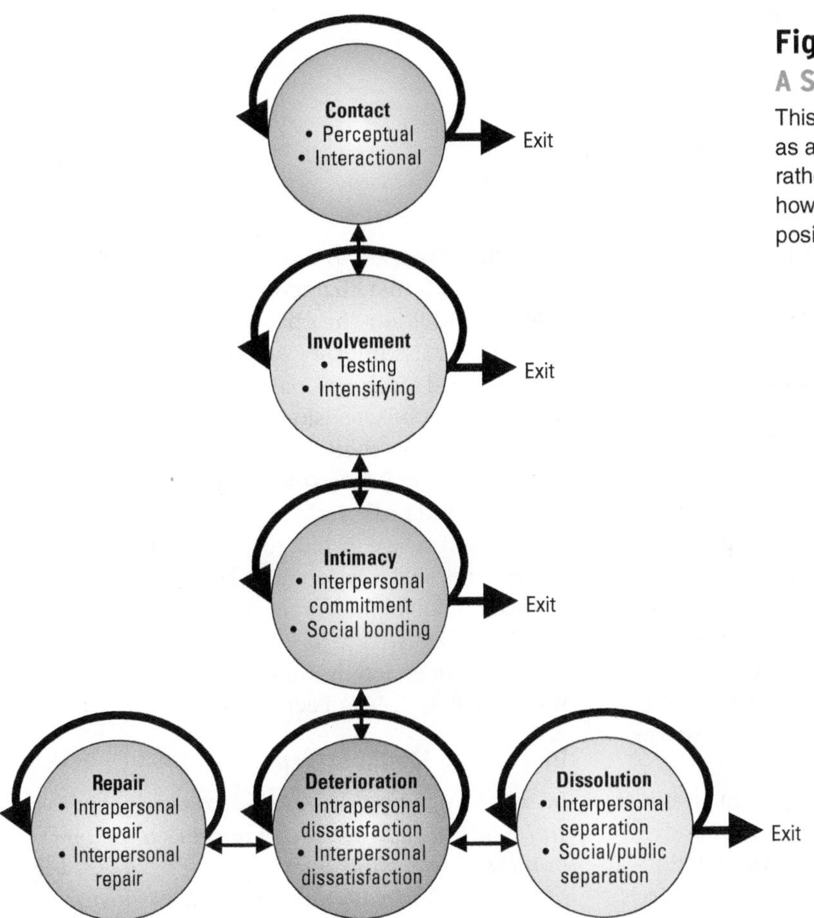

Figure 4.1

A Six-Stage Relationship Model

This model of relationships is best viewed as a tool for talking about relationships rather than as a specific map that indicates how you move from one relationship position to another.

the same level or stage—signify that any relationship may become stabilized at any point. You may, for example, remain at the contact stage without getting any further involved, a situation that exists among residents of many large apartment complexes.

Movement from one stage to another depends largely on your relationship communication skills—the skills you deploy to initiate and open a relationship, to present yourself as likable, to express affection, and to self-disclose appropriately—and in fact all the interpersonal skills you've been acquiring throughout this course (Dindia & Timmerman, 2003). Recognize that these skills will prove relevant in both face-to-face and in computer-mediated relationships; though the specific ways in which you express empathy, for example, will vary depending on you're expressing it with only written cues or with facial, vocal, and body as well as verbal cues.

Because relationships differ so widely, it's best to think of any relationship model as a tool for talking about relationships, rather than as a specific map that indicates how you move from one relationship position to another. This six-stage model is certainly not the only way you can look at relationships. Tables 4.1 (on page 89) and 4.2 (on page 90) depict models of different types.

Contact

At the **contact** stage, there is first *perceptual contact*—you see what the person looks like, you hear what the person sounds like, you may even smell the person. From this, you get a physical picture: gender, approximate age, height, and so on. If this is an online relationship, this initial perception relies on a different set of cues. Depending on your expectations for this relationship, you might develop a visual image based on the written messages exchanged; or, if you have audio and video capabilities, on the sound of the person's voice, facial features, the way the person moves, and so on. From these cues you develop a physical picture.

After this perception, there is usually *interactional contact*. Here the interaction is superficial and impersonal. This is the stage of "Hello, my name is

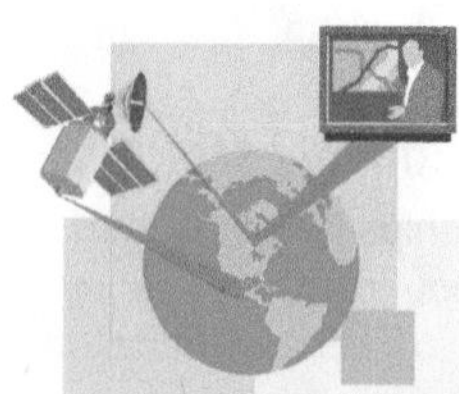

MEDIA WATCH

Parasocial Relationships

Parasocial relationships are relationships that viewers perceive themselves to have with media personalities (Rubin & McHugh, 1987; Giles, 2001). Some viewers develop these relationships with real media personalities—Katie Couric, Regis Philbin, Oprah Winfrey, or Dr. Phil, for example. As a result they may watch these people faithfully and communicate with them in their own imaginations. In other cases these relationships are with fictional characters—an investigator on *CSI*, a lawyer on *Law and Order*, or a doctor on a soap opera. In fact, actors who portray doctors frequently get mail asking for medical advice. And soap opera stars who are about to be "killed" frequently get warning letters from their parasocial relationship fans. Obviously, however, most people don't go quite this far.

Parasocial relationships develop from an initial attraction based on the character's social and task roles, then progress to a perceived relationship and finally to a sense that this relationship is important (Rubin & McHugh, 1987). The more you can predict the behavior of a character, the more likely you are to develop a parasocial relationship with that character (Perse & Rubin, 1989). In addition, the chat sessions that celebrities hold on the Internet help to foster the illusion of a real interpersonal relationship. And the screen savers of television performers make it difficult not to think of them in relationship terms when they face you every time you leave your computer idle for a few minutes.

As might be expected, research indicates that these parasocial relationships are most important to those who spend a great deal of time with the media, who have few interpersonal relationships, and who are generally anxious (Rubin, Perse, & Powell, 1985; Cole & Leets, 1999).

Increasing Media Literacy

In what ways do the media encourage parasocial relationships between viewers on the one hand and television and film characters on the other? In what ways does the culture encourage such relationships? All things considered, what do you think about parasocial relationships?

Joe"—the stage at which you exchange basic information that needs to come before any more intense involvement. This interactional contact may also be nonverbal, as in, for example, exchanging smiles, concentrating your focus on one person, or decreasing the physical distance between the two of you.

This is the stage at which you initiate interaction ("May I join you?") and engage in invitational communication ("May I buy you a drink?"). The invitational messages in computer-mediated communication may involve moving to a face-to-face meeting. According to some researchers, it's at this contact stage—within the first four minutes of initial interaction—that you decide if you want to pursue the relationship or not (Zunin & Zunin, 1972).

Physical appearance is especially important in the initial development of attraction, because it's the characteristic most readily available to sensory inspection. Yet through both verbal and nonverbal behaviors, qualities such as friendliness, warmth, openness, and dynamism are also revealed at the contact stage.

Not surprisingly, people make contact through various means. Table 4.3 provides the results of one survey on the major places at which couples (all of whom were Internet users) met.

Involvement

At the **involvement** stage a sense of mutuality, of being connected, develops. During this stage you experiment and try to learn more about the other person. At the initial phase of involvement, a kind of preliminary *testing* goes on. You want to see if your initial judgment—made perhaps at the contact stage—proves reasonable. So you may ask questions: "Where do you work?" "What are you majoring in?"

If you're committed to getting to know the person even better, you continue your involvement by *intensifying* your interaction. In this process you not only try to get to know the other person better, but also begin to reveal yourself. It's at this stage that you begin to share your feelings and your

"Clarifying" Your Relationship Résumé

Although you've been mostly honest in your two-month Internet relationship, you have padded your relationship résumé—lopped off a few years and pounds and made your temporary job seem like the executive fast-track. You need to come clean.

WHAT DO YOU SAY?
Through what channel?

Table 4.1
Knapp's Model of Relationship Stages

Try comparing the 6-stage model presented in Figure 4.1 with mark Knapp's 10-stage model, shown here. You'll find it helpful to read Knapp's more complete explanation of this model (see Knapp & Vangelisti, 2005). The first five stages of Knapp's model describe the processes of coming together and moving toward greater connection and intimacy.

- *Initiation* is the stage at which you first perceive and interact with the other person. Here you try to present yourself in a positive light and to open the channels of communication.
- *Experimenting* involves trying to learn about the other person.
- *Intensifying* involves interacting on a more personal and intimate level; your speech becomes more informal, and you use lots of terms that have meaning only for the two of you.
- *Integrating* consists of a fusion of the two individuals, a stage when mutual opinions and attitudes are cultivated.
- *Bonding* has to do with the social naming of the relationship; for example, as marriage or domestic partnership or exclusive partnership.

The next five stages describe the stages of coming apart and moving away from intimacy.

- *Differentiating* is the process by which the individuals begin to think of themselves as different and distinct from each other.
- *Circumscribing* involves restricting communication, perhaps to topics that are safe and will not cause conflict.
- *Stagnating* is the stage of inactive communication; when you do communicate it's with difficulty and awkwardness.
- *Avoiding* involves active physical separation and the absence of face-to-face interaction.
- *Terminating* involves the breaking of the bonds that once held the relationship together.

Source: Adapted from Mark L. Knapp and Anita L. Vangelisti, *Interpersonal Communication and Human Relationships* (5th ed.). (Boston: Allyn & Bacon, 2005), p. 35. Published by Allyn & Bacon, Boston, MA. Copyright © by Pearson Education. Adapted by permission of the publisher.

Table 4.2
Online Relationship Stages

This table represents one attempt to identify the stages that people go through in Internet relationships. As you read down the table, consider how accurately this represents what you know of online relationships. How would you describe the way Internet relationships develop?

Stage	Behavior
1. Curiosity	You explore and search for individuals through chat rooms and other online sources.
2. Investigation	You find out information about an individual.
3. Testing	You introduce various topics, looking for common ground.
4. Increasing frequency of contact	You increase the breadth and depth of your relationship.
5. Anticipation	You anticipate face-to-face interaction and wonder what that will bring.
6. Fantasy integration	You create a fantasy of what the person looks like and how the person behaves.
7. Face-to-face meeting	You meet face-to-face, and reality and fantasy meet.
8. Reconfiguration	You adjust the fantasy to the reality; you may decide to end the relationship or to pursue it more vigorously.
9. Already separated	If you decide to maintain the relationship, you explore ways you can increase the depth and breadth of communication to compensate for the long-distance relationship.
10. Long-term relationship	You negotiate the new relationship, whether it will be maintained in its online form or in a new face-to-face form.

Source: This table is adapted from Leonard J. Shedletsky and Joan E. Aitken, *Human Communication on the Internet* (Boston: Allyn & Bacon, 2004), p. 159. Published by Allyn & Bacon, Boston, MA. Copyright © by Pearson Education. Reprinted by permission of the publisher.

Table 4.3
Where People Meet

Here are the major places at which couples say they met.

Where?	How Many?
Work or school	38%
Through friends and family	34%
At a night club, bar, or social gathering	13%
Through the Internet	3%
At a religious institution	2%
In the same neighborhood	1%
At a recreational facility	1%
On a blind date or through a dating service	1%

Source: Data for this table come from the Pew Internet & American Life Project (Rainie & Madden, 2006).

Discovering Personal Information

You're becoming romantically involved with someone at work but before this relationship goes any further, you want to know about this person's HIV status and safe-sex practices. At the same time, you don't want to create a rift in the relationship.

WHAT DO YOU SAY?
Through what channel?

emotions. If this is to be a romantic relationship, you might date. If it's to be a friendship, you might share in activities related to mutual interests—go to the movies or to some sports event together.

And throughout the relationship process—but especially during the involvement and early stages of intimacy, partners continue testing each other. Each person tests the other—each tries to find out how the other feels about the relationship. For example, you might ask your partner directly how he or she feels; or you might disclose your own feelings on the assumption that your partner will also self-disclose; or you might joke about a shared future together, touch more intimately, or hint that you're serious about the relationship; or you might question mutual friends as to your partner's feelings (Bell & Buerkel-Rothfuss, 1990; Baxter & Wilmot, 1984).

Intimacy

One way to define **intimacy** is as a feeling that you can be honest and open when talking about yourself, that you can express thoughts and feelings you wouldn't reveal in other relationships (Mackey, Diemer, & O'Brien, 2000). At the intimacy stage, you commit yourself still further to the other person and, in fact, establish a kind of relationship in which this individual becomes your best or closest friend, lover, or companion. Your communication becomes more personalized, more synchronized, and easier (Gudykunst, Nishida, & Chua, 1987). Usually the intimacy stage divides itself quite neatly into two phases: an *interpersonal commitment* phase, in which you commit yourselves to each other in a kind of private way, and a *social bonding* phase, in which the commitment is made public—revealed perhaps to family and friends, perhaps to the public at large through a formal ceremony. Here the two of you become a unit, a pair.

In addition, in the intimacy stage you increase your display of **affiliative cues** (signs that show you love the other person), including head nods, gestures, and forward leaning. You give **Duchenne smiles**, smiles that are beyond voluntary control and that signal genuine joy (Gonzaga, Keltner, Londahi, & Smith, 2001). These Duchenne smiles give you crow's-feet around the eyes, raise up your cheeks, and puff up the lower eyelids (Lemonick, 2005).

Commitment may take many forms; it may be an engagement or a marriage, a commitment to help the person or to be with the person, or a commitment to reveal your deepest secrets. It may consist of living together or agreeing to become lovers. Or it may consist of becoming a romantic pair either in face-to-face or in online relationships. The type of commitment varies with the relationship and with the individuals. The important characteristic is that the commitment made is a special one; it's a commitment that you do not make lightly or to everyone. Each of us reserves this level of intimacy for very few people at any given time—sometimes just one person; sometimes two, three, or perhaps four. In computer-mediated communication, there is the potential for a much greater number of intimates.

One important characteristic of intimacy is that we talk more affectionately, more lovingly, more deeply. The accompanying Building Communication Skills box explores a particular type of intimacy talk, cherishing.

Deterioration

Although many relationships remain at the intimacy stage, some enter the stage of **relationship deterioration**—the stage that sees the weakening of bonds between the parties and that represents the downside of the relationship progression. Relationships deteriorate for many reasons. When the reasons for coming together are no longer present or change drastically, relationships may deteriorate. Thus, for example, when your relationship no longer lessens your loneliness or provides stimulation or self-knowledge, or when it fails to increase your self-esteem or maximize pleasures and minimize pains, it may be in the process of deteriorating. Among the other reasons for deterioration are third-party relationships, sexual

ASK THE RESEARCHER

Topic Avoidance

Recently I've started dating seriously, and I want to know if there are certain topics that are best avoided in romantic relationships. And while I'm at it, are there topics friends should avoid? Any suggestions?

Every disclosure comes with risk. In the worst-case scenarios, disclosure begets violent reactions. However, a recent study showed that people's responses to negative disclosures were consistently better than people thought they would be.

Avoidance of certain topics (for example, past relational partners, future of the relationship) can sometimes help relationships. But we also know that the strongest relationships are those in which there is relatively limited avoidance. A perfect example is friendships. A lot of friendships, especially ones with potential for romance, never develop into closer relationships because of people's tendency to avoid talking about the most important issue—the relationship. So, less avoidance is generally better, but it serves little purpose to discuss issues that you know will incite conflict.

Of course, avoiding disclosure of issues that would clearly be of interest to your partner (for example, infidelity) or your friend (for example, theft) is a different ball game and almost never advised. The key issue in those cases is how to best disclose an issue, not whether to do so.

For further information: Petronio, S. (Ed). (2000). *Balancing the secrets of private disclosures*. Mahwah, NJ: Erlbaum. Also Greene, K., Derlega, V. J., Yep, G. A., & Petronio, S. (2003). *Privacy and disclosure of HIV in interpersonal relationships: A sourcebook for researchers and practitioners*. Mahwah, NJ: Erlbaum. And Afifi, T. D., Caughlin, J., & Afifi, W. A. (in press). The darkside of avoidance and secrets in interpersonal relationships: Reasons to question the ideology of openness. In B. Spitzberg and B. Cupach (Eds.), *The darkside of interpersonal relationships*. Mahwah, NJ: Lawrence Erlbaum.

Walid A. Afifi (Ph.D., University of Arizona) is an associate professor of communication at the University of California, Santa Barbara, where he teaches courses in interpersonal and relational communication and conducts research in information seeking, topic avoidance, and health communication (w-afifi@comm.ucsb.edu).

dissatisfaction, dissatisfaction with work, or financial difficulties (Blumstein & Schwartz, 1983).

The first phase of deterioration is usually *intrapersonal dissatisfaction*. You begin to feel that this relationship may not be as important as you had previously thought. You may experience personal dissatisfaction with everyday interactions, and begin to view the future together negatively. If this dissatisfaction continues or grows, you may pass to the second phase, *interpersonal deterioration*, in which you discuss these dissatisfactions with your partner.

During the process of deterioration, communication patterns change drastically. These altered patterns are in part a response to the deterioration; you communicate as you do because of the way you feel your relationship is deteriorating. However, the way you communicate (or fail to communicate) also influences the fate of your relationship. During the deterioration stage you may, for example, increase withdrawal, communicate less, respond to computer messages more briefly and with greater delays, and self-disclose less.

The accompanying Understanding Theory and Research box examines relationship commitment, which greatly influences the course of relationship deterioration.

Repair

The first phase of the **relationship repair** stage is *intrapersonal repair*, in which you analyze what went wrong and consider ways of solving your relational difficulties. At this stage, you may consider

BUILDING COMMUNICATION SKILLS

Talking Cherishing

Cherishing behaviors are an especially insightful way to affirm another person and to increase favor exchange, a concept that comes from the work of William Lederer (1984). **Cherishing behaviors** are those small gestures you enjoy receiving from your partner (a smile, a wink, a squeeze, a kiss, a phone call). Prepare a list of 10 cherishing behaviors that you would like to receive from your real or imagined relationship partner. Identify cherishing behaviors that are:

a. specific and positive—nothing overly general or negative

b. focused on the present and future rather than on issues about which the partners have argued in the past

c. capable of being performed daily

d. easily executed—nothing you really have to go out of your way to accomplish

In an actual relationship each partner would prepare a list; then the partners would exchange lists. Ideally, each partner would then perform the cherishing behaviors the other had chosen during their normal activities. In time, these behaviors should become a normal part of your interaction, which is exactly what you'd hope to achieve.

Lists of cherishing behaviors will also give you insight into your own relationship needs and the kind of communicating partner you want.

changing your behaviors or perhaps changing your expectations of your partner. You may also weigh the rewards of your relationship as it is now against the rewards you could anticipate if your relationship ended.

If you decide that you want to repair your relationship, you may discuss this with your partner at the *interpersonal repair* level. Here you may talk about the problems in the relationship, the corrections you would want to see, and perhaps what you would be willing to do and what you would want the other person to do. This is the stage of negotiating new agreements, new behaviors. You and your partner may try to solve your problems yourselves, seek the advice of friends or family, or perhaps enter professional counseling.

You can look at the strategies for repairing a relationship in terms of the following six suggestions—which conveniently spell out the word REPAIR, a useful reminder that repair is not a one-step but a multistep process: Recognize the problem, Engage in productive conflict resolution, Pose possible solutions, Affirm each other, Integrate solutions into normal behavior, and Risk.

- *Recognize* the problem. What, in concrete terms, is wrong with your present relationship? What changes would be needed to make it better—again, in specific terms? Create a picture of your relationship as you would want it to be and compare that picture to the way the relationship looks now.
- *Engage* in productive conflict resolution. Interpersonal conflict is an inevitable part of relationship life. It's not so much the conflict that causes relationship difficulties as the way in which the conflict is approached. If it's confronted through productive strategies, the conflict may be resolved, and the relationship may actually emerge stronger and healthier. If, however, unproductive and destructive strategies are used, the relationship may well deteriorate further.
- *Pose* possible solutions. Ideally, each person will ask, "What can we do to resolve the difficulty that will allow both of us to get what we want?"
- *Affirm* each other. For example, happily married couples engage in greater positive behavior exchange; that is, they communicate more agreement, approval, and positive affect than do unhappily married couples (Dindia & Fitzpatrick, 1985).
- *Integrate* solutions into your life—make the solutions a part of your normal behavior.
- *Risk* giving favors without any certainty of reciprocity. Risk rejection by making the first move to make up or say you're sorry. Be willing to change, to adapt, to take on new tasks and responsibilities.

UNDERSTANDING *THEORY* AND *RESEARCH*

Relationship Commitment

An important factor influencing the course of relationship deterioration (as well as relationship maintenance) is the degree of commitment the individuals have toward each other and toward the relationship. Three types of commitment are often distinguished and can be identified from your answers to the following questions (Johnson, 1973, 1982, 1991; Knapp & Taylor, 1995; Kurdek, 1995):

- Do I want to stay in this relationship? Do I have a desire to keep this relationship going?
- Do I have a moral obligation to stay in this relationship?
- Do I have to stay in this relationship? Is it a necessity for me to stay in this relationship?

All relationships are held together, in part, by desire, obligation, or necessity, or by some combination of these elements. The strength of the relationship, including its resistance to possible deterioration, is related to the degree of commitment. When a relationship shows signs of deterioration and yet there's a strong commitment to preserving it, the individuals may well surmount the obstacles and reverse the process. In contrast, when commitment is weak and the individuals doubt that there are good reasons for staying together, the relationship deteriorates faster and more intensely.

Working with Theories and Research

- *Has commitment or the lack of it (from either or both of you) ever influenced the progression of one of your relationships? What happened?*

Dissolution

The **dissolution** stage, in both friendship and romance, is the cutting of the bonds tying you together. At first it usually takes the form of *interpersonal separation*, in which you may not see each other anymore or may not return messages. If you live together, you may move into separate apartments and begin to lead lives apart from each other. If this relationship is a marriage, you may seek a legal separation. If this separation period proves workable and if the original relationship is not repaired, you may enter the phase of *social or public separation*. In marriage, this phase corresponds to divorce. Avoidance of each other and a return to being "single" are among the primary identifiable features of dissolution. In some cases, however, the former partners change the definition of their relationship; for example, ex-lovers become friends, or ex-friends become "just" business partners.

The final, "good-bye," phase of dissolution is the point at which you become an ex-lover or ex-friend. In some cases this is a stage of relief and relaxation; finally, it's over. In other cases this is a stage of anxiety and frustration, of guilt and regret, of resentment over time ill spent and now lost. In more materialistic terms, the good-bye phase is the stage when property is divided and when legal battles may ensue over who should get what.

No matter how friendly the breakup, dissolution is likely to bring some emotional difficulty. Here are some suggestions for dealing with this:

- *Break the loneliness-depression cycle.* Avoid sad passivity, a state in which you feel sorry for yourself, sit alone, and perhaps cry. Instead, try to engage in active solitude (exercise, write, study, play computer games) and seek distraction (do things to put loneliness out of your mind; for example, take a long drive or shop). The most effective way to deal with loneliness is through social action, especially through helping people in need.
- *Take time out.* Take some time for yourself. Renew your relationship with yourself. Get to know yourself as a unique individual, standing alone now but fully capable of entering a meaningful relationship in the future.
- *Bolster self-esteem.* Positive and successful experiences are most helpful in building self-esteem. As in dealing with loneliness, helping others is one of the best ways to raise your own self-esteem.

BUILDING COMMUNICATION SKILLS

Repairing Relationships

Whether expert or novice, each of us tries to repair relationships—not only our own but also those of others. Here are three situations that call for repair. Can you use what you've read about here (as well as your own experiences, readings, observations, and so on) to come up with some reasonable repair advice? What specific suggestions would you offer to each of the people in these situations?

1. *Friends and colleagues*: Mike and Jim, friends for 20 years, have had a falling out over the fact that Mike supported another person for promotion over Jim. Jim is resentful and feels that Mike should have helped him; Mike feels that his first obligation was to the company and that he chose the person he believed would do the best job. Mike feels that if Jim resents him and can't understand or appreciate his motives, then he no longer cares to be friends. Assuming that both Mike and Jim want the friendship to continue or will do so at some later time, what do you suggest that Mike and Jim do?
2. *Coming out*: Tom, a junior in college, recently came out as gay to his family. Contrary to his every expectation, they went ballistic. His parents want him out of the house, and his two brothers refuse to talk with him. Assuming that all parties will be sorry at some later time if the relationship is not repaired, what would you suggest that each of the individuals do?
3. *Betraying a confidence*: Pat and Chris have been best friends since elementary school. Even now, in their twenties, they speak every day and rely on each other for emotional support. Recently Pat betrayed a confidence and told several mutual friends that Chris had been having emotional problems and had been considering suicide. Chris found out and no longer wants to maintain the friendship. Assuming that the friendship is more good than bad and that both parties will regret it if they don't patch up the friendship, what do you suggest that Pat and Chris do?

- *Seek the support of others.* Avail yourself of your friends and family for support; it's an effective antidote to the discomfort and unhappiness that occurs when a relationship ends.
- *Avoid repeating negative patterns.* Ask, at the start of a new relationship, if you're entering a relationship modeled on the previous one. If the answer is yes, be especially careful that you do not repeat the problems. At the same time, avoid becoming a prophet of doom. Do not see in every new relationship vestiges of the old. Use past relationships and experiences as guides, not filters.

Relationship Theories

Many theories offer insight into why and how we develop and dissolve our relationships. Here we'll examine six relationship theories: theories focusing on attraction, relationship rules, relationship dialectics, social penetration, social exchange, and equity. Two theories that address online relationships are highlighted in the accompanying Understanding Theory and Research box on page 96.

Attraction Theory

Attraction theory holds that people form relationships on the basis of **attraction.** You are no doubt drawn, or attracted, to some people and not to others. In a similar way, some people are attracted to you and some are not. If you're like most people, then you're attracted to others on the basis of four major factors:

Similarity

If you could construct your mate, according to the **similarity** principle, it's likely that your mate would look, act, and think very much like you

UNDERSTANDING *THEORY* AND *RESEARCH*

Online Relationship Theories

Here are two theories of online relationships that raise issues that are unique to online communication and that the other theories do not address.

- *Social presence theory* argues that the "bandwidth" (the number of message cues exchanged) of communication influences the degree to which the communication is personal or impersonal (Walther & Parks, 2002; Wood & Smith, 2005). When lots of cues are exchanged (especially nonverbal cues), as in face-to-face communication, you feel great social presence—the whole person is there for you to communicate with and exchange messages with. When the bandwidth is smaller (as in e-mail or chat communication), then the communication is largely impersonal. So, for example, personal communication is easier to achieve in face-to-face situations (where tone of voice, facial expressions, eye contact and similar nonverbal cues come into play) than in computer-mediated communication, which essentially contains only written cues.

  It's more difficult, the theory goes, to communicate supportiveness, warmth, and friendliness in text-based chat or e-mail exchanges because of the smaller bandwidth. Of course, as noted elsewhere, as video and audio components become more widely used this bandwidth will increase.
- *Social information processing* (SIP) theory argues, contrary to social presence theory, that whether you're communicating face-to-face or online, you can communicate the same degree of personal involvement and develop similar close relationships (Walther, 1992; Walther & Parks, 2002). The idea behind this theory is that communicators are clever people: Given whatever channel they have available to send and receive messages, they will make adjustments to communicate what they want and to develop the relationships they want. It is true that when the time span studied is limited—as it is in much of the research—it is probably easier to communicate and develop relationships in face-to-face interaction than in online situations. But SIP theory argues that when the interaction occurs over an extended time period, as it often does in ongoing chat groups and in repeated e-mail exchanges, then the communication and the relationships can be as personal as those you develop in face-to-face situations.

Working with Theories and Research

- *How would you compare the level of closeness that you can communicate in face-to-face and in online situations? Do you feel it's more difficult (even impossible) to communicate, say, support, warmth, and friendship in online communication than in face-to-face communication?*

(Burleson, Samter, & Luccetti, 1992; Burleson, Kunkel, & Birch, 1994). Generally, people like those who are similar to them in nationality, race, abilities, physical characteristics, intelligence, and attitudes (Pornpitakpan, 2003).

Research also finds that you're more likely to help someone who is similar in race, attitude, and general appearance. Even the same first name is significant. For example, when an e-mail (asking receivers to fill out surveys of their food habits) identified the sender as having the same name as the receiver, there was a greater willingness to comply with the request (Gueguen, 2003). Sometimes people are attracted to their opposites, in a pattern called **complementarity**; for example, a dominant person might be attracted to someone who is more submissive. Generally, however, people prefer those who are similar.

Proximity

If you look around at people you find attractive, you will probably find that they are the people who live or work close to you. People who become friends are the people who have the greatest opportunity to interact with each other. **Proximity**, or physical closeness, is most important in the early stages of interaction—for example, during the first days of school (in class or in dormitories). It decreases in importance, though always remaining significant, as the opportunity to interact with more distant others increases.

Reinforcement

Not surprisingly, you're attracted to people who give rewards or **reinforcements**, which can range from a simple compliment to an expensive cruise. You're also attracted to people you reward (Jecker & Landy, 1969; Aronson, Wilson, & Akert, 1999). That is, you come to like people for whom you do favors; for example, you've probably increased your liking for persons after buying them an expensive present or going out of your way to do them a special favor. In these situations you justify your behavior by believing that the person was worth your efforts; otherwise, you'd have to admit to spending effort on people who might not deserve it.

Physical Attractiveness and Personality

It's easily appreciated that people like physically attractive people more than they like physically unattractive people. What isn't so obvious is that we also feel a greater sense of familiarity with more attractive people than with less attractive people; that is, we're more likely to think we've met a person before if that person is attractive (Monin, 2003). Also, although culture influences what people think is physical attractiveness and what isn't, some research indicates that there are certain facial features that seem to be thought attractive in all cultures—a kind of universal attractiveness (Brody, 1994). Additionally, you probably tend to like people who have a pleasant rather than an unpleasant personality (although people will differ on what is and what is not an agreeable personality).

Relationship Rules Theory

You can gain an interesting perspective on interpersonal relationships by looking at them in terms of the rules that govern them (Shimanoff, 1980). The general assumption of **rules theory** is that relationships—friendship and love in particular—are held together by adherence to certain rules. When those rules are broken, relationships may deteriorate and even dissolve.

Relationship rules theory helps us clarify several aspects of relationships. First, these rules help identify successful versus destructive relationship behavior. In addition, these rules help pinpoint more specifically why relationships break up and how they may be repaired. Further, if we know what the rules are, we will be better able to master the social skills involved in relationship development and maintenance. And because these rules vary from one culture to another, it is important to identify those unique to each culture so that intercultural relationships may be more effectively developed and maintained.

Friendship Rules

One approach to friendship argues that friendships are maintained by rules (Argyle & Henderson, 1984; Argyle, 1986). When these rules are followed, the friendship is strong and mutually satisfying. When these rules are broken, the friendship suffers and may die. For example, the rules for keeping a friendship include such behaviors as standing up for your friend in his or her absence, sharing information and feelings about successes, demonstrating emotional support for a friend, trusting and offering to help a friend in need, and trying to make a friend happy when you're together. On the other hand, a friendship is likely to be in trouble when one or both friends are intolerant of the other's friends, discuss confidences with third parties, fail to demonstrate positive support, nag, and/or fail to trust or confide in the other. The strategy for maintaining a friendship, then, depends on your knowing the rules and having the ability to apply the appropriate interpersonal skills (Trower, 1981; Blieszner & Adams, 1992).

Romantic Rules

Other research has identified the rules that romantic relationships establish and follow. These rules, of course, will vary considerably from one culture to another. For example, the different attitudes toward permissiveness and sexual relations with which Chinese and American college students view dating influence the romantic rules each group will establish and live by (Tang & Zuo, 2000). Leslie Baxter (1986) has identified eight major romantic rules. Baxter argues that these rules keep the relationship together—or, when broken, lead to deterioration and eventually dissolution. The general form for each rule, as Baxter phrases it, is, "If parties are in a close relationship, they should . . .":

1. acknowledge each other's individual identities and lives beyond the relationship;
2. express similar attitudes, beliefs, values, and interests;
3. enhance each other's self-worth and self-esteem;
4. be open, genuine, and authentic with each other;
5. remain loyal and faithful to each other;
6. have substantial shared time together;
7. reap rewards commensurate with their investments relative to the other party; and
8. experience a mysterious and inexplicable "magic" in each other's presence.

Family Rules

Family communication research points to the importance of rules in defining and maintaining the family (Galvin, Bylund, & Brommel, 2007). Family rules concern three main interpersonal communication issues (Satir, 1983):

- What can you talk about? Can you talk about the family finances? Grandpa's drinking? Your sister's lifestyle?
- How can you talk about something? Can you joke about your brother's disability? Can you address directly questions of family history or family skeletons?
- To whom can you talk? Can you talk openly to extended family members such as cousins and aunts and uncles? Can you talk to close neighbors about family health issues?

All families teach rules for communication. Some of these are explicit, such as "Never contradict the family in front of outsiders" or "Never talk finances with outsiders." Other rules are unspoken; you deduce them as you learn the communication style of your family. For example, if financial issues are always discussed in secret and in hushed tones, then you can infer that you shouldn't tell other more distant family members or neighbors about family finances.

Like the rules governing relationships between friends and lovers, family rules tell you which behaviors will be rewarded (and therefore what you should do) and which will be punished (and therefore what you should not do). Family rules also provide a kind of structure that defines the family as a cohesive unit and that distinguishes it from other similar families.

Not surprisingly, the rules a family develops are greatly influenced by the culture. Although there are many similarities among families throughout the world, there are also differences (Georgas et al., 2001). For example, members of collectivist cultures are more likely to shield family information from outsiders as a way of protecting the family than are members of individualist cultures. As already noted, this tendency to protect the family can create serious problems in cases of wife abuse. Many women will not report spousal abuse, because they feel they must protect the family image and must not let others know that things aren't perfect at home (Dresser, 1996, 2005).

Family communication theorists argue that rules should be flexible so that special circumstances can be accommodated; there are situations that necessitate changing the family dinner time, vacation plans, or savings goals (Noller & Fitzpatrick, 1993). Rules should also be negotiable so that all members can participate in their modification and feel a part of family government.

Relationship Dialectics Theory

Relationship dialectics theory argues that people in a relationship experience dynamic tensions between pairs of opposing motives or desires. Research generally finds three such pairs of opposites (Baxter, 1988, 1990; Baxter & Simon, 1993; Rawlins, 1989, 1992):

- The tension between *closedness and openness* has to do with the conflict between the desire to be in a closed, exclusive relationship and the wish to be in a relationship that is open to different people. You like the exclusiveness of your pairing, and yet you want also to relate to a larger group.
- The tension between *autonomy and connection* involves the desire to remain an autonomous, independent individual and the wish to connect intimately to another person and to a relationship. This tension, by the way, is a popular theme in women's magazines, which teach readers to want both autonomy and connection (Prusank, Duran, & DeLillo, 1993).
- The tension between *novelty and predictability* centers on the competing desires for newness,

different experiences, and adventure on the one hand and for sameness, stability, and predictability on the other. You're comfortable with being able to predict what will happen, and yet you also want newness, difference, novelty.

The closedness-openness tension occurs most during the early stages of relationship development. The autonomy-connection and novelty-predictability tensions occur more often as the relationship progresses. Each individual in a relationship may experience a somewhat different set of desires. For example, one person may want exclusivity above all, whereas that person's partner may want greater openness. Sometimes a happy combination can be negotiated; at other times these differences are irreconcilable, with the result that the couple becomes dissatisfied with their relationship or dissolves it.

Perhaps the major implication of relationship dialectics theory is that these tensions will influence a wide variety of behaviors. For example, the person who finds the primary relationship excessively predictable may seek novelty elsewhere, perhaps with a vacation to exotic places, perhaps with a different partner. The person who finds the primary relationship too connected (even suffocating) may need physical and psychological space to meet his or her autonomy needs. As you can appreciate, meeting your partner's needs—while also meeting your own needs—is one of the major relationship challenges you'll face.

Social Penetration Theory

Social penetration theory is a theory not of why relationships develop but of what happens when they do develop; it describes relationships in terms of the number of topics that people talk about and their degree of "personalness" (Altman & Taylor, 1973). The **breadth** of a relationship has to do with the number of topics you and your partner talk about. The **depth** of the relationship involves the degree to which you penetrate the inner personality—the core—of the other individual. We can represent an individual as a circle and divide that circle into various parts, as in Figure 4.2. This figure illustrates different models of social penetration. Each circle in the figure contains eight topic areas to depict breadth (identified as A through H) and five levels of intimacy to depict depth (represented by the concentric circles). Note that in Circle 1, only three topic areas are penetrated. Of these, one is penetrated only to the first level and two to the second. In this type of interaction, three topic areas are discussed, and only at rather superficial levels. This is the type of relationship you might have with an acquaintance. Circle 2 represents a more intense relationship, one that has greater breadth and depth; more topics are discussed and to deeper levels of penetration. This is the type of relationship you might have with a friend. Circle 3 represents a still more

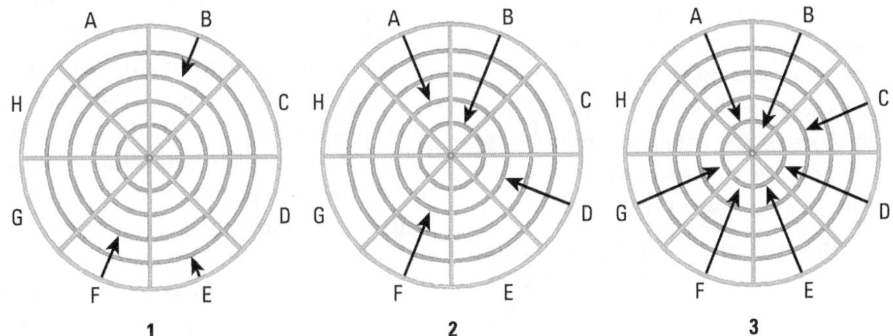

Figure 4.2
Models of Social Penetration
Can you visualize your own relationships in terms of these varying levels of depth and breadth? What can you do to increase both depth and breadth? What can you do to decrease both depth and breadth?

intense relationship. Here there is considerable breadth (seven of the eight areas are penetrated) and depth (most of the areas are penetrated to the deepest levels). This is the type of relationship you might have with a lover or a parent.

When a relationship begins to deteriorate, the breadth and depth will, in many ways, reverse themselves, in a process called **depenetration**. For example, while ending a relationship, you might cut out certain topics from your interpersonal communications. At the same time, you might discuss the remaining topics in less depth. In some instances of relational deterioration, however, both the breadth and the depth of interaction increase. For example, when a couple breaks up and each is finally free from an oppressive relationship, the partners may—after some time—begin to discuss problems and feelings they would never have discussed when they were together. In fact, they may become extremely close friends and come to like each other more than when they were together. In these cases the breadth and depth of their relationship may increase rather than decrease (Baxter, 1983).

Social Exchange Theory

Social exchange theory claims that you develop relationships that will enable you to maximize your profits (Chadwick-Jones, 1976; Gergen, Greenberg, & Willis, 1980; Thibaut & Kelley, 1986)—a theory based on an economic model of profits and losses. The theory begins with the following equation: Profits = Rewards − Costs.

- *Rewards* are anything that you would incur costs to obtain. Research has identified six types of rewards in a love relationship: money, status, love, information, goods, and services (Baron & Byrne, 1984). For example, to get the reward of money, you might have to work rather than play. To earn the status of an A in an interpersonal communication course, you might have to write a term paper or study more than you want to.
- *Costs* are things that you normally try to avoid, that you consider unpleasant or difficult. Examples might include working overtime; washing dishes and ironing clothes; watching your partner's favorite television show, which you find boring; or doing favors for those you dislike.
- *Profit* is what results when the rewards exceed the costs.

Using this basic economic model, social exchange theory claims that you seek to develop the friendships and romantic relationships that will give you the greatest profits, that is, relationships in which the rewards are greater than the costs.

When you enter a relationship, you have in mind a **comparison level**—a general idea of the kinds of rewards and profits that you feel you ought to get out of such a relationship. This comparison level consists of your realistic expectations concerning what you feel you deserve from this relationship. For example, a study of married couples found that most people expect high levels of trust, mutual respect, love, and commitment. Couples' expectations are significantly lower for time spent together, privacy, sexual activity, and communication (Sabatelli & Pearce, 1986). When the rewards that you get equal or surpass your comparison level, you feel satisfied with your relationship.

However, you also have a comparison level for alternatives. That is, you compare the profits that you get from your current relationship with the profits you think you could get from alternative relationships. Thus, if you see that the profits from your present relationship are below the profits that you could get from an alternative relationship, you may decide to leave your current relationship and enter a new, more profitable relationship.

Equity Theory

Equity theory uses the ideas of social exchange, but goes a step farther and claims that you develop and maintain relationships in which the ratio of your rewards relative to your costs is approximately equal to your partner's (Walster, Walster, & Berscheid, 1978; Messick & Cook, 1983). For example, if you and a friend start a business—you put up two-thirds of the money and your friend puts up one-third—equity would demand that you get two-thirds of the profits and your friend gets one-third. An *equitable relationship*, then, is simply one in which each party derives rewards that are proportional to their costs. If you contribute more toward the relationship than your partner, then equity requires that you should get greater rewards. If you both work equally hard, then equity demands that you should both get approximately equal rewards. Conversely, inequity will exist in a relationship if you pay more of the costs (for example, if you do more of the unpleasant tasks) but your partner en-

Achieving Equity

After thinking about equity, you realize that you put a lot more effort into the relationship; you pay significantly more of the costs than your partner. You want this imbalance corrected but at the same time don't want to create problems or destroy the relationship.

WHAT DO YOU SAY?
Through what channel?

joys more of the rewards. Inequity will also exist if you and your partner work equally hard but one of you gets more of the rewards.

Much research supports this idea that people want equity in their interpersonal relationships (Ueleke et al., 1983). The general idea behind the theory is that if you are underbenefited (you get less than you put in), you'll be angry and dissatisfied. If, on the other hand, you are overbenefited (you get more than you put in), you'll feel guilty. Some research, however, has questioned this rather neat but intuitively unsatisfying assumption and finds that the overbenefited person is often quite happy and contented; guilt from getting more than you deserve seems easily forgotten (Noller & Fitzpatrick, 1993).

Equity theory puts into clear focus the sources of the relational dissatisfaction we all hear about every day. For example, in a relationship both partners may have full-time jobs, but one partner may also be expected to do the major share of the household chores. Thus, although both may be deriving equal rewards—they have equally good cars, they live in the same three-bedroom house, and so on—one partner is paying more of the costs. According to equity theory, this partner will be dissatisfied because of this lack of equity.

Equity theory claims that you will develop, be satisfied with, and maintain relationships that are equitable. You will not develop, will be dissatisfied with, and will terminate relationships that are inequitable. The greater the inequity, the greater the dissatisfaction and the greater the likelihood that the relationship will end.

Though each relationship is unique, relationships for many people possess similar characteristics, and it is these general patterns that these theories tried to explain. Taken together, the theories actually explain a great deal about why you develop relationships, the way relationships work, the ways you seek to maintain relationships, and the reasons why some relationships are satisfying and others are not. With this awareness, you'll be in a better position to regulate and manage your own friendship, romantic, and family relationships.

REFLECTIONS ON ETHICS

Relationship Ethics

Ethics is a significant part of meaningful relationship communication. Relationships built and maintained on lies are not likely to survive in the long run. But there is more to relationship ethics than the injunction not to lie. For a beginning perspective, the ethical issues and guidelines that operate within a friendship, romantic, family, or workplace relationship can be reviewed with the acronym ETHICS—Empathy (Cheney & Tompkins, 1987), Talk rather than force, Honesty (Krebs, 1990), Interaction management, Confidentiality, and Supportiveness (Johannesen, 2001). As you read these guidelines, think about whether you and your relationship partners follow them.

Empathy: People in a relationship have an ethical obligation to try to understand what others are feeling and thinking from their point of view. This is especially important when relationship members from different cultures communicate.

Talk: Decisions in a relationship should be arrived at by talk, not by force—by persuasion rather than coercion.

Honesty: Relationship communication should be honest and truthful.

Interaction management: Relationship communication should be satisfying and comfortable and is the responsibility of all individuals.

Confidentiality: People in a relationship have a right to expect that what they say in confidence will not be made public or even whispered about.

Supportiveness: A supportive and cooperative climate should characterize interpersonal interactions in a relationship.

Ethical Choice Point

You're managing a work team of three colleagues charged with redesigning the company website. The problem is that Jack doesn't do any work and misses most of the meetings. You spoke with him about it, and he confided that he's going through a divorce and can't concentrate. You feel sorry for Jack and have been carrying him for the last few months, but you now realize that you'll never be able to bring the project in on time if you don't replace Jack. In addition, you really don't want to get a negative appraisal because of Jack; in fact, you were counting on the raise that this project was going to get you. What are your ethical obligations in this situation—to yourself? to the other team members? to your employer? What would you do?

Summary: Interpersonal Communication

In this chapter we looked at interpersonal relationships: some of the reasons we enter relationships, relationship stages, and the theories that try to explain what happens in an interpersonal relationship.

1. Interpersonal relationships may be characterized as those that are based on psychological data, involve explanatory knowledge, and rely on personally established rules.
2. Interpersonal relationships have both advantages and disadvantages. Among the advantages are that these relationships stimulate you, help you learn about yourself, and generally enhance your self-esteem. Among the disadvantages are that they force you to expose your vulnerabilities, make great demands on your time, and often cause you to abandon other relationships.
3. Most relationships involve various stages. Recognize at least these: contact, involvement, intimacy, deterioration, repair, and dissolution.
4. In contact there is first perceptual contact and then interaction.
5. Involvement includes a testing phase (will this be a suitable relationship?) and an intensifying of the interaction; often a sense of mutuality, of connectedness, begins.
6. In intimacy there is an interpersonal commitment, and perhaps a social bonding, in which the commitment is made public.
7. Some relationships deteriorate, proceeding through a period of intrapersonal dissatisfaction to interpersonal deterioration.
8. Along the process, repair may be initiated. Intrapersonal repair generally comes first (should I change my behavior?); it may be followed by interpersonal repair, in which you and your partner discuss your problems and seek remedies.
9. If repair fails, the relationship may dissolve, moving first to interpersonal separation and later, perhaps, to public or social separation.
10. Theories that focus on attraction, relationship rules, social penetration, social exchange, and relationship equity offer five explanations for what happens when you develop, maintain, and dissolve interpersonal relationships.
11. Attraction depends on four factors: similarity (especially attitudinal), proximity (physical closeness), reinforcement, and attractiveness (physical attractiveness and personality).
12. The relationship rules approach views relationships as held together by adherence to an agreed-on set of rules.

13. Social penetration theory describes relationships in terms of breadth and depth: respectively, the number of topics partners talk about and the degree of personalness with which the partners pursue topics.
14. Social exchange theory holds that we develop relationships that yield the greatest profits. We seek relationships in which our rewards exceed our costs, and we are more likely to dissolve relationships when costs exceed rewards.
15. Equity theory claims that we develop and maintain relationships in which each partner's rewards are distributed in proportion to his or her costs. When our share of the rewards is less than would be demanded by equity, we are likely to experience dissatisfaction and to exit the relationship.

Key Terms in Interpersonal Communication

affiliative cues
attraction
attraction theory
breadth
cherishing behaviors
comparison level
complementarity
contact
depenetration
depth
dissolution
Duchenne smiles
equity theory
interdependency
intimacy
involvement
parasocial relationships
proximity
reinforcements
relationship deterioration
relationship dialectics theory
relationship repair
rules theory
similarity
social exchange theory
social penetration theory

Thinking Critically about Interpersonal Communication

1. **Positive Behaviors.** One way to improve communication during difficult times is to ask your partner for positive behaviors rather than to try to stop negative behaviors. How might you use this suggestion to replace the following statements? (1) "I hate it when you ignore me at business functions." (2) "I can't stand going to these cheap restaurants; when are you going to start spending a few bucks?" (3) "Stop being so negative; you criticize everything and everyone."
2. **Sexual Relationships.** As noted earlier, different cultures look at relationships very differently. How do your own cultural beliefs and values influence what you consider an appropriate and an inappropriate relationship? Do your cultural beliefs and values influence what you consider appropriate relationship behavior? In what ways do your cultural beliefs and values influence what you actually do as a relationship partner (as friend, lover, or family member)?
3. **Turning Points.** Throughout the life of a relationship, there exist "turning points"—jumps or leaps that project you from one relationship level to another. Do men and women see turning points in the same way? For example, what turning points are most important to women? Which are most important to men?
4. **Flirting Online.** One research study found that women flirt online by stressing their physical attributes, whereas men flirt by focusing on their socioeconomic status (Whitty, 2003). Do you observe flirting on the Internet? If so, how would you describe the way men and women flirt?
5. **Internet Courage.** Anonymity often leads people to feel more courageous, enabling them to say or do things they would not say or do if their identity was known (Barrett, 2006). It may be argued that when communicating in chat rooms, where you can conceal your true identity, you're likely to be more assertive, take more chances, and risk possible failure than you would in face-to-face situations. Do you display "Internet courage"? Do others you know display "Internet courage"?

Log On! My Communication Lab

WWW.MYCOMMUNICATIONLAB.COM

Visit MCL for a variety of materials relevant to this unit, including self-tests (on beliefs about relationships, the type of relationship you prefer, and relationship commitment) as well as several exercises and discussions: Making Relationship Predictions, Relationship Theories and Relationship Movement, analyzing Stage Talk, Interpersonal Relationships in Songs and Cards, Relationship Repair from Advice Columnists, and Mate Preferences.

CHAPTER

5

Conflict

Taken from *Interpersonal Communication: Relating to Others*, Seventh Edition, by Steven A. Beebe, Susan J. Beebe, and Mark V. Redmond.

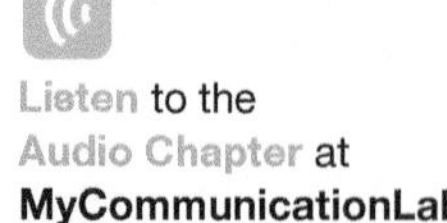
Listen to the
Audio Chapter at
MyCommunicationLab

Interpersonal conflict is a fact of life. Eventually, all relationships experience conflict. It's been estimated that people in stable, romantic relationships experience a conflict episode about twice a week.[1] You are more likely to have a quarrel with a romantic partner than with anyone else.[2] And the longer you know someone, the greater the likelihood that you'll experience conflict with that person, simply because you spend time together and know more about each other.[3] The key question of this chapter is, How can you best manage the inevitable conflict that occurs in your relationships with others?

Conflict management is not a single skill, but a set of skills. But to manage conflict effectively involves more than learning simple techniques. The best route to success in resolving conflict effectively is acquiring knowledge about what conflict is, what makes it happen, and what we can do about it. We will begin by defining conflict, then examine some of the myths about it and focus on some of its constructive functions. We will also discuss the relationship among conflict, power, and conflict management styles.

In addition, we will discuss how learning about your typical style of managing conflict can give you insight into managing interpersonal differences. And finally, we will build on our discussions of listening skills and verbal and nonverbal communication in the previous chapters to help you learn to manage the inevitable interpersonal conflicts that arise even in the best of relationships.

Conflict Defined

At the bedrock of all conflicts are differences—in goals, needs, and experiences. Unresolved and poorly managed interpersonal conflict is a significant predictor of an unsatisfactory interpersonal relationship. The opposite is also true: Partners in relationships in which conflict is effectively managed report being more satisfied with the relationship.[4] But precisely what is conflict? **Interpersonal conflict**, according to communication scholars William Wilmot and Joyce Hocker, includes four elements: It is (1) an expressed struggle (2) between at least two interdependent people (3) who perceive incompatible goals, scarce resources, or interference from others (4) and who are attempting to achieve specific goals.[5]

Conflict Elements

You probably don't need a textbook definition to determine whether you are experiencing conflict in a relationship. You know you're in conflict as you feel your emotions becoming aroused, as evidenced by an increased heart rate, muscle tension, and a raised voice.[6] Conflict can occur whether the issue is about something personal or nonpersonal, or about something outside the relationship.[7] Yet looking at the elements of conflict can help you understand both why conflict occurs and how to manage it.

An Expressed Struggle

You typically don't know that someone is upset with you until he or she expresses displeasure with a remark or by a nonverbal behavior such as a glare, a steely facial expression, or an emotion-laden tone of voice. The intensity of a conflict (as conveyed through the intensity of the emotion expressed) often correlates with the partners' perceptions of the importance of their unmet needs or goals. Sam Keltner developed the "struggle spectrum," shown in Figure 5.1, to describe conflicts ranging from mild differences to outright fights.[8] As conflict evolves in a relationship, it has the potential to escalate into physical abuse, especially in our most intimate relationships. One research team estimated that 50–60 percent of U.S. households have experienced at least minor forms of violence; there's evidence that in one out of every six romantic relationships, one partner has stalked the other.[9] Experts surmise that one reason violence is so prevalent in many relationships is that people don't have the skills to manage conflict.[10] They don't know how to express their relational struggle effectively.

Mild Differences | Disagreement | Dispute | Campaign | Litigation | Fight

Figure 5.1
The Struggle Spectrum
Used by permission of the National Communication Association.

Unresolved and poorly managed interpersonal conflict is a significant predictor of an unsatisfactory interpersonal relationship.

Between at Least Two Interdependent People

By **interdependent**, we mean that people are dependent on each other; what one person does or says affects the other.[11] If you were truly independent of someone, then what he or she did or said would have minimal effect on you. You are more likely to have conflict with people that you spend time with because you are connected to them in some way. Yes, you might have an emotional response to the anonymous driver who cuts you off in traffic, but the conflicts that weigh most heavily on us are those with people with whom we interact most frequently. And, as the old expression "it takes two to tango," suggests, it takes at least two people to have interpersonal conflict. You can certainly have intrapersonal conflict (conflict within yourself), but interpersonal conflict is between you and at least one other person.

Incompatible Goals, Scarce Resources, and Interference

Conflict often happens because two people want the same thing, but both can't have it, or because what one person wants is the opposite of what the other wants. Or, when resources (time, money, or something else) are scarce, there is more likely to be tension.[12] Whether it's a battle between former spouses who both want custody of the children, or a conflict over whether you spend the holidays with your parents or with your spouse's or partner's parents, when there are conflicting or incompatible goals or not enough of something to go around, or when someone is blocking what you believe is rightfully yours, conflict happens.

Achieving a Goal

People in conflict want something. As we noted, many conflicts occur because both people can't (or perceive that they can't) achieve their own goals. Understanding what the individuals in conflict want is an important step toward finding a way to manage the conflict. Most problems boil down to something you want more of or less of. Figuring out what you and the other person want more of or less of provides a starting point to getting to the end of conflict.

Conflict as a Process

Cathy was reading her e-book, enjoying a second cup of coffee, and listening to her favorite music. All seemed peaceful. Suddenly, for no apparent reason, her roommate Barb brusquely stormed into the room and shouted, "I can't stand it any more! We have to talk about who does what around here." Cathy was taken completely off guard. She had no idea her roommate was upset about the division of household chores. To her, this outburst seemed to come out of the blue; in reality, however, several events had led up to it.

Most relational disagreements have a source, a beginning, a middle, an end, and an aftermath.[13]

Source: Prior Conditions

The first phase in the conflict process is the one that sets the stage for disagreement; it begins when you become aware that there are differences between you and another person. The differences may stem from role expectations, perceptions, goals, or resources. In the previous example, Barb perceived that she and Cathy played different roles in caring for the household.

In interpersonal relationships, *many* potential sources of conflict may be smoldering below the surface. It may take some time before they flare up into overt conflict. Moreover, they may be compounded with other concerns, making them difficult to sort out. And it may not be just one conversation or issue that triggers conflict; multiple conflict "trip wires" may contribute to a conflict episode.[14]

Beginning: Frustration Awareness

At this stage, at least one of you becomes aware that the differences in the relationship are increasingly problematic. You may begin to engage in self-talk, noting that something is wrong and creating frustration. Perhaps you realize that you won't be able to achieve an important goal or that someone else has

RECAP Conflict as a Process

Prior Conditions	There are differences in background, experience, culture, attitudes, beliefs, values, opinions, or preferences.
Frustration Awareness	One individual becomes aware of differences. Thoughts and self-talk about the differences occur. The individual experiences frustration.
Active Conflict	The conflict is expressed; expression could range from a verbal expression of mild differences to physical violence.
Resolution	One or more of the individuals involved seek to manage the conflict. Not all conflicts are managed successfully or resolved.
Follow-Up	Individuals check to determine whether the conflict has been effectively and appropriately managed. They may need to revisit conflict management strategies.

resources you need to achieve it. Or you may become aware of differences in perceptions. Barb knew that Cathy's family always spent their weekends relaxing. All the members of Barb's family, in contrast, pitched in on weekends to get household chores done for the week. Barb may have recognized that difference, even as her frustration level rose.

Becoming aware of differences in perception does not always lead to increased frustration. But when the differences interfere with something you want to accomplish, your frustration level rises. Barb wanted to get the house clean so that she could turn her attention to studying for a test she had the next day. Cathy's apparent indifference to helping Barb achieve that goal was a conflict trigger.

Middle: Active Conflict

When you bring your frustration to the attention of others, a conflict becomes an active, *expressed struggle.*[15] If frustrations remain only as thoughts, the conflict is passive, not active. Active conflict does not necessarily mean that the differences are expressed with shouting or emotional intensity, although research suggests that if it is unmanaged, interpersonal conflict can escalate to interpersonal violence.[16] An expression of disagreement may be either verbal or nonverbal. Calmly asking someone to change an attitude or behavior to help you achieve your goal is a form of active conflict; so is kicking your brother under the table when he starts to reveal your secret to the rest of the family.

Cathy was not aware of the division of labor problem until Barb stormed into the room demanding a renegotiation of roles. Barb had been aware of her frustration for some time, yet had not acted on it. Many experts advocate not waiting until your frustration level escalates to peak intensity before you approach someone with your conflict. Unexpressed frustration tends to erupt like soda in a can that has just been shaken. Intense emotions can add to the difficulty of managing a conflict.

End: Resolution

When you begin to try to manage the conflict, it has progressed to the resolution stage. Of course, not all conflicts can be neatly resolved. Couples who divorce, feuding business partners who dissolve their corporation, or former lovers who go their separate ways have all found solutions, even though they may not be amicable ones.

After Barb's outburst, she and Cathy were able to reach a workable compromise about the division of their household labor. Cathy agreed to clean the house every other week; Barb promised not to expect her to do it on weekends.

Aftermath: Follow-Up

As Yogi Berra once said, "It ain't over 'til it's over." After a conflict has been resolved, the follow-up stage involves dealing with hurt feelings or managing simmering grudges, and checking with the other person to confirm that the conflict has not retreated into the frustration awareness stage.[17] Interpersonal relationships operate as transactive processes rather than as linear, step-by-step ones. Conflict does progress in stages, but you may need to resolve the same conflict again unless you confirm your understanding of the issues with your partner.

The Friday after their discussion, Cathy proudly showed off a spotless apartment to Barb when she

BEING Other-ORIENTED

When experiencing conflict with another person, identify some of the positive values or benefits of the conflict, and compare those with the costs or destructive nature of conflict. What could you do to increase the benefits and decrease the costs of conflict with others?

came home from class. Barb responded with a grin and a quick hug and privately resolved to get up early on Sunday morning so that she could go out to get Cathy pastries before she awoke. This kind of mutual thoughtfulness exemplifies a successful follow-up in a conflict.

Understanding the stages of conflict can help you better manage the process. You'll also be in a better position to make the conflict a constructive rather than a destructive experience. Conflict is **constructive** if it helps build new insights and establishes new patterns in a relationship. Airing differences can lead to a more satisfying relationship in the long run. David W. Johnson lists the following as benefits of conflict in interpersonal relationships. Interpersonal conflict

- Focuses attention on problems that may have to be solved.
- Clarifies what may need to be changed.
- Focuses attention on what is important to you and your partner.
- Clarifies who you are and what your values are.
- Helps you learn more about your partner.
- Keeps relationships interesting.
- Strengthens relationships by increasing your confidence that you can manage disagreements.[18]

Conflict can also be **destructive**. The hallmark of destructive conflict is a lack of flexibility in responding to others.[19] Conflict can become destructive when people view their differences from a win–lose perspective, rather than looking for solutions that allow both individuals to gain. There is clearly a dark side to conflict. Cyberbullying, hate crimes, stalking, aggressive verbal abuse, and physical abuse are some of the potential negative effects of escalating, unmanaged conflict. The Internet, smartphones, Skype, and YouTube make it easier to broadcast negative and destructive relational messages to more people at greater speed. A key purpose of this book, and specifically this chapter, is to identify sources of conflict *before* the relational turbulence becomes destructive. The principles, strategies, and skills we offer won't eliminate conflict, but they can help you manage it when it occurs in both face-to-face and electronically mediated relationships.

Conflict Triggers

Researchers have found that just as conflict typically follows a predictable path as it evolves, there are also some common causes that trigger conflict. A conflict trigger is a perceived cause of conflict. Note that we say, "perceived cause of conflict." When people communicate, especially during times of tension and conflict, perception becomes reality. What typically ticks people off? Here are some of the most common conflict triggers.

Criticism

Receiving criticism is one of the most frequently mentioned conflict triggers. One study found that young people especially are not pleased by criticism from their elders; the subjects were more likely to reject the criticism of family elders (parents or grandparents) than from non-family elders.[20] Some husbands have a heightened sensitivity to what they perceive as criticism from women—not just their wives in particular, but women in general.[21] That is, some men have a bias of treating *any* comment from *any* female as negative. This sensitivity to criticism been described as "empathic inaccuracy." The greater their "empathic inaccuracy," the more likely husbands were to respond to their wives with verbal aggression. Why does this happen? It's speculated that some men may have an insecure attachment style. If a husband is insecure about his relationship with others, especially women, he may be more likely to lash out verbally when receiving negative comments from women. The research found that men who could better empathize with their

"How many miles before our next fight?"

Michael Maslin/The New Yorker Collection/The Cartoon Bank

spouses and accurately infer that their spouses really did have specific and realistic points to make reported having more satisfying and happier relationships.

Feeling Entitled

If we believe we're entitled to something—whether "it" is a good grade in a class, a new car, or a relationship with someone—and we're denied getting what we think is ours, then conflict is a likely result.

Perceived Lack of Fairness

If we believe we have not been treated fairly or equitably, conflict is likely. "It's mine, not yours!" and "That's not fair!" are claims children make while playing with others in a sandbox; those same sentiments fuel conflict between adults, as well as international conflicts between nations.

More Perceived Costs than Rewards

Another trigger for conflict escalation in a relationship occurs when one person feels that he or she is getting less out of the relationship than the other person.[22] Over time, if the perceived burdens are greater than the joy of being in a relationship with someone, conflict ensues.

Different Perspectives

Researcher Lawrence Kurdek found that regardless of whether couples are heterosexual, gay, or lesbian, several topics or issues serve as conflict triggers: (1) power (who's in charge), (2) social issues (such as politics and religion), (3) personal flaws (such as using drugs or alcohol, smoking, or laziness), (4) distrust (concern about whether one person is telling the truth), (5) intimacy (differences about the frequency and timing of sex), and (6) personal distance (as evidenced by the amount of time each person commits to the relationship).[23] (Couples argue about other things, such as money, but money conflicts are often about power.) These "big six" appear to be common conflict themes across a wide variety of relationships.

> **BEING Other-ORIENTED**
>
> It's hard to be focused on others when you're under stress, tired, or worried about something. Have you noticed that you tend to experience more interpersonal conflict when either you or your communication partner are not at your best? What can you do to minimize conflict when you or others are fatigued or under stress?

Stress and Lack of Rest

When you are not at your physical best—when you're tired, stressed, or overworked—it may be wise to steer clear of situations that are likely to trigger disagreement. Before you know it, what you thought was just a casual remark can quickly escalate into conflict. The beginnings of vacations, when you and your friend, partner, or spouse may be at the peak of fatigue, are prime occasions for conflict. The end of a long work week may also be a time when it doesn't take much to turn a conversation into the Friday night fights. Not surprisingly, research has documented that being under the influence of alcohol or other substances that impair judgment increases the chances that conflict will erupt.[24]

Dialectical Tension

A **dialectical tension** stems from people's need or desire for two things at the same time.[25] The tension results in uncertainty and discomfort with the relationship. Here are two classic dialectical tensions experienced by many relationships

- *Being separate and connected.* You may have a desire to be both separate from other people and connected to them at the same time; we want our freedom, but we also want the comfort, predictability, and convenience of having someone who is a consistent part of our life. This desire can cause conflict if, for example, you want more freedom in a relationship, but your partner wants to keep closer tabs on what you are doing and where you are. You may feel a personal dialectical tension because you want both things *at the same time*—to be close to the other person and to have your freedom.
- *Feelings of being open and closed.* A second common dialectical tension is that we want and need various degrees of openness and closedness in our relationships. We want to share and disclose our thoughts and feelings, but we also want our privacy and secrecy.

The benefit of being aware of common conflict triggers is having the ability to spot them in your relationship before the conflict escalates into intractable tension that is more challenging to manage.

Conflict Myths

Although not all conflict is destructive to relationships, many cultures have taboos against displaying conflict in public. The prime experiences in life that shape how we learn to express and manage conflict occur in the families in which we grew up. It's in our families that we learn life lessons about relationships that remain with us throughout our days.[26] According to one researcher, many of us were raised with four myths that contribute to our negative feelings about conflict.[27] In some American families, conflict is expressed openly and often. But even if your experience has been different, reading about these prevailing myths may help you understand your or your partner's emotional responses to conflict.

Myth 1: Conflict Is Always a Sign of a Poor Interpersonal Relationship

It is an oversimplification to assume that all conflict is rooted in underlying relational problems. Conflict is a normal part of any interpersonal relationship.[28] Although it is true that constant bickering and sniping can be symptomatic of deeper problems, disagreements do not necessarily signal that the relationship is on the rocks. In fact, overly polite, stilted conversation is more likely to signal a problem than periodic disagreements.[29] The free expression of honest disagreement is often a hallmark of healthy relationships. Assertively and honestly expressing ideas may mean that a person feels safe and comfortable enough with his or her partner to disagree.

Myth 2: Conflict Can Always Be Avoided

"If you can't say anything nice, don't say anything at all." Many of us were taught early in our lives that conflict is undesirable and that we should eliminate it from our conversations and relationships. Yet evidence suggests that conflict arises in virtually every relationship.[30] Because each of us has a unique perspective on our world, it would be extraordinary for us *always* to see eye to eye with another person. Although such conflicts may not be intense, many differences of opinion punctuate our relationships with people we care about.[31]

Research suggests that contentment in marriage relates not to the amount of conflict, but to the way in which partners manage it.[32] Conflict is also a normal and productive part of interaction in group deliberations.[33] It is a myth that conflict is inherently unproductive and something to be avoided. It happens, even in the best of relationships.

Myth 3: Conflict Always Occurs Because of Misunderstandings

"You just don't understand what my days are like. I need to go to sleep!" shouts Janice as she scoops up a pillow and blanket and stalks off to the living room. "Oh, yeah? Well, you don't understand what will happen if I don't get this budget in!" responds Ron, who is hunched over the desk in their bedroom. It is clear that Ron and Janice are having a conflict. They have identified the cause of their problem as a lack of understanding between them, but in reality they *do* understand each other. Ron knows that Janice wants to sleep; Janice knows he wants to stay up and work. Their problem is that they disagree about whose goal is more important. This disagreement, not lack of understanding, is the source of the conflict.

Watch the Video "Power Moment" at **MyCommunicationLab**

Myth 4: Conflict Can Always Be Resolved

Consultants, corporate training experts, and authors of self-help books often offer advice about how to resolve conflicts so that all will be well and harmony will prevail. Some people claim that with the application of a few skills and how-to techniques, conflicts can disappear like a stain from a shirt laundered with the right kind of detergent. This is simply not true. Not all differences can be resolved by listening harder or paraphrasing your partner's message. Some disagreements are so intense and the perceptions so fixed that individuals may have to agree to disagree and live with it.

Conflict Types

At some time or another, many close relationships go through a conflict phase. "We're always fighting," complains a newlywed. But if she were to analyze these fights, she would discover important differences among them. According to communication researchers Gerald Miller and Mark Steinberg, most conflicts fit into one of three different categories: (1) pseudoconflict—triggered by a lack of understanding; (2) simple conflict—stemming from different ideas, definitions, perceptions, or goals; and (3) ego conflict—which occurs when conflict gets personal.[34]

Pseudoconflict: Misunderstandings

Will: Let's walk to the store.

Sean: No, it's too far. Let's drive.

Will: But the store is close.

Sean: No, it's not.

Will: Yes, it is. It's just off Market Street.

Sean: Oh, you mean the convenience store.

Will: Sure, that's exactly what I mean.

Sean: Oh, no problem. I thought you meant the supermarket.

Pseudoconflict is simply a misunderstanding. Your partner may communicate confusion by facial expressions or other nonverbal behavior. Pseudoconflict can be resolved if partners ask for clarification, listen between the lines, and work to establish a supportive climate.

BEING Other-ORIENTED

Listening for the unspoken message is especially important when experiencing conflict with another person. What are nonverbal cues that you can look for to provide information about what the other person may be feeling or experiencing? How do you know whether you have made accurate inferences when "listening between the lines"?

Pseudo means false or fake. **Pseudoconflict** occurs when we simply miss the meaning in a message. But unless we clear up the misunderstanding by asking for more information, a real conflict might ensue. Note that in this example, Will offers helpful information ("It's just off Market Street"), and Sean checks it with feedback ("Oh, you mean the convenience store").

How can you avoid pseudoconflict? A key strategy is to clarify the meaning of words and expressions that you don't understand. Keep the following strategies in mind to minimize misunderstandings before they occur:

- *Check your perceptions:* Ask for clarification of anything you don't understand; seek to determine whether your interpretation is the same as your partner's.
- *Listen between the lines:* Rather than voice their misunderstanding, people may express their uncertainty nonverbally. Look for puzzled or quizzical facial expressions from your partner. Or listen to his or her tone of voice to determine whether nonverbal behaviors are consistent with the verbal message
- *Establish a supportive rather than a defensive climate for conversation:* Avoid evaluating, controlling, using manipulative strategies, being aloof, acting superior, or rigidly asserting that you're always right. These classic behaviors are like pushing the button to increase defensiveness and misunderstanding.

Simple Conflict: Different Stands on the Issues

Simple conflict stems from differences in ideas, definitions, perceptions, or goals. You want to go to Disney World for your vacation; your spouse wants to go to Washington, D.C. Your spouse wants to fly; you would rather take the train. You understand each other, but you disagree.

A key to unraveling a simple conflict is to keep the conversation focused on the issues at hand so that the expression of differences does not deteriorate into a battle focusing on personalities.

To keep simple conflict from escalating into personal attacks, consider the following strategies:

- *Clarify your and your partner's understanding* of the issues and your partner's understanding of the source of the disagreement.
- *Keep the discussion* focused on facts and the issue at hand, rather than drifting back to past battles and unrelated personal grievances.
- *Look for more than just the initial solutions* that you and your partner bring to the discussion; generate many options.
- *Don't try to tackle too many issues at once.* Perform "issue triage"—identify the important issues, and work on those.
- *Find the kernel of truth in what your partner is saying.* Find agreement where you can.
- *If tempers begin to flare and conflict is escalating, cool off.* Come back to the discussion when you and your partner are fresh.

Ego Conflict: Conflict Gets Personal

A personal attack puts your partner on the defensive, and many people behave according to the adage "The best defense is a good offense." When you launch a personal attack, you are "picking a fight." And as Sue and Nadiya's exchange illustrates, fights that begin as pseudoconflict or simple conflict can easily lapse into more vicious **ego conflict**. And as each person in the conflict becomes more defensive about his or her position, the issues become more tangled. Research has found that when you are under stress, you are more likely to be verbally aggressive toward someone.[39] It can take

UNDERSTANDING OTHERS Adapting to Differences

Gender and Conflict

Since conflict is often rooted in differences, it's not surprising that gender differences can influence how conflict is managed.

One difference that influences how we manage conflict is whether we have an overall masculine style or feminine style when managing conflict. A person with a *feminine style* focuses more on relationship issues, whereas someone with a *masculine style* typically focuses on tasks.[35] People with a feminine style often interact with others to achieve intimacy and closeness. In contrast, people with a masculine style often interact to get something done or to accomplish something apart from the relationship. When pursuing a goal, people employing a masculine style tend to be more aggressive and assertive than those employing a feminine style.[36] The lists in this box summarize key differences that researchers have observed between feminine and masculine styles of responding to conflict. Note that individuals of either sex may employ some characteristics of both feminine and masculine gender styles.

Perceived Gender Differences in Responding to Conflict[37]

People with Feminine Styles . . .	People with Masculine Styles . . .
Are concerned with equity and caring; connect with and feel responsible to others.	Are concerned with equality of rights and fairness; they adhere to abstract principles, rules.
Interact to achieve closeness and interdependence.	Interact to achieve specific goals; they seek autonomy and distance.
Attend to interpersonal dynamics to assess relationship's health.	Are less aware of interpersonal dynamics.
Encourage mutual involvement.	Protect self-interest.
Attribute crises to problems in the relationship.	Attribute crises to problems external to the relationship.
Are concerned with the impact of the relationship on personal identity.	Are neither self- nor relationship-centered.
Respond to conflict by often focusing mainly on the relationship.	Respond to conflict by often focusing on rules and being evasive until a unilateral decision is reached.

Knowing your overall gender style and the style of the person with whom you are in conflict can help you respond and adapt to differing assumptions you may have about what the other person needs, wants, and expects.

Also, the overall attitude you have toward someone with a different gender style can influence how you manage conflict. One study found that men who expressed caring, positive, and protective attitudes toward women (in other words, had a more feminine style) were more likely to establish a warmer communication climate than were men who focused on the task and were less relationally skilled.[38] As the saying goes, "You can catch more flies with honey than with vinegar."

considerable time, skill, and patience to repair the damage of things you said in a moment of anger and frustration.

If you find yourself involved in ego conflict, try to refrain from hurling personal attacks and emotional epithets back and forth. Instead, take turns expressing your feelings without interrupting each other; then take time to cool off.[40] It is difficult to use effective listening skills when your emotions are at a high pitch. Marianne Mast and her colleagues found that when there are power differences between people, it's helpful to be more empathic—put

Watch the Video "Job Promotion" at **MyCommunicationLab**

RECAP Types of Conflict

	Pseudoconflict	Simple Conflict	Ego Conflict
What It Is	Individuals misunderstand each other.	Individuals disagree over which action to pursue to achieve their goals.	Individuals feel personally attacked.
What to Do	Check your perceptions. Listen between the lines; look for nonverbal expressions of puzzlement. Be supportive rather than defensive. Listen actively.	Clarify understanding. Stay focused on facts and issues. Generate many options rather than arguing over one or two options. Find the kernel of truth in what your partner is saying; emphasize where you agree.	Return to issues rather than personal attacks. Talk about a problem to be solved rather than a fight to be won. Write down rational arguments to support your position. Use "I" messages rather than "you" messages. Avoid contemptuous verbal or nonverbal messages.

yourself in the other person's position—to help establish a positive, interpersonally sensitive communication climate.[41] Being other-oriented, especially during ego conflict, can help you manage the conflict more effectively.

Here are additional strategies to consider when conflict becomes personal:

- *Try to steer the ego conflict back to simple conflict:* Stay focused on issues rather than personalities.
- *Make the issue a problem to be solved rather than a battle to be won.*
- *Write down what you want to say:* It may help you to clarify your point, and you and your partner can develop your ideas without interruption. But by all means avoid putting angry personal attacks in writing. Make your written summary rational, logical, and brief rather than emotion-laden.
- *When things get personal, make a vow not to reciprocate:* Use "I" messages ("I feel uncomfortable and threatened when we yell at each other.") rather than "you" messages ("You're such a creep. You never listen.") to express how you are feeling.
- *Avoid contempt.* To be contemptuous is to roll your eyes and sarcastically intone, "Oh, that's brilliant" to something your partner has said. Research has found that happy and satisfied couples rarely express contempt.[42] It doesn't mean there's no teasing, but caustic and corrosive contemptuous conversation is typically not present between people in a satisfying relationship.

Conflict and Power

Listen to "Power in Interpersonal Communication" at **MyCommunicationLab**

Often what we fight about is not what we're really fighting about. The topic of your argument may be anything from deciding which movie to see to something more significant, such as whether to have children. Yet underlying the surface issue may be a question about who has the power to make the decision. If, during an argument you or your partner says, "Who made you king?" or "What gives you the right to make this decision?" those comments are indicators that underlying the conflict is an issue of power. Power and conflict go hand in hand, because people often use the sources of interpersonal power available to them to achieve their desired outcome when conflict occurs.

Interpersonal power is the degree to which a person is able to influence or control his or her relational partner. During a conflict, you may not even be aware of how you are drawing on the power that you have, or that the other person is exerting power to influence you. Nonetheless, power issues are often the "back story" to the conflict.

Research has found gender differences in the way we use, interpret, and respond to power in our relationships.[43] Men's perception of whether they had power in a relationship was often not directly related to whether they were observed to dominate a conversation, nor did it correlate with what they actually did when talking with others. When women saw themselves as more powerful in a relationship, they sometimes surprisingly tended to view their partners as more dominant in the relationship. Perhaps when women perceived that their partner was dominant, they responded with increased power in response. Understanding principles of power and sources of power can give you greater insight into how you are using power to influence others to achieve your goals and how others are seeking to influence or control you, especially during conflict.

Underlying many interpersonal conflicts is the question of who has power to make decisions.

Power Principles

Most of us probably don't like to think that other people have power over us, but power is a fundamental element of all our personal relationships. Understanding the role of power in our relations with others can help explain and predict our thoughts, emotions, and behaviors, especially during relational conflict.

Power Exists in All Relationships

The definition of interpersonal communication presented in Chapter 1 suggests that *mutual influence* is an essential element any time you relate to others. When you talk, you are attempting to exert power over other people, if for no other purpose than to get them to listen to you. By definition, being in a relationship means letting someone have some influence on you and having influence on the other person.

Power Derives from the Ability to Meet a Person's Needs

If you can meet someone's need, then you have power. The degree to which one person can satisfy another person's interpersonal needs (for inclusion, control, and affection) as well as other needs (for food, clothing, safety, sex, money) represents the amount of power that person has.

In a **dependent relationship,** one person has a greater need for the partner to satisfy his or her needs; the power is out of balance and the person who depends on someone else to meet his or her needs has less power. One study of heterosexual romantic couples found that the partner with less emotional involvement in the relationship had more power, and this was generally the man.[44] The more we depend on one person to satisfy our needs, the more power that person has over us.

Both People in a Relationship Have Some Power

Although sometimes one person in a relationship has more power (influence) than the other, each person has some degree of power. When you were a child, your parents clearly had more power than you did; during conflicts, especially when you were quite young, they used their power to resolve conflicts in their favor. Now the power may be more balanced (or maybe not). When two people are satisfying each other's needs, they create an interdependent relationship; each person in the relationship has some amount of power over the other.

Power Is Circumstantial

Because our needs change, so does power. As you were growing up, you were very dependent on your parents and other adults. However, as you grew and developed skills, you no longer needed your parents to meet certain needs, and thus their power diminished. So the power balance ebbs and flows in a relationship over time and depending on circumstances.

Power Is Negotiated

Partners often negotiate which individual will have decision-making responsibility over what issues. But people can disagree as to who has power to do what. If one partner wants the power to control the TV remote and the other person also wants to have channel-changing power, conflict and tension are the result, unless some negotiation occurs. "OK, you decide what we watch between 6:00 and 8:00 P.M. and I'll control the remote the next two hours" may be one couple's way of negotiating the power. With power negotiated, the conflict is managed—unless one of the individuals wants to revisit who is in charge of the remote. If the negotiation is about something more weighty than who watches which TV program (such as sex, money, or children), the conflict can be more intense, and clearly more is at stake during the power negotiation.

Power Sources

Why does one person in a relationship have power over the other? Understanding the sources of power can help you analyze the power that you have and that others have over you. During conflict, being mindful of how people can influence you and how you may influence others can help you understand why some conflicts are managed as they are. A classic framework for identifying the sources of power was developed by researchers John French and Bertram Raven.[45] The five sources of power they identified are legitimate (or position) power, referent power, expert power, reward power, and coercive power.

Legitimate power is based on respect for a position that a person holds. Teachers, parents, law officers, store managers, and company presidents all have power because of the position they hold relative to other people. When a police officer tells you to pull off to the side of the road, you respond to this enactment of power by obeying the officer's command.

Referent power comes from our attraction to another person, or the charisma a person possesses. We let people we like influence us. We change our behavior to meet their demands or desires because we are attracted to them.

Expert power is based on a person's knowledge and experience. We grant power to those who know more than we do or have some expertise we don't possess. You recognize, for example, that your teenage son knows more about computers than you do, so you let him try his hand at solving a computer glitch. Such expertise can include knowledge about how to manage a relationship effectively. We grant power to partners who have more experience in relationships.

Reward power is based on another person's ability to satisfy your needs. There are obvious rewards, such as money and gifts, but most rewards are more interpersonal in nature. Reward power is probably the most common form of power in interpersonal relationships. Withholding rewards is actually a form of punishment, or what is called *coercive power.*

Coercive power involves the use of sanctions or punishment to influence others. Sanctions include holding back or removing rewards. If you have a high need for physical affection, your partner might withhold that affection if you do not comply with a given request. Punishment involves imposing something on another person that he or she does not want.

Power to Persuade

When we have power, we may use it to manage conflict in order to achieve our goals and meet our needs using compliance-gaining strategies. **Compliance gaining** involves taking actions in interpersonal relationships to gain something from our partners—to get others to comply with our goals.

People's level of power affects which compliance-gaining strategies they employ. People with more power can be more efficient in gaining compliance by using simple, more direct (and sometimes inappropriate) strategies to accomplish their goals.[46] Those with less power need to carefully consider which strategies they can use that won't result in negative consequences. For example, telling your boss that you want Friday night off or you'll quit might result in your no longer having a job. The appropriateness of compliance gaining varies according to our goals. For example, persuasive strategies involving either logic or emotion were seen as more effective in face-to-face interactions than in computer-mediated ones.[47] Communication scholar Kathy Kellerman compiled a list of fifty-six strategies that people might employ in trying to gain compliance (Table 5.1). Think about the last time you sought compliance from a friend, and see if you can identify the strategy or strategies you employed.

Compliance-gaining strategies are responsive to the ongoing, transactive nature of interpersonal relationships.[49] We plot strategies that develop over a number of interactions and modify them in accordance with others' responses. For example, before you ask to borrow money from your friend, you might first do a few favors for her during the day. Then if your friend says no to your request for a loan, you might remind her that she owes you for all you've done for her. If she still says no, you might offer to help her over the weekend with her class project. The type of relationship you have established with the other person will affect your strategy selection.

Power Negotiation

If you realize you don't have as much power as you'd like, you may want to renegotiate the balance

Table 5.1
Compliance-Gaining Strategies[48]

Accuse	Comment	Hint	Protest
Acknowledge	Complain	Inform	Question
Advise	Compliment	Insist	Remark
Apologize	Confess	Insult	Report
Approve	Confirm	Joke	Reprimand
Argue	Criticize	Justify	Request
Ask	Demand	Offer	Ridicule
Assert	Disagree	Order	Suggest
Assure	Disclose	Permit	Summarize
Attack	Excuse	Plead	Tell
Blame	Explain	Point out	Thank
Boast	Forbid	Praise	Threaten
Challenge	Forgive	Prohibit	Vow
Claim	Give	Promise	Warn

of power in a relationship. Defining who has power can be a source of conflict in interpersonal relationships, potentially even bringing about the end of a relationship. When a partner abuses power, ending the relationship may be warranted. Ideally, partners negotiate a mutually acceptable and rewarding power relationship. To negotiate or renegotiate power in a relationship, consider the following strategies.

Assess Needs

The first step to negotiating a satisfactory balance of power is to identify your needs and those of your partner. Knowing what you need and what the other person needs in the relationship can help you determine whether any negotiation or renegotiation of roles, responsibilities, and assumptions is warranted. Reflecting not just on your needs but also on the needs of the other person is an other-oriented strategy that can help you honestly and realistically start the negotiation process.

Identify Power-Based Conflicts

Examine your interpersonal conflicts for unresolved power issues. For example, in the first year of marriage, couples often argue about balancing job and family, about financial problems (including who spends money and on what), about the frequency of sexual relations, and about the division of household tasks.[50] These problems involve issues of power, control, responsibility, and decision making. Such issues exist in other relationships as well. Examine your relationships for recurring patterns of conflict, and try to determine the role that power is playing. Conflicts can result from unacceptable imbalances of power (the feeling that one or the other partner has too much), from equal amounts of power (with each partner attempting to influence the other), or as a reaction to a partner's attempts to exert control or to dominate.

Discuss Power Issues Directly

If you're not talking about what the real, underlying issue may be during a conflict—the issue of power—the conflict is unlikely to be managed permanently. Identification of the unmet needs that are fueling conflict should be followed up with conversation about who has, wants, and expects to have influence and control. But when talking about who has power and control in a relationship, it's vital to use the principles and skills of being supportive as well as effective listening and responding skills. Talking about who should have the power and influence in a relationship can be risky—like touching the third rail on a subway track that carries the electricity that propels the train. Some couples need a trained counselor or therapist to help them work through issues of power in their relationships. The more intense the unmet need that is affecting the power imbalance is,

Explore the Exercise "How Powerful Do You Feel?" at **MyCommunicationLab**

the greater the likelihood that help may be needed to address who has the influence in a specific situation.

Conflict Management Styles

What's your approach to managing interpersonal conflict: fight or flight? Do you tackle conflict head-on or seek ways to remove yourself from it? Most of us do not have a single way of dealing with differences, but we do have a tendency to manage conflict by following patterns that we have used before.[51] The pattern we choose depends on several factors: our personality, the individuals with whom we are in conflict, the time and place of the confrontation, and other situational factors. For example, if your boss gives you an order, you respond differently from the way you do if your spouse gives you an order. Virginia Satir, author of *Peoplemaking,* a book about family communication, suggests that we learn conflict response patterns early in life.[52] Ample research evidence supports Satir's conclusion.[53] How we manage conflict with others is related to how our family of origin dealt with conflict.

One of several classifications of **conflict styles** is a five-style model based on the work of K. W. Thomas and R. H. Kilmann that includes two primary dimensions: concern for others and concern for self.[54] These two dimensions result in five conflict management styles, shown in Figure 5.2. The five styles are (1) avoidance, (2) accommodation, (3) competition, (4) compromise, and (5) collaboration.

Avoidance

One approach to managing conflict is to back off and try to side-step the conflict. Typical responses from someone who uses this style are "I don't want to talk about it," "It's not my problem," "Don't bother me with that now," or "I'm not interested in that." The **avoidance** style might indicate that a person has low concern for others as well as for himself or herself. This is sometimes called the "lose–lose" approach to conflict. The person using the avoidance conflict style wishes the problem or conflict would go away by itself and appears uninterested in managing the conflict or in meeting the needs of the other person involved in the disagreement. People who avoid conflict may also just not like the hassle of dealing with a difficult, uncomfortable situation. Not dealing directly with conflict may also stem from being unassertive and unable to stand up for one's own rights.

Other times, people avoid conflict because they don't want to hurt the feelings of others. There may be times when avoiding a major blowup with someone is a wise strategy, but hoping the conflict will go away on its own may not always be the best plan.

Evidence suggests that husbands are more likely to avoid confrontation as a way of managing conflict with their wives. One research team argues that

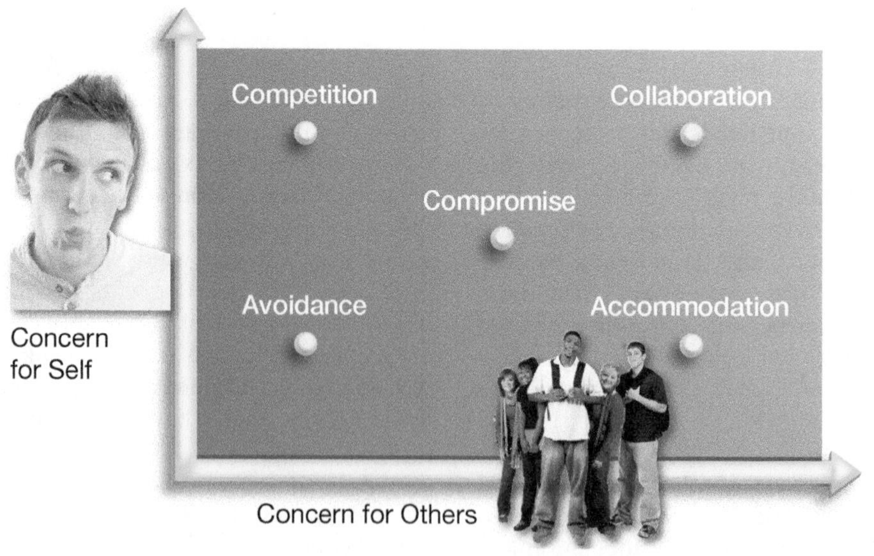

Figure 5.2
Conflict Management Styles
The five conflict management styles in relation to concern for others and concern for self.

males are likely to avoid conflict because of the way they process information, especially emotions.[55] Husbands may implicitly reason that it's better to keep quiet and avoid conflict than to speak up and try to sort things out; for them, the dissonance that results from speaking up is not worth the effort. Women, on the other hand, find avoiding the issues especially dissatisfying and irritating.[56]

One characteristic of an avoidant conflict management style is the **demand-withdrawal pattern of conflict management**. This is a communication pattern in which one person makes a demand and the other person avoids conflict by changing the subject or just walking away—he or she withdraws from the conflict.[57] The demand-withdrawal pattern is speculated to occur because one of the partners in the relationship wants to change the relationship and the other person does not; another reason may simply be that the person who withdraws may not care about the relationship. Yet another reason people withdraw is that they simply don't like to engage in conflict. Research has found that the demand-withdrawal communication pattern results in lower levels of relationship satisfaction.[58] We don't like it when a person makes demands and then refuses to talk about the issue.

The demand-withdrawal pattern can be found in marriages, dating relationships, and friendships, and between parents and children. Husband-and-wife couples are more likely to experience the demand-withdrawal pattern when they are talking about their relationship. Research that looked at how parents and teenagers managed their conflict found that the demand-withdrawal pattern was one of the *least* satisfying approaches to managing conflict.[59] Researchers have found that making repeated demands that aren't directly addressed, while also hurling put-downs at one another, results in a more distressed parent-teenager relationship. If you see that you're in a demand-withdrawal pattern of conflict, try to change the tone of the interaction so that it becomes a conversation rather than a shouting match or a standoff in which you both just stop talking. Make it a goal to keep the conversation going rather than making a demand that results in the other person just walking away.

In some respects, avoiding conflict could be perceived as uncooperative. However, there are some advantages to avoiding conflict. Doing so provides time for each person in the conflict to think about the issues, cool down, and ponder other approaches to dealing with the issues. If the conflict issue really is trivial, it may be advantageous not to throttle up the tension.

Avoiding conflict can also allow each person to save face. One of the ways people avoid conflict and try to de-escalate emotional tension is by being deliberately vague or ambiguous about what is causing the conflict. They provide general rather than specific feedback. Yet in certain situations people find a direct response more honest and competent than a vague one.[60] The trick is accurately reading a situation to know when to be vague and when to be specific.

There are also several disadvantages to avoiding conflict. If you avoid the conflict, you may be sending a message that you really don't care about the other person's feelings; you're more concerned about your own needs. Avoiding the conflict may also just make things worse. A conflict that was simply simmering may boil over if it's not tended to. And, of course, another disadvantage is that the issue remains unresolved. Like a lump in the throat, the conflict just sits there.

Accommodation

To accommodate is to give in to the demands of others. People may sometimes adopt an **accommodation** style because they fear rejection if they rock the boat. Sometimes, people who accommodate don't seem to get angry or upset; they just do what others want them to do. But, in reality, they also accommodate to serve their own interests—to get people to like them. This conflict management style

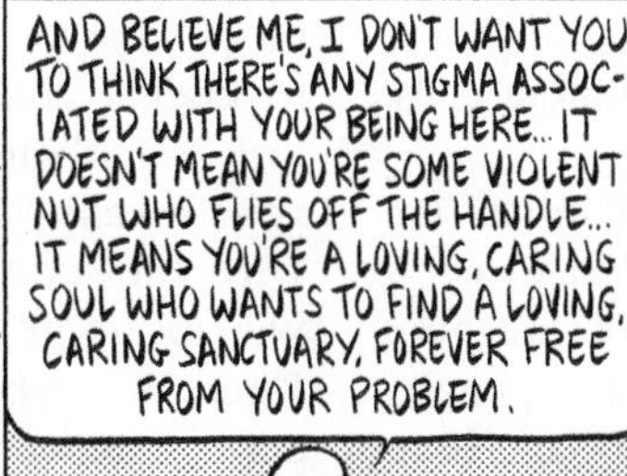

Stephan Pastis/Universal Uclick

is sometimes called the "lose-win" approach. If you consistently accommodate, you sacrifice your own needs so that someone else can win the argument.

Using the accommodation style has several advantages. For one thing, it shows that you're reasonable and you want to help. If the issue is a minor or trivial one, you may gain some credibility by just letting it slide. Of course, if you are wrong or have made a mistake, accommodation is an appropriate response.

There are disadvantages to accommodating, just as there are disadvantages to any conflict style. Throughout this book, we've stressed the importance of becoming other-oriented. But we've also noted that being other-oriented means considering the needs and position of the other person, without necessarily doing what the other person wants. Sometimes, a person may accommodate for self-protection rather than because he or she is genuinely interested in others. In the following exchange, note Luke's accommodation response to Martin:

Martin: Luke, I'm not in agreement with you on the QCN merger. I think the merger should be called off.

Luke: OK. Whatever you think is best. I just want you to feel good about your decision.

To accommodate can give the accommodator a false sense of security by producing a "pseudosolution"—one that doesn't really solve anything but just postpones the effort of seeking a solution to the problem. Also, if you consistently accommodate, you may diminish your power to the extent that others take advantage of you; the next time a conflict arises, the expectation may be that you'll give in and the other person will get his or her way again. In addition, if you accommodate too quickly, you short-circuit the possibility of finding a creative solution that is to everyone's liking.

Competition

"You're wrong!" shouts Ed. "Here's how to get our project in on time. We can't waste time in the library. We just have to write up what we have."

"But Ed," suggests Derrick, "the assignment calls for us to have three library sources."

"No. We don't have time. Just do it," Ed insists. Ed sees the issue as a competition that he must win.

Each of us has some need to control and also some need to be controlled by others. But people who have a **competition** conflict management style have a win-lose philosophy. They want to win at the expense of the other person, to claim victory over their opponents. They want to control others. They are typically not other-oriented; instead, they are focused on themselves.

People who compete often resort to blaming, or seeking a scapegoat, rather than assuming responsibility for a conflict. "I didn't do it," "Don't look at me," and "He made me do it" are typical blaming statements.

If these strategies do not work, people with a competitive style may try threats and warnings. *Threats* refer to actions that people can actually carry out.[61] Warnings are negative prophecies they cannot actually control. The boyfriend who says, "If you don't stop calling me names, I'm going to leave you," has issued a threat; he has the power to leave. If he were to say, "Don't call your parents names, or they'll write you out of their will," that would be a warning. In reality, he has no control over his partner's parents.

Obviously, threats are more powerful than warnings in changing behavior, and then only if the other person would genuinely find the threatened actions punishing or disruptive. If a parent threatens to ground a child, the child will take the threat seriously only if he or she knows the parent will carry it out.

Is it ever appropriate to compete with others? Yes, if you believe that your position is clearly the best approach and that anything short of achieving your goal would be harmful to you and to others.[62] In an election, someone will win and someone will lose. At the conclusion of a judicial trial, someone typically wins and someone loses. But even hard-fought elections and controversial trials have rules designed to maintain fairness for all involved in the conflict or decision. During often-emotional periods of competition, those involved nonetheless need to maintain an ethical concern for others.

Compromise

To compromise is to attempt to find a middle ground—a solution that somewhat meets the needs of all concerned. The word *somewhat* is important. Often, when people compromise, no one gets precisely what he or she wants; each has to give up a bit of what he or she had hoped to get. When trying to craft a compromise, you're really expecting to lose something and win something simultaneously; you also expect your partner to lose and win. That's why the **compromise** style is called "a lose/win-lose/win" approach to conflict. As shown in Figure 5.2, when you compromise, you have some concern for others as well as some concern for yourself. Research has found that college students are more likely to try a compromise conflict management style first than any other style.[63]

RELATING TO OTHERS E-Connections

Conflict Happens

Conflict happens not only during our face-to-face interactions but online as well. There are several reasons conflict may be even more likely to occur when we communicate online.

Managing Conflict Online

Reduced Nonverbal Cues

Because we may miss some of the subtle relational cues that exist in face-to-face situations, pseudoconflict in cyberspace can escalate from a mere misunderstanding to substantive differences (simple conflict). And if those differences become personal (ego conflict), the conflict is much more difficult to unravel.

Haste

Sometimes in our haste and informality, we tap out a message that is perfectly clear to us, but not to the recipient. Missed meaning because of a too-cryptic message often occurs online.

Flaming

Flaming occurs when someone sends an overly negative message that personally attacks someone else.[65] The flamer can further intensify the negative message by "shouting" the message in ALL CAPITAL LETTERS. People are more likely to use flaming language online than when talking in person.

The Disinhibition Effect

The tendency to escalate conflict online is called the **disinhibition effect**. Without another person physically in front of them, and with emotional tension rising, people tend to lash out—*they lose some of their inhibitions;* hence the term *disinhibition effect.*

Strategies for Managing Conflict Online

What should you do when you find yourself in an online conflict? Some of the same strategies that you would use when interacting in person can be useful, but there are other specific options to consider in cyberspace.

Avoid Counterflaming; Take Time to Cool Off

Because of the disinhibition effect, your first impulse may be to respond immediately with a reciprocal flaming message. But resist the temptation to fight fire with flaming fire. It may be cathartic to lash out in response to an unfair criticism or hurtful comment, but escalating the conflict makes it more difficult to manage.

Move to a Richer Medium

Consider interacting with the other person in a more media-rich context. If it's possible, talk to your communication partner in person; if that's not possible, reach for the phone to talk in real time rather than asynchronously.

Make Sure You Understand the Issues before Responding

Before you write or say anything further, reread the previous messages. Try to assume the role of an impartial mediator. Rather than looking for ways to justify your actions or feelings, read the messages as if you were looking at the information for the first time.

Paraphrase

Paraphrase what you understand your partner to be communicating. Then give the other person a chance to agree or disagree with your paraphrase. Don't make any further

(continued)

RELATING TO OTHERS E-Connections

(continued)

demands or requests until you're sure you comprehend the issues that are causing the controversy. Turn the conversation into one about clarification rather than about what you both want.

Increase Redundancy

To enhance clarity and understanding of your message, you may need to repeat key points and summarize what you'd like to have happen during the conflict. Being more redundant when reinforcing what you want to occur in the conflict can be helpful to ensure that your key ideas are being "listened to." It's helpful to slow the process down, especially when emotions may be running high; rather than piling on more details, make sure your essential points are clear.[66]

Use Caution When Trying to Lighten the Tone

In face-to-face contexts, humor can help break the tension. But when you're with someone physically, you can more accurately read your partner's nonverbal behavior to know when a joke is helping to reduce the tension and when it's not. Often what makes something funny is the timing of the joke's punch line, or the vocal or physical delivery of an intended humorous comment. Online, with limited nonverbal cues, what you think might reduce tension could escalate it.

Self Reflect

Take a "time out" to analyze your emotional reactions. Why are you getting upset and angry? Understanding why you've become upset can help you understand how to begin managing the conflict.

Put Yourself In the Other Person's Position

Use the other-oriented skill of decentering by asking yourself, "What was the other person thinking when he or she wrote that message?" Try to identify the thoughts that may have triggered the negative comments. Then, after considering the other person's thought process, empathize by asking yourself "What was the other person feeling?"

Conflict occurs both in person and online. Understanding that conflict may occur and rapidly escalate because of the disinhibition effect, and then implementing some of the suggestions presented here, may help you to cool a heated conflict and return your interaction to "room temperature."

Compromise has some advantages. It can be a good thing if a quick resolution to the conflict is needed. And it reinforces the notion that all parties involved share in equal power. Compromise can also be useful if what is needed is a temporary solution. And it has the advantage of helping everyone save face, because everyone wins at least something.

But if compromising results in each person giving in but no person feeling pleased with the compromise, then a more collaborative approach to managing the conflict may be appropriate.

Collaboration

To collaborate is to have a high concern for both yourself and others. People who use a collaboration style of conflict management are more likely to view conflict as a set of problems to be solved rather than a game in which one person wins and another loses.

The collaboration conflict style is best used when

- All sides of the conflict need fresh, new ideas.
- Enhanced commitment to a solution is important because all are involved in shaping the outcome.

- It's important to establish rapport and a positive relational climate.
- Emotional feelings are intense, and all involved in the conflict need to be listened to.
- It's important to affirm the value of the interpersonal relationship.

BEING Other-ORIENTED

Collaboration would be impossible if you failed to consider the thoughts and feelings of the other person. What are ways to identify the interests that you have in common with the person with whom you are in conflict? How can you determine where your goal overlaps with the other person's goal?

It may sound as though collaboration is always the best approach to managing conflict. However, there are times when its disadvantages may outweigh the advantages.[64] One of the biggest disadvantages is the time, skill, patience, and energy required to manage conflict collaboratively. If a solution is needed quickly, other approaches such as compromise may be best.

So, which style of managing conflict is best? The short answer to this question is "It depends." It depends on the outcome you seek, the amount of time you have, the quality of the relationship you have with the other people involved, and the amount of perceived power you and others have.[67] Each style has advantages and disadvantages; no style has an inherent advantage all of the time. The competent, other-oriented communicator consciously decides whether to compete, avoid, compromise, accommodate, or collaborate. Research suggests that most people find the following most uncomfortable: (1) no clear resolution to a conflict, (2) a conflict management process that is poorly managed, or (3) the avoidance of issues that they would like to discuss.[68] *There is no single conflict management style that "works" in all situations.* We do, however, strongly suggest that when time and other factors permit, a collaborative (win-win) conflict management style is worth exploring.[69] The conflict management skills presented in the final section of this chapter are anchored in a collaborative approach to managing conflict.

If both people who are involved in a conflict have a secure attachment style (meaning they were raised in a "secure" family that fostered trust, love, and support), then they are likely to use a collaboration or compromise style as apposed to a competing or avoiding style during conflict. If one person is "secure" and the other "insecure" in terms of attachment style, there is likely to be more mutual avoidance and withdrawal from untangling the issues. Researchers have also found that, overall, gay and lesbian couples used more mutual avoidance and withholding communication during conflict than did heterosexual couples.[70] Communication researcher Mitchell Hammer suggests that people from highly individualistic cultures (such as the predominant U.S. culture) prefer a conflict management style that is more direct in addressing the conflict-producing issues.[71] People in collectivistic cultures—those that emphasize group and team interests over individual interests—typically prefer a more indirect approach to addressing conflict. Hammer also suggests that our cultural preferences for expressing or restraining our emotions have an important influence on our

RECAP Conflict Management Styles

	The person who uses this style . . .
Avoidance	Withdraws from conflict; tries to side-step confrontation; finds conflict uncomfortable. A lose-lose approach to conflict.
Accommodation	Easily gives in to the demands of others; typically wants to be liked by others. A lose-win approach to conflict.
Competition	Dominates the discussion and wants to accomplish the goal even at the expense of others. A win-lose approach to conflict.
Compromise	Seeks the middle ground; will give up something to get something. A lose/win-lose/win approach to conflict.
Collaboration	Views conflict as a problem to be solved; negotiates to achieve a positive solution for all involved in the conflict. A win-win approach to conflict.

preferred conflict management style.[72] People from cultures that emphasize less explicit expression of emotions (Asian cultures, for example) will find intense emotional expressions of anger and frustration distracting and unproductive in managing conflict. Your culture has a strong influence on the degree to which you are direct or indirect when you communicate with others during conflict. Your culture also influences how emotionally expressive or restrained you are when you experience interpersonal conflict.

Conflict Management Skills

For many people, at the heart of enhancing the quality of interpersonal relationships is learning to manage conflict.[73] Managing conflict, especially emotion-charged ego conflict, is not easy. The more stress and anxiety you feel at any given time, the more likely you are to experience conflict in your relationships with others. When you are under stress, it's more likely that conflict will become personal and degenerate into ego conflict. And the opposite is also true: When you're rested and relaxed, you're less likely to experience conflict. But even while relaxed and with a fully developed set of skills, don't expect to avoid conflict. Conflict happens. The following skills can help you generate options that promote understanding and provide a framework for collaboration.[74]

Manage Your Emotions

For weeks, you have been working on a brochure with a tight deadline. You turned it over to the production department with instructions two weeks ago. Today, you call to check on its progress, and you discover that it is still sitting on the production coordinator's desk. You feel your anger begin to erupt. You're tempted to march into the production coordinator's office and scream at her, or to shout at her supervisor.

Try to avoid taking action when you are in such a state. You may regret what you say, and you will probably escalate the conflict.

Often, the first sign that we are in a conflict situation is a feeling of anger, frustration, fear, or even sadness, which sweeps over us like an ocean wave.[75] If we feel powerless to control our own emotions, we will have difficulty taking a logical or rational approach to managing the conflict. Expressing our feelings in an emotional outburst may make us feel better for the moment, but it may close the door to logical, rational negotiation.

"Cool! My new cell phone allows me to see your angry face as well as hear your angry voice."

Michael Maslin/Liza Donnelly

When we are emotionally charged, we experience physical changes as well. One researcher found that

> . . . our adrenaline flows faster and our strength increases by about 20 percent. The liver, pumping sugar into the bloodstream, demands more oxygen from the heart and lungs. The veins become enlarged and the cortical centers where thinking takes place do not perform nearly as well. . . . The blood supply to the problem-solving part of the brain is severely decreased because, under stress, a greater portion of blood is diverted to the body's extremities.[76]

Such changes fuel our fight–flight responses. If we choose to stay, verbal or physical violence may erupt; if we flee from the conflict, we cannot resolve it. Until we can tone down (not eliminate) our emotions, we will find it difficult to apply other skills. Let's look at some specific strategies that you can draw on when an intense emotional response to conflict clouds your judgment and decision-making skills.[77]

Be Aware That You Are Becoming Angry and Emotionally Volatile

One characteristic of people who "lose it" is that they let their emotions get the best of them. Before they know it, they are saying and doing things that they later regret. Unbridled and uncensored emotional outbursts rarely enhance the quality of an interpersonal relationship. An emotional purge may make you feel better, but your partner is likely to reciprocate, which will only escalate the conflict spiral.

Before that happens, become aware of what is happening to you. As we described earlier, your body will start to react to your emotions with an increased heart rate. Be sensitive to what is happening to you physically.

Seek to Understand Why You Are Angry and Emotional

Understanding what's behind your anger can help you manage it. Realize that it is normal and natural to be angry. It's a feeling everyone experiences. You need not feel guilty about it. Anger is often expressed as a defense when you feel violated or when you are fearful of losing something that is important to you. The conflict triggers presented on pages 109–110 can help you identify the source of your anger. Think about the last time you became very angry. Often, you experience a sense of righteous indignation when you are angry. You are being denied something you feel you should have.

Make a Conscious Decision About Whether to Express Your Anger

Rather than just letting anger and frustration build and erupt out of control, make a conscious choice about whether you should express your frustration and irritation. We're not denying that there are valid reasons for you to express anger and frustration, or suggesting that you should not express your feelings. Sometimes, there is no way to let someone know how important an issue is to you other than by forcefully expressing your irritation or anger. As these lines from William Blake illustrate, sometimes the wisest strategy is to be honest with others and express how you feel.

> I was angry with my friend:
> I told my wrath, my wrath did end.
> I was angry with my foe:
> I told it not, my wrath did grow.

If you do decide to express your anger, don't lose control. Be direct and descriptive. Keep your anger focused on issues rather than personalities.

Select a Mutually Acceptable Time and Place to Discuss a Conflict

If you are upset, or even tired, you risk becoming involved in an emotion-charged shouting match. If you ambush someone with an angry attack, don't expect him or her to be in a receptive frame of mind. Instead, give yourself time to cool off before you try to resolve a conflict. In the case of the lapsed deadline mentioned earlier, you could call both the production coordinator and her boss and schedule an appointment to meet with them later in the day. By that time, you could gain control of your feelings and also think the issue through. Of course, issues sometimes need to be discussed on the spot; you may not have the luxury of waiting. But whenever practical, make sure the other person is ready to receive you and your message. You may have heard the conventional wisdom "Never go to bed angry with your partner or spouse." Research suggests that the better application might be "Don't fight before bed." Couples who had experienced an "expressed struggle" conflict (more than just a mild difference of opinion) were less likely to sleep.[78]

> **BEING Other-ORIENTED**
>
> Identifying mutually agreeable approaches to managing a conflict is also a way to manage emotions. What other strategies have worked for you in managing your emotions during conflict?

Plan Your Message

If you are approaching someone to discuss a disagreement, take care to organize your message. Consider rehearsing what you will say. Identify your goal, and determine what outcome you would like; do not barge in and pour out your emotions.

> **BEING Other-ORIENTED**
>
> Saving face is giving the other person a way to maintain his or her dignity, even if his or her initial ideas and proposals are not accepted in the final resolution of a conflict. What strategies have you used to help others save face and maintain their personal dignity during conflict?

Breathe

One of the simplest yet most effective ways to avoid overheating is to breathe. As you become aware that your emotions are starting to erupt, take a slow, deep breath. Then breathe again. This can help calm you and manage the physiological changes that adrenaline creates. Deep breathing—the prime strategy women use to manage the pain of childbirth—can be a powerful way to restore calmness to your spirit. Focusing on your breathing is also one of the primary methods of meditation. We're not suggesting that you hyperventilate. But taking deep, slow breaths that not only fill your upper lungs but move your diaphragm—the muscle that moves as your lungs expand and contract—is an active strategy to help you regain rational control.

Monitor Nonverbal Messages

Your actions play a key role in establishing the emotional climate in any relationship. Monitoring your nonverbal messages can help to de-escalate an emotion-charged situation. Speaking calmly, using direct eye contact, and maintaining a calm, nonthreatening facial expression will signal that you wish to collaborate rather than control. Your nonverbal message should also support your verbal response. If you say you are listening to someone, but you continue to watch TV or work on a report, you are communicating a lack of interest in the speaker and the message.

Avoid Personal Attacks, Name Calling, and Emotional Overstatement

Using threats and derogatory names can turn a simple conflict into an ego conflict. When people feel attacked, they respond by protecting themselves. Research has found that when husbands and wives feel disconfirmed during conflict because of name calling or because their partner has made nasty comments, relational satisfaction significantly decreases.[79] It's not surprising that people don't like to be called names. Although you may feel hurt and angry, try to avoid exaggerating your emotions and hurling negative, personal comments at your partner.[80] If you say you are irritated or annoyed rather than furious, you can still communicate your emotions, but you take the harsh sting out of your description. We're not advocating that you be dishonest about how you are feeling; just don't overstate your emotions for dramatic effect. It may make you feel better, but it may make matters worse.[81]

Also avoid the bad habit of **gunny-sacking**. This occurs when you dredge up old problems and issues from the past, like pulling them out of an old bag or gunny sack, to use against your partner. Keep your focus on the issues at hand, not on old hurts. Gunny-sacking usually succeeds only in increasing tension, escalating emotions, and reducing listening effectiveness.

Take Time to Establish Rapport

Evidence suggests that you'll be more successful in managing conflict if you don't immediately dive in and attempt to sort out the issues with your partner.[82] Taking time to establish a positive emotional climate can pay big dividends; this is especially important if you're not well acquainted with the person you're having the conflict with. One study compared how effectively conflict was managed in two different groups.[83] In one group, the conflict negotiators spent time face to face, "schmoozing" and getting to know one another, before trying to negotiate a solution to a conflict. In the other group, the negotiators exchanged information via e-mail but did not meet face to face. The negotiators who spent time establishing a positive relationship in person were more successful in managing the conflict to everyone's satisfaction.

Even if you know the other person well, take some time to build rapport. Chatting about such seemingly innocuous topics as the weather or local events can help break the ice and provide a basis for a more positive conversational climate. A positive emotional climate is especially important when trying to sort through vexing, conflict-producing issues. Research has found that taking time to listen and thoughtfully respond to others during conflict goes a long way toward creating a positive climate that is more likely to enhance rather than detract from the accuracy of communication.[84]

Another way to establish rapport is to consider using appropriate humor to lighten the mood. One study found that using humor effectively during a period of emotionally infused conflict can help take the sting out of discussions of difficult topics.[85] But we offer this important caution: Be certain that what *you* think is funny will be perceived by *your partner* as humorous. Trying to make a joke out of something that your partner does not find funny can backfire. It's especially important to be other-oriented when using humor to defuse tense moments. Several researchers also note how important it is to help the other person in the conflict save face—not to leave the conversation feeling demoralized and humiliated.

Use Self-Talk

Kosta was chairing the committee meeting when Monique accused him of falsifying the attendance numbers at the last fine arts festival. Instead of lashing back at Monique, he paused, took a slow, deep breath, and thought, "I'm tired. If I snarl back, all we will do is escalate this issue out of proportion. I'll talk with Monique later, after we have both cooled down." Perhaps you think that talking to yourself is an eccentricity. Nothing could be further from the truth. Thoughts are directly linked to feelings,[94] and the messages we tell ourselves play a major role in how we feel and respond to others. Ask yourself whether an emotional tirade and an escalating conflict will produce the results you want. When Eleanor Roosevelt noted, "No one can make you feel inferior without your consent," she was acknowledging the power of self-talk to affect your emotional response to what others say and do.

As you read the discussion about managing emotions, you may wonder if it's ever useful or productive to express negative emotions, especially anger, overtly when negotiating an issue. One research study found that expressing your anger and frustration might be a productive conflict management strategy if you are negotiating with someone who simply offers no useful alternatives.[95] By expressing your irritation, you may motivate the other person to come up with better alternatives. In most cases, escalating emotional tension decreases the likelihood that the conflict will be managed smoothly and effectively. But sometimes, being honest in expressing

COMMUNICATION AND EMOTION How to Manage Anger: A "Hard" Emotion

When you are in a conflict with someone, you are likely to experience a strong emotional response. Researchers have identified three types of emotions that typically occur during conflict:

1. Hard emotions—feeling angry and irritated
2. Soft emotions—feeling hurt, sad, and vulnerable
3. Flat emotions—feeling indifferent, bored, or uninterested[86]

The emotion you *think* someone is expressing—hard, soft, or flat—has been shown to influence your own feelings and behavior during conflict. So monitoring your expression of emotion, as well as being aware of the emotions expressed by others, can help you better manage conflict.

Hard emotions are associated with assertions of power and control when someone is thought to be focusing on individual goals rather than collective or mutual goals.[87] If you perceive that your partner is expressing a hard emotion, you are likely to respond with more hostile or defensive thoughts and feelings.

A soft emotion is associated with an expression of vulnerability that stems from seeking to achieve a relationship goal.[88] When your partner expresses a soft emotion, you are likely to feel increased empathy for him or her.[89]

If you think your partner has a flat emotional response, you are likely to think he or she may just not care about the relationship.[90]

One of the biggest challenges when attempting to manage relational conflict is to manage the hard emotion of anger—whether you are expressing anger or your partner appears angry and upset. Having a better understanding of anger and its causes, symptoms, and appropriate ways to express it can be very helpful when managing conflict.[91]

What Is the Feeling Underlying Anger?

Anger is an emotional response to fear. Stated another way, anger is an outward response to an inward feeling of fear. And fear is often about losing something or not getting something we believe is rightfully ours. We may become angry, for example, if we fear we may lose our job or if we sense a relationship that is important to us may be dissolving. Anger also occurs when we feel someone is keeping us from what we want and have a right to have, or someone is unjustly blaming us for something or attacking us.

What Are the Best Ways to Manage Anger?

Some people may tell you it is a good idea to express your anger to the person who is making you angry: "Get your anger out—don't keep it bottled up." Assertively expressing what bothers you is appropriate when the other person is not aware that you are upset. But uncensored words of rage can escalate the anger you feel and also increase that of the other person.[92]

One research team offers these prescriptions for managing your own anger or coping with someone else's anger during conflict.[93]

- *Be determined not to get angry yourself.* If you know you are going to face someone who is likely to anger you or who will express hard emotions, prepare yourself before you meet with him or her. Assertively express your feelings, but make a promise to yourself not to "lose it" and allow the encounter to degenerate into a shout fest. Use some of the emotion management strategies we mention on pages 124–128 such as using a breathing technique and selecting a proper time and place to discuss the issue.

(continued)

COMMUNICATION AND EMOTION How to Manage Anger: A "Hard" Emotion

(*continued*)

- *Get on the same physical level as the other person.* One person should not be standing and the other sitting. Try to face each other eye to eye. You can also build rapport by trying to mirror the posture of the other person. Don't mimic your partner (this would probably make him or her more angry), but try to adopt a similar communication position.
- *Be silent.* If you are angry and afraid you might say something you'll regret, just be quiet and listen. Use self talk to keep from loudly lashing back at your partner.
- *Express your concern nonverbally by displaying soft emotions.* Because much of an emotional message is communicated nonverbally, use your facial expression and eyes to let the other person know you care about him or her. Communicate your empathy and support with your forward leaning body posture, sincere smile, and positive eye contact. Your communication partner will believe what you *do* more than what you *say.*
- *Make an appropriate empathic statement.* Saying "I would probably feel angry if I had experienced what you experienced" or "I think I can see why you are so upset" may help. But be careful not to say, "I know just how you feel" or "I know where you're coming from." For many people, those statements can seem patronizing.
- *Remind yourself that you control your own emotions.* Even though others may do and say things that can upset you, you are the only person who can control yourself and your response to others. Try to respond mindfully to others rather than just react emotionally to them.
- *Recognize that angry emotional outbursts rarely change someone's mind.* Exploding in an angry tirade may make you feel better for a moment by "getting it off your chest," but it usually does little to advance understanding and manage the issues at hand.

your bubbling frustration may nudge things along in a productive way, especially if there are no good options to discuss.

Manage Information

Because uncertainty, misinformation, and misunderstanding are often byproducts of conflict and disagreement, skills that promote mutual understanding are an important component of cooperative conflict management. The following specific suggestions can help you reduce uncertainty and enhance the quality of communication during conflict.

Clearly Describe the Conflict-Producing Events

Instead of just blurting out your complaints in random order, think of delivering a brief, well-organized minispeech. Offer your perspective on what created the conflict, sequencing the events like a well-organized story. Describe the events dispassionately so that the other person shares your understanding of the problem.

When Marsha almost had a car accident, she came home and told her husband, "Last week, you said you would get the brakes fixed on the car. On Monday, when you still hadn't taken the car in, you said you would do it on Wednesday. Now it's Friday, and the brakes are in even worse shape. I had a close call this afternoon when the car almost wouldn't stop. We've got to get those brakes fixed before anyone drives that car again."

Take Turns Talking

It's simple, yet powerful. Research has found that consciously taking turns when discussing a conflict increases the likelihood that the conflict will be managed effectively.[96] Although this strategy will not guarantee that the disagreement will be resolved, it does help establish a climate of mutual concern. When taking turns, it's also important to listen and remain calm when the other person is speaking.

"Own" Your Statements by Using Descriptive "I" Language

"I feel upset when you post the week's volunteer schedule without first consulting with me," reveals Katrina. Her statement is an example of **"I" language**, which expresses how a speaker is feeling. The use of the word *I* conveys a willingness to "own" one's feelings and the statements made about them.

And sometimes, to make sure your communication partner doesn't miss the subtlety of your owning your feelings by using an "I" message, it may be useful to extend your "I" message[97] by saying, for example, "I really don't want you to take this the wrong way. I really care about you. But I want you to know that when you take food from my plate, I feel uncomfortable. My sister sometimes did that when I was a kid, and I didn't like it."

One final tip about using "I" messages: Monitor your **"but" messages**. What's a "but" message? It's a statement that makes it seem as though whatever you've said prior to the word *but* is not truly the way you feel. Here's an example: "I love you. I really love you. But I feel really frustrated when you leave your clothes lying on every chair." A "but" message diminishes the positive sentiment you expressed with your "I" language. We're not suggesting that you never say *but,* only that you realize how the word may create noise for the listener; it may make your entire statement seem untrue.

Use Effective Listening Skills

Managing information is a two-way process. Whether you are describing a conflict situation to someone, or that individual is bringing a conflict to your attention, good listening skills will be invaluable.

Give your full attention to the speaker and make a conscious point of tuning out your internal messages. Sometimes, the best thing to do after describing the conflict-producing events is simply to wait for a response. If you don't stop talking and give the other person a chance to respond, he or she will feel frustrated, the emotional pitch will go up a notch, and it will become more difficult to reach an understanding.

Finally, remember to not only focus on the facts or details, but also analyze them so you can understand the major point the speaker is making. Try to use your understanding of the details to interpret the speaker's major ideas. Remember to stay other-oriented and to "seek to understand rather than to be understood."[98]

Check Your Understanding of What Others Say and Do

Respond clearly and appropriately. Your response and that of your conflict partner will confirm that you have understood each other. Checking perceptions is vital when emotions run high.

If you are genuinely unsure about facts, issues, or major ideas addressed during a conflict, ask questions to help you sort through them instead of barging ahead with solutions. Then summarize your understanding of the information; do not parrot the speaker's words or paraphrase every statement, but check key points to ensure that you have understood the message. Note how Ted adeptly paraphrases to check his understanding:

Maggie: I don't like the conclusion you've written to the conference report. It doesn't mention anything about the ideas suggested at the symposium. I think you have also misinterpreted the CEO's key message.

Ted: So if I understand you, Maggie, you're saying the report missed some key information and may also include an inaccurate summary of the CEO's speech.

Maggie: Yes, Ted. Those are my concerns.

BEING Other-ORIENTED

Being empathic is the core set of skills that allow you to be other-oriented. When you're involved in conflict with another person, what are the factors that hinder your ability to empathize with the other person? What actions and thoughts will enhance your skill in empathizing with another person?

Be Empathic

Understand others not only with your head, but also with your heart. To truly understand another person, you need to do more than catch the meaning of his or her words; you need to put yourself in the person's place emotionally. Ask yourself these questions: What emotions is the other person feeling? Why is he or she experiencing these emotions? Throughout this book, we have stressed the importance of becoming other-oriented. It's especially important to be other-oriented when you disagree with another person.[99] Trying to understand what's behind your partner's emotions may give you the insight you need to reframe the conflict from your partner's point of view. And with this other-oriented perspective, you may see new possibilities for managing the conflict.

Manage Goals

As you've seen, conflict is goal-driven. Both individuals involved in an interpersonal conflict want something. And for some reason, be it competition, scarce resources, or lack of understanding, the goals appear to be in conflict. To manage conflict, you must seek an accurate understanding of these goals and identify where they overlap.

Communication researchers Sandra Lakey and Daniel Canary found clear support for the importance of being sensitive to and aware of your communication partner's goals when trying to manage conflict.[100] People who were focused on the other person's goals were perceived as much more competent than people who weren't aware of what the other person wanted to accomplish. Another study found that stating the goal of developing a positive outcome for the other person, especially in a romantic relationship, makes you more likely to enhance the conflict management process.[101] Let's look at some specific strategies to help manage conflict by being aware of the other person's goals during conflict.

Identify Your Goal and Your Partner's Goal

After you describe, listen, and respond, your next task should be to identify what you would like to have happen. What is your goal? Most goal statements can be phrased in terms of wants or desires. Consider the following examples:

Problem	**Goals**
Your boss wants you to work overtime; you need to pick up your son from day care.	You want to leave work on time; your boss wants the work completed ASAP.
Your spouse wants to sleep with the window open; you like a warm room and sleep better with the window closed.	You want a good night's rest; your spouse wants a good night's rest.

Often in conflicts you will face balancing your goal against the goal of maintaining the relationship that you have with your partner. Eventually, you may decide that the latter goal is more important than the substantive conflict issue.

Next, it is useful to identify your partner's goal. In order to manage conflict, you need to know what the other person wants. Use effective listening and responding skills to determine what each of you wants and to verbalize your goals. Obviously, if you both keep your goals hidden, it will be difficult to manage the conflict.

Identify Where Your Goals and Your Partner's Goals Overlap

The authors of the best-selling book *Getting to Yes,* Roger Fisher and William Ury, stress the importance of focusing on shared interests when seeking to manage differences.[102] Armed with an understanding of what you want and what your partner wants, you can then determine whether the goals overlap. In the conflict over whether the window should be open or closed, the goal of both parties is the same: Each wants a good night's sleep. Framing the problem as "How can we achieve our mutual goal?" rather than arguing over whether the window should be up or down moves the discussion to a more productive level. If you focus on shared interests (common goals) and develop objective, rather than subjective, criteria for the solution, there is hope for finding a resolution that will satisfy both parties.

Manage the Problem

If you can structure conflicts as problems to be solved, rather than as battles to be won or lost, you are well on your way to finding strategies to manage the issues that confront you and your partner. Of course, as we have stressed, not all conflicts can be resolved. However, approaching the core of a

BUILDING YOUR SKILLS Communicating with Prickly People

Some people just seem to rub us the wrong way. They generate both friction and heat when we're trying to negotiate with them. In his popular book *Getting Past No,* William Ury suggests we try to change face-to-face confrontation into side-by-side problem solving.[103] Here are Ury's tips for managing conflict with difficult people, based on his review of negotiation literature.[104]

- *Go to the Balcony.* "Going to the balcony" is a metaphor for taking a time out. Take a moment to excuse yourself to cool off when someone pushes your buttons. Staying on the "main stage" to keep banging out a solution may be counterproductive.
- *Step to the Side.* Rather than continuing to debate and refute every argument, step to the side by just asking questions and listening. Change the dynamic of the relationship from a confrontation to a conversation.
- *Change the Frame.* Reframe by trying to see more than an either/or way of managing the conflict. Try to see it from a third, fourth, or fifth point of view. Change your overall perspective for viewing the conflict by not being you: Consider how someone else may view the issue.
- *Build a Golden Bridge.* To "build a golden bridge" is a metaphor for identifying ways to help the other person say yes by saving face. Find an alternative that allows the other person his or her dignity by using objective standards to find a solution.
- *Make It Hard to Say No.* Use information to educate rather than pummel the other person. As Ury puts it, bring people to their senses, not their knees. Help the other person understand the consequences of what he or she supports and the benefits of your alternatives.

Consider a conflict that you had with a prickly person that did not have a satisfying conclusion. How could you have implemented one or more of the five suggestions we've summarized from Ury's research? If it were possible to have a "do over" with this difficult person, what would you do differently? Use the following worksheet to help you identify alternatives for dealing with the prickly person in the situation you have in mind.

Go to the Balcony. At what point in the conflict could you have suggested a cooling-off period?

____

____

Step to the Side. Instead of adding new ideas and arguments, when and how could you have stepped to the side to listen and paraphrase?

____

____

Change the Frame. How could you have changed the frame of the conflict? What would have been a different way of looking at the issue that created the conflict?

____

____

Build a Golden Bridge. What could you have done or said that would have helped the other person save face?

____

____

Make It Hard to Say No. What could you have said or done that would have helped the other person see the benefits of what you were proposing?

____

____

____

conflict as a problem to be managed can provide a constructive way of seeking resolution. Structuring a conflict as a problem also helps to manage the emotion, and it keeps the conversation focused on issues (simple conflict) rather than personalities (ego conflict). How do you do that? We recommend three sets of skills: (1) use principled negotiation strategies, (2) use a problem-solving structure, and (3) develop a solution that helps each person save face.

Use Principled Negotiation Strategies

To use principled negotiation strategies is to use a *collaborative*, win-win framework, even as you acknowledge that there is a problem to be solved. Approaching conflict as a problem to be solved requires other-oriented strategies based on the following principles offered by Harvard researchers Roger Fisher and William Ury.[105]

Separate the People from the Problem. Leave personal grievances out of the discussion, describing problems without making judgmental or evaluative statements about personalities. But what do you do if the other person continues to be emotionally upset and makes the disagreement personal? Consider the following behaviors.[106]

1. Acknowledge the person's feelings.
2. Determine what specific behavior is causing the intense feelings.
3. Assess the intensity and importance of the issue.
4. Invite the other person to join you in working toward solutions.
5. Make a positive relational statement.

Focus on Shared Interests. Ask questions such as "What do we both want? What do we both value? Where are we already agreeing?" to emphasize common interests, values, and goals. If the discussions seem to be getting off track and conflict seems to be escalating, return to areas of mutual agreement.

Generate Many Options to Solve the Problem. You are more likely to reach a mutually acceptable solution if you identify many possible options rather than debate only one or two. Collaborators conduct research to find options, talk with other people for ideas, and use brainstorming techniques to generate alternative solutions.

Base Decisions on Objective Criteria. Try to establish standards for an acceptable solution to a problem; these standards may involve cost, timing, and other factors. Suppose, for example, that you and your neighbor are discussing possible ways to stop another neighbor's dog from barking throughout the night. You decide on these criteria: The solution must not harm the dog; it must be easy for the owner to implement; the owner must agree to it; it should not cost more than fifty dollars; and it must keep the dog from disturbing the sleep of others. Your neighbor says, "Maybe the dog can sleep in the owner's garage at night." This solution meets all but one of your criteria, so you call the owner, who agrees to put the dog in the garage by 10 P.M. Now everyone wins because the solution meets a sound, well-considered set of objective criteria.

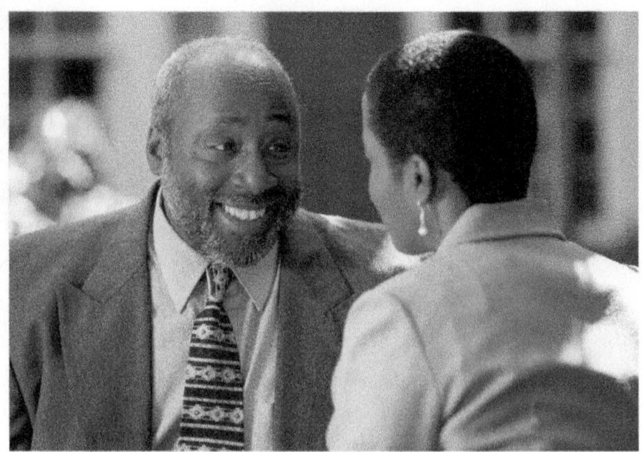

It's vital to be able to manage your emotions when you find yourself in an interpersonal conflict.

Use a Problem-Solving Structure

You can apply all the skills described so far to pursue a proven method for problem solving. The method is straightforward: Define the problem, analyze the problem's causes and effects, determine the goals you and your partner seek, generate many possible options, and then select the option that best achieves both your goals and those of your partner.

Define the Problem. Most problems boil down to something you or your conflict partner want more or less of.[107] For example, you may want more time, money, or freedom. Or you may want less interference, control, or criticism. To help you define the problem, renew your focus on your own and the other person's goals.[108] What do you want to happen, or not to happen?

Analyze the Problem. To *analyze* is to break something down into its components. With your partner, begin by describing the conflict-producing events in chronological order (see page 128). Then decide whether you're facing a pseudoconflict, a simple conflict, or an ego conflict (see pages 111–114). Attempt to ferret out symptoms, effects, and obstacles; decide whether the conflict stems from several sub-problems or from one major issue. As you proceed with your analysis, you and your partner may decide that you need more information to help clarify the issues.

Determine the Goals. To determine your own and your partner's goals, follow the suggestions on page 130. Also, generate objective criteria for a solution. The more measurable, verifiable, and objective the criteria, the greater the likelihood that you and your partner will be able to agree when the criteria have been met.

Generate Multiple Solutions. The more solutions you generate, the greater the probability that you can manage the conflict constructively. One way to generate options is through brainstorming.[109] Try the following suggestions:

1. Make sure the problem and the goals are clear to both of you.
2. Try to suspend judgment and evaluation temporarily; do not censor your thoughts.
3. Specify a certain time period for brainstorming.
4. Consider brainstorming ideas separately before meeting with your partner, or write ideas down before verbalizing solutions.
5. Try to develop at least one unique or far-out idea. You can always tame wild ideas later.
6. Piggyback your ideas onto those of your partner. Encourage your partner to use or modify your ideas.
7. Write down all the ideas suggested.
8. Review all ideas, noting ways to combine, eliminate, or extend them.

If the goal is to find the best way to manage the difficulty, it may take only one good idea to help move the conflict forward to a constructive resolution.

Select the Best Solution. It may take several attempts at defining the problem, analyzing issues, setting goals, and generating multiple ideas before a mutually agreeable solution emerges. It is always appropriate to recheck your understanding of the issues and goals.

If, after repeated attempts, you cannot arrive at a mutually acceptable solution, you may decide to keep trying. Or you may agree to take the issue to an impartial person who can help you identify conflict management strategies and solutions. At work, your immediate superior may be called in to help settle the matter. Or, occasionally, you may agree to disagree and drop it.

Making efforts to structure a conflict as a problem to be solved through mutual effort can keep the conversation focused on issues, so that the conflict does not escalate.

Develop a Solution That Helps Each Person Save Face

The concept of **face** refers to the positive self-image or self-respect that you and your partner seek to maintain.[110] The goal of managing conflict is not just to solve a problem, but to help work through relational issues with your partner, especially if your partner thinks he or she has "lost" the conflict. When seeking a solution to interpersonal problems, try to find ways for your partner to "win" while you also achieve your goal. Help your partner save face. Communication researcher Stella Ting-Toomey has conducted studies that emphasize the importance of face saving or maintaining a positive image, especially in collectivist cultures such as those in Asia, where maintaining face is especially important.[111]

How do you help someone save face and avoid embarrassment? Sometimes you can offer genuine forgiveness. Or you can offer explanations that help reframe the differences, perhaps suggesting that it was really just a misunderstanding that led to the disagreement.[112] Such face-restoring comments can help mend bruised egos. Finding ways to be gracious or allow your partner to save face is an important other-oriented approach to dealing with people. After a family feud between a mother and her teenage daughter, Mom might say, "You're right, I should not get so upset. I'm sorry I lost my temper. You're a great daughter." Admitting that you're wrong and offering an affirming, positive expression of support can begin to help heal a rift and help the other person save face.[113]

If you are the wronged person in the conflict and the person who instigated the conflict has apologized, then you have a choice to make: Do you forgive the person who offended you? The most common form of forgiveness is indirect forgiveness,[114] which occurs when a person does not explicitly tell someone that he or she is forgiven, but the resumption of normal relationships and communication patterns leads the other person to "understand" he or she is forgiven. You are more likely to indirectly forgive a friend than someone you are dating; dating couples report more conditional forgiveness ("I forgive you *if* you stop doing X"). If you forgive someone conditionally, it's more likely that the negative feelings of the conflict will linger longer. Directly forgiving someone without conditions is the most effective way to get the issue resolved for both of you.

Even though we have presented these conflict management steps as prescriptive suggestions, it is important to remember that *conflict is rarely a linear, step-by-step sequence of events.* These skills are designed to serve as a general framework for collaboratively managing differences. But if your partner does not want to collaborate, your job will be more challenging.

In reality, you don't simply manage your emotions and then move neatly on to develop greater understanding with another person. Sorting out your goals and your partner's goals is not something you do once and then put behind you. Time and patience are required to balance your immediate goal with the goal of maintaining a relationship with your partner. In fact, as you try to manage a conflict, you will more than likely bounce forward and backward from one step to another. The framework we've described gives you an overarching perspective for understanding and actively managing disagreements, but the nature of interpersonal relationships means that you and your partner will respond—sometimes in unpredictable ways—to a variety of cues (psychological, sociological, physical) when communicating. Think of the skills you have learned as options to consider, rather than as hard-and-fast rules to follow in every situation.

Watch the Video "Conflict Management" at **MyCommunicationLab**

Applying an Other-Orientation to Conflict Management

To manage differences with others, consider the conflict-producing issue or issues from the other person's point of view. We don't claim that an other-orientation will resolve all conflicts. As we noted earlier, it's a myth that all conflict can be resolved. But being other-oriented is an important element in managing differences and disagreements. The following five strategies drawn not only from this chapter but from the previous skill-development chapters distill the essence of being other-oriented.

- *Stop:* Socially decenter by taking into account the other person's thoughts, feelings, values, culture, and perspective. Stop making your arguments and concentrate on your partner's points. How is your partner "making sense" out of what has happened to him or her?
- *Look:* Monitor your partner's emotions by observing his or her nonverbal messages. Look for emotional cues in your partner's face; observe posture and gestures to gauge the intensity of the feelings being expressed.
- *Listen:* Listen both for the details and for the main points; also listen for tone of voice. Focus on the overall story your partner is telling.
- *Imagine:* Imagine how you would feel if you were in your partner's place. Based on your knowledge of the person you're in conflict with, as well as of people in general, imagine the conflict from his or her point of view.
- *Question:* If you need more information about what a partner has experienced or if there is something you don't understand, gently ask appropriate questions.
- *Paraphrase:* To confirm your understanding of your partner's point of view, briefly summarize the essence of what you think your partner is thinking or feeling.

No checklist of skills will magically melt tensions resulting from longstanding or entrenched conflicts. But honestly trying to understand both a person's position and the emotion behind it is a good beginning to developing understanding—a prerequisite to managing differences.

KEY TERMS IN CONFLICT

accommodation Conflict management style that involves giving in to the demands of others.

avoidance Conflict management style that involves backing off and trying to side-step conflict.

"but" message Statement using the word but that may communicate that whatever you've said prior to but is not really true.

coercive power Power based on the use of sanctions or punishments to influence others.

collaboration Conflict management style that uses other-oriented strategies to achieve a positive solution for all involved.

competition Conflict management style that stresses winning a conflict at the expense of the other person involved.

compliance gaining Taking persuasive actions to get others to comply with our goals.

compromise Conflict management style that attempts to find the middle ground in a conflict.

conflict style Consistent pattern or approach you use to manage disagreement with others.

conflict triggers Common perceived causes of interpersonal conflict.

constructive conflict Conflict that helps build new insights and establishes new patterns in a relationship.

demand-withdrawal pattern of conflict management Pattern in which one person makes a demand and the other person avoids conflict by changing the subject or walking away.

dependent relationship Relationship in which one partner has a greater need for the other to meet his or her needs.

destructive conflict Conflict that dismantles rather than strengthens relationships.

dialectical tension Tension arising from a person's need for two things at the same time.

disinhibition effect The loss of inhibitions when interacting with someone online that leads to the tendency to escalate conflict.

ego conflict Conflict in which the original issue is ignored as partners attack each other's self-esteem.

expert power Power based on a person's knowledge and experience.

face A person's positive perception of himself or herself in interactions with others.

flaming Sending an overly negative online message that personally attacks another person.

gunny-sacking Dredging up old problems and issues from the past to use against your partner.

"I" language Statements that use the word I to express how a speaker is feeling.

interdependent Dependent on each other; one person's actions affect the other person.

interpersonal conflict An expressed struggle between at least two interdependent people who perceive incompatible goals, scarce resources, or interference in the achievement of their goals.

interpersonal power Degree to which a person is able to influence his or her partner.

legitimate power Power that is based on respect for a person's position.

pseudoconflict Conflict triggered by a lack of understanding and miscommunication.

referent power Power that comes from our attraction to another person, or the charisma a person possesses.

reward power Power based on a person's ability to satisfy our needs.

simple conflict Conflict that stems from different ideas, definitions, perceptions, or goals.

Critical Thinking Questions

1. Think of a recent communication exchange with a friend, spouse, or coworker that began as a seemingly casual conversation but escalated into a conflict. Can you identify a reason for this, such as one or both of you feeling tired, stressed, or anxious? Is there anything you could have done to avoid the conflict? What cues might each of you have looked for to understand the other's mood?
2. Ethics: Is it ethical to mask your true emotions in order to get along with others? Is honesty in a relationship always the best policy? Explain your response.
3. Why is it important to identify conflict myths?
4. How might accepting one or more of the myths as true have an effect on your interpersonal relationships?
5. Pat and Chris have noticed an increase in the amount of conflict they are having in their romantic relationship. What are questions they could ask themselves to assess the type of conflict they may be experiencing?
6. If Pat and Chris are experiencing an increase in ego conflict, what are strategies that they could use to make the conflict more of a simple conflict rather than an ego conflict?
7. Examine several recent interpersonal conflicts for unresolved power issues. (For example, consider conflicts that have focused on managing money, household tasks, or intimacy.) What role did power play in the conflict? What type of power is it? Does one of you have more power over the other? How might you renegotiate that power imbalance?
8. Ethics: Are certain types of power more ethical to use during a conflict than others? Explain your answer, describing conditions that would justify the use of certain types of power.
9. Richard has an explosive temper. He consistently receives poor performance evaluations at work because he lashes out at those who disagree with him. What strategies might help him manage his emotional outbursts?
10. Have you experienced the disinhibition effect when communicating with others online? Was this in response to a blatantly negative message? Or was it your perception that you were being attacked? What was the result? How did you respond? What strategies could you have employed to avoid a conflict?
11. Although the chapter suggests that there are specific skills you could use to help manage conflicts and disagreements, are there disadvantages to premeditating how you will respond in a conflict?
12. How can you develop your skill in managing conflict without making it seem like you are using manipulative techniques to get your way?

Assessing Your Skills

Based on the discussion of conflict presented on pages 106–107, think of a recent conflict you had with someone or a conflict that is still ongoing. To help you better understand and manage the process, answer the following questions:

Prior Conditions Stage

- What were the prior conditions that led to the conflict?
- How long were some of the prior conditions simmering in the background?

Frustration Awareness Stage

- When did you become aware that you were frustrated and that your needs weren't being met or that there was an issue to resolve?
- When did you perceive that the other person was aware that a conflict might exist?

Active Conflict Stage

- What caused the conflict to move from frustration to active conflict?
- What type of conflict was (is) it—pseudoconflict, simple conflict, or ego conflict?

Resolution Stage

- What conflict management skills did you use (or are you and the other person using) to manage emotions, information, goals, or the problem?
- What conflict management skills could you have used, but didn't?

Follow-Up Stage

- Has the conflict been truly managed and resolved, or not? What leads you to that conclusion?
- Did you or the other person explicitly indicate that the conflict is over?

1. Think of a relationship you have had during which you treated one or more of the myths listed on pages 110–111 as true rather than as a myth. What was the effect of your belief or the belief of your partner on the way you managed conflict in your relationship?
2. Of the four myths listed in the chapter, rank order them from most important to least important, with a ranking of 1 meaning that buying into the myth would have the most serious consequences on a relationship. A ranking of 4 equals believing the myth would have the least impact on a relationship. Share your rankings with your classmates and discuss them.

Think of three different conflicts you have had with another person. Assess what type of conflicts each was.

1. How effectively did you manage the conflict?
2. What strategies listed on pages 112–114 did you use to manage the conflict?
3. Are there strategies that you could have used but didn't choose that would have helped you manage the conflict more effectively?

Statements about Conflict: Read each statement once, and on a separate piece of paper, indicate whether you agree (A) or disagree (D) with each statement. Take five or six minutes to do this.

1. Most people find an argument interesting and exciting.
2. In most conflicts, someone must win and someone must lose. That's the way conflict is.
3. The best way to handle a conflict is simply to let everyone cool off.
4. Most people get upset at a person who disagrees with them.
5. If people spend enough time together, they will find something to disagree about and will eventually become upset with each other.
6. Conflicts can be solved if people just take the time to listen to one another.
7. If you disagree with someone, it is usually better to keep quiet than to express your personal opinion.
8. To compromise is to take the easy way out of conflict.
9. Some people produce more conflict and tension than others. These people should be restricted from working with others.

After you have indicated whether you agree or disagree with the statements, ask a good friend, roommate, family member, or romantic partner to read each statement and indicate whether he or she agrees or disagrees. Compare answers and discuss the results. Use this activity as a way of identifying underlying assumptions you and the other person have about conflict. You could also do this activity in a small group. After comparing responses with others in the group, the entire group could seek to develop a consensus about each statement. If conflict occurs about a specific statement, use the principles of conflict management that are presented in the chapter to assist you in managing the disagreement.

Over the next week or so, keep a list of every conflict you observe or are involved in.

1. Make a note of what the conflict was about, whether there were underlying power issues (that you could detect), whether the conflict was resolved satisfactorily for both parties, and, if so, which strategies and skills were employed.
2. Could you identify a specific conflict management style that was used?
3. If the conflict involved you, did you use the style you typically use? Why or why not? Discuss your findings with your classmates.
4. Which of the skills sets (manage emotions, manage information, manage goals, manage the problem) are easier for you to use? Which are more challenging for you to implement?
5. On a scale of 1 to 10 rate yourself on each of the conflict management skills listed on pages 124–134. 1 = low and 10 = high. What are strategies you could use to increase your skill level of those items that received your lowest rating?

NOTES

1. S. A. Lloyd, "Conflict in Premarital Relationships: Differential Perceptions of Males and Females," *Family Relations* 36 (1987): 290–94.
2. M. Hicks and L. M. Diamond, "Don't Go To Bed Angry: Attachment, Conflict, and Affective and Physiological Reactivity," *Personal Relationships* 18 (2011): 266–84.
3. H. B. Braiker and H. H. Kelley, "Conflict in the Development of Close Relationships," in *Social Exchange in Developing Relationships,* edited by R. L Burgess and T. L Huston (New York: Academic Press, 1979), 135–68.
4. D. Cramer, "Relationship Satisfaction and Conflict Style in Romantic Relationships," *Journal of Psychology* 134 (2000): 337–41.
5. Our definition of conflict is adapted from W. Wilmot and J. Hocker, *Interpersonal Conflict* (New York: McGraw-Hill, 2007).
6. B. Fehr and C. Harasymchuk, "The Experience of Emotion in Close Relationships: Toward an Integration of the Emotion-in-Relationships and Interpersonal Script," *Personal Relationships* 12 (2005): 81–196; T. L. Zacchilli, C. Hendrick, and S. S. Hendrick, "The Romantic Partner Conflict Scale: A New Scale to Measure Relationship Conflict," *Journal of Social and Personal Relationships* 26, no. 8 (2009): 1073–96.
7. A. J. Johnson, "A Functional Approach to Interpersonal Argument: Differences Between Public-Issue and Personal-Issue Arguments," *Communication Reports* 22, no. 1 (2009): 13–28.
8. J. W. Keltner, *Mediation: Toward a Civilized System of Dispute Resolution* (Annandale, VA: Speech Communication Association, 1987); also see Wilmot and Hocker, *Interpersonal Conflict.*
9. For a review of literature about violence in relationships, see L. N. Olson and T. D. Golish, "Topics of Conflict and Patterns of Aggression in Romantic Relationships," *Southern Communication Journal* 67 (Winter 2002): 180–200.
10. D. J. Canary, W. R. Cupach, and R. T. Serpe, "A Competence-Based Approach to Examining Interpersonal Conflict: Test of a Longitudinal Model," *Communication Research* 29 (February 2001): 79–104; also see L. N. Olson and D. O. Braithwaite, "'If You Hit Me Again, I'll Hit You Back': Conflict Management Strategies of Individuals Experiencing Aggression During Conflicts," *Communication Studies* 55 (2004): 271–85; L. L. Marshall, "Physical and Psychological Abuse," in *The Dark Side of Interpersonal Communication,* edited by W. R. Cupach and B. H. Spitzberg (Hillsdale, NJ: Erlbaum, 1994), 281–311; Olson and Golish, "Topics of Conflict and Patterns of Aggression in Romantic Relationships," 41.
11. Wilmot and Hocker, *Interpersonal Conflict,* 8–15.
12. Olson and Braithwaite, "'If You Hit Me Again, I'll Hit You Back.'"
13. A. C. Filley, *Interpersonal Conflict Resolution* (Glenview, IL: Scott Foresman, 1975); R. H. Tumer, "Conflict and Harmony," *Family Interaction* (New York: Wiley, 1970); K. Galvin and B. J. Brommel, *Family Communication: Cohesion and Change* (New York: Addison Wesley Longman, 2000).
14. Olson and Golish, "Topics of Conflict and Patterns of Aggression in Romantic Relationships."
15. Wilmot and Hocker, *Interpersonal Conflict,* 10.
16. D. J. Canary, W. R. Cupach, and S. J. Messman, *Relationship Conflict: Conflict in Parent-Child, Friendship, and Romantic Relationships* (Thousand Oaks, CA: Sage, 1999).
17. Canary, Cupach, and Serpe, "A Competence-Based Approach to Examining Interpersonal Conflict."
18. Adapted from D. W. Johnson, *Reaching Out: Interpersonal Effectiveness and Self-Actualization* (Boston: Allyn & Bacon, 2000), 314.
19. M. Deutsch, *The Resolution of Conflict* (New Haven, CT: Yale University Press, 1973).
20. Y. B. Zhang and M. C. Lin, "Conflict-Initiating Factors in Intergenerational Relationships," *Journal of Language and Social Psychology* 28, no. 4 (2009): 343–63.
21. W. E. Schweinle, W. Ickes, and I. H. Bernstein, "Empathic Inaccuracy in Husband to Wife Aggression: The Overattribution Bias," *Personal Relationships* 9 (2002): 141–58; also see W. E. Schweinle and W. Ickes, "The Role of Men's Critical/Rejecting Overattribution Bias, Affect, and Attentional Disengagement in Marital Aggression," *Journal of Social and Clinical Psychology* 26, no. 2 (2007): 173–98.
22. A. M. Bippus, J. P. Boren, and S. Worsham, "Social Exchange Orientation and Conflict Communication in Romantic Relationships," *Communication Research Reports* 25, no. 3 (2008): 227–34.
23. L. A. Kurdek, "Areas of Conflict for Gay, Lesbian, and Heterosexual Couples: What Couples Argue About Influences Relationship Satisfaction," *Journal of Marriage and the Family* 56 (November 1994): 923–34: L. A. Kurdek, "Conflict Resolution Styles in Gay, Lesbian, Heterosexual Nonparent, and Heterosexual Parent Couples," *Journal of Marriage and the Family* 56 (August 1994): 705–22.

24. G. MacDonald, M. P. Zanna, and J. G. Imes, "An Experimental Test of the Role of Alcohol in Relationship Conflict," *Journal of Experimental Social Psychology* 36 (2000): 182–93.

25. L. A. Erbert, "Conflict and Dialectics: Perceptions of Dialectical Contradictions in Marital Conflict," *Journal of Social and Personal Relationships* 17 (2000): 638–59.

26. R. Dumlao and R. A. Botta, "Family Communication Patterns and the Conflict Styles Young Adults Use with Their Fathers," *Communication Quarterly* 48 (Spring 2000): 174–89; also see W. Aquilino, "From Adolescent to Young Adult: A Prospective Study of Parent-Child Relations During the Transition to Adulthood," *Journal of Marriage and the Family* 59 (1997): 670–86.

27. R. J. Doolittle, *Orientations of Communication and Conflict* (Chicago: Science Research Association 1976), 7–9.

28. Canary, Cupach, and Serpe, "A Competence-Based Approach to Examining Interpersonal Conflict."

29. D. H. Solomon, K. L. Knoblock, and M. A. Fitzpatrick, "Relational Power, Marital Schema, and Decisions to Withhold Complaints: An Investigation of the Chilling Effect of Confrontation in Marriage," *Communication Studies* 55 (2004): 146–67.

30. D. Canary, W. Cupach, and S. Messman, Relationship Conflict (Thousand Oaks, CA: Sage, 1995); J. Gottman, *What Predicts Divorce? The Relationship Between Marital Process and Marital Outcomes* (Hillsdale, NJ: Erlbaum, 1994).

31. Lloyd, "Conflict in Premarital Relationships."

32. E. H. Mudd, H. E. Mitchell, and J. W. Bullard, "Areas of Marital Conflict in Successfully Functioning and Unsuccessfully Functioning Families," *Journal of Health and Human Behavior* 3 (1962): 88–93; N. R Vines, "Adult Unfolding and Marital Conflict," *Journal of Marital and Family Therapy* 5 (1979): 5–14.

33. B. A. Fisher, "Decision Emergence: Phases in Group Decision Making," *Speech Monographs* 37 (1970): 60.

34. G. R Miller and M. Steinberg, *Between People: A New Analysis of Interpersonal Communication* (Chicago: Science Research Associates, 1975), 264.

35. C. M. Hoppe, "Interpersonal Aggression as a Function of Subject's Sex Role Identification, Opponent's Sex, and Degree of Provocation," *Journal of Personality* 47 (1979): 317–29.

36. Wilmot and Hocker, *Interpersonal Conflict;* also see S. W. Littlejohn and K. Domenici, *Engaging Communication in Conflict: Systemic Practice* (Thousand Oaks, CA: Sage, 2001).

37. J. M. Olsen, *The Process of Social Organization* (New York: Holt, Rinehart and Winston, 1978).

38. N. C. Overall, C. G. Sibley, and R. Tan, "The Cost and Benefits of Sexism: Resistance to Influence During Relationship Conflict," *Journal of Personality and Social Psychology* 101, no. 2 (2011): 271–90.

39. G. Bodenmann, N. Meuwly, T. N. Bradbury, S. Gmelch, and T. Ledermann, "Stress, Anger, and Verbal Aggression in Intimate Relationships: Moderating Effects of Individual and Dyadic Coping," *Journal of Social and Personal Relationships* 27, no. 3 (2010): 408–24.

40. S. L. Young, "Factors That Influence Recipients' Appraisals of Hurtful Communication," *Journal of Social and Personal Relationships* 21 (2004): 291–303; S. L. Young, T. L. Kubicka, C. E. Tucker, D. Chavez-Appel, and J. S. Rex, "Communicative Responses to Hurtful Messages in Families," *The Journal of Family Communication* 5 (2005): 123–40.

41. M. S. Mast, J. A. Hall, and K. Jonas, "Give a Person Power and He or She Will Show Interpersonal Sensitivity: The Phenomenon and Its Why and When," *Journal of Personality and Social Psychology* 97, no. 5 (2009): 835–50.

42. J. M. Gottman, "Repair and the Core Triad of Balance," in *The Marriage Clinic: A Scientifically-Based Marital Therapy,* edited by J. M. Gottman (New York: W. W. Norton & Company, 1999), 31–86.

43. N. E. Dunbar, A. M. Bippus, and S. L. Young, "Interpersonal Dominance in Relational Conflict: A View From Dyadic Power Theory," *Interpersona 2,* no. 1 (2008): 1–33.

44. K. Kellerman, "A Goal-Directed Approach to Gaining Compliance: Relating Differences Among Goals to Differences in Behaviors." *Communication Research* 31 (2004): 397–445.

45. J. R. P. French and B. H. Raven, "The Bases of Social Power," in *Group Dynamics,* edited by J. D. Cartwright and A. Zander (Evanston, IL: Row, Peterson, 1962), 607–22.

46. K. Kellerman, "A Goal-Directed Approach to Gaining Compliance."

47. E. V. Wilson, "Perceived Effectiveness of Interpersonal Persuasion Strategies in Computer-Mediated Communication," *Computers in Human Behavior* 19 (2003): 537–52.

48. K. Kellerman, "A Goal-Directed Approach to Gaining Compliance."

49. G. R. Miller and F. Boster, "Persuasion in Personal Relationships," in *A Handbook of Personal Relationships,* edited by S. Duck (New York: Wiley, 1988), 275–88; M. G. Garko, "Perspectives and Conceptualizations of Compliance and Compliance Gaining," *Communication Quarterly* 38, no. 2 (1990): 138–57.

50. M. G. Lawler and G. S. Risch, "Time, Sex and Money: The First Five Years of Marriage," *America* 184 (2001): 16–20.

51. M. A. Rahinn and N. R. Magner, "Confirmatory Factor Analysis of the Styles of Handling Interpersonal Conflict: First-Order Factor Model and Its Invariance Across Groups," *Journal of Applied Psychology* 80, no. 1 (1995): 122–32.

52. V. Satir, *Peoplemaking* (Palo Alto, CA: Science and Behavior Books, 1972).

53. A. F. Koerner and M. A. Fitzpatrick, "You Never Leave Your Family in a Fight: The Impact of Family of Origin on Conflict Behavior in Romantic Relationships," *Communication Studies* 53 (2002): 234–51.

54. R. Kilmann and K. Thomas, "Interpersonal Conflict-Handling Behavior as Reflections of Jungian Personality Dimensions," *Psychological Reports* 37 (1975): 971–80; K. W. Thomas and R. H. Kilmann, *Thomas-Kilmann Conflict Mode Instrument* (Tuxedo, NY: XICOM, 1974).

55. A. Buysse, A. De Clercq, L. Verhofstadt, E. Heene, H. Roeyers, and P. Van Oost, "Dealing with Relational Conflict: A Picture in Milliseconds," *Journal of Social and Personal Relationships* 17 (2000): 574–79.

56. T. D. Afifi, T. McManus, K. Steuber, and A. Coho, "Verbal Avoidance and Dissatisfaction in Intimate Conflict Situations," *Human Communication Research* 35 (2009): 357–83.

57. N. A. Klinetob and D. A. Smith, "Demand-Withdraw Communication in Marital Interaction: Tests of Interspousal Contingency and Gender Role Hypotheses," *Journal of Marriage and the Family* 58 (November 1996): 945–57; also see J. P. Caughlin and A. L. Vangelisti, "Desire to Change in One's Partner as a Predictor of the Demand/Withdraw Pattern of Marital Communication," *Communication Monographs* 66 (1999): 66–89.

58. L. M. Papp, C. D. Kouros, and E. M. Cummings, "Demand-Withdraw Patterns in Marital Conflict in the Home," *Personal Relationships* 16 (2009): 285–300.

59. J. P. Caughlin and R. S. Malis, "Demand/Withdraw Communication Between Parents and Adolescents as a Correlate of Relational Satisfaction," *Communication Reports* 17 (2004): 59–71.

60. R. Bello and R. Edwards, "Interpretations of Messages: The Influence of Various Forms of Equivocation, Face Concerns, and Sex Differences," *Journal of Language and Social Psychology* 24 (2005): 160–81.

61. J. T. Tedeschi, "Threats and Promises," in *The Structure of Conflict,* edited by R. Swingle (New York: Academic Press, 1970).

62. A. M. Czopp, M. J. Monteith, and A. Y. Mark, "Standing Up for a Change: Reducing Bias Through Interpersonal Confrontation," *Journal of Personality and Social Psychology* 90, no. 5 (2006): 784–803.

63. S. Dincyurek and A. H. Civelek, "The Determination of the Conflict Resolution Strategies of University Students That They Use When They Have Conflicts With People," *The Behavior Analyst Today* 9 (2009): 215–33.

64. Our discussion of the advantages and disadvantages of using different conflict management styles is based on material in Wilmot and Hocker, *Interpersonal Conflict.*

65. For an excellent review of the literature on flaming, see A. N. Joinson, *Understanding the Psychology of Internet Behavior: Virtual Worlds, Real Lives* (Houndsmill, England: Palgrave Macmillan, 2003), 64–77.

66. K. K. Stephens and S. A. Rains, "Information and Communication Technology Sequences and Message Repetition in Interpersonal Interaction," *Communication Research* 38, no. 1 (2011): 101–22.

67. L. Powell and M. Hickson, "Power Imbalance and Anticipation of Conflict Resolution: Positive and Negative Attributes of Perceptual Recall," *Communication Research Reports* 17 (Spring 2000): 181–90.

68. D. Cramer, "Linking Conflict Management Behaviors and Relational Satisfaction: The Intervening Role of Conflict Outcome Satisfaction," *Journal of Social and Personal Relationships* 19 (2000): 425–32.

69. D. A. Cai and E. L. Fink, "Conflict Style Differences Between Individualists and Collectivists," *Communication Monographs* 69 (March 2002): 67–87.

70. R. Dominque and D. Mollen, "Attachment and Conflict Communication in Adult Romantic Relationships," *Journal of Social and Personal Relationships* 26, no. 5 (2009): 678–96.

71. M. R. Hammer, "The Intercultural Conflict Style Inventory: A Conceptual Framework and Measure of Intercultural Conflict Resolution Approaches," *International Journal of Intercultural Relations* 29 (2005): 675–95.

72. Hammer, "The Intercultural Conflict Style Inventory."

73. Canary, Cupach, and Serpe, "A Competence-Based Approach to Examining Interpersonal Conflict."

74. Our discussion of conflict management skills is based on several excellent discussions of conflict management prescriptions. We acknowledge R. Fisher and W. Ury, *Getting to Yes: Negotiating Agreement Without Giving In* (Boston: Houghton Mifflin, 1991); R. Boulton, *People Skills* (New York: Simon & Schuster, 1979); D. A. Romig and L. J. Romig, *Structured Teamwork Guide* (Austin, TX: Performance Resources, 1990); O. Hargie, C. Saunders, and D. Dickson, *Social Skills in Interpersonal*

Communication (London: Routledge, 1994); S. Deep and L. Sussman, *Smart Moves* (Reading, MA: Addison-Wesley, 1990); Wilmot and Hocker, *Interpersonal Conflict;* M. D. Davis, E. L. Eshelman, and M. McKay, *The Relaxation and Stress Reduction Workbook* (Oakland, CA: New Harbinger Publications, 1982); W. A. Donohue and R. Kolt, *Managing Interpersonal Conflict* (Newbury Park: CA: Sage, 1992); O. Hargie (Ed.), *The Handbook of Communication Skills* (London: Routledge, 1997); Littlejohn and Domenici, *Engaging Communication in Conflict;* M. W. Isenhart and M. Spangle, *Collaborative Approaches to Resolving Conflict* (Thousand Oaks, CA: Sage, 2000); K. Sanford and A. J. Grace, "Emotion and Underlying Concerns During Couples' Conflict: An Investigation of Within-Person Change," *Personal Relationships* 18 (2011): 96–109.

75. Czopp, Monteith, and Mark, "Standing Up for a Change."
76. Boulton, *People Skills,* 217.
77. For additional strategies on managing emotion, see J. Gottman, *Why Marriages Succeed and Fail: And How You Can Make Yours Last* (New York: Simon & Schuster, 1994); J. Gottman, *The Seven Principles for Making Marriage Work* (New York: Crown, 1999). Also see Johnson, *Reaching Out.*
78. A. M. Hicks and L. M. Diamond, "Don't Go to Bed Angry: Attachment, Conflict, and Affective and Physiological Reactivity," *Personal Relationships* 18 (2011): 266–84.
79. J. A. Feeney, "Hurt Feelings in Couple Relationships: Towards Integrative Models of the Negative Effects of Hurtful Events," *Journal of Social and Personal Relationships* 21 (2004): 487–508.
80. Young, "Factors That Influence Recipients' Appraisals of Hurtful Communication."
81. H. Weger Jr., "Disconfirming Communication and Self-Verification in Marriage: Associations Among the Demand/Withdraw Interaction Pattern, Feeling Understood, and Marital Satisfaction." *Journal of Social and Personal Relationships* 22 (2005): 19–31.
82. J. Gottmann, *What Predicts Divorce? The Relationship Between Marital Process and Marital Outcomes* (Hillsdale, NJ: Erlbaum, 1994).
83. M. Morris, J. Nadler, T. Kurtzberg, and L. Thompson, "Schmooze or Lose: Social Friction and Lubrication in E-Mail Negotiations," *Group Dynamics: Theory, Research and Practice* 6 (2002): 89–100.
84. Dincyurek and Civelek, "The Determination of the Conflict Resolution Strategies of University Students That They Use When They Have Conflicts With People."
85. A. M. Bippus, S. L. Young, and N. E. Dunbar, "Humor in Conflict Discussions: Comparing Partners' Perceptions," *Humor* 24, no. 3 (2011): 287–303.
86. K. Sanford and A. J. Grace, "Emotion and Underlying Concerns During Couples' Conflict: An Investigation of Within-Person Change," *Personal Relationships* 18 (2011): 96–109.
87. Sanford and Grace, "Emotion and Underlying Concerns During Couples' Conflict."
88. Sanford and Grace, "Emotion and Underlying Concerns During Couples' Conflict."
89. Sanford and Grace, "Emotion and Underlying Concerns During Couples' Conflict."
90. Sanford and Grace, "Emotion and Underlying Concerns During Couples' Conflict."
91. K. Sanford, "Perceived Threat and Perceived Neglect: Couples' Underlying Concerns During Conflict," *Psychological Assessment* 22 (2010): 288–97.
92. Fisher and Ury, *Getting to Yes;* Boulton, *People Skills;* Romig and Romig, *Structured Teamwork® Guide;* T. Gordon, *Leader Effectiveness Training (L.E.T.): The No-Lose Way to Release the Productive Potential of People* (New York: Wyden Books, 1977).
93. Deep and Sussman, *Smart Moves.*
94. A. Ellis, *A New Guide to Rational Living* (North Hollywood, CA: Wilshire Books, 1977).
95. M. Sinaceau and L. Z. Tiedens, "Get Mad and Get More Than Even: When and Why Anger Expression Is Effective in Negotiations," *Journal of Experimental Social Psychology* 20 (2005): 1–9.
96. K. du Plessis and D. Clarke, "Couples' Helpful, Unhelpful and Ideal Conflict Resolution Strategies: Secure and Insecure Attachment Differences and Similarities," *Interpersona 2,* no. 1 (2008): 65–88.
97. A. M. Bippus and S. L. Young, "Your Emotions: Reactions to Expressions of Self- versus Other-Attributed Positive and Negative Emotions," *Journal of Applied Communication Research* 33 (2005): 26–45.
98. S. R. Covey, *The 7 Habits of Highly Effective People* (New York: Simon & Schuster, 1989), 235.
99. S. G. Lakey and D. J. Canary, "Actor Goal Achievement and Sensitivity to Partner as Critical Factors in Understanding Interpersonal Communication Competence and Conflict Strategies," *Communication Monographs* 69 (2002): 217–35.
100. Lakey and Canary, "Actor Goal Achievement and Sensitivity to Partner as Critical Factors in Understanding Interpersonal Communication Competence and Conflict Strategies."
101. For a review of goal setting and conflict management see J. L. Bevan, "Serial Argument Goals and

Conflict Strategies: A Comparison Between Romantic Partners and Family Members," *Communication Reports* 23, no. 1 (2010): 52–64.

102. Fisher and Ury, *Getting to Yes.*

103. W. Ury, *Getting Past No* (New York: Bantam Books, 1993); also see S. Hackley, "When Life Gives You Lemons: How to Deal with Difficult People," *Harvard Business School Publishing Corporation* (2004): 3–5.

104. For an excellent review and analysis of collaborative, side-by-side leadership research, see D. Romig, *Side by Side Leadership: Achieving Outstanding Results Together* (Marietta, GA: Bard Press, 2001).

105. Fisher and Ury, *Getting to Yes;* also see D. Yankelovich, *The Magic of Dialogue: Transforming Conflict into Cooperation* (New York: Simon & Schuster, 1999).

106. Fisher and Ury, *Getting to Yes.*

107. D. Romig, *Breakthrough Teamwork: Outstanding Results Using Structured Teamwork* (New York: Irwin, 1996).

108. Lakey and Canary, "Actor Goal Achievement and Sensitivity to Partner as Critical Factors in Understanding Interpersonal Communication Competence and Conflict Strategies."

109. The classic brainstorming approach was developed by A. E. Osborn, *Applied Imagination* (New York: Scribners, 1962).

110. E. Goffman, *Interaction Rituals: Essays on Face-to-Face Interaction* (Garden City, NY: Doubleday, 1967).

111. S. Ting-Toomey, "Face and Facework: An Introduction," in *The Challenge of Facework,* edited by S. Ting-Toomey (Albany, NY: SUNY Press, 1994), 1–14; S. Ting-Toomey, "Managing Intercultural Conflicts Effectively," in *Intercultural Communication: A Reader,* edited by L. A Samovar and R. E. Porter (Belmont, CA: Wadsworth, 1994), 360–72; also see S. Ting-Toomey and L. Chung, "Cross-Cultural Interpersonal Communication: Theoretical Trends and Research Directions," in *Communication in Personal Relationships Across Cultures,* edited by W. B. Gudykunst, S. Ting-Toomey, and T. Nishida (Thousand Oaks, CA: Sage, 1996), 237; Isenhart and Spangle, *Collaborative Approaches to Resolving Conflict,* 19–20.

112. V. Manusov, J. K. Kellas, and A. R. Trees, "Do Unto Others? Conversational Moves and Perceptions of Attentiveness Toward Otherface in Accounting Sequences Between Friends," *Human Communication Research* 30 (2004): 514–39.

113. M. L. McLaughlin, M. J. Cody, and H. D. O'Hair, "The Management of Failure Events: Some Contextual Determinants of Accounting Behavior," *Human Communication Research* 9 (1983): 102–25; Manusov, Kellas, and Trees, "Do Unto Others?"

114. A. J. Merolla, "Communicating Forgiveness in Friendships and Dating Relationships," *Communication Studies* 59, no. 2 (April-June 2008): 114–31.

Log On! My Communication Lab

WWW.MYCOMMUNICATIONLAB.COM

Listen to the Audio Chapter Summary at MyCommunicationLab
Study and Review the Flashcards at MyCommunicationLab

CHAPTER

6

Intercultural Communication

Taken from *Intercultural Competence: Interpersonal Communication Across Cultures*, Seventh Edition by Myron W. Lustig and Jolene Koester.

In the previous chapter, we provided an overview of the patterns that underlie all cultures. We described the nature of cultural patterns and the importance of beliefs, values, norms, and social practices in helping cultures to cope with problems. We now focus on specific conceptual taxonomies that are useful for understanding cultural differences.

We have chosen four different but related taxonomies to describe variations in cultural patterns. The first was developed by Edward Hall, who noted that cultures differ in the extent to which their primary message patterns are high context or low context. The second describes the ideas of Geert Hofstede, who identifies six dimensions along which cultures vary. The third taxonomy explains the ideas of Shalom Schwartz, who reasoned that there are three problems that all cultural groups must solve, which results in seven dimensions of culture. The fourth taxonomy, by a group of researchers collectively known as the GLOBE team, incorporates many of the previously described ideas and identifies nine dimensions of culture. Finally, we provide a synthesis of these four taxonomies and propose seven key features or dimensions that differ across cultures. These cultural dimensions are individualism versus collectivism, power distance, gender expectations, task versus relationship focus, uncertainty avoidance, harmony versus mastery, and time orientation.

As you read the descriptions of cultural patterns by Hall, Hofstede, Schwartz, and the GLOBE researchers, we caution you to remember three points. First, there is nothing sacred about these approaches and the internal categories they employ. Each approach takes the whole of cultural patterns (beliefs, values, norms, and social practices) and divides them in different ways.

Second, the parts of each of the systems are interrelated. We begin the description of each system at an arbitrarily chosen point, presupposing other parts of the system that have not yet been described. Cultural patterns are best understood as a unique whole rather than as an isolated dimension or characteristic, even if a given attribute is distinctive or predominates within a specific culture.

CULTURE CONNECTIONS

Iranian culture explicitly accepts certain types of deception and dissimulation. To begin with, the values of kindness, courtesy, and hospitality stand higher in many contexts than the values of frankness and honesty. Why tell the truth when feelings will be hurt? Why, indeed, linger on painful truths? Even deaths in the family may be concealed when circumstances are not conducive to informing the bereaved tactfully and supportively. It is important to note that this is not a case where honesty is not valued but where, given a certain type of dilemma in which honesty will cause pain, a kind deception is preferred—which would not be regarded as a lie, for real lies are very much condemned.

—Mary Catherine Bateson

Finally, individual members of a culture may vary greatly from the pattern that is typical of that culture. Therefore, as you study these approaches to cultural patterns, we encourage you to make some judgments about how your own culture fits into the pattern. Then, as you place it within the pattern, also try to discern how you, as an individual, fit into the patterns described. Similarly, as you learn about other cultural patterns, please remember that a specific person may or may not be a typical representative of that culture. As you study your own cultural patterns and those of other cultures, you improve the knowledge component of intercultural competence.

Hall's High- and Low-Context Cultural Taxonomy

Edward T. Hall, whose writings about the relationship between culture and communication are well known, organizes cultures by the amount of information implied by the setting or context of the communication itself, regardless of the specific words that are spoken.[1] Hall argues that every human being is faced with so many perceptual stimuli—sights, sounds, smells, tastes, and bodily sensations—that it is impossible to pay attention to them all. Therefore, one of the functions of culture is to provide a screen between the person and all of those stimuli to indicate what perceptions to notice and how to interpret them. Hall's approach is compatible with the other approaches discussed in this chapter. Where it differs is in the importance it places on the role of context.

According to Hall, cultures differ on a continuum that ranges from high to low context. **High-context cultures** prefer to use high-context messages, in which most of the meaning is either implied by the physical setting or is presumed to be part of the individual's internalized beliefs, values, norms, and social practices; very little is provided in the coded, explicit, transmitted part of the message. Examples of high-context cultures include Japanese, African American, Mexican, and Latino. **Low-context cultures** prefer to use low-context messages, in which the majority of the information is vested in the explicit code. Low-context cultures include German, Swedish, European American, and English.

A simple example of high-context communication is the interactions that take place in a long-term relationship between two people who are often able to interpret even the slightest gesture or the briefest comment. The message does not need to be stated explicitly because it is carried in the shared understandings about the relationship.

A simple example of low-context communication is now experienced by more and more people as they interact with computers. For computers to "understand" a message, every statement must be precise. Many computers will not accept or respond to instructions that do not have every space, period, letter, and number in precisely the right location. The message must be overt and very explicit.

Hall's description of high- and low-context cultures is based on the idea that some cultures have a preponderance of messages that are high context, others have messages that are mostly low context, and yet others have a mixture of both. Hall also describes other characteristics of high- and low-context cultures that reveal the beliefs, values, norms, and social practices of the cultural system. These characteristics include the use of indirect or direct messages, the importance of ingroups and outgroups, and the culture's orientation to time.

Use of Indirect and Direct Messages

In a high-context culture such as that of Japan, meanings are internalized and there is a large emphasis on nonverbal codes. Hall describes messages in high-context cultures as almost preprogrammed, in which very little of the interpretation of the message is left to chance because people already know that, in the context of the current situation, the communicative behaviors will have a specific and particular message. In low-context cultures, people look for the meaning of others' behaviors in the messages that are plainly and explicitly coded. The details of

A Japanese tea ceremony is an example of a high-context message. Nearly every movement, gesture, and action has significance to those who understand the "code" being used.

the message are expressed precisely and specifically in the words that people use as they try to communicate with others.

Another way to think about the difference between high- and low-context cultures is to imagine something with which you are very familiar, such as repairing a car, cooking, sewing, or playing a particular sport. When you talk about that activity with someone else who is very familiar with it, you will probably be less explicit and instead use a more succinct set of verbal and nonverbal messages. You will talk in a verbal shorthand that does not require you to be specific and precise about every aspect of the ideas that you are expressing, because the others will know what you mean without the ideas' specific presentation. However, if you talk to someone who does not know very much about the activity, you will have to explain more, be more precise and specific, and provide more background information.

In a high-context culture, much more is taken for granted and assumed to be shared, and consequently the overwhelming preponderance of messages are coded in such a way that they do not need to be explicitly and verbally transmitted. Instead, the demands of the situation and the shared meanings among the interactants mean that the preferred interpretation of the messages is already known.

Consider, as an example of high-context messages, an event that occurred in Indonesia. A young couple met, fell in love, and wanted to marry. She was from a wealthy and well-connected family, whereas he was from a family of more modest means, but the young couple did not regard this difference as a problem. So they shared their happy news with their respective families; shortly thereafter, the young man's parents were invited to the woman's home to socialize and to meet her parents. The social occasion was very cordial; the conversation was pleasant, and the two sets of parents were very gracious toward one another. At the appropriate time, the woman's parents served *nasi goreng* (fried rice) and star fruit, two foods that are very common in Indonesia. Finally, after an appropriate interval, the young man's parents thanked their hosts and left. Throughout the entire episode, the topic of the wedding was never broached. However, everyone knew that the wedding would never occur. After all, *nasi goreng* doesn't go with star fruit; the high-context and face-saving message that the woman's parents communicated, and that the man's parents clearly understood, was that they disapproved of the marriage.

Reactions in high-context cultures are likely to be reserved, whereas reactions in low-context cultures are frequently very explicit and readily observable. It is easy to understand why this is so. In high-context cultures, an important purpose in communicating is to promote and sustain harmony among the interactants. Unconstrained reactions could threaten the face or social esteem of others. In low-context cultures, however, an important purpose in communicating is to convey exact meaning. Explicit messages help to achieve this goal. If messages need to be explicit, so will people's reactions. Even when the message is understood, a person cannot assume that the meanings are clear in the absence of verbal messages coded specifically to provide feedback.

Importance of Ingroups and Outgroups

In high-context cultures, it is very easy to determine who is a member of the group and who is not. Because so much of the meaning of messages is embedded in the rules and rituals of situations, it is easy to tell who is acting according to those norms. As there are fixed and specific expectations for behaviors, deviations are easy to detect.

Another distinction concerns the emphasis placed on the individual in contrast to the group as a source of self-identity. In a high-context culture, the commitment between people is very strong and deep, and responsibility to others takes precedence over responsibility to oneself. Loyalties to families and the members of one's social and work groups are long-lasting and unchanging. This degree of loyalty differs from that found in a low-context culture, in which the bonds between people are very fragile and the extent of involvement and commitment to long-term relationships is lower.

Orientation to Time

The final distinguishable characteristic of high- and low-context cultures is their orientation to time. In the former, time is viewed as more open, less structured, more responsive to the immediate needs of people, and less subject to external goals and constraints. In low-context cultures, time is highly organized, in part because of the additional energy required to understand the messages of others. Low-context cultures are almost forced to pay more attention to time in order to complete the work of living with others.

As Table 6.1 indicates, Edward Hall's placement of cultures onto a continuum that is anchored by preferences for high-context messages and low-context messages offers a way to understand other variations in cultural patterns. A high-context culture chooses

Table 6.1
Characteristics of Low- and High-Context Cultures

High-Context Cultures	Low-Context Cultures
Indirect and implicit	Direct and explicit
Messages internalized	Messages plainly coded
Much nonverbal coding	Details verbalized
Reactions reserved	Reactions on the surface
Distinct ingroups and outgroups	Flexible ingroups and outgroups
Strong interpersonal bonds	Fragile interpersonal bonds
Commitment high	Commitment low
Time open and flexible	Time highly organized

to use indirect and implicit messages that rely heavily on nonverbal code systems. In a high-context culture, the group is very important, as are traditions, and members of the ingroup are easily recognized. Time is less structured and more responsive to people's needs. Low-context cultures are characterized by the opposite attributes: messages are explicit and dependent on verbal codes, group memberships change rapidly, innovation is valued, and time is highly structured.

Hofstede's Cultural Taxonomy

Geert Hofstede's impressive studies of cultural differences in value orientations offer another approach to understanding the range of cultural differences.[2] Hofstede's approach is based on the assertion that people carry mental programs, or "software of the mind," that are developed during childhood and are reinforced by their culture. These mental programs contain the ideas of a culture and are expressed through its dominant values. To identify the principal values of different cultures, Hofstede surveyed more than 100,000 IBM employees in seventy-one countries, and he has subsequently broadened his analysis to include many others.

Through theoretical reasoning and statistical analyses, Hofstede identified five dimensions along which dominant patterns of a culture can be ordered: power distance, uncertainty avoidance, individualism versus collectivism, masculinity versus femininity, and time orientation. Recently an additional dimension has been added: indulgence versus restraint. Hofstede's work provides an excellent synthesis of the relationships between cultural values and social behaviors.[3]

Power Distance

One of the basic concerns of all cultures is the issue of human inequality. Contrary to the claim in the U.S. Declaration of Independence that "all men are created equal," all people in a culture do not have equal levels of status or social power. Depending on the culture, some people might be regarded as superior to others because of their wealth, age, gender, education, physical strength, birth order, personal achievements, family background, occupation, or a wide variety of other characteristics.

Cultures also differ in the extent to which they view such status inequalities as good or bad, right or wrong, just or unjust, and fair or unfair. That is, all cultures have particular value orientations about the appropriateness or importance of status differences and social hierarchies. Thus **power distance** refers to the degree to which the culture believes that institutional and organizational power should be distributed unequally and the decisions of the power holders should be challenged or accepted.

Cultures that prefer small power distances—such as Austria, Denmark, Israel, and New Zealand—believe in the importance of minimizing social or class inequalities, questioning or challenging authority figures, reducing hierarchical organizational structures, and using power only for legitimate purposes. Conversely, cultures that prefer large power distances—such as those in Arab countries, Guatemala, Malaysia, and the Philippines—believe that each person has a rightful and protected place in the social order, that the actions of authorities should not be challenged or questioned, that hierarchy and inequality are

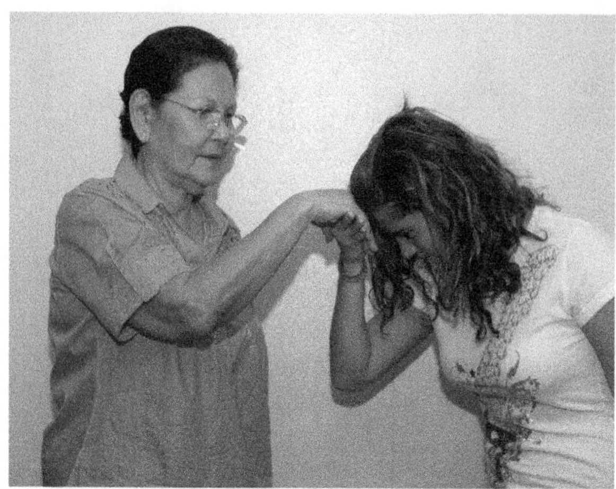

In the Philippines, large power distance is shown in this traditional gesture of greeting by a granddaughter to her grandmother.

appropriate and beneficial, and that those with social status have a right to use their power for whatever purposes and in whatever ways they deem desirable.

The consequences of the degree of power distance that a culture prefers are evident in family customs, the relationships between students and teachers, organizational practices, and in other areas of social life. Even the language systems in high power-distance cultures emphasize distinctions based on a social hierarchy.

Children raised in high power-distance cultures are expected to obey their parents without challenging or questioning them, while children raised in low power-distance cultures put less value on obedience and are taught to seek reasons or justifications for their parents' actions. Even the language of high power-distance cultures is more sensitive to hierarchical distinctions; the Chinese language, for instance, has separate terms for older brother, oldest brother, younger sister, youngest sister, and so on.

Students in high power-distance cultures are expected to comply with the wishes and requests of their teachers, and conformity is regarded very favorably. As a consequence, the curriculum in these cultures is likely to involve a great deal of rote learning, and students are discouraged from asking questions because questions might pose a threat to the teacher's authority. In low power-distance cultures, students regard their independence as very important, and they are less likely to conform to the expectations of teachers or other authorities. The educational system itself reinforces the low power-distance values by teaching students to ask questions, to solve problems creatively and uniquely, and to challenge the evidence leading to conclusions.

In the business world, managers in high power-distance cultures are likely to prefer an autocratic or centralized decision-making style, whereas subordinates in these cultures expect and want to be closely supervised. Alternatively, managers in low power-distance cultures prefer a consultative or participative decision-making style, and their subordinates expect a great deal of autonomy and independence as they do their work.

European Americans tend to have a relatively low power distance, though it is by no means exception-

CULTURE CONNECTIONS

The value systems of Australians and Americans combine competitive and cooperative strands, but in different ways. The Australian harmonizes them while the American sees them as mutually exclusive and is torn between them. Americans are always ready to put themselves in competition with the group or groups to which they belong; it is often "either the group or me." For the Australian it is "the group and me, with a great deal of personal privacy as well." Australians search for ways to collaborate with the competition while Americans seek ways to "beat" it. The American position seems to be that too much cooperation weakens one's advantage. This may stem, in part, from the different ways such values are inculcated. For example, much is made of mandatory participation in team sports in Australian schools. Americans place more emphasis on the outstanding individual and early on learn "spectatorism," with its powerful identification with the few superior performers. Social welfare legislation is much more comprehensive and more readily accepted in Australia than in the United States. The degree to which social welfare is a continuing social, political, economic, and ideological battleground in the United States surprises Australians.

—George W. Renwick

ally low. However, when European Americans communicate with people from cultures that value a relatively large power distance, problems related to differences in expectations are likely. For example, European American exchange students in a South American or Asian culture sometimes have difficulty adapting to a world in which people are expected to do as they are told without questioning the reasons for the requests. Conversely, exchange students visiting the United States from high power-distance cultures sometimes feel uneasy because they expect their teachers to direct and supervise their work closely, and they may also have been taught that it would be rude and impolite to ask for the kinds of information that might allow them to be more successful.

Uncertainty Avoidance

Another concern of all cultures is how they will adapt to changes and cope with uncertainties. The future will always be unknown in some respects. This unpredictability and the resultant anxiety that inevitably occurs are basic in human experience.

Cultures differ in the extent to which they prefer and can tolerate ambiguity and, therefore, in the means they select for coping with change. Thus, all cultures differ in their perceived need to be changeable and adaptable. Hofstede refers to these variations as the **uncertainty avoidance** dimension, the extent to which the culture feels threatened by ambiguous, uncertain situations and tries to avoid them by establishing more structure.

At one extreme on this dimension are cultures such as those of Denmark, Jamaica, India, and Ireland, which are all low in uncertainty avoidance and therefore have a high tolerance for uncertainty and ambiguity. They believe in minimizing the number of rules and rituals that govern social conduct and human behavior, in accepting and encouraging dissent among cultural members, in tolerating people who behave in ways that are considered socially deviant, and in taking risks and trying new things. Conversely, the cultures of Greece, Guatemala, Portugal, and Uruguay are among those that prefer to avoid uncertainty as a cultural value. They desire or even demand consensus about societal goals, and they do not like to tolerate dissent or allow deviation in the behaviors of cultural members. They try to ensure certainty and security through an extensive set of rules, regulations, and rituals.

Cultures must cope with the need to create a world that is more certain and predictable, and they do so by inventing rules and rituals to constrain human behaviors. Because members of high uncertainty avoidance cultures tend to be worried about the future, they have high levels of anxiety and are highly resistant to change. They regard the uncertainties of life as a continuous threat that must be overcome. Consequently, these cultures develop many rules to control social behaviors, and they often adopt elaborate rituals and religious practices that have a precise form or sequence.

Members of low uncertainty avoidance cultures tend to live day to day, and they are more willing to accept change and take risks. Conflict and competition are natural, dissent is acceptable, deviance is not threatening, and individual achievement is regarded as beneficial. Consequently, these cultures need few rules to control social behaviors, and they are unlikely to adopt religious rituals that require precise patterns of enactment.

Differences in level of uncertainty avoidance can result in unexpected problems in intercultural communication. For instance, European Americans tend to have a moderately low level of uncertainty avoidance. When these U.S. Americans communicate with someone from a high uncertainty avoidance culture, such as those in Japan or France, they are likely to be seen as too nonconforming and unconventional, and they may view their Japanese or French counterparts as rigid and overly controlled. Conversely, when these U.S. Americans communicate with someone from an extremely low uncertainty avoidance culture, such as the Irish or Swedes, they are likely to be viewed as too structured and uncompromising, whereas they may perceive their Irish or Swedish counterparts as too willing to accept dissent.

Individualism Versus Collectivism

Another concern of all cultures, and a problem for which they must all find a solution, involves people's relationships to the larger social groups of which they are a part. People must live and interact together for the culture to survive. In doing so, they must develop a way of relating that strikes a balance between showing concern for themselves and concern for others.

Cultures differ in the extent to which individual autonomy is regarded favorably or unfavorably. Thus, cultures vary in their tendency to encourage people to be unique and independent or conforming and interdependent. Hofstede refers to these variations as the **individualism–collectivism** dimension, the degree to which a culture relies on and has allegiance to the self or the group.

Highly individualistic cultures, such as the dominant cultures in Belgium, Hungary, the Netherlands, and the United States, believe that people are only

CULTURE CONNECTIONS

My job was managing the household. I told Joseph I didn't want any servants. Joseph wasn't listening.

"We can't afford servants," I protested....

"You'll like Kamau," he said. "He is a good man."

"It's not a question of liking," I said. "I don't want a cook. It's ridiculous for the two of us to have a cook and a yard man."

"A man in my position must have servants. It's expected. In America, I kept silent and learned your ways. Now you must learn."

"But servants, Joseph? It's so un-American."

He laughed and took my hand. "Kamau is of my age group—we were initiated together. We will help him. It is not a matter of choice." As it turned out, many things were not a matter of choice—my husband's monthly salary contributed to the school fees of several brothers or cousins and our garden was freely harvested by his family.

—Geraldine Kennedy

supposed to take care of themselves and perhaps their immediate families. In individualist cultures, the autonomy of the individual is paramount. Key words used to invoke this cultural pattern include *independence, privacy, self,* and the all-important *I.* Decisions are based primarily on what is good for the individual, not for the group, because the person is the primary source of motivation. Similarly, a judgment about what is right or wrong can be made only from the point of view of each individual.

Highly collectivist cultures such as those in Guatemala, Indonesia, Pakistan, and West Africa value a collectivist orientation. They require an absolute loyalty to the group, though the relevant group might be as varied as the nuclear family, the extended family, a work group, a social organization, a caste, or a jati (a subgrouping of a caste). In collectivist cultures, decisions that juxtapose the benefits to the individual and the benefits to the group are always based on what is best for the group, and the groups to which a person belongs are the most important social units. In turn, the group is expected to look out for and take care of its individual members. Consequently, collectivist cultures believe in obligations to the group, dependence of the individual on organizations and institutions, a "we" consciousness, and an emphasis on belonging.

Huge cultural differences can be explained by differences on the individualism–collectivism dimension. We have already noted that collectivistic cultures tend to be group-oriented. A related characteristic is that they typically impose a very large psychological distance between those who are members of their group (the ingroup) and those who are not (the outgroup). Ingroup members are required to have unquestioning loyalty, whereas outgroup members are regarded as almost inconsequential. Conversely, members of individualistic cultures do not perceive a large chasm between ingroup and outgroup members; ingroup members are not extremely close, but outgroup members are not as distant.

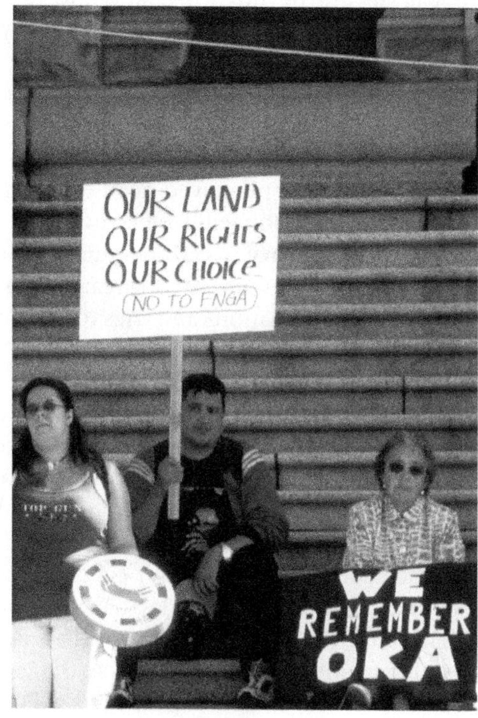

The importance of preserving one's cultural patterns is reflected in this protest against Canada's First Nations Governance Act.

Individualist cultures train their members to speak out as a means of resolving difficulties. In classrooms, students from individualistic cultures are likely to ask questions of the teacher; students from collectivistic cultures are not. Similarly, people from individualistic cultures are more likely than those from collectivistic cultures to use confrontational strategies when dealing with interpersonal problems; those with a collectivistic orientation are likely to use avoidance, third-party intermediaries, or other face-saving techniques. Indeed, a common maxim among European Americans, who are highly individualistic, is that "the squeaky wheel gets the grease" (suggesting that one should make noise in order to be rewarded); the corresponding maxim among the Japanese, who are somewhat collectivistic, is "the nail that sticks up gets pounded" (so one should always try to blend in).

Masculinity Versus Femininity

A fourth concern of all cultures, and for which they must all find solutions, pertains to gender expectations and the extent to which people prefer achievement and assertiveness or nurturance and social support. Hofstede refers to these variations as the **masculinity–femininity** dimension. This dimension indicates the degree to which a culture values "masculine" behaviors, such as assertiveness and the acquisition of wealth, or "feminine" behaviors, such as caring for others and the quality of life.

At one extreme are masculine cultures such as those in Austria, Italy, Japan, and Mexico, which believe in achievement and ambition. In this view, people should be judged on their performance, and those who achieve have the right to display the material goods that they acquired. The people in masculine cultures also believe in ostentatious manliness, and very specific behaviors and products are associated with appropriate male behavior.

At the other extreme are feminine cultures such as those of Chile, Portugal, Sweden, and Thailand, which believe less in external achievements and shows of manliness and more in the importance of life choices that improve intrinsic aspects of the quality of life, such as service to others and sympathy for the unfortunate. People in these feminine cultures are also likely to prefer equality between the sexes, less prescriptive role behaviors associated with each gender, and an acceptance of nurturing roles for both women and men.

Members of highly masculine cultures believe that men should be assertive and women should be nurturing. Sex roles are clearly differentiated, and sexual inequality is regarded as beneficial. The reverse is true for members of highly feminine cultures: men are far less interested in achievement, sex roles are far more fluid, and equality between the sexes is the norm.

Teachers in masculine cultures praise their best students because academic performance is rewarded highly. Similarly, male students in these masculine cultures strive to be competitive, visible, successful, and vocationally oriented. In feminine cultures, teachers rarely praise individual achievements and academic performance because social accommodation is more highly regarded. Male students try to cooperate with one another and develop a sense of solidarity, they try to behave modestly and properly, they select subjects because they are intrinsically interesting rather than vocationally rewarding, and friendliness is much more important than brilliance.

Time Orientation

A fifth concern of all cultures relates to its orientation to time. Hofstede has acknowledged that the four previously described dimensions have a Western bias, as they were developed by scholars from Europe or the United States who necessarily brought to their work an implicit set of assumptions and categories about the types of cultural values they would likely find. His **time-orientation** dimension is based on the work of Michael H. Bond, a Canadian who has lived in Asia for many years and who assembled a large team of researchers from Hong Kong and Taiwan to develop and administer a Chinese Value Survey to university students around the world.[4]

The time-orientation dimension refers to a person's point of reference about life and work. It ranges from long-term to short-term. Cultures with a long-term time orientation toward life include those of Germany, Japan, Russia, and South Korea. They all admire persistence, thriftiness, and humility. Linguistic and social distinctions between elder and younger siblings are common, and deferred gratification of needs is widely accepted. Conversely, cultures with a short-term orientation toward changing events include those from Australia, Colombia, Iran, and Morocco. These cultures have an expectation of quick results following one's actions.[5] The Chinese, for example, typically have a long-term time orientation—note the tendency to mark time in year-long increments, as in the Year of the Snake or the Year of the Horse—whereas Europeans typically have a short-term time orientation and aggregate time in month-long intervals (such as Aries, Gemini, Pisces, or Aquarius).

Indulgence Versus Restraint

Recently Hofstede has included an additional dimension to those previously described. Based on recent research, including ideas from Middle Eastern, Nordic, and Eastern European perspectives,[6] Hofstede has added the dimension of indulgence versus restraint to his taxonomy.

The **indulgence versus restraint** dimension juxtaposes hedonism with self-discipline. Indulgence—the view that pleasure and the enjoyment of life are very desirable—puts the focus on happiness as a way of life. Having fun, fulfilling one's appetites for delectable foods and drinks, indulging in social and sexual pleasures, and generally enjoying life by having pleasant and pleasurable experiences are characteristic. Cultures high on indulgence include those of El Salvador, Mexico, New Zealand, and Sweden. They all tend to encourage pleasure, enjoyment, spending, consumption, sexual gratification, and general merriment.

At the other extreme on this dimension are cultures that emphasize restraint. These cultures focus on self-discipline and believe that individuals should curb their urges and desires for unrestrained fun. Self-control, characterized as willpower, modesty, moderation, and self-discipline, is typical. Cultures high on restraint include those of Bulgaria, Italy, Morocco, and Pakistan. These cultures value the control of personal indulgences, they prefer to restrict "worldly" pleasures, and they discourage the seeking of enjoyments associated with leisure activities.

Comparing Hofstede's Dimensions

Hofstede's foundational work has been widely cited and appropriately praised for its importance, clarity, straightforwardness, simplicity, and excellence. Each of Hofstede's dimensions provides insights into the influence of culture on the communication process. Every culture, of course, forms an intricate and interrelated pattern; no one cultural dimension is sufficient to describe or understand this complexity.

The *hejab,* or head scarf, is worn by many Muslim women as a statement of their cultural values.

Hofstede's dimensions describe cultural expectations for a range of social behaviors: *power distance* refers to relationships with people higher or lower in rank, *uncertainty avoidance* to people's search for truth and certainty, *individualism-collectivism* to expected behaviors toward the group, *masculinity-femininity* to the expectations surrounding achievement and gender differences, *time orientation* to people's search for virtue and lasting ideals, and *indulgence-restraint* to psychological impulse control.

To guide you in understanding and using Hofstede's numerical data in the Resources section, let's use the United States as an example. There are important differences between *nations* and *cultures.* Though Hofstede's data focus on national characteristics, the information is best understood as representing the dominant culture within a nation or group. When Hofstede did his research, the dominant culture in the United States was European American.

A look at Hofstede's U.S. data reveals that European Americans tend to be at the extremes: low on power distance (–92), uncertainty avoidance (–93), and time orientation (–84) and high on individualism (195), masculinity (68), and indulgence (104). Translating Hofstede's data into specific cultural characteristics suggests a cultural orientation in which European Americans prefer to minimize status differences (power distance), encourage risk-taking (uncertainty avoidance), prefer short-term goals (time orientation), emphasize individual rights (individualism), value achievement (masculinity), and desire pleasurable consumption (indulgence).

Similar analyses can be done with data from other cultures. If two cultures have similar configurations on Hofstede's dimensions, they would likely have similar communication patterns; conversely, cultures that are very different from one another would probably behave dissimilarly. Note, however, that even cultures that are located very near others are not entirely similar; these differences underscore the importance of being cautious when making generalizations about cultures, even when they are within the same regions of the world (e.g., Latin America or the Middle East).

Time management, productivity, and communication all depend on the patterns of one's culture to define their importance.

Schwartz's Cultural Taxonomy

Another set of ongoing studies on differences in cultural patterns was conducted by Shalom Schwartz. He also began with Kluckhohn and Strodtbeck's premise (which is discussed more extensively in the previous chapter) that all cultures face common problems for which they must find a solution. Schwartz reasoned that there are three problems or issues that all groups must resolve.[7]

Schwartz's first problem is concerned with a cultural preference for the kinds of relationships and boundaries that ought to exist between individuals and the larger group. Schwartz calls this dimension **autonomy versus embeddedness**. At one extreme are cultures that value **autonomy**. In autonomy cultures, people are regarded as independent, and they are encouraged to express their unique preferences, tendencies, abilities, and feelings. Expressions of autonomy, Schwartz further reasoned, can occur in two ways, leading to two types of cultural autonomy: **intellectual autonomy** and affective autonomy. Cultures that value intellectual autonomy, such as those in France and Japan, promote and support people's independent pursuit of thoughts, ideas, and knowledge; curiosity, creativity, and a broadminded view of the world are all encouraged. Cultures that value **affective autonomy**, such as those in Denmark and England, encourage and reinforce each individual's pursuit of pleasurable emotional states, enjoyable feelings, varied experiences, and an exciting life.

In contrast to autonomy cultures, cultures that value **embeddedness** view people as nested within a collective social network. Identification with the group is a central concern, and maintenance of harmony in social relationships is paramount. Meaning in one's life is found primarily through identification with the group and through one's interpersonal relationships within that group. In embeddedness cultures, the preference is for one's routines, activities, goals—indeed, one's entire life—to be shared communally. Anything that might threaten or disrupt the sense of ingroup solidarity could be viewed as a threat. Consequently, in cultures such as those in Nigeria and Pakistan, the ideals of predictability, obedience to traditional authorities, maintenance of social order, and respect for elders' wisdom are usually central concerns.

The second cultural problem that Schwartz addresses is that people must organize and coordinate their activities in a way that preserves and fulfills the needs and goals of the social group. That is, within every culture, each person's survival requires that people must work together productively, must consider and adapt to the needs and wants of others, must coordinate and manage their actions with those of others, and must do their fair share of helping with the activities that are communally required. Schwartz calls this dimension **egalitarianism versus hierarchy**. At one extreme are **egalitarian** cultures, which encourage people to view others as social and moral equals who voluntarily choose to work together as peers to fulfill shared interests. People in egalitarian cultures, such as those in Spain and Belgium, are taught to be concerned about the welfare of others, to cooperate, and to be responsible and honest about helping others. At the other extreme are **hierarchy** cultures, which see the unequal distribution of social, political, and economic power as legitimate and desirable. People in hierarchy cultures, such as those in Thailand and Turkey, are taught to defer to those with higher status and to value authority, humility, and social power.

Schwartz's third cultural problem, which he calls **harmony versus mastery**, deals with people's orientations to social and natural resources. **Harmony** cultures encourage acceptance and blending into the natural and social worlds, as humans are seen as an integral part of nature. The view of this cultural orientation, which is held by the dominant cultures in Italy and Mexico, is to accept rather than to change, to fit in rather than to exploit, and to limit rather than to control. **Mastery** cultures encourage their members to direct and control the natural and social worlds. One's goals can be achieved most effectively by changing and adapting the social and natural environments. The view of this cultural orientation, which is held by the dominant cultures in China and India, is that

CULTURE CONNECTIONS

A powwow arena is a place for celebration by Native Indian people. It is an opportunity for Native Indian people from all parts of North America and Canada to share their music and their communal beliefs in the nature of life. As one powwow host stated before an initiation ceremony for a young girl, "This circle (the powwow arena) is the Creator's circle. It's a sacred place." For many Native Indian people, attending a powwow has the same characteristics as attending church. However, most Anglos usually cannot see the analogy. A "religious" service has different qualities for Anglos, and the celebratory atmosphere of powwows, as well as the presence of contests and vendors and grandstands, makes it difficult for many Anglos to recognize the sacred nature of what is occurring in front of them. Further, when Anglos behave inappropriately at powwows by being scantily clad or by walking into the arena to take pictures, few Native people will overtly criticize their actions. This is especially true when visitors are perceived as "guests." Numerous times I was encouraged to move ahead of Navajos when waiting in line for activities, told as they moved aside, "You're our guest." There may often be disapproving glances toward the Anglos, especially from the elderly Indians, but no direct confrontations. Except for children and some teenagers, most Native peoples at the powwows wear long pants or long skirts and do not expose their bodies unnecessarily.

—Charles A. Braithwaite

one should be self-sufficient, self-assertive, daring, ambitious, and, ultimately, successful.

In sum, Schwartz maintains that there are three primary cultural dimensions: autonomy versus embeddedness, egalitarianism versus hierarchy, and harmony versus mastery. Each cultural dimension identifies alternative solutions to a central problem that every culture must resolve. Whereas each dimension represents a continuum of possible cultural responses, a culture's tendency to prefer one pole of a given dimension means that the opposite pole is less emphasized and therefore less important to that culture. Figure 6.1 depicts the relationships among Schwartz's value orientations.

There you will find information about many cultures, grouped by geographic region. As we suggested about Hofstede's information, Schwartz's data can also be used to understand the tendencies of cultures that are of interest to you. Our earlier caution still applies: no one cultural dimension is sufficient to describe or understand the complexity of cultural differences.

The GLOBE Cultural Taxonomy

A recent and very impressive study of differences in cultural patterns was conducted by Robert J. House and his team of more than 170 investigators.[9] This ongoing research effort is called Project GLOBE, which is an acronym for Global Leadership and Organizational Behavior Effectiveness. To date, the team has collected information from nearly 20,000 middle managers in 61 cultures.

The GLOBE research program builds on the work of Hofstede and on that of Kluckhohn and Strodtbeck (which is described in the previous chapter). Nine dimensions are used to describe the dominant patterns of a culture: power distance, uncertainty avoidance, in-group collectivism, institutional collectivism, gender egalitarianism, assertiveness, performance orientation, future orientation, and humane orientation. The first six GLOBE dimensions are based on the work of Hofstede. The dimensions of power distance and uncertainty avoidance are identical in the two taxonomies. Hofstede's individualism–collectivism dimension has been separated into two GLOBE components: in-group collectivism and institutional collectivism. Similarly, Hofstede's masculinity–femininity dimension has been divided into two components: gender egalitarianism and assertiveness. The remaining three GLOBE dimensions are based on the work of Kluckhohn and Strodtbeck. The GLOBE's performance orientation dimension relates to Kluckhohn and Strodtbeck's world-orientation dimension. The future orientation dimension is based on Kluckhohn and Strodtbeck's concept of time and the distinctions among past-, present-, and future-oriented cultures. The GLOBE's humane orientation dimension is anchored in Kluckhohn and Strodtbeck's view of human nature, especially their

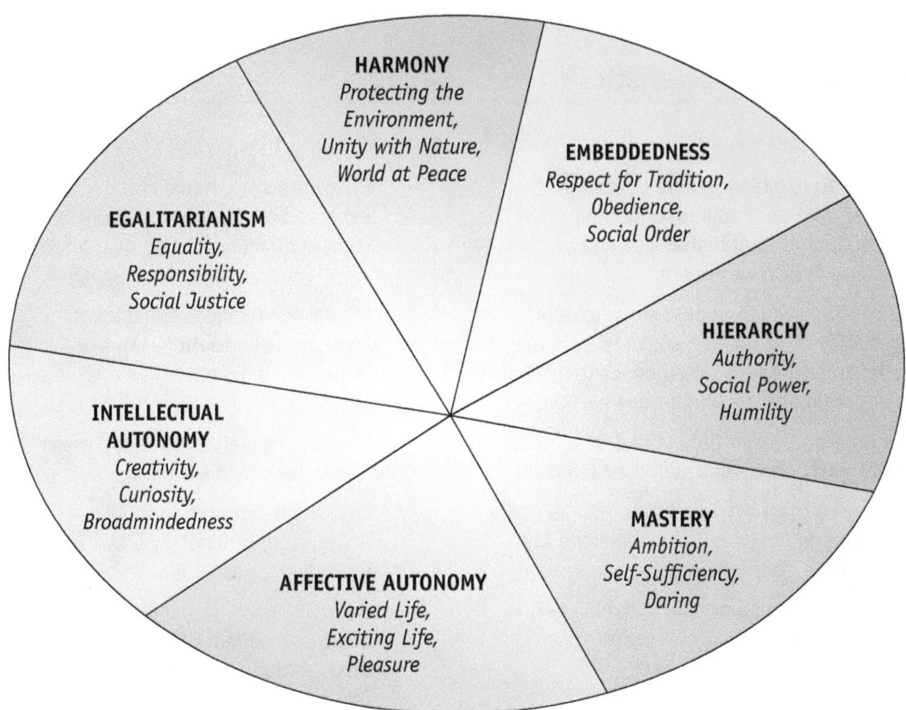

Figure 6.1
Schwartz's Cultural Value Orientations[8]

CULTURE CONNECTIONS

Ghote wanted to say that his name was Ghote, and that it was spelt with the H as the second letter. But he knew at least something about Americans. They believed in informality.

"I am Ganesh," he said. "Ganesh."

"Well, this is how it is, Gan," Hoskins said. "I'm the guy who picked up the trail of the Shahaneye kid and I'm the guy who found the ashram. So I'm in a position to inform you that I know as much about that little piece of ass as anyone. And you can take my word for it, she's not going to leave that place any time soon. She's gone off on a religion kick, and that's the way she's gonna stay."

Ghote, his head still thickly muzzy from his long flight, felt as if a hammer was being repeatedly banged down on the top of his skull. But he had to make some sort of a reply.

"Yes, Mr Hoskins," he began, "I very well understand what is the position, but—"

"Listen, if we're gonna work together on this case we're gonna have to work as a team. So you're gonna have to call me Fred. In this United States we don't stand on ceremony. You're just gonna have to learn that."

"Yes," Ghote said.

He wished with all his might that this yammering giant could simply vanish into thin air. But he was dependent on the fellow. Without him he would have the greatest difficulty getting to the ashram at all. He did not even know its address, just that it was not in Los Angeles but somewhere outside. He could make inquiries if he had to, and in the end he would find it. But if he was to act at all quickly Fred Hoskins stood, giant-like, squarely in his path.

"Fred," he said. "Yes, I will call you Fred."

—H. R. F. Keating

Table 6.2
GLOBE Dimensions and Cultural Characteristics[10]

Dimension	Cultural Characteristics	Sample Items
Power Distance	The degree to which people believe that power should be stratified, unequally shared, and concentrated at higher levels of an organization or government.	Followers are (should be) expected to obey their leaders without question.
Uncertainty Avoidance	The extent to which people strive to avoid uncertainty by relying on social norms, rules, rituals, and bureaucratic practices to alleviate the unpredictability of future events.	Most people lead (should lead) highly structured lives with few unexpected events.
In-Group Collectivism	The degree to which people express pride, loyalty, and cohesiveness in their families.	Employees feel (should feel) great loyalty toward this organization.
Institutional Collectivism	The degree to which a culture's institutional practices encourage collective actions and the collective distribution of resources.	Leaders encourage (should encourage) group loyalty even if individual goals suffer.
Gender Egalitarianism	The extent to which people minimize gender role differences and gender discrimination while promoting gender equality.	Boys are encouraged (should be encouraged) more than girls to attain a higher education. (scored inversely)
Assertiveness	The degree to which people are assertive, confrontational, and aggressive in social relationships.	People are (should be) generally dominant in their relationships with each other.
Performance Orientation	The extent to which people encourage others to improve their task-oriented performance and excel.	Students are encouraged (should be encouraged) to strive for continuously improved performance.
Future Orientation	The degree to which people engage in future-oriented behaviors such as planning, investing in the future, and delaying gratification.	Most people live (should live) in the present rather than for the future. (scored inversely)
Humane Orientation	The degree to which people encourage others to be fair, altruistic, friendly, generous, caring, and kind.	Most people are (should be) generally very tolerant of mistakes.

distinction that cultures may regard humans on a continuum ranging from inherently "good" to inherently "bad." Table 6.2 provides the nine cultural dimensions studied in the GLOBE research, their cultural characteristics, and sample items. The information in this table provides a useful reference guide to help you understand the GLOBE ideas more easily.

Power Distance

As Hofstede suggested, one of the basic concerns of all cultures is the issue of human inequality. Cultures differ in the extent to which they view status inequalities as desirable or undesirable. Thus power distance refers to the degree to which cultures believe that social and political power should be distributed disproportionately, shared unequally, and concentrated among a few top decision makers.

High power-distance cultures, such as those in France, Argentina, and Nigeria, believe it is very appropriate to have differences among social classes. Upward mobility ought to be limited, because people already occupy their correct places in the social hierarchy. The decisions of the powerful authorities should be met with unchallenged acceptance.

Conversely, low power-distance cultures like those in Australia, Denmark, and Albania believe it is important to minimize or even eliminate social class differences. Upward mobility is high, because an equal opportunity for each person is an overriding goal. Questioning and challenging the decisions of authorities is regarded as each person's duty and responsibility, as only through such challenges will social and political power be used well.

Uncertainty Avoidance

All cultures need to have some degree of predictability in their social worlds. While complete certainty can never be achieved, humans could not survive in a world of total and chaotic uncertainty. Thus cultures vary in the degree of predictability they prefer. These variations constitute the uncertainty avoidance dimension, which is the extent to which cultures feel threatened by the unpredictability of the future and therefore try to establish more structure in the form of rules, regulations, rituals, and mandatory practices.

Cultures such as those in Sweden, Switzerland, and China are relatively high on uncertainty avoidance. Therefore, they prefer to avoid uncertainty as a cultural value, desire or even demand consensus about societal goals, and do not tolerate dissent or allow deviation in the behaviors of cultural members. They try to ensure certainty and security through an extensive set of instructions about how one ought to behave. As a result, cultures that are high on uncertainty avoidance prefer to develop many ways to control people's social behaviors. These controls exist as formal regulations and as informal rules about acceptable conduct, and they also include elaborate rituals and religious practices that have a precise form or sequence.

Cultures such as those in Russia, Bolivia, and South Korea are relatively low on uncertainty avoidance. Therefore, they have a higher tolerance for uncertainty and ambiguity and are much more comfortable with the unpredictability of life. Consequently, rules and regulations are kept to a minimum, dissent is tolerated, and deviance is more likely to be regarded as peculiar or eccentric rather than as threatening.

In-Group Collectivism

The in-group collectivism dimension is similar to what Hofstede calls individualism-collectivism. Individualistic cultures have low in-group collectivism, whereas collectivistic cultures rate high on this dimension.

In-group collectivism reflects the degree to which people express pride, loyalty, and solidarity with their family or similar group. In cultures with high in-group collectivism, individuals take pride in and define their sense of self—quite literally, their sense of who they are—in terms of their family or similar group. That is, people's identities within collectivistic cultures are closely tied to their ingroups, and strong group memberships are both required and desired. As the African saying suggests, in collectivist cultures "I am because we are." Representative cultures that are high on in-group collectivism include those in Georgia, Morocco, and the Philippines.

In individualistic cultures—those that are low on in-group collectivism—the independence and autonomy of the individual is an overriding feature. People's identities within individualistic cultures are separate from, and perhaps very distant from, those of the group. Group membership is often regarded as voluntary, and allegiance with one's ingroup—even with one's family—is not expected to be overly strong. Included in this category are such cultures as those in New Zealand, Finland, and the Netherlands.

Institutional Collectivism

Another aspect of the dimension that Hofstede called individualism-collectivism is concerned with the basis upon which decisions are made and the group's resources are allocated. The dimension of **institutional collectivism** represents the degree to which cultures support, value, and prefer to distribute rewards based on group versus individual interests.

In cultures that are high on institutional collectivism, decisions that juxtapose the benefits to the group with the benefits to the individual nearly always base the decision on what is best for the group. Thus, in cultures like those in Qatar and Japan, group activities are typically preferred to individual actions.

In cultures that are low on institutional collectivism, decisions are based on what is good for the

Within Massai culture, which is high on institutional collectivism, there is a strong identification with the tribe. Here, a group of Massai women live in a communal village.

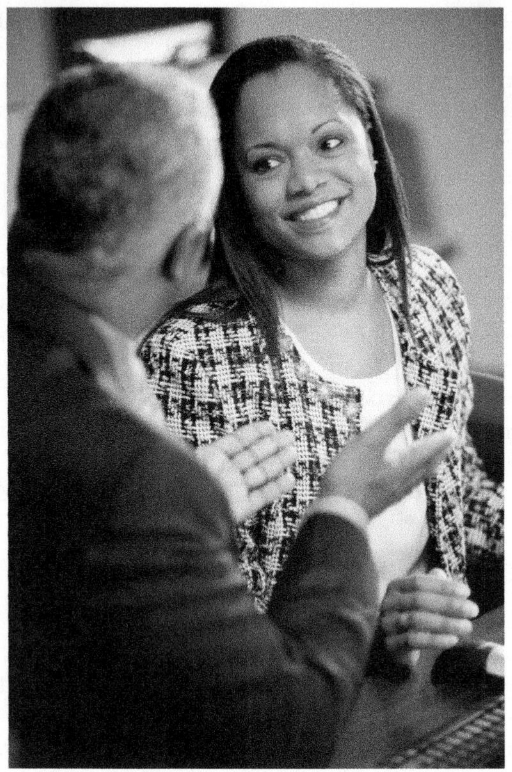

Gender egalitarianism, which minimizes differences among men and woman, is evident in this conversation between two business people.

individual, with little regard for the group. Because the person is the primary source of motivation, individual autonomy and actions tend to dominate. Thus, in Italy and Greece, decisions are based on individual merit rather than on collective involvement.

Gender Egalitarianism

If you carefully read the description of Hofstede's masculinity-femininity dimension, you will note that it combines two related attributes that, in the GLOBE project, have been separated into separate dimensions: a belief in equality between women and men and a preference for forceful assertiveness. The first of these attributes is called **gender egalitarianism** and is the extent to which a culture minimizes differences in gender expectations for men versus women.

Cultures such as those in Hungary and Poland, which are near the midpoint of the gender egalitarianism dimension, believe that gender equality is preferred, that men and women should be treated in the same way, and that unequal treatment solely because of one's biological sex or gender constitutes discrimination and should not occur. Conversely, cultures like those in Austria and Egypt, which are low in gender egalitarianism, engage in unequal treatment of men and women. In this view, there are inherent differences between men and women, and these differences require dissimilar expectations and treatments. Rather than regarding these fundamental differences negatively, cultures that are low on gender egalitarianism view the divergence in gender roles and expectations as normal and natural.

Assertiveness

Another concern of all cultures, which also requires every culture to find a solution, pertains to the cultural preference for dominance and forcefulness or nurturance and social support. This **assertiveness** dimension describes the extent to which people value and prefer tough aggressiveness or tender nonaggressiveness.

Cultures high on the assertiveness dimension value strength, success, and taking the initiative. Competition is good, winning is desirable, and rewards should go to those who are victorious. People are encouraged to be competitive, visible, and successful. Representative cultures include those in Germany and Hong Kong.

Conversely, cultures low on the assertiveness dimension value modesty, tenderness, warm relationships, and cooperation. Competition is bad, a win-lose orientation is unacceptable, and rewards should be shared among all. Nurturance and social support are important, as are modesty, cooperation with others, and a sense of solidarity. Friendliness is much more important than brilliance. Typical of this orientation are the cultures in Kuwait and Thailand.

Performance Orientation

The degree to which a culture encourages and rewards people for their accomplishments is called the **performance orientation** dimension. Depending on the culture, some people might be regarded as superior to others because of who they are—the "correct" family background, age, gender, birth order, or school—whereas others may acquire status based on personal achievements such as the amount of education, success in business, physical strength, occupation, or a wide variety of other characteristics.

In high performance-oriented cultures, such as those in Canada and Singapore, status is based on what a person has accomplished. Schooling and education are critical to one's success, people are expected to demonstrate some initiative in work-related tasks, and expectations are high. Conversely, in low performance-oriented cultures, like those in

Colombia and Guatemala, status is based on who you are. Attending the "right" school is important, as are family connections, seniority, loyalty, and tradition.

An important component of performance orientation is people's preferred relationship to the natural and spiritual worlds. As Kluckhohn and Strodtbeck suggested in the previous chapter, some cultures view nature as something to be conquered and controlled, others see themselves as living in harmony with nature, and still others view themselves as subjugated to nature.

High performance-oriented cultures assert their dominance over nature, and they try to shape the world to fit their needs. Getting the job done is far more important than maintaining effective relationships, for what really matters is the task-related results that show what someone has accomplished. People in high performance-oriented cultures value competitiveness, assertiveness, and achievement. In contrast, people in low performance-oriented cultures feel more controlled by nature and want to live in harmony with the natural and spiritual environments. Maintaining effective relationships is more important in such cultures than is getting the job done; what matters most are cooperation, integrity, and loyalty.

Another important distinction related to performance orientation is Edward Hall's concept of low-context versus high-context messages, which we discussed earlier. High performance-oriented cultures tend to be low context; they prefer to use messages that are clear, explicit, and direct. They also have a monochronic approach to time; time is valuable and limited, events are sequential, and punctuality is preferred. Conversely, low performance-oriented cultures use high-context messages more often; their intent is to avoid direct confrontations and maintain harmony in their relationships.

Future Orientation

Locating one's world in time—and thereby giving structure, coherence, and significance to events—creates order and meaning in people's lives. The extent to which a culture plans for forthcoming events is the **future orientation** dimension. Related slightly to Hofstede's long-term dimension and very directly to Kluckhohn and Strodtbeck's ideas on time orientation, the future orientation dimension describes the degree to which cultures advocate long-term planning and deferred gratification or the deeply felt satisfaction that comes from experiencing the simple pleasures of the present moment.

Cultures *differ*, of course, in the extent to which they prefer to focus on the future rather than on the spontaneity of the present. Those high in future orientation, such as Iran and Hong Kong, believe that current pleasures are less important than future benefits, so they believe in planning, self-control, and activities that have a delayed impact. Cultures like those in Portugal and Venezuela are low in future orientation and thus prefer to enjoy fully the experiences currently under way; they like to live "in the moment" and are less constrained by doubts about the past or concerns about the future.

People from cultures that are high in future orientation want to save money and other resources. They believe in strategic planning, and they value economic success. People from cultures that are low in future orientation are more likely to spend now rather than save for later. They view material and spiritual achievements as opposing goals, and they prefer the latter.

Humane Orientation

The final GLOBE dimension, **humane orientation**, refers to the extent to which cultures encourage and

CULTURE CONNECTIONS

At the other end of the line is Vitalie, a blogger, one of the few in Moldova. He seemed like someone who could shed some light on Moldovan misery. We agree to meet the next day. Vitalie asks me if I know any good restaurants. This strikes me as odd, since he's lived here all of his life and I've been in Moldova for about one hour. I take this as a discouraging sign about the culinary prospects in Moldova. Later, someone explained that in Moldova the relationship between host and guest is reversed. It is the guest's obligation to make the host feel at ease. Reverse hospitality. One of the many peculiar customs in this country.

—Eric Weiner

reward their members for being benevolent and compassionate toward others or are concerned with self-interest and self-gratification.

Cultures high in humane orientation value expressions of kindness, generosity, caring, and compassion, and people who express social support for others are admired. Members of humane-oriented cultures are expected to help others financially and emotionally, to share information that others may need, to spend time with others, and to offer empathy and love. Representative cultures include those in Zambia and Indonesia.

Cultures low in humane orientation value comfort, pleasure, satisfaction, and personal enjoyment. People from low humane orientation cultures are expected to confront personal problems by themselves, and they are concerned primarily with individual gratification. Typical of this orientation are the cultures of Spain and white South Africa.

Comparing the GLOBE Dimensions

Cultural patterns represent a universal social choice that must be made by each culture and that is learned from the family and throughout the social institutions of a culture: in the degree to which children are encouraged to have their own desires and motivations, in the solidarity and unity expected in the family, in the role models that are presented, and throughout the range of messages that are conveyed.

Additional numerical information about sixty-one cultures on the GLOBE dimensions can be found in the Resources section at the back of this book. The regional groupings organize the cultures in the GLOBE studies by geographic areas. As we suggested previously, the data can be used to understand the tendencies of cultures that are of interest to you.

The GLOBE research expands our understanding of cultural patterns. By providing updated information on a wide range of cultures, and by revising and expanding the cultural dimensions that are relevant, this effort substantially increases our understanding of cultures and of intercultural communication. To provide just one example of the usefulness of the expanded GLOBE dimensions, consider the information about the Japanese culture on the dimensions of institutional collectivism and in-group collectivism. Whereas the Japanese are extremely high in institutional collectivism (+222), they are below the average for in-group collectivism (−68). This information clarifies why decisions in Japan are most often made, and resources among the Japanese are typically distributed, in a very collectivist fashion, but the collective group for the Japanese—that is, the group with which people identify most closely—is not necessarily the family but rather the organization, the nation, or some other social unit. New Zealanders, Swedes, and Danes, among others, have patterns on these two dimensions that are similar to the Japanese; Greeks, Guatemalans, Colombians, and others have the opposite pattern.

A Synthesis of Cultural Taxonomies

We began this chapter by noting that each attempt to identify the fundamental ways that cultures can differ—that is, the core ideas of Kluckhohn and Strodtbeck (in the previous chapter), Hall, Hofstede, Schwartz, and the GLOBE team—takes the whole of cultural patterns and divides them in different ways. Yet we are sure you noticed that there are many commonalities in these approaches.

One idea that is central to each of these approaches was first discussed in the previous chapter. Kluckhohn and Strodtbeck noted that all cultures face a common set of problems for which they must find solutions. Based on the ideas presented in this chapter, we now have a more refined basis for suggesting what those fundamental cultural problems might be, and therefore what aspects of culture would likely make one cultural group similar to or different from another.

Based on the extensive scholarly research that is discussed in this chapter and the previous one, we suggest that there are seven universal problems, and therefore seven cultural dimensions, that are fundamental to understanding a culture. Each dimension can be viewed as a continuum of choices that a culture must make. To avoid confusion, we label these dimensions by their commonly used names, when such a name exists. Each label describes one or both of the end points—the extremes—of the continuum. The cultural dimensions are: individualism versus collectivism, power distance, gender expectations, task versus relationship, uncertainty avoidance, harmony versus mastery, and time orientation.

Perhaps the most essential issue that all cultures must confront involves the requirement for *a balance between the needs of individuals versus the priorities of the group.* The **individualism–collectivism** dimension highlights this important issue. Scholars such as Harry Triandis have suggested that the individualism-collectivism dimension is, by far, the most important attribute that distinguishes

CULTURE CONNECTIONS

Balinese culture is one of the most methodical systems of social and religious organization on earth, a magnificent beehive of tasks and role and ceremonies. The Balinese are *lodged,* completely held, within an elaborate lattice of customs. A combination of several factors created this network but basically we can say that Bali is what happens when the lavish rituals of traditional Hinduism are superimposed over a vast rice-growing agricultural society that operates, by necessity, with elaborate communal cooperation. Rice terraces require an unbelievable amount of shared labor, maintenance and engineering in order to prosper, so each Balinese village has a *banjar*—a united organization of citizens who administer, through consensus, the village's political and economic and religious and agricultural decisions. In Bali, the collective is absolutely more important than the individual, or nobody eats.

—Elizabeth Gilbert

one culture from another[11]; thus it is not surprising that it appears in each of the previously discussed taxonomies.

Another universal issue faced by all cultures involves *expectations about the behaviors of people with higher or lower status.* This **power-distance** dimension emphasizes the cultural choices related to equality versus hierarchy. Both the value of status differences (how important they are) and the basis of status differences (the characteristics that give someone increased status) are culturally based.

A third issue that all cultures must confront involves their *beliefs about appropriate behaviors for men and women.* This **gender expectations** dimension includes both expectations about suitable role behaviors—to what extent, for example, are men and women encouraged to be assertive or nurturing—and expectations about the preferred similarities or differences in the behaviors of men and women.

A fourth cultural issue requires a *balance between task-related and relationship-building activities.* This **task-relationship** dimension involves a cultural choice that emphasizes the relative importance of task concerns (getting the job done) and relational concerns (maintaining good social relationships) among the cultural members.

A fifth concern of all cultures arises through the culture's efforts at *coping with the unknown.* This **uncertainty avoidance** dimension highlights cultural choices that involve a preference for impulsiveness versus predictability, and it therefore emphasizes the culture's desire for risk versus caution.

A sixth cultural issue entails *locating the culture in space and place.* The **harmony–mastery** dimension is concerned with a culture's approach to its physical and material environments. Cultural preferences on this dimension can range from complete acceptance of and "fitting into" the natural world to a preference for absolute control and conquest of the physical environment.

The final cultural issue, which is general and overarching, is concerned with *locating the culture in time.* This **time-orientation** dimension includes four very different types of problems that arise from the passage of time: the culture's preferred *goals,* which can range from short term to long term; its *emphasis,* which can focus on past, present, or future moments; its *use,* which involves a penchant for organizing activities one-at-a-time or many-things-at-once; and the culture's preferred *rhythm* for pacing activities, which can range from a view that time is open and flexible to one in which time is highly structured and organized.

Table 6.3 highlights the correspondence between the seven universal problems we have identified, the cultural dimensions that address them, and the cultural taxonomies that we discussed previously. As you can see, there is substantial commonality across the taxonomies. But they also differ in what they emphasize, in the distinctions they regard as significant, and in the terminology they use to feature these universal cultural issues.

Figure 6.2 summarizes the range of cultural orientations that can occur on these seven dimensions. Taken together, these seven dimensions provide a culture-general "map" or framework that can be filled in with culture-specific information. This gives you an accessible way to understand specific cultural patterns.

Table 6.3
A Synthesis of Cultural Taxonomies

Synthesis of Taxonomies	Kluckhohn & Strodbeck	Hall	Hofstede	Schwartz	Globe
Individualism–Collectivism	Social Relations Orientation	Context	Individualism–Collectivism	Autonomy vs. Embeddedness	Ingroup Collectivism; Institutional Collectivism
Power Distance	Social Relations Orientation	Context	Power Distance	Egalitarianism vs. Hierarchy	Power Distance
Gender Expectations	Social Relations; Self-Orientation	Context	Masculinity–Femininity	—	Gender Egalitarianism; Assertiveness
Task Relationship	Activity Orientation	—	Indulgence–Restraint	Intellectual Autonomy; Affective Autonomy	Performance Orientation; Humane Orientation
Uncertainty Avoidance	—	Context	Uncertainty Avoidance	—	Uncertainty Avoidance
Harmony–Mastery	World Orientation	—	—	Harmony vs. Mastery	—
Time Orientation	Time Orientation	Context	Time Orientation	—	Future Orientation

Individualism ———— Collectivism
High Power Distance ———— Low Power Distance
Gender Expectations
Men Assertive ———— Men Nurturing
Women Assertive ———— Women Nurturing
Men, Women Equal ———— Men, Women Unequal
Task Focus ———— Relationship Focus
Uncertainty Avoidance ———— Uncertainty Seeking
Harmony with Environment ———— Mastery of Environment
Time Orientation
Goals: Short-Term ———— Long-Term
Emphasis: Past ———— Present ———— Future
Use: One-at-a-Time ———— Many-Things-at-Once
Rhythm: Open, Flexible ———— Structured, Organized

Figure 6.2
Cultural Orientations

Cultural Taxonomies and Intercultural Competence

The major lesson in this chapter is that cultures vary systematically in their choices about solutions to basic human problems. The taxonomies offer lenses through which cultural variations can be understood and appreciated, rather than negatively evaluated and disregarded. The categories in these taxonomies can help you to describe the fundamental aspects of cultures. As frames of reference, they provide mechanisms to understand many intercultural communication events. In any intercultural encounter, people may be communicating from very different perceptions of what is "real," what is "good," and what is "correct" behavior. The competent intercultural communicator must recognize that there will be cultural differences in addressing the seven universal cultural issues, and these differences will always be a factor in intercultural communication.

The taxonomies allow you to use culture-specific knowledge to improve intercultural competence. First, begin by seeking out information about the cultural patterns of those individuals with whom you engage in intercultural communication. To assist your analysis and understanding of the culture, use the seven cultural dimensions as an organizing framework for the information you gather, and create a profile of the culture's preferred choices. Libraries and the Internet are natural starting places for this kind of knowledge. So, too, are representatives of the culture. Engage them in conversation as you try to understand their culture. Most people welcome questions from a genuinely curious person. Be systematic in your search for information by using the categories thoroughly. Think about the interrelatedness of the various aspects of the culture's patterns.

Second, study the patterns of your own culture. Because you take your beliefs, values, norms, and social practices for granted, stepping outside of your cultural patterns by researching them is very useful. You might want to describe the preferences of your own culture by using the seven universal cultural dimensions as a framework for your analysis.

The third step requires only a willingness to reflect on your personal preferences. Do your beliefs, values, norms, and social practices match those of the typical person in your culture? How do your choices coincide with and differ from the general cultural description?

Finally, mentally consider your own preferences by juxtaposing them with the description of the typical person from another culture. Note the similarities and differences in beliefs, values, norms, and social practices. Can you predict where misinterpretations may occur because of contrasting assumptions about what is important and good? For example, the European American who shares the culture's preference for directness would inevitably encounter difficulties in communication with a typical member of the Japanese culture or a typical Latino cultural member. Similarly, knowing that you value informality, and usually act accordingly, can help you to monitor your expressions when communicating with someone from a culture that prefers formality. Viewing time as linear often causes problems in communication with people from cultures with other orientations to time. Interpretations of behavior as "late," "inattentive," or "disrespectful," rather than just "different," can produce alternative ways of viewing the ticking of the clock.

SUMMARY

This chapter first discussed four important taxonomies that can be used to describe cultural variations. Edward Hall placed cultures on a continuum from high context to low context. High-context cultures prefer messages in which most of the meaning is either implied by the physical setting or is presumed to be part of the individual's internalized beliefs, values, norms, and social practices; low-context cultures prefer messages in which the information is contained within the explicit code.

Geert Hofstede described six dimensions along which dominant patterns of a culture can be ordered: power distance, uncertainty avoidance, individualism–collectivism, masculinity–femininity, time orientation, and indulgence–restraint. The power-distance dimension assesses the degree to which the culture believes that institutional power should be distributed equally or unequally. The uncertainty avoidance dimension describes the extent to which cultures prefer and can tolerate ambiguity and change. The individualism–collectivism dimension describes the degree to which a culture relies on and has allegiance to the self or the group. The masculinity–femininity dimension indicates the degree to which a culture values assertiveness and "manliness" or caring for others and the quality of life. The time-orientation dimension refers to a long-term versus short-term orientation toward life and work. The indulgence–restraint dimension contrasts pleasure-seeking with self-restraint.

Shalom Schwartz maintained that there are three aspects of culture that are primary: autonomy versus embeddedness, egalitarianism versus hierarchy, and harmony versus mastery. Each of these cultural continua identifies alternative solutions to a central problem that every culture must resolve. The autonomy–embeddedness dimension is concerned with preferences for an individual versus collective orientation; the egalitarianism–hierarchy dimension is concerned with preferences for power and control; and the harmony–mastery dimension emphasizes the culture's approach to the social and natural worlds.

The GLOBE researchers identified nine dimensions of culture. The power-distance and uncertainty avoidance dimensions are similar to those that Hofstede described. In-group collectivism and institutional collectivism refine Hofstede's individualism–collectivism dimension; in-group collectivism is concerned with family loyalty, whereas societal collectivism refers to group-oriented actions. Gender egalitarianism and assertiveness refine Hofstede's masculinity–femininity dimension; gender egalitarianism is about equality between men and women, while assertiveness is about social dominance. Performance orientation refers to task- or work-related accomplishments, future orientation is about preferences for delayed versus immediate gratifications, and humane orientation is concerned with fairness and generosity.

Our synthesis of the various cultural taxonomies proposes seven cultural dimensions: individualism versus collectivism, power distance, gender expectations, task versus relationship, uncertainty avoidance, harmony versus mastery, and time orientation. Each of these dimensions is based on—and is therefore similar to—the analogous ideas of Kluckhohn and Strodtbeck, Hall, Hofstede, Schwartz, and the GLOBE researchers.

The ideas presented in this chapter and in the previous one offer alternative lenses through which cultures can be understood and appreciated. Taken together, these two chapters provide multiple frames of reference that can enhance your knowledge, motivations, and skills in intercultural communication.

Key Terms

affective autonomy
assertiveness
autonomy
autonomy versus embeddedness
egalitarian
egalitarianism versus hierarchy
embeddedness
future orientation
gender egalitarianism
gender expectations
harmony
harmony versus mastery
hierarchy
high-context cultures
humane orientation
individualism–collectivism
indulgence versus restraint
in-group collectivism
institutional collectivism
intellectual autonomy
low-context cultures
masculinity–femininity
mastery
performance orientation
power distance
task-relationship
time-orientation
uncertainty avoidance

FOR DISCUSSION

1. What does Edward Hall mean when he refers to culture as a "screen" for its members?
2. Describe how each of Hofstede's dimensions of cultural patterns is displayed within your culture.
3. Does Schwartz's taxonomy coincide with your own intercultural experiences? Explain.
4. Consider the following two philosophical statements: "I think; therefore, I am" and "I am because we are." What do these two statements reveal about the underlying cultural values of those who use them?
5. Compare your own values with the GLOBE's cultural values for the "typical" person from your culture. In what ways are they the same? Different? What might this suggest about intercultural communication?

FOR FURTHER READING

Jagdeep S. Chhokar, Felix C. Brodbek, and Robert J. House (eds.), *Culture and Leadership across the World: The GLOBE Book of In-Depth Studies of 25 Societies* (Mahwah, NJ: Erlbaum, 2007). A companion to the earlier GLOBE book, this volume provides in-depth qualitative information about the dimensions of culture.

Edward T. Hall, *Beyond Culture* (New York: Anchor Books, 1989). Describes, in great detail, the cultural variations among high- and low-context cultures.

Geert Hofstede, Gert Jan Hofstede, and Michael Minkov, *Cultures and Organizations: Software of the Mind: Intercultural Cooperation and Its Importance for Survival,* 3rd ed. (New York: McGraw-Hill, 2010). Hofstede's recent and most comprehensive book, which extensively describes his ideas about the dimensions on which cultures can vary.

Robert J. House, Paul J. Hanges, Mansour Javidan, Peter W. Dorfman, and Vipin Gupta (eds.), *Culture, Leadership, and Organizations: The GLOBE Study of 62 Societies* (Thousand Oaks, CA: Sage, 2004). A momentous work that presents ground-breaking research on the current practices and value dimensions that differ among cultures. Provides extensive quantitative evidence for cultural variations on the nine GLOBE dimensions.

Shalom H. Schwartz, "A Theory of Cultural Value Orientations: Explication and Applications," *Measuring and Mapping Cultures: 25 Years of Comparative Value Surveys,* ed. Yilmaz Esmer and Thorleif Pettersson (Boston: Brill, 2007), 33–78. A concise and useful summary of Schwartz's research on cultural values.

NOTES

1. Edward T. Hall, *Beyond Culture* (Garden City, NY: Anchor, 1977).

2. Geert Hofstede, *Culture's Consequences: Comparing Values, Behaviors, Institutions, and Organizations across Nations*, 2nd ed. (Thousand Oaks, CA: Sage, 2001); Geert Hofstede, *Cultures and Organizations: Software of the Mind* (London: McGraw-Hill, 1991); Geert Hofstede, Gert Jan Hofstede, and Michael Minkov, *Cultures and Organizations: Software of the Mind: Intercultural Cooperation and Its Importance for Survival*, 3rd ed. (New York: McGraw-Hill, 2010).

3. Denise Rotondo Fernandez, Dawn S. Carlson, Lee P. Stepina, and Joel D. Nicholson, "Hofstede's Country Classification 25 Years Later," *Journal of Social Psychology* 137 (1997): 43–54; Bradley L. Kirkman, Kevin B. Lowe, and Cristina B. Gibson, "A Quarter Century of *Culture's Consequences*: A Review of Empirical Research Incorporating Hofstede's Cultural Values Framework," *Journal of International Business Studies* 37 (2006): 285–320.

4. Data from twenty-two countries were originally reported in: Chinese Culture Connection, "Chinese Values and the Search for Culture-Free Dimensions of Culture," *Journal of Cross-Cultural Psychology* 18 (1987): 143–164. See also Hofstede, Hofstede, and Minkov (2010).

5. Hofstede, *Cultures and Organizations*, 164–166; *Culture's Consequences*, 360.

6. Hofstede, Hofstede, and Minkov, *Cultures and Organizations*; Geert Hofstede, Gert Jan Hofstede, Michael Minkov, and Henk Vinken, "VSM 08: Values Survey Module 2008 Manual," 2008. Accessed May 5, 2011, from http://geerthofstede.com/research—vsm/vsm-08.aspx; Ronald Inglehart (ed.), *Human Values and Social Change: Findings from the Values Surveys* (Boston: Brill, 2003); Ronald Inglehart, Miguel Basañez, Jaime Díez-Medrano, Loek Halman, and Ruud Luijkx, *Human Beliefs and Values: A Cross-Cultural Sourcebook Based on the 1999–2002 Values Surveys* (Mexico: Siglo XXI Editores, 2004); Ronald Inglehart, Miguel Basañez, and Alejandro Moreno, *Human Values and Beliefs: A Cross-Cultural Sourcebook. Findings from the 1990–1993 World Values Survey* (Ann Arbor: University of Michigan Press, 1998); Ronald Inglehart and Pippa Norris, *Rising Tide: Gender Equality and Cultural Change around the World* (Cambridge: Cambridge University Press, 2003); Michael Minkov, *What Makes Us Different and Similar: A New Interpretation of the World Values Survey and Other Cross-Cultural Data* (Bulgaria: Klasika y Stil, 2007); Peter B. Smith, "Book Review: Michael Minkov, What Makes Us Different and Similar: A New Interpretation of the World Values Survey and Other Cross-Cultural Data," *International Journal of Cross Cultural Management* 8 (2008): 110–112.

7. Our description of Schwartz's ideas is based on the following: Ronald Fischer, C.-Melanie Vauclair, Johnny R. J. Fontaine, and Shalom H. Schwartz, "Are Individual-Level and Country-Level Value Structures Different? Testing Hofstede's Legacy with the Schwartz Value Survey," *Journal of Cross-Cultural Psychology* 41 (2010): 135–151; Johnny R. J. Fontaine, Ype H. Poortinga, Luc Delbeke, and Shalom H. Schwartz, "Structural Equivalence of the Values Domain across Cultures: Distinguishing Sampling Fluctuations from Meaningful Variation," *Journal of Cross-Cultural Psychology 39* (2008): 345–365; Sonia Roccas, Lilach Sagiv, Shalom H. Schwartz, and Ariel Knafo, "The Big Five Personality Factors and Personal Values," *Personality and Social Psychology Bulletin* 28.6 (2002): 789–801; Lilach Sagiv and Shalom H. Schwartz, "Value Priorities and Readiness for Out-Group Social Contact," *Journal of Personality and Social Psychology* 69 (1995): 437–448; Shalom H. Schwartz, "Individualism-Collectivism: Critique and Proposed Refinements," *Journal of Cross-Cultural Psychology* 21 (1990): 139–157; Shalom H. Schwartz, "Universals in the Content and Structure of Values: Theoretical Advances and Empirical Tests in 20 Countries," *Advances in Experimental Social Psychology*, ed. Mark P. Zanna, Vol. 25 (San Diego: Academic Press, 1992), 1–65; Shalom H. Schwartz, "Are There Universal Aspects in the Structure and Content of Values?" *Journal of Social Issues* 50 (1994): 19–45; Shalom H. Schwartz, "Beyond Individualism-Collectivism: New Cultural Dimensions of Values," *Individualism and Collectivism: Theory, Method and Applications*, ed. Uichol Kim, Harry C. Triandis, Cigdem Kagitçibasi, Sang-Chin Choi, and Gene Yoon (Newbury Park, CA: Sage, 1994), 85–119; Shalom H. Schwartz, "Value Priorities and Behavior: Applying

a Theory of Integrated Value Systems," *The Psychology of Values*, ed. Clive Seligman, James M. Olson, and Mark P. Zanna (Mahwah, NJ: Erlbaum, 1996), 1–24; Shalom H. Schwartz, "Values and Culture," *Motivation and Culture*, ed. Donald Munro, John F. Schumaker, and Stuart C. Carr (New York: Routledge, 1997), 69–84; Shalom H. Schwartz, "Values and Behavior: Strength and Structure of Relations," *Personality and Social Psychology Bulletin* 29 (2003): 1207–1220; Shalom H. Schwartz, "Evaluating the Structure of Human Values with Confirmatory Factor Analysis," *Journal of Research in Personality* 38 (2004): 230–255; Shalom H. Schwartz, "Mapping and Interpreting Cultural Differences around the World," *Comparing Cultures: Dimensions of Culture in a Comparative Perspective*, ed. Henk Vinken, Joseph Soeters, and Peter Ester (Boston: Brill, 2004), 43–73; Shalom H. Schwartz, "A Theory of Cultural Value Orientations: Explication and Applications," *Comparative Sociology* 5 (2006): 137–182; Shalom H. Schwartz, "A Theory of Cultural Value Orientations: Explication and Applications," *Measuring and Mapping Cultures: 25 Years of Comparative Value Surveys*, ed. Yilmaz Esmer and Thorleif Pettersson (Boston: Brill, 2007), 33–78; Shalom H. Schwartz, "Studying Values: Personal Adventure, Future Directions," *Journal of Cross-Cultural Psychology* 42 (2011): 307–319; Shalom H. Schwartz and Anat Bardi, "Influences of Adaptation to Communist Rule on Value Priorities in Eastern Europe," *Political Psychology* 18 (1997): 385–410; Shalom H. Schwartz and Anat Bardi, "Moral Dialogue across Cultures: An Empirical Perspective," *Autonomy and Order: A Communitarian Anthology*, ed. Edward W. Lehman (Lanham, England: Rowman & Littlefield, 2000); Shalom H. Schwartz and Anat Bardi, "Value Hierarchies across Cultures: Taking a Similarities Perspective," *Journal of Cross-Cultural Psychology* 32 (2001): 268–290; Shalom H. Schwartz and Klaus Boehnke, "Evaluating the Structure of Human Values with Confirmatory Factor Analysis," *Journal of Research in Personality* 38 (2004): 230–255; Shalom H. Schwartz, Gila Melech, Arielle Lehmann, Steven Burgess, Mari Harris, and Vicki Owens, "Extending the Cross-Cultural Validity of the Theory of Basic Human Values with a Different Method of Measurement," *Journal of Cross-Cultural Psychology* 32 (2001): 519–542; Shalom H. Schwartz and Tammy Rubel, "Sex Differences in Value Priorities: Cross-Cultural and Multimethod Studies," *Journal of Personality and Social Psychology* 89 (2005): 1010–1028; Shalom H. Schwartz and Lilach Sagiv, "Identifying Culture-Specifics in the Content and Structure of Values," *Journal of Cross-Cultural Psychology* 26 (1995): 92–116; Shalom H. Schwartz, Markku Verkasalo, Avishai Antonovsky, and Avishai Sagiv, "Value Priorities and Social Desirability: Much Substance, Some Style," *British Journal of Social Psychology* 36 (1997): 3–18; Peter B. Smith, Mark F. Peterson, and Shalom H. Schwartz, "Cultural Values, Sources of Guidance, and Their Relevance to Managerial Behavior: A 47-Nation Study," *Journal of Cross-Cultural Psychology* 34 (2002): 297–303; Peter B. Smith and Shalom H. Schwartz, "Values," *Handbook of Cross-Cultural Psychology*, ed. John W. Berry, Marshall H. Segall, and Cigdem Kagitçibasi, 2nd ed. Vol. 3. Social behavior and applications (Boston: Allyn and Bacon, 1997); Naomi Struch, Shalom H. Schwartz, and Willem A. van der Kloot, "Meanings of Basic Values for Women and Men: A Cross-Cultural Analysis," *Personality and Social Psychology Bulletin* 28 (2002): 16–28; Christin-Melanie Vauclair, Katja Hanke, Ronald Fischer, and Johnny Fontaine, "The Structure of Human Values at the Culture Level: A Meta-Analytical Replication of Schwartz's Value Orientations Using the Rokeach Value Survey," *Journal of Cross-Cultural Psychology* 42 (2011): 186–205; Evert van de Vliert, Shalom H. Schwartz, Sipke E. Huismans, Geert Hofstede, and Serge Daan, "Temperature, Cultural Masculinity, and Domestic Political Violence: A Cross-National Study," *Journal of Cross-Cultural Psychology* 30 (1999): 291–314.

8. Our discussion of the GLOBE research is based on the following: Neal Ashkanasy, Vipin Gupta, Melinda S. Mayfield, and Edwin Trevor-Roberts, "Future Orientation," *Culture, Leadership, and Organizations: The GLOBE Study of 62 Societies*, ed. Robert J. House, Paul J. Hanges, Mansour Javidan, Peter W. Dorfman, and Vipin Gupta (Thousand Oaks, CA: Sage, 2004), 282–342; Neal M. Ashkanasy, Edwin Trevor-Roberts, and Louise Earnshaw, "The Anglo Cluster: Legacy of the British Empire," *Journal of World Business* 37 (2002): 28–39; Gyula Bakacsi, Takács Sándor, Karácsonyi András, and Imrek Viktor, "Eastern European Cluster: Tradition and Transition," *Journal of World Business* 37 (2002): 69–80; Dale Carl, Vipin Gupta, and Mansour Javidan, "Power Distance," *Culture, Leadership, and Organizations: The GLOBE Study of 62 Societies*, ed. House, Hanges, Javidan, Dorfman, and Gupta, 513–563; Mary Sully De Luque and Mansour Javidan, "Uncertainty Avoidance," *Culture, Leadership, and Organizations: The GLOBE Study*

of 62 Societies, ed. House, Hanges, Javidan, Dorfman, and Gupta, 602–653; Deanne N. Den Hartog, "Assertiveness," *Culture, Leadership, and Organizations: The GLOBE Study of 62 Societies*, ed. House, Hanges, Javidan, Dorfman, and Gupta, 395–436; P. Christopher Earley, "Leading Cultural Research in the Future: A Matter of Paradigms and Taste," *Journal of International Business Studies* 37 (2006): 922–931; Cynthia G. Emrich, Florence L. Denmark, and Deanne N. Den Hartog, "Cross-Cultural Differences in Gender Egalitarianism," *Culture, Leadership, and Organizations: The GLOBE Study of 62 Societies*, ed. House, Hanges, Javidan, Dorfman, and Gupta, 343–394; Michele J. Gelfand, Dharm P. S. Bhawuk, Lisa Hisae Nishii, and David J. Bechtold, "Individualism and Collectivism," *Culture, Leadership, and Organizations: The GLOBE Study of 62 Societies*, ed. House, Hanges, Javidan, Dorfman, and Gupta, 437–512; Vipin Gupta and Paul J. Hanges, "Regional and Climate Clustering of Societal Cultures," *Culture, Leadership, and Organizations: The GLOBE Study of 62 Societies*, ed. House, Hanges, Javidan, Dorfman, and Gupta, (178–218; Vipin Gupta, Paul J. Hanges, and Peter Dorfman, "Cultural Clusters: Methodology and Findings," *Journal of World Business* 37 (2002): 11–15; Vipin Gupta, Gita Surie, Mansour Javidan, and Jagdeep Chhokar, "Southern Asia Cluster: Where the Old Meets the New?" *Journal of World Business* 37 (2002): 16–27; Paul J. Hanges and Marcus W. Dickson, "Agitation over Aggregation: Clarifying the Development of and the Nature of the GLOBE Scales," *Leadership Quarterly* 17 (2006): 522–536; Paul J. Hanges, Marcus W. Dickson, and Mina T. Sipe, "Rationale for GLOBE Statistical Analyses," *Culture, Leadership, and Organizations: The GLOBE Study of 62 Societies*, ed. Robert J. House, Paul J. Hanges, Mansour Javidan, Peter W. Dorfman, and Vipin Gupta (Thousand Oaks, CA: Sage, 2004), 219–233; Paul J. Hanges, Julie S. Lyon, and Peter W. Dorfman, "Managing a Multinational Team: Lessons from Project Globe," *Advances in International Management* 18 (2005): 337–360; Geert Hofstede, "What Did GLOBE Really Measure? Researchers' Minds Versus Respondents' Minds," *Journal of International Business Studies* 37 (2006): 882–896; Robert J. House, Mansour Javidan, Paul Hanges, and Peter Dorfman, "Understanding Cultures and Implicit Leadership Theories across the Globe: An Introduction to Project GLOBE," *Journal of World Business* 37 (2002): 3–10; Robert J. House, Paul J. Hanges, Mansour Javidan, Peter W. Dorfman, and Vipin Gupta (eds.), *Culture, Leadership, and Organizations: The GLOBE Study of 62 Societies* (Thousand Oaks, CA: Sage, 2004); Robert J. House and Mansour Javidan, "Overview of GLOBE," *Culture, Leadership, and Organizations: The GLOBE Study of 62 Societies*, ed. House, Hanges, Javidan, Dorfman, and Gupta, 9–28; Jon P. Howell, José DelaCerda, Sandra M. Martínez, Leonel Prieto, J. Arnoldo Bautista, Juan Ortiz, Peter Dorfman, and Maria J. Méndez, "Leadership and Culture in Mexico," *Journal of World Business* 42 (2007): 449–462; Mansour Javidan, "Performance Orientation," *Culture, Leadership, and Organizations: The GLOBE Study of 62 Societies*, ed. House, Hanges, Javidan, Dorfman, and Gupta, 239–281; Mansour Javidan and Markus Hauser, "The Linkage between GLOBE Findings and Other Cross-Cultural Information," *Culture, Leadership, and Organizations: The GLOBE Study of 62 Societies*, ed. House, Hanges, Javidan, Dorfman, and Gupta, 102–121; Mansour Javidan and Robert J. House, "Leadership and Cultures around the World: Findings from GLOBE: An Introduction to the Special Issue," *Journal of World Business* 37 (2002): 1–2; Mansour Javidan, Robert J. House, and Peter W. Dorfman, "A Nontechnical Summary of GLOBE Findings," *Culture, Leadership, and Organizations: The GLOBE Study of 62 Societies*, ed. House, Hanges, Javidan, Dorfman, and Gupta, 29–48; Mansour Javidan, Robert J. House, Peter W. Dorfman, Paul J. Hange, and Mary Sully de Luque, "Conceptualizing and Measuring Cultures and Their Consequences: A Comparative Review of Globe's and Hofstede's Approaches," *Journal of International Business Studies* 37 (2006): 897–914; Jorge Correia Jesuino, "Latin Europe Cluster: From South to North," *Journal of World Business* 37 (2002): 81–89; Hayat Kabasakal and Muzaffer Bodur, "Arabic Cluster: A Bridge between East and West," *Journal of World Business* 37 (2002): 40–54; Hayat Kabasakal and Muzaffer Bodur, "Humane Orientation in Societies, Organizations, and Leader Attributes," *Culture, Leadership, and Organizations: The GLOBE Study of 62 Societies*, ed. House, Hanges, Javidan,

Dorfman, and Gupta, (Thousand Oaks, CA: Sage, 2004), 564–601; Mark F. Peterson and Stephanie L. Castro, "Measurement Metrics at Aggregate Levels of Analysis: Implications for Organization Culture Research and the GLOBE Project," *Leadership Quarterly* 17 (2006): 506–521; Peter B. Smith, "When Elephants Fight, the Grass Gets Trampled: The GLOBE and Hofstede Projects," *Journal of International Business Studies* 37 (2006): 915–921; Erna Szabo, Felix C. Brodbeck, Deanne N. Den Hartog, Gerhard Reber, Jürgen Weiblere, and Rolf Wunderer, "The Germanic Europe Cluster: Where Employees Have a Voice," *Journal of World Business* 37 (2002): 55–68.

9. See C. Harry Hui and Harry C. Triandis, "Individualism-Collectivism: A Study of Cross-Cultural Researchers," *Journal of Cross-Cultural Psychology* 17 (1986): 225–248; Harry C. Triandis, *The Analysis of Subjective Culture* (New York: Wiley, 1972); Harry C. Triandis, *Culture and Social Behavior* (New York: McGraw-Hill, 1994); Harry C. Triandis, *Individualism & Collectivism* (Boulder, CO: Westview, 1995); Harry C. Triandis and S. Arzu Wasti, "Culture," *The Influence of Culture on Human Resource Management Processes and Practices*, ed. Dianna Stone and Eugene Stone-Romero (New York: Earlbaum, 2008), 1–24.

10. Adapted from: Schwartz, "A Theory of Cultural Value Orientations: Explication and Applications," 142; Shalom H. Schwartz, *Cultural Values Influence and Constrain Economic and Social Change*, Unpublished Manuscript; Shalom H. Schwartz, *Cultural Value Orientations: Nature & Implications of National Differences*, Unpublished Manuscript; Shalom H. Schwartz, "Values: Cultural and Individual," *Fundamental Questions in Cross-Cultural Psychology*, ed. Fons J. R. van de Vijver, Athanasios Chasiotis, and Seger M. Breugelmans (New York: Cambridge University Press, 2011), 473; Christin-Melanie Vauclair, Katja Hanke, Ronald Fischer, and Johnny Fontaine, "The Structure of Human Values at the Culture Level: A Meta-Analytical Replication of Schwartz's Value Orientations Using the Rokeach Value Survey," *Journal of Cross-Cultural Psychology* 42 (2011): 188.

11. Adapted from: House, Hanges, Javidan, Dorfman, and Gupta.

CHAPTER

7

Rhetorical Theory

Taken from *Modern Rhetorical Criticism*, Third Edition, by Roderick P. Hart and Suzanne Daughton.

The Rhetorical Perspective

Because as they cut it was that special green, they
decided
To make a woman of the fresh hay. They wished to
lie in green, to wrap
Themselves in it, light but not pale, silvered but not
grey.
Green and ample, big enough so both of them could
shelter together
In any of her crevices, the armpit, the join
Of hip and groin. They—who knew what there was
to know about baling
The modern way with hay so you rolled it up like a
carpet,
Rather than those loose stacks—they packed the
green body tight
So she wouldn't fray. Each day they moulted her to
keep her
Green and soft. Only her hair was allowed to ripen
into yellow tousle.

The next weeks whenever they stopped cutting
they lay with her.
She was always there, waiting, reliable, their green
woman.
She gathered them in, yes she did,
Into the folds of herself, like the mother they hadn't
had.
Like the women they had had, only more pliant,
more graceful,
Welcoming in a way you never just found.
They not only had the awe of taking her,
But the awe of having made her. They drank beer
Leaning against the pillow of her belly
And one would tell the other, "Like two Adams
creating."

And they marveled as they placed
The cans at her ankles, at her neck, at her wrists so she
Glittered gold and silver. They adorned what they'd
made.
After harrowing they'd come to her, drawing
The fountains of the Plains, the long line
Of irrigating spray and moisten her up.
And lean against her tight, green thighs to watch
buzzards
Circle black against the pink stain of the sunset.

What time she began to smolder they never
knew—
Sometime between night when they'd left her
And evening when they returned. Wet, green hay
Can go a long time smoldering before you notice.
It has a way
Of catching itself, of asserting that
There is no dominion over it but the air. And it
flares suddenly
Like a red head losing her temper, and allows its
long bright hair
To tangle in the air, letting you know again
That what shelters you can turn incendiary in a
flash.
And then there is only the space of what has been,
An absence in the field, memory in the shape of a
woman.
[Macdonald, 1985:75–6]

This is not, mainly, a chapter about poems. It is a chapter about rhetoric and the rhetors who create it, as well as criticism and the critics who perform it. It is a chapter that invites careful attention to the messages of daily life. This chapter encourages us to pick and probe at messages designed to influence human thoughts and actions. It invites careful attention to such **rhetorical artifacts,** that is, the leftovers of rhetorical acts: the records that remain and can be re-examined after the speech, letter, debate, editorial, or performance has been created and in some cases, ended. Because it is a chapter about **rhetoric,** it is a chapter about the art of using language to help people narrow their choices among specifiable, if not specified, policy options. Not a very sophisticated definition, perhaps, but one that has its intuitive attractions. For example, we know, intuitively, that the poem above involves a special use of language. But is it language designed to *narrow* the choices of other people? Not in an obvious sense. Our day-to-day experience with obvious forms of rhetoric — advertising, political speeches, televised evangelism—tells us that if poet Cynthia Macdonald is attempting to persuade us of something specific, she has chosen a strange tack indeed.

Admittedly, Macdonald uses language well—beautifully, in fact. She paints her pictures with dexterity, creating for us the simple beauty of the bountiful pasture she describes, allowing us to hear the casual conversations of the laboring brothers, inviting us to feel the alternating softness and hardness of the carefully baled hay. Poet Macdonald also evokes rich feeling states: the brothers' feelings of entitlement, sensual comfort, and loss; the wonder of watching nature's earthen blackness blend into the "pink stain" of her sunsets; the catch in the breath as the brothers realize that their feelings of control were illusory. Macdonald, then, gives us precisely what a good poet often gives us—old thoughts thought anew, old feelings felt anew—but does she give us rhetoric?

Many scholars have argued in the affirmative. Any use of language, Richard Weaver claims, is sermonic. "We are all of us preachers in private or public capacities. We have no sooner uttered words than we have given impulse to other people to look at the world, or some small part of it, in our way" [2001:1360]. Influential literary critic and rhetorical theorist Kenneth Burke told us that "effective literature could be nothing else but rhetoric" [1931:210]. Literary scholar Wayne C. Booth authored a germinal text entitled *The Rhetoric of Fiction* [1961] that presumed the persuasiveness of literature. And in their encyclopedic anthology of Western rhetorical theory, *The Rhetorical Tradition,* Patricia Bizzell and Bruce Herzberg [2001] note that disagreement over the proper description of the relationship between what the Ancient Greeks called rhetoric and poetic has been going on since, well, the time of the Ancient Greeks. "Even if, as many critics have argued, there is a distinction between the 'contemplative' goal of literature and the 'active' goal of rhetoric, literature frequently uses persuasion and argumentation. . . . [Throughout history,] the independence of rhetoric and poetic has been asserted and defended just as frequently as their interrelatedness" [Bizzell & Herzberg, 2001: 1193].

So it seems that poetry may be rhetorical, and rhetoric may be poetic. But does that mean that poetry should be subjected to rhetorical criticism? Some of it certainly would yield rich insights. A careful reading of "Two Brothers in a Field of Absence," for example, could note the shift to the second-person form of address in the final stanza: "before you notice," "letting you know again / That what shelters you can turn incendiary in a flash." Such changes, in which the reader is suddenly placed in the role of an eyewitness, signal a subtle but powerful turn toward the rhetorical. This use of "you" implies that although the brothers had mistakenly tried to assert dominion over a woman, the reader can be expected to know better—or at least, to learn from their example. Another clue that could support such an interpretation is the poem's title, "Two Brothers in a Field of Absence." French feminists and others, following the work of Sigmund Freud and Jacques Lacan, have noted that in Western patriarchal culture, "woman" has often been (mis)understood to be symbolic of a castrated man (and therefore less than a man), because of her "absence" of male genitalia [Bizzell & Herzberg, 2001:1225]. But here, the "absence" or loss is caused by the woman's refusal to live under male domination, which essentially negates male power. Macdonald thus removes the "castration" from "castration anxiety," pointing toward the real prize: "dominion." (Most women don't want male anatomy, they want self-determination.)

But our interpretation of Macdonald's poem offers arguable implications rather than clearly specified policy options. We take the position here that poetry, while at times highly rhetorical, can differ from rhetoric. As with any other medium of communication, several of which we will explore in this chapter, certain examples or artifacts will be more likely to reward a careful look than others. In its written form at least, poetry often assumes a contemplative reader, one who has time to reread and rethink. Rhetoric is an active art; it cannot trust its audience to mull over its meaning long after the message has been delivered. Poetry may thus have the luxury of being elliptical and enigmatic, at times challenging even basic understanding. Rhetoric takes no such chances.

Certainly, any given message or artifact can be highly poetic or highly rhetorical, or both at once. The two are not mutually exclusive, nor are they even different ends of the same continuum. As meteorologists tell us, temperature and humidity combine to create our physical experience of heat or cold. Likewise, the degrees of rhetorical and poetic artistry in a message combine to create our experience of memorable and moving discourse. Shakespeare's version of Marc Antony's famous speech ("I come to bury Caesar, not to praise him. . .") is clearly high on both scales, since it remains a classic example of gorgeous prose that, just incidentally, uses irony so masterfully as to incite a riot. On the other hand, the listings in the residential phone book are comparatively low on both measures. The following speech, while obviously an example of what the Greeks called *epideictic* rhetoric (ceremonial speech that praises or blames), would score lower on the poetry index.

> Mr. Speaker, I rise to celebrate a victorious day for West Genessee High School as both the men's and women's lacrosse teams captured the New York State Lacrosse Division 1, Class A Championship titles. It was a memorable day that will go down in history for the Wildcats, as both teams soared triumphantly to the top.
>
> The day began as the women's team traveled to Cortland, New York to defend their

> state title, and this is exactly what they accomplished. . . . Later that afternoon at Hofstra University, the men's lacrosse team regained the State title with an exciting 10–9 victory. As Coach Mike Messere stated "It was one of the most exciting games I've seen."
>
> West Genessee Lacrosse has always had the reputation for a stellar program, and as displayed this past weekend, the program continues to generate gifted athletes. These students work hard year-round to master the sport, and because of their relentless hard work, dedication, and passion for the game, they came out true champions.
>
> I am proud of these devoted athletes, and I commend the coaching staff, parents, and entourage of supporters who traveled this long road with them. This type of outcome does not happen overnight, nor is it the result of just one season. It takes years of dedication to get such results, and this entire team should be proud of their accomplishments. [Walsh, 2002: E1055]

Any person of aesthetic sensibility will be almost embarrassed by the stark contrast between Cynthia Macdonald's mellifluous lines and Representative James Walsh's banal sports reporting in the halls of the U.S. Congress. In contrast to Macdonald, who demands thoughtful reconsideration from her readers, Walsh makes us squirm with his tedious pontificating ("The day began. . ."), his tiresome clichés ("both teams soared triumphantly to the top. . ."), and his ponderous overstatements ("It was a memorable day that will go down in history. . ."). Unrequired pontificating, tiresome clichés, ponderous over-statements. This is rhetoric. Or at least some of it. The worst of it, perhaps. But every day, in every profession, people like James T. Walsh produce rhetoric, much of it trivial, some of it important, all of it purporting to help others sort through their choices.

Modern Rhetorical Criticism invites us to study why the *Congressional Record* is filled with such stuff, why Representative Walsh's constituents were flattered by his blandishments, and why his colleagues in the House smiled benignly when he read his remarks into the *Record.* Because he operates as something of a classic persuader here, Walsh tries to "cut off" the many options for response available to his audience. Walsh's **policy options** are clearly specified ("let's congratulate the Wildcats"), whereas Cynthia Macdonald never tells her audience exactly what she expects them to *do* as a result of reading her poem. This lack of specificity is what makes reading verse such a pleasure: It gives us room to wander; it permits a vacation from choosing between this concrete possibility and that concrete probability. Representative Walsh, in contrast, is all business.

But must all rhetoric be as pedestrian and self-serving as James Walsh's? Clearly not. Human history has been written by great people creating great messages for social betterment. Often, these great statements have seemed more poetic than pragmatic, as satisfying to the heart as to the head. Consider, for example, the following artifact. The exiled Tibetan Buddhist leader, His Holiness the Dalai Lama, wrote an essay for the British-based magazine, *Caduceus.* In that essay, he asks,

> How are we to achieve world peace? Through anger, hatred, the arms race? No. True world peace can be achieved only through mental peace. And mental peace is based on the understanding of or conviction in the importance of compassion and the concept of impermanence. Through such an understanding or conviction one can then genuinely practice tolerance and respect for others and recognize that all human beings are brothers and sisters, even though we may be different in terms of our ideological, political or economic system. These are secondary issues. The most important thing is that we are all the same human beings wishing for happiness and seeking to avoid suffering. We are interdependent because we need each other for our very survival. . . . In order to achieve genuine, lasting world peace, we must first develop peaceful relations with others, and I believe we can only achieve that if we have inner peace within ourselves. . . .
>
> Our ultimate goal should be the demilitarization of the entire planet, but to achieve that, first some kind of inner disarmament is necessary. The key. . .is inner peace and the foundation of that is a sense of understanding and respect for each other as human beings, based on compassion and love. Some may dismiss compassion and love as impractical and unrealistic, but I believe their practice is the true source of success. Compassion is, by nature, peaceful and gentle, but it is also very powerful. It is a sign of

> true inner strength. To achieve it we do not need to become religious, nor do we need any ideology. All that is necessary is for us to develop our basic human qualities. [Dalai Lama, 2002:10]

This is hardly Walsh-like discourse. A great man, not an average man, is expressing himself. And he is writing of great matters, not of expedient matters. Like poet Macdonald, the Dalai Lama draws on our most basic human commonalities, and uses simple language with elegance. But there is an awkwardness to his language also. He repeats himself, at times using more words than he really needs. The Dalai Lama's message could use a little editing: smoother flow, less redundancy.

But to call for such changes would be to miss the point of this rhetorical artifact, for the Dalai Lama had no intention of producing poetry. In the context of war and terrorism, he wanted one thing: to communicate his simple truth about the most profound bedevilment of the human condition. His eloquence derived from the emotional investment he made in his message, from his personal experiences as a refugee, and from the powerful simplicity of his logic. All of this made for an *artistry* not seen in Representative Walsh's celebration of high school lacrosse but it also made for an *insistence* not apparent in Cynthia Macdonald's poem. In short, the Dalai Lama mustered as much artistry as his insistence would allow.

Modern Rhetorical Criticism will probe these subtleties of human interaction. The chapter presents practical techniques for uncovering the wishes and schemes hidden in public discourse and shows how important answers arise when one asks the right questions. It details a number of theoretical perspectives for "taking apart" the messages we hear each day so that we can better appreciate why, rightly or wrongly, the James Walshs of the world far outnumber the Dalai Lamas and the Cynthia Macdonalds. But before considering these perspectives, let us consider what rhetoric is and what it is not.

The Arts of Rhetoric

The premises in this chapter are threefold: (1) Rhetoric is a special sort of human activity; (2) it takes a special kind of practice to understand it; and (3) by understanding it, one acquires a special perspective on the world itself. We can get some sense of the special nature of rhetoric by contrasting the messages above. After reading Macdonald's poem, for example, each reader has a unique set of feelings and expectations. Macdonald develops many images, trips off many associations. She seems to demand nothing in particular from us as readers. Walsh, in contrast, clearly seeks universal agreement from his audience about a narrowed set of choices. He takes pains to provide background for his audience, uses language in highly conventional ways, mentions specific names and dates and places, is obvious when identifying good (victory) and evil (failure), and tells his audience what he wishes them to do next (applaud).

There is also a purposiveness in Walsh's remarks that is missing in Macdonald's poem. Walsh seems less patient than Macdonald; he is almost boorish in his concern that we get his story straight. Macdonald, in contrast, seems more willing to let us find our own story within her story. She wants us to be different after reading her poem but she seems content to let *us* explore the dimensions of that difference. Both rhetoric and poetry tell a story, but the rhetor (that is, the one who uses rhetoric) takes special pains to be sure that the moral of the story is clear to the audience.

But what is the moral of Cynthia Macdonald's story? Some might be unconvinced by the feminist reading we offer above, and see this poem as a naturalistic foray into the primitive connections between humans and their agricultural products. Others might see Macdonald as a retrograde sexist, celebrating a masculine world of physical dominance in which woman becomes a pliable object to be freely manipulated by men.

Any of these interpretations are possible, and they are the sorts of things that critics debate about. But the important thing to note here is that *the poet herself does not resolve these disputes.* All critics need to offer textual evidence to support their claims. Apart from providing clues in the poem that support one interpretation more than another, the poet keeps her own counsel, content to provoke questions in her readers but not to answer them.

Like poetry, rhetoric is an art. Like poetry, rhetoric creates a story out of nothing, using words to bring to life feelings we may have forgotten, plans we may not have considered. As we see in Walsh's speech, rhetoric uses common ideas, conventional language, and specific information to influence audiences' feelings and behaviors. The story rhetoric tells is always a story with a purpose; it is never told for its own sake.

Given our definition of rhetoric above, every rhetorical task involves five basic moves: (1) the rhetor tries to exert change by using **symbols** (verbal and nonverbal communication) rather than nonsymbolic forces (like guns or torture); (2) the rhetor must come to be regarded as a **helper** rather than an exploiter; (3) the rhetor must convince the audience that new **choices** be made; (4) the rhetor must **narrow** the audience's options for making these choices, even though (5) the rhetor may become subtle by not **specifying** the details of the policies advocated.

Thus, the user of rhetoric peddles choices, even though most people naturally resist making choices unless forced to do so. And if forced to do so, people also naturally resist having their search for a solution prematurely constrained by someone else. So persuasion takes work: The rhetor must "help" without appearing gauche or paternalistic and the rhetor must establish that the world is not yet fundamentally right (hence requiring new choice-making by the audience) but that it can soon be set right by making the (narrowed) choice the rhetor endorses.

The average TV commercial tells this tale a thousand times daily, with Young Heterosexual being driven to insecurity (and choice) by the desire to make the Best First Impression on Ideal Romantic Partner. Knowing Voiceover arrives on the scene with the perfect answer in a pack of new Narrowed Choice gum. Lust proceeds on its merry course, we are led to believe, and choice-making recedes into the background until Unmanageable Hair strikes fifteen minutes later. Not all persuasion is this predictable, of course, but all of it involves the art of managing choices.

If rhetoric is an art, it is an art that sometimes differs from the arts of poetry and painting. It is an art with these characteristics:

1. *A cooperative art*. Rhetoric is an art that brings rhetors and audiences together. It cannot be done in solitude. To speak by oneself in a closet is of course possible but hardly normal. Rhetoric makes little sense unless it is made for others. After all, the reactions of other people will be its measure: their votes, their purchases, their conversions, their affection. And so rhetoric is a transactive art because it brings two or more people together in an atmosphere of potential change.

   By sharing communication, both rhetors and audiences open themselves up to each other's influence. In that sense, communication is not something that is *done* to others. Rather, it is something that people choose to do to themselves by consenting to communicative contact. By agreeing to rhetorical exchange, says Arnold [1972:16], people acknowledge their dependence upon one another. In the world of rhetoric, a rhetor succeeds only when he or she can induce an audience to "contribute" their knowledge, feelings, and experiences about the matter in question. The rhetorical critic studies such invitations to cooperate.

2. *A people's art*. Rhetoric is an ordinary art. Its standards of excellence are the standards of ordinary people. Rhetoric is rarely as graceful or as lilting as poetry because the people for whom it is made are too busy to bother with grace and lilt. Rhetoric works within the constraints of everyday logic. The heroes in rhetorical history are people like Louisiana populist Huey Long, who severely mangled the King's English whenever he spoke but who was loved by his constituents because of it, not in spite of it. Rhetoric is often neither pretty nor fetching, although it can be both. At times it is even heavy-handed, although it tries never to be seen as such. At its best, rhetoric is ordinary language done extraordinarily.

3. *A temporary art*. Normally, rhetoric is rooted in the age of its creation. The people who create rhetoric speak today's language, not yesterday's. Such rhetors use time-bound examples, time-bound statistics, time-bound jargon, caring little how it will sound tomorrow. That is why most of the rhetoric we hear each day sounds more like James Walsh's than Abraham Lincoln's. Or, more precisely, that is why only one or two of Lincoln's speeches continue to be re-read today. The remainder of his speeches dealt with issues and personalities that no longer concern us. Only on a few occasions did he turn rhetoric into poetry. Like the Dalai Lama, Lincoln knew that most rhetoric was meant to be consumed, not savored.

4. *A limited art*. As Bitzer [1968] reminds us, rhetoric is only deployed when it can make a difference. Rhetoric cannot really move mountains, which is why so few people stand at the bases of mountains to orate. Similarly, for years Palestinians could not move Israelis by speaking to them and that is why, sadly, they often did not try. Neither of these situations was "rhetorical" in Bitzer's sense because human discourse could not seem to change them. Rhetoric can do much, but it cannot do everything.

5. *A frustrating art.* There are no laws of rhetoric. There are important guidelines but little else. To be effective in persuasion one must cultivate a sensitivity to what the ancient Greeks called *kairos:* the ability to use the right argument and the deft phrase at precisely the right time. As Miller [2002:xii] notes, *kairos* is the principle of timely, creative response to the particular situation as well as "adaptation and accommodation to convention, expectation and predictability." When deciding what to say, the rhetor always swims in a sea of uncertainty because (1) people normally argue only about uncertain matters (e.g., Should gay marriage be permitted?) rather than about that which is fixed (e.g., the inevitability of death) and because (2) people are so complex, so changeful, and so ornery about so many matters. Thus, when thumping for more funding for the space shuttle, a NASA spokesperson must often leave the best scientific arguments at home because it is ordinary citizens and their representatives, not scientists, who fund space missions. Rhetoric, then, deals with the probable, the best case that can be made under limited circumstances. It is used to decide the undecided question and to solve the unsolved problem [Bryant, 1972:20–1]. People talk when they can think of nothing else to do but feel that they must do something.

6. *A generative art.* Contemporary writers [e.g., Cherwitz and Darwin, 1995] tell us that rhetoric produces most of what passes for everyday knowledge. They claim that rhetoric helps us learn what other people think (e.g., whether or not space funding should be increased) and also to learn our *own* minds about things (e.g., the old saying that one never really knows something until one can teach it to someone else). By arguing with one another we produce what is called social knowledge, which determines much in human affairs.

Today in the United States, for example, witches are no longer burned, African Americans are no longer limited to plantation employment, and Japanese Americans are no longer interned. But in other eras, *when other arguments prevailed,* such "truths" were taken for granted and, more important, were used as the basis for social policy. So rhetoric never produces True Truth. It produces partial truth, truth for these times and these people. As Johnstone [1969:408] says, "the only way to tell whether what I have is a truth or a falsehood is to contemplate its evocative power," that is, its power to secure the agreement of others. And lest we think that such social knowledge is not really knowledge, we need only reflect upon the comparatively recent history of witches, African Americans, and Japanese Americans.

The Range of Rhetoric

One way of understanding rhetoric is to consider what it is and what it is not or, better, *how much* of a thing it is and *how much* of another thing it is not. In Figure 7.1, "the rhetorical" is depicted as an area bordering on other domains but one that is nonetheless special. For example, rhetoric resembles science in that both the scientist and the rhetor want to be taken seriously. The persuader wants the audience to believe that calamity will in fact strike unless the rhetor's warnings are heeded. Like the scientist, the persuader marshalls evidence (e.g., the testimony of experts, certain statistical trends, etc.), uses this evidence to comment upon some real, not imagined, feature of the observable world (e.g., "overpopulation will inundate the infrastructure of this city"), and then employs this package of arguments to support a policy recommendation (e.g., "we must put an immediate moratorium on building permits"). But even though both the scientist and the persuader seek to make things demonstrably true, the persuader is willing to treat the perceptions of *ordinary people* as the acid test of demonstratedness. The scientist, in contrast, normally is expected to meet a more exacting standard of truth (empirical verifiability, the judgments of experts,

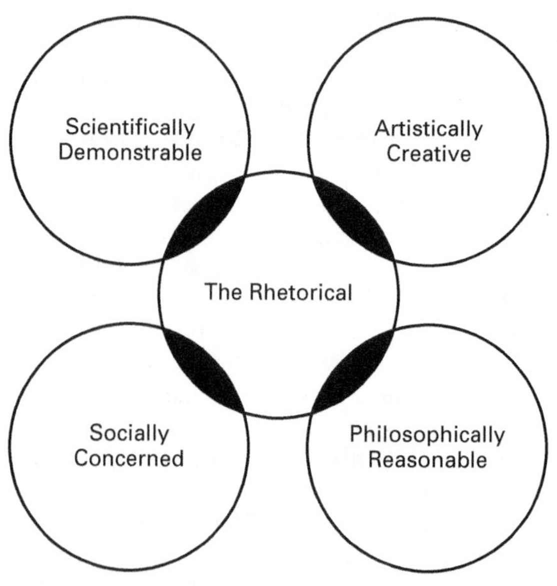

Figure 7.1
Realm of the Rhetorical

experimental replication, etc.), while the persuader's truth is often fifty-one percent truth: the majority judgment of ordinary citizens. For most persuaders on most issues, fifty-one percent truth is sufficient.

As we have mentioned above, the persuader, like the poet, is artistically creative. Both use symbols to breathe life into ideas. Neither uses tangible tools (like pick axes) to change tangible phenomena (like rocks). Rather, both the artist and the persuader use their imaginations to engage their audience's imaginations. But as we have noted before, the persuader's creativity is often exercised in behalf of decidedly short-term gains (i.e., assent on the particular issue at hand) and the persuader, because he or she is a "narrower," is unlikely to give an audience the intellectual freedom normally permitted them by the artist. It is also true that the imagination of the persuader is not likely to be as uncontrolled as that of the traditional artist because, as we have said, rhetoric is a *social* art. It does little good for the rhetor to take flights of fancy unless the audience can come along as well.

The persuader also tries to be philosophically reasonable, to insure that an argument makes the kind of *patterned* sense that will be understood by others. The rhetor typically avoids the incomplete mental image, the sudden self-interruption, or the discordant use of language that lends excitement to more purely artistic endeavors. It is also true, however, that the persuader typically uses what works and is less scrupulous in argumentation than the philosopher. The rhetor uses, in Aristotle's terms, all the means of argument available, not just those recommended in the logic books.

There is a special logic to persuasion, a psycho-logic, and it is to these informal methods of reasoning that the practical rhetor most often pays homage. Thus, as Morrison [1992] points out, it even makes "sense" at times for rhetors (e.g., GLBT, or Gay/Lesbian/Bisexual/Transgendered folks) to challenge accepted categories of sexual identity in order to shock audiences into "queer" ways of seeing and being. The logic of persuasion is sometimes a curious logic.

Finally, the persuader is socially concerned, at least in part. The persuader is a public person, seeking to change not just one life but many lives. When abandoning solitude, the persuader promises that many people's lives will be improved in some important way. But the persuader is not a social worker. As McGee [1975] says, persuaders present *their* versions of what "the people" believe, often taking great liberties with public opinion when doing so. Thus, the persuader's social concern is limited to his or her private version of the ideal life, a life in which everyone owns a Dodge truck or votes a straight Socialist ticket. The persuader wants to make a particular kind of change, a public change. Those who dream social dreams need the aid of others.

Because it borders on so many worlds, the realm of rhetoric is powerful. The rhetor draws upon each of these worlds and yet steps back from each simultaneously, seeking to become a poet, but a poet of practical consequences, a scientist, but a scientist unencumbered by footnotes. The persuader also becomes an easygoing logician and a social worker with an eye on the bottom line. By blending these roles skillfully as, say, Hillary Rodham Clinton did when serving as First Lady, persuaders become highly influential. For this reason alone they bear watching. Watching them is the job of the rhetorical critic.

The definition of rhetoric provided above is obviously a generous definition, one designed to encompass a variety of messages. Included within this broad definition would be the television docudrama, the cooing of lovers on a park bench, the scientific treatise, the invocation at the City Council meeting, the reprimand from the boss at work, the presidential address, the college lecture, the adolescent's whining during dinner, the blockbuster movie, the top sergeant's welcome to boot camp, the sermon from the pulpit, the Diet Coke commercial, the psychiatrist's counseling session, and much else.

All of these situations require the use of language and all of them can result in both obvious and nonobvious forms of influence. Indeed, it is a hallmark of the critical perspective that all messages be examined carefully, *especially* those that seem to lie outside the realm of rhetoric. The most basic job of the rhetorical critic is to be able to discover *when* rhetoric is being used in the first place. Persuaders, after all, do not always own up to their profession. Often, they would like to be mistaken for a scientist or a poet or a philosopher. By keeping a sharp eye peeled for the essential features of rhetoric, however, the critic can discover when rhetoric has come to call.

Normally, three features make a message rhetorical: (1) **delineations of the good,** (2) **resonance for a particular audience,** and (3) **clear or clearly implied policy recommendations.** (We conceive "policy" here in its broadest sense, including proposals of marriage, requests for repentance, voter solicitations, and much else.)

For example, Table 7.1 presents three similar-yet-different lists of events ranging from the obviously rhetorical to the less obviously rhetorical. As

Table 7.1
Types of Rhetorical Events

Messages	More Obviously Rhetorical	Ambiguous	Less Obviously Rhetorical
Photographs	An Appalachian shack	The White House	A South Sea hut
Telephone call	From Handicapped Workers of America	From a son at college	From a rich friend
Drama	Guerrilla theatre	Off-Broadway drama	Broadway musical
Signs	On a highway billboard	At an hourly parking lot	On a restroom door
Commercials	About hamburgers from Wendy's Restaurants	About drugs from the National Basketball Association	About Picasso from the National Museum of Art
Magazines	*Michigan Militia Report*	*Harper's*	*Time*
Guided tours	At Budweiser plant	At Lincoln Memorial	At Yellowstone National Park
Humor	Political jokes	Ethnic jokes	Animal jokes
Poetry	Langston Hughes	Wallace Stevens	E.E. Cummings
Trip directions	From Big Al to his car lot	From a new boyfriend to his lake cabin	From Rand McNally to Salt Lake City
Statistics	From International Association of Oil Producers	From Mobil Oil Corp.	From U.S. Department of Energy
Music	Folk songs	Church hymns	Rhythm and blues
Football	Halftime pep talk	TV color commentary	Cheerleaders' cheers
Storytelling	Religious testimonials	Folklore	Fairy tales

one moves from right to left, notice how the events change in subtle yet important ways, increasingly lending themselves to more immediate and powerful rhetorical uses. In the case of the photographs, for example, it is not hard to imagine how the picture of an Appalachian shack could be used in the hands of a community activist seeking federal funding. Such a picture presents a special invitation to the viewer to think *now* about matters of right and wrong. The fact that this is an "American" shack makes Americans especially uncomfortable because it calls into question certain aspects of the national dream. Perhaps because of this audience resonance, policy recommendations seem to jump out of the picture for many Americans ("Let us put a stop to this kind of poverty" or "Why don't those people get a job and live better?").

The picture of the White House is more ambiguous. One can imagine the photograph being used in patriotic ways in the United States ("the seat of our democracy") and quite differently by hardliners in Iran ("lair of the Great Satan"). It could be used for comedic effect on Comedy Central ("The Prez's house") or for purely crass boosterism on a multicolored flyer ("Bring your convention to Washington. Hotel rates have never been lower").

The South Sea hut, in contrast, might lend itself to any number of case-makings. Previous rhetoric in the U.S. culture, at least, seems not to have marked it yet for special use and hence the image makes fewer immediate and specific demands on us. (Should it be used for a travel brochure? In connection with religious missionary work? As a symbol of exploitation in the developing world?)

As one moves from right to left in Table 7.1, one gets the feeling that (1) the rhetor's exact purposes for persuasion become less ambiguous, (2) perhaps as a result, the emotions of the rhetor lie increasingly close to the surface, (3) increasingly specific "policies" are being recommended to the audience or at least broadly hinted at ("Give now," "Follow the Word"), (4) the question of essential good and evil has become less of a question, and (5) finding an "ideal audience" for the message would become easier because fewer and fewer people can fill the bill as the rhetoric heats up. In short, as we move from right to left, things become more rhetorical.

This is not to say, of course, that we should turn our backs on less obvious rhetoric. Indeed, critics have become increasingly interested in these subtler messages precisely because most people (that is, most potential audience members) are oblivious to the *hints* of good and evil or *implied* policy recommendations buried within them. Thus, for example, critics have looked at painting as rhetorical action [Helmers, 2001], at sanitized racism in letters-to-the-editor [Lacy, 1992], and at U.S. memorial sites as evidence that rhetoric requires material form [Blair, 1999]. Throughout this chapter, we will look for rhetoric in all of its haunts and hideaways.

The Functions of Rhetoric

Thus far, we have discussed what rhetoric is and what it is not, where it can be found, and what shapes it takes. It now remains for us to examine what rhetoric *does,* how it functions in human society. Of course, we will be studying the uses of rhetoric throughout this chapter but here, briefly, we can examine some of its less frequently noticed uses.

1. *Rhetoric unburdens.* People make rhetoric because they must get something off their chests, because the cause they champion overwhelms their natural reticence. Rhetors refuse to let history take its slow, evolutionary course and instead try to become part of history themselves. The history they make may be quite local in character (e.g., picketing a neighborhood abortion clinic), but rhetorical people typically do not hang back. They sense that the world around them is not yet set and so they approach it aggressively, often convinced that they can make a difference, always convinced that they must try.

Savoy magazine, which catered to an upscale African American readership, added activist/comedian/entrepreneur/actor Dick Gregory to its "Hall of Fame," citing the following rationale:

> Because he's the only man we know who has run for president *and* shined shoes. . . . Because when he got his girlfriend Lil pregnant, he married her because his mama said he should, and he has stayed married for 43 years. Because he made white folks laugh at their own foibles and prejudices until their sides ached. Because he lived by his beliefs, even when the price was his freedom. . . . Because his failed campaign for mayor of Chicago paved the way for a young Carl Stokes, the nation's first black mayor of a major city. . . . Because he had the audacity to name his book *Nigger* and then invited white folks to "take a *Nigger* home tonight." Because he embodied The Movement. [2001–2002: 34]

This list catalogues a range of historical and contemporary values of African American culture. The rhetor is confident that readers will respond to the familial appeal, addressing African Americans as an extended family in need of preservation ("mama said he should," "white folks" as outsiders). Politically, the rhetor takes for granted a shared commitment to uplifting the race (paving the way for a black mayor) and achieving social justice (being imprisoned for one's beliefs, "The Movement"). The conservative emphasis on marriage is contrasted with the belief that at times, one should behave audaciously in order to shock and draw attention to oppression ("take a *Nigger* home tonight"). Different as they are, however, each sentence asserts without qualification or apology. In order to see oneself in this target audience, the reader is expected, even required, to approve of each item listed.

In a sense, then, communication is a kind of presumptuous imposition on other people. When A tries to persuade B, for example, A affirms that (1) something is wrong in B's world and (2) that A can fix it. Thus, if it is true that the poet is an escapist, it is also true that the rhetor is an infiltrator. Naturally, the arrogance of the rhetorical act is normally well disguised by the practicing persuader who is, after all, only there to "help" ("You owe it to *yourself* to sign this contract," "The *disabled* do indeed appreciate your contribution"). Still, a rhetorical engagement is no less intrusive just because its intrusions have been camouflaged.

2. *Rhetoric distracts.* When speaking, a rhetor wants to have all, not just some, of our attention. To get that attention, the rhetor must so fill up our minds that we forget, temporarily at least, the other ideas, people, and policies important to us. Naturally, we do not give our attention freely, so it takes rhetoric at its best to sidetrack us. One way of doing so is for the rhetor to control the premises of a discussion. As McCombs and Shaw [1972] demonstrated some years ago, the power of the mass media derives not so much from their ability to tell us what to think but what to think about. When choosing to report on industrial lead poisoning, for example, a

local T.V. station simultaneously chooses *not* to cover the crowning of the Peach Queen or the win-loss record of the local Double A farm club. By "setting the agenda" in this fashion, by controlling the premises pertaining to newsworthiness, the media can thus influence any conclusions drawn from those premises.

Similarly, in his study of military training camp "jodies," or work songs, Knight [1990] discovered that they did more than simply help the time pass on a long march. By examining jodies as a rhetorical performance, Knight illustrated that these deceptively simple songs served to socialize young men to kill without hesitation or remorse. So the rhetor asks the audience to think about this topic, not that one, to try out this solution, not that endorsed by the rhetor's opponent. In this sense, rhetoric operates like a good map. Maps, after all, have a distinctive point of view: They "favor" interstate highways (by coloring them a bright red) over rural roads (often a pale blue); they emphasize urban areas (blotched in yellow) over small towns (tiny dots); they adapt their appeals to vacationers (by highlighting Yosemite) rather than to truckers (no diners are listed). Like the rhetor, the roadmap bristles with integrity, implying by the precision of its drawings that it provides the complete story: all the highway news that's fit to print.

Rhetoric, too, tries to narrow our latitudes of choice without giving us the feeling that we are being thereby hemmed in. Rhetoric tries to control the *definition* we provide for a given activity ("Your church offering isn't a monetary loss; it's a down payment on heaven") as well as the *criteria* we employ to solve a problem ("Abortion is not a religious issue; it's a legal one"). By also emphasizing one rhetor *category* over another (e.g., George W. Bush as commander-in-chief vs. George W. Bush as failed entrepreneur), persuaders invite us to focus on this and not that, on here and not there, on now and not then.

3. *Rhetoric enlarges.* In some senses, modern persuaders are like the heralds of old. They move among us singing the siren song of change, asking us to consider a new solution to an old problem (or an old solution to a problem of which we were unaware). Rhetoric operates, then, like a kind of intellectual algebra, asking us to equate things we had never before considered equatable. Thus, for example, Adolph Hitler rose to fame (and infamy) by linking German nationalism with increased militarism and Germany's economic woes with Jewish clannishness. These were corrupt equations but for him they were useful ones.

Often, the **associations** encouraged by rhetoric are no less sophisticated, or honorable, than those created by Adolph Hitler. Nevertheless, these linkages are the workhorses of persuasion. So, for example, some manufacturers of personal computers now virtually assure unwary parents that computing skills will translate instantly into educational achievement for their children. It is interesting to note that persuaders rarely ask for major expansion of their audiences' worldviews. They imply that only a slight modification is in order. Persuasion moves by increments of inches.

Often, persuaders **disassociate** ideas in order to expand the viewpoints of their audiences. So, for example, Bankamericard changed its name to Visa in the early 1970s so that the more international flavor of the new name would offset the growing anti-Americanism found in Western Europe at the time. Similarly, American Indian writers have used what Powell [2002] calls "rhetorics of survivance" (a combination of survival and resistance). Such writers adopt the contemporary ways of speaking about Indian-ness and yet respond to those ideas critically, in order to "reimagine what it could mean to be Indian" [p. 396]. It becomes the persuader's task to demonstrate that any such alterations are a natural extension of thoughts and feelings the audience *already* possesses and that any such new notions can be easily accommodated within the audience's *existing* repertoire of ideas. That is why rhetoric is called an art.

4. *Rhetoric names.* To understand the power of rhetoric we must remember that creatures and non-creatures alike (people, frogs, rocks, bicycles) are born without labels. People are, as best we know, nature's only namers. And they name things with a vengeance: Newman's Own Spaghetti Sauce; Sri Lanka; black holes; the Utah Jazz; Nirvana. People take their naming seriously: Newly enfranchised Americans have anglicized their names to ward off discrimination; professional women have retained their original surnames to avoid being seen as the property of their mates; and the fate of captured Taliban and Al Qaeda "detainees" hung on whether they were considered "prisoners of war" and therefore protected under international law.

No doubt, naming is as important as it is because meaning is such a variable thing. A tornado-ravaged town, after all, is but wind and torment until it is publicly labeled by the appropriate official as a

"Federal Disaster Area." Some executions spawn massive religious movements (e.g., the death of Jesus Christ) or excite political passions (e.g., that of Oklahoma City bomber Timothy McVeigh), while other executions are met with mere curiosity (e.g., that of Gary Gillmore, the first person to be executed in recent times). The facts in each of these capital punishment cases were different, of course, but so too was the rhetorical skill of the partisans who labeled the executions.

The naming function of rhetoric helps audiences become comfortable with new ideas and provides audiences with an acceptable vocabulary for talking about these ideas. Through rhetoric, "white flight schools" are transformed into "independent academies," "labor-baiting" becomes the "right-to-work," a "fetus" is seen as an "unborn child," "suicide" is replaced by "death with dignity," and a vague assemblage of disconnected thoughts and random social trends is decried as "secular humanism." A major challenge for the rhetorical critic, then, is to study how namers name things and how audiences respond to the names they hear.

5. *Rhetoric empowers.* Whom does it empower? Traditionally, the answer to this question has been "public speakers." Western rhetors, those with the political power in their culture, have often tended to be already privileged in a variety of ways by virtue of being white, heterosexual, male, and economically secure. As a result, rhetoric (especially public address) has been blamed for the oppression of women and poor people of all races, and men of color as well. This led to dialogue among several feminist rhetoricians. Condit [1997], Foss, Griffin, and Foss [1997], and Downey [1997] articulated and disputed claims about the extent to which rhetoric requires cooperation (a value often identified with feminism), whether definitions of "eloquence" needed broadening, and the centrality of interdependence to our understandings of rhetoric, gender, and feminism.

Those who decry the art of rhetoric sometimes do so because its users embrace many truths, not just one. Traditionally, teachers of rhetoric have encouraged us to consider alternative modes of expressing ourselves and not to just settle on the first thought that comes to mind. This attitude sometimes brings censure to rhetoric. Those who embrace absolute standards of right and wrong have always had problems with rhetoric because, above all, rhetoric encourages flexibility. Flexibility, in turn, provides options: to address one audience or several; to mention an idea or avoid it; to say something this way, not that way; to tell all one knows or only just a bit; to repeat oneself or to vary one's response. Rhetoric encourages flexibility because it is based on a kind of symbolic Darwinism: (1) rhetors who do not adapt to their surroundings quickly become irrelevant; (2) ideas that become frozen soon die for want of social usefulness.

Such flexibility, in turn, permits continual growth, for the individual as well as for society. Rhetorical theorists contend that the possible ways of making an idea clear are as numerous as the potential audiences to receive them [Hart and Burks, 1972]. Moreover, because it encourages adaptability, rhetoric permits personal evolution for rhetors as well. Both 1960s feminist Gloria Steinem and consumer advocate Ralph Nader continued to be prominent in later decades not because they changed their beliefs fundamentally, but because they found new *ways* of telling their truths as they matured.

Social power, then, often derives from rhetorical strength. Grand ideas, deeply felt beliefs, and unsullied ideologies are sources of power too but, as Plato told us, none of these factors can be influential without a delivery system, without rhetoric. Purity of heart and a spotless record for integrity are assets to a political rhetor but they are hardly enough to sustain a campaign unless those qualities are *shared* with the voters. As Bryant [1972:23] remarks, if they are to be used with confidence "a bridge or an automobile or a clothes-line must not only *be* strong but must *appear* to be."

6. *Rhetoric elongates.* What does rhetoric make longer? Time. Time, that most precious of all substances, can be extended—or, more accurately, seems to be extended—when rhetoric is put to use. Consider the Reverend Martin Luther King, Jr. When he spoke at the March on Washington in 1963, King certainly knew that civil rights laws would not be enacted just because he mounted the public platform. *But King succeeded in making the future seem to be the present* because his appeals reached so deeply into people's souls and because his futuristic images were painted so vividly: "I have a dream. . .that one day, right here in Alabama, little black boys and black girls will be able to join hands with little white boys and white girls as sisters and brothers. I have a dream today!" [King, 1964:374].

Naturally, King's speeches did not cause immediate legal and social changes. But for his followers, the devastations of the past commanded less of their attention when they listened to him describe future possibilities. In his presence, audiences lingered in the future and felt better because of it. As Hart [1984a:764] says, rhetoric can become a "way station for the patient."

Most persuaders sell the future when trying to move audiences to a better place, a happier circumstance. Whether it is robust health through Herbalife, a slimmer figure with Healthy Choice, or tax cuts with George W. Bush, rhetoric transports us, momentarily at least, across the boundaries of time. Admittedly, this is a kind of surrogate or false reality. But genuinely effective rhetoric makes such criticisms of literal falseness seem small-minded. When tempted with visions of untold wealth via Amway or a glorious afterlife via Jesus, many people relax their guards.

It is also true that rhetoric can be used to appropriate the *past.* When doing so, of course, skilled persuaders do some historical housecleaning. Thus, as Warner [1976] tells us, most patriotic celebrations in the United States omit from their oratory stories of ethnic or religious persecution. Rhetors on such occasions steer clear of these unquestionable historical facts because ceremonial rhetoric has its own upbeat story to tell. Rhetoric tells a *selective* history, taking us back in time for a brief, heavily edited tour of that which was. But as the good eulogist knows, not everything about the dearly departed needs to be told at the funeral. The eulogist reminds us of the deceased's grandest virtues, his or her most endearing qualities, because only the best of the past can make the present seem less tragic. So, while rhetoric often tells literal lies, most of us would have it no other way.

Conclusion

In this chapter, we covered the essentials of rhetoric. We have seen that rhetoric has a combination of features not found in other creative arts like painting and music and poetry. Rhetoric's creations are practical creations and because they are the creations of real people living in the real world, rhetoric is a controversial thing to study. Many people do not like rhetoric, which is to say, they like their own rhetoric best. But human beings have little choice but to use and respond to rhetoric if they wish the world to be different than it is. Jonas Salk may have invented a vaccine for polio but no further vaccines will be discovered at the Salk Institute unless its fundraising goes well. Neal Armstrong may have set foot on the moon but he was permitted to do so only because congressional arms were twisted by the space lobby in the United States. Similarly, those Americans who enjoy riding on an interstate highway system or watching rock videos should thank the structural and acoustic engineers who made such marvels possible but they should thank, too, the rhetorical engineers whose persuasive appeals generated the funding needed to nurture those inventions along.

So rhetoric is with us, for both good and ill. It is with us because most worthwhile ideas come from groups of people working in concert. For religions to thrive there must be apostles. For ideas to be understood there must be teachers. For justice to be served there must be lawyers. To turn our backs on rhetoric would be to turn our backs on the sharing of ideas and hence any practical notion of human community. So rhetoric is with us because it must be with us.

Tips for the Practicing Critic

1. Although some argue that "everything is rhetorical," a definition that excludes nothing is useless. Certainly, every message has some element(s) that may be interpreted as rhetorical. Determine whether the message in question fits our working definition.
2. After determining that the piece of discourse meets these definitional standards, try to isolate elements in the text (specific words and phrases, structural placement/order of ideas, ways of referring to self and intended audience, etc.) that illustrate the rhetor's purpose and/or bias.
3. Note that in the analysis of the Dalai Lama's message, we focused on what was most important *in this situation and at this time.* Rather than *simply* reading the text, noting its flaws, and concluding that it "needs editing," the critic takes into account the emotional power of the essay. This far outweighed any minor editorial problems, which were probably not even noticeable to its intended readers. Keep in mind that close reading of the text is necessary, but not sufficient, for good criticism. Be sure to "step back" and look at the different situational elements of the message. At different times, different features of the message and its environment carry more persuasive force.

BUILDING COMMUNICATION SKILLS

Tips for the Practicing Critic

1. Although some argue that "everything is rhetorical," a definition that excludes nothing is useless. Certainly, every message has some element(s) that may be interpreted as rhetorical. But in early critical work, it will be best to determine whether the message in question fits our working definition.
2. After determining that the piece of discourse meets these definitional standards, try to isolate elements in the text (specific words and phrases, structural placement/order of ideas, ways of referring to self and intended audience, etc.) that illustrate the rhetor's purpose and/or bias.
3. Note that in the analysis of the Dalai Lama's message, we focused on what was most important *in this situation and at this time.* Rather than *simply* reading the text, noting its flaws, and concluding that it "needs editing," the critic takes into account the emotional power of the essay. This far outweighed any minor editorial problems, which were probably not even noticeable to its intended readers. Keep in mind that close reading of the text is necessary, but not sufficient, for good criticism. Be sure to "step back" and look at the different situational elements of the message. At different times, different features of the message and its environment carry more persuasive force.

Rhetoric and Persuasion: An Introduction to Argument and the Rhetorical Situation*

The process of identity formation is largely about the struggle to control our meaning, to construct an identity consonant with our values, and to defend that identity against the misinterpretations and misappropriations of others. We are assaulted on a daily basis by various pitches for readymade identities proffered by advertisers, employers, writers, and propagandists. While these appeals often come disguised as information, entertainment, advice, or recommendations to purchase a good or service, they all promise to transform us. In this regard, the process of identity formation exemplifies all rhetorical processes. How I go about defining and defending my sense of self is not significantly different from how I go about defining and defending my sense of "justice" or "the good." In fact how I define justice and the good is a remarkably good indicator of my self-definition. And my capacity to resist, oppose, and entertain divergent beliefs—to understand my ways of talking about the world "in terms of" alternative ways of talking about the world—is a fundamental expression of my humanity.

Why Persuasion Matters Today

Our identity has not always been such a problematic matter. While our incorrigible tendency to go astray, a condition known to our Puritan ancestors as "innate depravity," has always meant that we might lose our souls, our essences, our citizenship, our membership in a family or community, or whatever other status fixed our identities, we were assured a reasonably unproblematic existence so long as we "behaved" by observing the laws and conventions appropriate to our place in a fixed order. Absent a fixed order that assigns everything a value, meanwhile, we are free to construct and choose our identities; but with that freedom comes the necessity of evaluating and negotiating our options. Which means in turn that our beliefs, values, relationships, status, and all the things that matter most deeply to us are also subject to negotiation and evaluation.

Obviously, not everyone would agree with this conclusion. Many people subscribe to systems of belief that, for them at least, fulfill the role of the old fixed orders in laying out their priorities and defining their choices. None of these systems is, however, universally subscribed to and there are few if any places left on earth where the inhabitants may freely ignore the alternatives. No matter how secure people may be in their faith that their particular system

*The following material taken from *Rhetoric: A User's Guide* by John D. Ramage.

is absolute and universal, no matter how strongly they may believe that everyone *ought* to join them in subscribing to their particular doctrine, getting others who do not share their beliefs to cooperate with them—and some form of cooperation is always required—or to adopt their beliefs means they must either use force or persuasion. And as recent history amply illustrates, when dominant belief systems attempt either to ignore alternative belief systems or to coerce them into compliance with their own, they pay a very high price for their intolerance. As media, modern transport, and the globalization of commerce combine to shrink the world, we have little choice but to acknowledge alternative belief systems and to take them into account in making decisions. Increasingly, matters that were once determined by authority now must be submitted to discussion and negotiation.

Rhetoric as a Pluralistic, versus Relativistic, Activity

For some people, the above description of the world might be dismissed as "relativism," a doctrine with which, as we've seen, rhetoric has long been associated. But relativism involves more than the disavowal of one absolute value system and a tolerance for multiple belief systems. Relativism also holds that it is impossible to "converse" across belief systems, that the denizens of different belief systems cannot modify each other's views, and that it's futile to try. Moreover, relativism also leaves open the possibility that each individual may constitute an independent, autonomous belief system, leaving each one of us free to pursue our own interests, under no obligation to accommodate others' interests or to reconcile our ends with anyone else's. (Ironically, the proponents of rugged individualism, a form of relativism on stilts that might with equal justice be termed "brawny subjectivism," are among those most exercised by the specter of relativism—or at least by everyone else's relativism but their own.) If rhetoric really were reducible to relativism, it would be a tawdry business indeed. But it's not. First of all, rhetoric can't be reduced to any sort of radical subjectivism (formerly known as solipsism) because of its inherently social nature. A rhetorician espousing radical subjectivism makes as little sense as a pope espousing atheism. To the extent that either were successful, they would soon be out of jobs; in the first instance, people would no longer have a motive to communicate with others whose reality was, after all, chimerical, while in the second instance, people would no longer have a need for an institution to intercede on their behalf with a deity who didn't exist. Moreover, even less radical forms of subjectivism are incompatible with the inner dynamic of rhetoric. As we've seen, truth for rhetoric can't be reduced to an agreement between a word in my head and a thing in the world. Truth for rhetoric is a public matter requiring agreement among people. Indeed, the most fundamental motive for practicing rhetoric is to achieve identification across differences of class, race, gender, nationality, ideology, age, or any of the other numberless ways we have devised to divide ourselves up categorically. Which is why Kenneth Burke sometimes characterizes persuasion as courtship, whereby we use all manner of guile in the amorous pursuit of the Other, an endeavor at once morbidly self-interested and gloriously selfless. Burke's metaphor transforms difference from a disability into a virtue—"Vive la difference!"—and a goad to identification.

Given its thoroughly social basis, rhetoric can more accurately be described as pluralistic rather than relativistic. Because of their mutual opposition to absolutism, pluralism and relativism are sometimes confused, but while relativism emphasizes the differences among individuals and classes of peoples, pluralism emphasizes the commonalities. Because of this emphasis, pluralism holds out the possibility that different "sorts" of people may achieve identification with one another and thereby tolerate each others' differences in the name of cooperation. But in saying that categorical differences among people may be bridged in a pluralist world, we are not suggesting that people will be less passionate in their commitment to their faiths and beliefs, or less ardent about proselytizing on behalf of those beliefs. In a pluralist world, people simply accept that there is no universal court of appeal in which they can prove the rightness of their position, no master vocabulary that will assign *their* meanings to the world. Unless we are willing to impose our views on others by force, we have to work out among ourselves views that are mutually acceptable and represent us as fully as possible in a given circumstance. Truths arrived at through such a process, while they may not be absolute or universal, are not capricious or subjective in the way that relativist truths may be.

In the best of all possible worlds, rhetoric would be unnecessary because human beings would recognize their fundamental kinship and arrive automatically at conclusions that best harmonized their superficial differences. In the worst of all possible worlds—and here we have considerably more experience to draw on—rhetoric would be useless because right would be determined by might. Any given system of belief would be as absolute and universal as the power possessed by those subscribing to the system. Those critical of rhetoric tend to contrast its ways to those that would prevail in the best of all possible worlds; those supportive of rhetoric tend to contrast its ways to the ways that would prevail in the worst of all possible worlds. Rhetoric viewed as an alternative to force and coercion is considerably more attractive than rhetoric viewed as an alternative to sweet reasonableness. To borrow an epigram from Kenneth Burke's *A Rhetoric of Motives,* rhetoric understood in the first way is dedicated *ad bellum purificandum,* "to the purification of war." Recognizing the inevitability of difference, competition, even enmity among people who live "in the state of Babel after the Fall"(ROM, 23) Burke uses rhetoric to transcend strife and transform it into dialectic. Wars are won by transforming enemies into casualties; wars are "purified" by transforming those same enemies into interlocutors.

The Conceptual Range of Persuasion: From Coercion to Pure Persuasion

So let us start from the perspective of rhetoric as an alternative to coercion and an old joke. The late comedian Jack Benny was famous for his skinflint ways. Much of his humor centered on his unwillingness to spend or loan money. In one particular comedy sketch on his weekly TV show, Jack is locked out of his house, peering in through a window to see if he can get his wife, Mary, to let him in. Suddenly a masked man appears and sticks a gun in Benny's back: "Your money or your life!" he barks. A lengthy silence ensues. Benny looks thoughtfully upward. More time passes.

> "I said, 'Your money or your *life!*' " the robber demands, this time more loudly.
>
> "I'm *thinking!* I'm *thinking!*" Benny sputters at last.

The crux of the joke lies in the fact that Benny hears a proposition where virtually any rational person would hear a command. For Benny, the gunman is offering up for his consideration a claim of the sort Aristotle called "deliberative" involving a decision about some future—and the future is now in this case—action. Clearly the speaker/gunman favors the course of action in which Benny gives up his money, hence his prominent use of a persuasive tool touted by Chinese leader Mao Tse-tung, who once opined that truth is most reliably found "at the end of a gun." From a rhetorical standpoint, the weakness of the gunman's argument lies in his failure to account for the unorthodox views about life and money of his immediate audience. For the miserly Benny, the two possess roughly equal value, thereby neutralizing the gunman's most forceful persuasive appeal. Presumably, as he stands there with his hands raised, a gun in his ribs, Benny is busily "proving opposites" in his head, working out the costs and benefits for each of his two choices for future action.

What this joke illustrates is the sometimes blurry line separating persuasion from coercion. What distinguishes the above case from most cases where the line between the two is blurred has to do with the direction of the confusion. It's not typically the audience who transforms overt acts of coercion into persuasive appeals; it's typically the speaker/author who sets about masking coercion as persuasion. Coercion, when it takes the form of a symbolic act, relies primarily on the suppression of alternatives. In its strongest form it presents as fait accompli, necessary, or inevitable what is in reality contingent and subject to human agency. It turns "could" into "must" or "should" or "did" without acknowledging its sleight of hand. In more diluted forms it simply loads the dice strongly in favor of a conclusion by distorting or withholding reasonable alternative conclusions. One of the distinguishing marks of our age is the increasingly sophisticated and subtle way in which coercion may be disguised as persuasion.

In saying that coercion must be distinguished from persuasion, we don't mean to suggest that one can construct a simple binary—persuasion (good) versus coercion (bad)—that does justice to their subtle interactions. Rather, we would argue that coercion lies at one end of a continuum marking the range of persuasive practices. In its pure form, it would lie off the end of that continuum just as pure persuasion would lie just beyond the opposite end of that continuum. But in their pure form, coercion and persuasion are rare indeed. Torture—which Aristotle, not normally known for his sense of humor, refers to, deadpan, as an "inartistic proof"—is about as purely coercive as it gets. But coercion can take far less obvious forms. Take for example one of my favorite philosophical oddities, Pascal's Wager, a sort of pseudological proposition aimed at persuading people to declare their faith in God. According to the wager, there are two possibilities regarding God's existence: God does or does not exist. In turn there are two possible attitudes to adopt toward God's existence: I can believe or disbelieve. That gives rise to four possible combinations, four possible outcomes: I believe, God exists, and I exult in heaven after having lived a happy life full of faith; I believe, God does not exist, but I've spent a lifetime being happily deceived and in the end there's no heaven or hell anyway; I don't believe, God exists, and after a hopeless existence I go to hell; I don't believe, God doesn't exist, who cares? The absence of wiggle room here, the insistence on four and only four alternatives when more seem possible (e.g., who's to say an agnostic can't have a cheerful mortal existence?), inclines me to place it toward the coercive end of the continuum, though clearly no one is torturing me or sticking a gun in my ribs to gain my assent. It's the sort of fear-based argument that entices some of us to buy elaborate home security systems or to move to gated communities. It's hard to imagine anyone sustaining a profound faith based on the motives assumed by Pascal's Wager.

At the other end of the continuum, a complex play like *Death of a Salesman* persuades in a way that is probably about as noncoercive as possible, as evidenced by the long and continuing debate over its meaning and the values it promotes. But what about a teacher in a classroom using a series of questions similar to Pascal's to lead students to predetermined understanding? How does one avoid using coercion to move students reliably from a position of ignorance about a subject to an understanding already possessed by the teacher? This example may seem somewhat of a stretch if our model of education is, say, an intro to biology course in a contemporary American university. But what if our model were a nineteenth-century biology course promoting "eugenics," the pseudoscience of human breeding, or a German biology classroom during the time of the Third Reich when "Nazi biology" was being taught? The line between coercion and persuasion may not always be bright, and in an attempt to better understand when we cross it we'll consider a range of persuasive acts along the continuum from pure coercion to pure persuasion and note some of the traits that distinguish them from one another.

The Continuum of Persuasive Practices: From Propaganda to Literature

In imagining such a continuum we immediately need to give up the notion that it might be exhaustive. Persuasion takes countless forms. Moreover, any form of persuasion we may think to place along our continuum will itself constitute a "minicontinuum" of practices distinguished by similar means. Advertising, thus, may be deceptive to the point that its claims are legally actionable, or it may be a relatively straightforward presentation of comparable data from independent sources about price and performance reflecting favorably on the advertiser's product. And literary works may range from those that engage our critical faculties and require deep reflection about our values and choices to "novels of ideas" so heavily loaded toward a particular ideology that they are barely distinguishable from political tracts. Our neat continuum, thus, is perhaps more profitably pictured as a series of overlapping horizontal lines, each representative of one sort of practice.

By way of simplifying our task, we'll limit ourselves to three representative forms of persuasive practice. On the left end, where coercion predominates, we place propaganda; in the middle, where persuasion dominates but coercion lurks around the edges, we place legal reasoning; and on the far right, where persuasion approaches purity, we place literary texts. Clustered around the three points on our continuum one could place various allied practices. Near propaganda, thus, one might position marketing, advertising, salesmanship, talk radio call-in shows, political campaign speeches, and the like; near legal reasoning, one might place parliamentary debate, classroom lectures, and point-counterpoint TV and radio discussions among informed discussants; near literary texts, one might place various ceremonial speeches and sermons, extended essays, and small-group discussions aimed at achieving consensus.

What characteristics of propaganda cause us to place it on the left end of the continuum? How does legal reasoning end up to the right of propaganda and why would literary texts outflank legal reasoning? A number of different considerations play into these judgments. Most of the differences are of degree, not kind. Thus, for example, just to the right of coercion but on the same scale, many people, starting with the Greeks, have placed "advantage-seeking" or *pleonexia;* in theory, those who practice propagandistic persuasion are strongly motivated by a desire to seek advantage for themselves and their cause. Those who write literary texts, on the other hand, are sometimes depicted as having transcended advantage-seeking, in the name of truth and beauty for their own sake. While there's some justice in this division of rhetorical practices, it's far too neat. After all, even Gandhi sought "advantage" for his beliefs and to that end wrote an autobiography that is simultaneously a serious literary work and a passionate argument whose intriguing subtitle, *The Story of My Experiments with Truth,* underscores its rhetorical sophistication. (In determining what makes a text "literary," we do not require it to be fictional or purely imaginative work; any carefully crafted work, be it fiction, memoir, autobiography, essay, and so forth, that engages us and offers up "equipment for living"—even sometimes defective equipment—would be considered "literary.") It's not that literary texts never seek advantage for anything, it's just that the advantages sought are more likely to exceed the author's self-interests.

The seeming godlike aloofness of literary authors from worldly concerns stems less from their moral superiority than from the demands of their craft. When ideas are dramatized they are necessarily more elusive, less single-pointed. Our attitudes toward them will be complicated by our attitudes toward the characters who hold and express them and those who oppose them. If one experiences Willy Loman as pathetic and deluded, one will view the ideas he represents differently from another who sees him as nobly tragic. (And if our interpretation is based on a performance of the play, it will rest in turn on the interpretation of the character by the director and the actor who embodies the character.) To dramatize ideas is to submit them to dialectic encounter with other ideas, and if audience interest is to be held by these encounters, there must be some rough equality among them, some chance that the "losing" proposition may prevail, may be right. Burke refers to the requirements of craft depicted here as "self-interference" and sees it in turn as the dominant characteristic of pure persuasion. Whatever an individual's interests may be at the outset of creating a literary text, her devotion to her craft will force her to accommodate those interests to the needs of her text. Which, again, is why writing a literary text is an exemplary "Act" for Burke, who emphasizes how the act of writing can eventually render the agent a servant of her own act.

Propagandists, meanwhile, practice a form of self-interference that, ironically enough, improves their odds of realizing their self-interests. They make adjustments to texts almost exclusively on the basis of the effect of those changes on an audience. The propagandist relies on "cunning," to use Burke's terminology, to "address" an audience. The starting point of the propagandist's argument is always whatever an audience most strongly believes or most fervently wishes to be true; and the conclusion of that argument is always what the propagandist already knows to be true. Audience beliefs are rarely challenged, or complicated; rather, they become the means through which the propagandist realizes his ends. No matter how contrary the propagandist's ends may be to the audience's beliefs, the two will be made to appear consonant with each other such that subscribing to the propagandist's ends seems the surest way for the audience to act in the name of their beliefs. Which is why propagandists and advertisers study their audiences so acutely, reading and performing extensive research, forming "focus groups" to test appeals, conducting opinion polls, and so forth; as a general rule, the more to the left a persuasive activity is situated, the more thoroughly and scientifically do the practitioners study their audiences, not so as to learn *from* them but so as to find out how best to take advantage *of* them. (Among legal reasoners in the middle of our persuasion/coercion continuum, those at the left end of things would include the litigators who hire expensive jury consultants to help them select jurors most likely to sympathize with their client and arguments most likely to work on their client's behalf.)

While propagandists may sincerely believe that the doctrine or product they promote will best serve their audience—and one of the crucial differences between propagandists and advertisers is the former's sincere belief in their cause—their first commitment is to the doctrine or product rather than to the happiness of their audience. Thus when the first propagandists—or at least the first to self-identify as such—went forth on behalf of the Catholic Church to convert people to Catholicism, promoting the acceptance of church doctrine as a necessary condition for salvation was a higher priority for the propagandists than the salvation of souls. And when various Marxist economies of Eastern Europe began floundering in the mid-twentieth century, propagandists did whatever they could to save the doctrine responsible for misdirecting the Marxist countries' economic policies, however disastrous the consequences for the people to whom they promoted that doctrine.

Another important distinguishing characteristic among persuasive activities concerns their manner of presentation and what that manner reveals about their respect for audience autonomy. Propagandists' narrowly partisan visions often reflect a disdain for their audience's intelligence. The goal of propaganda is to induce "Motion" in an audience, to bypass critical thought, and to cause an audience to respond *reflexively,* in the manner of an involuntary muscle movement, rather than *reflectively,* in the manner of an informed citizen. The more we move to the right, the more texts invite us to react critically and reflectively, and the less they are directed to us en masse as a member of a carefully researched cohort. Texts on the right end of our continuum address us as individuals free to respond differently to their message, and invite us to engage in conversation by way of negotiating those differences. Just as the way of rhetoric encourages us to slow the production of symbolic acts by taking into account the particulars of our circumstances, the products of pure persuasion force slower, "thicker" readings of themselves on us through self-referentiality and dialectic. To echo a familiar theme, the way in which texts are constructed determines their manner of construal.

Conversely, propagandists view the persuasive occasion not as a conversation but as a monologue, both in its manner of construction and in its manner of presentation. Propagandists start out knowing the truth, the right way of doing things, and see their function as "propagating" truth in much the way that people used to plant crops by propagating seeds. They don't see themselves as being responsible for testing and questioning the truths they propagate (modifying or hybridizing their "seeds"), any more than they see themselves as responsible for presenting their truths in a manner that invites others to test or question them. They don't consult various sources of information and different viewpoints to construct their arguments, and in fact they often make a point of ignoring "bad news" or any information that disrupts their settled view of things; "proving opposites" is not for them. Propagandists select data and viewpoints solely on the basis of their conformity to the orthodoxy in whose name they propagandize and then dress them up to look like the orthodoxies of their audience. By the same token, advertisers rarely question the social utility or relative worth of a product they've been hired to sell and seldom solicit the views of those who might be critical of the product. They target the audience most likely to buy the product; analyze their tastes, preferences, and beliefs; and do their best to associate the product with the audience's norms.

The law, meanwhile, exhibits a more complex relationship between audience and the construction of arguments. While lawyers are infamous for stretching arguments as far as they can in favor of their clients' interests, the structure of law makes it impossible for them to ignore contrary views in the process of constructing their own. They must anticipate opposing arguments, not to mention intervention from the bench if they fail to observe legal protocols for presentation of evidence, questioning of witnesses, and so forth. Witnesses, unlike unnamed sources in propaganda or paid spokespersons in ads, must give their testimony under oath. And whereas advertisers and propagandists are judged solely by popular reception of their "product," legal judgments are rendered by informed third parties, judges, and/or juries, who have been privy to arguments on both sides of the case. And those judgments, unlike the popular responses to advertising and propaganda, are unambiguous. While litigators may certainly tailor their arguments to the psychology of a given jury and the predilections of a given judge, they cannot construct arguments that ignore inconvenient points or the arguments of the opposition in the process. In effect, the law is an adversarial process constructed so as to *require* "interference" and to limit the legal reasoner's ability to seek advantage for their clients or to spin responses to their arguments.

While legal arguments are constrained by these external requirements, literary texts are constrained by the inherent requirements of literary craft, which force the author to "listen" to the divergent voices of her characters if her text is to be plausible and engaging. So, not only is there increasing "interference" with a writer/speaker's self-interest as we move from left to right across the continuum, the source of that interference is increasingly from within, increasingly the upshot of a creative act.

What the above analysis suggests is that "self-interference" is something of a misnomer. In the act of "interfering" with our established beliefs and assumptions, we generate new ideas and insights. By forcing ourselves to accommodate divergent views, even if doing so forces us to challenge the beliefs and assumptions of our audience, we are forced to engage our creative powers and enrich our arguments. While this process does not guarantee that the argument we produce will win the day with a given audience—propagandists' and marketers' more narrowly conceived arguments, which are often carefully and scientifically targeted at a given segment of the population, may be extremely persuasive—we are more likely to discover new ways of thinking about issues, new ways of representing and solving problems, new ways of identifying with our audience than we would have if we scrupulously accommodated our audience's existing beliefs, assumptions, and tastes.

It's this inventive power of argument that Aristotle calls attention to when he famously defines rhetoric as "the faculty of observing in any given case the available means of persuasion." Had he called rhetoric "the faculty of creating the winning argument every time," he would have been guilty of the crassest advantage-seeking of the sort that serious people charge against rhetoric. And in the process he would have slighted the distinctive power of rhetoric to discover new reasons, new solutions. To be sure, Aristotle goes on to emphasize the importance of effective argument and offers numerous techniques for winning over audiences by appealing to their beliefs and prejudices. But one's first responsibility is actively to seek out all the possible arguments that might be made, pro and con, in response to a given proposition, a practice that may well force one to change or modify one's argument. In effect, this first commandment of rhetoric represents the same sort of obligation to "self-interfere" that was previously identified with pure persuasion.

Make no mistake, rhetoric is always concerned with the effectiveness of arguments at persuading audiences, always operates under the assumption that people construct arguments in order to seek advantage of some sort and that ineffective arguments that fail to persuade audiences are more often deserving of judicious amendment than unswerving loyalty. But in discovering/observing all available means of persuasion, one not only discovers more arguments, one puts oneself in a position to discover "better" arguments that not only are more likely to win the day, but are more likely to serve the interests of all parties to a controversy. For whatever reason, one may not choose that better argument; rhetoric does not require one to choose it, and has no power to enforce such a requirement. But insofar as others are empowered by their understanding of rhetoric to oppose our arguments and do choose the better argument, our own argument may not fare well or last long in the marketplace of ideas.

How to Observe in Any Given Case the Available Means of Persuasion

Like most creative activities, finding the available means of persuasion is largely a matter of attending to those "given circumstances," the very contingencies that at first blush appear to be inhibiting one's creative capacity. Circumstances are like the rules of a game—the squares on a chessboard, the moves assigned to each of the pieces, the definition of winning—in combination with the progress of a particular game at a particular point in time—the position of the pieces on the board at various stages of play. One's strategy will flow from the limits imposed by these rules and by the prior moves made by each player. We calculate our possibilities, invent our moves and strategies, based on our close observation of all these seeming necessities. Each of the particulars comprising our given circumstances constitutes a "problem" that must be solved. But in the act of solving each of these problems, we define our task more clearly. Articulating the particulars of one's circumstances turns up multiple ways of representing those circumstances, many different "gists" that suggest many different strategies to pursue. In the case of our chess analogy, a player may consult various models of the game in progress selected from among previously played games that followed similar paths. This process of charting and naming one's situation turns out to be a very powerful discovery tool, and over the centuries numerous systems have been developed to help one work out, in a more or less systematic way, the potential means at one's disposal in a given situation. Like chess players who've studied their own games and the games of others in order to devise sets of strategies appropriate for various circumstances, rhetoricians too have devised their own stock of strategies useful in recurrent situations and roughly similar circumstances.

Rhetoric is more or less a "science of single instances" such that no formula could be conceived that would be adequate for every possible instance. We likened the practice of rhetoric to the practice of the law insofar as each operates on a case-by-case basis even while each also recognizes many commonalities among cases that allow one to generalize about strategies and principles. In rhetoric, "cases" are typically referred to as "rhetorical situations." By studying a broad array of rhetorical situations, rhetoricians have devised many strategies and principles useful in discovering "the available means of persuasion" in a given situation. The various elements of a rhetorical situation constitute "places" we can look for new insights into the matter at hand. But before considering some of those strategies and principles, a word needs to be said about the vexatious nature of the rhetorical situation.

Those who are vexed by the nature of the rhetorical situation question the extent to which such situations are objective, independently existing entities, sitting there waiting for us in a more or less solid form, and the extent to which the rhetorical situation is constructed by a person free to define the situation as she wishes. Our response should be by now predictable: It's a bit of both. Like Wordsworth's view of reality, "half perceived and created," a given situation may be perceived as rhetorical, as calling for a persuasive response of some sort, or it may be perceived as simply the way things are and as such, not corrigible through rhetorical means. Two different people might look at the same state of affairs and legitimately reach opposite conclusions about it. But having deemed a given situation rhetorical, I must persuade others that my naming is appropriate. And insofar as both the situation I am characterizing and the people I am addressing are not mere creatures of my desires, I may have my work cut out for me. The things I name may not behave in a manner consistent with the names I give them; the people I address may be unwilling to entertain, let alone grant, my claims or share my vocabulary. There is, as we've noted, an indelible strain of "recalcitrance" in the world. Even in a socially constructed world, "saying doesn't make it so" unless one happens to be a magician or a denizen of Alice's Wonderland.

The nature of the rhetorical situation is perhaps best understood on the model of identity discussed previously. There will certainly be an element of "given-ness" about the situation, elements already there, already formed, resistant as anvils to our importuning. And often as not the situation will arrive with a readymade label or labels already attached, courtesy of those privy to the situation, or similar situations, before us. But to the extent the situation in question involves human judgment we still are free to redefine it, reconstruct the problem, and persuade others that our reconstruction is better than the prevailing constructions. As we review the various elements of the rhetorical situation, we'll try to keep in mind this "tripartite" model of identity insofar as it characterizes the various elements.

Elements of the Rhetorical Situation

In what follows, we'll enumerate the elements of the rhetorical situation and exemplify each of those elements using a variety of examples, but always including one example taken from the 2003 State of the Union Address delivered by President George W. Bush. We'll be reading that address with the sort of close attention that's usually reserved for poems and other extremely complex and prestigious verbal artifacts of "high culture." We do so both to illustrate how consideration of the rhetorical situation deepens our understanding of an argument, allowing us to recognize its strengths and weaknesses, and also to show how any text, even an apparently simple one performing a job of work in the everyday world, can possess intricacies of construction and complexities of form not immediately detectable to the casual listener/reader. Drawing once again on the language of the law, these extended analyses of the president's address are labeled "sidebars" in honor of the conferences judges and lawyers sometimes hold out of earshot of the jury and courtroom audiences. They are asides to the main proceedings, but may play a crucial role in the determination of a case's outcome.

The Rhetorical Act

The first element of any rhetorical situation is the *rhetorical act* itself, which is usually, but not always, a verbal construct of some sort. The act can be further broken down into the act's *message* and its *medium* (sometimes referred to as *agency*). In "charting" the rhetorical situation, message is most fully treated under two rubrics: stases and Toulmin schema. Because it is the most obvious element of the rhetorical situation, it may seem as if all other elements are subservient to the message, as if their importance is strictly a function of their influence on the message. In fact, all of the elements may play this role, serving simultaneously as the whole of the rhetorical situation and a part. It is, once again, a matter of perspective. No single part is understandable except insofar as it is understood "in terms of" another part. (Ideally all the parts will be understood in terms of each other, but the process can only occur one pair at a time.) The tendency of the parts of the rhetorical situation to appear at once independent and interdependent is illuminated by Burke's analogy of a hand, whereby the elements, like fingers, "in their extremities are distinct from one another, but merge in the palm of the hand" (*GOM*, xxii). For now, we'll be talking about the elements as if they existed independently of one another, though when it comes time to actually apply the terms to situations, it will be clear how interdependent they are.

Act as Message: Presence and Coherence

Since message will be discussed at length later on, we'll touch here on just two factors relevant to this element of the rhetorical situation: the language choices one makes in articulating one's message, in particular the degree to which one uses very specific, sensory language to embody one's message and lend it greater "presence," and the overall coherence of the message, the extent to which it all hangs together for an audience. (In ancient times, these matters would be discussed under the rubrics of *pathos* and *logos*.) Presence, as the term implies, has to do with the effects of a message on the sensibilities of its audience. In the broadest sense, presence results from the selection of what to discuss and what to ignore in one's argument. Anything that makes it into the argument can be said to have at least minimal presence. But in the stronger sense of the term, "presence" refers to examples, metaphors, illustrations, anecdotes, extended analogies, well-known allusions, and detailed descriptions—all the traditional storytellers' tools—that put the message immediately before the audience and invite their identification (*pathos*) with it. If one wishes to appeal to hearts as well as minds, if one wishes an audience not merely to assent to one's message but to act on it, one is well advised to imbue one's message with presence. In some circumstances, data, particularly when presented in a graphic form, can be said to possess presence. Or if data are presented in a particularly imaginative fashion, they can lend presence to an argument. Take, for example, the following: "If every SUV owner in America were to switch to a hybrid automobile, the subsequent reduction in our annual demand for oil would be equivalent to the amount we currently buy each year from Saudi Arabia." To the extent that arguments rely too heavily on presence—frequently the case in advertising—the effect may be to obscure the point of the argument by crossing the line from *pathos* to *bathos,* drowning the audience's sensibilities in sentiment and sensory detail rather than merely touching those sensibilities.

A coherent message is a logical message. But by itself logic, as we shall see, is an incomplete measure of coherence. In particular, logic treats coherence as a purely internal affair. So long as the parts of an argument do not contradict one another, logic calls it sound. But rhetorical coherence requires us to take external as well as internal relationships into account and demands more of internal relationships than mere noncontradiction. In addition to the consistency of a message's parts with one another, rhetoric considers the effectiveness of the parts' arrangement, and the relevance of the parts to the whole. A point that does not contradict an overall message may still be criticized as being irrelevant or barely relevant, or as being situated inappropriately given its importance to the whole argument.

Thus, while it may be perfectly logical for a church spokesperson to say, as a Phoenix spokesperson did, that the counseling and transfer of priests accused of child molestation was consistent with the Catholic Church's general policy stressing rehabilitation, few people found the statement persuasive in the context of an argument about the legal and moral culpability of the priests. The point made by the spokesperson is mostly irrelevant to the latter argument; it was as if a large energy company accused of defrauding ratepayers were to defend its actions by saying that company policies did not prohibit fraud. And had the spokesperson placed this claim at the conclusion of her defense of the church, she would have compounded her error by situating a weak claim in a place where audiences pay particularly close attention. According to the classic principle of Nestorian order, we expect to find the most important points in an argument in the conclusion, the part people are most likely to remember, just as we expect to find the most important information in a sentence at its end (sometimes referred to as the "emphatic" position in a proposition). By the same logic, one is advised to place one's weakest or least-important points in the middle of an argument or in the "second" position after one has completed the second-most carefully attended portion of an argument, the opening, and well before the conclusion.

Coherence viewed as an external matter, meanwhile, may be thought of as a message's plausibility. If a message fails to conform to our overall sense of how the world works, it is unlikely to be persuasive. If an example is chosen to illustrate a principle and the choice strikes us as inappropriate or unrepresentative, we are likely to be skeptical about the principle being illustrated. Thus when opponents of federal estate tax on inheritances (which they dubbed "the death tax" to lend it a grim bit of presence) protested that the tax was bad because it prevented family farms from being passed on from one generation to the next, their protest was initially greeted sympathetically, thanks in part to the central place of family farms to the American *mythos.* But when no actual instances of the tax preventing a farm from being inherited could be found in the "heartland" state of Iowa, death tax opponents quickly moved on to other examples, none of which were drawn, it should be said, from the one class of people indubitably impacted by the tax—offspring of the nation's wealthiest 2 percent, who stood to inherit their family fortunes.

I cite this particular example because of my own experience growing up on a family farm. I found the example implausible on the face of it primarily because most of the family farms I grew up around were barely solvent, and none would ever have come close to the considerable dollars in assets that one must possess before estate taxes even begin to kick in. Some farmers are, to be sure, "land rich" to the point that they may appear to meet the inheritance tax thresholds, but in most cases they owe much of—sometimes more than—their land's worth to lenders they borrow from to get their crops in and harvested each year. Occasionally, farmland skyrockets in value when a city begins encroaching on it and developers bid to replace cornfields with subdivisions or shopping malls. But most states have provisions whereby such land continues to be taxed at its considerably lower value as farmland for as long as it is used for that purpose. The only way for it to be affected by "death taxes" is if its owners choose to get out of farming voluntarily. (In a recent Arizona case, a well-known family farm did precisely this; the owners claimed they were being "forced" out of farming not because they were losing money, but because they stood to make millions more selling to a developer than they could make from their agricultural operations.) To the extent that any argument relies on implausible examples—understanding that our sense of the plausible is influenced by our personal experiences and must eventually be tested against a wider sampling of experience—it will strike us as incoherent. The disconnect between the claim and the example is not a logical disconnect, it is a veridical one. The example doesn't "ring true," rendering us skeptical of the entire argument. If one's examples are implausible, they had best be obscure.

Act as Medium: The Physical Means of Transmission and Genre

Every rhetorical act must be expressed through a given *medium:* spoken, written, digital, electronic, visual, and so forth. Whatever form it takes, there will be an extraverbal dimension to that act—pitch, gestures, fonts, papers, sets and backdrops, lighting, costume, visual accompaniments, and so forth—and in some cases, the rhetorical act may be entirely extraverbal. In many realms, including diplomacy, finance, politics, and the law, persuasive messages are routinely sent via actions and decisions. Refusing to meet with a country's leaders face-to-face, demanding instead to meet with them through third parties, is a way of telling the country in question that they are less powerful than you and that you are not happy with them. Lowering interest rates is the Fed's way of signaling investors that they have little to fear from inflation. Awarding a huge settlement in a corporate fraud case allows a jury to "send a message" to potential perpetrators that they should rethink their business practices. Even criminals may indicate the nature of their displeasure with their victims by the manner in which they choose to "whack" them.

Every medium affects the messages it transmits. Every medium has its own set of protocols that must be observed, or else violated judiciously and mindfully by the author of a rhetorical act. Before participating in an Internet listserv, for example, one is well advised to lurk for a bit, observing how formally or informally people address each other, who is deferred to and who is ignored, how long people are allowed to go on about the matter at hand, how new threads are introduced, etc. Because of the nature of the medium and the circumstances in which messages are read, Internet communication generally encourages a more time-sensitive, terse style over more conversational or "chatty" styles. At the same time, the strong sense of community that develops among members of a listserv over time may render participants more tolerant of individuals "thinking out loud" about common problems without requiring them to reach some sort of closure. By the same token, a political speech given on TV and a live speech given over a handheld microphone on the quad of a university campus will require different deliveries. A speech that strikes one as inspirational when heard live in a large open space may strike one as strident and overly emotional when seen on a TV screen in the more intimate space of one's living room, particularly if crowd noises have been filtered out through the use of sensitive microphones and the camera remains "tight" on the speaker. While every message in some sense exceeds its medium, there is no question that one's message, verbal and extraverbal, will have to be adjusted to its medium for maximum effectiveness.

In addition to the physical medium of our persuasive messages, they all may be assigned to a readymade category of message known as a genre. Everything from office memos to State of the Union Addresses are read and responded to within the context of the history and conventions associated with that particular genre. A funeral oration full of invective against the deceased will probably not go over well with the assembled loved ones, even if the slurs are largely true and the loved ones might agree, "off the record," that the deceased was a most disagreeable fellow. When faced with an anomalous persuasive message that we can't immediately assign to a familiar genre, when we don't know what "sort" of message we're processing, we may well have great difficulty understanding, let alone assenting to, the piece's message. Some genres, particularly those aimed at narrow audiences of specialists or those associated with formal ceremonial occasions, are more rigid than others. One has, thus, considerably less latitude in constructing a National Institutes of Health proposal than in constructing an editorial calling for a change in tax policy.

Agent and Ethos

The second element of any rhetorical situation is the person doing the persuading, the *agent.* The quality of any act is tied to the perceived quality of the act's agent, his or her *ethos.* Are they trustworthy people? Do they have the appropriate credentials and experience to speak to the issue? What is their "history" on the issue? Are they identified strongly with a particular interest? Agents do not arrive on the scene tabula rasa, absent prejudices, ideologies, beliefs, allegiances, etc., that predispose them to view the situation in certain ways. They arrive on the scene as members of a given socioeconomic class, gender, ethnicity, nationality, age group, and so forth. They may well have already taken positions on the issue at hand or on similar issues, and desire to remain true to their previously expressed convictions and consubstantial with those who have shared their views in the past. Their need to at least appear to be consistent and thereby trustworthy people means that their response is to some extent predictable, even inevitable. They may, after all, be required to reach certain conclusions—or rewarded, sometimes lavishly, for persuading others to reach those conclusions—by those who employ them. All of these would be considered "given" factors that influence a person's

MEDIA WATCH

2003 State of the Union Address (SOUA)—Its Message and Medium

The 2003 State of the Union Address, given by President George W. Bush, promises to go down in history as one of the most controversial State of the Union Addresses ever delivered. Not that there is a great deal of competition among such addresses for the title "most controversial." As a genre, State of the Union Addresses may occasion mild controversy, but seldom the sort of animus, long-term angst, and prolonged scrutiny this one occasioned. They usually serve as an opportunity for the president to celebrate legislative accomplishments, blunt criticism of failures or shortcomings, and announce new initiatives in the broadest and most agreeable of terms. But President Bush used this address to prepare the nation for a controversial war against Iraq and its leader, Saddam Hussein. This particular aspect of his address will be the primary focus of our analysis.

The State of the Union Address is delivered before a joint session of Congress and on live national television amidst a good deal of pomp and circumstance. The Joint Chiefs of Staff, the members of the Supreme Court, and a number of other worthies are in attendance, often in full regalia. In recent years, it has become pro forma for the members of the president's party to erupt in applause at key junctures of his speech, signaled by his rising intonation followed by a pause and a resolute gaze across the room. It is, in sum, a curious hybrid of state ceremony and stump speech. The address usually covers a lot of ground in a fairly brief period of time, which means that few extended arguments are developed. The speech mostly serves to announce the executive branch's agenda, its self-graded scorecard, and its spin on pending issues. More extended arguments are left to other venues and other occasions.

While ostensibly delivered directly to those in attendance, the more critical audience for the speech is the television audience. Winning over the millions of television viewers is seen as a necessary condition for getting Congress to act on the president's agenda. Hence the applause, however heartfelt by the members of the president's party, serves a function similar to that of a laugh track on a sitcom. Just as the laugh track signals us that the just-delivered line is funny and invites us to chuckle along, the applause signals us that something significant has just been said and invites us to nod along. Like the "call-and-response" of a church sermon, the "pronouncement-and-applause" of the address usually follows a predictable rhythm. Once that rhythm is established, a break or departure, like a break or departure from the pattern of a poem or song, typically signals a particularly important passage.

In the case of the 2003 State of the Union Address, the interjections of applause come very quickly in the beginning, every 40–50 words. They then lengthen out to 50–200-word intervals until, near the end of the speech, the president begins a long narrative, over 900 uninterrupted words, enumerating the evidence of Saddam Hussein's duplicity and evil intentions. In contrast to earlier "sound-bite" proclamations, this applause-free interval frames the passage in a lengthy, steepled silence that implies a rapt audience hanging on every word and lends great weight to the president's words. Appropriately situated near the speech's conclusion, it serves as the high point and climax. The remainder of the speech serves as a denouement or "sorting out" of the type one encounters in the fifth act of a play. A response is announced (we will not wait until danger is imminent), the future is foretold (yet-to-be-taken diplomatic steps are outlined, and allusion is made to American forces assembling in the region), and a stirring call to action is issued.

Given the president's desire to win popular support for the Iraq war, and given the urgency of that desire—troops were already gathering in Kuwait, budget estimates for conducting such a war had already been submitted, and "military consultants" to news organizations had been on talk shows stressing the importance of invading before the heat of Iraq's summer set in—it is not surprising to find him lending great "presence" to several key points through graphic presentation. Thus, in order to underscore the futility of the U.N. presence in Iraq, and to dismiss U.N. weapons inspectors' contentions that no weapons of mass destruction were to be found in Iraq, the president likens the inspections to a "scavenger hunt" conducted by 108 inspectors "across a country the size of California." And to underscore the threat posed by the weapons putatively being hidden by Saddam Hussein, he ticks them off by name, quantity, and killing potential. Thus he mentions "25,000 liters of anthrax; enough to kill several million people," and "38,000 liters of botulinum toxin; enough to subject millions of people to death by respiratory failure." He goes on to say that "intelligence officials estimate" that Hussein possesses raw materials adequate to produce up to "500 tons of sarin, mustard and VX nerve gas" capable of killing "untold thousands" more, and "nearly 30,000 munitions capable of delivering chemical agents." And finally, by way of linking the Iraqi threat to the disaster of 9/11, and bringing the litany of threats and dangers to an apocalyptic finish, he calls

continued

upon his audience to "Imagine those 19 hijackers with other weapons and other plans, this time armed by Saddam Hussein. It would take one vial, one canister, one crate slipped into this country to bring a day of horror like none we have ever known." While he goes on to dismiss the idea that America should wait until a threat is "imminent" to act, he clearly establishes a strong sense of imminent peril in his lengthy, uninterrupted, graphic depiction of a threat, a threat posed not by a nation but by a single unstable and evil person, Saddam Hussein, who is named seventeen times in the passage cited above, and who allows us to put a face at last to a faceless enemy and "shadowy terrorist networks" that are everywhere and nowhere.

Just as he highlights his bill of particulars against Saddam Hussein by breaking the rhythm of his talk, by placing it toward the end of his address, and by lending it particularly strong presence through metaphors, numbers, examples, and a hypothetical scenario lifted from the script for a summer blockbuster, the president downplays some less happy information by slipping it seamlessly into the classic "second" position, by avoiding any of the devices that might lend it presence, and by, in some cases, avoiding any mention of it altogether. Given the remarkable brevity of the bad tidings and their position within the speech, one would be excused for overlooking them altogether. After a ceremonial opening statement and a portentous allusion to "the decisive days that lie ahead," the president gives an upbeat start to his address by citing four major accomplishments from his administration's two years in office. Refusing to deem these accomplishments "a good record," he concedes they constitute "a good start" but now calls for some "bold steps" vis à vis the economy, which was sputtering. The bad economic news is delivered in a fifty-word passage bracketed by applause lines that blends neatly into the happier passages that precede and follow it. The sentence that announces the shift goes like this: "After recession, terrorist attacks, corporate scandals and stock market declines, our economy is recovering." It's a rhetorically masterful sentence. The causes of the sputtering economy are consigned to the past, assigned no human agency, and dropped into the beginning of the sentence, while the declaration of recovery is put in the emphatic position at the end. After conceding that the pace of the recovery is too slow, the president then tackles the unhappy news about unemployment. Again, the bad news comes in a dependent clause at the beginning of the sentence— "With unemployment rising,"—while the rest of the sentence offers a solution to the problem in a series of mounting statements that end with a vivid image and a ringing applause line—"our nation needs more small businesses to open, more companies to invest and expand, more employers to put up the sign that says, 'Help Wanted.' " The president then goes on to outline the steps that will bring about this happy result, beginning with his proposed tax cuts.

persuasiveness regardless of what he or she actually says or writes. Those same givens may also cause an agent to modify his or her usual personality and to adopt a readymade persona—bellicose leader, thoughtful statesman—more appropriate to the occasion.

But more often than not, what a person actually says or writes will probably have the greatest bearing on our willingness to credit them with a strong *ethos.* We've already mentioned some features of the message that will render it more or less effective, and we will later take up other factors that bear on the content of an argument. But *how* agents deliver the message—the tone or voice, the persona their words and/or gestures conjure up for us—is crucial to our ability to identify with their position. One of the most obvious elements of the message that influences our view of agents is their characterization of those with whom they disagree. The use of highly charged, prejudicial language on the one hand, or the failure to qualify carefully their certitude about the claims they make on the other will cause us to question whether they have "interfered" with their personal interests sufficiently to construct sound arguments. To be sure, all of the above practices may be mimicked by propagandists skillful in the art of counterfeiting the manner and arguments of reliable people. So, while absence of these practices justifies one's skepticism about agents, their presence should not render us completely credulous regarding said agents' reliability.

Rhetorical Scene

Before there's an *agent* or a *rhetorical act,* there's a scene, a particular time and place and a context, that gives rise to both. The characteristics of such a scene can be articulated with reasonable clarity; but, as we shall see, determining just what elements of the scene may be relevant to one's argument and identifying the proper "scope" of the scene is a considerably more difficult matter. By its nature a rhetorical scene is one that demands a response of us. What might otherwise be heard as a straightforward descriptive statement—e.g., "America liberated Iraq"—is heard as a claim, a contention that

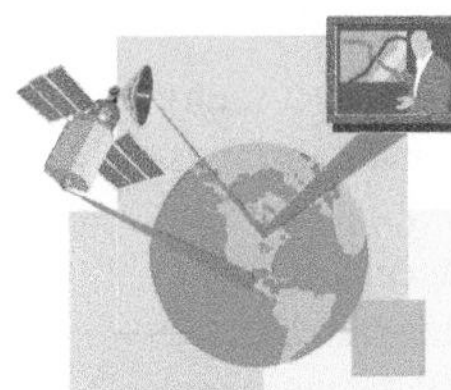

MEDIA WATCH

SOUA and Presidential Ethos

By virtue of being the democratically elected leader of the world's most powerful nation, George W. Bush possesses a great deal of credibility. The stature of his office was dramatically underscored by the deference shown to the president when he entered the chamber to give his address, the eagerness with which legislators—who must be seated well before the president's formally announced entrance—from both sides of the aisle reached out to shake his hand. Moreover we routinely grant presidents a presumption of expertise in whatever matter is before them. To varying degrees, we also grant them a presumption of disinterestedness in their conduct of the nation's business. We hope that presidents will rise above party affiliation to do what's best for the country. While some presidents, like Richard Nixon, never managed to persuade the nation of their objectivity, others, like Ronald Reagan, managed it handily and earned enormous political capital as a result. In the case of George W. Bush, his *ethos* had suffered some blows in his early days of office, including his election. Opinion polls and a sampling of editorials of the time suggest that he was a controversial leader when he gave the address and would subsequently become an extremely controversial figure, even a "polarizing" figure in the eyes of some. Indeed, the impact of this particular speech and the subsequent questioning of it by his political opponents played a major role in his increasingly controversial reputation.

When he came into office, after a tightly contested, very heated race that required Supreme Court intervention to determine the outcome, the president was perceived to lack a mandate for his agenda. His standing in the polls inched inexorably downward, thanks largely to a bad economy, until the events of 9/11. After 9/11, the president's stature and his favorable ratings in the polls shot up. A nation was reminded that he was not only President of the United States, but Commander-in-Chief of the armed forces. He eagerly took on a role he himself referred to as that of a "war president," promising, and delivering, bold and decisive responses to the terror attack. In short order terrorist training camps in Afghanistan were destroyed and Taliban leaders were neutralized. While many Americans had questioned his credentials prior to and during the elections, citing his relatively brief career in state politics, his spotty record in business, and his oft-questioned service in the Texas Air National Guard during the Vietnam conflict, his quick response to 9/ll and his stirring verbal challenges to the terrorists won over many Americans. He used his popularity in the months leading up to the speech to gain support for military action against Iraq. But he paid a price for his advocacy as his favorable ratings in the polls declined, in part, to be sure, because of a weak economy, but also because of the public's uncertainty about Iraq's place in the war against terrorism and their puzzlement over the failure of other world leaders to endorse our cause. By the time America actually went to war two months after his address, the president's approval ratings hovered around the lackluster 50 percent level that he had experienced prior to 9/11.

So, while the president certainly benefited from the status of his office and the trappings of power and prestige that framed his presentation, these "givens" would not by themselves be enough to persuade a skeptical electorate that an invasion of Iraq was justified. As his polling figures showed, he was not speaking from a position of strength. Many of his longtime critics questioned his objectivity, citing in particular his personal antipathy toward Saddam Hussein, who had once plotted to kill his father, former President George H. W. Bush. Others cited the fact that a number of key figures in his administration had called publicly for the overthrow of Iraq years earlier. His critics conjectured that he was using the events of 9/11 as rationalization for a war that they felt was unjustified but to which he had been committed long before the terrorist attack. Given his diminished popularity and the depth of the suspicions about his motives, the speech itself would have to compensate for a weakened *ethos*. The president would have to project a trustworthy, competent figure through his presentation and offer solid grounds for the war.

While frequently criticized for his shortcomings as a public speaker, particularly in spontaneous situations where his tendency to invent words and pretzel logic sometimes raised eyebrows and crossed eyes, the president's style served him well on TV. His flat, nasal east Texas accent marked him as a man of the people, belying his patrician upbringing and his Ivy League education. And while some commentators were exasperated by his predilection for mangled syntax and tortuous logic, many ordinary Americans were more appalled by those who ridiculed his speech, perhaps remembering their own unhappy experiences with middle school "Grammar Nazis," and identified with his plight. His unpolished speaking style was well suited to television, an intimate medium that put him directly in people's living rooms, where folksiness often works better than eloquence, and where nuanced messages may well be lost on audiences conditioned by the dynamics of television to listen for sound bites and laugh lines and to ignore the tedious middle bits.

A final note on the role of the agent in the persuasiveness of the State of the Union Address concerns

continued

questions about the way the president qualified, or failed to qualify, several of his claims about the danger posed by Iraq. A number of people questioned the claimed existence of weapons of mass destruction prior to the war. And yet, several times the president presented as matters of fact claims about Iraq's WMD and ties to al-Quaida that were later shown to be matters of conjecture. While we may never know the proper degree of certainty that should have been accorded these claims, absolute certainty seems a stretch by any reckoning. And we also may never know just who was finally responsible for overstating the certitude of such claims. Many people around the world assumed that Saddam Hussein had such weapons, and when asked by the president if such weapons would be found in the wake of a war, former CIA director George Tenet famously exclaimed that it would be a "Slam dunk!" Whatever the source or magnitude of the overstatements, they found their way into the president's address. Thus, at one point he declares that "From three Iraqi defectors we know that Iraq, in the late 1990s, had several mobile biological weapons labs." The only questionable part of this statement is the "we know" locution. We had been told by Iraqi defectors, whose credibility was questioned at the time by some in the intelligence community, that such labs existed. Unless the sources were infallible, the "we know" conclusion is unearned. Likewise the president states flatly that "The dictator of Iraq is not disarming. To the contrary, he is deceiving." Based on what was ultimately found in Iraq, it appeared that Saddam Hussein had, for whatever reason, been disarming. Almost certainly, he was also deceiving. The evident certainty of the second claim apparently led many to "deduce" the equal certainty of the first claim. While those contributing information to the speech had initially examined the record and set about "proving opposites" concerning the proper conclusions to be drawn, they eventually decided to come down on one side and ignore the other.

Offering probable truths as certain truths should certainly undermine the *ethos* of the president and would normally earn his address a place on the coercive end of our persuasion/coercion continuum. A couple of factors mitigate the severity of our judgment without exculpating his act. First of all, the State of the Union Address, for all its pomp and circumstance, is understood to be closer in spirit to a campaign speech than a speech to the nation occasioned by world events. Which is why networks who carry the address are obligated afterward to present rebuttals from the opposition party. We don't necessarily look for balanced presentations from presidents offering State of the Union Addresses. Moreover, when presidents speak on formal occasions, it is widely understood that they speak as representatives of their administration, and that the speeches they deliver are the product of many hands. Certainly they bear a strong measure of personal responsibility for the truthfulness of their remarks, but they necessarily rely on staff and agency heads to provide them with accurate information on which to base their conclusions. When faulty conclusions are drawn from information, one cannot assign definitive responsibility for the problematic statements without being privy to the information.

Moreover, even if one were to conclude that the president's address constituted a piece of propaganda, that judgment is not necessarily fatal. After all, our own Declaration of Independence, which is at one level the ringing birth pronouncement of a new nation, is at another level a first-rate piece of propaganda, a sly appeal to the world community, particularly France, to help us out in our struggle with England. Indeed, according to Jacques Ellul, one of our most astute students of propaganda, the use of propaganda is not limited to tyrannies and dictatorships. Democratic governments too will resort to propaganda in order to influence public opinion, to secure "the consent of the governed," or simply to ensure their political survival. Without popular consent, no democratic government can execute its policies. Yet policies must be stable to be effective and public opinion (as witnessed by the notable dips and surges in the president's approval ratings over a brief period of time) is famously fickle. Every democratic government will on occasion use persuasive practices from across the entire continuum, including classic marketing and advertising techniques, spin control, and, yes, propaganda, to gain support for its policies. But no president who relies heavily or even significantly on propaganda techniques to win the day with the electorate can long retain his ethos. So while the existence of propaganda in his speech should not be considered fatal to George W. Bush's *ethos,* evidence that he relied significantly on propaganda would be.

According to Ellul, use of propaganda to influence public opinion is especially prevalent in the area of foreign affairs. While many Americans are acutely aware of the impact that policy decisions about the economy might have on their personal lives, and most of us can judge over time if economic policies are working or not, most of us are considerably more dependent on our government to sort out foreign policy for us. We simply don't have much access to the information on which foreign policy decisions are made, and the moral and political complexity of decisions arising from that information tends to be greater by an order of magnitude than domestic policy decisions. And when foreign policy decisions involve questions of war, democratic governments are particularly prone to using propaganda. No other political decision requires a stronger public commitment or signifies a higher expression of national interest. Moreover, members of the public both care more passionately about war and feel a greater sense of personal responsibility for its consequences. Which is why unpopular wars can mobilize political opposition so quickly and so massively and why politicians take such special care to gather popular support for declarations of war. Which is also why throughout history the most egregious uses of propaganda by American administrations have been associated with foreign affairs generally and wars most especially.

matters to us and to which more than one response is possible. Moreover, there can be no final certainty about the rightness of any of these responses, either because there's insufficient knowledge or information to demonstrate their truth beyond all doubt, or because the responses rest on incommensurable assumptions incapable of amending one another. In many cases, both conditions apply. But for whatever reason, we feel compelled to offer up a response. Perhaps because our self-interests are threatened or served, perhaps because we feel we can construct a response not yet offered, perhaps because our position or office requires us to offer a response, perhaps because a value or belief we subscribe to strongly is challenged. Typically, the issue has about it some sense of urgency, a decision point, a window of opportunity, a recurring cost, an ongoing struggle whose outcome hangs in the balance. Whatever the goad, it is sufficient for us to overcome our inertia or our willingness to wait until a perfect and definitive solution is possible and to set about committing ourselves to a rhetorical act. The particulars of the scene will determine the particulars of that act, but in general a rhetorical scene will motivate us to seek cooperation from others in the form of identification with our views. In some cases, that may mean that we ask them to take some form of action or to change their minds radically. But in many cases we may be seeking simply to increase our audience's adherence to an attitude they hold less strongly than we or decrease their adherence to one we oppose more strongly than they.

While one may at first blush think of a scene as the most concrete, the most thoroughly "given" element of a rhetorical situation, it turns out to be extremely amorphous and highly manipulable. What is the proper "circumference" in space and time of the scene? How far back do we seek historical precedents? How far afield do we look for analogous situations? How far aloft do we pursue applicable principles? Different fields of knowledge and disciplines provide more or less readymade answers to such questions, but in many cases it's a judgment call that each of us must make anew with each rhetorical act, and seldom will an audience be privy to the criteria used to make that judgment. Our attention will be directed to some things and not to others, but rarely will the principle of selection be articulated or justified. Just as point of view indiscernibly guides our perception of events in a novel or movie, the determination of scene in a rhetorical situation indiscernibly orients our perception of the issue at hand.

On the rare occasions when a scene's scope becomes an explicit issue, it's usually because a critic has contested its scope, charging it with a failure to take the "larger context" adequately into account. A larger context, in the language of this study, refers to the choices we make in attempting to define our subject "in terms of" other matters—especially precedents, analogues, and principles. When we wrestle with the question of what is singular about this particular issue and what is connected in time and space to other matters, we are determining the proper scope of our argument.

Proponents of gay marriage, for example, will include as part of the issue's larger context the precedent of "antimiscegenation" laws that withered away in the last third of the twentieth century. Like the ban on gay marriage, state bans on interracial marriage had existed for many years in this country and over time had been normalized through custom. It was considered "unnatural" for people of different races to marry and have children. While such bans were more prevalent and more sedulously observed in some regions of the country than in others, they were widely accepted or at least tolerated. But in the wake of the civil rights movement and the striking down of many laws promoting discrimination on the basis of race, the bans on interracial marriage were also struck down, culminating in a 1987 Supreme Court decision that ended them completely. Proponents of gay marriage point out that, by the same token, many of the laws allowing discrimination against homosexuals, including laws criminalizing gay sexual behaviors, have been struck down, which in their view opens the way for same-sex couples to marry. Opponents of the measure of course stress the differences between same-sex and interracial marriage and look to religious proscriptions against homosexuality, thereby in their view "outflanking" their opponents and enlarging the relevant context even further. Whether in fact religious proscriptions trump legal tolerance is an issue that continues to play out as this is written.

Audience as Scenic Element

The most crucial element of scene is *audience*. Indeed, the most distinctive feature of rhetoric as a way of understanding is the role of audience in shaping discourse and determining truth. In choosing to treat audience as an element of scene rather than as an independent element of the rhetorical situation, we may seem to downplay its significance. In some people's eyes, all other rhetorical questions can be reduced to questions about the effect of our choices on our audience. For many of these folks, to lump audience in with other scenic considerations is to trivialize it. That's certainly not our intent. Our approach here simply reflects our desire to balance rhetoric's concern for audience with its concern for invention, the extent to which rhetoric is practiced in order to persuade an audience to believe or do whatever is consistent with our aims, and the extent to which it is practiced to discover more and better arguments. Audience is one means, the most important means, of finally determining which line of argument to pursue, which reasons and what evidence to put forth, but it is not the only one. And more importantly, our choice is not between pandering to a "given" audience's norms and beliefs or constructing new and better arguments. Audiences too are constructed as well as given and readymade. We can appeal to an audience's basest nature or we can appeal to their "best selves"; we can challenge their most questionable assumptions or we can reinforce those assumptions. Indeed, as we've seen, those who do the most to alter their arguments to suit their audiences, who demand the least of their audiences in the way of transformation, are most likely to persuade audiences to acts and beliefs that ill-serve audience interests.

All of which is not to suggest that one ignores actual audiences. Saying that an author must modify a rhetorical act in recognition of the genre and the medium within which it operates is to acknowledge the power of audiences. The conventions imposed by genres and media are grounded in audience expectations and limitations. Audiences self-select according to the types of media they choose, the shows they watch, the commentators they listen to, the advertisements they attend to, and the books, newspapers, journals, and magazines they read. Clearly, one would have to have a death wish to ignore those audience expectations. Just as clearly, we have to determine who our primary audience might be, who has the greatest say in the outcome of an issue, and how good our access to that audience is. Not every audience will be prepared to hear what I have to say, no matter how passionate I am about an issue and even, in some cases, no matter how much I may know about the issue.

MEDIA WATCH

SOUA and Scene

Some elements of the "scene" for the State of the Union Address have already been mentioned in the discussion of the president's *ethos* and the lingering skepticism about his motivations. This overlap between scene and agent illustrates the earlier noted difficulty of treating the various elements of the rhetorical situation as separable. In this case, the prior actions of the agent help construct the audience's understanding of the scene, which affects their take on the message. In what follows, the scene, or larger context for the address, will first be considered from the perspective of the president, who attempted to link his justification for military action against Iraq as firmly as possible to 9/11 even as he also supported the principle of preemptive war; it will also be considered from the perspective of the president's critics who challenged such links and questioned the wisdom of launching a preemptive war. Further, the president's strategy for dealing with a heterogeneous audience will be inferred from the manner in which he constructed his message.

In his 2002 State of the Union Address, the president helped set the "scene" for his linkage of Iraq to 9/11 by referring to Iraq as part of an "axis of evil" that included Iran and North Korea. Specifically, he cited the three countries' commitment to securing weapons of mass destruction (WMD) and the possibility that they would supply terrorists with such weapons. While this reference creates a precedent for the references in his 2003 address, it also poses a problem insofar as he now needs to distinguish the threat posed by Iraq from the threat posed by the other two nations—if we must now go to war with Iraq, why aren't we also going to war with Iran or North Korea? In his 2003 address, thus, he again mentions Iran and North Korea (he refrains, however, from naming the leader of either country, even though North Korea's leader Kim Jong Il was widely viewed as even less stable than Saddam Hussein), but only after suggesting that "Different threats require different strategies." In the case of Iran, says the president, our strategy has been to support Iranian citizens who protest their country's policies. In the case of North Korea, he says, our strategy has been to seek cooperation from other countries in the region in imposing economic sanctions and isolating North Korea from the rest of the world. But in light of the fact that we had every reason to believe that Iran and North Korea's nuclear weapons programs were far more advanced than Iraq's, the decision to single out Iraq seems puzzling. Until differences in the level and type of threat posed by the three countries have been elaborated, it's difficult to evaluate the different strategies to which they gave rise.

continued

The above argument assumes that proving Saddam Hussein a threat to our national interest and to our security was sufficient to justify a call for war. While that may be true, it is not an argument designed to appeal strongly to American idealism. Indeed, by carefully limiting any discussion of tangible sacrifice—the address contains no references to the financial costs of the war and makes only vague reference to "the brave Americans who bear the risk" of battle and the "days of mourning" that war brings—the president's argument appeals less to his audience's sense of nobility than to its sense of self-preservation. Certainly throughout much of his long apostrophe on Iraq, the president pays far more attention and lends considerably more presence to the threat posed by Iraq than to matters of duty and sacrifice.

Which brings us then to his conclusion and his most ambitious attempt to "ethicize" the war. In building to his conclusion, the president twice refers to the coming war in these terms: "If war is forced upon us. . . ." He immediately goes on to clarify that the necessity for war arises not just from mere self-preservation, but from a higher obligation, a "call of history [that] has come to the right nation." We are the right nation because of our willingness to "exercise power without conquest, and [to] sacrifice for the liberty of strangers." More importantly, we seek liberty for others in "God's" name, who has given it as a "gift to humanity." In the next-to-last line of his address, he brings this line of his argument to a swelling climax: "We do not claim to know all the ways of Providence, yet we can trust in them, placing our confidence in the loving God behind all of life and all of history." If much of his earlier argument constitutes a powerful secular appeal to his audience's fears and interests, this last appeal is designed to resonate with a long-standing and powerful national *mythos,* a belief stretching back to the Puritans, that America is God's favored land, that in realizing our "manifest destiny" we realize God's designs. Against the backdrop of this "larger context," the war in Iraq is transformed from a preemptive strike to a political necessity, and finally a holy obligation. To be sure, this message is more likely to resonate with some in his audience than with others; indeed, some are more likely than others to hear it all. Because religious references are quite common in the conclusion of presidential addresses, many in the president's audience doubtless heard his words as more ceremonial than substantive. But the members of the president's "base," his core political constituency, may well have heard it as the most meaningful appeal of the address.

CHAPTER

8

Informative Speaking

Taken from *Public Speaking: Strategies for Success*, Seventh Edition, by David Zarefsky.

In this chapter you'll learn about:

- Planning Your Strategy
  - Defining Your Specific Purpose | Informing Your Audience
  - Clarifying Your Informative Goal
- Informative Strategies
  - Defining | Reporting | Describing
  - Explaining | Demonstrating | Comparing
- Encouraging Retention

Now that we have explored delivery, audience analysis, research, reasoning, organization, and language, we are ready to bring these skills together into a complete speech. To do so, we should revisit two related concepts: purpose and strategy. A speech is designed to achieve a purpose, and strategic planning is the process of deciding how your speech can best do that.

We examine seven different kinds of purpose:

- Providing new information or sharing a perspective
- Setting the agenda
- Intensifying or weakening a feeling
- Strengthening commitment to a position
- Weakening commitment to a position
- Converting the audience away from one belief and toward another
- Inducing a specific action

Now the question is which strategies are most appropriate for achieving these purposes?

Planning Your Strategy

Broadly speaking, speech goals are achieved through the strategies of informing, persuading, and entertaining. These are sometimes mistaken as resulting in three fundamentally different kinds of speeches. In fact, though, because successful sharing of information also affects people's attitudes, informing and persuading occur together. Likewise, a successful persuasive speech is also entertaining and enjoyable to listen to, and an entertaining speech usually also conveys new information.

The broad strategies overlap, then, and they do not exclude each other. So if your assignment is to present "an informative speech," this does not mean that you should avoid saying anything entertaining or persuasive. Rather, you should achieve your purpose primarily through strategies of informing.

Defining Your Specific Purpose

What happens if the assignment does not specify a purpose? Or what if you are speaking outside the classroom setting? Then you must decide what you want to achieve (for example, to teach people something new, to get them to contribute money to a cause, or to make them laugh). You will need to assess how the audience and the occasion create opportunities or constraints. Finally, based on this analysis, you will define your specific purpose.

For example, suppose that many of your listeners believe that the Internet should be regulated to protect children from indecent material. Your own opinion is exactly the opposite, and you would like to change their minds. But you know (or will learn in the next chapter) that people do not usually make major changes in their beliefs because of a single speech. You also realize that although most of your listeners use the Internet frequently, they lack a basic grasp of the decentralized and transnational structure of the Web that makes regulation of the Internet so difficult. Finally, you will be speaking at an educational conference that is exploring how better to use the Internet in elementary school classrooms. All of these factors lead you not to try to convert your audience but to seek the more realistic goal of providing new information about the Internet. You hope that this new information, in turn, will weaken the audience's commitment to the view that the Internet should be regulated, but that is not your goal for this speech. Believing that your audience must be informed before it can be persuaded, you have chosen to provide new ideas or perspective.

However, sometimes an audience must be persuaded before it can be informed. Consider another example. During the Cold War years, most Americans approached foreign policy issues from the premise that the world was locked in a mortal struggle between freedom and communism. Information about world events was understood within the framework provided by this dominant assumption.

Informing her audience about the extent of child labor practices, this speaker draws on information from the Department of Labor.

For a speaker even to discuss independent nationalism in Eastern Europe, it first was necessary to challenge the prevailing view that all of Eastern Europe was a monolith dominated by the Soviet Union. In order to share information effectively, it first was necessary to change listeners' attitudes.

Informing Your Audience

In this chapter, we are concerned with informing. **Informative strategies** presume that a principal goal of the speech is to share ideas with the audience. They rely on the metaphor of the speaker as teacher and the speech as a lesson. The speaker is expected to be clear, accurate, and interesting. Listeners are asked to be attentive, to understand what is being said, and to modify their knowledge and belief systems to take this new information and perspective into account. Informative speeches share information about objects, processes, events, and concepts.

In a speech about the microscopic world around us, Kimo Sanderson made his classmates think about something they had previously ignored:

> There are millions of living creatures in your house right now. They crawl through your carpet, reproduce under your bed, and snack in your closet. When examined under a microscope, they look like creatures from your worst nightmares. They are dust mites, and we live with them every day.

In her speech about pharmacists and the idea of a "conscience clause," Krupa Shah introduced her audience to a developing controversy:

> Every day, every hour, every minute, someone steps inside a pharmacy that holds the medicines to fill nearly every prescription a doctor can write. I say "nearly," of course, because there may be times when the pharmacy runs out of a certain drug or maybe the pharmacist just doesn't want to give it to the patient. Wait! Running out of a drug seems legitimate, but the latter seems odd. However, it is possible, and it is possible because pharmacists have what is called a "conscience clause," which allows them to refuse certain prescription requests based on their own moral concerns.

Informative strategies do not explicitly ask listeners to believe or do any particular thing. Rather, they ask that listeners alter their understanding of a subject. Sometimes this can be done by taking new information into account, such as when one learns that the local community was founded by immigrants 150 years ago. At other times, listeners' understanding is changed because they see the subject in a different light, such as when confusing instructions for filling out a tax form are made clear, or when the speaker explains the counterintuitive fact that the Panama Canal is farther east on the Pacific side than on the Atlantic side (the canal mainly runs north–south).

Of course, learning something new might stimulate listeners to take action. For example, imagine that you heard a speech about fuel economy standards for automobile manufacturers, knowing very little about the scientific, ecological, and economic details of this important issue. The speaker's purpose was to share information about the significant global decrease in oil consumption that could be achieved by a modest increase in the average fuel efficiency of American cars and trucks. The speaker did not actually call on you to do anything; the goal was only to make you aware of an issue you previously had neglected. But it would not be surprising if, after hearing such a speech, you paid more attention to how many miles per gallon your car gets. The speech might also prompt you to take fuel economy into consideration the next time you buy a car, and even to urge legislators to support tougher standards for automakers. In the next chapter, we will contrast informative strategies with strategies of persuasion, which seek to influence listeners' beliefs, values, or actions.

Informative speeches come within the public forum for two reasons. First, they provide information enabling audiences to think and decide about matters that affect people generally. Second, having the

RHETORICAL WORKOUT

Keep Your Informative Goal in Mind

You are working on an informative speech about the International Space Station (ISS). You assume it is common knowledge that the ISS is a research laboratory in space with an international crew, even if most of your audience may not know any more details. Think about the informative goals presented in this chapter.

1. If your goal is to *provide new information or perspective,* how useful or interesting might each of the following be: (a) a list of countries that have contributed to the ISS; (b) a demonstration of how to look up NASA's website; (c) data on the size of the station and what kinds of equipment are aboard; (d) information about which countries built each part of the station? Explain why.
2. If your goal is *agenda setting,* how useful might each of the following be: (a) a report that the life span of the ISS is due to end in 2015; (b) information that experiments on the station are vital to understanding how living in space affects humans; (c) figures for how much funding for the ISS comes from the United States? Explain why.
3. If your goal is to *create positive or negative feeling,* how useful might each of the following be: (a) a poll showing that few Americans are interested in the ISS; (b) information about recycling innovations tested on the station; (c) an anecdote about how NASA named a treadmill on the station after comedian Stephen Colbert? Explain why.

information may enable the public to decide what to do about these matters. The speech on fuel economy standards illustrates both of these points.

Clarifying Your Informative Goal

Two of the speech purposes to be discussed in Chapter 9 rely primarily on informative strategies: providing new information or perspective and agenda setting. Information is essential if you are to induce listeners to think about something new, to view it from a unique perspective, or to take into account something they had previously ignored. In addition, the purpose of creating positive or negative feelings relies heavily on both informative and persuasive strategies, as well as on entertaining.

Providing New Information or Perspective

Common knowledge about a subject is often quite general. It is widely acknowledged, for example, that many eligible voters in the United States do not vote. But most people have little understanding of what lies behind this statement—whether the percentage of voters has been increasing or decreasing, how participation varies among different groups, factors that tend to increase or limit participation, the relationship between registration and voting, and so on. One informational goal for a speech would be to enrich the audience's common knowledge about voting rates, moving listeners from a broad understanding to a more detailed awareness of the issue.

Sometimes a speaker's objective is not merely to supply more details but to update and revise the audience's common knowledge. Part of what people generally believe may be mistaken, and social knowledge changes with the times. There is probably no clearer example than what people in the United States "know" about Russia. For most of the period from 1945 to 1990, people "knew" that the Soviet Union (which included Russia) was engaged in a deadly economic and political struggle with the United States. But in the years after 1990, people came to "know" that this was no longer the case. Since the rise to power of Vladimir Putin in the early 2000s, Americans have once again modified what they "know" about Russia. If not a deadly adversary of the United States, that nation is now seen as an economic and diplomatic rival.

The question of what Americans "know" about Russia came up again during the 2012 presidential election campaign, when Republican presidential hopeful Mitt Romney alleged that Russia was the number-one security threat and ideological adversary of the United States. His claim was vigorously denied by both the Russian president and the Obama administration, who assigned that ranking instead to the international terrorist network al-Qaeda.

You probably will not be able to alter your listeners' perspective so dramatically as in this example. But if your speech about the Internet gives listeners information that leads to a new way of thinking about "indecency," you probably will have accomplished a similar purpose.

Checklist 8.1
Speech Purposes and Strategies

1. Purposes achieved primarily through informative strategies
   - ☐ Providing new information or sharing a perspective
   - ☐ Agenda setting
2. Purposes achieved through a combination of informative and persuasive strategies
   - ☐ Creating positive or negative feeling
3. Purposes achieved primarily through persuasive strategies
   - ☐ Strengthening commitment to a position
   - ☐ Weakening commitment to a position
   - ☐ Converting the audience away from one belief and toward another
   - ☐ Inducing the audience to perform a specific action

Agenda Setting

A speaker whose purpose is **agenda setting** wants to create awareness of a subject that listeners did not know about or think about before, thus putting it on the agenda of topics that warrant their concern. Until fairly recently, for example, the majority of Americans simply didn't think about whether there was a pattern to the race or ethnicity of drivers who are stopped by police officers and searched in an effort to reduce crime. Most Americans went about their errands, assuming that if a person was stopped and searched by an officer, that person was rightly suspected of engaging in illegal activity. But many African American drivers who have been pulled over and searched without reasonable cause have protested against "racial profiling," the practice of making traffic or other investigative stops on the basis of a person's race or ethnicity. As a result, the subject now warrants our attention, and increasing numbers of people are becoming aware of the problem. Speakers and writers focused attention on a topic that had been ignored, and at some point it was put on the agenda. The September 11, 2001, terrorist attacks added yet another dimension to the issue, as people who had not thought one way or another about profiling during security screening at airports had to consider how it was being used to combat terrorism.

Creating Positive or Negative Feeling

It borders on cliché to say that information gives people power. Knowledge and understanding enable people to perform competently and to make intelligent choices. Providing information empowers listeners to feel better about their ability to control their lives. Ellen Benson, for example, did not think that she was good at managing her time. She never seemed to have enough time to get everything done; tasks took much longer than she thought they should, and she often forgot what she needed to do. But then she attended a speech about time management skills, and the speaker's information helped Ellen to understand her problems and gave her some techniques to manage time better. After the speech, she told a friend, "I feel like this speech has given me a new way to take control of my own life." The speech had created a positive feeling.

The ability to make intelligent choices is also a source of power. Informative speeches do not tell the audience which option to choose. But if they lay out the costs and benefits of alternatives, they may help listeners to form criteria for making a decision. By resolving a difficult question, people feel better both about the subject and about themselves.

To provide new information or perspective, set the agenda, or create positive or negative feeling, you will rely on informative strategies. We now will consider some of the primary informative strategies, most of which can be used to achieve any of the three goals.

Informative Strategies

For ease of explanation, we examine informative strategies one at a time, as though speakers used only one strategy in a given speech. Although that is possible, most speeches combine a number of strategies to achieve the speaker's purpose and to make it more likely that listeners will remember the information.

Defining

The strategy of **defining** uses this process to clarify a term or concept that is vague or troublesome. Or definition may be used to introduce a new or unexpected way of viewing the subject, so that the speech can develop the details and implications of this new approach.

Definition is unnecessary when a term's meaning is clear-cut. It is necessary, though, when a concept is not clear at all, as when new technical terminology makes its way into general usage. In the early 2000s, when computer-mediated interaction came into widespread use, most people suddenly needed to learn a new vocabulary: texting, Facebook, social networking sites, friend (as a verb), tweeting, and so on. A speech entitled "Deciphering Social Networking"—which included definitions of such terms—would have been well received. In this case, defining would serve as the means to provide new information or perspective. In the example about racial profiling, definition serves as a means of agenda setting, because understanding the meaning of the term helps audiences to think about the problem.

At other times, definition is used to create a positive feeling. Student Sonia Rubenstein, for example, believed that many of the unfortunate racial incidents and cases of "hate speech" on college campuses arose partly because the key concept "affirmative action" was misunderstood. She used the strategy of definition to clarify the concept and to establish a preferred meaning:

> Mention the term *affirmative action,* and some people will tell you that it means special recruiting efforts to attract minorities and women. Others say it means identifying a specific goal for the number of minorities and women to be hired. Still others think it means reserving a specific number of places for minorities and women. And people speak so often of the mechanics of affirmative action that they lose sight of the goal: We all benefit from the perspectives offered by a culturally diverse student body. If we keep track of that goal, then the best way to think of affirmative action is as special efforts to seek out qualified students who will enable us to achieve the goal.

Intelligent discussion is unlikely when the participants have different ideas of what they are talking about. For that reason, Sonia's goals were to identify different possible meanings, to explain the implications of accepting one meaning or another, and to describe a preferred point of view. She made definition the focus of her speech and organized the body like this:

I. Affirmative action has multiple meanings.
  A. It may mean aggressive recruiting.
  B. It may mean numerical goals.
  C. It may mean tie-breaking preferences.
  D. It may mean quotas.

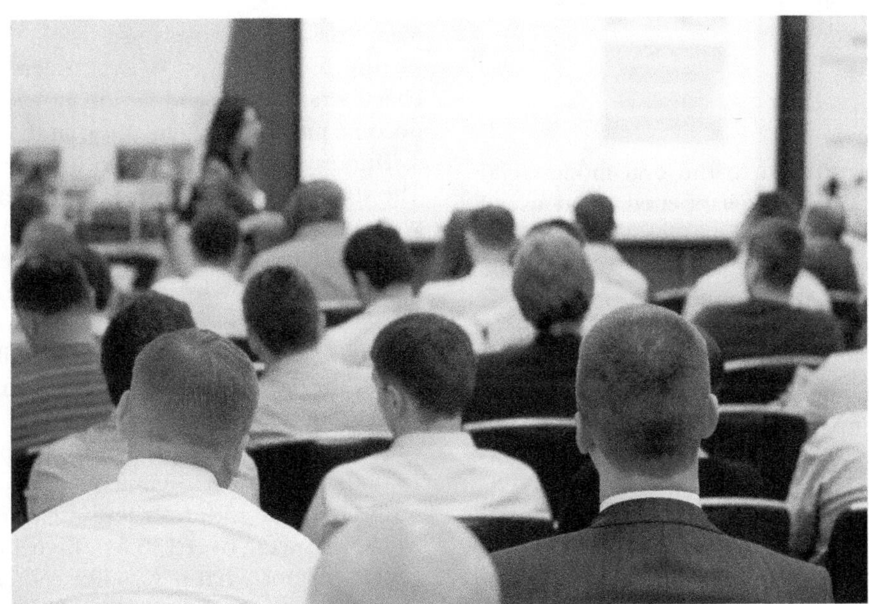

When the subject about which you are informing listeners is complex, charts, drawings, and pictures can aid in the explanation.

II. Selecting a meaning makes a difference.
    A. It will influence how actively the government takes an interest in the question.
    B. It will clarify whom affirmative action seeks to help.
    C. It will determine whether it is fair to place at a disadvantage people who have not themselves caused previous discrimination.
    D. It will influence how actively committed we should be to the goal.
III. Affirmative action really means aggressive recruiting.
    A. This meaning is consistent with our belief that people should be evaluated as individuals, not as groups.
    B. It is consistent with our belief that decisions should ultimately be made on the basis of merit.
    C. It recognizes the historical underrepresentation of minorities and the fact that qualified minority candidates may not be identified through normal means.

In this example the speaker uses definition to identify and explain a preferred meaning. Such definitions are not neutral; they shape how we view or think about a subject. In educating listeners about a definition, the speaker is also influencing them to think about the topic in a particular way, and to prefer one definition over another. This illustrates why the purposes of informing and persuading cannot be strictly separated. Although the strategy of definition is intended mainly to be informative, definitions also are persuasive.

Reporting

Reporting is journalism in the oral mode. It answers the question "What happened?" and usually does so in strict chronological order with little overt analysis or interpretation. Select this strategy if your analysis of audience, occasion, and purpose suggests that you need to explain a complex event by identifying each of its components.

If you were giving a speech about the recent trip to India by a group of students to build a house for a low-income family, and your goal was to share what happened, the body of the speech would report the major events of the trip:

I. Travel to India
    A. Who was part of the group
    B. Arrival at airport
    C. Coping with jet lag
II. Meeting charity organizers
    A. Why the low-income housing is needed
    B. Who will benefit from the housing
    C. Understanding cross-cultural differences
III. Building the house
    A. Where the house is located
    B. What materials were used
    C. How long it took to build
IV. Arrival of the new occupants
    A. What the new occupants thought of the house
    B. What the charity organizers thought of the house
V. Returning to campus
    A. What student participants thought of the experience
    B. How to participate next year

Reporting is primarily a means to provide new information or perspective, but it can also contribute to other goals. Knowing about this trip might lead listeners to think about sponsoring others. Moreover, although the image of reporting is that it is purely factual, usually far more has occurred than can be conveyed in a relatively short speech. Selecting which items to include and which to leave out therefore involves the speaker in making subjective judgments; in turn, these can influence what listeners think about the topic. Even reporting, then, is not a purely informative strategy.

Describing

Many passages in novels use words to try to paint a picture of the scene. When readers can "see" the characters, setting, and action in their minds, they become more actively involved in the novel.

Painting a mental picture involves description. The strategy of **describing** can benefit a speech as well as a novel.[1] In a speech about travel to the French Riviera, we are unlikely to hear a set of arguments about why we should go. Rather, the speaker will develop so appealing an image of the Riviera that we will *want* to go. Similarly, a speech about the 2011 earthquake and tsunami that hit Japan might mention not only the fact that the earthquake was magnitude 9.0 or that more than 15,000 people lost their lives, but could also describe the fear and destruction caused by tsunami waves that were over 130 feet high, in order to convey a sense of what it was like rather than just reporting what happened. In this way, description achieves the purpose of creating positive or negative feeling.

CHOOSE A STRATEGY: Using Informative Strategies

The Situation

You are preparing an informative speech for your class on how immigration reform might affect your classmates. In your research, you have found several studies and personal stories that speak to economic, political, and social impacts. Your informative goal is to place the issue of immigration reform on the agenda and raise the awareness of your audience about this complex issue. Now think about the informative strategies presented in this chapter.

Making Choices

1. Would defining be an appropriate informative strategy for your topic? Why or why not?
2. Which of the following strategies seems well suited to your topic: reporting, describing, or explaining, or some combination of these? What are the potential benefits or drawbacks of each strategy?
3. If you wanted to include a demonstration of some aspect of this topic, what might you be able to include? What would you need to do to your larger topic in order to include such a demonstration?
4. What might you compare your topic to in order to help your audience understand it better?

What If . . .

How would your answers above be affected by the following conditions?

1. Your audience is a group of recent immigrants. Or your audience is a group of anti-immigration activists.
2. Your informative goal is to provide new and updated information for your audience.

A mental picture becomes vivid through its details. Instead of a general reference to a person, an effective speaker describes the color of the eyes or hair, whether the person was standing erect or leaning against a post, the expression on the person's face, and so on. But a steady stream of details quickly becomes tedious, so the speaker selects details that evoke a larger picture. The expression on the person's face, for example, might convey a certain attitude. In a speech about the professor who had the greatest influence on her life, student Janet Wickstrom described many such details to her audience:

> I walked into Professor Alvarez's office and immediately noticed her desk. Or, rather, I noticed that I couldn't see her desk. One corner was piled high with new books. The telephone was covered with reminder notes. Students' papers and memos were strewn across the desk. There was yesterday's newspaper opened to the crossword puzzle. A napkin with crumbs from a leftover bagel was on top. Somewhere nearby was a coffee cup. Class notes were piled on top of the computer. A grade book was buried underneath a stack of paper. "What a desk," I thought. Yet I soon would discover that behind that desk was the most organized woman I ever have met.

Describing is an especially useful strategy when you believe that listeners will share your appraisal of the details, once you mention them, and that they will regard them as signs or examples of some characteristic that you could not observe or report directly—such as, in this example, the generalization that first appearances can be deceptive. Stated directly, the claim would seem a cliché. But if it is developed indirectly through detailed description, listeners' interest in the details will help them to appreciate the generalization.

Explaining

Beyond simply defining a term or making an idea precise, speakers sometimes want to share with an audience a deeper understanding of events, people, policies, or processes. This is done through explanation, which goes beyond reporting to consider

STRATEGIES FOR SPEAKING to Diverse Audiences

Respecting Diversity Through Informing

Information is not neutral. How people understand information is affected by their backgrounds and perspectives. These strategies will help you in presenting information to a diverse audience.

1. Consider how your audience members' beliefs and experiences influence what can be considered informative. For instance, speaking about evolution for an audience of biologists may be considered informative, whereas speaking for an audience of creationists may require persuasive strategies.
2. When providing new information or perspective, recognize that anyone's perspective on a topic is influenced by one's culture. Speaking about women's rights to an audience raised in a male-dominated culture requires awareness of your audience's expectations. You cannot assume that the audience shares your perspective.
3. Acknowledge that cultures may differ with respect to what topics legitimately can be placed on the agenda. Sometimes the topic itself may alienate the audience. In order to assure good will, remember that some topics may require greater sympathy than others.
4. Do not knowingly bias audience members' views. Insofar as possible, present all sides of an issue.

different views of what happened, to ask how or why it happened, or to speculate about what it means or implies.

For example, if you wanted to explain the 1962 Cuban missile crisis to listeners who were not yet born and who don't really understand that event, you would not simply report what took place from October 16 to October 28, 1962. You would discuss such topics as how and why Soviet missiles were placed in Cuba, why Americans regarded them as so threatening, what options for a response were weighed by President Kennedy and his advisers, how the crisis was resolved, and what it meant for U.S.-Soviet relations at the height of the Cold War. If your explanation is successful, listeners not only will know more of the facts but also will grasp the significance of the crisis and will appreciate why the issues it raised have fascinated people for over 50 years. In this example, you would be both providing new perspectives on the missile crisis and setting an agenda by encouraging listeners to think critically about what they might otherwise have regarded as just a series of facts.

Speeches that explain events or people often begin simply and then build toward greater richness or complexity. In contrast, speeches that explain policies or processes generally proceed in the opposite direction. Ever since 1980, for example, the diplomatic relationship between the United States and Iran has been either poor or nonexistent. A speaker who wants to explain why the United States does not have diplomatic relations with Iran in 2012 would have to break this simple concept down into its components: the 1979 overthrow of the U.S.-backed shah, how Israel is both a friend of the United States and an enemy of Iran, how nuclear development is understood as an aggressive act to the United States and an act of national sovereignty for Iran, and so on. Only by understanding these components well could listeners really understand why the United States and Iran do not have diplomatic relations in 2012 and what types of barriers stand in the way of future relations.

Speeches explaining a difficult concept should distinguish between its essential meaning and other meanings that may be associated with it but that are less central.[2] Similarly, speeches that explain a process proceed by breaking down complex operations into a simple sequence of steps. For example, because public opinion polls are reported so often in the news, you might want to speak about how such polls are conducted. You would explain all the steps in the process: the framing of the questions, identification of the population to be sampled, procedures for obtaining responses from the sample, recording and coding of responses, performing statistical analyses, and interpreting significant results. After hearing your speech, listeners will not be able

Sometimes explanation is not enough—the speaker must show listeners how to do something. The speech of demonstration enables listeners to view a process so that they may be able to repeat it themselves.

to design and conduct polls themselves but they will recognize and understand the key steps in the polling process.

Demonstrating

Sometimes, it is not enough to explain a process; it is necessary as well for the audience to see it. Or sometimes, the goal is not just for listeners to understand something; the object is to enable them to do it themselves. In such a case, a speaker may offer a demonstration, describing a seemingly mysterious or complicated procedure as a series of fairly simple steps performed in a particular order. Such a speech that demonstrates how to cook a meal, how to wallpaper a room, how to prepare a simple tax return, or how to organize a cluttered desk demystifies the topic for listeners, so that they learn to do something that they could not do before. The speech obviously provides new information; in making the subject less mysterious to listeners, it also helps to create a positive feeling.

Demonstration could be the only focus of a speech, or it could be part of a speech that employs other strategies as well. In either case, as you prepare the demonstration, the following considerations are particularly important:

1. Do listeners really need to see the process to understand it? If not, a demonstration may seem superfluous or boring; but if so, a demonstration will be strategically essential.
2. Is the subject precise enough that it can be demonstrated in the time available? Complicated operations, such as rebuilding an automobile engine, can't possibly be covered in a single speech. And even without a time limit, it's unlikely that an audience will attend to, much less remember, a long demonstration about how to rebuild an engine. However, such topics as how to make an apple pie, how to plan one's study time, and how to pack a suitcase efficiently lend themselves well to brief demonstrations.
3. Are the steps of the process clear, distinct, and in proper sequence? Listeners will not understand what they are supposed to do if your instructions are vague or incomprehensible or if you demonstrate the steps out of order. Start at the beginning, and go through all the steps leading to the finished product. Do not skip any necessary steps, and do not duplicate steps.
4. Are your actions and your verbal instructions coordinated? Avoid any long gaps in the speech while you are doing something or waiting for something to happen. You will lose both the continuity of the speech and the audience's attention if you must pause and wait for results. This problem often weakens a demonstration of how to cook something.

Demonstration speeches usually benefit from visual aids.

Comparing

The final informative strategy is comparing, which seeks to clarify for listeners the similarities and differences between the items compared. It can be used to make things seem more similar than an audience had imagined. For example, computer platforms are often thought to be quite different from one another, but a speech comparing features of two leading systems, PC and Mac, could convince the audience that they are so similar that anyone who knows one can learn the other quickly. Alternatively, a comparison might heighten awareness of differences between things thought to be alike. If listeners think that all systems of parliamentary procedure are basically the same, they might learn otherwise by hearing a speech that compares different systems. Or the strategy could accomplish both of these purposes. A speech comparing the curriculum in engineering with that in liberal arts could make listeners aware of both similarities and differences that they had not recognized.

Another use of the strategy of comparing is to decide in what category something should be placed. Deciding whether Social Security is basically an insurance program or basically a welfare program could be helped by a speech exploring its similarities to and differences from each of those concepts.

Finally, comparing can provide listeners with a basis for making a choice. The speaker does not tell them what to do or urge them to accept one perspective over another but instead identifies the options available and compares the benefits and costs.

The public debate about affirmative action in university admissions policies provides a good example. In 2003, the Supreme Court heard arguments in two separate cases from two students who believed that they were denied admission to the University of Michigan as a result of reverse discrimination. Opponents of affirmative action have suggested some alternatives to it, such as focusing on economics rather than race, and adopting "affirmative access" that guarantees state university admission to top high-school seniors from any high school in the state. Other opponents have called for race-neutral admissions policies. Supporters of affirmative action believe that it is still necessary to take race into account in order to achieve a truly equal educational opportunity. A speech of comparison might increase public understanding by identifying the problem, describing the proposed options, and determining the strengths and weaknesses of each. The purpose of the speech would not be to urge any particular choice, but to make the alternatives clear so that listeners could apply their own criteria in deciding and forming a judgment about what action should be taken once the Supreme Court announced in the spring of 2012 that it would reexamine the issue. The body of such a speech might be organized this way:

I. Subjective individual review of each applicant is a possible solution.
   A. It offers certain benefits.
   B. It poses certain drawbacks.
II. Race-neutral admissions is a possible solution.
   A. It offers certain benefits.
   B. It poses certain drawbacks.
III. Admissions focused on economic diversity is a possible solution.
   A. It offers certain benefits.
   B. It poses certain drawbacks.
IV. "Affirmative access" guarantees of admission to all top students is a possible solution.
   A. It offers certain benefits.
   B. It poses certain drawbacks.
V. Race-conscious admissions for a limited time period is a possible solution.
   A. It offers certain benefits.
   B. It poses certain drawbacks.
VI. Summary: The choices that we must consider are subjective review of individual applications, race-neutral admissions, admissions focused on economic diversity, "affirmative access," and race-conscious admissions for a limited time period.

The principal purpose of this speech was to provide new information for listeners unfamiliar with alternatives to affirmative action. A secondary purpose might well be to create a positive feeling of sympathy for the complex nature of the issue.

Finally, remember that speakers often combine these informative strategies. A speech may both report what happened and attempt to interpret what it means, or may both explain and compare, or may both define and describe, or may both demonstrate and explain. Always, however, the goal is to share understanding and insight in order to provide new information or perspective, set an agenda, or create a positive or negative feeling.

Encouraging Retention

It might be said that the true test of learning is not how much knowledge or insight one takes in but how much one retains. There are cases in which the speaker seeks only an immediate response. If the purpose of the speech is to convince people to donate to a fund-raising effort, then the immediate response—Did people actually give money?—may be the sole test of success. But with informing, it is different. Speakers want the audience not only to attend to and understand what they said but also to remember it.[3]

Over a century ago, psychologists explained what is called the **forgetting curve**. This concept is applied to public speaking in Figure 8.1, where the horizontal axis represents the amount of time after the speech and the vertical axis shows the percentage of content that is remembered. As you can see from the fast-falling curve, a large portion of the speech is forgotten quickly; the line begins with a sharp negative slope and then levels out later. The forgetting curve applies both to the main points of the speech and to the sources of information. Over a short period of time, listeners quickly forget what was said. We might say that the information conveyed in a speech typically has a short half-life. Indeed, this is the biggest constraint on the effectiveness of informative strategies.

Although the forgetting curve typically takes the shape shown in Figure 8.1, the sharp decline does not have to appear at the same place on the graph. It is possible to "shift the curve upward," to increase the likelihood that listeners will remember more content at any given time:

1. Fortunately, the methods used to increase attention apply to retention as well.
2. Compared with passively receiving information, active listening requires a higher level of participation. And because participation enhances motivation, it should be no surprise that active involvement by listeners (rather than just passive hearing of the speech) increases the chances that they will remember the message.
3. Retention is also strengthened through **reinforcement**, a response by the speaker that rewards the listener and thereby strengthens the listener's positive attitudes toward the speech. In the public speaking classroom, listeners often reinforce speakers. If audience members nod their heads in agreement whenever a speaker expresses an opinion, the speaker is likely to increase the number of opinion statements.

As a speaker, though, you also can use reinforcement strategically to ensure that the audience remembers the message. As you learned in Chapter 10, if your organizational pattern enables listeners to anticipate what will come next and the subsequent development of your speech confirms their guess, then by confirming their expectation you reward their shrewd judgment.

You can also reinforce audience members by how you refer to them. Saying "we" instead of "you" conveys the message that you identify with listeners and regard them as your equals; you signal that you respect their thoughtful judgment. In his historic speech on election night in 2008, Barack Obama

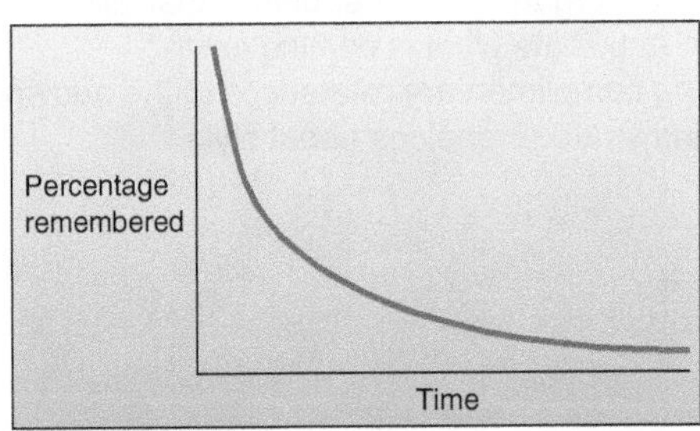

Figure 8.1
The Forgetting Curve

A Question of ETHICS

The Ethics of Informing

If information is empowering, even more empowering is the opportunity to present information. The speaker chooses what information to share and what to omit, how to describe the information, and how to explain what it means. Under what conditions can the exercise of this power result in unethical manipulation of the audience? Can any speaker be truly neutral in presenting information? If not, is it ethical to distinguish informing from persuading? Why or why not?

repeatedly avoided referring to himself, and focused on "we" rather than "I." This usage reinforced the beliefs of listeners that they were in the know and had participated actively in making the election result possible. Explicit references to them within the speech may have the same effect. A speaker whose transition says, in effect, "Since you've followed this complex topic so far, I'm sure you can see why the next point is valid," is speaking well of the audience and providing reinforcement. This, along with strategies that draw attention and encourage active listening, will shift the forgetting curve and improve the odds of ensuring retention.

Parallel wording makes it easier to remember ideas, vivid language will keep a description in the listener's mind, and simple sentences enable a listener to follow the message and focus more easily on what is being said. These elements help to make ideas not only more readily understood, but also more likely to be remembered. They are strategic resources that can be used to achieve any informative purpose.

SUMMARY

Speeches that rely mainly on informative strategies do not seek directly to influence listeners' actions, yet it would be unfair to say that they have no persuasive effects.

Informative strategies achieve several speech purposes:

- Provide new information or perspective
- Agenda setting
- Create positive or negative feeling

Based on analysis of the audience, occasion, and purpose, you can select appropriate informative strategies, including a combination of the following:

- Defining: clarifying a term or concept or introducing a new way to view the subject
- Reporting: relating what happened with little analysis or interpretation
- Describing: characterizing or evoking a mental image of the subject
- Explaining: sharing a deeper understanding beyond reporting
- Demonstrating: showing a process as steps in a particular order
- Comparing: clarifying similarities and differences between items

Listeners quickly forget much of what was said in a speech, so you will want to encourage and reinforce retention by doing the following:

- Providing information that draws attention
- Using an organizational structure that allows listeners to anticipate what is coming next
- Making complimentary references to the audience
- Making strategic choices about style

Discussion Questions

1. In the public speeches that you've heard lately, were informative strategies or persuasive strategies dominant? Consider speeches from outside the public speaking classroom, such as the following:
   - A presidential address
   - A speech at a protest rally
   - A lecture in your history class
   - An oral research report presented by a student in another class
   - The closing argument in a trial

   Were any of these speeches completely devoid of persuasive strategies? Were any completely devoid of informative strategies? Can a speaker inform listeners without influencing them in some way? Can a speaker persuade listeners without providing information?
2. Speakers encourage retention by reinforcing listeners, by drawing their attention, and by encouraging them to listen actively. Two strategies for doing these things are (a) to provide a clear organizational pattern and (b) to refer to "we" instead of "you." What other strategies help a speaker to encourage retention in a speech with a primarily informative goal? Discuss the strategies that in your experience were most effective in making you remember the message long after the speech was over (e.g., visual aids, audience participation, etc). Do the means of making the speech memorable distract from its message?
3. The lectures of a college professor are a form of informative speech. Discuss what distinguishes a good lecture from a poor one. Might other factors, such as class size or topic, create different requirements for an effective informative speech?

Activities

1. Watch a news report on television. In what ways is it like a speech to inform? In what ways is it different? Can you take anything from this model to help you create speeches with informative strategies?
2. Create one of the following:
   a. A speech of explanation about the process of developing informative strategies in speeches
   b. A speech of comparison that discusses informative and persuasive strategies
   c. A speech of definition about the concept of "strategic planning" in speech preparation
   d. A speech of explanation about five strategies that you plan to use in your next speech to increase the audience's retention of information.
3. Outline a speech describing one side of a controversy, and then outline a speech detailing the other side. Put these two together to create a speech, informing your audience about the complexity of a particular controversy. If your purpose is to inform without bias, to what might you need to pay attention? Where might bias potentially lie? At the level of words, sentences, overall structure, etc.?

KEY TERMS

agenda setting
defining
describing
forgetting curve
informative strategies
reinforcement
reporting

NOTES

1. For more about description in speeches, see Gerard A. Hauser, "Empiricism, Description, and New Rhetoric," *Philosophy and Rhetoric* 5 (Winter 1972): 24–44. Fear can be instilled through description as well. For one example, see Brian Jackson, "Jonathan Edwards Goes to Hell (House): Fear Appeals in American Evangelism," *Rhetoric Review* 26 (2007): 42–59.
2. For a fuller discussion of explanatory discourse, see Katherine E. Rowan, "Informing and Explaining Skills: Theory and Research on Informative Communication," *Handbook of Communication and Social Interaction Skills,* eds. John O. Greene and Brant R. Burleson, Mahwah, NJ: Erlbaum, 2003, pp. 419–430.
3. For more about retention, see Robert L. Greene, *Human Memory: Paradigms and Paradoxes,* Mahwah, NJ: Lawrence Erlbaum, 1992. For retention in visual media, see John J, Hale, "The Visual Superiority Effect: Retention of Audiovisual Messages," *International Journal of Instructional Media* 36 (2009): 275–86.

CHAPTER

9

Invention

Taken from *Public Speaking: Strategies for Success*, Seventh Edition, by David Zarefsky.

In this chapter you'll learn about:

From your audience analysis, you know as much as you can about your listeners, and now you are ready to make the choices that will shape your speech. These choices involve *strategic* decisions; that is, decisions about what will best achieve your purpose. But first you need to know what your purpose is; and to decide that, you need to know what your **topic** is.

For many students, deciding what to talk about is the hardest part of a speech assignment. Fortunately, when you speak outside the classroom, elements in the situation will often make that decision for you. These elements may include:

- *Commitment to a cause.* Suppose, for example, that you are committed to a specific public issue, such as the fight against global warming. The issue itself defines your topic, and your personal commitment determines why it is important for you to speak.
- *Reputation.* Your experience and knowledge may lead to an invitation to speak about a specific topic. If you are an expert on Cascading Style Sheets (CSS), for example, a group of Web developers might invite you to speak at a meeting about new techniques for designing blogs. If you instead discussed U.S. foreign policy, or the pleasures of sailing, or the need for reform in the university, you would not be meeting your responsibility to the audience.
- *Occasion.* Many speeches are delivered on ceremonial occasions. If you are accepting an award, the award and what it represents will decide your topic. If you are delivering a eulogy, the achievements of the person who died become the subject of the speech. If you are roasting a coworker who is about to retire, your subject matter will be humorous traits or events involving that person.

Sometimes, a classroom-speaking assignment will specify the topic. More typically, in class the choice of topic will be left to you, with the understanding that you will address an audience of people your age, in your school. You probably will be more effective if you talk about something that interests you rather than an assigned topic that has been chosen by someone else.[1] In the classroom, it is particularly important that you size up the situation and then stand up for what interests you, for what you believe, and can share with others.

Outside of class, the primary occasion when you will have freedom in choosing your topic occurs when the audience is interested in hearing *you,* almost regardless of what you have to say. Such an open-ended invitation may arise out of respect for your achievements, interest in your experiences, curiosity about your personality or general approach, or the desire to learn whatever is on your mind.

In short, selecting a topic is a complex matter. Sometimes speakers analyze the audience and then select a topic that will attract listeners. Sometimes they pick a topic first because it is important to them, and then analyze the audience so that the speech can be adapted to listeners. And sometimes topics are thrust upon them by the situation, in which case they can decide how to mold the speech in the most appropriate way.

What Makes a Good Topic?

If the topic of your speech is dictated by the issue, occasion, or audience, it is easy to decide what will make a good topic: whatever is pertinent and appropriate to the situation. You talk about what you were asked to discuss or about what the issue or occasion seems to require. You are not completely captive to the situation, because how you shape your speech will influence listeners' perceptions of the situation. But at the most basic level, your understanding of the situation will govern what you need to talk about.

But what should you talk about if you have complete freedom to select the topic? Table 9.1 identifies some potential speech topics, and the following criteria will help you to decide whether the topic you have in mind is a good one. (As you read, you might want to apply these criteria to the topics listed in Table 9.1.)

Importance to the Speaker

A good topic is one that matters to you. If you do not care about the subject, it will be very hard to make it interesting or important to the audience. Consider how the following three students used their personal interests to develop good speech topics:

- Melanie Nehrkorn listened to several of her friends complain that during city housing inspections, their landlord had to hide the fact that they lived off campus because a city ordinance limited the number of unrelated people who could share an apartment. Fearing that this might happen to her and others, Melanie used her public speaking opportunity to explain the city ordinance and why it threatened to hurt her fellow students who wished to live off campus. She wanted both to inform her audience about this controversial ordinance and to persuade them to campaign for its repeal.
- Elisabeth Pinkerton was at a movie theater with friends when someone's cell phone began ringing during the show. This was not the first time this had happened. Elisabeth was appalled by this person's rudeness and lack of consideration for others. She used her speech class to share information about cell phone etiquette with her classmates.
- Phillip Marcus was angry. During a closed-book exam in a sociology class, he saw another student sending a text message to his roommate seeking help on three of the questions. At first he was stunned by what he regarded as outrageous conduct; then he became upset that his work and the work of other honest students was devalued by

Table 9.1
Sample Speech Topics

Public Issues	Personal Experience	Significance of an Occasion
Stem cell research	Lifeguarding	Commencement
Health-care costs	Snowboarding	Death of friend
Video game violence	Sign language	Wedding
Northwest logging	Yoga	School election
Gay rights	Poetry writing	Presentation of award
Internet Privacy rights	International travel	Office party
Affirmative action	Volunteering at a homeless shelter	
Nuclear proliferation	Digital filmmaking	
AIDS epidemic	Political campaigning	
Third World debt	Hot-air ballooning	
Dependence on fossil fuels	Tutoring	
Terrorism		

this incident. He decided to give a speech in his public speaking class to make others aware of what was happening, to evoke in them similar feelings of anger, and to channel their emotions toward doing something about cheating. How Phillip chose his topic and developed his strategy will be seen throughout this chapter.

In choosing a topic of personal interest, you must be careful that your own interest does not harden into bias. You must be able to discuss the subject impartially and must recognize the value of other people's points of view.

Interest to the Audience

Even though the topic matters to you, you still must gain the interest of the audience. Audiences will be interested if your topic provides new information they can use, if it offers a solution to a puzzle or problem that affects them, if it connects what is unfamiliar to what they know, or if it reports stories or experiences similar to their own. Phillip Marcus decided that his story of the student who was cheating on the exam would interest others and also would arouse their anger.

Keep in mind as well that an audience's strong interest in the topic potentially may lead to *mis*communication as a result of selective perception. For example, when a manager addresses employees to describe the company's new policy about personal telephone calls and Internet use on the office's computer network, the audience has a strong interest in the message because it clearly will affect them. But there is also a risk that the audience will feel threatened or will believe that the company has become less friendly and may misperceive the message. Their personal interest may actually weaken their ability to listen critically.

Worthy of Listeners' Time

A related criterion is that the topic should be something that listeners regard as worth hearing about. If the topic is frivolous or trivial, they may feel that they have wasted their time by listening to you, especially if they came voluntarily and could have been doing something else. Unless there is something unique about the approach, a topic such as "How to open a beer can" probably would not meet this test. This does not mean that your topic must be profound or deadly serious; light-hearted humor or new insights on familiar subjects can work very well in a speech. The question to keep in mind is whether the audience will feel that what you have had to say was worth their attention and time.

RHETORICAL WORKOUT

Estimate Audience Interest in Your Topic

You learn about a type of storm called a derecho (deh-REY-cho), a damaging straight-line windstorm that often occurs within a band of thunderstorms. Although you haven't heard of a derecho before, you find out that it has some similarities in scope and destructiveness to tornadoes. You wonder if this could be a topic of interest to your class for your next speech. Think about the following criteria:

- Does the topic provide new information to your class audience? Do you think they already know about the topic? Why or why not?
- You learn that derechos can occur in your region and that people can take certain measures to protect themselves from the storms. Do you think this information would be useful to your audience? Why or why not? What if derechos rarely occur in your area?
- Does the topic offer a solution to a puzzle or problem that affects your audience? Why or why not?
- Does the topic offer a way to connect something unfamiliar to what your audience already knows? Explain.
- You do some early research and find several stories about people who have been through derechos and what damage the storms did. Do you think these stories could relate to experiences of your classmates? Why or why not?

Appropriateness of Scope

A speaker has to cover the topic to an appropriate degree within the time available. A topic that includes a very large number of points that can be covered only superficially—for example, a five-minute analysis of U.S. foreign policy—should probably be avoided. Similarly, a very narrow topic that can be covered completely in a very short time—such as a description of how to stop when in-line skating—is probably not a good choice either.

Even in a five-minute speech, you might discover that you are repeating yourself several times. Although the topic of cheating on exams might invite a long philosophical discussion of ethics and morality, it also could be focused enough to be covered in a short speech. It is a good topic because it offers rich possibilities for the development of ideas without excessive repetition.

Appropriateness for Oral Delivery

Sometimes, a topic can be developed better in an essay than in a speech. Because readers proceed at their own pace, they can reread any passage that is difficult to understand. But a speech is delivered in real time and at the same pace to all listeners, some of whom will not be able to recall it after delivery. Listeners who miss a particular link in a speaker's chain of ideas cannot replay it; if the link was critical, the rest of the speech might become meaningless.

Topics that depend on technical formulas or elaborate arguments are usually better presented in print than in oral delivery. Still, if a speaker's main ideas and examples are planned carefully and presented clearly, even technical and complex topics can be understood by a nonspecialist audience.

Appropriateness to the Rhetorical Situation

Even when the rhetorical situation does not completely determine your topic and you have a range of choice, still it is important that the topic fit the rhetorical situation. A humorous topic is not appropriate if the situation calls for solemnity; a secular topic is not appropriate at most religious functions; and a topic that does not present a problem is inappropriate if the situation calls for a problem-solution speech.

This does not mean, however, that it is inappropriate to discuss topics that are controversial. Topics that are faith based or that relate to personal or public morality are examples of these. They involve issues that many people regard as central to their identity, and people can be expected to disagree—sometimes sharply. The very fact that these topics are important and controversial makes them appropriate for the public forum. The question is not whether to select them but how to develop them. Even when you have strong convictions, your audience will likely be heterogeneous. You should remember that others will disagree with you. They are not likely to be swayed, and you are not likely to succeed, with a display of intolerance for competing views, bigotry, or closed-mindedness.

There also are topics that have been addressed so many times that—even though the subject may be important—it may seem that there is little new to be said. If that really is the case, these topics will not be appropriate to the rhetorical situation because speaking about them probably will not add to what listeners have heard already, and so will not inspire listeners to be attentive and interested. Examples include the dangers of smoking, capital punishment, whether abortion should be outlawed, and

A Question of *ETHICS*

Appropriate Topics

In choosing a topic, it is important to think about the situation in which you will speak. Imagine that you will be speaking at a high-school graduation and that you feel very strongly about an upcoming gubernatorial election in the state. Is it ethical for you to engage in political advocacy on this occasion? Would your answer be different if the audience were voluntary instead of captive? How does the nature of the situation as a high-school graduation affect your answer? On the other hand, because you feel strongly about the matter, is it ethical to suppress your own feelings just because of the specific situation? How do you resolve a tension between articulating your own convictions and deferring to the expectations of the situation?

Checklist 9.1
Characteristics of a Good Topic

- Importance to the Speaker: Does the topic matter to you?
- Interest to the Audience: Will the topic gain and hold the audience's interest?
- Worthy of Listeners' Time: Will your listeners feel the topic is worth their time to hear about?
- Appropriateness of Scope: Is the topic manageable within the time available?
- Appropriateness for Oral Delivery: Can the topic be understood from a speech or is it too complex?
- Appropriateness to the Rhetorical Situation: Does the topic recognize and respond to the constraints imposed by the rhetorical situation?
- Clarity: Is the topic one that your audience can easily identify?

the abolition of the Electoral College. You should not necessarily avoid speaking on such topics, unless your instructor has ruled them out of bounds, but you should recognize that you will have a greater burden to offer a fresh perspective to your audience, not to just tell them what they already know. Speaking on hackneyed topics is not likely to be productive.

Clarity

Finally, of course, the speaker should make the topic clear to all listeners. Speakers often fail to refine their topics sufficiently, and the result is a confused jumble of poorly connected ideas. If you are confused about the ideas in your speech, you can be sure that your audience will be confused, too. Even if you think you understand the topic, the fact that you know more about it than the audience does may lead you to present it in a way that is beyond comprehension. For this reason, you should always strive to understand and be sensitive to the audience's level of knowledge.

How to Choose a Good Topic

What you have just read about the *general* characteristics of a good speech topic may still leave you wondering what the right topic is *for you.* This section offers some suggestions to help you identify a good topic.

Conduct a Personal Inventory

It is time to ask some questions about yourself.

What Public Issues Do I Care About?

Public issues are those that concern people generally. Because most audience members are likely to be affected by these issues, they often make good speech topics—but only if you yourself also care about them. It is important, then, to be aware of current events and to think about how you and others are affected by them.

Suppose you decide that the topics of animal rights, homelessness, child abuse, and shifting ethical standards really matter to you. But you are not very interested in international trade, health care financing, and school voucher systems. You probably could develop the first group of topics into effective speeches; the second group would probably not inspire you.

Which of My Experiences Might Be Generalizable?

Everyone has had unique experiences, but these do not always make good speech topics. If audience members do not believe that your experience could happen to them, they may react to your speech with the same boredom that many people feel when watching someone else's home videos. However, if something about your experience can be generalized so that others can imagine themselves in the same situation, you may be onto a good topic.

The fact that you work a part-time job and cannot become full-time, so the company can avoid offering you full medical benefits, might matter only to you. But if you can generalize the experience—for example, to the anxiety that many people share about rising medical costs or to the advantages of health insurance that is not linked to employment—your experience might make a good topic. Audience members who don't care at all about your job might still become interested in a speech about a more general problem that they share. Likewise, Phillip Marcus's anger at seeing a classmate cheat could be generalized if he relates the experience so that listeners can imagine how they would feel if it had happened to them.

Which of My Interests Overlap with Those of the Audience?

Another question to ask in your personal inventory is whether you share a common interest in any topic with your listeners. If so, you'll have a good match. You will have an incentive to speak about the topic, and they will be motivated to listen.

Sometimes, the match may be exact. For example, you may find that both you and your audience are interested in the Beatles because no musical group in the past 50 years has been so successful. At other times, you will have to match a specific interest with a more general category. For example, you are interested in the Beatles, and your audience is interested in rock stars of the past generation. In that case, you'll want to relate the more specific to the more general, explaining how the Beatles exemplify the general subject of rock stardom. If you can do that, you have a good topic.

Brainstorm

If your personal inventory did not uncover a good topic for your speech, you can try **brainstorming**, a mental exercise in which you identify the first things that come to mind when you are presented with a given term or category. Do not censor your thoughts; just record them without evaluation. For example, you might divide a sheet of paper into columns with such category headings as "Heroes," "Places to Visit," "Hobbies," and "Favorite Books." (These are just examples, of course; pick whichever categories you want to explore through brainstorming.) Under each heading, jot down the first five things that occur to you. For example, you might list five heroes or five characteristics of a hero, or you might name five places you have visited or five places you hope to visit. Do not stop to evaluate your ideas; write down whatever first comes to mind. Then study the list to see whether you can find any patterns. You may discover, for example, that your lists of heroes, places to visit, hobbies, and favorite books all include items related to the Civil War. Because you seem to have an interest in the Civil War, some aspect of that could become your speech topic.

Brainstorming works well when you can identify a group of categories, as in the previous example. ***Topoi*** (a Greek term meaning "commonplaces" or "common topics") can be used to form the categories in the first place. As the term suggests, *topoi* are general headings for subject matter. Among Aristotle's *topoi* were "war and peace" and "legislation." Today, the *topoi* of public life might include the economy, science and technology, public finance, social policy, education, and the environment, among others. The *topoi* of the college experience might include classes, residential life, social activities, extracurricular organizations, independent study, and community service. Under each of these categories you can identify potential topics for speeches.

You also can try casually browsing through newspapers, magazines, and the Internet, writing down notes about topics that interest you. Even if you have not given much thought to these topics before, perhaps now you can see how they could lead to a good speech. Being informed about current events and thinking about material covered in your other classes may also help you to brainstorm possible speech topics.

Narrow the Topic

The final step in selecting a good topic is to narrow it so that it fits the situation. If your speech is limited to only 10 minutes, for example, you could not begin to explore a topic like "America's Shifting Ethical Standards." But suppose that you narrowed the topic down to the specific standard of honesty, then narrowed that to cheating as an example of dishonesty, and then narrowed that to cheating by college students and finally to "Cheating on This Campus." *Now* you could cover the topic within the allotted time, and your topic would relate to the broader subject that caught your interest in the first place.

Narrowing the topic means sharpening your focus so you concentrate on only some part of a broad topic. It is like pouring the topic through a funnel: What goes into the large end is too much to manage,

Checklist 9.2
Steps in Choosing a Good Topic

1. Conduct a personal inventory.
   - What public issues do I care about?
   - What experiences have I had that might be generalizable?
   - Which of my interests overlap with those of the audience?
2. Brainstorm and browse through published or online materials.
3. Narrow the topic so that it can be covered adequately within the time available.

but what comes out the small end can be focused effectively. Time constraints are one obvious reason to narrow the topic. But you also should narrow it to be sure that you can learn enough about the topic before your speech is due and to be sure that the topic fulfills your specific assignment. You can still allude briefly to the topic's larger implications without attempting to develop them in depth.

Figure 9.1 illustrates one approach to narrowing a topic. Beginning with the most general statement, the speaker narrows through a series of steps, dividing the general topic until a topic of manageable scope is selected. For the sake of clarity, Figure 9.1 does not include all of the possible subdivisions; nor is the seven-step sequence in Figure 9.1 the only way to narrow this or any other topic. It is meant to illustrate the thought processes involved in narrowing a very general topic to manageable scope. It also shows how one very general topic can yield a large number of different specific topics for speeches.

Whatever else you do, resist any urge to postpone selecting a topic. If you wait until the last minute, you won't have time to inventory your interests, to brainstorm, and to narrow the topic appropriately.

Developing a Strategic Plan

So far, we have examined the elements that *create* a rhetorical situation (audience, occasion, speaker, and speech). And now that you understand how to select a topic, it is time to consider how your speech will *respond* to the rhetorical situation.

Any speech will affect or change the situation in some way. This change should be strategic, not random; the speech is planned so that it becomes the means to a desired end. Consequently, a crucial early step in preparing to give a speech is to discern your purpose, any factors that might limit your strategies, and the options and opportunities available.

In preparing to respond to the rhetorical situation, you need to develop a **strategic plan** that identifies the purpose of your speech, the constraints on it, and the opportunities it provides (see Figure 9.2). Then you select the best means to achieve your purpose, execute them, and evaluate the results.

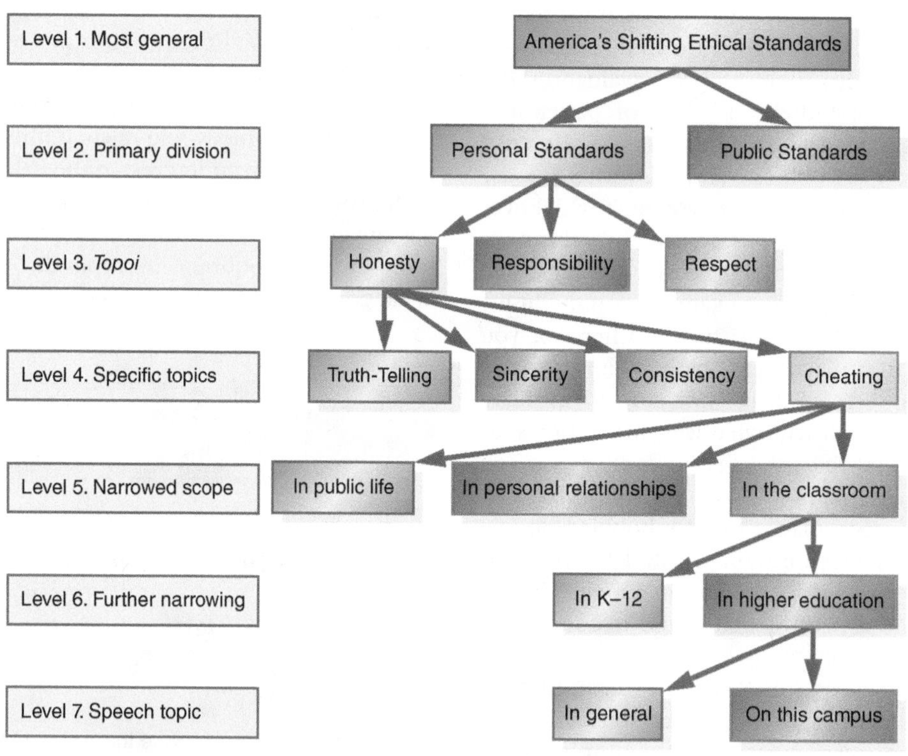

Figure 9.1
Narrowing a General Topic

Identifying the Purpose

The classroom assignment to "make a speech" may mislead you into thinking that fulfilling the assignment is an end in itself. This approach courts disaster, however, because strong public speeches have a clear sense of **purpose**. The speaker plans to achieve a particular goal and wants the audience to respond in a specific way. A speaker's purpose provides the criteria that determine whether the speech was successful or not.

We saw earlier that speeches traditionally are classified as ceremonial, deliberative, or forensic, depending on their purpose. Ceremonial speeches entertain but also celebrate shared values and strengthen commitments to them. Deliberative speeches explore what public policy ought to be. And forensic speaking seeks justice with respect to past events. In addition the general purposes of a speech are informing, persuading, and entertaining.

Both of these conceptions of purpose are useful, and yet both are limited. For example, many speeches combine deliberative and ceremonial elements, and it is not uncommon for a single speech to both inform and persuade. For the rest of our study, then, we will use a more precise classification that identifies seven common speech purposes.[2]

1. Providing new information or perspective
2. Agenda setting
3. Creating positive or negative feeling
4. Strengthening commitment
5. Weakening commitment
6. Conversion
7. Inducing a specific action

Providing New Information or Perspective

Sometimes, the audience generally knows about a topic but is unfamiliar with its details. Your goal as speaker may be to fill in such gaps by providing new information. For example, listeners may be aware that U.S. political campaigns are expensive, but they may not know that costs are escalating, or the reasons for this trend and its implications, or whether there are practical alternatives. Thus, the purpose of a speech about campaign finance might be "to deepen and enrich the audience's understanding of campaign costs."

Alternatively, listeners may be accustomed to thinking about a topic only from a certain **perspective**, or point of view. For example, in his 2005 commencement speech at Stanford University, Steve Jobs, CEO of Apple Computer, spoke about getting fired at age 30. He said:

> I didn't see it then, but it turned out that getting fired from Apple was the best thing that could have ever happened to me. The heaviness of being successful was replaced by the lightness of being a beginner again, less sure about everything. It freed me to enter one of the most creative periods of my life.

Changing listeners' perspectives about a subject may alter beliefs and values relating to it. At the very least, it may convince listeners that the subject is more complicated than they thought and that how they think about the topic is affected by the perspective from which they view it.

Agenda Setting

One purpose of a speech is **agenda setting**, causing people to think about a topic that they previously

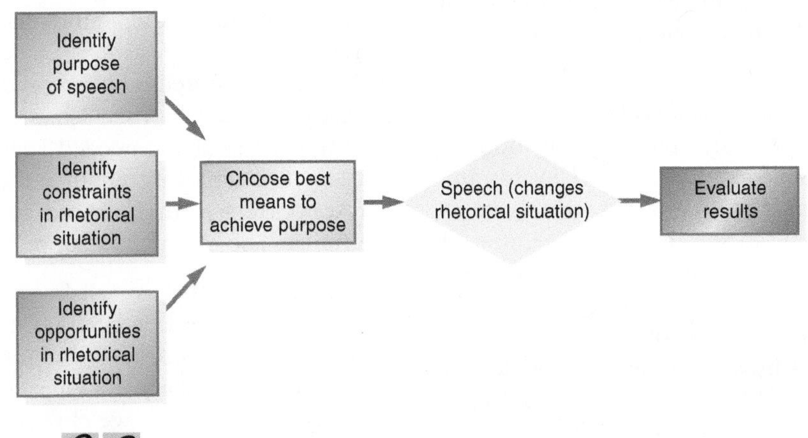

Figure 9.2
A Strategic Plan for a Speech

knew little about or ignored. The goal of the speech is to put the topic "on the agenda," to draw attention to it. Many environmental threats, for example, were not taken seriously until advocates put them on the agenda by speaking about them.

Maria Rogers, a first-year college student, heard her parents rave about seeing Alaska glaciers "calve," or break off large chunks of ice into the sea. She was concerned that this beautiful sight might actually be a sign of global warming, and she gave a speech to encourage her listeners to think about this serious issue:

> My parents went on an Alaskan cruise last summer, and when they returned they kept raving about the spectacular "calving" of glaciers along the Alaskan coast. These enormous sheets of ice break off, or "calve," at the sea's edge, making a spectacular display as they splash and crash into the icy blue water to the delight of hundreds of cheering tourists. The passengers on deck responded with wild applause, but when I heard about it I listened with deep concern, and then I started doing some research into the causes and effects of global warming. I read scientific reports that, unfortunately, justified my concern. And today I want to encourage you to pay serious attention to this growing threat.

Creating Positive or Negative Feeling

Sometimes a speaker's goal is more general: to leave the audience with a positive or negative feeling about the occasion, the speaker, or the message. Political candidates, even as they discuss specific policy issues, are often really more interested in making listeners generally feel good or bad about themselves or the world.

Student speaker Craig Hinners prepared a speech of this type when he took a short, nostalgic look at the Chicago elevated train, called the El by locals:

> On the El, you are always entertained. If you gaze out the window, you are treated to an intimate look at the lives of people whose backyards and windows face the tracks. If you set your sights inside the train, you can see and hear the stories of people from all walks of life—office workers, mothers with children, old men. You glance at the bright color of gum casually placed on the back of the seat by a teenager who no longer tasted its flavor, and hear the sound of old vehicles and snow-damaged tracks.

Craig's purpose was not to get listeners to do anything about the El, or even to change their beliefs about its run-down condition; rather, he wanted to share a wistful, comfortable feeling with them.

This speaker needs a strong strategic plan to stay lighthearted while also addressing serious issues regarding gaming on Native American reservations.

Likewise, many ceremonial speeches aim to evoke or strengthen common bonds by reference to a shared event or experience. The speakers wish to have the audience feel as they do, most often in a positive way. The audience's general attitude, not a belief or action, is the measure of success.

Strengthening Commitment

Many speeches are like "preaching to the converted"; they are delivered to listeners who already agree with the speaker. In such cases, the goal is to motivate audience members to become even more strongly committed. It is one thing to casually favor a candidate's election to office, but it is quite another thing to contribute money to the candidate's campaign, to display the candidate's poster on one's lawn, or to mobilize friends to vote for the candidate on Election Day. Increasing the intensity of listeners' commitment makes them more likely to act on their beliefs.

Narrowly defeated in the Democratic presidential primaries in 2008, then-Senator Hillary Clinton sought, even as she conceded victory to then-Senator Barack Obama, to strengthen the commitment of her supporters to their shared goals and vision of the future. She offered her supporters these words:

> I understand that we all know this has been a tough fight. The Democratic Party is a family, and it's now time to restore the ties that bind us together and to come together around the ideals we share, the values we cherish, and the country we love.
>
> We may have started on separate journeys—but today, our paths have merged. And we are all heading toward the same destination, united and more ready than ever to win in November and

> to turn our country around because so much is at stake.

These sentiments helped to convince Clinton's supporters to transfer their commitment to Obama and to see the man whom they had seen as an adversary now as an ally.

Weakening Commitment

Speakers also sometimes want to reduce the intensity of listeners' commitment to a belief—not so much to get them to change their minds as to acknowledge some sense of *doubt.* Recognizing that an issue has more than one legitimate side may be the first step in *eventually* changing people's minds. Even if listeners remain committed to their position, a reasonable but contrary argument may weaken their support for it. Although you may believe, for example, that higher defense spending is necessary, you may at least think twice about it after hearing a speech that argues that much defense spending is wasted.

Dorothy Hurst knew that her listeners strongly believed that the United States should withdraw all troops from Afghanistan immediately. She also knew that a single 10-minute speech was unlikely to change their belief. But she might be able to chip away at their position if she could show convincingly that an immediate withdrawal would endanger American troops and further destabilize an already fragile Afghan government. She focused not on whether to withdraw troops, but when.

> I know that most of you think that the United States should withdraw all of our troops from Afghanistan immediately. I do not stand here today to dispute the facts that our military is strained, our intelligence agencies have failed, and that our public is weary of war. Rather, I want to call your attention to another set of facts that receive less attention in our media. The Middle East remains a highly volatile region, as we saw during the 2011 "Arab spring," and I believe that maintaining a reasonable-sized force in Afghanistan would generate great strategic benefit to the U.S. Before you rush to judgment against this viewpoint, I ask that you at least consider the risks of leaving Afghanistan completely and immediately; they may be greater than the risks of staying a few years longer.

Conversion

Although it happens rarely on the basis of a single speech, sometimes listeners actually *are* persuaded to change their minds—to stop believing one thing and to start believing another. In short, listeners are converted. **Conversion** involves the replacement of one set of beliefs with another set that is inconsistent with the first. For example, a listener who believes that homeless people are to blame for their condition might be persuaded by a speaker that homelessness reflects faulty social policy, not faulty individuals.

Student speaker Rachel Samuels converted some of her audience by explaining the need for adult teachers to censor high school newspapers. Her classmates initially bristled at the idea of curtailing students' freedom of speech, but when Rachel demonstrated that libel lawsuits could bankrupt the public school system, they began to understand her position:

> The editing of high school newspapers is not government censorship of political or religious speech. Rather, it is editing by an authority to avoid the danger of libel lawsuits. In the world outside high schools, editors often keep journalists from printing the whole story in order to protect citizens' privacy. High school newspapers should be no different.

Inducing a Specific Action

The last purpose we will consider is the most specific and most pragmatic. Often, speakers do not really care about the beliefs and attitudes of individual listeners, as long as they can persuade people to take a specific action—to make a contribution, to purchase a product, to vote for a specific candidate, and so on.

When the goal is action regardless of the reason, the speaker may use widely different appeals. One listener may be induced to vote by the argument that it is a civic duty; another may favor a particular candidate's economic proposals; a third may know one of the candidates personally. The speaker does not care whether listeners have the same reasons for voting; all that matters is that they be prompted to take the same action.

Sunny Lin, a student who was once stranded in inclement weather waiting for a campus shuttle bus, gave a speech urging students to organize a more effective shuttle system for the college campus. She started with an appeal to her audience's concern for public safety:

> While the current shuttle system is meant to transport students across campus at night in order to keep them safe from criminals and predators, 20 minutes between buses is too much time. It takes only a couple of minutes to be robbed or assaulted while waiting for a bus.

Although this was a strong argument, Sunny didn't think that it would motivate all the students. Knowing that others might be moved more by an appeal to the school's reputation, Sunny described the trends in campus shuttle systems at other colleges:

> Other colleges with campuses known for rough terrain, bad traffic, and poor weather have shuttles that run every 10 minutes and provide students with multiple routes to increase transportation options. It's about time our school implements a shuttle program on par with other colleges.

Sunny figured that still other listeners might petition for a better shuttle system if they thought a new system would benefit them directly:

> Some of the most important buildings on campus aren't even on the current shuttle route. A new schedule and the addition of more bus routes would make it possible, for instance, to get to the student union. Think of how much easier it would be to take advantage of the food and entertainment opportunities if you could take a bus to the student union instead of walking in the cold, wet weather.

Sunny's only real concern was whether audience members would participate in a push for a new shuttle system. She didn't care whether they were motivated by safety concerns, school spirit, or personal convenience. She used multiple appeals to achieve her purpose with as many listeners as possible.

These seven categories of purpose certainly do not exhaust the possibilities, but they illustrate some common reasons why people give a speech.[3] Identifying your purpose is a critical step that will help you plan strategies to accomplish your goal.

Identifying the Constraints

After you identify the specific purpose of your speech, the next step in developing a strategic plan is to identify the constraints within which you must maneuver. As noted earlier, constraints are factors beyond your control that limit your options. Constraints may arise from:

- Audiences in general
- Your specific audience analysis
- Your *ethos* as a speaker
- The nature of your topic
- The rhetorical situation

From Audiences in General

The attention span of most listeners is limited, and it has shrunk over the years. Today, most audiences begin to get restless when a speech exceeds 20 or 30 minutes. And even when listeners are generally attentive, the degree of attention varies. At one moment, your speech may be the most important thing on their minds; at another moment, something you say may trigger an unrelated thought; and at yet another moment, listeners may be distracted by something else altogether.

You can help the audience remember your main ideas by phrasing them simply, organizing them in a structure that is easy to follow, and repeating them during the speech. Another strategy is to use interesting examples and to choose language that captures attention.

Besides having limited attention spans, audiences tend to have a high opinion of themselves and naturally resist being talked down to. They may believe that they have exerted great effort or even done you a favor by coming to hear you speak. You should always show respect to the audience and recognize that they will be the ultimate judges of your speech.

From Your Specific Audience Analysis

You also will be constrained by the analysis you performed of your specific audience. Your audience analysis may tell you that some appeals are out of bounds and that others are far more likely to succeed. For example, the manager who speaks to employees about the company's strained economic conditions has many choices; to succeed, however, she or he *must* deal with the fact that workers are worried about losing their jobs. This fear, identified through audience analysis, is an important constraint on what the manager can say.

From Your *Ethos* as a Speaker

The audience's perceptions of the speaker's character, or *ethos,* are another important constraint. If listeners see you as competent to discuss the subject, as trustworthy, as dynamic and energetic, and as having goodwill toward them, you enjoy a positive *ethos.* You want to evoke positive assessments of your *ethos* because an audience's perceptions of your character strongly affect whether that audience will be influenced by what you say.

Even a generally positive *ethos* can constrain you, however, because then you must craft a speech that sustains or builds on the audience's high expectations. When, in a 2004 speech to the National Association for the Advancement of Colored People

(NAACP), well-loved comedian Bill Cosby harshly criticized African Americans for a lack of responsible parenting, his remarks created a firestorm of controversy and debate. People had grown to expect lighthearted humor from this TV icon, and his serious tone surprised many who heard, read, or watched the speech. But Cosby's qualifications as a trained educator and his identity as one of America's most recognized fathers put him in a position to speak credibly on this important topic. Even though Cosby's cultural critique was vicious, he did not present a serious lecture but instead peppered the speech with dozens of jokes and witty observations about his own culture. Although Cosby's *ethos* is positive, he still must work within its constraints.

If, for whatever reason, your *ethos* is generally perceived as negative, then your challenge is either to change it or to overcome it. When President Bill Clinton acknowledged that he had been involved in an inappropriate sexual relationship with a White House intern, after having earlier denied it, he found subsequently that many people suspected him of dishonesty whenever he spoke. His negative *ethos* was a constraint on his effectiveness. He tried to overcome it by focusing his speeches instead on the strength of the economy and society during his administration.

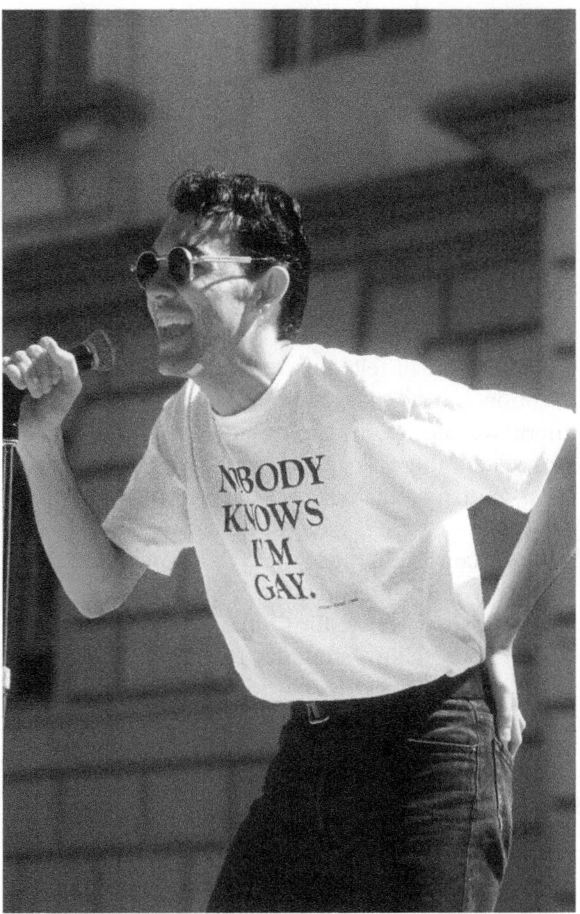

This speaker's strategic plan should recognize the constraint that his audience may be deeply divided and have strong emotions about his topic.

From the Nature of Your Topic

Some topics constrain a speaker more than others do. A highly technical subject that is difficult to make interesting challenges the audience's attention span even more than usual. And a topic that seems far removed from listeners' concerns is unlikely to spark and hold their interest.

In such cases, the challenge is to plan strategies that evoke and heighten interest. This is what student John Casey did in speaking about the research under way in the university's laboratories. Rather than droning on about details of antibodies and peptides, he made the topic interesting by describing the scientific community's quest for a "magic bullet" to cure cancer.

From the Rhetorical Situation

Every speech is a one-shot effort to influence the audience, but the occasions when a single message will change anyone's attitudes are few. For example, a classroom speech about abortion is unlikely to convince strong believers on either side to change their basic beliefs. Moreover, a speaker's range of stimuli is limited to only words and, sometimes, visual aids. Yet most cases of successful persuasion involve multiple messages and a variety of stimuli—verbal, visual, and experiential. Of course, a one-shot effort may be more likely to succeed when your goal is to reinforce the commitment that listeners already feel. Even so, a speaker should never overestimate the effect that a single speech can have on an audience.

We see, then, that a speaker cannot plan a speech with complete freedom. The constraints imposed by the audience, the audience analysis, the speaker's *ethos,* the topic, and the rhetorical situation must all become part of the strategic plan. Then the challenge is to be creative and find opportunities within these limits.

Identifying the Opportunities

Your opportunities as a speaker result from the assets that you bring to the situation and from the choices that you *are* able to make.

Your first and most important asset is that you should have an *information advantage* over listeners; you are likely to be better informed about the topic than they are. This may offset the constraints that the audience imposes. After all, you selected the topic because it matters to you, and you have researched it. You have given the topic sustained attention, and so you should be able to awaken interest in it, to provide new information about it, and to explain difficult concepts.

A second opportunity arises from your *audience analysis*. It will tell you something about the composition and attitudes of your specific listeners. Furthermore, almost any topic can be presented in various ways; there is no single "correct" approach. Your audience analysis will enable you to plan the strategies that are most likely to succeed.

For example, suppose that you know that, despite threats of legal penalties, large numbers of college students share music files online. You want to persuade your fellow students that they should not share digital music files with each other because they may be doing so illegally, and you expect strong opposition from students who would see your proposal as a limitation of their freedom. So you might suggest that this limitation is justified:

> College students today are logged on and linked in like no generation in history. It requires no effort to rip, copy, download, upload, or send digital music files to each other. With a few clicks, we can enjoy the latest single from our favorite artists and bands. But where we get our music is not just a matter of convenience—it's also a matter of dollars and cents. When we share music downloads without obtaining the proper rights, then we are listening and distributing in direct violation of the artist's rights and, in more stark terms, we are breaking the law. Good music costs money to create, produce, and distribute, and illegal file sharing sabotages the very thing we are trying to enjoy.

Although these justifications seem reasonable, they depend on values such as sympathy for artists and respect for the law. This argument probably would be more effective in reinforcing the commitment of listeners who already believed in upholding copyright laws than in converting people who are not particularly bothered by this legal transgression but are disturbed by what they see as limitations on their freedom. To reach these listeners, a strategy of stressing the personal benefits of not

CHOOSE A STRATEGY: Identifying Constraints and Opportunities

The Situation

You are preparing a speech for your class on three things that people can do to improve or maintain their health. You want to pick three ideas that are significant and feasible for your audience to implement.

Making Choices

1. What do you know about your class audience that could constrain or limit the kinds of health measures you choose to talk about? How could their age, current health, level of activity, and economic status affect how they respond to your topic?
2. Suppose you personally follow the health measures you will talk about in your speech. How might this contribute to your *ethos*?
3. In your research, you will learn that exercise can help prevent many more serious diseases that you realized. You assume that your audience already knows that exercise is good for them but that some people still don't do it. What opportunities for your speech does this information give you?

What If . . .

How would you change the way you choose which three health measures to discuss if your audience was:

1. A group of senior citizens
2. A kindergarten class

What are some constraints and opportunities you might encounter with each of these audiences?

sharing music files illegally might be more effective. For them, you might add:

> And not only that, we ourselves benefit from our restraint. How? First, a profitable music industry has the money to search out and develop new talent, expanding the pool of artists from which you can choose. Second, we avoid the potential nightmare of major lawsuits, confiscated computers, and network blackouts. And finally, since not every musician is a multi-platinum artist, we ensure that artists are paid fairly for their creativity, talent, and hard work. Asking that we refrain from illegal music file sharing is not really a curtailment of our freedom: it's an opportunity to show that we don't take our Internet access for granted and to show our support and desire for more music from innovative artists who will be secure in their ability to make music and make a living, too.

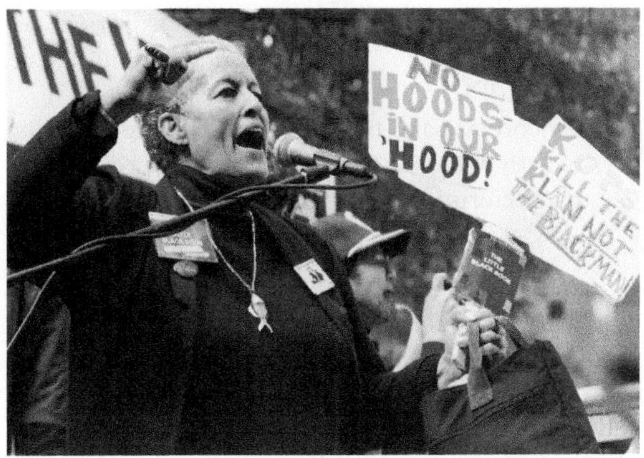

The thesis statement sums up what you most want listeners to remember. It should be possible to translate the thesis statement into a slogan for a poster.

Selecting the Means

If you have been thinking strategically, by this point you have articulated the purpose of your speech and have identified your constraints and opportunities in proceeding toward that goal. The final step in strategic planning is to select the means that you will use to achieve your purpose. In many respects, this decision is the most important, because it touches on virtually every aspect of your speech.

- How will you lead your audience in reasoning through to the conclusions you want to establish?
- How will you structure the speech?
- What supporting materials will you use?
- What choices will you make about wording, emotional language, and repetition?
- How will you actually present the speech?

All these matters will be explored in later chapters, but here you should recognize that each of them involves a choice that can be made either by accident or by design. The essence of strategic planning is to avoid accident and to design means that are most appropriate for achieving your purpose.

Developing the Purpose Statement and the Thesis Statement

From this understanding of strategic elements—purpose, constraints, and opportunities—you can begin to construct the skeleton of your speech. You have already determined the topic. The next steps are to formulate a clear statement of purpose and a thesis for the speech.

The Purpose Statement

Our earlier discussion suggested seven general categories of purpose: agenda setting, providing new information, weakening commitment, and so on. Review those categories to determine which one best describes the overall purpose of your speech. That description is your **general purpose statement**. Then you need to develop a **specific purpose statement**. This focuses on the outcome of your speech by specifying what you want to achieve—or what you want the audience to take away from the speech—and for that reason it is audience centered. It follows from the seven general purposes described earlier; those general purposes are made more specific by relation to a particular topic.

For example, if you were going to discuss cheating at the university, you might proceed as follows:

TOPIC:	Cheating at the university
GENERAL PURPOSE:	To provide new information
SPECIFIC PURPOSE:	To inform listeners of widespread cheating on this campus

The specific purpose is an instance of the general purpose, to provide new information. Notice that the specific purpose statement has three important characteristics.

1. It focuses on the audience rather than on the speaker. It identifies the outcome you seek, not how you will achieve that outcome.
2. It summarizes a single idea. Although some speeches are complex and have more than one

purpose, you are likely to be more effective if you can state your purpose as a single succinct idea.

3. It is precise and free of vague language. It tells exactly what you are trying to achieve, so you can determine whether you succeed.

Next, think critically about your specific purpose statement. Remember that listeners are giving their time and energy to hear you speak, and ask yourself whether your specific purpose is worthy of their efforts. If you are telling them only things that they already know, if your purpose is too grand to be achieved in the time available, if the topic is too technical or seems trivial, listeners are unlikely to pay close attention. In that case, of course, you cannot achieve your purpose.

The Thesis Statement

The final step in preparing the overall design of the speech is to identify the **thesis**, a succinct statement of the central idea or claim made by the speech. Whereas the specific purpose statement indicates what you want the audience to *take from* the speech, the thesis statement indicates what you want to *put into* it. The purpose statement identifies the desired audience reaction; the thesis statement succinctly summarizes the content of the speech in a single sentence that you most want listeners to remember. Here is how the thesis statement about campus cheating might evolve:

TOPIC:	Cheating at the university
GENERAL PURPOSE:	To provide new information
SPECIFIC PURPOSE:	To inform listeners of widespread cheating on this campus
THESIS STATEMENT:	Far more students engage in cheating than most of us think.

Notice how the topic (itself the result of a narrowing process) has been narrowed into a thesis statement that summarizes exactly what the speech will say.

Many of the tests of the specific purpose statement also apply to the thesis. Both should be stated in a single phrase or sentence. Both should be worded precisely. And both should fit the time available and other constraints in the situation.

Occasionally, a speaker does not state the thesis explicitly, relying instead on all the supporting ideas to imply it. There are advantages and disadvantages to letting the audience determine the exact thesis. If listeners participate actively in figuring it out, they are likely to stay interested in the speech and perhaps may even be more likely to accept the thesis. However, if the thesis is not stated, the audience might not identify it accurately, or different listeners might identify different theses. Even though accomplished speakers sometimes trust the audience to identify the thesis, students of public speaking are well advised to state it explicitly.

Analyzing the Thesis Statement

The thesis statement governs various choices about the content of a speech. By analyzing your thesis statement, you can determine your choices.

Identifying the Issues

First, you must identify the issues contained within the thesis statement. People often use the term *issue* quite loosely, as when they say, "Don't make an issue of it." But the term has a more precise meaning. An **issue** is a question raised by the thesis statement that must be addressed in order for the thesis itself to be addressed effectively.[4]

Issues are identified by posing questions about your thesis statement. Because the statement is so simple and brief, it always leaves much unsaid. By raising questions about the thesis statement, you'll discover what it seems to take for granted. Then your speech can flesh out these underlying assumptions and show that they are correct, giving listeners reason to accept the thesis statement itself.

Consider the thesis statement in the example above: "Far more students engage in cheating than most of us think." It seems straightforward. But notice what happens when we ask questions about the statement:

"Far more students"	How many? Is that number more than we think? Is it "far more"?
"Engage in cheating"	What is covered by the term cheating? And what must one do to "engage in" it?
"Than most of us think"	Who are "most of us"? What do "most of us" think? Why do we think this?

These questions identify the issues in the thesis statement. You may decide that some of the answers

STRATEGIES FOR SPEAKING to Diverse Audiences

Respecting Diversity Through Your Topic Selection and Strategy Development

Some topics work better than others for a diverse audience. Likewise, identifying your purpose and selecting a strategy are affected by the need to reach listeners with diverse backgrounds and perspectives. These strategies will help you to consider diversity at these key stages of speech planning.

1. Select a topic that is relevant to people of diverse interests rather than one that will be meaningful to only a narrow segment of your audience.
2. Emphasize points of commonality with your audience that do not rely on cultural stereotypes.
3. Keep in mind the diversity of your audience when identifying your opportunities and constraints. For example, "the role of faith in public life" will have a different mix of opportunities and constraints for secular than for evangelical audiences.
4. Remember that different levels of commitment may exist within the audience. Discussing certain issues may be more important for your audience's identity. For instance, discussing the issue of wearing headscarves in school will garner different levels of commitment from an audience of Muslim women than from secular U.S. men.

are obvious or that some can be covered together. You may decide not to take them up in the same order in the speech. But these essentially are the questions you'll need to answer if you want listeners to accept that "far more students engage in cheating than most of us think."

Now consider a thesis that is not yet well formed. Bill Goldman wanted to explore whether "voting in local elections is a worthwhile effort for me as a student." He had not yet framed an explicit thesis, but even this more broadly phrased statement can be questioned to discover the issues. Bill had to think about what "worthwhile" means for a student, whose stake in local elections is usually small; he also had to think about what "effort" is required to vote and why even that is an issue. He then began to question whether it was "harder" for him to vote than for others or harder than it "should" be. Gradually, he came to believe that low voter turnout can be explained by the fact that voting is inconvenient. This process of discovering issues helped Bill both to refine and to test his thesis statement.

Finally, consider the example of Angela Peters, who wanted to talk about the college admissions process to an audience of high school juniors. After doing some research, she might begin to develop her speech like this:

TOPIC:	The college admissions process
GENERAL PURPOSE:	Weakening commitment to a position
SPECIFIC PURPOSE:	To cause listeners to doubt their belief that admissions decisions are made rationally
THESIS STATEMENT:	Most colleges and students lack clear criteria for making admissions decisions.
ISSUES:	1. What are "most colleges"? Who are "most students"? How do we know? 2. What makes the criteria for admissions clear or unclear? 3. What are a college's or a student's criteria? Are they "clear" or not? 4. What are the admissions decisions about which we are concerned?

Now Angela can complete her research by looking for the answers to these specific questions. When she speaks about "the college admissions process," she will know what she wants to say, and she will have the supporting material she needs to weaken listeners' commitment to the belief that admissions decisions are made rationally.

Why Identify the Issues?

Analyzing the topic to identify the issues is important for several reasons. First, it enables you to determine what the speech must cover. Without knowing the issues, you risk giving a speech that listeners will dismiss as being beside the point.

Recall that Bill Goldman initially wanted to explore whether "voting in local elections is a worthwhile effort for me as a student." Through the process of discovering issues, he eventually came to believe that many students are dissuaded from voting in local elections because of the inconvenience of voting. At this point, his topic became "Why students don't vote," and his thesis was "Because voting is inconvenient, many students don't vote." He was able to document that, across the country, students are reluctant to vote in their adopted communities. He also was able to show that polling places may be in obscure locations, that lines are too long, and that paper ballots often are complex and tedious. He proposed as his solution that students be allowed to vote from their apartments or dorm rooms using the Internet. This solution seemed appropriate *as he described the problem,* but he did not really analyze the issues and causes fully. His thesis statement was too vague and did not consider alternative explanations.

After the speech, an audience member challenged whether Bill had really thought through the problem. The listener pointed out that, because people will endure inconvenience if they believe that the rewards justify it, perhaps the perceived benefits of voting in local elections do not outweigh the cost of inconvenience. The listener suggested that a more significant cause for students' failing to vote might be the lack of identification with a community that they do not regard as a permanent "home" but instead as a temporary "way station." They might prefer to register at home rather than at school. Students' lack of identification with the surrounding community perpetuates their disinterest in local politics, which in turn discourages students from learning more about the issues that are relevant to the community. Had Bill analyzed his thesis more carefully, he might have seen that the costs and benefits of voting were likely to be an issue, and he would have been prepared to address this.

A second reason to analyze the thesis statement is to direct your research, which otherwise could be endless. Combing your own experience and ideas, talking with others, and investigating library resources could go on indefinitely. A search of books and articles in just a single library will probably turn up hundreds of sources that have something to say about voting rates (and on the Internet, an unfocused search will yield truly unmanageable results).

One way to make your research task manageable is to focus your inquiry. By analyzing your thesis to determine the issues, you can better decide what and how to research. For example, in giving a speech about voting rates, you may decide that the key issue you want to explore relates to voting at state and local levels. As a result, you would not pay much attention to the vast literature comparing turnout rates among countries or turnout rates in national elections. Your research would focus on the issues you have identified.

A third reason to identify the issues is that doing so may lead you to modify your thesis. If your initial thesis is "Students are too busy to vote," analyzing the issues might convince you that your thesis should be "Students are too lazy to vote" or "Students are too confused to vote" or "Students feel that they have no reason to vote." The differences among these statements are obvious. Which one (or more) claim you try to develop and defend in the speech will be influenced by your analysis of what the issues really are.

Finally, as you will see in Chapter 10, analyzing your thesis is also helpful when you turn to organizing your speech.

RESEARCHING THE SPEECH

In this chapter, you will learn how to investigate your topic so that you can speak about it intelligently. Because you are making claims on listeners' time and attention, both you and they will want to be confident that you know what you're talking about.

The process of finding supporting material for your speech is **research**. Just as you do research in order to decide which service plan is best for your cell phone or whether to buy a car, you look for material that will support the claims you want to make in your speech. Research is closely linked to the process of **analysis**. On the one hand, the available materials guide you in identifying the issues related to your topic. On the other, searching for material without knowing which issues you need to investigate is pointless.

Sometimes, analysis precedes research. This is the right sequence when you already know what your thesis statement is. You then determine which questions must be answered in order to make that statement, and you go to find the answers. Sometimes, though, you don't yet know your thesis statement; you know only the topic. Angela Peters wanted to talk about the college admissions process (topic), but she didn't know enough about it to be sure of what she wanted to say (thesis). In this case, she should begin not with analysis but with research. She needs a general understanding of the topic before she can frame the thesis statement. Then she should analyze her thesis statement as described in Chapter 9 and, finally, return to research for answers to the specific questions she identified.

Strategic Perspectives on Research

Whether your research precedes or follows your analysis, you will want it to accomplish three basic goals:

1. To develop or strengthen your own expertise on the topic
2. To find the evidence that will support your ideas
3. To make your ideas clear, understandable, and pertinent to your audience

Keep in mind that these different goals may not all be achieved by the same kind of material. If you conceive of the research process too narrowly, you may find that you have obtained great background knowledge but have no specific material to include in your speech. Or you may find that your evidence is clear and meaningful in the context in which you found it, but it may mean little to your audience without that context.

Like every other aspect of public speaking, research involves strategic choices. You simply cannot find out all there is to know about every possible aspect of your speech topic. Consequently, you will have to decide the following:

- How much general background reading to do and what sources to select for this purpose.
- What issues in your speech will require specific supporting material.
- What types of supporting material you will need and where you should go to find it.
- How much supporting material you need to find.

Unsuccessful speakers often make these choices haphazardly. For example, after an Internet search yields a large number of source citations, one speaker tracks down the first two or three she can find, and she stops as soon as she has enough to fill the speaking time she has been allotted. But she never considers whether she has the best kinds of support or the right amount of it. Or, because another speaker's personal experience is relevant to his topic, he does not bother looking for other types of supporting material. He doesn't think about whether an audience will find his personal experience adequate or credible.

To be successful, instead of acting in such an unplanned way, you should make these choices—like all others—in light of your audience and your purpose. What will your audience expect? What claims might listeners be expected to accept without evidence? Will examples or statistics be more likely to lead them to accept your thesis? At what point would you provide so much evidence that it overwhelms them?

In the classroom, this thought process may be simplified by the details of the speech assignment. You may be asked, for instance, to give a speech with at least five pieces of supporting material of at least three different types. These are arbitrary instructions, not an all-purpose formula. Their purpose is to expose you to the range of possible supporting material and to give you practice using it. But outside the classroom, you will have to make these choices based on the particular rhetorical situation you face.

Types of Supporting Material

To do research for your speech, you first have to decide which types of supporting material you need. The following seven types illustrate the array of possibilities:

1. Personal experience
2. Common knowledge
3. Direct observation
4. Examples
5. Documents
6. Statistics
7. Testimony

Personal Experience

Sometimes, you can support your ideas on the basis of your own experience. Suppose your topic concerns the difficulties that first-year students have in adjusting to college life. You might well illustrate your main points by referring to your own first college days. If you were speaking about volunteerism, your experience in tutoring elementary school students or working in a soup kitchen would certainly be relevant. Student speaker Mitch Grissom used a personal story to introduce his speech about student protests against the continuing war in Afghanistan:

> Probably everyone in this class has an opinion on the war in Afghanistan. Some of you might think it was a good idea poorly executed, and others might think it was a bad idea tragically fabricated.

> I have my own ideas on Afghanistan, too. Last month, I participated in a student protest against the war, and a guy from my dorm came up to me afterward to say he didn't know I was a radical. I smiled and rolled up my left sleeve, exposing the shrapnel scars on my arm. I told him I wasn't a radical; I was just a veteran who had served in Afghanistan.

Mitch gained credibility—and the audience's attention—because he knew what he was talking about. He used his experience to illustrate his main points, and because his listeners could relate to him, they found his experience pertinent to them as well.

Those are the strategic benefits of using personal experience to support your ideas. Of course, audience members must be able to relate to your experience or they will not think it meaningful to them. For this reason, only rarely should a speaker rely on personal experience as the *only* type of supporting material.

Common Knowledge

An often-overlooked type of supporting material is **common knowledge**, the understandings, beliefs, and values that members of a society or culture generally share. Such beliefs are sometimes called "common sense." Some writers use the term *social knowledge* to emphasize that we know these things to be true on the basis of broad social consensus.[5]

Common knowledge is often expressed in the form of *maxims,* such as "what happens here, stays here," "this is no time for business as usual," or "if you want something done right, do it yourself." Sometimes, common knowledge takes the form of *generally held beliefs.* For example, whether correctly or not, most Americans believe that large government programs don't work, that taxes are too high and definitely should not be increased, that the Cold War is over, and that God plays a role in their lives. Common knowledge also is expressed in *value judgments,* such as the importance of protecting the environment, the commitment to a right to privacy, and a preference for practical solutions over ideological disputes.

One student speaker used common knowledge as supporting material when he said:

> Everybody knows that youth is a time for experimenting, for doing adventurous things. That's why you should consider signing up for study abroad.

When asked later, audience members agreed with the speaker's assertion that young people are adventurous and willing to try something new.

Common knowledge is not always correct, of course; people certainly can believe things that "ain't so." But common knowledge has the status of **presumption**—that is, we consider it to be right until we are shown otherwise. Precisely because the knowledge is "common" and widely shared, it can often be strategically useful as supporting material.

Direct Observation

Sometimes, you can support your claim on the basis of simple, direct observation—the heart of the scientific method. If you are speaking about whether drivers obey basic traffic laws, you can stand near a traffic light or stop sign and count how many drivers ignore these signals. If you are speaking about the widespread use of texting, you can keep track of how often you communicate with your friends by text rather than phone or e-mail (or in person). Student speaker Susan Anderson used direct observation to support her claim that students are taking unnecessary risks by not wearing bicycle helmets:

> You've seen them. They're big, oval-shaped, and odd-looking. And they sit on top of bicyclists' heads to reduce the risk of head injury in the unfortunate event of an accident. At least, that's what they're intended to do—but only if you wear them. Today I saw 27 students on bicycles, but only five—that's right, five—of them were wearing helmets. The other 22 students may not know this, but they were unnecessarily risking their lives.

This form of evidence appeals to the common cultural value that "seeing is believing." Susan's point gained credibility because she was reporting what she had seen with her own eyes. Direct observation is not just a recollection of personal experience; it can be verified by others. Usually, direct observation results from a deliberate decision to gather evidence that might support your point, but occasionally it is powerful because you saw something by accident—such as an act of crime—while you were doing something else.

Examples

When you offer an example, you make a general statement more meaningful by illustrating a specific instance of it. This form of supporting material helps to make an abstract idea more concrete. You can provide this kind of support for a claim by using a brief example, a hypothetical example, an anecdote, or a case study.

Brief Example

If you wanted to support the claim that the structure of the United Nations does not adequately reflect the current balance of power in the world, you might cite as an example the fact that Germany and Japan—despite their economic strength—do not have permanent seats on the Security Council. You might cite as another example the dominance of the General Assembly by Third-World nations. And you also might cite the United Nations' inability to compel member nations to pay their assessments. You would not develop any of these examples in detail; however, they are important to your speech because *together* they support your claim that the structure of the United Nations is outmoded.

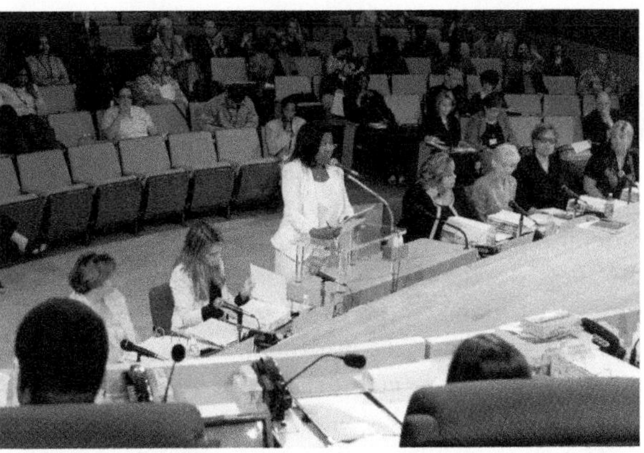

Referring to a specific example can help you to explain the claims you are making, as this speaker does when addressing members of the city council.

Hypothetical Example

In using a hypothetical example to support a claim, you ask listeners to *imagine* themselves in a particular situation. You might say the following:

> Suppose that year after year you spent more money than you took in. What would you have to do about that?

Listeners might conjure up images of severe cuts in their budget, selling their home or car, or even bankruptcy. You then could use this example to help the audience understand the difficult choices Congress makes in fashioning the federal budget.

Anecdote

An anecdote, or story, allows you to develop an example in greater detail. If your topic is the frustration of dealing with a bureaucracy, you might tell a story about someone's failure to get a problem resolved within the system. You could describe the maze of telephone inquiries and form letter replies and your hero's trek to the appropriate agency, only to be directed to the wrong office. Finally reaching the appropriate official, the person is patronized by a clerk who says, "According to our records, you are dead." Such an extended, engaging story would illustrate your point and help the audience relate to the issues.

Case Study

You often can support a general claim by zeroing in on one particular true case and discussing it in detail. If your topic is about whether campus codes to regulate offensive speech can be effective, you might describe one or two campuses that have tried this approach and then argue that their experiences illustrate whether such codes are workable in general. If you believe that making Election Day a national holiday would increase voter turnout, you might support your claim by drawing on case studies of nations where Election Day is a holiday. During recent political campaigns, candidates frequently have used this form of support when they showcase specific families they said would benefit more from their tax and spending proposals than from their opponent's.

Notice that all these types of examples work by relating a part of something to the whole. By examining a particular instance of whatever is being discussed, you may be able to support claims about the topic as a whole.

Documents

Word processing programs often identify anything they produce as a document, and Web pages are also sometimes called documents. But as a type of supporting material, the term **document** has a more specific meaning. It refers to primary sources that can establish a claim directly, without the need for opinion or speculation.

A person's will is a document specifying what will happen to his or her possessions after death. This document takes priority over someone's opinion about what the deceased "really wanted." Likewise, a lawyer who wants to know what the copyright law is will not ask for a colleague's opinion; he or she will look up the text of the act passed by Congress. If you want to know who has the authority to set the dues for the campus film society, you'll consult the society's bylaws—another example of a document.

Documents can be a valuable source of supporting material. The Declaration of Independence is often quoted to support the belief that there are natural rights. For many people, the Bible is the document most often quoted. In the investigation of Watergate, the 1972 break-in at the offices of the Democratic National Committee in Washington, D.C., the key documents were tape recordings. Transcripts of news interviews, television shows, or court proceedings are also documents, as are contracts and loan agreements. Even a bus schedule or weather report is a document.

The student who spoke about cheating on campus referred to a university document to show that academic dishonesty would not be tolerated:

> According to the student handbook we got as freshmen, cheating is "a serious breach of our commitment to ethical behavior as students" and will be punished with "a failing grade in the class and possible expulsion from the university."

Documents can be a solid form of evidence if your audience regards them as trustworthy—and if you quote them accurately. The exact words of a document provide a record that is not skewed by the opinions and interpretations of others.

Statistics

Supporting materials presented in quantitative form, as statistics, are especially useful when the scope of the topic is vast. They make it possible to generalize beyond a few specific examples and hence to make a powerful statement about larger populations. If you are speaking about your family or your college class, the scope of the topic is narrow enough that you probably don't need statistical support; you can just provide a set of examples or case studies. When your topic involves the state or the nation, however, one or two examples are unlikely to represent the diversity of the population.

Statistics are numbers that record the extent of something or the frequency with which something occurs; they take such forms as medians, averages, ratios, indices, and standardized scores. Such numbers become meaningful when they are compared with a baseline or other pattern to show a relationship between the two. For example, you might sup-

CHOOSE A STRATEGY: Using Research to Support Your Speech

The Situation

Residents and business owners in the town where you live have established a grassroots community organization to convince the city council to ban smoking in local restaurants and bars. Your state doesn't have smoke-free laws in force; therefore, it is up to you and your fellow committee members to prove to city government leaders and other business owners—especially bar owners, where smoking is commonplace—that such a ban will not result in a drop in revenue. You and other group members recognize that environmental tobacco smoke provides a serious health risk to nonsmokers and has been associated with increases in rates of cancer, respiratory conditions, and cardiovascular problems. Your group plans to present your case at the next city council meeting, and you have been appointed spokesperson.

Making Choices

1. What questions do you need to answer in order to provide evidence to back up your proposal?
2. What sources of information will you use to research your case?

What If . . .

Suppose that your research shows that a loss in revenue is possible.

1. With one of your key arguments lacking support, what additional information should you get to support your overall case?
2. What other arguments might you make based on the evidence, and how might you support them?
3. What will you do with information that does not support your case?

port a claim by comparing the median family income for different professions or different ethnic groups or different nations.

Statistics can be misleading. If they sound too strange to be true, they may not be accurate. Therefore, you need to understand how they were derived and exactly what they mean. If your audience is likely to doubt the truth of a statistic, you will need to support it in the speech more than you will for a statistic listeners are likely to accept.

Although statistical statements take a great variety of forms, the following four types are especially valuable for supporting material in speeches.

Simple Enumeration

The most basic form of a statistic is a single number. For example

> A total of 35 faculty members on our campus have won teaching awards.

Such statistics have the virtue of simplicity, but they may be difficult to interpret without more knowledge of the context. Having 35 winners of teaching awards on the faculty means one thing at a small college with only 60 faculty members, but it means something different for a large public university with 3,000 people on the faculty.

Interpreting simple enumerations can be tricky. For example, in the spring of 2003, President George W. Bush said that under his tax cut proposal, "92 million Americans would receive an average tax reduction of $1,083," The figure for the average tax reduction—the mean—was mathematically correct, but the average was skewed by a small number of very large reductions. Indeed, 50 percent of all taxpayers would see a tax cut of $100 or less.[6] Because context shapes our understanding of simple enumerations, you want to be very careful not just to accept them at face value, but to place them in appropriate contexts.

Surveys and Polls

Suppose your topic was about how most Americans regard the public education system. In theory, you or someone else could interview all Americans and then tabulate the results. But not even the Census Bureau has been able to find and count all Americans, and the time and expense involved would make the task impossible. Moreover, the data would be obsolete by the time you completed your survey.

Instead, you can *infer* the attitudes of people as a whole from the attitudes reported by a sample of the population, as long as the sample is representative of the whole. In the case of public opinion about the performance of the U.S. Congress, a 2011 Gallup Poll reported that 86 percent of the sample interviewed said that they were dissatisfied with the way Congress is handling its job. That statistic would be used like this in a speech:

> The Gallup Poll reports that 86% of its sample are dissatisfied with Congress. Since it used a random sample, we can conclude that about 86% of the whole country—six out of every seven people—give Congress a failing grade.

Surveys and polls are widely used in the physical and social sciences and to gain information about public opinion on matters of policy. Not all are equally reliable, however. Check how the sample was selected; a random sample is more likely to be representative of the whole population than is a sample in which people of any particular viewpoint are more likely to be included. Check the wording of the questions asked to make sure that they are not slanted to encourage one answer rather than another. Check the reported margin of error to see whether the results reported might have occurred just by chance. And check the organization sponsoring the survey or poll to be sure that it does not have a vested interest in the outcome.

Rates of Change

Often, what is noteworthy about a statistic is not its absolute size, but its rate of change. For instance, it may be more important to know that the national debt more than doubled during the period from 2000 to 2013 than to know the total dollar amount of the debt. Similarly, knowing that medical costs have increased at a much faster rate than personal income since 2000 may be more useful than knowing either of the exact amounts. And knowing that the world's population is doubling faster and faster may have greater implications than knowing the total population. Speakers often can illustrate and emphasize such dramatic rate changes through visual aids.

Rates of change show what is happening and can help an audience compare the situation to a known benchmark. By themselves, however, statistics may not tell much and may easily mislead others.[7] For example, one student speaker supported the claim that the university was not promoting affirmative action by citing what seemed like an important statistic:

> Did you know that fewer African Americans were admitted to this school this year than last year? There's no excuse for that! It proves that this school has no commitment to diversity.

The speaker had fallen into a statistical trap, however, by failing to note that the *total* number of students admitted was lower this year than last. The

RHETORICAL WORKOUT

Assess Types of Supporting Information

You are researching a speech about the safety issue of maple-wood baseball bats used in Major League Baseball (MLB). You know that a number of players and fans have been injured, some seriously, by sharp pieces of wood that hit them after a maple bat shattered during its use in a game. You learn that bats made of ash wood don't break as easily as maple. You also read that MLB and the Players Association, which represents professional baseball players, did a study in 2008 and came up with new recommendations in 2009. Your speech will look at the issues surrounding the problem of shattering maple bats, the safety solutions proposed in 2009, and whether the new recommendations have made a difference in safety.

What types of supporting material might be applicable to your speech?

1. *Personal experience:* Suppose you've played baseball for several years. Is this experience worth mentioning? Why or why not?
2. *Common knowledge:* Are there any kinds of common knowledge you could draw on? What about the topic might connect with the shared beliefs or values of a classroom audience?
3. *Direct observation:* How useful would the following experiences be for informing your speech: (a) You once watched a craftsperson make a baseball bat. (b) You were at a baseball game when a bat broke and flew across the field, although it didn't hit anyone. (c) Last summer you went to a Major League game.
4. *Examples:* What kinds of examples would help support your speech?
5. *Documents:* How useful would the following documents be for your speech: (a) a press release announcing the findings of the 2008 study; (b) a video of a bat breaking; (c) a brochure about collectible bats that aren't for game use; (d) a letter from a bat manufacturer protesting the new rules.
6. *Statistics:* You find a statistic that says 2,232 bats broke during Major League games from July to September 2008. What are some other types of statistics and information you might need to find in order to put this number in context?
7. *Testimony:* You find an article that quotes some bat makers who think the new rules have no scientific merit. What types of information about the article, the bat makers who are quoted, and the new rules might help you decide the credibility of this testimony?

percentage of African American students in the entering class was actually slightly higher and had increased for three years in a row.

Experiments

Experiments are controlled tests of the effect of one thing on another. They are conducted by comparing situations that are essentially similar except for the factor being tested. A claim that secondhand smoke leads to lung cancer, for example, would be supported by comparing the cancer rates of two groups that were similar in all essential respects except that one had been exposed to secondhand smoke and the other had not. It could be used in this way in a speech:

> Two groups of people were basically alike—same city; same mix of age, race, and gender; same overall health; same income; in fact, alike in just about every way you can imagine, except one: One group was regularly exposed to secondhand smoke and the other was not. And the group that was exposed had significantly higher rates of cancer. Guess why.

Similarly, the claim that African American drivers are stopped by police officers in a particular neighborhood more often than are Caucasian drivers could be tested by sending the same model car through the same neighborhood at the same time of day at the same speed with drivers who differ only in the color of their skin.

Testimony

Testimony is information or an opinion that is expressed by someone other than the speaker.

Checklist 9.3
Testing the Strength of Supporting Material

1. Personal experience
   - Are you sure your memory is reliable?
   - Is your experience generalizable?
   - Will others interpret it the same way?
2. Common knowledge
   - Are you sure the audience shares it?
   - Are you sure it is correct?
3. Direct observation
   - Are you sure of what you saw?
   - Do you have any bias?
4. Examples
   - Are they representative?
   - Are there enough of them?
5. Documents
   - Can they be trusted?
   - Are they properly interpreted?
   - Is the context made clear?
6. Statistics
   - Are appropriate measures used?
   - Are they reliable and valid?
   - Have they been interpreted properly?
7. Testimony
   - Does the person have access to the data?
   - Is the person expert on the subject?
   - Is the person reasonably objective?

When using testimony, you rely on someone else's judgment, and so you need to assess that person's competence and credibility. You may also need to convince the audience that your source is knowledgeable and trustworthy.

Factual Testimony

Facts are pieces of information that can be proved true or false. Speakers often support ideas by reporting facts that were gathered by others, such as quoting the secretary of state about developments in the Middle East, or quoting a public health expert about the dangers of secondhand smoke, or quoting a campus security officer about the number of crimes reported last year. When you quote facts, you are implying that you cannot verify the information yourself but are willing to accept it because you think the source is credible.

Opinion Testimony

Opinions are beliefs formed from experience and judgment. When you offer another person's opinion to support a claim, you are indicating that someone whose judgment is trusted, whose expertise is valued, or who is in a better position to know than most people are has reached a certain conclusion. You are asking the audience to accept that conclusion because of the person's expertise, judgment, or knowledge. Thus, you might quote an expert in Middle Eastern politics to support a point about the peace process in that region, or you might quote campus security officers about whether the campus is a safe place to be after dark.

When using opinion testimony for support, consider whether the audience will know and trust the person you are quoting. You may have to establish why your source's opinion is more valuable than the average person's.

Tools for Locating Supporting Material

Now that you know about the *types* of supporting material, what tools can you use to find it? Some common research tools are search engines, electronic databases, catalogs, and indexes.

Search Engines

The easiest way to begin research is on your computer. Anyone with Internet access and a Web browser can conduct online research, but locating a specific piece of information tucked somewhere within the over 185 million active websites can be a daunting task. Most researchers therefore use search engines, such as Google, Yahoo!, or Bing to navigate this sea of data. Search engines employ slightly different algorithms, which are constantly being refined, so you may not want to limit yourself to only one search engine.

Search engines respond to the directions they are given, so you should be as precise as you can in directing the search. To generate more accurate results, it is helpful to use search commands, such as quotation marks around phrases or the command "AND" between related keywords. Different search engines may have different commands, and it is important to realize that a search engine is only as good as the questions you ask. Therefore, you may also wish to dig deeper into the "Advanced Search" functions of a search engine.

The search engine will generate lists and brief descriptions of websites containing the terms you

STRATEGIES FOR SPEAKING to Diverse Audiences

Respecting Diversity Through Research

Using a variety of research sources will help you to find and to recognize diverse perspectives on your topic. These strategies will help you to do appropriate research in light of the diversity of your audience.

1. Go beyond U.S.-based media sources, particularly if your topic is international in scope.
2. Be aware of the partisanship of your media sources. Include both "liberal" and "conservative" perspectives on your topic.
3. Consider the "voices" you quote in your speech. Are they all male? American? Over age 55? Be sure you are presenting diverse and relevant perspectives.
4. Consider how to treat radical or "fringe" voices. Should they be discredited because they attract few supporters? Does treating them in the same way as "mainstream" voices give them too much weight? Should they be excluded if they are hateful? Or does the pursuit of diversity dictate that all voices should be heard?

entered. Usually these will be arranged in order of potential relevance to your request or else according to the frequency with which they are consulted (or "hit"). You then click on the link to the website and peruse it for the information you are seeking. Keep in mind, though, that advertisements and other "sponsored" sites may pop up. The sites that are "hit" most often are not necessarily the most credible.

Electronic Databases

A search engine will direct you to websites that are available to anyone. Although these sites can be a good source of general information, you often can find more reliable, detailed, or pertinent information in subject-specific electronic databases. These provide full-text entries and abstracts from a wide range of academic and popular sources. Some databases are free and available to the public, like those listed in Table 9.2. Many, however, are available only on a subscription basis, and the cost of a subscription for an individual would be prohibitive. Fortunately, your college or university library most likely maintains subscriptions to many electronic databases in different fields of study. Some common databases are JSTOR, EBSCOhost, Project MUSE, and Lexis/Nexis. You may well be able to access these databases from your own computer by connecting to the library through the Internet; check with your reference librarian.

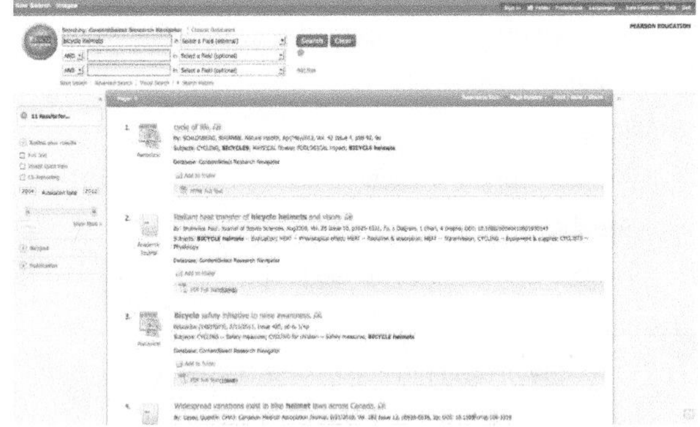

The search page of the EBSCOhost electronic database.

Catalogs

All libraries maintain catalogs of their collections, usually electronic catalogs that are searchable. If you have Internet access, you can likely connect to your college or university catalog and search by subject, author, title, or keywords to see what library resources are available. You may be able to connect to your local public library as well. In either case, you can contact a reference librarian if you need assistance.

In addition to the resources in your own library, you can check the holdings of more than 10,000 libraries worldwide by using WorldCat. This site (http://www.WorldCat.org) also offers varying degrees of access to databases, collections, library help, and other services.

Indexes

Newspapers, periodicals, and government publications publish indexes, many of which are available

Table 9.2
Electronic Databases

Source	Description	URL
ipl2 (*combines the Internet Public Library and the Librarians' Internet Index*)	Indexes online newspapers, magazines, and special collections.	www.ipl.org
Fed World Information Network	Index of local, state, and federal agencies.	www.fedworld.gov
Libweb	Links to library collections around the world.	www.lib-web.org
Bio.com	Database of famous people.	www.biography.com
American Rhetoric	Texts of famous American orators.	americanrhetoric.com
USA Services	Access to government documents.	www.usa.gov
THOMAS	Library of Congress site for learning about Congress and government.	thomas.loc.gov
State and Local Governments on the Net	Servers for each of the 50 states, with links to various branches of state government agencies, county or city servers.	www.statelocalgov.net
E-journals	Electronic journals organized by topic.	www.e-journals.org
White House	Links to White House documents.	www.whitehouse.gov
Fed Stats	Links to statistics from over 100 federal agencies.	www.fedstats.gov
Arts and Letters Daily	Media links, including magazines, newspapers, and wire services.	www.aldaily.com

online and are searchable by author, title, subject, or key terms. These indexes will direct you to specific articles or reports on subjects of your interest.

Newspaper Indexes

Many major national newspapers have their own indexes, including the *New York Times* (probably the most comprehensive), the *Wall Street Journal* (especially good on business and economic issues), the *Christian Science Monitor,* the *Washington Post* (particularly on matters of national politics), the *Chicago Tribune,* and the *Los Angeles Times.*

Periodical Indexes

The most common index to periodicals is the *Reader's Guide to Periodical Literature.* This easy-to-use subject index can be found in virtually every library. With few exceptions, though, it indexes only popular, general-interest periodicals. More specialized indexes are also available. The *Bulletin of the Public Affairs Information Service* is useful for topics dealing with public policy issues. The *Social Sciences Index* and the *Humanities Index* can point you to journals and periodicals relating to these many disciplines. The *Business Periodicals Index* can help you research topics about the economy and business conditions, and the *Index to Legal Periodicals* covers law reviews and journals. The *Communication and Mass Media Index* includes hundreds of journals devoted to that topic. Finally, the *International Index to Periodicals* can guide you through journals published in other countries. Full-text versions of many periodical articles can be found through electronic services such as JSTOR and EBSCOhost.

Government Publication Indexes

The most comprehensive federal index is the *Monthly Catalog of U.S. Government Publications,* in which titles are arranged alphabetically under the government agency that published them. There also is a subject index, which usually would be the place to start. Although the *Monthly Catalog* is the most comprehensive index, it is not annotated. You will have to guess from the issuing agency and the title whether the document is of interest to you.

At your library, you may be able to access digital material that is available only by subscription.

The *Congressional Information Service* is an especially valuable index to congressional publications because it includes abstracts, or brief summaries, of their contents. Again, the subject index lists entry numbers that you can use to look up the abstracts. The *Congressional Information Service* includes all publications of the legislative branch: hearings, committee reports, commissioned studies, and other documents. It does not index the executive or judicial branch, and it does not cover years before 1970. But for matters currently before Congress or that have been considered in the recent past, it is an invaluable index. Other indexes to federal government publications include the *Congressional Record Index*, the *American Statistics Index*, and the *Index to U.S. Government Periodicals.*

Supplementing the Tools

Even though most of the tools you will use can be accessed electronically, you may want to supplement them by physically going to the library. First, many sources are still not available electronically, and the library will have hard-copy versions of books, periodicals, and government publications. Second, if the library has open stacks (meaning that you can get the books you want rather than depending on library staff to get them for you) you can browse and discover material on your topic that is shelved near the book you want but that you might not discover otherwise. Third, you will be able to access digital materials that are available only by subscription if they can't be accessed from your own computer. And fourth, you will be able to consult with librarians who can give you valuable help on your topic and sometimes can direct you to reference materials of which you otherwise would be completely unaware.

Sometimes, the best source of supporting material is other people. Interviews enable you to ask the exact questions you need to have answered, and the give-and-take of the interview routine permits follow-up discussion. Moreover, people sometimes will make statements in an oral interview that they would not be willing to make in print or on the Internet. You will learn more about interviewing later in this chapter.

Sources of Supporting Material

The tools described previously will lead you to the sources of your supporting material. These include periodicals, newspapers, books, reference works, government publications, other materials available online, and interviews. Many of these sources are available in both electronic and print formats, and they will be considered here without regard to the format in which you find them.

Periodicals

Periodicals (sometimes called *serials*) are published at regular intervals—usually weekly, monthly, or quarterly—and have the advantage of being more up to date than books.

General-Interest Periodicals

These are usually sold on newsstands and by subscription, and they thus circulate widely; examples include *Time, Newsweek, U.S. News & World Report,* and *People.* Periodicals such as these may have useful information about current events, but their coverage of issues is fairly brief and not deep, with the exception of feature articles. Given their mass circulation, they may be useful in identifying topics of interest and prevalent attitudes among many readers.

Other general-interest periodicals are more focused journals of opinion that delve more deeply into issues and often espouse a particular point of view. Examples include *The American Prospect* and *Progressive* (liberal) and *Commentary* and *National Review* (conservative). Consult sources such as these when you are interested in a particular political perspective on your topic. Other opinion journals, such as *Atlantic* and *Harper's,* tend to represent more diverse and eclectic viewpoints.

Special-Interest Periodicals

These are intended for readers who have particular interests, which may be as broadly defined as business (*Fortune* and *Bloomberg BusinessWeek*) or pop music (*Rolling Stone* and *Spin*) or may be as narrowly focused as snowmobiles, digital imaging, or coin collecting. Whatever your topic is, you probably can find a periodical that is devoted to it. Some are aimed at specific demographic groups—based on age, gender, ethnicity, and so on—and even cities, for that matter, are the focus of magazines named after them.

Technical Periodicals

These are written primarily for specialists in a given field. Scholarly journals are the obvious example, with one or more publications dedicated to most academic disciplines: *American Political Science Review, Journal of the American Medical Association, Journal of American History, American Bar Association Journal, Quarterly Journal of Speech,* and so on. Colleges and universities also sometimes publish scholarly journals, such as *Critical Inquiry* and *Yale Review.* Law reviews also fit into this category. Although journals such as these are intended mainly for subject-matter specialists, they sometimes include material that can be very helpful for a speech, such as the results of surveys, experiments, and historical and critical analyses conducted by experts in various fields.

Newspapers

Newspapers remain an important source of information that you can use for your speeches. Besides reporting the latest news, many newspapers analyze and interpret it and publish related feature articles, columns, and editorials. Your own daily newspaper will be a helpful source. Especially if you live outside a major metropolitan area, though, it's a good idea to consult newspapers that cover current events and opinions more comprehensively than your local paper does. This is particularly important if you are doing research on topics of national or international significance.

Books

Both general and specific books about your topic—as well as anthologies of essays by different authors—can be valuable sources of supporting material. If the book is not available electronically, its call number—which you can obtain from the digital catalog—will tell you where to find it on the library shelves.

Sometimes, particularly if your library is small, you may run across a citation to a book that your library does not have. Fortunately, most libraries can arrange an interlibrary loan, using specialized indexes to help you identify other libraries that have the book and borrowing it for you. Be aware, however, that this takes time. If you anticipate needing books that your library doesn't have, request them far ahead of when you will need them for your speech. The librarian in charge of interlibrary loans can explain the procedure and time frame to you.

Reference Works

Reference works are not intended to be read from start to finish; they do not develop a sustained argument or claim, and they usually are not written in narrative form. Rather, they are convenient collections of facts and information. In print form, they typically are shelved in a special section of the library, where a reference librarian can help you. Online, they are a convenient source for finding information quickly. Some of these sources will be familiar to you already; others may not be.

- *Dictionaries* not only tell you the definitions of a word but also trace its origin and usage. Besides general dictionaries, you can find specialized dictionaries that identify the terms and usage within particular fields, such as finance or medicine.
- *General encyclopedias* can sometimes be found in print form, but today many are accessible

online. One of the largest and most viewed sites on the Web is the encyclopedia Wikipedia. Within general guidelines, anyone can contribute to it or revise entries, which makes the site accessible but also allows for easy corruption of data and misrepresentation of facts. That does not mean that all Wikipedia entries are inaccurate; many are comprehensive and adequately documented. You cannot be sure of the accuracy, so you need to verify facts, cross-check stories, and investigate the identity of the author. Wikipedia can be useful as a starting point to develop background knowledge, to locate primary sources, and to formulate research questions that you can try to answer by consulting other sources, even if you do not quote from it directly.

- *Specialized encyclopedias and handbooks* are subject-specific and contain brief essays that will give you an overview of a subject. Examples include the *Encyclopedia of Philosophy,* the *Handbook on Race and Ethnicity,* the *International Encyclopedia of Communications,* and the *Handbook of the Supreme Court of the United States.* If you're looking up a subject that is not the main focus of your speech, the encyclopedia or handbook may be all you need. If you need a deeper understanding, the handbook or encyclopedia often will have bibliographical references that will steer you to other subjects.
- *Abstracts* are short summaries of articles or books related to a particular discipline. Many academic and professional groups publish abstracts of the articles appearing in their current journals. By reading abstracts instead of entire journals, you can discover which articles include material that may be useful.
- *Fact books* are compilations of statistical information that you can consult when you need specific data to support a point in your speech. Almanacs, for example, are published every year and supply up-to-date facts about an enormous range of subjects.
- *Biographical references* identify particular individuals and outline their backgrounds and achievements. *Who's Who* is the best-known biographical reference, but a vast number of such sources can tell you about both contemporary and historical figures.
- *Compilations* and *yearbooks* are edited collections of material of a given type. For example, *Editorials on File* is a digest of selected newspaper editorials arranged by topic; it is published regularly and then compiled into a yearbook each year. Other examples of such compilations are *Facts on File* and *Congressional Quarterly Almanac,* an especially useful guide to the status of issues currently before the U.S. Congress. *Congressional Quarterly* also publishes a pamphlet called *CQ Researcher,* which examines a different issue of public interest each week. This compilation of facts and opinions includes background information, editorials about each side of the issue, and a bibliography of important books and articles to help you start researching the issue.
- *Atlases* provide geographical information, including the exact location and physical characteristics of specific sites, cities, and regions.
- *Collections of quotations* are useful both for tracking down the origin of popular sayings and for finding maxims or brief quotations related to a particular topic.
- *Book previews* will alert you to forthcoming books that may be relevant to your topic. You can find previews through such services as Amazon.com and books.google.com.

Government Publications

Many college and university libraries are government depositories, which means that they regularly receive copies of most federal (and sometimes state) government publications. Some also include the publications of foreign governments and of the United Nations.

Covering virtually every public issue, government publications include bulletins, reports, pamphlets, research studies, congressional deliberations, judicial opinions, and agency publications. Often, however, these are not indexed in the general digital catalog or in other online tools. If your speech topic is of concern to government bodies, you are well advised to visit the Government Publications section of your library and to consult with the librarian in charge.

Other Materials Found Online

Many documents that are hard to find otherwise are posted online and can be located through the use of search engines. These include papers presented at professional meetings, conference proceedings, position papers, working documents and archives of groups and organizations, and unpublished essays and manuscripts. These often can provide valuable background, lend a behind-the-scenes perspective on a topic, and give you access to specialized information. They should be viewed with some caution, however, because there often is no quality control in the selection of materials to post.

Table 9.3
Examples of Subject-Specific Websites

Site	URL
Macworld	www.macworld.com
American Psychological Association	www.apa.org
Internet Movie Database	www.imdb.com
Susan G. Komen for the Cure	www.komen.org
U.S. Green Building Council	www.usgbc.org
Presidential Rhetoric	www.presidentialrhetoric.com

In addition, millions of individuals, companies, associations, professional organizations, and government agencies maintain websites to provide information and links to related sites. The home page for a university's website, for instance, might contain links to such topics as admissions, degree requirements, departments and curricula, events and activities, and recent news. Table 9.3 lists some examples of subject-specific websites. Also, many people maintain blogs on which they post their thoughts and invite comments from others. Blogs can permit extended discussion of an issue. Because websites and blogs are often self-published, they will vary greatly in quality and should be used with caution.

Interviews

It is not only national and international experts who provide valuable interviews. The manager of the local department store has a perspective on how economic conditions affect consumer confidence. Faculty members have expertise on a variety of issues in every academic discipline. And fellow students can tell you about all aspects of campus life, including, say, how changes in funding for student loans may affect their educational plans. The following guidelines will help make your interviews effective.

Prepare for the Person

Learn as much as you can about the people you plan to interview. How long have they held their current position? What experiences have they had with the subject? Are they prominently identified with an issue or aspect of your topic? Are they well known, or will you need to establish their credentials?

Prepare for the Subject

It is a waste of your sources' time if you ask them very general questions or seek information that you can get easily in other ways. Don't let the interview substitute for your own background reading and research. For instance, if you were interviewing a local banker about the influence of the national economy on your town, you should not need to ask such a basic question as "Can you tell me the definition of a recession?" Make sure that you understand basic concepts that are likely to come up in the interview so that you can focus your questions on unique information that your source can provide.

Prepare for the Format

An interview is a particular kind of communication event that proceeds through questions and answers. Before the interview, formulate your questions carefully so that they are not vague and not leading or hostile. Your questions should be simple and direct and should not anticipate answers or favor any particular viewpoint. Give your sources the opportunity to make their own judgments, to explain why they think as they do, and to comment on different points of view that others may have expressed.

Also be aware that different types of questions elicit different types of information. A **closed question** limits the respondent to a fixed number of choices, such as "Would it be more efficient for campus security to invest in (1) an escort system or (2) a shuttle bus?" This type of question directs the respondent to pick one option from those you have offered, which is helpful when you want to commit the person to a definite position. A closed question also allows you to count and compare the answers of different respondents, because they all choose from the same list of answers. However, closed questions do not reveal much about respondents' thinking and opinions.

In contrast, an **open-ended question** does not limit or direct the person's response, as in "What do you think should be done to enhance campus security?" Although an open-ended question does permit full expression of opinions, the answer may stray far from the information you most need for your speech, and you may have to refocus the interview.

Conduct the Interview Competently

Being a competent interviewer includes such basic matters as arriving on time, reminding the person who you are and the purpose of your interview, and thanking him or her for taking the time to help you. But competence also includes the ability to adjust your questions in response to the flow of the

Having specific questions prepared for your subject will help with the flow of the interview, but also be open to answers that may lead you in an unexpected direction.

interview itself. The person may say something that answers several of your questions or parts of them, or a comment may bring up a question that you had not planned on asking. Do not regard your questions as rigid and inflexible; adjust them as the interview evolves. However, if the interviewee seems to ignore a question, you may need to ask it again, perhaps phrasing it differently. Or, you may need to ask a **follow-up question** that explores the implications of a previous response. Finally, you must take care to reach an agreement with the respondent about what information, if any, you can quote directly and what information is solely for your own use.

Take Notes or Record the Interview

Don't assume that you will remember everything important that is said during an interview. Arrive prepared, with notebook in hand, so you can keep track of important points. If you prefer to record the interview, be sure to ask ahead of time whether that will be all right; no one should be recorded without permission. Think carefully about recording the interview, however. Although it does free you from the burden of note taking and ensures an accurate record of the interview, it also may make the respondent more guarded and less candid, knowing that every word is being "recorded for posterity."

Determine What to Use in Your Speech

Not everything that you obtain in an interview will be useful in your speech; nor should the interview be your sole source of information. As you assemble materials for the speech, ask yourself which points can be supported most effectively by the interview and which points can be supported just as well by other sources. For example, you may decide to rely on printed sources for general or statistical information about your topic and then draw on the interview for opinion testimony and for real-world examples.

Checklist 9.4
Guidelines for Interviewing

- Prepare for the person.
- Prepare for the subject.
- Prepare for the format.
- Conduct the interview competently.
- Take notes or record the interview.
- Determine what information to use.

Evaluating Evidence

From whatever source your supporting materials were obtained, you want to be sure that your evidence is credible—that it should be taken seriously and given weight by an audience of reasonable people. Unfortunately, not all supporting materials will meet this standard.

Potential Deficiencies in Evidence

Several factors can make evidence deficient. Poor evidence may be:

- *Unavailable for inspection:* In some cases, the evidence is kept secret and its quality cannot be assessed.
- *Inaccurate or uncertain:* Some evidence may be false or misleading. It may report inaccurately or out of context. The source of the evidence may be unknown.
- *Not credible:* The source may not be credible, whether because of inexperience or bias.
- *Not from a relevant expert:* The source may be speaking outside his or her field of expertise, as when a distinguished scientist offers opinions about the salary structure in baseball.
- *Inconsistent:* The evidence may be internally inconsistent—for example, one part of the evidence might assume that college students have significant discretionary income while another part of the evidence assumes that their budgets are strapped.
- *Contradicted:* The evidence may be contradicted by the best evidence from other sources.
- *Outdated:* The evidence may be out of date, supplanted by more recent evidence. Some matters are timeless, but for others recency is crucial. For example, in discussing how many nations in the world have the capability to develop nuclear weapons, it makes a difference whether the evidence comes from 2004 or 2014.
- *Irrelevant:* If the evidence is completely true but does not help to advance the speaker's main claim, then it is not strong evidence. The supporting material must be relevant to the point it claims to support.

You can use Checklist 9.5 to help test the credibility of your supporting material.

The Quality of Internet Evidence

There are additional concerns that relate to evidence obtained from the Internet. The Internet has been described as the most democratic means of publishing there is. Virtually anyone can post virtually anything on the Web. As a consequence, there is almost no editorial or quality control except whatever is exercised by the producer of the site. An online version of a printed publication—an electronic copy of a print journal article, for example—can be assumed to reflect the same editorial judgment as the printed publication itself. At the other extreme, an individual's personal website may not have been checked at all. And some organizations whose mission is to promote a particular viewpoint can be deceptive, presenting propaganda as if it were scholarship.

Search engines attempt to distinguish between reliable and unreliable websites, but they cannot do so perfectly. And whether the site looks "professional" is not a reliable indicator either, because it is easier to design a sophisticated-looking site than it is to produce a book. In fact, sophisticated websites that look like those of easily recognized organizations have been created for the purpose of coaxing individuals to reveal their Social Security and credit card numbers in order to facilitate identity theft. This, of course, is fraud.[8] Extra vigilance is needed to be sure that you take only reliable evidence from the Web. For these reasons, the responsibility to evaluate Internet evidence rests with you. We need, therefore, to note some special precautions about supporting materials from electronic sources. The following questions are especially pertinent:[9]

- **Does the site meet the basic standards of credibility?** At a minimum, a credible website should contain the name of the sponsor, identification of expert and believable author(s) or contributor(s), and information that is current, appropriate, and capable of being checked for accuracy.
- **Who set up the website?** If you cannot tell who sponsors the site, be suspicious of its contents. People or organizations with an ax to grind can disguise their motivations or identity, leading you to regard biased information as though it were neutral. One clue to a site's reliability is its *domain name*—the last portion of its URL. As a general rule, URLs that end in .gov (government agency) or

Checklist 9.5
Testing the Credibility of Supporting Material[10]

- Is the evidence available for inspection?
- Is the evidence accurate?
- Is the source credible?
- Is the source making statements within his or her expertise?
- Is the evidence internally consistent?
- Is the evidence contradicted by the best evidence from other sources?
- Is the evidence recent enough?
- Is the evidence relevant to the point that it supports?

.edu (educational institution) may be more reliable sites than those ending in .org (organization) or .com (commercial source).

- **What are the source's credentials?** To determine whether the author has expertise on the subject, you should check a credentials page. You may need to trace back in the URL (Internet address) to find one. If the author has a specific agenda or ideology, take that into consideration when you evaluate the source.
- **What is the purpose of the website?** If the goal is to sell a product or service or to campaign for an individual or a point of view, you should examine the content more skeptically than if the goal is simply to provide information. Sometimes the site's purpose will not be apparent from its title and the name of the source. You will need to read through the material on the site in order to form a judgment.
- **Does the content appear to reflect scholarship?** Scholarly work generally provides documentation for claims, indicates where information was obtained, describes limits of the data and does not overstate claims, considers alternative viewpoints on matters of opinion and describes these alternatives accurately, honors context, and relies on critical thinking skills. If the site contains excessive claims of certainty, presents ideas out of context or without documentation, and suppresses alternative views, it is more likely to be biased advocacy or propaganda.
- **Can you confirm the information?** If you find information on the Web that seems to make your case airtight or to refute someone's ideas conclusively, be careful. A good general rule is to check electronic information against other sources. Even if you can't find the exact same facts or ideas, what you obtain from the Web should be compatible with what you learn from people or in print.
- **When was the site last updated?** One of the chief virtues of the Web is that it can supply up-to-the-minute information about current topics. Often, however, sites are not updated regularly, and the information becomes obsolete. If you cannot tell when a site was last updated, that may be a reason to be wary of its content.

A Plan for Research

Researching for a speech can seem overwhelming. At first, the topic may seem so vast that you don't know where to begin. You may not be able to think of any people you should interview, or you may identify so many people that you don't have time to question them all. The resources of a major library can be daunting, and specialized indexes may only compound the problem by revealing an even larger mass of material to consider. Also, the Internet sources you checked might include thousands of citations. How can you possibly go through them all?

A research strategy can make these burdens manageable. Just as you need to understand your speech goals and the means to achieve them, you need to approach research strategically. The following suggestions will help you devise a research strategy.

Start Early

Don't wait until the last minute to begin preparing your speech. Research does take time and involves a certain amount of trial and error. The sooner you begin thinking about and working on the speech, the better.

Determine Where You Need to Go

Your topic may require you to do research on the Internet, in the library, in the field, or with a combination of these tools. The analysis of the issues related to your topic should help you determine which questions you need to answer and which kinds of research will help you answer them. Keep those questions in mind as you do your research.

Bring Necessary Materials and Supplies

It's frustrating (and often embarrassing) to arrive at the research site and discover that you don't have the materials you need. For example, if you are conducting interviews, you may need an audio recorder and batteries as well as a notebook and pen. In the library, you may need a laptop, a USB flash drive, notecards or paper, and pencils or pens. You also will need to be prepared to pay for the use of a copier. Think ahead.

Learn the Library's Layout

You do not want to waste valuable research time figuring out how the library is arranged and where things are located. You should know your way around. Learn where to find the digital catalog terminals, the reference room, and the stacks. Find out where periodicals, newspapers, and government publications are kept. Learn whether copiers and computer labs are available and what the library's hours and procedures are. If your library offers an orientation tour, arrange to take it before you begin intensive research for your speech. And do not be

A Question of *ETHICS*

Ethics and Research

Research is important to a speech because it ensures both that the speech is accurate and that you are credible. Using external sources, testimony, and data all increase your and the audience's knowledge of a topic. But the more you rely on others, the less room you have for your own analysis and conclusions. What is more, it may seem that you are just a conduit for other people's ideas. Is this ethical? Is there a point at which a speech suffers from too much information and citation? Do you have a responsibility to make sure your ideas are your own? Even if you appropriately cite every source in your speech, is it truly your speech if it is merely a well-crafted series of citations, quotations, and statistics gathered from other places? Conversely, is it ethical to expect any audience to accept your conclusions just on your own say-so? Why or why not?

afraid to ask librarians questions, because they usually are knowledgeable about the library's resources and genuinely helpful.

Develop a Preliminary Bibliography

Consult the various indexes and reference works described in this chapter to develop a list of potential sources. To save time later, this preliminary bibliography should include the URL or other online locator, or the call numbers or other identifying numbers you will need to locate the material.

Set Priorities Within the Bibliography

The order of items in your bibliography probably will not reflect the order in which you want to read the materials. Decide what is most important to locate right away. It may be a particular aspect of the topic or a certain kind of source.

Read Progressively

If you are not yet very familiar with your topic, begin by reading general works to gain a background understanding of key terms, major issues, and the origins and development of the subject. This background will prepare you for in-depth reading about the specific issues that you will highlight in your speech. Finally, there probably are particular claims or arguments for which you will need support: a specific example, a particular statistic, or a certain piece of testimony. As you proceed through your research, be clear about what level of understanding you seek. In general, if you find yourself reading about the same points repeatedly in different sources, it is time to move on to a more specialized level of research.

Read Selectively

Very likely, you will discover far more information than you can read—or even skim—in the time you have to prepare your speech. The key is to be selective in what you read. For example, check the dates of available sources. For some topics, such as how soon the economy may pull out of a recession, very recent material is crucial. For other topics, such as the origins of the Social Security system, older material may be more valuable. If the date seems inappropriate for your purpose, don't bother consulting that source.

Read Efficiently

Doing research is not like reading a novel; you want to read quickly and efficiently, not from start to finish. The goal is to identify which elements of a document or source are most pertinent for your speech. Skim material, looking for key words and a general sense of the context. Use guides—such as the subheadings and specific pages on a website, or a book's table of contents, index, and headings—to determine which sections to read carefully and which you may skim or skip. Stay alert, however; efficiency is not haste, and you do not want to make a wrong turn somewhere that causes you to misunderstand the context of key points.

Be Open to New Ideas

Even though you are researching with a particular goal in mind, keep open the possibility that your investigation may change your perspective or uncover something about your topic that you had not considered. You might discover issues that you did not originally anticipate, and you might even decide to change your thesis statement.

Use Multiple Sources and Evidence of Various Types

Your speech will be less credible if all the supporting material comes from a single source or is of one type. If you use a single source to support your claims, the audience may think that you are simply parroting the thoughts of someone else. For example, one student's speech about recycling presented the same information, in the same order, as did a pamphlet that had been distributed to every student on campus. Not only did this student bore the audience with information they already had, but she made them angry because they thought she was trying to avoid the work of amassing evidence from different sources, evaluating it, and arranging it creatively for their benefit.

Likewise, the speech will be less interesting if all your evidence is of the same type. A mix of examples, testimony, statistics, and other types of support not only will hold the audience's attention but also will add credibility to your claims by suggesting that the same conclusion was reached through several different methods.

Protect Against Plagiarism

Avoid **plagiarism**, which is usually thought of as the use of someone else's words as though they were your own. But the same warning applies to using someone else's *ideas* as though they were yours. In either case, the plagiarist both misrepresents himself or herself and steals the intellectual property of another.

Most people recognize that plagiarism is wrong. When it happens, it usually is unintentional. A student organizes her speech in exactly the same way as a magazine article on the same subject without identifying the article and either doesn't realize it happened or doesn't recognize that it is a form of plagiarism. Another student thinks he is paraphrasing his source, but in fact is engaged in almost direct quotation without saying so. Because he identified the source, he may not think this is plagiarism, or he may not realize how close his speech stays to the original. A third student gives a speech basically reporting what a single source said without identifying the source because the student's speech was not a direct quotation. He, too, has misrepresented another person's thinking by treating it as his own idea. Each of these examples is a form of plagiarism.

How can you protect against plagiarism while doing your research? First, don't limit yourself to a single source. The need to bring together several different sources should reduce any unconscious tendency to stick too closely to the text. Second, as you take notes, paraphrase except when the exact words of the source are important to quote. In this way, you'll cast your notes in your own words right from the beginning. Third, organize your notes without any of the sources immediately at hand, so you won't be tempted to follow someone else's organizational structure. Finally, whenever you draw upon one of your notes to use it in the speech, be sure you identify the source.

Checklist 9.6
Research Strategy Checklist

- Start early.
- Determine where you need to go.
- Bring necessary materials and supplies.
- Learn the library's layout and the locations of various materials.
- Develop a preliminary bibliography.
- Set priorities within the bibliography.
- Read progressively.
- Read selectively.
- Read efficiently.
- Be open to new ideas.
- Use multiple sources and evidence of varous types.
- Protect against plagiarism.
- Keep a speech material file.
- Know when to stop.

Keep a Speech Material File

Sometimes you will find materials that could be useful in a speech while you are doing something else—reading the newspaper, watching television, conversing with others, or studying for other courses. Don't lose track of this material or assume that you can find it when you need it. If you think that you may want to talk about a subject later in the term, begin now to save relevant material as you come across it.

Experienced speakers develop a **speech material file**. The file might be a notebook in which you jot down ideas, quotations, stories, poetry, or interesting examples. It might be a file of clippings from newspaper or magazine articles. More likely, it will be an electronic file that you keep on your computer with documents, images, and links that you find interesting or potentially useful. The form of the file is not as important as the habit of keeping one. You will be pleasantly surprised by how much easier it is to prepare a speech when you do not have to start from scratch, when you already have materials about topics that interest you.

Know When to Stop

Research is an ongoing activity, and you can always learn more about any topic—especially if you enjoy the subject and like doing research. But there comes a point at which you must stop collecting evidence and assemble the speech, which, after all, has limits of time and scope. Besides, you want to leave enough time for the other steps of preparation; further research will only tell you more about what you already know—and more than you can possibly tell the audience. Considerations such as these should help you to determine when it is time to move on to the other steps of speech preparation. As you develop the speech, you can return to research as needed to fill specific holes.

Taking notes from different sources in your own words will enable you to integrate material from different sources and avoid the risk of plagiarism.

Note Taking

No matter how thorough or extensive your research is, it will do you little good if you forget what you learned or where you learned it. Sometimes, something will seem so vivid or so obvious that you cannot imagine forgetting it, but most people remember far less than they think they will. Experienced speakers have learned to keep track of their speech material by establishing a system of note taking. Be guided by whatever works best for you, but the following suggestions should help you to establish an effective note-taking system.

Use a Flexible System

Recording each idea, statistic, example, quotation, and the like on an individual note card or sheet of paper is better than taking continuous notes about different topics or taking notes in a spiral notebook or other bound book. A flexible system is one that makes it easy to sort and rearrange material in organizing the speech, to locate related materials, and to discard items that you decide not to use. Taking notes on a computer may be the most flexible system, as long as you can rearrange the notes easily when developing the speech.

When taking notes from electronic sources, you can follow the same methods described here—copying material from the monitor onto note cards or sheets of paper. There are also programs that enable you to take notes electronically, such as EndNote and Zotero.

Include Full Bibliographic Citations

A "full" citation contains all the material needed to find the source from which you took notes. This step may seem time-consuming, but you can make it more efficient through careful use of abbreviations. In any case, it should not be omitted. First, you often will need to go back to the original source to verify your notes, to check their context, or to compare them with other sources. Second, the bibliographic information will often be helpful in evaluating the strength of evidence or in choosing among different sources of evidence. It takes far more time and effort to find the source a second time than to note its full bibliographic citation while doing research.

Standard guides for citing sources cover both print and electronic sources. Whatever citation system you use, it is important to use it consistently. (See Table 9.4 for some examples.)

The purpose of citation is to allow someone to obtain information from the sources you used. Unlike print materials, a document on the Internet can appear, disappear, or be revised without any warning. For this reason, you need to include information on when a source was posted on the Internet (if that is available) and, for some citation styles, on when you obtained the information. If you think that the Internet source may play a large role in your speech, it is a good idea either to print or to download the electronic document, preserving it in the form in which you consulted it.

Citing sources in notes or a bibliography is an essential part of your research. When you cite the source orally, during the speech itself, the process is a bit different. We will consider that issue in Chapter 10, when we discuss incorporating supporting materials into the speech and the presentation outline.

Decide Whether to Quote or to Paraphrase the Source

Unless an exact quotation is necessary, you can paraphrase, to summarize the gist of the idea in your own words. That way, you will be less likely

Table 9.4
Bibliographic Formats

American Psychological Association (APA)—References

Type of Source	Sample Format
Book	White, R. C., Jr. (2009). *A. Lincoln: A biography.* New York, NY: Random House.
Chapter from an edited book	Hauser, G. A. (2008). Rethinking deliberative democracy: Rhetoric, power, and civil society. In T. F. McDorman and D. M. Timmerman (Eds.), *Rhetoric and democracy: Pedagogical and political practices* (pp. 225–264). East Lansing, MI: Michigan State University Press.
Magazine or newspaper article (online)	Stolberg, S. G., & Zeleny, J. (2009, September 10). Obama, armed with details, challenges Congress. *The New York Times.* Retrieved from http://www.nytimes.com.
Magazine or newspaper article (print)	Stolberg, S. G., & Zeleny, J. (2009, September 10). Obama, armed with details, challenges Congress. *The New York Times,* p. A1.
Journal article (online)	Howell, B. W. (2008). Reagan and Reykjavik: Arms control, SDI, and the argument from human rights. *Rhetoric & Public Affairs, 11,* 389–415. doi: 10.1353/rap.0.0045
Journal article (print)	Bostdorff, D. M. (2009). Judgment, experience, and leadership: Candidate debates on the Iraq war in the 2008 presidential primaries. *Rhetoric & Public Affairs, 12,* 223–277.
Web page	Mehltretter, S. A. (2009). John F. Kennedy, "Inaugural Address," 1961. *Voices of Democracy.* Retrieved from http://www.voicesofdemocracy.umd.edu/documents/Mehltretter-Kennedy.pdf.
Personal interview*	*Interviews are not listed in References. Cite in outline or text as: (O. Winfrey, personal communication, August 15, 2009).

Modern Language Association (MLA)—Works Cited

Type of Source	Sample Format
Book	White, Ronald C., Jr. *A. Lincoln: A Biography.* New York: Random, 2009. Print.
Chapter from an edited book	Hauser, Gerard A. "Rethinking Deliberative Democracy: Rhetoric, Power, and Civil Society." In *Rhetoric and Democracy: Pedagogical and Political Practices.* Ed. Todd F. McDorman and David M. Timmerman. East Lansing: Michigan State UP, 2008. 225–64. Print.
Magazine or newspaper article (online)	Stolberg, Sheryl Gay, and Jeff Zeleny. "Obama, Armed with Details, Challenges Congress." *New York Times.* New York Times, 10 Sept. 2009. Web. 3 Jan. 2010.
Magazine or newspaper article (print)	Stolberg, Sheryl Gay, and Jeff Zeleny. "Obama, Armed with Details, Challenges Congress." *New York Times* 10 Sept. 2009, natl. ed.: A1. Print.
Journal article (online)	Howell, B. Wayne. "Reagan and Reykjavik: Arms Control, SDI, and the Argument from Human Rights." *Rhetoric and Public Affairs,* 11.3 (2008): 389–415. *Project Muse.* Web. 10 Sept. 2009.
Journal article (print)	Bostdorff, Denise M. "Judgment, Experience, and Leadership: Candidate Debates on the Iraq War in the 2008 Presidential Primaries." *Rhetoric and Public Affairs* 12 (2009): 223–77. Print.
Web page	Mehltretter, Sara Ann. "John F. Kennedy, 'Inaugural Address,' 1961." *Voices of Democracy.* U of Maryland, 2009. Web. 3 Jan. 2010.
Personal interview	Winfrey, Oprah. Personal interview. 15 Aug. 2009.

Note: For citations of online sources, MLA lists two dates. The first is the date of online publication and the second is the date you accessed the source.

accidentally to plagiarize. In any case, your note-taking system should signal to you at a glance whether a note is quoted or not. A good method is to enclose the words of others in quotation marks but to omit them from your own paraphrases or summaries.

Clearly Identify Deletions and Additions in Quoted Material

Sometimes, the quotation you want to use is interspersed with other material that is unrelated to your purposes or is longer than you want to quote. At other times, the quotation may not be clear unless you add some words—for example, to identify the reference of a pronoun in the quotation.

When you use a quotation, you must make certain that all deletions and insertions are faithful to the context of the original source. Your notes should identify any variations from the exact text of the quotation. The most common practice is to identify deletions in your notes with an ellipsis (a series of three dots, like this: . . .) and to identify insertions in notes with brackets (like this: [ ]). It is important to use brackets rather than parentheses, because parentheses would indicate that the inserted words were in the original source. (In the speech itself, use changes in pitch or rate to identify insertions or deletions.)

Take Notes Only Once

If you take notes in longhand, be sure that you write legibly so that you do not have to recopy or type the notes. Duplicate note taking is a waste of time. Increasingly, laptop computers are used for note taking at the library, which overcomes the problem of unclear handwriting. A computer also lets you take notes in continuous fashion and later print them out on separate sheets of paper, as recommended earlier. Or you may keep your notes in electronic files that you can search and manipulate as needs arise.

SUMMARY

You can choose your own topic if:

- A classroom assignment permits it.
- People are interested in hearing you, regardless of the subject you wish to address.

Topic choice is beyond your control if:

- Your commitment to a specific cause impels you to speak.
- Your reputation on a given subject leads you to speak out.
- The occasion calls for a speech on a particular topic.
- A classroom assignment specifies the topic.

The initial steps in preparing a speech are as follows:

- Choosing a topic, if the choice is up to you.
- Developing a strategic plan for designing the speech, reflecting a clear sense of purpose and identifying your constraints and opportunities.

When you are able to choose your own topic, your speech will be more effective if

- The topic matters to you.
- You can make the topic interesting to the audience.
- The topic is worth the listeners' time.
- The scope of the topic fits the time available.
- The topic is appropriate for oral delivery.
- The topic is appropriate to the rhetorical situation.
- The topic is clear.

As aids in selecting a topic, you should

- Conduct an inventory of your interests and those of the audience.
- Use brainstorming and general reading.
- Narrow the topic so that it can be addressed adequately within the time available.

Strategic planning—identifying objectives to be sought and the means for achieving them—develops an overall strategy for responding to the rhetorical situation, including

- Identifying the purpose
- Identifying the opportunities
- Identifying the constraints
- Selecting the means

Shaping your plan for the speech is guided by its specific purpose:

- Providing new information or perspective
- Agenda-setting (raising issues for consideration)
- Creating positive or negative feeling
- Strengthening commitment to a position
- Weakening commitment to a position
- Changing listeners' minds
- Inducing a specific action by audience members

Constraints limit what you can do in achieving your purpose; they result from

- Audiences in general
- Your analysis of the specific audience
- Your ethos as a speaker
- The nature of your topic
- The fact that a speech is a one-shot appeal that is primarily verbal

On the other hand, opportunities to achieve your purpose arise from the facts that

- You will know more about your topic than listeners do.
- You may draw on and respond to the audience's attention and values.

The process of formulating your strategic plan enables you to identify

- The general purpose statement
- The specific purpose statement
- The thesis statement

You might modify these statements as you learn more about the subject and refine your audience analysis, but they will influence the following strategic decisions:

- What you need to know about the topic in order to establish that the thesis is true
- Which main ideas you need to develop to establish the thesis
- Which inferences must be made to link the main ideas to the thesis
- How best to organize your development and support of the thesis
- Which elements in the design of the speech will make listeners most comfortable about accepting the thesis statement

We will focus on these important strategic choices in the next several chapters.

Research is the process of locating the supporting materials to be used in the speech.

Types of supporting materials include the following:

- Personal experience
- Common knowledge
- Direct observation
- Examples
- Documents
- Statistics
- Testimony

Tools for finding supporting materials, in the order most people use them, are the following:

- Search engines
- Electronic databases
- Catalogs
- Indexes

These tools can be supplemented by visiting the library or by interviewing people.

Sources of supporting material, whether obtained electronically or in hard copy, include the following:

- Periodicals
- Newspapers
- Books
- Reference works
- Government publications
- Other materials found online, such as individual or corporate websites, conference proceedings, archives, and unpublished writings
- Interviews

Potential deficiencies in evidence include the following:

- Evidence unavailable for inspection
- Inaccurate or uncertain evidence
- Evidence that is not credible
- Evidence not from a relevant expert
- Inconsistent evidence
- Contradicted evidence
- Outdated evidence
- Irrelevant evidence

Strategic questions to ask about Internet evidence are as follows:

- Does the site meet the basic standards of credibility?
- Who set up the website?
- What are the source's credentials?
- What is the purpose of the website?
- Does the content appear to reflect scholarship?
- Can you confirm the information?
- When was the site last updated?

The process of researching a speech can be managed by developing a plan for research. Such a plan includes the following:

- Beginning early
- Being clear about what is needed and where it can be found
- Setting priorities
- Reading progressively and efficiently
- Taking useful notes
- Keeping full bibliographic citations
- Maintaining a speech material file
- Knowing when to stop

A full citation of a source contains all the material needed to find the source. This is important because

- You may want to go back to the original source.
- The bibliographic information may be helpful in evaluating the evidence or in choosing among different sources.
- Someone else may want to obtain information from the sources you used.

A note-taking system

- Should be flexible so you can rearrange notes.
- Should distinguish between quotations and paraphrases.
- Should clearly identify additions or deletions in quoted material.
- Should not require duplicative effort.

Discussion Questions

1. When a small liberal arts college decided to change its core curriculum, the issue of core requirements became important to students in a public speaking class, many of whom spoke about that topic. Discuss the issues in this rhetorical situation that seemed to call for speech.
2. How do the purpose of a speech and its subject matter relate to one another? Discuss the speech purposes described in this chapter, and identify some potential topics for each purpose.
3. Imagine that you are giving a six- to eight-minute speech to a group of fraternity members in which your purpose is to weaken their commitment to the idea that alcohol is desirable at parties. What constraints and opportunities do you face in this situation? How will you use those constraints and opportunities in your strategic plan for this speech?
4. Now imagine that you are giving a six- to eight-minute speech to a meeting of Students Against Drunk Driving in which your purpose is to strengthen their commitment to the idea that alcohol is dangerous at parties. How do the constraints and opportunities of this situation differ from those in item 3? In what ways would your strategic plan for this speech be different?
5. Think of a speech or other presentation that you have seen or heard that lacked a clear thesis. What are some of the common pitfalls of a speech without a well-defined thesis—from the perspective both of the speaker and of the audience?
6. Which types of supporting material would you need to back up the thesis "Video games have too much violence"? Evaluate each type of supporting material, and determine which part of the thesis each type would best support.
7. What types of sources do you find most and least credible? Why?
8. With a group, discuss the pros and cons of the following sources of supporting material, including the situations in which each type would be most appropriate:

   Personal experience

   Interviews

   Library research

   Internet
9. In what situations might you want to use blogs as evidence? If a blog and a printed editorial say essentially the same thing, which is preferable? Why?

ACTIVITIES

1. Choose a good topic for a speech in this class. In doing so, conduct a personal inventory and use finding aids such as brainstorming and source browsing. Share topics with a classmate. In what ways does your classmate's topic appeal or not appeal to you? Is your classmate's topic narrow enough? Why or why not?
2. Produce a list of constraints and a list of opportunities for the topic you have chosen (in activity 1). Consider the audience, the occasion, the speaker, and the speech. In a few paragraphs, describe your purpose and how you are going to achieve it within the bounds of these constraints and opportunities.
3. Provide the following information about your speech:

   TOPIC:

   GENERAL PURPOSE:

   SPECIFIC PURPOSE:

   THESIS STATEMENT:

   Evaluate each of these decisions, explaining why you made the choices you did.
4. Make a list of topics that you think are hackneyed. What makes them hackneyed topics? Will such topics always remain hackneyed? If not, how might you apply a fresh perspective to them?
5. In researching a thesis of your choice, find an example of each type of supporting material. Test the strength of each type to determine which material would best support your thesis.
6. Conduct an interview, following the guidelines offered in this chapter.
7. Pick a clearly defined, narrow topic that you know little about. Brainstorm what research resources you would best consult. Use Internet search engines and your library to come up with an annotated bibliography of five sources that you would use in writing the speech, explaining how each source would strengthen your speech.

KEY TERMS

agenda setting
analysis
brainstorming
closed question
common knowledge
conversion
document
follow-up question
general purpose statement
issue
open-ended question
perspective
plagiarism
presumption
purpose
research
specific purpose statement
speech material file
statistics
strategic plan
testimony
thesis
topic
topoi

NOTES

1. See Craig R. Smith and Paul Prince, "Language Choice Expectation and the Roman Notion of Style," *Communication Education* 39 (January 1990): 63–74.
2. This classification system is original. We will use this more precise system of purposes for the remainder of our study.
3. For another list of purposes, see Sonja K. Foss and Karen A. Foss, *Inviting Transformation: Presentational Speaking for a Changing World,* Prospect Heights, IL: Waveland Press, 1994, pp. 10–16.
4. Classical rhetoric addresses the subject of issue identification as "stasis theory." For more on modern approaches to classical stasis theory, see Sharon Crowley and Debra Hawhee, *Ancient Rhetorics for Contemporary Students,* 5th ed., New York: Pearson Longman, 2011; Richard Johnson-Sheehan, *Writing Proposals: Rhetoric for Managing Change,* 2nd ed., New York: Longman, 2007; and Allen H. Brizee, "Stasis Theory as a Strategy for Workplace Teaming and Decision Making," *Journal of Technical Writing and Communication* 38 (December 2008): 363–85.
5. Thomas B. Farrell, "Knowledge, Consensus, and Rhetorical Theory, " *Quarterly Journal of Speech* 62 (February 1976): 1–14.
6. The misleading statistics about the tax cut proposal are described in David E. Rosenbaum, "The President's Tax Cut and Its Unspoken Numbers," *New York Times,* February 5, 2003, p. A23.
7. For more on the misuse of statistics, see Joel Best, *Damned Lies and Statistics: Untangling Numbers from the Media, Politicians, and Activists,* Berkeley: University of California Press, 2001.
8. For an example of this problem, see Ylan Q. Mui. "Justice Dept. cracks down on Cyber Monday scams," *Washington Post,* November 28, 2011 (http://www.washingtonpost.com/business/economy/justice-dept-cracks-down-on-scams-on-cyber-monday/2011/11/28/gIQA1clz5N_story.html?tid=pm_business_pop.
9. Some of the problems with doing electronic research are explained in Steven B. Knowlton, "How Students Get Lost in Cyberspace," *New York Times,* "Education Life" section, November 2, 1997: 18, 21. There are also online sources offering good suggestions for evaluating Internet evidence. Two examples are wps.pearsoncustom.com/ph_hss_mycomplab_25/75/19245/4926917.cw/content/index.html and www.tarleton.edu/departments/library/library_module/unit8/8internet_lm.htm.
10. These tests for evidence are adapted from James A. Herrick, *Argumentation: Understanding and Shaping Arguments,* 3rd ed. (State College, Pa.: Strata, 2007), 73–80.

CHAPTER 10

Organizing the Speech

Taken from *Public Speaking: Strategies for Success*, Seventh Edition, by David Zarefsky.

In this chapter, you'll learn about:

- Why Is Organization Important?
- Selecting the Main Ideas
  - Identifying Your Main Ideas | Choosing Among Main Ideas | Criteria for Selecting the Main Ideas | Characteristics of the Main Ideas
- Arranging the Main Ideas
  - Factors Affecting Arrangement | Patterns for Arranging Main Ideas | Choosing the Organizational Pattern
- Selecting and Arranging Supporting Materials
  - Selection of Supporting Materials | Arrangement of Supporting Materials
- Introductions: Beginning the Speech
  - The Purposes of an Introduction | An Example of an Introduction | Types of Introductions Strategies for Preparing an Introduction
- Conclusions: Ending the Speech
  - The Purposes of a Conclusion | An Example of a Conclusion | Types of Conclusions Strategies for Preparing a Conclusion
- Transitions: Connecting the Elements of a Speech
  - The Purposes of Transitions | Elements of Effective Transitions | Strategies for Preparing Transitions
- From Ideas to Outline
- The Preparation Outline
  - What Does a Good Outline Look Like? Outlining the Body of the Speech | Outlining Introductions and Conclusions | Outlining Transitions | Citing Supporting Materials in the Outline
- Sample Preparation Outline
- The Presentation Outline
  - Guidelines for the Presentation Outline Use of Note Cards | Reference to Supporting Materials | Use of Stage Directions | Using an Outline in Rehearsal
- Sample Presentation Outline

If you have used all the strategies suggested in Chapter 9 for investigating your topic, you now should have a better understanding of the issues that are implicit in your thesis. You also should have located a variety of supporting materials for your ideas—examples, statistics, testimony, and so forth. You have probably investigated many more ideas than you can discuss in the time available, and you very likely have located far more supporting materials than you can use. For all this effort, your ideas and materials may show no evident pattern and may not seem to fit together well. What, then, do you do with all the ideas you have explored and all the evidence you have gathered?

Identifying and locating material for the speech is not enough; you also need to organize it in strategic ways that advance your purpose. **Organization** is the selection of ideas and materials and their arrangement into a discernible and effective pattern. This process is so crucial that we will discuss it in three chapters. Here, we will focus exclusively on the body of the speech. Then we will consider introductions, conclusions, and transitions. Finally we will learn how to apply the principles of organization in outlining your speech.

Why Is Organization Important?

To help orient new students to the college, the counseling office offers a program in which seniors give speeches about how to develop good study habits. The first speaker, Burt Wilson, maintained that "good habits depend on several important factors. For one thing, you have to avoid procrastination. Good reading skills are also helpful to college students. Oh yes, and by the way, you also need to be self-motivated." The incoming students looked puzzled and unconvinced; they stopped taking notes, and no one asked questions. The very next speaker, Laura Simmons, covered the same ground, but she said: "Good study habits depend on a balance of skills plus motivation. On the one hand, you have to develop good reading skills; on the other hand, you need to overcome procrastination. You can do both if you focus on the priorities that motivate you to study." The audience responded very differently to Laura's speech; they took notes and asked a number of questions when she finished.

This example illustrates that audiences will understand, remember, and be influenced by an organized message more than by a disorganized one. The reason is obvious. Careful listening is difficult under any circumstances, and it is even more difficult when listeners cannot tell where the speaker is going or how the parts of the speech relate to one another. An idea or example that is not connected to anything else is easy to forget.[1] The mental energy that listeners use in reconstructing a confused or disorganized speech is not available for absorbing and reflecting on its main points.[2] Moreover, even critical listeners may resent this additional work of listening to a disorganized speech and may express their resentment by resisting the message.[3]

Beyond such basic considerations about the audience, a speaker should recognize that form itself is persuasive. The ability to follow a speaker's organizational pattern is important for several reasons:

- *Recall.* An audience can better remember the main ideas of a speech when the speaker presents them in a recognizable pattern. For example, the past/present/future pattern encourages listeners to remember the first idea if they can connect it mentally to the heading "past."
- *Active listening.* Effective organization engages listeners' attention and helps them to ignore or override distractions.
- *Personal satisfaction.* Being able to anticipate what's coming next makes listeners feel that they are "in the know." If the speaker has just discussed recent issues in intercollegiate athletics, for example, they may believe that the next natural step is to discuss the merits of a playoff system for college football. If that indeed is the next main idea, they are likely to feel personal satisfaction at having "called it right."[4]

Organization is important for the speaker as well. In Chapter 9, you were introduced to the idea of *strategic planning* for a speech. In any rhetorical situation, the goal is to respond to your constraints and to take advantage of your opportunities to achieve your purpose. Organization is a major strategic resource as you make decisions about the number and order of ideas, how you group them, what you call them, and how you relate them to the audience.

For a political candidate to hold the attention of students in an informal setting, it's especially important that the speech be well organized and easy to follow.

Moreover, in planning your speech, organization can be a guide to check that you haven't accidentally left anything out. For example, noticing that your speech covers both the past and the present of your topic, you recognize that the audience will be likely to think, "But what about the future?" During your presentation, too, keeping the organization in mind can prevent the embarrassment of suddenly forgetting about the next point.[5]

Organization has two basic components: *selection* and *arrangement.* We will discuss each component with respect both to the main ideas of the speech and to the supporting materials.

Selecting the Main Ideas

As you remember from Chapter 9, the thesis statement is the principal claim of your speech, the statement you want listeners to accept. When you ask questions about your thesis statement, you identify the issues that you must address in order to establish the thesis. **Main ideas** are the claims that address the issues in your thesis statement, and they are the major divisions of the speech. You'll see that main ideas are signaled in the speech outline by Roman numerals.

Identifying Your Main Ideas

The first step is to identify the main ideas in your speech. To do that, you must determine the possible main ideas from which you could choose. You can do so either (1) from your thesis or specific purpose or (2) from patterns in your research.

In either case, your answers will be affected by the current status of the topic in the public forum: what aspects or issues people generally are considering, which matters are accepted and uncontested and which are in dispute, which questions seem central and which seem peripheral.

From Your Thesis or Specific Purpose

Stuart Kim used this approach to identify his main ideas in a speech seeking to persuade the audience to contribute to the United Way. Like many college students, Stuart was a community-service volunteer; he tutored reading and math at an after-school center for children from low-income families who had no parent at home during the day. Stuart enjoyed the work and felt that he was really helping the children, but toward the end of the year he was startled to learn that the center would have to close. It was funded by the United Way, and contributions were down. Appalled that "his" children would have nowhere to go, Stuart decided to speak to community groups and urge them to support the United Way. He used his public speaking classmates as a test audience to practice the speech.

Because Stuart's purpose was to persuade the audience to contribute to the United Way, he thought immediately of several ideas that he needed to address. He would have to tell listeners what the United Way is, that the agencies it supports (such as Stuart's after-school center) were important and valuable, that other sources of funding were not readily available, and that the United Way needed and merited *their* support. If the speech failed to address any of these elements, the audience was unlikely to be persuaded to donate money. Stuart regarded these as the main ideas, and he divided the speech into corresponding sections:

I. The United Way is a federation of health, recreational, and social service agencies.
II. The activities of these agencies are important and valuable to our community.
III. These activities cannot be continued unless we support the United Way.

In this example, Stuart was able immediately to see the main ideas that derived from his thesis and purpose. But sometimes the connection is not so obvious. If Stuart had not identified his main ideas at once, he might have worked them out by quizzing his thesis statement, using the method you learned in Chapter 9:

TOPIC:	The United Way		
GENERAL PURPOSE:	Inducing a specific action		
SPECIFIC PURPOSE:	Convincing listeners to give money to the United Way		
THESIS:	Everyone should contribute to the United Way.		
ISSUES:	1. Everyone	→	Why me?
	2. Should contribute	→	Why? What does it do?
	3. The United Way	→	What is it?
MAIN IDEAS:	1. The United Way needs and merits your support.		
	2. The United Way supports important and valuable programs.		
	3. The United Way is an umbrella organization to raise money for social service programs.		

Looking over this list, Stuart would probably decide to put main idea 3 first in the speech and to end with main idea 1. Why? Because listeners need to know what the United Way is before they can decide whether to support it and because the direct appeal in main idea 1 provides a strong conclusion. Applying these analytical steps, Stuart would derive the same main ideas that he was able to recognize instinctively.

Checklist 10.1 contains some of the standard questions to ask about a thesis statement in order to identify your main ideas.

Checklist 10.1
Questions to Help Identify Main Ideas

- What does it mean?
- How to describe it?
- What are the facts?
- What are the reasons?
- How often does it occur?
- What are the parts?
- What is the reasoning?
- Why is it strange?
- What are the objections?
- Compared with what?

From Patterns in Your Research

Another approach to identifying main ideas is to observe patterns in the research that you have completed. If the people you interview and the literature you read repeatedly mention certain subjects, those may well be the main ideas about your topic.

For example, suppose that almost everything Stuart Kim read about the United Way mentioned its low administrative costs and suggested that its reliance on volunteers meant that most of the money raised can be spent directly on providing services. This idea may not have emerged from Stuart's initial conception of a strategy, and yet it may be very important to include the idea in the speech. It suggests that it is better for people to contribute to the United Way than to support a host of individual charities that do not use their funds as efficiently.

Choosing Among Main Ideas

Whichever method you use to identify main ideas, you are likely to have more ideas than you have time or energy to pursue—and more than your audience will be willing and able to consider.

Suppose, for example, that Stuart's research suggested all the following points:

- The administrative costs of the United Way are low.
- Organizations in the United Way must be nondiscriminatory.
- The United Way had its origins in charitable organizations of the late nineteenth century.
- Some groups within the public object to the programs of certain United Way organizations.
- The United Way is staffed largely by volunteers.
- It is not clear whether someone who lives in one community but works in another should support the United Way at home or at work.
- The United Way substitutes a single annual campaign for what otherwise would be continuous solicitation for each of the member agencies.
- The alternative to supporting the United Way is to expand the government's social welfare programs.

Each of these topics could be discussed at length, and each might be supported by a variety of materials. Yet no speech of reasonable length could address them all. Therefore, like most speakers, Stuart will need to select from among the possible main ideas which ones to use in his speech.

Criteria for Selecting the Main Ideas

Most speeches cover between two and five main ideas. Although there is no magic to these numbers, they do generally represent what an audience expects and can likely follow and remember.

If you have derived more than five main ideas from your thesis and purpose and from your research, you can reduce their number and select which ideas to include by asking two questions:

- Is this idea really essential to the speech?
- Can a more general statement combine several ideas?

Is This Idea Essential?

In researching a speech, you may discover many interesting things about your subject that are, frankly, sidelights. Although they may be fascinating to you, they distract from your specific purpose. For example, knowing that the United Way developed from nineteenth-century charitable organizations may reveal quite a bit about American attitudes toward charity or about how organizations evolve. But remember that Stuart Kim's purpose is to persuade audience members to donate money. Most people don't need to know about the United Way's origins and history in order to decide whether to contribute. Likewise, if Stuart's goal is only to persuade people to give, it may not matter whether they do so at work or at home.

This first criterion is often difficult to apply. Speakers are reluctant to omit ideas that interest them, and valuable research time seems wasted if the results do not find their way into the speech. Material that does not directly relate to your topic and purpose is nonessential. Including nonessential material may distract the audience and prevent you from achieving your ultimate purpose. It is necessary, then, to be hard-nosed and to subject all potential main ideas to this rigorous test: If an idea—no matter how interesting—is not essential to your specific purpose, it does not qualify as a main idea and should be excluded.

Can Several Ideas Be Combined?

When you find yourself considering a large number of main ideas, consider whether some of them are not main ideas at all but illustrations of, or support for, more general statements. You may be able to combine what you thought were distinct main ideas into one general statement, thereby reducing the number. Your thesis should suggest these more general statements into which you could combine elements.

In the United Way example, the low administrative costs, the nondiscriminatory policies, and the convenience of a single annual campaign might turn out not to be separate main ideas but examples to support a general statement such as "The United Way is the best way to contribute to charity." The three statements all answer the question "Once I've decided that it's important to make a charitable con-

Audience members listen attentively to a presentation that is well organized and easy to follow.

tribution, why should I do so through the United Way?" That question is a longer form of "Why me?" which was derived from the thesis statement. All these examples could support the main idea, "The United Way merits *your* support."

Characteristics of the Main Ideas

Unfortunately, just cutting the number of main ideas—as difficult as that is—may still result in a speech that does not seem complete, coherent, or persuasive. It is also important that the selected main ideas have the following characteristics.

Simplicity

Because the main ideas serve as memory aids for both speaker and audience, they should be stated simply and succinctly so that they can be remembered. "The United Way is efficient" is a better statement of a main idea than is "The United Way has low administrative costs, economies of scale from combining campaigns, and simple distribution mechanisms." As a general rule, a main idea should be stated in a single short sentence.

Discreteness

Each main idea should be separate from the others. When main ideas overlap, the structure of the speech becomes confusing, and it is difficult to remember what was said under each main heading. For example, if one main idea is "The United Way supports agencies that meet social needs" and another main idea is "The United Way supports health and recreational agencies," the two ideas overlap; they are not discrete. After all, health and recreation are also among our social needs. Such a structure will not be clear to listeners, and the speaker will not know where to put supporting material.

Parallel Structure

When possible, main ideas should be stated in similar fashion. Sentences should have the same grammatical structure and should be of approximately the same length. This principle, known as **parallel structure**, makes the pattern easy to follow and to remember. For example, Stuart Kim might use this pattern:

> The United Way is effective.
>
> The United Way is efficient.
>
> The United Way is humane.

In this example, *effective, efficient,* and *humane* are the key terms that listeners are asked to remember.

Balance

Taken together, the main ideas should not be loaded toward one particular aspect of the subject. Rather, they should add up to a balanced perspective. In the preceding list, each of the three key terms refers to a different aspect of the United Way: what it accomplishes, what it costs, and what values it represents. These are three different factors that would affect the decision to contribute, and together they offer a balanced perspective. If, on the other hand, three or four main ideas related to the United Way's finances and only one dealt with its underlying values, the organization of the speech would appear unbalanced. Finances would be covered in detail, but other important aspects of the topic would be treated superficially or ignored.

Coherence

Coherence means that the separate main ideas have a clear relationship and hang together; listeners can see why they appear in the same speech. If Stuart Kim wished to persuade listeners to contribute to the United Way but offered one main idea about the origins of charitable organizations, another about efforts to extend the United Way to Eastern Europe, another about controversial agencies that the United Way supports, and another about accounting procedures, it is hard to imagine how the speech could be coherent. These topics are not clearly related to each other (except that they all involve the United Way), and they do not come together to support any conclusion—certainly not the ultimate claim that "you should contribute to the United Way."

Completeness

Finally, the main ideas taken together should present a complete view of the subject, omitting nothing of major importance. If Stuart wants to convince the

Checklist 10.2
Characteristics of Main Ideas

- Are my main ideas **simple** and succinct?
- Is each main idea **discrete,** or separate from the others?
- Are the main ideas stated in a **parallel structure?**
- Are the main ideas **balanced** in perspective?
- Are the main ideas **coherent** and clear?
- Do the main ideas, taken together, offer a **complete** view of my topic?

audience to contribute to the United Way but fails to explain what the organization does with the money it receives, the pattern of main ideas would not be complete. Most people who make charitable gifts want to know how their contributions are used.

Arranging the Main Ideas

After selecting the main ideas for your speech, the next step is deciding upon their order—which ideas to put first, last, or in the middle. We'll look at the factors you should consider in arranging your main ideas and then at a variety of organizational patterns that you can use.

Factors Affecting Arrangement

Are the Main Ideas Dependent?

Ideas can be arranged in a pattern that makes them either *dependent* or *independent.*

Logically dependent ideas are like links in a chain, because the strength of each depends on all the others. If one link is broken, the chain is destroyed. Here is such a chain of logically dependent main ideas:

1. If we develop regulations for campus speech, they will necessarily be vague.
2. If regulations are vague, people will not know whether or not the regulations apply to them.
3. If people are unsure whether regulations apply to them, they will hesitate to speak out about controversial issues.
4. If people do not speak out about controversial issues, intellectual debate is undermined.

The links in this chain need to be arranged precisely as shown if the audience is to follow the speaker's reasoning.

Logical dependence is common in telling a story. With obvious exceptions (such as flashbacks), you should relate events in the order in which they occurred so that listeners can follow the plot. Likewise, if you arrange ideas in a spatial pattern—talking, for example, about colleges in different regions of the country—then you need to maintain that pattern of geographical movement. You might move from east to west or from west to east, but you would not want to zigzag from New England to the Southwest and then to the mid-Atlantic states.

In contrast, **logically independent ideas** stand alone, and the truth of each in no way rests on the others. Again, using the example of a proposed code to regulate campus speech, here is a logically independent pattern of reasoning:

> Campus speech codes are unacceptably vague.
>
> Campus speech codes discourage the airing of controversial issues.
>
> Campus speech codes bring bad publicity to the college.

This speaker also wishes to oppose campus speech codes, but notice the difference in the structure of main ideas. In this case, each idea bears *independently* on the conclusion. Any one of these claims by itself could give the audience good reason to oppose speech codes, regardless of the other claims. Speech codes are undesirable if they are too vague, *or* if they chill the discussion of controversial issues, *or* if they bring unfavorable publicity.

A dependent pattern of reasoning can be risky, because the defeat of any one link will cause the chain to break. But a dependent pattern also offers advantages. It is highly coherent and easy to follow. And if each link is established successfully, the force of the overall pattern may cause the whole chain to seem even stronger than the sum of its links.

The choice of a dependent or an independent pattern is influenced most strongly by your thesis statement. Use whichever pattern is more effective in establishing your claim for your audience. But one thing is certain: If your main ideas are dependent on each other, their arrangement is virtually decided. You can begin at either end of the chain, but you must connect the ideas in order, link by link. With an independent pattern, however, you do not have to present the main ideas in any particular order. In that case, additional questions will arise.

Are Some Main Ideas Relatively Unfamiliar?

Because most people comprehend unfamiliar ideas by linking them to familiar ideas, you may wish to begin your speech with a main idea that is already familiar to listeners. This will attract their interest and get them thinking about your topic. Then you can move to the less familiar ideas, knowing that the audience is working with you.

Your audience analysis may suggest that most people realize that campus speech codes attract adverse publicity but that they may not be familiar with the vagueness of such codes and may not have thought about their effect on the airing of controversial issues. You therefore might begin with the familiar idea that campus speech codes attract negative publicity, making the point that this is just the tip of the iceberg. Speech codes also have two less

When you have a strong idea that you plan to present emphatically, as this speaker does, should it be placed first or last in your speech?

obvious problems: They are too vague to be administered fairly, and—even worse—they stifle discussion of controversial issues. If your audience analysis is correct, you have succeeded in arranging the ideas from most familiar to least familiar.

There is another reason to begin with the familiar. If your first main idea were completely unfamiliar to the audience, it would be much more difficult for listeners to grasp. You might distract them by making them stop to think about what you mean by "the inherent vagueness of speech codes," and they might miss your next point. On the other hand, discussion of a familiar main idea can be used to explain a less familiar idea. For example, knowing that listeners might quickly recognize that campus speech codes cause adverse publicity, you might ask why the publicity is so adverse. This question would provide a natural transition into your second, less familiar idea.

Should the Strongest Idea Come First or Last?

This question comes into play when two conditions are met: when the main ideas are independent and when they are not equally strong. A "strong" idea is one that will seem compelling to an audience of critical listeners. An idea is not considered strong if it does not make much difference to listeners—even if it is true and well supported.

Should you present your strongest main idea first in order to make a strong first impression on the audience? Or should you present it last, to end with a bang and leave the audience on a positive note? Many researchers have studied the relative merits of a **primacy effect** (strongest idea first) versus a **recency effect** (strongest idea last), but the results are inconclusive because too many other factors also influence the impact of arrangement.[6] However, if one idea seems weaker than the others, you should present it in a middle position rather than either toward the beginning or toward the end.

Often, the strength of an idea depends not on any inherent feature of the idea itself, but on how well the idea sits with the audience. Therefore, your audience analysis is not finished when you first select a topic, purpose, thesis, and strategy; the audience affects all major decisions about speech preparation and delivery.

Patterns for Arranging Main Ideas

In theory, you can arrange main ideas in an infinite number of patterns, but several common patterns are easy for an audience to follow, and they work well for a variety of topics. You first should focus on these general patterns, which are described next. Then, if your topic, purpose, or audience seems to call for a different pattern, you can develop your own.

Chronological

The passage of time is the organizing principle in the chronological approach. The units of time (most often the past, the present, and the future) become the main ideas. For example, in discussing the topic of "Discrimination Against Female Sports Reporters," student Jordan Breal organized her speech this way:

I. Female sports reporters received little credit for their work until the 1930s.
II. Female sports reporters were not allowed into press rooms until the 1970s.
III. Female sports reporters were not allowed into locker rooms until the late 1970s.
IV. Treatment of female sports reporters leaves much room for improvement in the future.

This example proceeds in normal chronological order, beginning with the past and ending with the future. But you can start at any point in the chronology. For example, you might decide that a speech about AIDS should begin with a discussion of the current crisis in Africa, then move backwards in time to examine the origins of AIDS, and conclude with a discussion of the future of AIDS research and possible cures.

Spatial

Whereas chronological order organizes main ideas according to time, spatial order arranges them according to place or position. A speech might begin with the aspects of the topic that are nearest and then proceed to the aspects that are farther away. This pattern might work well for a speech about the effects of a strong national economy, in which the main points include the following:

I. A booming economy increases the individual's spending power.
II. A booming economy supports state and local projects.
III. A booming economy improves the federal budget.

Another common spatial arrangement would be to present ideas literally in geographic order:

I. A booming economy helps farmers in the South.
II. A booming economy helps manufacturing in the Midwest.
III. A booming economy helps the oil industry in the Southwest.
IV. A booming economy helps technology industries in the Northwest.

Categorical (Topical)

In the categorical pattern, each main idea that you identified in analyzing your topic becomes a major division of the speech. For example, in researching the Hindu religion, student Anuj Vedak learned that Hindus hold many distinct beliefs, including a belief in karma as a guide to treating others ethically, a belief in reincarnation for those who have died, and a belief in Nirvana as the soul's act of attaining salvation. Each of these topics can become a major heading in a speech. Because a categorical pattern has no required order (e.g., from past to present or from left to right), it is important that main ideas be stated in parallel fashion and that they be easy to recognize and remember. The major headings for a speech on Hinduism might be the following:

I. Hindus believe in karma as a guide to ethical behavior.
II. Hindus believe in reincarnation as the process of rebirth for the deceased.
III. Hindus believe in nirvana as the soul's act of attaining salvation.

This pattern is also called *topical* because it derives from the *topoi.* As we saw in Chapter 9, these are obvious or typical categories for organizing subject matter. They usually will have an obvious or standard structure. "People, places, and events" is an example of a set of *topoi,* as is "economic, military, and political aspects."

Cause-Effect

Cause-effect is also an organizational pattern, and it can proceed in either direction. You can focus on causes and then identify their effects, or you can first identify effects and then try to determine their causes. For example, a speech about global warming might proceed like as follows:

I. Factories, refineries, power plants, and cars emit vast amounts of carbon into the Earth's atmosphere.
II. Industrialized societies generate so much atmospheric carbon that they are effectively wrapping the Earth in a heating blanket.
III. As the Earth's surface temperatures rise, fundamental and irreversible shifts in our planet's climate patterns are occurring.

Or, rather than moving from cause to effect, you might proceed from effect to cause:

I. We are becoming more vulnerable to the effects of global warming and climate change.
II. This effect results from the release of carbon into the atmosphere from the world's factories, refineries, power plants, and cars.
III. Widespread use of carbon-based fossil fuels is a major source of the problem.

The choice between these two arrangements would be governed by which topics you wanted to present first and last, not by anything intrinsic to the cause-effect organizational pattern.

Problem-Solution

A variation of the cause-effect pattern is one that focuses on problems and their solutions. A speech using this pattern first lays out the dimensions of the problem and shows why it is serious; then it considers one or more potential solutions. It may simply report on the various possible solutions or it may proceed to explain why a particular solution is best. For example, a speech about the difficulties of the campus parking system might be structured like as follows:

I. There is a shortage of parking spaces near the main classroom buildings.

A Question of *ETHICS*

Ethics and Organization

The desire to organize our thoughts and make them easily memorable for our audiences is natural. But what if our organizational patterns distort the subject matter of our speech? Suppose we would like to deliver a speech in a chronological pattern, explaining the historical development of the topic, but that history would not allow for some of the more critical information that might show up in a categorical pattern. For example, the history of the civil rights movement often focuses on major achievements since the 1960s rather than on the internal tensions within the movement or the extent and ferocity of resistance to it. Or suppose we select a categorical pattern but the categories are not really separate from one another. What are our ethical responsibilities to our subject, and how can these be reconciled with our strategic interest in effective organization? How do we negotiate these tensions?

II. As a result, many students must walk almost a mile from their cars to their classes.
III. In the short term, expanding the campus bus service, and in the long term, building a central parking garage would solve the problem.

The development of the first two major headings would establish that there is a problem, perhaps by claiming that the current situation is unsafe for students attending evening classes. Possibly after considering other solutions, the speaker would claim in the third main idea that these problems can be overcome by a combination of expanded bus service and construction of a parking garage.

Often, problems are not self-evident to an audience. A speaker has to motivate listeners to feel that some important need is not being met before they will regard a situation as a problem. A variation on the problem-solution pattern, then, is to emphasize *psychological order.* The speaker first motivates listeners to perceive a problem and then provides the means to satisfy that feeling by identifying a solution. If Stuart Kim had chosen this approach in speaking about the United Way, his speech might have been organized as follows:

I. We all have a responsibility to others.
II. This responsibility includes financial support for the social service organizations that help others.
III. Giving to the United Way helps us to meet our responsibilities.

In this example, the first step is to arouse an attitude, motive, or desire among the audience members. Subsequent steps then refine that motivation and show how it can be satisfied by a particular action.

Comparison and Contrast

Sometimes it is easiest to examine a topic by demonstrating its similarities to, and differences from, other topics with which the audience is likely to be familiar. From your studies of American history, for example, you know that women and racial and ethnic minorities have sometimes been subjected to prejudice and discrimination in the workplace. Your speech might be organized to compare the experiences among these groups:

I. Women often are not promoted to senior positions because executives do not think they will remain on the job while raising children.
II. Mexican Americans, in many parts of the country, are hired only for the most menial jobs.
III. Earlier, German Americans and Japanese Americans were fired from their jobs because employers thought them to be unpatriotic.
IV. Today, immigrants from the Middle East are denied access to some jobs because they are categorically suspected of involvement in terrorist activities.
V. African Americans have been limited in work opportunities because many whites believe that they do not want to work.

Now the question is whether you want to highlight the differences or the similarities among these

RHETORICAL WORKOUT

Shape and Organize Main Ideas

You are working on an informative speech about zero waste and are ready to choose and arrange your main ideas. Your *general purpose* is to provide new information, and your *specific purpose* is to inform listeners of what zero waste means and what initiatives have been successful. You write this thesis: "Zero waste initiatives are making a difference for a better environment."

1. Use the criteria for selecting main ideas to assess the points below. Which ideas seem essential to your speech? Which can be combined into fewer general statements?
   - Zero waste initiatives have proven to reduce pollution.
   - Zero waste means eliminating waste in all stages of a product's life.
   - Initiatives are under way in nearly 20 countries.
   - Not creating waste is more environmentally friendly than recycling it.
   - The quantity of garbage in landfills has gone down in areas using zero waste initiatives.
   - At least five U.S. states have adopted zero waste initiatives.
   - A zero waste economy is based on recovering resources and can create jobs.
2. Using the principle of parallel structure, create three main ideas out of the above list. Is the grammatical structure of each main idea the same? Are the three main ideas approximately the same length? If not, revise the sentences to fit these requirements.
3. Does each of your three main ideas stand alone, as a *logically independent idea,* or are all three like links in a chain, as *logically dependent ideas?* Explain. If they are logically dependent, write them down in the order they need to appear in your speech.
4. Which organizational pattern would be best suited to your three main ideas: chronological, spatial, categorical (topical), cause-effect, problem-solution, comparison and contrast, or residues? Why? Apply the pattern to your three main ideas. Is the result logical and effective? Why or why not?

groups. You might select either of the following as your last main idea:

VI. Although some groups have managed to overcome the effects of discrimination and have succeeded in the workplace, others have not been so lucky.

or

VI. Although the experiences of these groups are very different, they have one factor in common: Society's prejudice places an artificial ceiling on their economic opportunities.

In either case, the earlier main ideas are brought together in the last one, which shows either how differences outweigh similarities or the reverse.

Residues

A final organizational pattern is to arrange the speech by process of elimination. This pattern works well when there are a finite number of possibilities, none particularly desirable, and you want to argue that one of them represents "the least among the evils." For example, in a political campaign in which you find no candidate particularly appealing, you could use this pattern to rule out all but one candidate, whom you then support as being the least objectionable.

Student speaker Jennifer Aiello used organization by residues to get her classmates to consider seriously the proposal that gun manufacturers should be required to install locks on guns. She arranged her main ideas to rule out the other options available to society:

> No one wants freedom infringed upon. And no one wants to have to pay more for a gun. But let's consider the alternatives. Does anyone want more children to have access to guns that take virtually no effort to use? Does anyone want to attend more funerals of children shot dead while at school? Does anyone want to see more six-year-olds lying in critical condition in hospital beds because they thought their parents' handgun was a

Checklist 10.3
Basic Organizational Patterns

- **Chronological:** Can my topic be broken down into units of time?
- **Spatial:** Can my topic be organized according to place or position?
- **Categorical (topical):** Is my topic best organized according to my existing main ideas? If so, are my main ideas in parallel form?
- **Cause–effect:** Can my topic be organized around causes and effects?
- **Problem–solution:** Does my topic suggest a problem that can be organized around its possible solutions?
- **Comparison and contrast:** Can I examine my topic by showing similarities to or differences from other topics?
- **Residues:** Does my topic lend itself to a process-of-elimination pattern?

toy? Does anyone want to see parents, friends, and family mourning another unnecessary death?

By ruling out each of these other alternatives, Jennifer was able to convince many of her audience members that putting locks on guns was a proposal worthy of their reflection.

Choosing the Organizational Pattern

The organizational patterns described here do not exhaust all the possibilities, but they illustrate that you have many options from which to choose.[7] How should you decide which organizational pattern to use in your speech? Does it matter, for example, whether you use a cause–effect pattern or a comparison and contrast pattern? How do you know whether, say, the costs and benefits of voting are more important than the convenience of voting? Questions like these require you to think strategically. The answers are complex and must take into account your subject, your purpose, your audience, and your culture.

Based on Your Subject

Certain subjects lend themselves to particular organizational patterns. For example, because the collapse of communism in Eastern Europe is a historical event, it has a dramatic structure that would be emphasized by telling a story in chronological order. However, a speech about the components of air pollution would more likely suggest a topical pattern—unless, perhaps, it was being delivered to an audience of environmental historians who would be more interested in understanding when and how these components became serious national problems.

Based on Your Purpose

Your purpose or strategy also influences the selection of an organizational pattern. For instance, if you want to urge the audience to lobby for updated privacy laws that better protect consumers against online identity theft, an analytical pattern that emphasizes the problems and solutions will be especially appropriate because it will focus attention on the specific proposal for which you want listeners to lobby. In contrast, if your purpose is to show that the protection of a person's online identity is very different from the traditional practice of maintaining personal privacy, a comparison and contrast pattern probably would make more sense.

Based on Your Audience

Your audience is another influence on the arrangement of your speech. For example, listeners who have paid little attention to developments in relations between Russia and Ukraine probably would be more interested in an overview of events since the fall of the Soviet Union than in a detailed analysis of oil and gas supply agreements between the two countries. But an audience composed mostly of people with family origins in either Russia or Ukraine might be strongly interested in hearing about developments in their "old countries." And listeners who are involved in foreign policy issues probably would be most interested in the implications of changes since the Orange Revolution and the political ascent of Vladimir Putin. These differences can help you decide which points to put first and last.

Based on the Culture

Finally, the culture will affect your organizational pattern. For example, mainstream American culture is strongly oriented toward pragmatism, and so a pattern that focuses on problems and solutions would resonate well for many listeners. But other cultures and subcultures have a much greater concern for ideology, for myth and ritual, for narrative, or for authority; the preference for these values would affect the pattern of analysis.

Joanna Watkins was about to address an audience with a high proportion of Asian students. She had studied some Roper Poll surveys about dominant values among various cultural groups in the United States and had learned that many Asians value family

STRATEGIES FOR SPEAKING to Diverse Audiences

Respecting Diversity Through the Organization of the Body of Your Speech

A sense of form is achieved in different ways for different cultures. Here are strategies to respect the diversity of the audience when organizing the body of the speech.

1. Acknowledge the presuppositions of your audience members. Analyze your audience, but be careful not to stereotype cultures by assuming that one's culture completely determines one's response to your speech.
2. Organize your ideas according to what you believe will appeal to the majority of your audience, but do not rely heavily on a structure that might alienate parts of your audience.
3. Consider whether cultures differ in their approach to space; for example, Hebrew and Arabic texts read from right to left. If you use spatial order in your speech, do not automatically move from left to right.
4. Consider whether cultures differ in their approach to time. For example, tradition remains an important source of authority for many, giving greater weight to the past, while some regard tradition as a hindrance to progress and give greater weight to the present.
5. Consider whether cultures differ in their approach to consistency. For example, Taoism celebrates *wu wei* ("action without action"), a concept that seems impossible to understand in the world of science, embracing opposites rather than regarding inconsistency as a logical error. You may not be able to assume that by identifying an inconsistency you have discredited an opposing argument.
6. Consider whether cultures differ in their dominant mode of reasoning; for example, prizing cause-effect thinking or prizing narrative and myth.

and group loyalty and mutual support more than such mainstream American values as competitiveness and individual achievement. Because Joanna's topic was about how to get ahead in college, she needed to arrange her speech carefully. In this case, a highly pragmatic cause-effect pattern—which might be just right in other situations—would probably be inappropriate.

Joanna chose to include material about the value of close friendships and the sense of community that often develops among Asian college students. At the same time, she was careful not to stereotype her audience or to assume that "all Asians think alike." She did not say, "Since most of you are Asian, let me talk about group loyalty," and she was careful also to include at least some appeals based on pragmatic values, too.

Clearly, no organizational pattern is automatically "right" for any given speech. You need to think critically about the implications and effects of any pattern and choose an arrangement that suits your strategy. Moreover, although we have considered these basic patterns as though they were mutually exclusive, you obviously can combine them. For instance, you could use a chronological pattern, but at each step in the chronology you might examine developments topically or by reference to causes and effects. Or you could organize your speech using both a topical pattern and comparison and contrast. In theory, the potential combinations of patterns are limitless. Particularly when audience members have different cultural backgrounds, value systems, and priorities, a creative combination may be most effective.

Selecting and Arranging Supporting Materials

Most main ideas are sufficiently complex that they involve several supporting ideas or **subheadings**. The supporting material that you located following the guidelines in Chapter 9 will usually support these subheadings, which in turn will support the main ideas. Subheadings are chosen and arranged using the same methods that we have described for main ideas. Moreover, many of the same considerations also apply to the materials you will use to support your main ideas and subpoints. In Chapter 9, you studied research tech-

CHOOSE A STRATEGY: Organizing Your Speech

The Situation

You and a number of other students are dismayed by your university's decision to limit Internet access to certain sites on campus. You've been attending rallies against the policy and have been invited to speak at the next student government meeting about your objections.

Making Choices

1. How should you decide what main points you want to relay to your audience, and in what order should you present them?
2. What do you know about the school board's position that would affect your organizational choices?
3. What kind of supporting material would be important to include—and where in the speech should you include it?

What If . . .

How would your organizational decisions change if the following were true?

1. There was evidence of illegal Internet activity among the student population.
2. The university had asked for student feedback before making the decision to limit Internet access.

niques to help you locate supporting materials; now, you should consider which materials to select and how to arrange them.

Selection of Supporting Materials

How Much?

Probably the most important question, and the hardest to answer, is "How much support is enough?" You need to offer enough evidence to establish your claims but not so much that the speech becomes repetitive and boring. But how do you know what is the right balance?

The only all-purpose answer to this question is, "It depends."[8] It depends, most of all, on your audience analysis. In examining listeners' prior understanding of your topic, you may find that your main idea is one with which they are likely to agree. If so, a relatively modest amount of support will be enough. But if the audience is likely to find your main idea controversial, you will need more support to convince doubters.

For example, a speaker who tells a college audience that the legal drinking age should be lowered to 18 is probably "preaching to the choir." These listeners have likely already accepted the claim, and so the speaker needs only a few pieces of reliable supporting material. But a speaker who tells the same audience that the legal drinking age should be kept at 21 will probably need to supply much more evidence to convince listeners that the disadvantages of change would outweigh the benefits. In contrast, if the audience were composed of older people, the reverse would likely be true: The speaker who wants to raise the drinking age might need less supporting material than the speaker who wants to lower it.

Besides listeners' beliefs about the specific topic, their common knowledge and experience will affect

Checklist 10.4
Selecting Supporting Materials

- Does the supporting material meet tests of strength for its type? (These are given in this chapter.)
- Will the supporting material be easily understood?
- Is the supporting material vivid and interesting?
- Is the supporting material consistent with other things you know?
- Will the supporting material be efficient to present?
- Can the supporting material be easily cited in the speech?

how much supporting material you need. Also, if they are skeptical by nature, you will want to add more support. If they are impatient or are not good listeners, you will want to keep the speech short and the supporting materials simple. If they are accustomed to asking questions after a speech, you will want to anticipate their major questions and to incorporate supporting material that prepares you to answer them.

The general principle to follow is: The greater the distance between the audience's current views and the position you wish listeners to adopt, the more supporting material will be required. Yet you also must be careful not to stereotype or to assume that all listeners would identify their position on an issue in the same way.

In any case, supporting material should not be redundant; each piece of evidence should add something new to the speech as a whole. The testimony of three different people who say exactly the same thing is not likely to be higher in value than one person's testimony. Nor will you strengthen the speech by citing the same example from multiple sources.

What Kind?

Regarding the types of supporting materials to use, the general goal is to aim for variety. The speech should not depend entirely on statistics, on testimony, on examples, or on primary documents. The reasons are simple. First, you are more likely to hold the audience's interest by varying the types of evidence you offer. Although it is important that the audience be able to anticipate your general pattern, too much repetition induces boredom. Second, different listeners will be persuaded by different kinds of evidence. If your audience is heterogeneous, then using a variety of support helps you to strike a responsive chord among many different listeners.

What Criteria?

Having decided how much and what types of support you need, you still face other choices. For example, you may have decided that testimony is the form of support you need and that one quotation from an expert will be enough. But your research may have accumulated the testimony of four or five experts. How do you decide which one to use? Similarly, you may have found multiple examples, various statistical measures, or more primary documents than you might need.

What criteria can you use to assess these supporting materials?

1. *Apply the criteria for strength of supporting material that were given in Chapter 9.* For instance, with regard to testimony, you should ask which authority has the greatest expertise on the subject, which statement is most recent (if timeliness is a factor), and so on. With respect to examples, you want to use a case that is representative. And if you are choosing among pieces of statistical evidence, consider the reliability and validity of each.
2. *Select the supporting material that is easiest to understand.* If listeners have to work hard to understand and remember your supporting material, they will be distracted from the focus of your speech.

   This can be a special concern with respect to statistical evidence. Complicated or overly precise statistics may be hard to comprehend orally, and using them may require some minor editing. For example, rather than reporting that the federal budget deficit is projected to be $4,267,153,697,000 over a 10-year period, you might report the projection as "more than $4 trillion." Rather than "significant at the 0.001 level," you might say, "These are results we would get by chance only one one-thousandth of the time."
3. *Select vivid or interesting supporting material when you can.* Less interesting material requires the audience to give it greater concentration, which again will distract from your main ideas.
4. *Select supporting material that is consistent with other things you know.* If you use material that challenges commonly held beliefs, you should be prepared to defend it and explain why the audience should not reject it out of hand.
5. *Select supporting material that will be efficient to present.* In general, a short anecdote is better than a long narrative, if they make the same point. And a statistical measure with categories that are clear is more useful than one that needs lengthy explanations.
6. *Select supporting material that can be cited easily in the speech.* Unlike a written mode, you cannot supply a full bibliographic citation orally. But you do want to give enough information so that a listener knows where you got

the material. An "oral footnote" that refers to "Secretary of State Clinton in last January's issue of *Foreign Affairs*" is a good example. This chapter provides more guidance on creating oral citations to include in your presentation outline.

Arrangement of Supporting Materials

Just as the main ideas of a speech can be arranged according to a variety of patterns, so, too, can the supporting materials that establish each main idea. The same considerations—your purpose and your strategy—govern the arrangement of main ideas and of supporting materials.

Suppose, for example, that for a main idea you want to demonstrate that the percentage of deaths from car crashes linked to alcohol use declined over a certain period of time. Because your objective is to demonstrate a rate and direction of change, a chronological pattern might serve best. It would enable you to "take a snapshot" of how many crash fatalities were linked to alcohol at different points in time. You could show your audience that in 1990, 51 percent of accident fatalities were linked to alcohol; that it was down to 43 percent by 1994; and that by 2004 it was 39 percent (see Table 10.1). By arranging these "snapshots" in chronological order, you can convey the message of ongoing progress.

For another example, suppose you want to establish that alienation from politics is a nationwide occurrence. You might use a spatial pattern, drawing on examples from the East, the Midwest, the South, and the West. In yet another speech, you might want to emphasize trends in the training and preparation of popular music singers. You could use a topical pattern to focus on each singer you want to discuss or a comparison and contrast pattern that would let you demonstrate important similarities and differences among the singers.

Table 10.1

Total Traffic Fatalities versus Alcohol-Related Traffic Fatalities, 1990–2004.

Calendar Year	Total Killed in Alcohol-Related Crashes		Total Killed in All Traffic Crashes	
	Number	**Percent**	**Number**	**Percent**
1990	22,587	51	44,599	100
1991	20,159	49	41,508	100
1992	18,290	47	39,250	100
1993	17,908	45	40,150	100
1994	17,308	43	40,716	100
1995	17,732	42	41,817	100
1996	17,749	42	42,065	100
1997	16,711	40	42,013	100
1998	16,673	40	41,501	100
1999	16,572	40	41,717	100
2000	17,380	41	41,945	100
2001	17,400	41	42,196	100
2002	17,524	41	43,005	100
2003	17,105	40	42,884	100
2004	16,694	39	42,836	100

Source: National Highway Traffic Safety Administration FARS data.

You also can combine the patterns of arrangement in a single speech. In discussing the apathy of American voters, you might use both a chronological and a spatial pattern, as follows:

I. Voter apathy has become a growing concern.
   A. During the years before World War I, voter turnout was high.
   B. In the modern age, the height of voter participation came in 1960.
   C. Since 1960, there has been a slow but steady decline in political participation.
   D. By 1996, voter turnout was at the lowest level since 1924.
   E. Even in the razor-thin election of 2000, turnout rose only slightly.
   F. Even in 2008, while turnout among younger voters rose, the overall voter turnout remained a full 10 percentage points below its 1960 peak.

II. Voter apathy is widespread.
   A. It can be found in the East.
   B. It can be found in the Midwest.
   C. It can be found in the South.
   D. It can be found in the West.

Such a combination, aside from clarifying each main idea in the most appropriate way, also brings variety to the speech—a desirable objective in itself.

The body of the speech is certainly its most important part; it takes up the most time, and it expresses and supports the main ideas. But if a speaker launches directly into the first main idea and ends abruptly after the last, you probably would think something was strange, perhaps even insulting, about the speech. It would be like joining a conversation that was already well along, missing the beginning completely. The ending would seem abrupt, too—like reading a book that was missing its last few pages or walking out of a movie in its last minutes. You would be surprised that the speaker had stopped, because the speech would not seem "finished."

Listeners expect a beginning, a middle, and an end. They expect to be guided into a topic, not dropped in its midst, and they expect the discussion to conclude naturally. Audiences notice when a speaker departs from this customary sense of form; if they are not disturbed by it, they at least are likely to be distracted.

In this chapter, we will explore the two elements of a speech that surround its body: the introduction and the conclusion. We will focus on the purposes of these elements, some common types, and strategies for preparing them. Finally, we will look at how speakers use transitions to connect the introduction, body, and conclusion and thus give the speech a dynamic quality.

Introductions: Beginning the Speech

Both daily life and studies in the psychology of persuasion tell us that first impressions are extremely important. When you meet someone new, you quickly form impressions about that person, often based on little more than superficial characteristics such as the person's clothing and hairstyle, or car, or way of speaking. Many first impressions are likely to prove durable; they will influence how you interpret what this person says and does.[9]

The Purposes of an Introduction

The **introduction** is the beginning of the speech, which affects listeners' first impressions of the speaker and prepares them for the speech. It gives the audience clues about the speaker's personality, intentions, style, and overall perspective. And it prepares the audience for the speech by giving clues about what will follow.

The overall purpose of using your introduction to prepare the audience can be broken down into four specific goals:

1. To gain the attention and interest of your audience
2. To influence the audience to view you and your topic favorably
3. To clarify the purpose or thesis of your speech
4. To preview the development of your topic

Gaining the Attention and Interest of Your Audience

The introduction should make the audience want to hear what will follow. Accomplishing this goal is critical because, like someone switching television channels, listeners can choose whether to pay attention. Even when the audience cannot escape a speaker physically, individuals can decide whether to be active listeners.

The primary way to make listeners pay attention is to convince them that what follows will be interesting. An effective introduction suggests to listeners that they will be stimulated by the speech. A lively narrative, startling or unexpected information, or a personal experience that listeners can identify with will suggest that the speech will be interesting and thus warrants attention.

Influencing the Audience to View You and Your Topic Favorably

It is not enough merely to get the audience's attention. Indeed, a speaker can easily gain attention by appearing overbearing, pompous, or dogmatic.

The introduction aims to influence the audience to view you and your topic favorably so that listeners will be sympathetic and attentive. You can create a favorable first impression as follows:

- Be well prepared and confident, thereby establishing positive *ethos* (credibility).
- Identify with the predispositions of the audience.

Like most generalizations, this one needs to be qualified a bit. Sometimes, a speaker will choose deliberately not to gain the audience's favor. For example, a dissenter who feels the need to speak out against the majority opinion may intentionally make an audience hostile by, say, accusing them of denying rights to those who are less powerful. Even though the immediate audience is unlikely to be persuaded by such a direct attack, the dissenter may, in fact, be addressing those listeners primarily to gain the attention and favor of some other audience. The real intended audience is composed of people who will hear about the speech and conclude that the dissenter is a person of courage and principle for venturing into hostile territory. This audience, of course, will then be favorably disposed toward the speaker and the topic; the dissenter will have gained both their attention and their goodwill.

Clarifying the Purpose or Thesis of Your Speech

Listeners are more likely to follow your speech and be influenced by it if you clearly identify what you want them to believe or to do. Most introductions include an explicit statement of the speaker's thesis or purpose, as in the following examples:

> I will argue that the United States cannot compete economically without strengthening public education.
>
> After you consider the facts, I hope you will call the Red Cross and volunteer to donate blood.

Speakers often state their purpose only after making introductory remarks that gain the audience's interest and make listeners favorably disposed. But, sometimes speakers can *assume* that the audience is interested and favorably disposed. For instance, a speaker addressing the student government, who discusses the benefits of student government, surely could assume interest and motivation on the part of the audience. In this case, the entire introduction might focus on an explicit statement of purpose.

Previewing the Development of Your Topic

Besides capturing the audience's attention, influencing them to view you and your topic favorably, and clarifying your purpose, the introduction also previews how you will develop your topic in the body of the speech. Classical theorists of public speaking refer to this step as the **partition**; the speaker divides the body of the speech into selected categories for discussion.[10] For example, a speaker might say:

> First I will explain how higher education got into financial trouble, then I will describe the consequences of this for students and faculty, and finally I will tell you what we can do about it.

Basically, the speaker has revealed the pattern for the body of the speech (in this case, a problem-solution pattern) and what the major headings will be. As we saw in this chapter, such a "road map" helps listeners to follow the speaker's thinking and to anticipate what will come next.

An Example of an Introduction

Only your own imagination and creativity limit you in devising an introduction that achieves the four primary goals. Let's look at how one student used her introduction to prepare the audience.

Michelle Ekanemesang was the third speaker in her public speaking class. To gain her listeners' attention (after all, they had already heard two speeches), she walked to the podium, paused, looked at the audience, and then suddenly dropped a large book on the floor. The resounding thud brought all eyes to Michelle as she began to speak: "Just as easily as that book fell to the floor, the innocence of a child can crash." Then, walking around to the front of the podium to retrieve the book, Michelle continued:

> However, unlike this book, a child's innocence cannot be picked up and placed back on the

pedestal where it was. Children today encounter many experiences that challenge their innocence. Along with gangs, guns, and drugs, they also face another monster that is not so well publicized: sexual abuse. Approximately one child out of four is sexually abused by the age of 18. That would be four people in this classroom. Today, I want to discuss the causes and effects of childhood sexual abuse as well as to offer some tips about preventing it and what to do if you or a child you know has been a victim of sexual abuse.

Michelle's book-dropping trick could have turned into a resounding flop if she had not explained how it connected to her speech. She quickly and effectively gained her listeners' attention and then maintained it by saying that some of them might be victims themselves, thereby emphasizing the personal relevance of her topic. From the outset, it was clear that Michelle was going to talk about the horrors of child abuse. She took a serious tone of outrage and influenced the audience favorably toward her treatment of the subject. Her final statement in the introduction then clearly previewed which main topics the audience could expect her to cover: the causes, effects, prevention, and treatment of childhood sexual abuse.

Types of Introductions

Several types of introductions show up frequently in successful speeches, and you should be aware of them in order to decide whether they will be effective for your speech and audience.

In deciding which type of introduction to use, always try to relate the introduction directly to your speech, as Michelle did. If you quote someone famous or tell a story without showing how that connects to the speech itself, the introduction may soon seem out of place. The speech, after all, should be a unified whole. The introduction and the conclusion should work together with the body of the speech to create the response or action that you desire.

Identifying with Your Audience

One obvious way to build goodwill and capture the audience's interest is to draw on something that you share—a common experience, common acquaintances, common values, or common goals. If listeners perceive you as being basically like themselves, they usually form a good first impression of you. And their interest should be high because, in effect, you may be telling them something about themselves or be speaking on their behalf.

Student speakers often find it easy and effective to identify with their audience because, typically, they do share many common experiences with their listeners. One student began a speech about the disillusionment felt by many of America's less fortunate youth by making a reference to a popular Hollywood movie:

> Many of you may have seen the hit movie *The Matrix*. This high-budget film paints America as one huge computerized box in which we all are trapped, with no real control of our lives and no say in our futures. We are just digits in an artificially intelligent matrix—added, subtracted, multiplied, and divided at the will of a supercomputer. When my friends and I first saw the movie, we felt strangely numb and powerless, but the feeling only lasted a few minutes. But for many of America's less fortunate youth, this is the only feeling they know.

Having gained the interest and goodwill of the audience by identifying with them, and having stated the thesis, the speaker was then well positioned to complete the introduction by previewing how the feelings of disempowerment among America's disadvantaged youth would be developed in the speech.

Referring to the Speech Situation

Another way to establish common bonds with an audience and to strike an appropriate opening note is to refer directly to the situation. Many speeches are delivered on ceremonial occasions (for example, commencement addresses, wedding toasts, speeches of welcome or farewell), and these often are introduced effectively by an explicit reference to the occasion.

Similarly, speeches that happen to be given on a significant anniversary might make reference to the date. For example, a student speaking on September 11, 2013, might begin this way:

> Twelve years ago today, our generation and our country lost some of its innocence. Even though we were very young, none of us will ever forget the image of the planes crashing into the World Trade Center. That action started what President George W. Bush called a "war on terror." Twelve years later, do we feel safer or more secure? Can we deter or stop terrorists? In short, are we winning the war?

The speaker could go on to state the thesis and preview its development:

> I do not think we are. Our airports are safer, but our transportation system and our industrial base are vulnerable.

Telling an interesting story with enthusiasm is often a good way to dispose the audience favorably toward the speaker and the speech.

Similarly, Rachel Venegas used the beginning of final examination week as an opportunity to point out a disturbing trend in student study habits:

> With finals beginning, students all over campus will be frantically trying to absorb every bit of knowledge from their courses or putting the finishing touches on their papers. But during these cram sessions, students tend to put their academics before their own health, especially by neglecting sleep. One way to bypass the urge to sleep, and an increasingly popular option, is the use of drugs meant to treat Attention Deficit Hyperactivity Disorder. Despite the serious side effects, many college students continue to take these drugs, prescribed or not, without knowing fully the risks of their misuse.

Other situational factors also can be the touchstone for an effective introduction. For example, the location of the speech might be important, as it was when Martin Luther King, Jr., began his famous address "I Have a Dream." Dr. King's introduction noted that he stood symbolically in the shadow of Abraham Lincoln; he was delivering his address from the Lincoln Memorial.

Referring to a previous speaker might be a natural introduction to your own speech. If your reference endorses or builds on something a previous speaker said, it creates a bridge between the two speeches and a seemingly logical flow to the discussion. And if the previous speaker was competent and credible, you even may inherit the audience's favorable disposition toward that speaker.

However, your reference does not have to support the previous speaker. In fact, that speech might provide the ammunition needed for you to disagree with something the speaker said. In this case, your introduction is both a bridge that maintains continuity and a stop sign that signals the differences between the two of you. For example, imagine that a student in a public speaking class just spoke about the ways in which Steve Jobs and Apple have revolutionized the personal computer, praising Jobs's vision and imagination. By coincidence, the next speaker had planned to condemn the overdependence by technology companies on foreign labor. Adapting the introduction to fit this situation, the second speaker could say:

> Many consider high-tech companies, such as Apple, to be ahead of their time, but in at least one respect they are dangerously behind the times: their dependence on exploited foreign labor.

Stating Your Purpose

Sometimes, an introduction that explicitly states your purpose can be very helpful, especially if the audience is captive or is known already to be favorably disposed to your ideas. This approach is also effective when your thesis is startling or unexpected:

> In the next hour, many children in this town will suffer from abuse and neglect. We will see why this happens. Then I want you to volunteer one day a week to help stop this.

Your direct challenge will probably make the audience take notice, because you've alerted them that you expect something of them, and so they are likely to pay attention in order to decide whether or not to grant your request.

Stating the Importance of Your Topic

Another effective opening device is to alert the audience to the significance of your topic before actually stating what the topic is. For example, a speech about preventing AIDS might begin with the statement "I have information that literally can save your lives." Similarly, a speech about purchasing a home might begin with "Today, I want to discuss the most important financial decision most of us will ever make."

This type of introduction demands the audience's attention. Just by saying that your topic is important, you ask people to take notice. This strategy also has an element of mystery, which leads the audience to wonder just what it is that is so critical. Be aware, however, that this approach has been overused, and audiences sometimes react to such claims by being skeptical. A speaker who opens with "This speech could change the course of your life" may actually prompt listeners to think, "Oh, sure; I've heard that before."

If your speech has a formal title, be sure that its specific wording is accurate and complete. Then your introduction can "unpack" the title to forecast what will follow and to highlight your main points. In 1984, Governor Mario Cuomo of New York illustrated this introductory strategy in a speech at the University of Notre Dame:

> I would like to begin by drawing your attention to the title of this lecture: "Religious Belief and Public Morality: A Catholic Governor's Perspective." I was not invited to speak on "Church and State" generally. Certainly not "Mondale versus Reagan." The subject assigned is difficult enough. I will try not to do more than I've been asked.

Governor Cuomo then proceeded to state his perspective and to indicate how he planned to develop his ideas.

Citing Statistics, Making Claims

Listeners sit up in interest when a speaker cites startling statistics or makes a surprising claim. Their astonishment on hearing the information causes them to pay attention. For example, to introduce the topic of poverty in the Navajo Nation, a student might begin:

> The Navajo Nation is the largest Indian reservation in the United States. It has a population of 235,000 and covers an area of 16.2 million acres. But the largest Indian reservation in America is not thriving as well as some of the country's smallest towns. According to a recent Bureau of Indian Affairs report, the unemployment rate in the Navajo Nation is almost 58 percent. Only 22.5 percent of Navajo homes have any telephone service, and many of the lines are too old to support modern Internet communication.

This type of introduction works best when the statistics are accurate but not well known—when there is a gap between what listeners think they know and what is actually the case. Statistics can show that our common assumptions are not accurate, that a problem is greater than we know, that a condition we viewed as worsening is actually improving, and so on. But the risk with this approach is that listeners may become defensive about their predispositions. Rather than considering the possibility that academic dishonesty really is more serious than they thought, for example, they may react by doubting the statistics or by denying the claim. You certainly want to encourage listeners to think critically; but if their very first response to your introduction is to doubt what you say, it will be difficult to build goodwill and regain their interest.

Telling a Story

Speakers often begin with an anecdote—an extended illustration or example that is cast in narrative form. A speaker introduces the topic by relating a personal experience or something that happened to others. For example, when Elie Wiesel, Holocaust survivor, novelist, and Nobel Peace Prize winner, gave a speech at the White House in April 1999 on "the perils of indifference," he began by relating the story of a young boy who had been rescued from a Nazi concentration camp by American soldiers:

> Fifty-four years ago to the day, a young Jewish boy from a small town in the Carpathian Mountains woke up, not far from Goethe's beloved Weimar, in a place of eternal infamy called Buchenwald. He was finally free, but there was no joy in his heart. He thought there never would be again.
>
> Liberated a day earlier by American soldiers, he remembers their rage at what they saw. And even if he lives to be a very old man, he will always be grateful to them for that rage, and also for their compassion. Though he did not understand their language, their eyes told him what he needed to know—that they, too, would remember and bear witness.

The power of an anecdotal introduction lies in its narrative form. The story is engaging, and the chronological sequence is easy to follow. A narrative is concrete—it involves specific characters in a particular situation—and therefore listeners can attend to it with less effort than is needed to follow something more abstract.

One potential drawback in using an introductory anecdote is that it may overshadow the preview of your topic or even the body of the speech. It may be so interesting that it distracts attention from your main points. To avoid this, use an anecdote that leads directly into your thesis statement and parti-

CHOOSE A STRATEGY: Weighing the Types of Introductions

The Situation

You are in charge of bringing a documentary about a charity to a local cinema. Before the movie starts, you will make a few comments about why you support the charity. You know that your main points will be that the charity directly benefits the community, it addresses a significant need, and it depends solely on donations. Now you want to create an attention-getting introduction.

Making Choices

1. Of the 10 types of introductions discussed in this chapter, what are some types that seem well suited to your topic and speech situation? Why?
2. You know the audience already supports the charity and you want to strengthen their commitment. Which type of introduction do you think would be more effective, (a) identifying with your audience or (b) stating your purpose? Why?
3. Suppose the charity has helped a member of your family through a tough time. What are the potential benefits and drawbacks of telling a story about your family member in your introduction?

What If . . .

How would your choices be affected by the following?

1. The film showing is to raise awareness for an audience that isn't familiar with the charity.
2. You are speaking at the end of a documentary festival and others have made similar introductions.

tion. Try to create unity between the anecdote and the main points so that each reminds the audience of the other.

Using an Analogy

Closely related to the anecdote is an analogy, which, is a comparison. An analogy draws attention to the similarities or the differences between two objects, events, or situations. A speaker can use an analogy to clarify an unfamiliar subject by comparing the subject with something else that the audience already understands. For example, a speech describing the pros and cons of school vouchers might compare public and private schools with retail stores and parents and their children with consumers. In this way, the unfamiliar issue of school vouchers can be explained in the more familiar terms of shopping.

Like anecdotes, analogies help to make abstract concepts concrete. They are especially useful in introducing technical material to listeners who are not specialists in the speaker's field. For example, to inform his audience, consisting of senior citizens unfamiliar with the Internet, about search engines, student Stan Barkers began with the following analogy:

> When borrowing a book from the public library, the first thing you do is consult the card catalog, which used to be housed in a large wooden cabinet but now is online and accessible with a computer. Whether the "cards" are typed on paper or captured electronically on a computer screen, the process still works the same: you use a catalog to find where the book is located, then you proceed along the shelf and get the book. A search engine uses a process very similar to the way in which you've always searched for a book in the library. Instead of looking up an author or title, the search engine identifies key words and looks for them in billions of documents that are posted on the Internet. So it may be helpful for us to think of a search engine like Google as the Internet's card catalog.

This analogy translated what could be an unfamiliar process—using a search engine to research on the Internet—into a process that the audience easily could grasp.

During World War II, President Franklin D. Roosevelt was gifted at using analogies to explain the complexities of foreign policy to average voters. Discussing why, in 1940, the United States should lend (rather than sell) war materials to Great Britain and its allies, he offered the analogy of a man whose neighbor's house was on fire. When the neighbor ran up to ask for a garden hose, the man did not first demand payment; instead, he gave the hose to the neighbor on the promise that it would be returned when the threat was past. In just this way, Roosevelt reasoned, the United States should approach lending supplies to cash-strapped allies. This simple analogy both explained and dramatized the president's perspective, and it helped make his case with the public.

Analogies are persuasive (and thus advance the purposes of an introduction) because most listeners find it easy to focus on similarities and differences. To be effective, though, an analogy should be fairly simple and direct, like Roosevelt's. A complex comparison will force your listeners to puzzle out just what it is that you think is similar about the two things, and they will be distracted from the body of your speech. And if your analogy is too farfetched, or if it assumes key similarities without considering significant differences, listeners' first impressions of you may be negative, and they may not take your main ideas seriously. For example, several people objected to Stan Barkers's analogy, because people use card catalogs to find specific books, not to see all the places that a particular word or phrase is used.

Asking a Rhetorical Question

What's a rhetorical question? Like the sentence you just read, a **rhetorical question** is one that you do not expect listeners to answer (even if they could). You ask the question simply to cause an audience (or a reader) to think about the answer.

A rhetorical question may prompt listeners to imagine themselves in some other time, place, or situation. For example, in urging white Americans to be sensitive to the role of race in the lives of African Americans, a student speaker might begin by asking,

> How would you feel if, at the time you were born, your earning capacity and life expectancy were automatically reduced for no reason but the color of your skin?

Then, to preview the development of the speech, the student might ask,

> Why is it that, more than 50 years after *Brown v. Board of Education,* educational opportunities still are not equal?

The first question gets the audience to empathize with African Americans, and the second question previews the development of the speech. Because the goal is to make the audience think, the speaker in this case would probably not state the thesis explicitly yet.

The pitfall in asking rhetorical questions is that speakers have overused or misused this device. Some may ask an introductory question merely to ask it, rather than to induce listeners to imagine a situation or to preview the speech. An even greater risk is that listeners will answer the question in their minds—with an answer that is different from what the speaker wants to discuss. In the worst case of all, someone in the audience may shout a response that undermines the entire introduction. One student began a speech about popular films of the 1960s by asking, "What do you think of when you hear the name 'James Bond'?" From the rear of the classroom another student called out, "A third-rate movie."

Sometimes you may ask a question that you do want listeners to answer orally, perhaps to get them actively involved in the development of your ideas or to start a pattern of questions and answers. In that case, you should pause after asking the question to give them time to reply. If they remain silent, you may even need to add a comment such as "This is not a rhetorical question" or "I really want to know your answer." The danger here is the reverse of the one above: your listeners may stay silent even though you want them to speak.

Quoting Someone

Starting with a quotation is especially common and useful in sermons; the scriptural quotation then serves as the text on which the sermon is based. In secular settings, too, speakers often open with a quotation that captures the essential idea they intend to develop. For example, student speaker Clayton Hottinger introduced a speech on AIDS in South Africa by saying:

> "Cry aloud for the man who is dead, for the woman and children bereaved. Cry, the beloved country, these things are not yet at an end." So said anti-apartheid activist Alan Paton in a time of hatred and strife for South Africa, but now that trouble is over, right? Sadly, South Africa still has reason to cry, not because of apartheid, but because of a growing infection that might be mankind's greatest enemy: AIDS.

Student speaker Andrea Richards introduced a speech on cultural diversity by saying:

> In a famous speech in 1963, President Kennedy said, "If we cannot now end our differences, at least we can help make the world safe for diversity." President Kennedy was talking about ideo-

logical diversity, but today we need to apply his insight to the growing issue of racial, ethnic, and cultural diversity.

The quotation does not have to come from a famous person. It might be a simple statement such as this one:

> My father once told me that when someone says, 'It's not about the money,' then it's about the money. This is how I feel about all the politicians who keep insisting that they won't use negative campaigning.

Quoting an opposing viewpoint is a variation of this type of introduction. Abraham Lincoln did this superbly in a famous speech he made at Cooper Union in 1860. He began by quoting what his political rival, Stephen A. Douglas, had said about the intentions of the country's founders; then Lincoln used the Douglas quotation to highlight and advance his own thesis and main points.

Beginning a speech with a quotation is such a common introductory device that whole books of short quotations are published for this purpose. The warning about introductory quotations, however, is exactly the same as for anecdotes and analogies: Your introduction must relate directly to what you plan to say in your speech. If the audience cannot see the connection clearly, the introduction will seem superfluous and, therefore, will be counterproductive. A good test is to ask yourself whether the quotation will lead naturally to your thesis statement and partition and then to the body of the speech.

Using Humor

A very common introductory device is to begin the speech with a humorous reference or a joke. When it works, humor relaxes the audience, influences listeners to view the speaker favorably, and disarms skeptics. It also tells both the speaker and the audience to keep their perspective about the topic and not to take themselves too seriously.

Despite all these advantages of humor, the worst advice for preparing the introduction to a speech is that "every speech should start with a joke." Humor is not always appropriate to the subject (or the occasion or the audience), and the joke does not always relate directly to the speech. And sometimes a joke may not be as funny to your audience as it is to you. Especially with a culturally diverse audience, it is easy for a joke to backfire—to offend rather than to amuse. Despite the frequency with which accomplished speakers tell jokes, beginning speakers who have any doubt about them should avoid this type of introduction.[11]

Checklist 10.5
Types of Introductions

- Identifying with the audience
- Referring to the speech situation
- Stating the purpose
- Stating the importance of the topic
- Citing statistics or making claims
- Telling a story (anecdote)
- Using an analogy
- Asking a rhetorical question
- Quoting someone
- Using humor

This survey of the types of introductions is extensive, but it is not meant to be complete.[12] Anything can be used to begin a speech if it will achieve the four purposes of an introduction: gaining your audience's interest, influencing listeners to think well of you and your topic, clarifying your purpose or central theme, and previewing how you will develop the topic. The great variety and range of introductory devices, however, does not mean that you should select one hastily or without care. The introduction is clearly critical in making an effective speech, and you should prepare it as carefully as you do the body and the conclusion.

Strategies for Preparing an Introduction

The multiple purposes of an introduction and the great variety of ways to achieve them may seem daunting, but the following strategies and suggestions should help you plan a successful introduction for your speech.

Prepare the Body of the Speech First

Just as this book explains how to organize the body of the speech before focusing in this chapter on introductions and conclusions, you should follow that same sequence in preparing your speech. After all, it helps to know what you are introducing. Having already prepared the body, you now know what your main ideas are and how you will develop them. That information will help you craft an appropriate introduction that prepares the audience effectively. Another good reason to follow this strategy is that you will be less likely to delay preparing the entire speech just because you haven't yet thought of the "perfect" introduction.

Relate the Introduction to the Body

Keep in mind that the introduction has to prepare your listeners and then lead them naturally into the body of your speech. The connection between the introduction and the body should be clear and direct. A particular anecdote, joke, or quotation might well arouse your audience's interest, but if it seems unrelated to your main points, it may not lead listeners in the direction you intend. Indeed, some introductions—no matter how engaging—may undercut your purposes, weakening the entire speech.

Keep the Introduction Brief

Remember that the focus of the speech is on the main ideas that you will develop in the body; the introduction should lead listeners to these ideas, not obscure them. A too-long, too-strong introduction could turn into the tail that wags the dog, running away with the speech and ultimately confusing your audience. Some speechwriters advocate that an introduction should take 10 to 20 percent of the total time for the speech. Although this text resists such precise measurement, the key point remains: Limit the length of your introduction so that it does not become a speech in itself.[13]

Make the Introduction Complete

Although exceptions exist, most introductions include the following elements: a device to gain your listeners' interest and to dispose them favorably toward you as a speaker, a statement of your thesis or purpose, and a preview of how you will develop the topic.

Keep a File of Potential Introductions

In developing an introduction, you will doubtless run across ideas, quotations, examples, and other materials that are not immediately useful but that you can imagine shaping into an introduction for a future speech. Keep track of such materials. Do not rely on memory to recall them or find them at just the moment you need them. You might keep a folder on your computer where you will enter introductory material arranged by topic, adding new entries as you find them. Perhaps you might even download audio and video clips. Just as you learned about keeping a speech material file to aid in your research (Chapter 9), you should keep track of potential introductions as well. Then, when you start preparing your next speech, you already will have resources and will not have to depend entirely on either memory or inspiration.

Be Guided by the Examples in This Book

In this chapter, you have studied the most frequently used types of introductions; the appendix and other speeches in the book also illustrate a variety of introductions. Consider these examples not as models to be followed blindly, but as guidelines to help you think creatively about the best way to introduce your particular speech.

Plan the Introduction Word for Word

Especially in the opening lines of the speech, you want to be sure that you say exactly what you intend. An extemporaneous opening is risky even for very confident, very experienced speakers, unless they have thought very carefully about the introduction first, because no one can entirely control the speech setting and circumstances. Nor is it wise to carry a written script to the podium, planning to read the introduction aloud. A good first impression is unlikely when your face is buried in notes. Instead, prepare and practice your opening words carefully so that you can begin speaking with confidence and good effect.

Preparing and practicing the introduction word for word will enable you to create the clearest, most compelling first impression on the audience. Moreover, knowing exactly what you are going to say at the beginning of your speech will give you greater confidence and a sense of security. So armed, you can overcome the anxiety that even experienced speakers feel when they stand to address an audience.

Conclusions: Ending the Speech

Just as you want to begin your speech on the right note, so do you want to develop an appropriate, effective ending. A speech should neither end abruptly nor trail off into oblivion. As we did with introductions, we will approach conclusions by focusing on their purposes and their types and then looking at some strategies for preparing them.

The Purposes of a Conclusion

Like your introduction, your **conclusion** needs to accomplish several specific goals:

- Signal that the end is coming
- Summarize the main ideas
- Make a final appeal to the audience

Signaling That the End Is Coming

Perhaps the most basic function of the conclusion is to signal to listeners that the speech is ending. No doubt you have heard a speaker who seemed to be finishing several times before the speech actually ended. Such a speech has "false conclusions"—misleading signals that the end is near. Summary statements, the use of the word *finally,* and similar cues alert the audience that the speech is wrapping up. But if you send such signals prematurely, you will confuse listeners and may even arouse their impatience when the speech does not end as expected.

You probably also have heard a speaker who ended so abruptly that you were surprised. Suddenly, although you thought the speaker was still developing a major idea, he or she came to the end of a sentence, said, "Thank you," and sat down. Somehow, that approach did not seem right either.

In both cases, the speakers failed to provide a satisfying sense of closure. If you confuse listeners with false endings or surprise them by stopping abruptly, your conclusion has not completed the sense of form. Listeners do need to be signaled that it is time to draw together their perceptions about the speech, but you should send this signal only at the appropriate time.

Summarizing the Main Ideas

A second important purpose of the conclusion is to draw together the main ideas in your speech in a way that helps listeners to remember them. Even trained and experienced listeners rapidly forget what they have heard. If you want the audience to remember what you have said, you need to issue reminders at appropriate points throughout the speech. And no place is more appropriate for a **summary** than the conclusion.

To end a speech about the messages embodied in popular music, for example, you might summarize by saying, "As we have seen, popular music tells us about our own values, about our relationships with others, and about our obligations to nature, society, and the next generation." A summary does not exactly repeat the main ideas, and it certainly does not reprise their development. Rather, it reminds the audience of key points, often by highlighting particular words or phrases in a way that listeners can remember—as in the parallel structure of the three "about" phrases in this example.

An effective summary, then, is an aid to memory. By including a summary in your conclusion, you will increase the chances that listeners will recall your main ideas correctly.

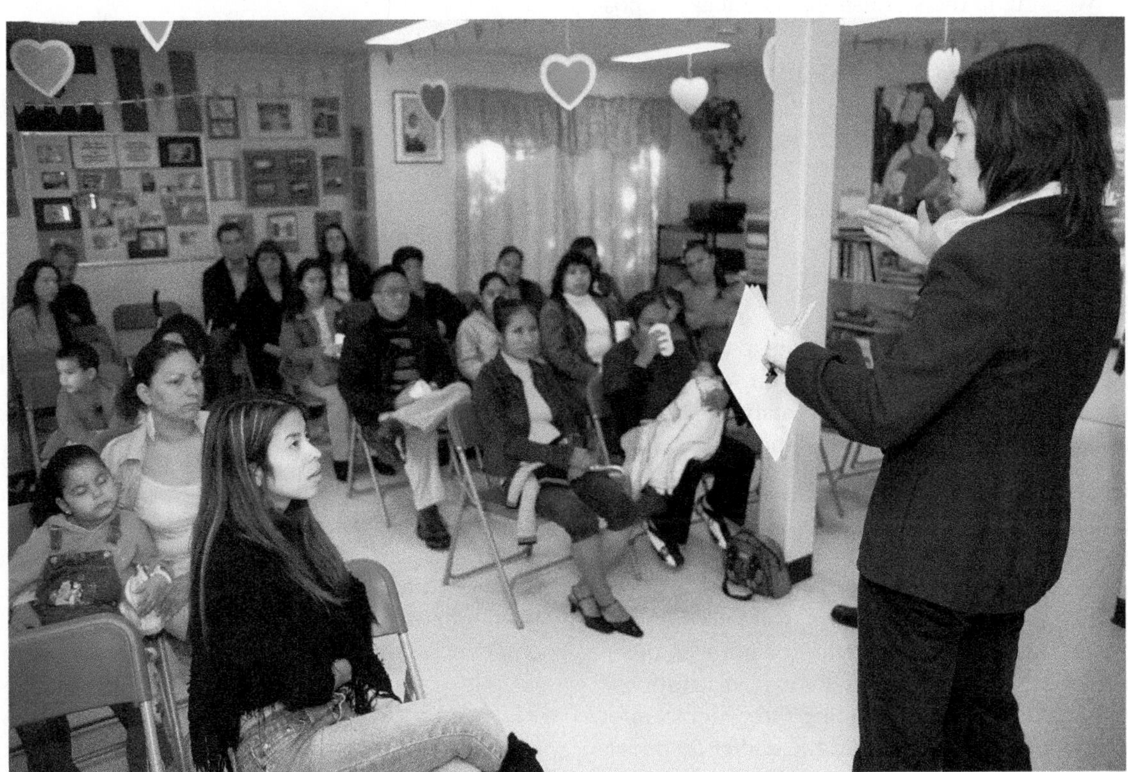

An effective conclusion will reward the audience's attention by completing the form of the speech, drawing the ideas together, and making clear what listeners should believe or do.

Making a Final Appeal to the Audience

The conclusion is also an opportunity to say exactly what response you want from the audience. It is your last chance to remind listeners about whatever you want them to think or do as a result of your speech.

Sometimes a speaker wants listeners to take a very specific action, such as signing a petition, donating money, writing to their legislators, or purchasing a particular product. At other times, the desired response is a belief rather than an action. For example, suppose you want the audience to agree that the current president and administration have set a correct course in foreign policy matters. You are not asking listeners to take any specific action, but you do want them to be favorably disposed toward the president's international policies. Your conclusion might say, "I hope I've convinced you that the president's foreign policy is on the right track." Although you are not asking for anything directly, you do want to intensify or to change your listeners' beliefs. Either response may lead to actions later.

Sometimes the response you seek may be even more general, as in these four examples of concluding remarks:

- The next time you consider buying running shoes from one of these companies, consider the people working in the sweatshops who make it possible for you to get an affordable deal.
- You may not agree with me that Michael Phelps is the world's best athlete, but I hope you will appreciate the dedication and perseverance of professional swimmers.
- There are strong arguments on both sides of the abortion debate. I ask that you think about what I have said and come to your own conclusion about what you believe.
- You may not decide to hop a plane to the slums of Bangladesh as I did, but maybe you will consider other spring break travel alternatives that will make a difference in the lives of the less fortunate.

None of these concluding statements calls for action, and yet each of them asks listeners to "do" something: to become more aware of something they had not recognized or to think critically about something they had accepted.

Virtually any speech—whether or not it is billed as a "persuasive" speech—asks for some response from the audience. In developing the conclusion of a speech, your goal is to make the audience understand exactly what response you seek.

An Example of a Conclusion

Here's how Michelle Ekanemesang ended her classroom speech about online sexual predators:

> So remember that we must commit ourselves to keeping children safe from the scourge of online sexual predators. These psychologically damaged men and women use a bag of tricks to deceive, lure, and abuse their prey—innocent children who will bear emotional and physical scars for a lifetime. We can blunt the weapons of online sexual predators by equipping children in our community with the education and knowledge they will need to detect, report, and foil the plans of sexual predators. I hope the information I've shared with you today will not fall on deaf or apathetic ears; please mention the tools I've discussed to a young person in your life. Remember that prevention is always better than a cure!

Michelle's first concluding sentence hinted to the audience that her speech was coming to an end. The next two sentences summarized the points she had made in the body of her speech. Finally, she asked the audience to take action and help stop online sexual predators by passing on the information that children need in order to prevent this form of sexual abuse.

Types of Conclusions

You already know that the types of introductions can be developed in various ways to achieve your purpose. The same is true for conclusions. Indeed, some of the following types of conclusions mirror the types of introductions you have studied; others introduce new elements into the speech.

Summarizing

We observed earlier that one purpose of the conclusion is to summarize the main points of the speech. Sometimes, summary is the *dominant* purpose. In that case, the concluding summary would be more extended than in the preceding examples. It would remind the audience not only about major topics addressed but also about the details of your argument, even repeating some memorable thematic phrases. Such an extensive concluding summary may need a "miniconclusion" of its own, to avoid ending abruptly or trailing off into insignificance.

In contrast, sometimes a succinct, bare-bones restatement of key phrases may make the most rousing finish. Consider the following conclusion from a speech by President George W. Bush outlining his strategy for responding to the terrorist attacks of September 11, 2001:

> Fellow citizens, we'll meet violence with patient justice—assured of the rightness of our cause, and confident of the victories to come.

The first part of the sentence captures the essence of Bush's policy, and the two clauses after the dash (note their parallel structure!) are a brief but powerful reminder of the attitudes the president sought to represent and to evoke.

Quoting Someone

Just as many speeches begin with a quotation, so many end with one. In both cases, remember to tie the quotation clearly to your speech. A concluding quotation, however, may also go beyond your central ideas and give the audience something to think about; the risk of confusing listeners is much lower at the conclusion, because they have already heard your main points.

Student speaker Kim Davis found a quotation that succinctly summed up her ideas in a speech about gays in the military. Quoting a gay soldier who had been discharged for his sexual preference, she read:

> "They gave me a medal for killing two men, and a discharge for loving one."

Closing quotations should be like this one—a few neatly balanced, memorable words that sum up your central idea or advance your main purpose.

Making a Personal Reference

Particularly if your speech is about impersonal or abstract issues, it may be appropriate in the conclusion to personalize the issues by making reference to yourself. Such a concluding device (1) illustrates your own identification with the subject—you embody the ideas and values in the speech—and (2) encourages the audience to identify with you. In this way, listeners might imagine that they have the same feelings you have about the topic.

Student Romila Mushtag used this type of conclusion effectively after arguing that hate speech should not be outlawed on campus. She ended the speech by showing the audience a handwritten racist note that had been taped to her locker door.

RHETORICAL WORKOUT

Conclude Your Speech

You've written the body and introduction of your speech demonstrating how to ride a snowboard. Your purpose is to teach your audience a few basics about snowboarding. Think about some types of conclusions and how they could work with this speech.

1. *Summarizing:* How could an extended summary of your main "how-to" points benefit your listeners?
2. *Quoting someone:* Suppose you find three catchy quotations and you want to use one as a conclusion. How appropriate or interesting do you think each of the following might be: (a) a snowboarding instructor on how knowing the basics increases your safety; (b) a first-time snowboarder on how much fun he had learning; (c) a professional snowboarder on how much she practices.
3. *Making a personal reference:* How might concluding with a personal reference or story affect your audience?
4. *Challenging the audience:* How could you use your conclusion to challenge your listeners?
5. *Offering a utopian vision:* Suppose you chose this topic because you enjoy snowboarding and you find it to be good exercise. How could you turn these elements into a conclusion that offers a utopian, positive vision to your audience?
6. What are some potential strengths and weaknesses of each type of conclusion? Which type would you use for this speech? Why?

By revealing that she had been victimized by hate speech and yet would defend someone's right to use such speech, she demonstrated a level of integrity that the audience couldn't help endorsing and trying to emulate. Her personal reference made listeners identify with her—and with the ideas in her speech.

Challenging the Audience

Particularly when your speech asks the audience to do something, concluding with a direct challenge may be effective. This type of conclusion not only creates a common bond between speaker and audience but also transfers to the audience some of the responsibility for achieving the speaker's goals. For example, student speaker Todd McCullough, after summarizing his main ideas, ended a speech about the need for environmentally and economically responsible automobiles with this challenge:

> We need to use our power as consumers to purchase vehicles that are fuel efficient and to boycott the continued production of gas-guzzling vehicles. We are here at college to get an education so we can go out and make a living. We cannot afford to watch as our paychecks are devoured by our automobiles. It is time to rise up and demand fuel-efficient vehicles.

Offering a Utopian Vision

Closely related to challenging the audience is this type of conclusion, which offers an idealized, positive vision of what can be achieved if only the audience will work together with the speaker. Rather than focusing on the challenge itself, however, this approach emphasizes the results of meeting the challenge successfully. The vision is called "utopian" not to dismiss it, but to emphasize that it usually transcends the immediate, practical world. One of the most famous examples of a conclusion containing a utopian vision is Martin Luther King, Jr.'s "I Have a Dream" address, delivered in 1963 at the March on Washington.

Abraham Lincoln also used this type of conclusion often. After warning of the perilous situation facing the Union in 1861, at the time of his first inaugural address, Lincoln confidently predicted in his conclusion that "the mystic chords of memory, stretching from every battlefield and patriot grave to every living heart and hearthstone all over this broad land, will yet swell the chorus of the Union, when again touched, as surely they will be, by the better angels of our nature." Yes, clouds may darken the sky at the moment, Lincoln was saying, but he promised his listeners that together they could achieve positive results in the fullness of time.

Checklist 10.6
Types of Conclusions

- Summarizing
- Quoting someone
- Making a personal reference
- Challenging the audience
- Offering a utopian vision

(In addition, many of the types of introductions in Checklist 10.5 can also be used as concluding devices.)

Even speeches about less momentous topics may conclude by envisioning how things will be once a problem is solved or a goal is achieved. Offering a utopian vision is particularly effective when the speaker is calling on the audience to make sacrifices or to take risks to achieve a distant goal. By predicting ultimate success, the utopian vision assures listeners that what the speaker is calling for will be worth the efforts they make.

Besides these specific types of conclusions, notice that many of the introductory approaches discussed earlier also can be used for the conclusion, including narratives, anecdotes, and rhetorical questions.[14] In the same way, some types of conclusions can be adapted effectively for use in an introduction. A quotation or a personal reference, for instance, can be as powerful at the beginning of the speech as at the end.

Strategies for Preparing a Conclusion

Several of the earlier suggestions for preparing an introduction apply as well to preparing a conclusion:

- Work on the conclusion after developing the body of your speech; again, it helps to know what you are concluding.
- Connect the conclusion clearly to the body of the speech so that listeners will grasp how it relates to your main ideas.
- Keep the conclusion relatively brief so that it does not detract from the speech itself.
- Aim for a complete conclusion, including both a wrap-up of your major ideas and a clear indication of how you want listeners to respond.
- Summarize your argument memorably; then tell the audience what belief or action you seek.

The following additional guidelines and suggestions will help you develop an effective conclusion.

Be Sure That It Truly Is the Conclusion

This first principle is simple to state but no less important for that. As you begin to develop the conclusion, take care to put it at the end of the body, and lead the audience naturally into your summary and final appeal.

Recall once more that listeners get distracted or confused when a speech departs from customary structure. On the one hand, avoid any wording that might signal a false (premature) conclusion. You certainly do not want your audience to applaud when, after several false endings, you finally say, "In conclusion . . . ," as actually happened to Arkansas Governor Bill Clinton at the 1988 Democratic convention. On the other hand, indicate clearly when you are ready to move from the body of your speech to its conclusion.

Return to Your Introductory Device When Possible

One way to enhance the sense of form and unity in a speech is to conclude by referring again to the device you used in the introduction. If you began with a quotation, you may be able to repeat that same quotation in your conclusion, teasing a different meaning from it now that the audience has heard how you developed your topic. If your introductory device was an anecdote or a rhetorical question, your conclusion might return to that same device and embellish it based on the ideas you developed in your speech.

Of course, this suggestion cannot always be followed. The ideas in the speech may have moved far beyond where they were in the introduction, and returning to the introductory device would seem jarring ("Isn't this where we came in?"). But when you can return to the introduction, listeners will feel that the speech hangs together well, that it has a satisfying sense of structure.

Practice the Conclusion

The inspiration of the moment is no more dependable at the end of a speech than at the beginning. Just as you developed your introduction word for word, so should you prepare a conclusion by writing out key phrases and sentences that summarize your ideas and make a strong appeal. In addition, practice the conclusion orally. Your speaking rate is likely to slow down by the end of the speech; you probably will pause briefly between the body and the conclusion; and specific words and phrases will need careful emphasis. Practicing the conclusion out loud a few times before you present the entire speech will help you craft both its content and its ultimate effect.

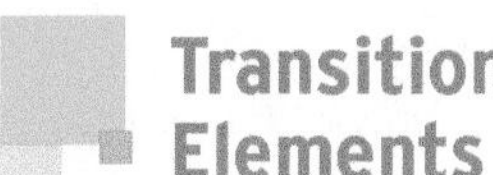

Transitions: Connecting the Elements of a Speech

Introduction, body, and conclusion—these structural elements seem so static that, in planning one of them, you can easily forget how dynamic a speech actually is. From beginning to end, the speech represents movement. You begin with a set of ideas and a strategic objective; by moving through the ideas, you also move toward achieving the objective. Similarly, listeners begin with a certain level of understanding about the subject and a certain disposition toward you as speaker; careful listening and thinking move them through the speech as well.

This dynamic movement of both speaker and listeners is achieved by—and depends on—connections that the speaker provides to bridge any gaps between elements. **Transitions** connect the introduction to the body, connect the main ideas within the body, and connect the body to the conclusion.

The Purposes of Transitions

The most important purpose of transitions is to create this sense of movement. They also help listeners follow the speaker's movement and remember what the speaker said. Equally important, transitions keep the speaker from lapsing into nervous mannerisms that would accentuate the gaps between ideas.[15]

Even accomplished speakers sometimes neglect to think about transitions. They may organize the body of the speech carefully, labor to devise an effective introduction, and craft a compelling conclusion; yet they assume that transitions will spring up spontaneously. Facing the audience, however, their spontaneous connections may be as pedestrian as "My next point is . . ." or "Next, let me discuss. . . ." The movement is halting; the sense of form is unclear.

Even worse is a speaker who bridges gaps and moves forward on the basis of sheer nervous energy and repetition. You probably have heard a speaker who punctuated every pause with "Umm . . ." or "like . . . ," or who completed every thought with "Okay" or "Right?" or who moved to each new point with "Now, then. . . ." Such mannerisms can become so obvious and distracting that the audience starts counting them rather than listening to the speech.

From your experience as a listener, then, you know that an effective speaker understands the nature of transitions and includes them consciously to create movement and form. The rest of the chapter focuses on how to provide such connections in your speeches.

STRATEGIES FOR SPEAKING to Diverse Audiences

Respecting Diversity Through Introductions and Conclusions

Introductions and conclusions are important places to recognize and adapt to the diversity of the audience. Here are some strategies that will enable you to do so:

1. Consider the variety of strategies for building goodwill with your audience. Strive to identify with them early in your speech, but recognize that you will have to make a conscious decision in your introduction about how to do so.
2. Humor is an excellent way either to build goodwill with your audience or to alienate them. Demeaning individuals or cultural groups through humor should be avoided.
3. Offer "utopian visions" that enable listeners to imagine themselves as you ideally want them to be, emphasizing common values or themes that transcend diverse cultures.

Elements of Effective Transitions

We cannot list and describe "types" of transitions, as we could with introductions and conclusions. Transitions have three basic elements: an internal summary of what has been completed, a link to what is coming next, and an internal preview of the new idea. These three elements sometimes will be found in isolation, but a complete transition will include them all.

Internal Summaries

Like a concluding summary at the end of the speech, an **internal summary** draws together the central points that were discussed within the body of the speech or even within the discussion of one main idea, serving both to aid memory and to signal closure to those points. The following are simple examples of internal summaries:

1. In a speech recommending that your college switch from a quarter to a semester system:

   So, as we've seen, abandoning the quarter system would permit students to take classes that last longer, allowing them to learn more about a particular subject and reducing the pressures they face.

2. In a speech arguing that both students and faculty would benefit if the school offered more sections of closed classes:

   I hope I've made it clear that one benefit of additional sections of closed courses is more individualized attention. The faculty will be able to answer more questions in class and students will get prompt feedback.

3. In a speech about current campaign finance laws:

   So the current campaign finance laws really do pose a serious problem, because they encourage influence peddling, because they encourage legislators to forego their legislative work to engage in time-consuming fundraising, and because they lessen public confidence in government's ability to represent the interests of ordinary working people.

4. In a speech about multiculturalism:

   As I see it, then, our commitment to cultural diversity came about through this and other key incidents that embarrassed us by showing the limitations of our perspective.

Each of these internal summaries wraps up one main idea of the speech. It gives the audience a brief reminder of the idea and also signals the point of completion.

Links

Links are connections from one idea to the next. Some links are subtle and are established through careful word choice; others are explicit.

The construction *not only . . . but also* is an example of a subtle link. It moves from the point that was just discussed to the one that is coming up next, as in "Not only are closed classes bad for the students but also they're bad for the faculty." The speaker thus links two ideas that previously were separate in the speech.

Conjunctions such as *in addition, furthermore,* and *moreover* have the same effect. They suggest the cumulation of ideas, linking the ideas by hinting

A Question of ETHICS

Ethical Introductions and Conclusions

Introductions and conclusions are important because they set the tone for the speech and consolidate the ideas of the speech in a memorable way. Speakers should be creative in developing their introductions and conclusions. But what if the tone or nature of the introduction or conclusion is different from that of the body of the speech? For example, does a light-hearted or engaging story in the introduction distort the audience's response to the body of the speech that is the somber explanation of the latest economic crisis? Does the speaker have an ethical responsibility not to deviate from the body of the speech when crafting the introduction and conclusion? Is it ethical to create a tone in the introduction that gets the audience interested, and then to change the tone or nature of the argument within the speech? Or is this just a matter of artistic creativity and not ethics? What are the benefits, drawbacks, and ethical concerns raised by placing ideas in the introduction and conclusion that do not appear elsewhere in the speech?

that the one to come will build on the one just considered. In contrast, conjunctions such as *however, nonetheless,* and *on the other hand* signal that the speaker is going to move from one point of view to an opposing viewpoint or in some way will qualify or limit the force of what was just said.

Sometimes links are more explicit. The speaker who finishes one idea with an internal summary and then says, "But here's the proverbial fly in the ointment," is announcing that the point just made is about to be rendered troublesome or problematic or that something calls it into question. And the speaker who says, "It's not enough to focus on the cost of higher education; we also have to be concerned with quality," is telling the audience that they need to consider one more important factor.

How subtle or explicit should a particular link be? That depends on several factors. If the connection seems obvious and listeners can be expected to see it without help, an explicit link may be insulting. But if the connection between points is complex or seems to contradict common sense, an explicit link may be appreciated. Audiences can follow narrative and chronological links more easily than they can follow analytical links. Similarly, links based on "common knowledge" and general understanding do not have to be as explicit as links that require specialized knowledge or training.

Internal Previews

A preview is a compressed version of what the speaker is about to develop; it prompts the audience to anticipate what is coming. The introduction will probably preview your main ideas. Similarly, an **internal preview** will help prepare your audience to follow along every time you introduce a new main idea. Here are some examples of how to do that, corresponding to the examples of internal summaries that you recently read:

1. In your speech on abandoning the quarter system, an internal preview might point out,

   One of the most important reasons is that in a semester system students will have a longer time to learn what is offered in each course.

2. In your speech arguing for more sections of closed courses, an internal preview between the first and second main points might tell the audience,

   The second reason to have more sections is that the faculty will be able to give each student more attention.

3. In your speech about campaign finance laws, the body of the speech might start with an internal preview of the first major argument:

   Some argue that campaign finance laws no longer pose a serious problem. I don't agree, and let me tell you why.

4. In your speech about multiculturalism, an internal preview might signal that you are going to tell a story about how cultural diversity became a concern on campus.

Whether obviously or subtly, each of these internal previews tells the audience what to expect—each is a kind of early alert system for the audience.

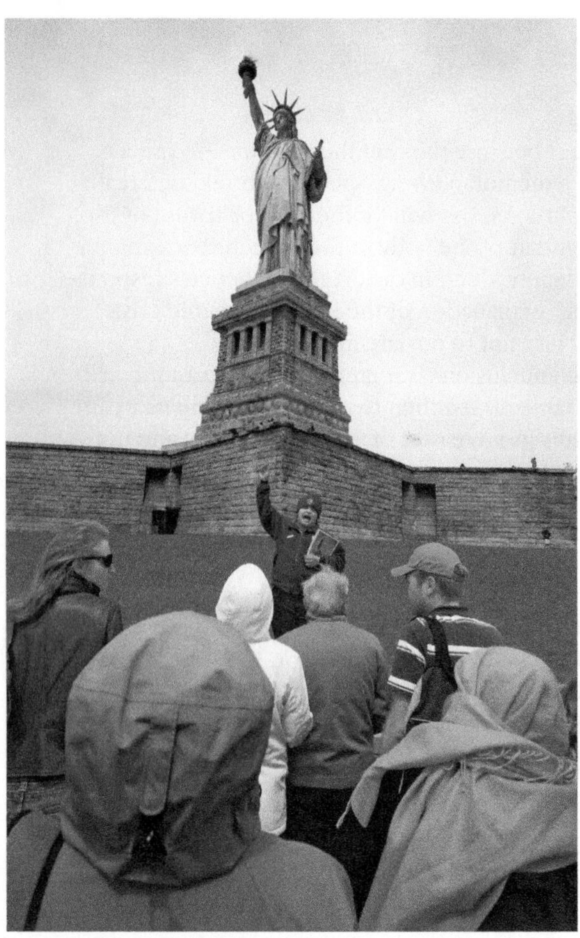

After discussing the history of the Statue of Liberty, speaker signals a transition to considering its artistic features. Notice how the verbal transition is matched by gesture corresponding to the outstretched arm on the statue.

An internal preview signals that listeners should get ready to move on to a new aspect of the speech, and it provides clues about the nature of the movement or the new aspect itself.

Whether previewing or summarizing the entire speech or just a part, you can use repetition and restatement to alert the audience that you are beginning or ending one of your key points. For example, the first internal preview described above might be elaborated as follows:

> One reason to abandon the quarter system is that students will have longer to learn what is offered in each course. More time to learn means less rush. Let me explain why this is so.

Similarly, the second internal summary above might be drawn out in this way:

> I hope I've made it clear that one benefit of additional sections of closed courses is more individualized attention. The faculty will be able to answer more questions in class, and students will get prompt feedback. Opening up more sections of closed courses will truly help our teachers to interact more with us and that, in turn, will benefit us.

Complete Transitions

As we have suggested, not every element of every transition need be made apparent. But a complete transition would include an internal summary of the point being concluded, a link to connect it to the next point, and an internal preview leading into the new point. For example, a complete transition in the speech about abandoning the quarter system might go like this:

> So there's no doubt that students will benefit from the change. Abandoning the quarter system will give them more time to write papers and study for final exams and will reduce their level of pressure and stress. [*Internal summary*] But students aren't the only ones who will gain from this change. [*Link*] The faculty will gain two benefits as well. Let me tell you about them. [*Internal preview*]

If you think that such a complete transition somehow seems stilted or unnatural, think again after imagining how a speech would be hurt by a really awkward transition such as this one:

> Uh, okay. Enough about that. Time to move on. Uh, okay. Oh yes, let me discuss . . .

This speaker completely sacrificed a sense of smooth progression of ideas, one of the most important contributions that transitions make to the speech.

Strategies for Preparing Transitions

Besides deciding how explicit to make each transition and whether to use repetition to emphasize the transition, consider the following brief suggestions.

Identify Main Ideas Succinctly

In internal previews and internal summaries, quickly and clearly identify the main idea being referred to; that will make it easier to remember. Rather than restating an idea completely, use a memorable word or phrase to highlight it in the transition.

Use Parallel Structure If Possible

When related ideas are identified in a similar or parallel fashion, that repeated pattern may make the link more memorable. Whenever possible, internal

Checklist 10.7

Transitions: Critical Thinking and Strategic Planning

1. Questions to ask yourself: At this point in my speech:
   - Do my listeners need a reminder or an alert about how far I've come?
   - Do my listeners need a reminder of how my last point relates to my next?
   - Do I need some verbal markers to help me and my listeners follow my outline?
   - Will my listeners follow my ideas better if I give them a brief preview?
2. If the answer is "Yes," here are some things worth doing:
   - Construct brief phrases that identify main ideas in the speech, and use them as markers and reminders at key intervals.
   - Set up your points in parallel structure whenever possible. Check your outline to help you do this.
   - Include verbal signposts that briefly show where you are and what comes next.

previews and internal summaries should use one of the organizational patterns described in this chapter.

Use Signposting

Signposting is the use of verbal cues to alert the audience to where you are in the speech. If you say that you will discuss three advantages of something, in previewing each advantage it will be helpful to identify it as "first," "second," or "third." Listeners will have no doubt that you have completed the discussion of one advantage and are about to talk about the next; and they also will clearly perceive the structure that you intended. Similarly, you can use pauses, repetition, and changes in speaking rate, pitch, or volume as signposting to guide the audience.

OUTLINING THE SPEECH

A speech **outline** is simply a display of the organizational pattern of the speech. If you already have selected one of the organizational patterns discussed earlier, the outline will record your choices and let you check that you have made them correctly. Sometimes, however, you may not have a specific organizational plan in mind. Developing the outline will enable you to decide which organizational plan is best. In either case, however, the outline serves several purposes. It helps you to:

- *Be sure that you have covered the topic adequately,* that you have not included irrelevant material, and that your ideas are developed in the right proportion so you don't spend too much or too little time on any one idea.
- *Clarify and choose the best organizational strategy* for your speech.
- *Check your organizational pattern* to see that it is sensible and consistent. It lets you determine easily whether the main ideas support your thesis statement, whether your reasoning is strong, whether the supporting materials are linked to your claims, and whether the overall design of the speech advances your purpose.
- *Become familiar with the claims you want to make* and the order in which you plan to make them.

From Ideas to Outline

Suppose that you've done quite a bit of research on your topic and have given it a good deal of thought, but you're not sure exactly how you want to organize it. A few basic steps will help you to develop the outline:

1. List the ideas you plan to develop in the speech. If you were discussing the drawbacks of the electoral college, for example, you might have a list like this:

   Exaggerates influence of small states
   Romney needn't campaign in Alabama in 2012
   Denies voice to the minority within each state
   Supports false stereotypes about states
   Excludes the campaign from much of the country
   Democratic votes in Texas didn't count for anything in 212
   Denies democratic principle of majority rule
   Red states aren't dramatically different from blue states
   Harrison won in 1888 though Cleveland had more popular votes
   Obama could ignore Illinois in 2008 and 2012
   Red and blue states are not internally homogeneous
   Republican votes in California didn't count for anything in 2012
   Bush won in 2000 though Gore had more popular votes

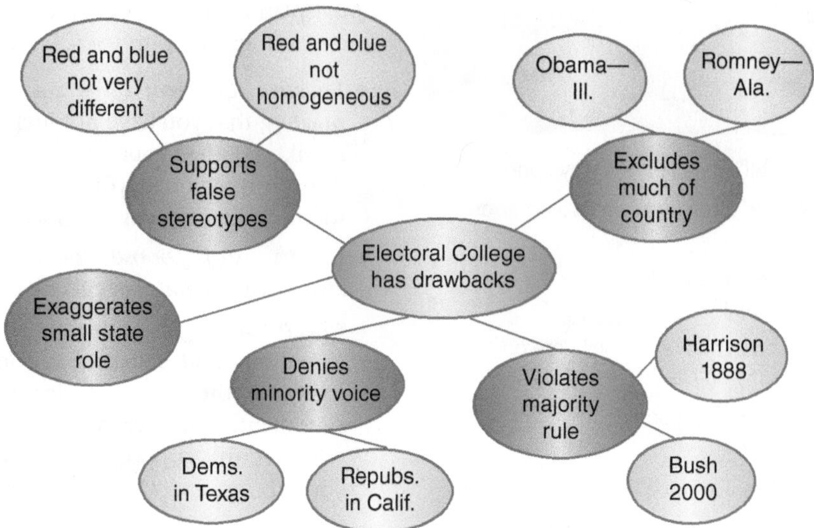

Figure 10.1
Mapping the Main Ideas

These are the ideas that have emerged from your research and thought about the topic.

2. Determine which of these ideas subsume other ideas. Rearrange the list so that you group together ideas that are closely related. For example, "Harrison won in 1888 though Cleveland had more popular votes" and "Bush won in 2000 though Gore had more popular votes" are both supporting points for the idea "Denies democratic principle of majority rule."
3. Diagram the relationships among the ideas. One excellent way to do so is by mapping. A map of the above list is diagrammed in Figure 10.1. The circles connected directly to the thesis statement are the main ideas. Moving outward, the circles that are linked to them will be the supporting ideas. (If we proceeded to more subordinate levels of support, the map would continue to expand outward.)

   If you don't want to draw a concept map, you might simply draw lines among the ideas in your list, to connect those that go together. Either way, you will develop clusters that represent the main ideas of the speech. As noted in Chapter 9, most speakers will want to have between two and five main ideas, because having more will risk losing the audience's attention and comprehension. If you find that you have more than five main ideas, it may mean that you are trying to do too much in the speech. Or it may mean that some of your ideas still can be combined—that you haven't yet gone to the level of main ideas.
4. Determine the order in which you want to discuss the main ideas. You probably will want to use one of the organizational patterns in this chapter, because they are easy for listeners to follow, unless there is a good reason to develop a novel plan for your particular speech.

Now you are ready to translate the results of your mental exercise into the form of an outline. Speakers depend on outlines at two stages: when they put the speech together and when they deliver it. Each stage requires a different kind of outline. The **preparation outline** is used in composing the speech and is developed in enough detail to show how each idea and piece of evidence fits into the overall structure. The **presentation outline**, or speaking outline, is simpler and briefer and is used as a memory aid while you deliver the speech. Although the character and use of these outlines are different, the preparation outline should lead naturally into the presentation outline.

The Preparation Outline

In making your preparation outline, you pull together many of the subjects you studied in previous chapters. You decide on your purpose and thesis statement; you identify the issues and supporting material; and you organize the introduction, body, and conclusion. As you develop your ideas, you plan a strategy for your speech, thinking about what to put where and why. You think critically, inspecting the outline to ask which sections of the speech are complete and which need further development. Outlining a speech is like exercising; it is a "rhetorical workout" that helps you get in shape.

The preparation outline is relatively formal. If your instructor has asked for an outline of your speech, it is the preparation outline that you should submit. Usually, you should write it in complete sentences so that anyone reading the outline can make reasonable guesses about what your speech includes. Student speakers sometimes think of the preparation outline as drudgery. "After all," they might say, "I took this course to learn how to speak, not how to write outlines." And it is true that some very accomplished speakers can do without a fully developed outline. But for beginning speakers, the preparation outline is extremely important and you should approach it with care. It enables you to clarify your own thinking, to be sure that the structure of your speech is clear, and to rehearse on paper the main ideas you will develop and the relationships among them. On the other hand, once you have the structure of the speech in place, you should leave the preparation outline aside and work on the presentation outline. Be careful that you do not simply read the speech from the preparation outline. That could interfere with your ability to establish contact with, and receive feedback from, the audience.

What Does a Good Outline Look Like?

An outline indicates the hierarchy of importance of ideas within a speech. Typically, the main ideas are signaled by Roman numerals, and each successive level of less central ideas is designated first by capital letters, then by Arabic numerals, and finally by lowercase letters.[16] In short, you proceed from the ideas most central to your thesis to those least central, indenting each level appropriately. The overall structure of your outline would look something like this:

I. Main idea
   A. Supporting idea (subheading)
   B. Supporting idea (subheading)
      1. Supporting material (evidence)
      2. Supporting material (evidence)
   C. Supporting idea (subheading)
      1. Supporting material (evidence)
         a. Backing for the supporting material
         b. Backing for the supporting material
      2. Supporting material (evidence)
   D. Supporting idea (subheading)
II. Main idea

An outline may extend to additional detail, of course, with deeper indentations for each level of organization. But if the structure of a speech is that complex, the audience probably will not be able to follow it carefully. If your preparation outline needs more than four levels of importance, your thesis is probably too broad and unfocused.

Outlining the Body of the Speech

The following principles will help you construct your preparation outline.

Statement of Topic, General Purpose, Specific Purpose, and Thesis

hese elements, discussed in Chapter 9, should be displayed above the outline. By keeping them in view as you develop the outline, you can check the emerging plan against the goals it is designed to achieve. For a speech about the quality of Campus Food Service, you might precede the outline with the following:

TOPIC:	Campus Food Service
GENERAL PURPOSE:	Conversion
SPECIFIC PURPOSE:	To convince listeners that the often-criticized Campus Food Service is really quite good
THESIS:	Campus Food Service is vastly underrated.

Complete Sentences

One function of the preparation outline is to test the clarity and precision of your claims. Sometimes you may have a general idea of what you want to say but are unsure of the exact idea you want to express. By writing the outline in complete sentences, rather than just highlighting general topics, you will force yourself to specify exactly what claims you want to make. This will make you less likely to "talk around the subject" when you deliver the speech.

For example, if your outline simply says "Voting bad," you would have little idea what you really want to say—other than that there is something negative about voting patterns. In contrast, the complete sentence "Voting in presidential elections has declined over time" is much more precise and focuses your attention on your essential message.

Subordination

A primary purpose of the preparation outline is to map out the relationships between claims and supporting materials. The outline should clearly show **subordination**; supporting materials for a given idea should be outlined as indented under that idea. If you designate the main idea with Roman numerals, for example, then you should identify its supporting ideas (subheadings) with capital letters. It is easy to mistake subheadings for main ideas or for supporting material when your outline does not show their subordinate structure.

Look again at this fragment of an outline from earlier in this chaper:

I. Voter apathy has become a growing concern.
  A. During the years before World War I, voter turnout was high.
  B. In the modern age, the height of voter participation came in 1960.
  C. Since 1960, there has been a slow but steady decline in political participation.
  D. By 1996, voter turnout was at the lowest level since 1924.
  E. Even in the razor-thin election of 2000, turnout rose only slightly.
  F. Even though there were many new voters in 2008, the turnout rate did not change very much.
II. Voter apathy is widespread.
  A. It can be found in the East.
  B. It can be found in the Midwest.
  C. It can be found in the South.
  D. It can be found in the West.

Details about the voting in different eras would be subordinate to a claim that voter apathy has increased over time. Likewise, information about voting rates in different regions of the country would be subordinate to a main idea about the geographic spread of the problem. Each subheading supports the idea under which it is indented. The distinction between main and supporting ideas helps to make the subordinate structure clear and easy for an audience to follow.

Coordination

Closely related to the principle of subordination is **coordination**: Ideas with the same level of importance should be designated with the same symbol series—all with Roman numerals, or all with capital letters, and so on. Items so designated are parallel, or coordinate, statements.

The preceding outline appropriately identifies the two statements "Voter apathy has become a growing concern" and "Voter apathy is widespread" as main headings. These are equally important ideas, and they are both parts of an overall topical organization that coordinates two aspects of the topic: chronology and geography. It would be a mistake to label as main headings "Voter apathy has become a growing concern" and "It can be found in the South." These statements are not united by a topical plan and might even be said to conflict, because the first statement implies a national problem and the second focuses on a single region. In the same way, it would be a mistake to label "Voter apathy has become a growing concern" as a main idea and "Voter apathy is widespread" as a supporting point, because the second point is on equal footing with the first, not subordinate to it.

It is easy to see in the abstract that these patterns are in error. But it is also easy to make these types of errors when you are not consciously thinking about outlining and organizational schemes—especially if, say, you happen to find compelling supporting material about voting rates in the South. As you compose your preparation outline, ask whether the ideas that you have designated with the same symbol series are really *coordinate*—whether they are of the same importance and (often) parallel in structure.[17]

Activity 1 at the end of the chapter provides an opportunity to practice the principles of coordination and subordination.

Discreteness

Each element of the outline should express only one idea, so that you do not mix together themes that should be developed separately. "Voter apathy is growing and widespread" would not be a good entry in your outline because it combines themes that would be clearer for your audience if they were developed one at a time.

As a general rule, you should have at least two entries at any level of subordination—if there is a "capital A," for example, then there also should be (at least) a "capital B." The reason is that an idea cannot be subdivided into only one part. A single entry at any level of subordination usually is a sign either that something is missing in your analysis or that you have regarded as a subpoint what really is a main idea (in which case your "capital A" really should be "Roman numeral II."

Some teachers of public speaking regard this general rule as an absolute prohibition against single entries, but there are cases in which an exception might be justified. For instance, you may wish to discuss a general idea and illustrate only one specific dimension. If you examine carefully the outline structure of this book, you will find a few cases where there is only one subpoint. Still, the general rule is a

RHETORICAL WORKOUT

Format a Preparation Outline

Read Jaimie Sakumura's speech, "Immigration," in the Appendix. Then take apart the body of the speech and put it into the format of a preparation outline. For example, Jaimie's first main idea is at the beginning of her second paragraph. In a preparation outline, where you use complete sentences, the main idea would look like this:

I. Let me begin by telling you why treating illegal immigrants as felons is an inhumane and impractical way to deal with this problem.

Using the outline format under "What Does a Good Outline Look Like?" plug in the following items from Jaimie's speech. Be sure to write out the ideas in complete sentences.

- What are the other two *main ideas*?
- The first *supporting idea* for main idea number I is "Not providing illegal immigrants with the opportunity to obtain citizenship is, first of all, completely impractical." What *supporting materials,* or evidence, does Jaimie cite to back up this supporting idea? What other supporting idea(s) and supporting materials does Jaimie use in discussing her main idea number I?
- Fill in the supporting ideas and supporting materials for main ideas II and III.
- Look at the overall outline you have just created. Is each supporting idea *subordinate* to, or beneath, its main idea? Are ideas of equal weight designated as *coordinate,* or parallel, statements, with the same level of numbering?
- Is each element of the outline *discrete,* expressing only one idea?
- Based on the preparation outline, does the body of Jaimie's speech look balanced? Do the main ideas each have a similar number of supporting ideas? Does each supporting idea have supporting material (evidence) to back it up?
- How do you think creating a preparation outline as you write your speech could help you organize your ideas?

good guideline to follow when developing your first preparation outline. You can experiment with deviation later.

Outlining Introductions and Conclusions

Including the introduction and conclusion of your speech in the preparation outline is fairly straightforward. They are developed as separate sections of the outline, and the primary numerical divisions identify the elements of the introduction and conclusion. For the introduction, these elements typically include the following:

I. Attention-getting device.
II. Statement of thesis or purpose.
III. Preview of the speech.

(The introduction also seeks to create a favorable impression, but that is an overall effect to achieve, not necessarily an individual component of the introduction.)

And for the conclusion, the key elements usually are as follows:

I. Summary of main ideas.
II. Action desired from audience.
III. Closure device.

Checklist 10.8

Principles for Outlining the Body of the Speech

- ☐ Complete sentences (in preparation outline)
- ☐ Subordination
- ☐ Coordination
- ☐ Discreteness

Here is how you might outline the introduction and conclusion of the speech about Campus Food Service:

Introduction

I. **Attention-getting device:** [*Take on persona of student going through food service line.*] "Oh great! Another meal at Campus Food Service. Let's see . . . what do I want? What is that? Uh . . . no mystery meat tonight, thanks. What? Chicken again. There's some pasta. Ugh, it looks like three noodles and a gallon of water. That's it. I'm ordering in tonight." This is a common but misguided student reaction.

II. **Thesis:** Campus Food Service, however, is vastly underrated.

III. **Preview:** By explaining how Campus Food Service keeps costs to a minimum, keeps offering a good variety, keeps a democratic system sensitive to the needs of the consumer, and keeps maintaining high-quality standards, I am going to prove that Campus Food Service is the best meal program for students.

Conclusion

I. **Summary:** The Campus Food Service plan is a fair way for students at the university to eat. It keeps charging students a low price for meals, keeps offering a wide variety of food selections, keeps trying its best to meet the student's needs, and keeps maintaining freshness and taste standards.

II. **Action step:** The next time you hear people making ill-founded complaints about Campus Food Service, don't hesitate to set them straight.

III. **Closure:** We are just left with one problem, though. Now that we know all the benefits of eating at Campus Food Service, what are we going to complain about at dinner?

Outlining Transitions

The preparation outline will also help you check the flow of your reasoning and the structural "joints" of your message. Look over the outline to check that the sections naturally link to one another. Is it clear, for example, that B is the next logical step after A? Can you envision how you will wrap up the discussion of idea I and then move to idea II?

If you need to make the transitions of your reasoning explicit, incorporate them into your preparation outline. The easiest way to do this is to make parenthetical notes between the items in the outline that the transition will link. In the example about voter apathy, you might include an explicit transition between items I and II in the body of the speech. The relevant part of the preparation outline might look like this:

D.

(Transition)

II.

Citing Supporting Materials in the Outline

You also can use the preparation outline to fit supporting materials into the speech. You can do so physically, by sorting your note cards according to the designations on your outline. For instance, you could put in one pile all the notes that bear on item I-A in the outline; separate piles would contain notes that relate to items I-B, II-A, and so on. This process has two obvious benefits; you can:

1. *Evaluate the supporting materials* for a given idea in the speech and can select which evidence to include.
2. *Discover which ideas still lack supporting materials,* indicating that further research may be needed.

After you have selected supporting materials, incorporate them into the outline. The following three alternative ways to do this all have both benefits and drawbacks:

1. *Reproduce the supporting material immediately below the idea to which it relates.* This approach most closely resembles what you will do in the speech and is probably easiest for a reader of the outline to follow; but it will make your outline longer and may disrupt the clarity of its structure.
2. *Use footnotes in the outline, and then reproduce the supporting materials at the end.* This method preserves the clarity of your structure, but you'll have to flip back and forth between the outline and the supporting materials.
3. *Attach a bibliography indicating the sources of supporting materials.* This approach will keep your structure clear and will let a reader of the outline know, in general, where supporting materials came from; but it will not match up specific evidence with specific ideas.

Even if you cite supporting materials in the outline, you often will need a bibliography at the end. It will identify all the sources you consulted in preparing the speech, whether or not you cite or quote them directly. Several different guides offer information on how to cite sources, ranging from the *Chicago Manual of Style* to the style manuals of the American Psychological Association (APA) and the Modern Language Association (MLA). You may be instructed as to which guide to use or the choice may be left up to you. Whichever you use, however, use it consistently. As you take notes (discussed in Chapter 9), be sure to take down the information required by the style manual you use. Review the bibliographic formats discussed in Chapter 9 (see Table 9.4 on pages 252).

Sample Preparation Outline

Here is an example of a preparation outline for a speech by Christopher Chiyung, a student at Northwestern University. In the margin alongside the outline are comments, questions, and suggestions. As you review the outline, consider its strengths and weaknesses and how you might improve it in response to the marginal notes. This outline is not presented as "perfect," but as an actual student outline, with both strengths and weaknesses, for you to review and analyze.

Preparation Outline

Microlending in Evanston: by Christopher Chiyung

GENERAL PURPOSE: To persuade the audience to support microloans in Evanston, Illinois.

SPECIFIC PURPOSE: To get people who are unfamiliar with microfinance to begin thinking about it and to strengthen the commitment of those who already support it.

THESIS: Microlending in Evanston is crucial to allow depressed businesses to survive, institutions to be adequately funded, and the standard of living to rise.

Introduction

This may seem to be a trite attention-getting device, because the quotation is frequently used and because the speech really is not about teaching people how to do something.

I. **Attention-getting device:** "Give a man a fish, feed him for a day; teach a man to fish, feed him for a lifetime." This maxim relates directly to a sustainable practice that isn't as well known as it should be.

This step is not always included, but it is here because a technical term needs to be defined.

II. **Definition.** Microfinance is based on the premise that low-income individuals are capable of lifting themselves out of poverty if given access to financial services.

Building one's *ethos* is often done implicitly, but it is made explicit here because of the speaker's direct personal involvement with the issue.

III. **Personal credibility.** As a member of Northwestern's premier microfinance organization, Lending for Evanston and Northwestern Development (LEND), I have researched the microfinance model's feasibility and have seen its far-reaching and long-lasting positive impact in the community.

This is a clear statement of the thesis and suggests that the speaker will advocate a point of view, not just present both sides of an issue.

IV. **Thesis:** Microlending in Evanston is crucial to allow depressed businesses to survive, institutions to be adequately funded, and the standard of living to rise.

This is an unusually brief preview, suggesting that the structure of the speech will be simple and easy to follow.

V. **Preview:** First I will tell you why we all should support microfinance and then I'll show how you can become involved.

Body

I. Microloans in poor areas have led to success.

There are only two examples here, but notice how they are varied: rural vs. urban, foreign vs. domestic.

A. In Bangladesh, 48 percent of the poor using microcredit were able to rise above the poverty line, versus only 4 percent of those without access to microcredit. [CITE GLOBAL ENVISION STUDY]

Notice how Christopher combines examples with an analogy, and then uses another example to support the analogy. This is a strong combination of evidence and reasoning.

B. Microloans in St. Louis have also been successful. [CITE MARKETWATCH]

C. West Evanston shares similar problems. [ANALOGY OF BARBERS & PAINTERS TO FARMERS & ARTISANS]

D. There is a personal example of success in west Evanston [GIGI AT EBONY BARBERSHOP]

[*TRANSITION:* While these success stories are wonderful, they are few and far between, for one reason: there aren't enough microfinance institutions.]

Christopher is hoping that the 4 percent figure, being so small, will speak for itself. There is an implicit value judgment that this is nowhere near enough.

II. Microfinance institutions need your support because they lack sufficient funding.

A. The existing 10,000 microfinance institutions reach only 4 percent of the potential market worldwide. [WORLD BANK]

B. Many small businesses and community organizations in the United States simply do not have access to credit or financing. [ANNIBALE—CITI MICROFINANCE & COMMUNITY DEVELOPMENT]

The visual aids become an additional form of support because the audience might not be able to remember the statistics.

C. These graphs illustrate how little funding is available.

Notice how this transition contains all the elements: internal summary of the previous idea, a link (reference to "other benefits"), and a preview of what is coming next.

[*TRANSITION:* In other words, microfinance institutions really need help in order to reach more people. But what other benefits are there besides growing small businesses? One is widespread financial stability from being employed.]

III. Microfinance brings up the standard of living and creates jobs.

A. In Rwanda, a gas station owner was able to hire additional workers. [CNN CORRESPONDENT GAYLE LEMMON]

Notice how the support for this main idea consists entirely of examples. Why might Christopher have made this choice? Is it a wise move? Do the examples meet the tests for this kind of evidence?

B. In Sarajevo, a textile entrepreneur was able to start a company employing 20 people who could now afford to send their children to school. [GAYLE LEMMON]

C. In St. Louis, microloans for appliances, car repairs, and college tuition allows repairmen and local businesses to thrive.

D. There is a sort of unexplainable positive energy that surrounds microfinance and helps to reinvigorate communities. [CITE BRIDGET McDERMOTT FLOOD, INCARNATE WORD FOUNDATION]

This transitional statement is a double negative. It might be confusing.

[*TRANSITION:* However, this is not to say that microfinance doesn't have its own set of criticisms.]

IV. The risks of supporting microfinance are not significant.

If the audience is likely to be thinking critically, it can be advantageous to acknowledge that there are criticisms of your proposal. Are these representative of the objections that might be made to it?

A. Naysayers argue that microfinance institutions often fail to engage the communities where they work. [CITE foodfirst.org]

B. Bringing people up to the poverty line is not enough; they need to be able to invest in themselves. [CITE HARVARD CRIMSON STUDY]

C. Although microfinance cannot do everything, it still can make a significant difference.

Conclusion

A succinct statement of the main ideas in the body of the speech. This should make it easier for the audience to remember.

I. ***Summary:*** Although the debate over microfinance continues, the most important facts to remember are that microfinance has proven successful in a decent number of cases, the institutions can use any means of financial support, and the positive effects aren't confined to just a small sphere.

II. ***Call to action:*** Please donate to LEND and spread awareness of the organization. It is a great way to understand the economic divide between Evanston's lakefront mansions and those struggling to make it on the west side.

Notice how the conclusion returns to the theme of the introduction, tying the speech together.

III. ***Final plea:*** The best thing you can do is to become a member next school year. In this way, we all could teach others how to fish, and we'd never have to just give the fish away.

Notice that all the sources came from the Internet and all were accessed on the same date. Is this a problem? Why or why not? Does the fact that there is a wide variety of types of sources make a difference?

Compare the format of Christopher's source entries to the citation style required by your instructor. What changes or corrections are needed to comply with that style?

Bibliography

Baker, Meredith C. "Show Me the Money" [Opinion]. *The Harvard Crimson.* Web. November 9, 2011.

"Kiva—About Microfinance." *Kiva—Loans That Change Lives.* Web. November 9, 2011.

Lemmon, Gayle Tzemach. "Why Think Small When It Comes to Women in Poor Nations?" *CNN.com Breaking News, U.S., World, Weather, Entertainment & Video News.* Web. November 9, 2011.

"The Limits of Microcredit—A Bangladesh Case." *Food First/Institute for Food and Development Policy.* Web. November 9, 2011.

McFarland, Holly. "The Basics of Microfinance/Global Envision." *Global Envision/The Confluence of Global Markets and Poverty Alleviation.* Web. November 9, 2011.

"St. Louis Microfinance Conference Showcases Positive Impact of Providing Financial Services to Low-Income Families, Communities." *MarketWatch—Stock Market Quotes, Business News, Financial News.* Web. November 9, 2011.

The Presentation Outline

As important as the preparation outline is, you probably will not want to use it during your speech. It is cumbersome and wordy; and it may encourage you to read the outline as though it were a manuscript, rather than speaking extemporaneously and adapting to the situation. Therefore, when you are satisfied with the preparation outline, you should develop a presentation, or speaking, outline. This will be the main source of notes you'll use during the speech itself.

Guidelines for the Presentation Outline

Some basic principles will help you develop a useful speaking outline.

Match Structure of Preparation Outline

This first principle is the most obvious. The whole point of carefully developing the preparation outline is to devise a clear and meaningful structure for the speech. The outline from which you speak, therefore, should follow the same pattern.

A Question of *ETHICS*

Ethics in Outlining

Because the presentation outline is always simpler than the preparation outline, you will be forced to make choices and edit out some information. How do you know what this crucial information is? What if you must trim your notes down anyway? What sort of ethical concerns might this pose? How can you minimize such concerns? If the audience is providing feedback suggesting that they are confused or need more information. Is it the speaker's responsibility to adapt to this audience response? Does having a presentation outline deter the speaker from being flexible? Can following the outline mean defaulting on one's ethical responsibility to the audience? How can the speaker negotiate responsibilities both to the outline and to the audience?

Use Key Words

The complete sentences that you used in the preparation outline will distract you in the speaking outline; there will be too much to stop and read while you are speaking. Instead, the speaking outline should use key words that remind you of your ideas. For example, the preparation outline for the speech about voter apathy might be translated into this presentation outline:

I. Growing
  A. Before WWI
  B. 1960
  C. After 1960
  D. 1996
  E. 2000
  F. 2008
II. Widespread
  A. East
  B. Midwest
  C. South
  D. West

Each key word should recall to your mind the complete statement that appears in the preparation outline. If a key word does not reliably prompt your memory, change the key word.

Using small note cards is a practical way to keep simple cues in front of you as you speak.

Include Introduction, Conclusion, and Transitions

Just as your preparation outline includes entries for the introduction, the conclusion, and transitions, your speaking outline can have separate sections for the introduction and the conclusion and can show transitions as parenthetical notes. In keeping with the keyword nature of the speaking outline, however, state these as briefly as possible, with only enough detail to ensure that you will remember them.

There are two exceptions to this general statement. Because the exact wording of your introduction and conclusion may be important to create the desired initial and final impressions, the attention-getting step in the introduction and the closure-developing step in the conclusion may be written out word for word or even committed to memory.[18]

Your speaking outline may refer to transitions in the form of parenthetical notes, such as "(Cause-effect link here)," "(On the other hand)," and the like. These will remind you of how you intend to signal transitions, thereby making the movement through your outline apparent to listeners.

Use of Note Cards

Most speakers find it better to use note cards than large sheets of paper for the speaking outline. Note cards are more compact, sturdier, easier to rearrange, and less distracting. You can set them on the lectern (if you are using one) or hold them in one hand without limiting your freedom of movement or gesture. You can outline each Roman numeral on a separate note card, or you can put your entire speaking outline on a single card. But be sure not to overload your note cards with overly small writing that will be hard for you to read while speaking. Some classroom assignments may limit you to a single note card so that you will make your key-word outline as simple as possible.

Reference to Supporting Materials and Oral Citations

The presentation outline should cue you about which supporting materials to use. If the actual materials are not simple enough to remember, put them on separate note cards. If you are speaking at a lectern, you can stack the cards in the order you'll use them. If not, you may want to hold them with your speaking outline cards.

Here is a simple illustration of how you might identify supporting materials in your speaking outline:

III. Voting not thought important
- A. Makes no difference—[quot. from Dionne book]
- B. No real choice—[on-campus interviews]

Point A would remind you to read the quotation that supports idea III (you can write the quotation on a separate note card or put it on a visual aid so that you don't need to handle a large book). Point B will similarly remind you to recount your informal talks with people on campus who said that there is no real difference between the major political parties and hence no reason to vote.

When you quote from source material, you need to cite the source, but an oral citation has less detail than a written bibliography entry. Exact dates, volume numbers of periodicals, lengthy titles and subtitles, and specific page numbers usually will not be necessary. Audience members will be unlikely to remember all of this information (though occasionally these elements will be necessary in order to put quoted matter into context).

CHOOSE A STRATEGY: Creating a Presentation Outline

The Situation

Choose a short speech from the Appendix or from the website http://americanrhetoric.com. Imagine that you have written it and will be delivering it to your class. Consider how you could create a presentation outline that would help you give the speech.

Making Choices

1. Choose an idea from the speech and identify if it is a main idea, a supporting idea, or supporting material (evidence). What are some key words you could use for this idea in your presentation outline?
2. Identify the speech's introduction and conclusion. Would you choose to include these in your presentation outline by using key words or by writing them out word for word? Why?
3. Of the supporting materials in the speech, what are some that you might want to include separate note cards for? Why?
4. Think about your delivery of an earlier speech or about presentation skills you want to work on. What kinds of stage directions would you include in your outline (slow down, pause, take a breath, gesture, eye contact, etc.)?

What If . . .

How would your choices be affected by the following:

1. You are limited to using three note cards for your speech.
2. Your speech contains many statistics.
3. You will be speaking without a lectern/podium.

Govenor Rick Perry of Texas reads his speech from a teleprompter. Since you will speak extemporaneously, use a presentation outline on note cards to remind you of the big ideas.

The general guideline is that you should provide a full enough citation to enable an audience member to *evaluate* the quotation and to *find* it, should he or she so choose. In most cases, this will include the following:

- The name of the person being quoted
- A brief mention of his or her qualifications if they are not obvious
- The date, at least the year
- The title of the book, name of the journal or newspaper, or identity of other source

Here are some examples of oral citations:

1. "The columnist E.J. Dionne, in his 2004 book *Why Americans Hate Politics,* says..."
2. "Secretary of State Hillary Rodham Clinton was quoted in the July 1, 2012, *New York Times* ..."
3. "Constitutional law scholar Erwin Chemerinsky, writing in the 2011 *Harvard Law Review* ..."
4. "The Bureau of Labor Statistics unemployment rate, as reported on CNN on October 5..."
5. "According to the 1964 speech by protest leader Mario Savio archived on American-Rhetoric.com, . . . "

The easiest way to prepare oral citations is to put them on the note cards you will use with the presentation outline. Example 1 above might be put on the top of your note card as follows:

E.J. Dionne—columnist—2004—*Why Americans Hate Politics* (book)

Use of Stage Directions

Your speaking outline also can include reminders to yourself, as long as they are brief and don't interfere with the structure. Reminders like the following will alert you to things you plan to do during the speech:

I. Growing [REPEAT]
  A. Before WWI [SLOW DOWN]
  B. 1960
  C. After 1960
  D. 1996
  E. 2000
  F. 2008
  [SUMMARIZE/PAUSE]

II. Widespread [REPEAT]
  A. East
  B. Midwest
  C. South
  D. West
  [RESTATE POINT]

Your stage directions also can include cues to remind you when to refer to visual aids. In this way, your presentation outline not only will remind you of the structural pattern of the speech, but also will help you to coordinate your actions during its delivery.

Using an Outline in Rehearsal

In Chapter 11, you will learn how to practice presenting your speech. The speaking outline plays an important role in rehearsal. Be sure that its key words remind you of all the solid thinking you've done and the supporting material you've found. If a key word doesn't immediately prompt you to recall the details, change the key word to one that will. As you rehearse, it will become easier to see and remember the relationship between key words and the overall structure you have devised. Also, keep your preparation outline handy; you'll want to check during rehearsal that you are not leaving any gaps and that all your careful work is included in the speaking outline.

Sample Presentation Outline

Here is the presentation outline for Christopher Chiyung's speech on microfinance. If you compare it to the preparation outline, you will see how complete sentences have been reduced to key words, how essential stage directions have been included, and how key lines in the introduction and conclusion have been written out. As before, marginal comments are included alongside the outline. Study these to determine what is strong in the outline and what could be improved.

Presentation Outline
"Microlending in Evanston": by Christopher Chiyung

Introduction

I. **Attention-getting device:** "Give a man a fish, feed him for a day; teach a man to fish, feed him for a lifetime." This maxim relates directly to a sustainable practice that isn't as well known as it should be.

II. **Thesis:** Microlending in Evanston is crucial to allow depressed businesses to survive, institutions to be adequately funded, and the standard of living to rise.

III. **Preview**

Some key words might be in order here so the speaker will recall the key points in the preview.

Body

I. Effectiveness
   A. Empirical evidence from Bangladesh [GLOBAL ENVISION]
   B. MarketWatch in St. Louis
   C. Business in west Evanston [ANALOGY]

[*TRANSITION*: Success stories ar not as prevalent as they could be.]

II. MFIs lacks sufficient funding
   A. 10,000 MFI's = only 4 percent of market [WORLD BANK]
   B. MFI's in United States lack access to credit or financing [ANNIBALE]
   C. Graphs

[*TRANSITION*: Other benefits as well]

Notice that there is no need to reproduce the content of the quotations so long as Christopher has their text easily at hand.

III. Raising standard of living
   A. Creating jobs worldwide [LEMMON quote]
   B. Widespread benefits; health and education [SHERRADEN quote]
   C. Not just individuals; also communities [FLOOD quote]

Again, some key words here would help Christopher to remember what limitations he plans to discuss.

[*TRANSITION*: Acknowledge limitations but outweigh]

Conclusion

Do you think Christopher will remember the essential points of the summary? It might be helpful to include key words here.

I. ***Summary***

II. ***Closure:*** Please donate to LEND and spread awareness. It is a great way to understand the socioeconomic divide between Evanston's lakefront mansions and those struggling to make it on the west side.

III. ***Final plea:*** Even better, join next school year. Then we could all teach others how to fish, not just give the fish away.

Notice how the speaking outline follows exactly the structure of the preparation outline, while substituting key words for complete sentences and ideas. This is likely to be a valuable memory aid during the speech without getting in Christopher's way.

STRATEGIES FOR SPEAKING to Diverse Audiences

Respecting Diversity Through Outlining the Speech

Even a seemingly mechanical process such as outlining reflects important strategic choices. These strategies will remind you how the diversity of the audience affects outlining and organization.

1. Use your outline to make sure that each of your points is treated fairly and uses balanced sources. If you discover any biases, make sure that they are intentional and chosen in light of your specific audience.
2. Pay attention to how well your speech holds together. Using your outline, consider whether your points will connect as obviously for your audience as they do for you. Do your connections or does your order depend upon implicit knowledge that your audience may not share?
3. Recognize that cultures may be differently sensitive to the order in which ideas are arranged. For example: Are points of disagreement valued more than consensus? Is analyzing problems more important than identifying solutions? Is linear progression expected more than indirect progression?

SUMMARY

Organizing the body of the speech involves two sets of choices regarding main ideas as well as supporting materials:

- What to include
- What pattern of arrangement to use

Organization helps both the audience and the speaker, because:

- Form itself is persuasive.
- A recognizable form makes content easier to remember.
- Listeners can anticipate what is coming next and feel satisfied when they are right.
- Structure is an aid in preparing the speech and in remembering what comes next.

Main ideas are chosen by reference to:

- The speaker's strategy and purpose
- The themes most frequently identified in research

Main ideas should have these characteristics:

- Few in number
- Simple in phrasing
- Parallel in structure
- Coherent
- Complete in their treatment of the topic

Arranging the main ideas raises questions such as the following:

- Their dependence on one another
- The value of beginning with the familiar
- The importance of first and last impressions
- The nature of the audience

Several of the most common organizational patterns are as follows:

- Chronological
- Spatial
- Categorical (topical)
- Cause–effect
- Problem–solution
- Comparison and contrast
- Residues

Guided by audience analysis, speakers should select supporting material that is

- Tested for strength
- Easy to understand
- Vivid and interesting
- Consistent with what already is known
- Efficient to present
- Easy to cite in the speech

The same factors that govern arrangement of main ideas also affect arrangement of the supporting material.

The introduction shapes the audience's first impressions; its purposes are as follows:

- To gain attention and interest
- To influence the audience to view the speaker and topic favorably
- To state the thesis or purpose of the speech
- To preview how the speech will be developed.

Some common types of introductions include the following:

- Identifying with the audience
- Referring to the speech situation
- Stating the purpose of the speech
- Stating the importance of the topic
- Citing statistics and making claims
- Telling a story (anecdote)
- Using an analogy
- Asking a rhetorical question
- Quoting someone
- Using humor

The introduction should be

- Prepared after the body of the speech is well in hand
- Related to the body
- Brief but complete
- Worded (and practiced) carefully

The purposes of the conclusion are as follows:

- To complete the speech and signal to the audience that the end is near.
- To summarize the main ideas.
- To make a final appeal to listeners, asking them for a particular belief or action.

Among the common types of conclusions are the following:

- Summarizing
- Quoting someone
- Making a personal reference
- Challenging the audience
- Offering a utopian vision

Guidelines for planning a conclusion are similar to those of the introduction. When possible, the conclusion should return in some way to the introductory device.

Transitions serve to

- Give a sense of movement or progression to the speech by guiding listeners from one point to the next.
- Help the audience remember the main points and the structure of the speech.
- Reduce a speaker's distracting mannerisms in attempting to move from one idea to the next.

Transitions should have these characteristics:

- They should be succinct.
- They should use parallel structure if possible.
- They should provide signposting to guide the audience.

A complete transition includes three elements:

- Internal summary
- Link
- Internal preview

However, not all elements are presented explicitly in every transition.

Outlines display the formal structure of the speech in terms of numbers and letters.

The outline allows you to do the following:

- Visualize the form of the speech
- Check your reasoning and organizational pattern

The preparation outline:

- Is usually written in complete sentences.
- Includes separate sections for the introduction, body, and conclusion, each with separate numbering for the major divisions.
- Reflects coordination and subordination of ideas.
- Avoids overlap.
- Includes transitions as parenthetical comments.
- Includes citations within the outline or at the end in footnotes, a reference list, or a bibliography.

Because the preparation outline can be long and cumbersome, a presentation outline (sometimes called a *speaking outline*) is used during delivery. This outline:

- Follows the form of the preparation outline
- Is written in key words, not complete sentences
- Is reproduced on note cards
- Includes supporting material on separate note cards
- Includes information to be included in oral citations.
- May include notes about stage directions

The sample preparation and speaking outlines provided in this chapter show some of the issues to be addressed in order for the parts of a speech to come together into a well-planned, purposeful presentation.

Discussion Questions

1. In this chapter, we examined Stuart Kim's strategic plan to select and organize main ideas for a speech to convince listeners to donate to the United Way. But what would Stuart's speech be like if he faced a different rhetorical situation? Imagine that he is planning to speak to fellow volunteers at a year-end gathering to celebrate the United Way. Using the list of ideas that Stuart developed in his research, and drawing on your own imagination, discuss the selection and arrangement of appropriate main ideas for such a speech.
2. Which organizational pattern would you recommend for each of the following rhetorical situations? Why?

   To inform an audience of high school students about their college options

   To explain the history of your state capital to a group of German tourists

   To teach a group of coworkers how to use a new computer program

   To strengthen the commitment of fellow party members to a candidate's campaign

   To persuade an audience of restaurant and bar owners that smoking should be banned in public spaces

   To introduce an award-winning journalist who is about to give a lecture at a school assembly
3. What is the best organizational strategy for your next speech in this class? Gather in groups of four or five, and discuss your strategic plan with your classmates. Answer the following questions about each group member's strategy:
   a. Do the main ideas satisfy the criteria of simplicity, discreteness, parallel structure, balance, coherence, and completeness?
   b. Which other organizational patterns might be more suitable for the purpose and audience of this speech?
   c. Which type of supporting material is needed to develop each main idea in the speech?
4. Identify the basic organizational pattern used in a speech shown or presented in class. In small groups, discuss the benefit of a particular organizational pattern for this speech, and also think about alternative organizational patterns that might have worked well for that speech.
5. a. Which type of introduction would be most effective in each of the following speech situations?
      - A speech introducing the recipient of a lifetime achievement award
      - An informative speech to classmates about how to improve study skills
      - A speech to warn boaters about the dangers of "mixing water and alcohol"
      - A speech to strengthen volunteers' commitment to helping the homeless
      - A speech to reverse opposition to the death penalty

   b. In those same speech situations, which type of introduction would be least appropriate? Why?
6. What does an introduction need in order to prepare the audience effectively for the speech? Meet in small groups to answer this question. Each group member will present the introduction to a speech, and the other group members then will guess the speaker's purpose, the rhetorical situation, and the content of the speech. After everyone has made a guess, the speaker will reveal the actual purpose, situation, and content so that the group can compare intent and effect and then discuss ways to improve that introduction.
7. Which factors should a speaker consider when deciding how complete to make a particular transition? Discuss how the following constraints and opportunities might or might not influence your decision:
   - Your main points are organized in a dependent pattern.
   - Your main points are organized in an independent pattern.
   - You are moving between main ideas in the speech.
   - You are moving between subpoints within a main idea.
   - You are giving a speech that teaches a difficult concept to a group of students.
   - You are giving a speech to a group of protesters that enumerates well-known reasons to reinforce their commitment to the movement.

8. Many speakers write speeches without first developing an outline. How does the construction of an outline help a speaker to prepare a better speech? What are the disadvantages of creating an outline?
9. When developing an outline, how do you determine which ideas are subordinate to others? How do you determine which ideas are coordinate? As a class, construct an outline of this chapter, and discuss how it demonstrates the principles of subordination and coordination.
10. In small groups, share the preparation outline for your next speech with your classmates. Discuss the following questions:
    - Do the main ideas support the thesis?
    - Are the main ideas parallel and on the same level of importance?
    - Do the subpoints support the claims made in the main ideas?
    - Are the subpoints parallel and on the same level of importance?
    - Are there places where transitions are especially needed?

ACTIVITIES

1. Select the main ideas for your next speech.
   a. Use Checklist 9.1 to generate a list of potential main ideas.
   b. Subject each idea in the list to the tests described in this chapter: Is the idea essential? Can a more general statement combine several main ideas?
2. Arrange the main ideas for your next speech.
   a. Choose an organizational pattern and explain why it is more fitting than the other patterns discussed in this chapter.
   b. Write a paragraph or two to justify the pattern that you have selected. In doing so, ask yourself the following questions:

      Are the ideas dependent on or independent of one another?

      Are you beginning with the familiar or with the unfamiliar?

      Are the first and the last ideas strongest?

      Why is this pattern most appropriate for your audience and purpose?
3. Select the supporting material for your next speech.
   a. Apply the general principle described on page 275 to determine how much supporting material you need.
   b. Choose the supporting material that you will use to develop each main idea in the speech.
   c. Using the criteria in Checklist 9.4, write a sentence or two to explain why you have chosen each piece of supporting material.
4. Using the presentation note cards from one of your previous speeches for this course, design a new organizational pattern. Since the content of your speech has remained the same, but the order is different, decide whether this reorganization affected the meaning or effectiveness of the speech. Try to imagine other audiences and situations in which your new organizational pattern might be desirable.
5. On a copy of a speech manuscript you have retrieved from the library or the Internet, do the following:
   a. Mark the passages in the text that make up the introduction, conclusion, and transitions. What do these markings tell you about the organization of the speech?
   b. Identify the strategies used in the introduction and in the conclusion.
   c. Closely examine at least one transition in the speech. Is it complete? Can you identify the internal summary, link, and internal preview?
   d. Evaluate the effectiveness of the introduction, conclusion, and transitions. What makes them effective or ineffective? How would you improve them?
6. Create three potential introductions and conclusions for your next speech. Choose the best one of each, and explain why you think it is best.
7. Follow the instructions in Checklist 10.7 to plan strategic transitions for your next speech.
8. Using the three introductions that you wrote for activity two, read each to a group of other students. Together, make a list of positive aspects (to repeat) and mistakes (to avoid).

9. Take an essay that you have written for another class and create an outline in order to turn this written essay into a speech. Switching outlines with a partner in class, use this chapter's discussion of outlines to critique the structure of your partner's outline.
10. Construct a preparation outline for your next speech. Then, annotate your outline, explaining why you made the decisions that you made. Model the page layout of your outline after the sample preparation outline at the end of this chapter, using marginal notes to describe your strategic choices.
11. Create a speaking outline for your next speech, and use it to rehearse. Practice and modify the speaking outline until your delivery becomes smooth.
12. Some of the marginal comments on Christopher Chiyung's outlines in this chapter identify problems with the outline. Modify the preparation and speaking outlines to correct these problems.
13 Examine the outlining features of any common word processing program. Explain how they reflect and how they differ from the principles discussed in this chapter. Is there any difference between writing an outline by hand and using a computer program?

KEY TERMS

coherence
conclusion
coordination
internal preview
internal summary
introduction
logically dependent idea
logically independent idea
main ideas
organization
outline
parallel structure
partition
preparation outline
presentation (speaking) outline
primacy effect
recency effect
rhetorical question
signposting
subheadings
subordination
summary
transition

NOTES

1. Experiments show that an audience retains more of a message that is organized than of one that is not. See Ernest C. Thompson, "An Experimental Investigation of the Relative Effectiveness of Organizational Structure in Oral Communication," *Southern Speech Communication Journal* 26 (Fall 1960): 59–69.
2. Research confirms that organized speeches are comprehended more fully than unorganized speeches. See Arlee Johnson, "A Preliminary Investigation of the Relationship between Message Organization and Listener Comprehension," *Communication Studies* 21 (Summer 1970): 104–107.
3. One study suggests that an unorganized persuasive message may actually produce an effect that is opposite to what the speaker intended. See Raymond G. Smith, "An Experimental Study of the Effects of Speech Organization upon Attitudes of College Students," *Communication Monographs* 18 (November 1951): 292–301. Another study simply concludes that an extremely unorganized speech is not very persuasive. See James C. McCroskey and R. Samuel Mehrley, "The Effects of Disorganization and Nonfluency on Attitude Change and Source Credibility," *Communication Monographs* 36 (March 1969): 13–21.
4. Rhetorical theorist Kenneth Burke envisions form as "the creation of an appetite in the mind of the auditor, and the adequate satisfying of that appetite." See "Psychology and Form," *Counter-Statement,* Berkeley: University of California Press, 1931.
5. One study demonstrated that speakers who have a plan and practice that plan have fewer pauses in their speeches. See John O. Greene, "Speech Preparation and Verbal Fluency," *Human Communication Research* 11 (Fall 1984): 61–84.
6. See Howard Gilkinson, Stanley F. Paulson, and Donald E. Sikkink, "Effects of Order and Authority in an Argumentative Speech," *Quarterly Journal of Speech* 40 (April 1954): 183–92; and Halbert E. Gulley and David K. Berlo, "Effect of Intercellular and Intracellular Speech Structure on Attitude Change and Learning," *Communication Monographs* 23 (November 1956): 288–97. For a more recent look at how these questions affect other aspects of our lives, see Jaime Murphy, Charles Hofacker, and Richard Mizerski, "Primacy and Recency Effects on Clicking Behavior," *Journal of Computer-Mediated Communcation,* 11 (January 2006), 522–35.
7. For a few more ideas, see James A. Benson, "Extemporaneous Speaking: Organization Which Inheres," *Argumentation and Advocacy* 14 (Winter 1978): 150–55.
8. Some researchers who have tried to determine experimentally the place of evidence in a speech have concluded that there are just too many variables (such as the prior beliefs of the audience members, the credibility of the speaker, and the different types of evidence) to draw deterministic conclusions. See Kathy Kellermann, "The Concept of Evidence: A Critical Review," *Argumentation and Advocacy* 16 (Winter 1980): 159–72; and Richard B. Gregg, "The Rhetoric of Evidence," *Western Journal of Speech Communication* 31 (Summer 1967): 180–89.
9. Although first impressions may be durable, even such "first-impression bias" may be overridden. See Tanya Kraljic, Arthur G. Samuel, and Susan E. Brennan, "First Impressions and Last Resorts: How Listeners Adjust to Speaker Variability," *Psychology Science* 19 (April, 2008): 332–38.
10. Classical theorists often used words such as this, from the language of architecture, to describe the organization of speeches. See Leland M. Griffin, "The Edifice Metaphor in Rhetorical Theory," *Communication Monographs* 27 (November 1960): 279–92.
11. For more on the effects of humor in speeches, see C. R. Gruner, "Advice to the Beginning Speaker on Using Humor—What the Research Tells Us," *Communication Education* 34 (April 1985): 142–47. For a contemporary view on risqué humor and the varieties of interpretation open to an audience, see Lisa Glebatis Perks, "Polysemic Scaffolding: Explicating Discursive Clashes in Chappelle's Show," *Communication, Culture & Critique* 3 (June, 2010): 270–89.
12. For another list of introduction types, see Richard Whately, *Elements of Rhetoric,* Carbondale: Southern Illinois University Press, 1963, originally published 1828, pp. 170–72.
13. One early study found that, on average, introductions made up 9 percent of the total speech and conclusions made up 4 percent. See Ed Miller, "Speech Introductions and Conclusions," *Quarterly Journal of Speech* 32 (April 1946): 181–83.

14. For a discussion on the use of metaphor in conclusions, see John Waite Bowers and Michael M. Osborn, "Attitudinal Effects of Selected Types of Concluding Metaphors in Persuasive Speeches," *Communication Monographs* 33 (June 1966): 148–55.
15. Research shows that transitions make it easier for listeners to comprehend a speech. See Ernest Thompson, "Some Effects of Message Structure on Listeners' Comprehension," *Communication Monographs* 34 (March 1967): 51–57.
16. For another way of creating preparation outlines, see Collin Rae, "Before the Outline—The Writing Wheel," *Social Studies* 81 (July–August 1990): 178.
17. If you are having trouble with the mechanics of outlining, see James Gibson, *Speech Organization: A Programmed Approach,* San Francisco: Rinehart Press, 1971.
18. It has been shown that apprehensive speakers are less likely to follow the strategy that they had planned for the introduction of a speech. See Michael J. Beatty, "Public Speaking Apprehension, Decision-Making Errors in the Selection of Speech Introduction Strategies and Adherence to Strategy," *Communication Education* 37 (October 1988): 297–311. By including a detailed introduction in your speaking outline, you may be more likely to follow your plan, despite apprehension at the beginning of a speech. See, for example, Christina G. Paxman, "Map Your Way to Speech Success: Mind Mapping as a Speech Preparation Technique," *Communication Teacher* 25 (January 2011): 7–11.

CHAPTER

11

Effective Delivery

Taken from *Public Speaking: Strategies for Success*, Seventh Edition, by David Zarefsky.

In this chapter you'll learn about:

- Characteristics of Effective Presentation
- The Voice in Presentation
  - Volume | Pitch | Rate | Pauses | Articulation and Enunciation | Pronunciation | Inflection
- The Body in Presentation
  - Physical Appearance | Movement | Gesture | Facial Expression
- Modes of Presentation
  - Impromptu Presentation | Memorized Presentation | Manuscript Presentation | Extemporaneous Presentation
- Practicing for Speech Presentation
  - The Presentation Outline | Mental Rehearsal | Oral Practice | Simulation

People who fear speaking in public are usually anxious about some aspect of oral presentation. "What will I do with my hands?" "What if I forget my speech?" "How will I know if I'm talking too fast?" "Suppose I start shaking and can't control it?" Concerns such as these often lead people to avoid public speaking altogether.

In some ways, it would make sense to defer a discussion of presenting the speech until after we had learned more about selecting and researching a topic, testing the reasoning, and organizing the speech. But since many beginning speakers are most concerned about presentation, it actually makes sense to focus on it first.

There is a potential drawback here. Strange as it seems, one of the *least* effective ways to improve your presentation is to concentrate on it directly. If you are self-conscious about what to do with your hands, for example, thinking about them will make you feel even more awkward—they'll suddenly seem like 50-pound weights. Worrying about using your hands will distract you (and your audience) from the subject of your speech. In fact, the best way to improve your presentation is to keep your attention on the speech and on the audience.

Why, then, should you study presentation now if it might make you even more self-conscious? Because, by learning about the aspects of presentation and by practicing certain strategies, you can train yourself to speak "naturally" and confidently even if you are nervous about facing an audience. You will be more effective at your own approach to speaking.

Presentation is also called **delivery**; the two terms are used interchangeably to refer to how the voice and body help create the effect a speaker wants. The same ideas, even the same words, can elicit different reactions from an audience, depending on how you present them. Delivery, then, is much more than simply a way to "embellish" a speech. *How* a speaker says something affects what is really said, and so it also affects *what* listeners actually hear and understand.

Characteristics of Effective Presentation

A delivery style that contributes positively to the overall effect of your speech has three main characteristics:

1. *Effective delivery seems natural and uncontrived.* It does not call attention to itself or divert attention from the ideas in the speech.
2. *Effective delivery helps the audience to listen to, understand, remember, and act on the speech.* Listening carefully and critically to a speech is difficult; your presentation, if well done, can make it easier for your audience. For example, perhaps by lowering your voice, you can make the audience listen more carefully when you state your main idea. Or well-timed pauses may signal the transitions in your argument, making it easier to follow. Or a gesture that points to the audience may help you personalize your call for action in the conclusion of the speech.
3. *Effective delivery builds a sense of community between speaker and audience.* In most situations, the speaker wants to identify with listeners and symbolize that they are all members of the same speaking/listening community. In other words, the speaker wants to show **empathy** with listeners, to give them a sense that he or she knows what they think and can feel what they feel. Empathy is usually achieved through a presentation that invites audience members to listen and suggests that the speaker cares about them.

This chapter looks closely at how both your voice and your body can enhance the presentation of your speech and to help you build the desired relationship with listeners.

The Voice in Presentation

Unlike a singer, a speaker doesn't cultivate the voice as an end in itself, just to be expressive. Rather, a speaker uses the voice to advance the overall purpose of the speech.[1] Vocal cues are among the audience's earliest evidence in judging a speaker's *ethos*.

Seven dimensions of the voice can be drawn on to enhance your effectiveness as a speaker: volume, pitch, rate, pauses, articulation and enunciation, pronunciation, and inflection (see Table 11.1). Any vocal pattern—no matter how pleasant it first sounds—can easily become monotonous and distracting. Just as in conversation, to keep a speech interesting and to keep the audience listening, you want to create variety in the seven dimensions of your voice.

Volume

Volume refers to loudness; the higher the volume, the louder the voice. But how loudly should you speak? That will depend on the size and the shape of the setting and on whether you use a microphone. As a beginning speaker, you probably should err on the side of greater volume rather than of less (as long as you don't scream), in order to help convey a sense of self-confidence. To check and adjust your volume in any setting, watch listeners' reactions carefully when you begin to speak.

Besides regulating the overall loudness of your voice, remember to vary the volume at key points in the speech. You can emphasize an idea either by speaking louder or by lowering your voice. In both cases, listeners renew their attention because the vocal variety signals that they should listen carefully. By changing your volume, you can either understate an idea or overclaim it, depending on your purpose and the situation.

Feedback

Most audiences will let you know quickly if they cannot hear you, and their feedback will help you decide how loudly to speak. Also pay attention to the volume of other speakers and to how the audience reacts to them.

Students Brad Cummings, Alicia Lee, and Rosa Dominguez all gave classroom speeches on the same day. Brad was first, and he began in a very soft voice. Listeners had so much trouble hearing him that they moved forward in their seats and even cupped their ears with their hands. Unfortunately, for the first two minutes of his speech Brad looked only at his notes, and he missed the signal from the audience that he should speak more loudly. Alicia noticed the problem and was determined to avoid it when she spoke. But she overcompensated, speaking in a booming voice that made some listeners so uncomfortable that they actually pushed their chairs farther away and covered their ears. When Rosa's turn came, she knew that her volume should be somewhere between Brad's and Alicia's.

Amplification

If the audience is large, you can choose to use a microphone to amplify your voice; this gives you the option of speaking at lower volumes. It takes some practice to use a microphone effectively, however. You need to speak more slowly and to articulate words more distinctly so that they will not become slurred through amplification. Position your mouth a few inches from the microphone, and speak directly into it. If you hear static or noises or your voice feeds back to you, move farther from the microphone and speak more softly. Don't wait until the time of your speech to test the microphone, and make sure that it is turned on if you plan to use it. You'll undercut the power of your introduction if you have to stop to ask, "Can everyone hear me?"

Because most classroom speeches are not amplified, you need to learn to project your voice adequately by controlling volume and the other dimensions of vocal quality. But because so many auditoriums, large meeting rooms, and outdoor rallies

Table 11.1
Dimensions of Vocal Quality

Vocal Dimension	Description
Volume	Loudness
Pitch	Placement on the musical scale
Rate	Speed; number of words per minute
Pauses	Silences for emphasis or transition
Articulation and enunciation	Clarity and distinctness of individual sounds or words
Pronunciation	The accepted way to sound a given word
Inflection	The sound pattern for a sentence as a whole

require the use of amplification, you also should look for opportunities to practice speaking with a microphone.

Pitch

When we say that someone's voice is "high" or "low," we are referring to its **pitch**—the placement of the voice on the musical scale. A soprano has a higher pitch than a bass. The pitch of a voice is determined by the speed with which sound waves vibrate. The faster the vibration, the higher the pitch—and voice.

As shown in Figure 11.1, the normal pitch for any speaker is within a fairly narrow range. But extending higher- and lower-than-normal pitch is a larger range within which both speaker and listeners will be comfortable. You can raise or lower your pitch within this range for emphasis, and listeners will still find it pleasant to hear you. The widest range that the speaker is physically able to produce includes extreme pitches that are difficult for an audience to listen to. Extremely high pitches grate on the ears, like fingernails scratching a chalkboard; and extremely low pitches are distorted and too resonant, which most listeners also find displeasing.

Probably the most distracting pitch for listeners is a **monotone**—a very narrow, unchanging range that is used for the entire speech. Audiences quickly tire of it, and they tune it out; some people even fall asleep, lulled by the droning voice of the speaker. Because most people have a wider range of comfortable pitches than they customarily use, there's no reason to speak in a monotone. By varying your pitch, you can sustain the audience's interest, signal transitions in the speech, and emphasize important ideas.

If you record yourself delivering a speech, you may well discover that your pitch is higher than it sounds to you when you are speaking. Two factors account for this. First, your ability to hear your own voice is always distorted. Second, pitch rises under stress, and giving a speech is stressful for many people. The key to a pleasant pitch is to relax as much as possible. Control your breathing so that you have enough air to complete each sentence, relax your shoulder muscles, and project your voice from deep in your body rather than forcing it from your throat.

Rate

Rate is the speed at which a person speaks. The average rate is between 120 and 150 words per minute, but successful speakers vary considerably. John F. Kennedy typically spoke at a faster rate than did Ronald Reagan, and yet both presidents were immensely persuasive speakers.

Stereotype suggests that there also are distinct regional variations in rate—Southerners talk slower than Midwesterners do, and Easterners talk faster. In fact, regional differences in rate are much less dramatic than they used to be, partly because people move more often and partly because radio and television have created a national audience. Today, for example, many Southerners have just as rapid a speaking rate as anyone else.

Two factors that we considered in connection with pitch—stress and variety—also apply to rate.

Stress

Like pitch, rate goes up when a person is under stress. Students who practice their speech and time it to fill the 10 minutes required by the assignment may be surprised that the speech takes only 6 minutes when they deliver it in class. This happens not because they timed it inaccurately or forgot a large portion of the speech but because they sped up their rate under the stress of presentation.

Racing through your speech makes it difficult for the audience to follow and comprehend your ideas; listeners simply don't have time to process and react to what they hear. The remedy, as with pitch, is to control your breathing and relax. Pause frequently for breath, taking in enough air to complete each statement. And remember to watch for feedback from the audience since you also want to avoid speaking too slowly. A speech delivered at a very

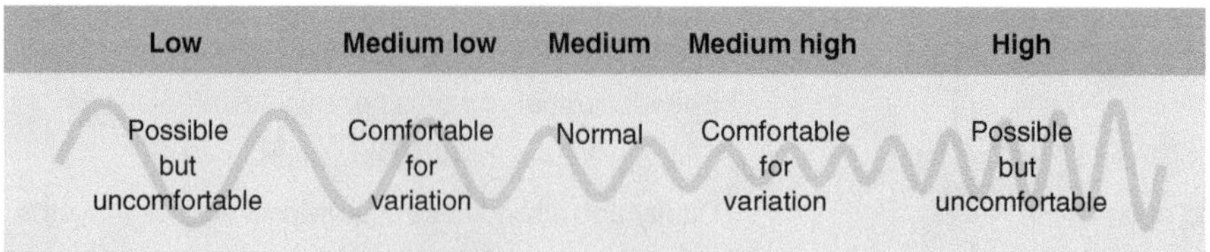

Low	Medium low	Medium	Medium high	High
Possible but uncomfortable	Comfortable for variation	Normal	Comfortable for variation	Possible but uncomfortable

Figure 11.1
Ranges of Pitch

slow rate will tire listeners and will invite distractions by giving them time to think about things other than your ideas.

Variety

Just as a monotonous pitch can seem boring, so too a monotonous, unchanging rate can displease listeners. A speaker who utters every word and sentence at the same rate—no matter how significant or suspenseful the ideas are—gives no clues about what's really important. All ideas receive about the same treatment, and listeners tend to tune out.

Beginning speakers sometimes think that the only way to vary rate is to speed up at critical places in the speech. In fact, *both* speeding up *and* slowing down can convey movement or suspense and can compel attention and interest. Indeed, the choice of rate may itself communicate a message. Slowing down suggests that the speaker is serious and that every word matters; the audience had better pay attention. It may also create a mood such as calmness or sadness or may suggest that the speaker thinks the ideas are difficult to grasp. Speeding up may propel a narrative forward or may evoke feelings of suspense, excitement, or outrage.

Most speakers vary their rate less than they think they do, and most could benefit by cultivating greater variety. Exercises in which you read a sentence or a list of words at differing rates will help you see how variety in rate can enhance interest in the message. Record yourself reading part of a famous speech at different rates. The playback may surprise you by showing that changes in rate may change meaning as well. This exercise should also give you a sense of which "normal" rate is most comfortable for you personally.

Pauses

Pauses are the brief silences within a speech. Although it may seem strange to include silence among the dimensions of voice, silence as well as speech can be highly communicative. The message in a pause is one of completeness and transition.

Properly used, pauses enhance a speech in two ways. First, they emphasize what the speaker said, providing a kind of nonverbal underlining. While the speaker is silent, listeners can think about what they have just heard, storing the thought in memory. A speaker who never pauses will move on to a new idea before listeners can make sense of the last one—and can unintentionally convey that all ideas are equally important or that none is really important. Without pauses, the audience will remember less and will be influenced less.

Second, pauses mark transitions in a speech. Because speaking doesn't have "punctuation marks," pauses—and variety in pitch and rate—can serve that function, telling the audience that the speaker has ended a section and is about to move on to a new topic or idea. This gives the audience time to absorb what was just said before switching again to active listening. It also gives speakers time to collect their thoughts before moving to the next idea.

Simple as the concept of pauses might seem, like the other dimensions of voice, pausing requires practice to be used effectively. You will want to avoid the following common problems.

Pausing too Often

A pause can signal the end of a paragraph in a speech, but that signal will be undercut if you also pause for every comma or semicolon. Too many pauses make a speech jerky and make the speaker seem nervous. Use pauses sparingly for effect.

Pausing at the Wrong Places

Because pauses are like punctuation marks, use them at the same places in the text as you would write the marks for which they stand. Pausing in the middle of sentences or ideas can confuse listeners and make comprehension difficult.

However, powerful effects sometimes can result from unusual pausing. One of the most memorable speeches of the twentieth century was delivered by Dr. Martin Luther King, Jr., on August 28, 1963. Standing in front of the Lincoln Memorial in Washington, D.C., he summoned his audience to work peacefully to attain civil rights for African Americans. He inspired listeners with his vision of the American Dream, closing with lines adapted from the song "America."

Instead of pausing after each sentence, Dr. King stopped briefly after each refrain of "Let freedom ring," building intensity and creating the musical effect of a crescendo. His midsentence pauses emphasized the repeating pattern in his examples and let the audience know what to expect next.

Not Pausing Long Enough

Uncomfortable with silence, speakers are notoriously poor judges of how long their pauses are; most imagine them to be much longer than is the case. Again an audio recording is a valuable aid. Time your recorded pauses, and compare them with how long you thought you paused when you spoke. All pauses should be relatively brief, of course, but the effects of a one-second pause and a five-second pause are considerably different.

Using Vocalized Pauses

Sounds such as "uh" and "umm" are **vocalized pauses**, meaningless sounds that a speaker produces during moments of silence. These almost always arise from nervousness and can be highly distracting to listeners. (Have you ever been in an audience that began to count the speaker's "uhs" and "umms"?) Sometimes vocalized pauses are words or phrases such as "like," "you know," "now then," "right?" and "okay?" Such repetition is a nervous response; the speaker is uncomfortable stopping for even a few seconds.

Whether syllables or words, vocalized pauses call so much attention to themselves that they interfere with the message. The remedy is easy to state but difficult to carry out: When you pause, *be silent.* Again, an audio recording is useful, because most speakers are not aware of their vocalized pauses. Listen to yourself, and discover how often you vocalize during a pause. If you do it frequently, make a mental note to *remain silent.*

Articulation and Enunciation

The related concepts of articulation and enunciation have to do with precise, distinct speech. **Articulation** refers to the clarity of *individual sounds;* **enunciation** refers to the distinctness with which *whole words* are sounded.

Articulation

For native speakers of English, common articulation problems include difficulty in forming the *th* sound (saying "dese" instead of "these") and dropping the final *g* from a word ("workin' " and "makin' "). Articulation can be improved through specific vocal exercises for particular sounds. The easiest way to diagnose articulation problems is to have someone else listen with you to a recording of your speech and to identify any sounds that call attention to themselves.

Not everyone articulates in the same way, of course. Speakers whose native language is not English, for example, often have difficulty with standard English articulation. Their goal should be not to articulate like native English speakers but to articulate clearly enough that they can be heard and understood. By the same token, listeners should make reasonable efforts to understand speakers whose articulation patterns are unfamiliar. In our increasingly diverse society, we all meet people who "speak differently." We should not allow cultural differences in articulation to block successful communication.

Enunciation

The distinctness with which *words* are sounded is another aspect of clarity that speakers need to consider. One specific problem is the tendency to slur words together. This is common in informal settings, where "I'm gonna," "Whaddaya know?" and "Howya doin'?" may replace "I am going to," "What do you know?" and "How are you doing?"[2] In a speech, however, such lack of enunciation will seem inappropriate; unless it is being used for effect, it is likely to influence negatively the audience's perception of the speaker.

The other extreme to avoid is being too precise in enunciation, saying each word so distinctly that you seem artificial and condescending to the audience. Speaking too distinctly not only distracts attention from the message but also may arouse negative feelings in listeners, who believe the speaker is either being snobbish or "hamming it up."

Pronunciation

Even when a word is familiar to the eye, we sometimes wonder how it should be sounded. Correct **pronunciation** refers to the accepted way to sound any given word. This includes such matters as which syllable to accent, whether to sound a vowel as short or long, and which optional consonant sound to use (for example, whether to give a *c* a hard sound, like a *k,* or a soft sound, like an *s*).

The Importance of Proper Pronunciation

First, the meaning of a spoken word may depend on its pronunciation, and mispronouncing it may prevent listeners from sensing which meaning you intend. The word *desert,* for example, means something different when you accent the first syllable (noun = "hot, dry place with lots of sand") than when you accent the second syllable (verb = "to abandon"). Second, like some of the other dimensions of vocal quality, mispronunciation calls attention to itself and may overshadow your ideas and message. Third, faulty pronunciation reflects negatively on a speaker's *ethos;* listeners may (mistakenly) get the impression that the speaker is ignorant or incompetent and hence is not to be trusted.

The phrase "proper pronunciation" may conjure up images of Eliza Doolittle, the British street vendor in *My Fair Lady* who could not speak "the king's English" and was stigmatized because of her lower-class **dialect**, or pronunciation pattern. Today in the United States, however, people are more likely to recognize and to accept that pronunciations vary according to geography (and according to economic

RHETORICAL WORKOUT

Exercise Your Voice

Go to a space (your room, an empty classroom, etc.) where you can practice using the different dimensions of your voice. Use this sentence from President Franklin D. Roosevelt's first inaugural speech to practice: "**Our greatest primary task is to put people to work.**" (The full text of this speech can be found at AmericanRhetoric.com.)

- **Volume:** First, speak the sentence at your normal speaking volume, as if you were talking to a friend just a few feet away from you. Then, speak it as loudly as you can without shouting. Now imagine what size of audience would fit in the space where you're practicing. Speak the sentence at a volume that would allow this audience to hear you clearly.
- **Pitch:** Speak the sentence using a fake, exaggerated high pitch—in a falsetto as if you had just inhaled helium. Then use a very low voice, an exaggerated bass, as if you were the announcer in a movie trailer. Try several levels in between, including your normal speaking voice. Is your normal pitch closer to the high end or the low end? What range of pitches do you think is most comfortable for your imagined audience to listen to?
- **Rate:** Say the sentence as fast as you can without skipping or slurring any words. Say it as slowly as possible without making it sound unnatural. Say part of the sentence quickly and the other part slowly. Try a few different rates and combinations. What rate or variety of rates makes the sentence sound best to your ear?
- **Pauses:** Say the sentence with a pause after the word "task." Say it again, pausing after "is." Does either sound better to you? Say the sentence with no pauses. How does this compare? If you pause after "greatest," does the pause make an interesting emphasis or does it sound awkward? Insert a vocalized pause such as "okay" somewhere in the sentence. How do you think your audience would respond to it?
- **Articulation and enunciation:** (a) Articulation: Change the sentence to "Our greatest primary task is putting people to work." Speak the sentence and drop the "g" in "putting"—say "puttin' people to work." Say the sentence again and articulate the "ing" precisely. How do these different ways of articulating the "ing" sound affect the impact of the sentence? (b) Enunciation: Try saying the sentence so it sounds like "Our greatest primary goal is taput people tawork." Now say it and carefully enunciate "to put" and "to work" as separate words. How do these different ways of enunciating words affect the impact of the sentence?
- **Pronunciation:** Practice pronouncing "our" in two different ways: (1) say "our" to rhyme with "are," then (2) say "our" to rhyme with "hour." Do you think either pronunciation is incorrect? Does either sound better to you? What if you were to pronounce "put" as "putt"? How would that change the meaning of the sentence?
- **Inflection:** Say the sentence with an inflection pattern that raises the pitch toward the end, as though it were a question: "Our greatest primary goal is to put people to work?" How does it change the meaning of the sentence? Now say the sentence several times, emphasizing a different word each time. Which words make sense to you to stress? What is the difference between stressing "our" and stressing "goal"?

and social class, among other cultural factors). We are more likely to hear speakers with a variety of dialects, and so we are less likely to view such differences as highly unusual.

On the other hand, just as slang is sometimes inappropriate, it remains important to speak standard American English in highly formal situations, where any sort of dialect may be seen as a distraction.

Pronunciation and Audience Analysis

In thinking about pronunciation and dialect, analyze your audience in relation to yourself, asking the questions listed in Checklist 11.1. Depending on your answers, design a strategy for your speech as suggested in the checklist.

Cultural diversity is a feature of many audiences. Even though dialects have become more familiar and less distinct, the acceptance of cultural diversity may, at times, require overcoming strongly held preconceptions.

Checklist 11.1

Pronunciation and Audience Analysis

Questions to Ask:

- Am I culturally different from most of my immediate listeners? If so, how might this affect their impressions of me and my speech?
- How do cultural differences affect my ability to achieve the goals of my speech?
- Does my pronunciation make me vulnerable to stereotyping by the audience? Conversely, is there a danger that I may stereotype the audience?

Strategic Decisions to Consider:

- Should I confront stereotyping, either directly or indirectly?
- How should I try to manage the impression that my pronunciation might give the audience?
- Should I modify my volume or rate, the amount of explanation I provide, or any of my supporting material?

Inflection

Articulation, enunciation, and pronunciation relate to the sound of individual syllables and words. **Inflection** is a similar concept except that it applies to the sentence as a whole. Appropriate inflection is important for the same reasons we have already discussed: Without it, you risk distracting listeners' attention, distorting your message, and damaging your credibility.

For example, one normal inflection pattern is to raise the pitch toward the end of a question and to lower the pitch toward the end of a statement. Speakers who reverse this pattern sound strange, and the audience may have trouble figuring out what they mean. Some speakers are so unsure of themselves that they raise their pitch after nearly every statement, hoping to discover whether the audience understands and agrees with their point. But this inflection pattern only makes ideas more difficult to follow, because they sound like questions rather than statements. In addition, the speakers appear to be unsure of themselves and overly tentative about whatever they say.

A given sentence may have more than one correct inflection pattern, and yet its meaning will change greatly depending on which pattern is used. Student Jordan Rivers, for example, was extolling the merits of a particular brand of breakfast cereal and confidently told the audience, "Nothing makes a better breakfast than this brand." He thought this statement was strongly positive, and so did most listeners. But Jordan was surprised to discover that a few audience members understood this remark differently, concluding that they really would be better off eating *nothing* for breakfast than eating this brand of cereal. Careful attention to inflection, taking care to stress the word *better* as well as the word *nothing,* would have given the audience a better clue about which meaning Jordan intended.

In general, think about the audience when you work on improving your speaking voice. Watch for feedback to ensure that your volume, pitch, rate, and degree of pauses are comfortable for listeners and to see that your enunciation, articulation, and pronunciation make your ideas clear. To avoid distracting from your message, aim for a presentation voice that has variety, that seems natural, and that captures and holds listeners' attention.

The Body in Presentation

Just as the voice gives the speaker important *auditory* and *verbal* resources, the body provides equally valuable *visual* resources. Not surprisingly, the same general principles relating to the voice in presentation also apply to the body. The speaker's body is used to enhance the message, not to call attention to itself. The body and its movements influence listeners' first impressions of the speaker and, hence, their willingness to take the speaker seriously. And changes in body placement and movement can mark transitions in the speech and add enough variety to keep the audience interested in and focused on the message.

Physical Appearance

Even before you begin to speak, audience members are forming impressions of the sort of person you are. This happens quickly and on the basis of superficial judgments, but those judgments are durable. Consequently, you want to avoid doing anything that will make you seem unprepared, incompetent, or unreliable.

Before You Speak

Consider the physical arrangement of the speaking space before deciding such things as how to approach the podium and what to wear. Is the setting large and impersonal or small and intimate? How formal or informal is the setting (and occasion)? Will you be able to establish eye contact with listeners, or will you be far away from them and speaking with a microphone?

Your appearance to an audience at an outdoor rally will be far different from how you appear to the same audience in a cathedral. Similarly, the settings for a retirement banquet, a business meeting, a commencement address, and a medical lecture are all different and can influence how the audience perceives you. Whenever possible, then, you should examine the speaking space and practice in it before presenting your speech.

Approaching the Speaking Space

Your physical appearance begins to create impressions as you walk to the front of the speaking space. If you start speaking while you walk, before facing the audience, you may seem in a hurry to finish and so unsure of yourself that you won't look the audience in the eye. Likewise, if you shuffle uncertainly toward the front, the audience may think you lack confidence and don't know what you are talking about. Such assumptions may be wrong, of course, but they affect your *ethos* and can create a "credibility deficit" that you'll have to overcome.

No matter how you feel about speaking, create the best first impression that you can. Walk firmly and purposefully to the front, pause to collect your thoughts, look directly at the audience, and then begin with confidence. Your body acts as a visual aid for the speech—the audience will be looking at you. Try to make your body's message match and reinforce the message of your words.

Clothes and Grooming

What you wear and your personal appearance—everything from hairstyle to footwear—are the stuff of first impressions and will affect your *ethos*. A badly dressed, unkempt speaker easily becomes the focus of attention and distracts the audience from the message. If you constantly push hair out of your face, wear a baseball cap that makes eye contact impossible, or fiddle with keys or jewelry, you practically beg the audience to focus on the distractions rather than the speech. Sometimes clothing choices can even send messages that contradict your thesis and tarnish your *ethos*. For example, wearing army fatigues during a speech promoting pacifism or wearing a popular brand of running shoes during a speech about the shoe company's questionable labor practices could send mixed messages to your audience.

Usually a speaker wearing in-line skates will not be dressed appropriately, but if the speech is about how in-line skates work, the attire may be just right.

Typically, speakers dress a bit more formally than audience members do.[3] The general public may attend a speech in sports attire, but the speaker is a major figure and is expected to look the part. In recent years, this unwritten dress code has relaxed considerably, allowing our choice of clothes to adapt to a variety of situations more effectively. When President George W. Bush threw out the first pitch at a baseball game, it would have been odd to see him in a suit. Yet President Bush dressed in a suit and tie when addressing the public formally—when he wanted to project a serious image. So do many business and entertainment speakers.

Sometimes, a speaker will want to make a cultural statement through unusual clothing and hairstyle and will resent any advice about adapting to the audience's expectations. For example, Sergey Brin, the founder of Google, frequently appears in public in jeans and tennis shoes. Other executives of technology companies may do the same, as a way to emphasize that their corporate culture is quite informal and that there is no hierarchy. You may be tempted to do this, too. But here, as elsewhere, audience analysis is critical; plan your personal appearance to advance your strategic goals.

Movement

How and where you position your body while speaking can also enhance or distract from the message. When student speaker Rachel Samuels stood behind the large, heavy podium in her classroom, only her head was visible. Recognizing the problem, Rachel stepped away from the podium to present her speech.

Even if the height of the podium does not affect your appearance this way, it's a good idea to step away from it occasionally. Many beginning speakers grip the podium tensely as though steering a car that is out of control. This may give you a sense of security, but it also puts a barrier between you and the audience. Instead, if you loosen your grip and step away from the podium at points in the speech, your body language will provide visual cues. For example, you can signal transitions in the speech by moving a step or two forward or to the side. And by moving toward the audience, you can show your trust and break down any imaginary walls between you and listeners.

The 1992 presidential debates among Bill Clinton, George Bush, and Ross Perot were the first that included one "Town Hall" format in which citizens in the audience asked questions. At one point, when Bill Clinton was asked how the federal budget deficit had affected him personally, he did not respond right away. First he took a few steps toward the questioner and established eye contact. Although he was actually speaking to a television audience of millions, Mr. Clinton seemed to be responding to this citizen one on one. The unstated message was that they had a common bond. And because Mr. Clinton had to face the cameras to answer his questioner, television viewers also felt that he was responding directly to them—and had a bond with them. Although this debate took place over 20 years ago, it still is the model for the "Town Hall" format. In contrast, in the 2008 "Town Hall" debate, the candidates seemed to move aimlessly on the stage and neither John McCain nor Barack Obama established a personal connection with members of the audience.

Although purposeful, planned movement will benefit your presentation, constant or aimless movement will be a great distraction. A speaker who moves all around the room for no apparent reason puts a burden on listeners; it's up to them to follow the movements and maintain eye contact. Many will simply stop trying—and stop listening as well. Speakers also should avoid shifting their weight from side to side, rocking on their feet. Like vocalized pauses, this nervous response calls negative attention to itself.

Speakers who use natural and relaxed gestures while speaking can enhance listeners' interest in and comfort with the message.

Just as you should not begin speaking until you have reached the front of the room and sized up the audience, do not gather up your notes and start returning to your seat while you are still speaking. The audience will not have a chance to absorb your final thoughts, and your conclusion will be weakened. You also will give the impression that speaking to them was painful and that you want to finish as soon as possible. Take your time, and take control of the situation. When you do return to your seat, walk confidently without calling attention to yourself.

Gesture

The term **gesture** refers to the movement of hands and arms during the speech as a means of emphasis. Many speakers are especially self-conscious about their hands and what to do with them while they speak. Some put their hands into their pockets—not to create an informal, conversational tone, but just to get them out of the way. These speakers usually seem tense, as though they are tightly clenching something buried deep in their pocket. Other untrained speakers fidget, moving their hands and arms aimlessly as a nervous reaction. One nervous student had a tendency to rotate his arms and hands in big circles so that he looked more like an orchestra conductor than a public speaker. Because such movements are not coordinated with the speech, they call attention to themselves and detract from the message.

In contrast, a well-timed, purposeful gesture heightens the power of both your text and your voice. But what is such a gesture like? Centuries ago, theorists of public speaking believed that certain gestures went naturally with particular words or ideas. They wrote manuals illustrating hundreds of gestures and their matching words so that speakers could learn the gestures by rote and perform them automatically when reciting the matching text.[4] Today, this approach is considered nonsense; such a presentation is so artificial and contrived that it seems funny.

Even so, not all speakers are naturally expressive with their hands. Whether you use many or few gestures does not matter; what matters is that your gestures support your message, and not draw attention away from it. If you made a video of yourself in informal conversation, you probably would discover gestures that you are unaware of—they simply come out naturally when you talk. A few possible uses of gestures are to emphasize the importance of a point, to suggest balance or opposition ("on the one hand," "on the other hand"), and to position ideas in space and time.[5]

Above all, gestures used in presentation should appear natural. Achieving this is less a matter of memorizing gestures than of becoming familiar with the general rhythm of gesture. It has three steps:

1. The **anticipation step**, in which you bring your hands to a position from which a gesture can easily be made. If you are gripping the podium or handling several pages of notes, gesturing will be difficult and awkward. You need to be in a position that lets you execute a gesture naturally.
2. The **implementation step**, the few seconds in which you execute the gesture. Typically, your hands will be somewhere between the waist and shoulders, an area that eases natural motion and is also visible to audience members. Perhaps most important in implementing the gesture is to *follow it through.* Untrained speakers often make a half-gesture, raising a hand partway without completing the motion. Such a gesture has little purpose or effect. It suggests that the speaker is nervous.
3. The **relaxation step**, in which you return your hands to their normal position—whether at your side, in front of you, or resting gently on the podium. Without this step, you risk being trapped in continuous gesture. If your hands are in the visual space where gestures take place and you haven't returned them to rest, you may find yourself gesturing repeatedly and in the same way for every word or idea. That, of course, dilutes the power of the gesture.

Finally, don't worry too much about gestures. Although "what to do with my hands" is a concern for many speakers, the issue is relatively unimportant. Gestures tend to take care of themselves as long as you avoid distracting mannerisms, practice the three steps of gesture, and concentrate on your message.

Facial Expression

The speaker's facial expressions are another powerful element of nonverbal communication that can heighten or detract from the speech. Obviously, a smiling speaker communicates something much different from a frowning one. But someone who smirks or grins throughout a serious presentation will seem out of place and hence not believable, as will a speaker who delivers a lighthearted message but shows no facial expression at all. Again, it is valuable either to record your speech or to have someone observe you practicing it. Discover whether your facial expressions are consistent with and support the message in your text.

Making Eye Contact

One aspect of facial expression, **eye contact**, deserves special attention. Speakers who do not look the audience in the eye may lose credibility. In mainstream American culture, not looking at someone is widely thought to mean that the person is lying or has something to hide. Speakers from cultures with different norms about eye contact may be misunderstood and misjudged by an American audience.

Another important point is that eye contact lets you see how the audience is responding to the speech; it provides feedback. Listeners' facial expressions often indicate whether the message is clear or needs explanation, whether claims seem persuasive or not, and so on. Such feedback helps you adjust your presentation to fit the audience while you speak. But if you stare at your notes or gaze at the back wall, you cannot engage your audience and take advantage of feedback.

Maintaining Eye Contact When Using Notes

How can you maintain eye contact if you are using notes? It takes practice, but the idea is to glance down at your notes during the brief moments when you pause and then to gracefully resume eye contact when you start to speak again. Having notes that are in large print and easy to read will help you. What you want to avoid are jerky movements of your head and eyes between your notes and your audience, and looking down at your notes while you're stating or explaining your main ideas.

Speaking to a Large Audience

Maintaining eye contact with a large audience presents problems. You can't look at everyone, but if you focus only on nearby listeners, those farther away will feel left out. And if you keep turning your head mechanically from side to side, the constant sweeping movements will be a distraction, and you won't really make eye contact with anyone. The remedy is not to fix on particular audience members but to focus on general areas of the audience. Mentally divide listeners into three or four groups, and shift your focus among them to correspond to transitions in the speech. This lets all listeners feel—to some degree—that you are talking directly to them, and you can monitor the groups for feedback. At the same time, your shifting focus helps to signal transitions in the speech.

By resting your hands lightly on the podium rather than gripping it for dear life, you will be relaxed and your hands will be free for gesture.

Speaking for the Camera

Different problems arise when speaking either in front of a camera or for the camera. You *may* be addressing a much larger audience, but when you focus on the camera, you are speaking only to a single "listener" who provides no direct feedback through eye contact. If you are speaking to a group of people but are also being recorded on video, you must choose to give one audience priority over the other. For instance, if the immediate audience is more important, focusing on the camera will stifle your ability to distribute your eye contact effectively; the live audience may feel ignored. But if you are more concerned with the virtual audience, moving your eyes away from the camera may make you seem shifty, detracting from the recorded speech. Think about the difference between YouTube videos that were created for an Internet audience and the speeches you give in class. In the YouTube videos, the speaker purposefully addresses the camera, thinking of the audience watching the video online. But in class you will try to engage with your live audience precisely by not focusing exclusively on any one person. This is a trade-off. Moreover, trying to address both live and virtual audiences can detract from your appeals to either.

Being Dynamic

One important component of *ethos* is dynamism. A dynamic speaker is one who appears animated and enthusiastic. Eye contact, smiles, and especially variety in facial response are a few signs of enthusiasm. Although trained actors may be able to "fake" a sense of animation, most speakers cannot. The easiest way to convey the impression that you are animated and enthusiastic about your topic and about speaking to your audience is for you to actually feel that way. As we saw in Chapter 9, this is an important consideration in audience analysis and topic selection.

Modes of Presentation

Most theorists identify four general modes of presentation: impromptu, memorized, manuscript, and extemporaneous. No matter which mode you choose, you can use voice and body to enhance the presentation, but the modes also involve choices that can strengthen or weaken the speech.

Impromptu Presentation

When you have little or no time to prepare specifically for a speech, you make an **impromptu presentation**. Perhaps someone at a meeting says something that inspires you to respond, and so you raise your hand to offer your views. You thereby give a speech seemingly without any preparation at all. In fact, you may have "spent a lifetime" preparing for that speech. The issues are important to you, and you've thought about them a great deal. But you never imagined that you would be speaking about them on this particular occasion.

Structure an impromptu presentation as simply and clearly as possible. Because you do not have a chance to plan the speech in detail, you may become entangled in the web of your thoughts. The

CHOOSE A STRATEGY: Presenting Your Speech

The Situation

You are a teacher at a grade school and your principal has asked you to present the new curriculum plan to the parents in your community and also to answer any questions they may have regarding these changes. There have been several major additions to the curriculum, and you want to make sure that each change is explained clearly to the parents. You will be presenting in the school gymnasium where a microphone and podium will be set up the evening of your speech—which is two weeks from today.

Making Choices

1. Which presentation mode do you plan to use? Why? What are the benefits and/or drawbacks of this mode?
2. How will you incorporate the podium into your presentation, if at all? Will you use the microphone? Why or why not?
3. How will you prepare for your speech? How will you prepare to answer the audience's questions?

What If . . .

How would your presentation strategies change if the following were true? Would your mode of presenting change? Would your practice strategies change? Why or why not?

1. You are presenting to a group of parents in a small classroom.
2. You have met each of the parents on an individual basis and know that they support the curriculum changes.
3. You have met with each of the parents on an individual basis and know that they do not support the curriculum changes.
4. Your principal planned to make this presentation but has become ill at the last minute. You need to give this presentation tomorrow.

key is to focus on a very small number of main ideas, previewing and summarizing them so that listeners have no doubts about your thesis or how the ideas develop it. Impromptu speaking also often takes cues from previous speakers, referring to their specific points and suggesting how their message relates to yours.

Memorized Presentation

A **memorized presentation** is the opposite of impromptu; you pay such close attention to your text that you commit it to memory. This mode of speaking was highly valued in the past. School children studied famous orations and recited them by rote. Great orators often wrote out their entire speeches and then committed them to memory.

Today few theorists advise anyone to memorize a speech. Besides the unnecessary investment in energy, speaking from memory has other problems. First, you might not take feedback into account and adapt to the audience's needs. Second, if you write and then memorize a speech for oral delivery, the recital may be stiff and stilted. It will sound memorized, which quickly causes an audience to lose interest. Finally, a memorized text raises concern about what might happen if you forget a line. Some speakers can ad-lib and patch things up quickly, but many become flustered; having forgotten the memorized words, they don't know what to say.

Although memorized presentation is generally discouraged, it can be helpful to memorize the first few sentences of your introduction and the last few sentences of your conclusion. Then you will begin the speech confidently and end it solidly, without trailing off. And if you want to use a particular phrase or line in the speech, you might commit that to memory and plan where it would fit best. But the practice of memorizing an entire speech has fallen into disuse—deservedly.

STRATEGIES FOR SPEAKING to Diverse Audiences

Respecting Diversity Through the Presentation of Your Speech

Your voice will affect how easily people will hear you, and your gestures will mean different things in different cultures. Here are strategies that will help you to consider audience diversity when presenting your speech.

1. **Volume:** Adjust your volume to your audience. Some cultures (such as people from Thailand) normally speak at a lower volume than do Americans. Yet if you are speaking to people with hearing impairments, you will need to speak louder.
2. **Gestures:** Consider how certain hand gestures may mean different things for different cultures. For instance, putting your forefinger to your thumb means "O.K." in the United States but can be offensive in Mexico or Syria.
3. **Stereotyping:** Using slang or false dialects that may stereotype your audience members can also be offensive.
4. **Speaker and audience:** Recognize that different cultures have different expectations about the physical relationship between speaker and audience.

Manuscript Presentation

Like a memorized speech, **manuscript presentation** also involves a text that is prepared word for word, but the speech is read rather than delivered from memory. This speaking mode is useful in highly formal situations, when specific wording is critical. The president of the United States uses manuscript presentation for the State of the Union address and for most speeches about major policies. The risk of saying the wrong thing is too great to rely on other presentation modes. Many leaders in business, labor, and community organizations use manuscript presentation when they speak in high-stakes situations where their precise wording is extremely important. Major presentations at corporate or academic meetings also are often read from manuscript.

Manuscript presentation also is useful when precise timing is important, as when speaking on radio or television. This was clearly illustrated in 1952, when vice presidential candidate Richard Nixon appeared on television to defend himself against charges of financial irregularities. He ended by urging listeners to express support for him by writing to the Republican National Committee. But Mr. Nixon was not speaking from manuscript, and he ran out of time as he was telling the audience where to write. Millions of listeners were able to respond anyway, but if you watch a recording of that speech, you will see how awkward the ending is.

Although manuscript presentation may be appropriate in these specific circumstances, as a general rule it is not the best mode. First, reading a paper aloud is not the same as speaking directly to an audience. It is very difficult to write in an oral style. Audiences recognize the difference and are less attentive; the manuscript interferes with direct communication between the speaker and listeners.

Second, very few people are well trained in the art of reading aloud. Even a text that is rich in imagery, that identifies with the audience, and that offers solid argument may be negated if it is read indifferently or with vocal patterns that do not match the intent of the message.[6]

Third, presenting a speech from manuscript makes it difficult to maintain eye contact and profit from feedback. Accomplished speakers sometimes can do it—taking in a sentence or two of their text and then gracefully looking up and speaking to the audience. But many speakers do this awkwardly, which is distracting at best, and they often lose their place in the text.

Extemporaneous Presentation

A speech that is prepared and rehearsed but is neither written out nor memorized is called *extemporaneous presentation.* This mode is recommended for most speakers and speeches, because it encourages a conversational quality and is flexible enough to permit adaptation to feedback. Extemporaneous speaking is not impromptu; the speaker has outlined and planned the speech carefully, has a specific structure in mind, and probably uses prepared notes during presentation. But no word-for-word text exists in advance of delivery, and the speech is not memorized or read aloud.

The advice that you develop a preparation outline and a presentation outline assumed an extemporaneous mode of presentation. The preparation outline helps you identify your main ideas, their relation to each other and to your thesis, and the order in which to present them. The presentation outline includes enough key words to help you keep the ideas straight and to present them as intended. As you practice the speech, you will try out different ways of verbalizing the ideas, getting a sense of how the speech sounds and what you mean. But you will not memorize or write down the specific wording (other than introductory and concluding sentences). Speaking extemporaneously lets you discuss ideas informally and conversationally. Your focus will be on ideas rather than on specific words, making it easier to maintain eye contact and modify your message in response to feedback.

Practicing for Speech Presentation

The idea of practicing to appear natural may not seem quite so strange, now that we have explored how the speaker's voice and body can be used in a planned way to bring about that result. Yet the easiest way to fail at the goal is to focus too much on your voice or body rather than on what you are going to say and on what you are trying to achieve.

Thinking consciously about your strategic objectives—what you wish to share with the audience, how you want to affect listeners, or what you want audience members to believe or do after hearing your speech—should focus your attention on the purpose of the speech. If you keep content and purpose clearly in mind, then you can practice using your voice and body to *contribute* to those goals rather than to be ends in themselves.[7]

The most important advice about practice is to begin early. Skills of presentation take time to perfect, and you will learn them best when you are relaxed, not tense. Unless the assignment really calls for an impromptu speech, waiting until the last minute is never a good idea. Things will not seem to fall into place. The speech may seem disorganized or not artfully crafted; or the content and presentation may be out of sync; or the gestures, movement, and vocal variations may be distracting. Admittedly, the advice to start early on a task is easier to give than to follow, but it will pay great dividends in the case of speech presentation.

Each person takes a unique approach to practicing a speech, and you should find methods that work well for you. In general, however, a four-step process is likely to be effective:

1. Develop the presentation outline.
2. Mentally rehearse the speech.
3. Practice the speech orally.
4. Simulate the speech setting.

The Presentation Outline

Develop your presentation outline and talk it through several times. By referring only to the outline, you should be able to articulate your main ideas and the links in your thought. Each key word should trigger a more complete thought. If this does not happen, revise the presentation outline to include more key words, different words, or a different structure.

This is also the time to write out or memorize any portion of the speech for which exact language is essential, such as a few introductory sentences or your conclusion. You might include your thesis statement, if you want to have its precise wording in front of you. Although excessive memorization is discouraged, some parts of even an extemporaneous speech depend on exact wording, and this is the time to develop the words you plan to use.

Mental Rehearsal

Picture an imaginary audience, and run through the speech in your mind while holding this image. Try to see yourself in the speaking situation, and think through what you would say. As you rehearse mentally, you may hit upon a particular transitional phrase or may discover the most effective way to

Practicing in the room where you will speak can make you more comfortable—even if it is an empty auditorium.

A Question of ETHICS

Ethics in Delivery

Speakers reveal how invested they are in their speeches by the way they present speeches to an audience. What responsibilities do speakers have with respect to performance? Is it ethical, for example, to assume a natural, conversational, informal stance if you really are hostile toward the audience? Is it ethical to badger or "browbeat" an audience when doing so can wear down their resistance? If an animated delivery leads an audience to accept a position the speaker knows to be weak, is that ethical? Is it ethical to mask your real anxieties by appearing to be confident? Similarly, when we are listeners, to what extent do we allow the presentation of a speech to affect our judgment of the speaker and the message? Do we trust a speaker who has memorized the speech more or less than a speaker who uses notes? More or less than a speaker who reads a manuscript? Does the effect of presentation on our judgments raise any ethical issues?

express an idea clearly. Speakers who skip the step of mental rehearsal often fail to consider the big picture of how the speech will look and sound when everything comes together. As a result, the speech may seem fragmented or unnatural to an audience.

Oral Practice

Practice the speech orally, several times, under a variety of conditions. Distributed practice (brief periods of practice spread over time) is likely to be more effective than massed practice (a few lengthy sessions shortly before you speak).

For the first few times, deliver the speech with no one else present. Although this will not give you feedback, you will become sensitive to the sound of the speech, to its length and timing, and to opportunities to enhance your use of voice and body. Because you are both speaker and listener, you'll want to satisfy yourself that everything fits together correctly.

Then practice with a small group of friends. Even two or three people are enough, if you trust them to give candid reactions that might improve the speech. This stage of practice will let you actually share your thoughts with others and see how the speech is affected by having an audience present. Use such "early reviews" to check whether the design of the speech will achieve your purpose. Ask especially whether listeners got a clear sense of your thesis, whether the speech moved clearly from one point to another, whether you spent too much or too little time on anything, and whether the speech seemed too slow or too fast. Raise any other specific concerns you have about the speech. One study found that speakers who practiced before an audience received higher evaluation scores on their speeches than those who did not.[8] The more feedback you get from these first listeners, the stronger your final presentation will be.

Checklist 11.2
Practicing the Speech

1. Develop the presentation outline.
   - ☐ Talk through the outline several times.
   - ☐ Write out or memorize any portion for which exact language is essential.
2. Mentally rehearse the speech.
3. Practice the speech orally:
   - ☐ With no one else present.
   - ☐ With a small group of friends.
   - ☐ On video if possible.
4. Simulate the speech setting.

Record your presentation, if possible, and study it to see how the speech looks and sounds to others. This step makes many people uncomfortable, because they think they look and sound different from what the video reveals. But try to set aside such feelings, focusing instead on what listeners will see and hear. For example, if the video shows that you are looking only at your notes and are not making eye contact, you can correct this by the time you deliver the speech. The video also might reassure you about some aspect of performance, such as gestures—perhaps they appear more natural than you thought. Look for positive feedback as well as negative; the video can build your confidence even as it reveals areas that need improvement.

Simulation

Either practice the speech in the room where you'll speak, or simulate that setting as closely as possible. For instance, if you will be speaking in a large auditorium, practicing there or in a similar space will show you how much you should exaggerate gestures and movement so that they can be seen at a distance. If the setting will be smaller and more intimate, you may need to practice modulating your voice so that you don't seem to be shouting. And if you will be using a microphone, practicing with it will help you control and adapt your voice in ways that avoid distortion and slurring. Finally, this step will make you more comfortable with the setting so that, when the time comes, you can focus on your audience and your message.

SUMMARY

An effective delivery style should:

- Seem natural and not call attention to itself or detract from the message.
- Help the audience listen to, understand, remember, and act on your speech.
- Build a sense of community between speaker and audience.

The speaker's voice:

- Is a resource for the speaker.
- Gives the audience insights into the speaker's personality.
- When varied, keeps listeners interested and suggests emphases within the speech.

Dimensions of voice that can enhance a speech:

- Volume
- Pitch
- Rate
- Pauses
- Articulation and enunciation
- Pronunciation
- Inflection

The speaker's body and movements:

- Are visual resources for the speaker.
- Influence listeners' first impressions of the speaker.
- Can indicate transitions in the speech.

Resources of the body that can enhance a speech:

- Physical appearance
- Movement
- Gesture
- Facial expression

Modes of presentation:

- Impromptu
- Memorized
- Manuscript
- Extemporaneous (usually preferred)

Speech presentation is improved by practice:

- Develop the presentation outline.
- Mentally rehearse.
- Practice orally with feedback.
- Simulate the speech setting as closely as possible.

Discussion Questions

1. How does delivery vary according to purpose? In what ways might delivery be different for a eulogy, an instructional speech, and a speech of dissent?
2. In what ways does delivery style contribute to or detract from a speaker's strategy? Discuss and compare the strategies and styles of some famous speakers—for example, Hillary Clinton, Michele Bachmann, Steve Jobs, Jesse Jackson, Jon Stewart, George W. Bush, and Barack Obama. Discuss both their manuscript delivery in formal televised speeches and their extemporaneous delivery in more informal settings.
3. In what ways might you improve your delivery? Each student should present a short introduction to a familiar person or thing, and classmates should then discuss the strengths and weaknesses of the presentation. Focus especially on aspects of delivery that the speaker is unlikely to recognize by examining a recording, such as articulation, enunciation, and pronunciation.

Activities

1. Select a passage from a speech that you can obtain in manuscript form. Record yourself presenting this passage first at a very slow rate, then at a moderate rate, and finally at a quick rate. Then vary the rate *within* the passage, slowing down or speeding up as needed to best convey the message. Repeat this process, varying the volume of your delivery. Listen to the recording of these variations, and identify how changes in rate and volume affected the presentation.
2. Write out the introduction and conclusion of your next speech. Before you practice the delivery of these sections, decide where you want to include pauses and which words you want to emphasize by changes in volume and pitch. Record yourself and listen to see if these decisions worked as you planned. If not, try to determine why.
3. Watch a video of yourself presenting a speech. Pay close attention to your delivery style—your volume, rate, and pitch variations; whether you use vocalized pauses; your eye contact, posture, and gestures; and so on. List the things about your delivery style that currently detract from your message and that you would like to improve. How might you go about improving them?

Key Terms

anticipation step
articulation
delivery
dialect
empathy
enunciation
eye contact
gesture
implementation step
impromptu presentation
inflection
manuscript presentation
memorized presentation
monotone
pauses
pitch
pronunciation
rate
relaxation step
vocalized pauses
volume

NOTES

1. For an excellent overview of the physiology of the voice mechanism and a wide selection of exercises to improve the speaker's voice, see Linda Gates, *Voice for Performance,* New York: Applause Books, 2000.
2. For a humorous treatment of the tendency to slur words, see William Safire, "Slurvian," *New York Times Magazine* (Sept. 17, 2000): 37, 40.
3. Studies have shown that a speaker's attractiveness has an influence on the persuasiveness of the message. Attractiveness can be achieved at least partly through clothing and grooming. See Shelly Chaiken, "Physical Appearance and Social Influence," *Physical Appearance, Stigma, and Social Behavior: The Ontario Symposium,* vol. 3, ed. C. Peter Herman, Mark P. Zanna, and E. Tory Higgins, Hillsdale, NJ: Lawrence Erlbaum, 1986, pp. 143–77.
4. For examples of this, see John Bulwer, *Chirologia: Or the Natural Language of the Hand;* and *Chironomia: Or the Art of Manual Rhetoric,* first published 1644, ed. James W. Cleary, Carbondale: Southern Illinois University Press, 1974; and Gilbert Austin, *Chironomia: Or, A Treatise on Rhetorical Delivery,* first published 1806, ed. Mary Margaret Robb and Lester Thonssen, Carbondale: Southern Illinois University Press, 1966.
5. For more discussion of gestures in informal conversation and in speeches, see Naomi Jacobs and Alan Garnham, "The Role of Conversational Hand Gestures in a Narrative Task," *Journal of Memory and Language* 56 (February 2007): 291–303.
6. Researchers Herbert W. Hildebrandt and Walter W. Stevens discovered this rather accidentally when trying to determine whether extemporaneous or manuscript delivery was more effective. See their "Manuscript and Extemporaneous Delivery in Communicating Information," *Communication Monographs* 30 (November 1963): 369–72.
7. It is important to remember that delivery should match the speaker's material, intent, and personality. See Harry W. Bowen, "A Reassessment of Speech Delivery," *Communication Quarterly* 14 (November 1966): 21–24.
8. Tony E. Smith and Ann Bainbridge Frymier, "Get 'Real': Does Practicing Speeches Before an Audience Improve Performance?" *Communication Quarterly* 54 (February 2006): 111–25.

CHAPTER

12

Language and Persuasion

Taken from *Persuasion, Social Influence, and Compliance Gaining*, Fifth Edition by Robert H. Gass and John S. Seiter.

When William Shakespeare wrote, "A rose by any other name would smell as sweet," he found an eloquent way to note that words and the things they represent have no necessary connection. Indeed, you can't change a flower's scent just by renaming it "armpit" or "manure." That being said, sometimes the names we give things affect how we react to those things. For example, because we attach meanings to words and names, we might react differently to a woman named Rose than we would to a man with the same name. As another illustration, consider the story of Adolf Hitler Campbell, a 3-year-old from Hunterdon County, New Jersey, whose parents were unable to get a supermarket to write the child's name on his birthday cake, presumably because of the connotations associated with such an infamous name. After meeting with resistance, the family, including Adolf's little sister, JoyceLynn Aryan Nation Campbell, hightailed it to Pennsylvania, where a Wal-Mart employee was willing to produce their cake ("Three-year-old Hitler," 2008).

These examples illustrate an interesting property of language that is one of the main themes of this chapter. Specifically, because we associate meanings with words, words have the power to influence us. Indeed, the maxim "The pen is mightier than the sword" is correct. Words are the primary means of persuasion. They not only affect our perceptions, attitudes, beliefs, and emotions but they also create reality.

Because words are so important in the process of persuasion, the purpose of this chapter is to examine words and their effects on social influence. We begin by discussing the nature of symbols and of meaning, which are integral to understanding the relationship between language and persuasion.

Symbols, Meaning, and Persuasion: The Power of Babble

What is a *symbol*? A very basic definition is that a symbol is something that represents something else. Names are a good example. Your name represents who you are, just as the word *pig* represents an animal with a curly tail and slimy snout.

As noted above, one important characteristic of symbols is that they are arbitrary. In other words, symbols have no necessary connection to what they represent, although we sometimes seem to forget this. For example, S. I. Hayakawa (cited in Adler, Rosenfeld, & Towne, 1995) told the story of a little boy who thought that pigs were called pigs because they are so dirty. The word *pig*, however, has no direct connection to the curly-tailed animal, just as your name, although it may seem to fit, has no necessary connection to you. That is, when your parents were trying to decide what to call you, there was nothing written in stone that said you had to be given a certain name. You could just as easily have been called Binky or Unga Bunga. Don't laugh—the singer Frank Zappa named his children Moon Unit and Dweezil, and when tax authorities told a Swedish couple that they had to give their 5-year-old son a name or pay a fine, the couple named the child Brfxxccxxmnpcccclllmmnprxvclnmckssqlbb11116 ("The best and worst," 1996). As wrong as such names might seem, however, they're not. When it comes to finding representations of things, there's not one "right" word or symbol.

Because they are arbitrarily connected to what they represent, a second characteristic of symbols is that they are conventionalized, which means that if we want to use a symbol to communicate to someone else, we have to agree on the symbol's meaning. Without some measure of agreement on the meanings of words, communication and persuasion would be difficult, if not impossible. If you've ever tried to communicate with someone who speaks a different language, you know this is true.

Connotative and Denotative Meaning: That's Not How I See It

Up to this point, we've noted how important it is for communicators to agree on the meaning of the symbols they use. With that said, however, we are certain that, without telepathy, total agreement on the meaning of symbols is impossible. Of course, the degree to which people agree may depend on the type of meaning with which we're concerned. There are at least two meanings for every word. The first, the *denotative* meaning, is a word's direct, explicit dictionary definition.

The second type of meaning, *connotative*, refers to the thoughts and emotions associated with a word. As you might expect, the connotations associated with words vary widely from person to person. To illustrate, let's return to pigs. Although all of us might agree on the denotative meaning of the word *pig* (i.e., curly-tailed animal with snout), our attitudes associated with the word may be quite different. For instance, compared to a farmer's child who grew up sloppin' hogs, a person who grew up reading books or watching movies about cuddly, talking pigs, such as Wilbur from *Charlotte's Web* or Babe from the movie *Babe*, would probably have a different view of pigs. In contrast, the members of some religious groups, Jews and Muslims, are forbidden to eat pork, which is perceived as unclean. Not long ago, in fact, a woman in Israel was sentenced to 50 years for depicting Allah as a pig.

As persuaders, it is important to recognize that the meanings of words are subjective. As scholars in the field of communication are fond of saying, "Meanings are in people, not in words." Effective persuaders are aware of this and attempt to adapt their messages accordingly.

Ultimate Terms: Speak of the Devil

Although connotative meanings tend to be more subjective than denotative meanings, sometimes the connotations associated with certain words are shared by large groups of people (i.e., societies and cultures). As a result, such words can be powerfully persuasive tools for motivating people. This is especially true of what Richard Weaver (1953) labeled *ultimate terms*, which are words or phrases that are highly revered, widely accepted, and carry special power in a culture. According to Weaver, there are three types of ultimate terms. The first, *god terms*, carry the greatest blessing in a culture and demand sacrifice or obedience (see Foss, Foss, & Trapp, 1985; Hart, 1997). When Weaver wrote, he used terms such as *fact* and *progress* as examples of god terms. Modern-day god terms include *family values*, *critical thinking*, and *teachable moment*.

In contrast to god terms, Weaver argued that some terms, which he labeled *devil terms*, are perceived by a culture as associated with the absolutely abhorrent and disgusting. Examples of past devil terms include *communism*, *Nazi*, and *fascist* (Foss et al., 1985). Today, terms such as *dead-beat dad*, *racist*, *terrorist*, *child molester*, *sweat shop*, and *hate crime* might be considered devil terms. Because such terms represent what is evil or detestable to a culture, they can also be extremely persuasive (Hart, 1997).

Finally, Weaver labeled a third type, *charismatic terms*. Unlike god and devil terms, which are associated with something observable, charismatic terms, much like a charismatic person, have a power that in some ways is mysteriously given (Foss et al., 1985):

> "Freedom" and "democracy" are charismatic terms in our culture. We demand sacrifice in the name of these terms, yet the referents most of us attach to them are obscure and often contradictory. In fact, Weaver says, we may resist the attempt to define such terms, perhaps fearing that a term defined explicitly will have its charisma taken away. (p. 66)

What becomes clear, then, is that although god, devil, and charismatic terms have power, their ability to persuade is not stable; the connotations associated with such terms may change over time. For instance, calling someone a communist today would not have the same impact as it did in the days of Senator Joseph McCarthy.

Considering the power of ultimate terms, it is not surprising that politicians spend considerable amounts of money discovering the "right" terms to use in their ads and speeches. By way of example, Lemann (2000) noted that politicians use focus groups in order to discover specific words that should and should not be used in campaigns. The people in such groups watch ads and speeches while moving dials from right to left, indicating when they like or dislike what they are hearing and seeing. As a result, politicians learn an entirely new vocabulary of god and devil terms. For example, based on his research with focus groups, Frank Luntz, a political consultant, advises his candidates to say

> "Department of Defense" instead of "Pentagon," "opportunity scholarships" instead of "vouchers," "tax relief" instead of "tax cuts," and "climate change" instead of "global warming." The terms "Washington" and "I.R.S.," Luntz says, always play as super-negative and should be attached to a policy you want to turn people against. "Prosperity" is super-positive. In general, words starting with an "r" or ending with an "-ity" are good—hence "reform" and "accountability" work and "responsibility" really works. (Lemann, 2000, p. 100)

Politicians might also use language to create other images. For instance, following the September 11 attacks on the World Trade Center and Pentagon, George W. Bush used words such as *evil*, *those people*, and *demons* to characterize people of Arab/Middle Eastern descent. Merskin (2004) argued that Bush's speeches were carefully constructed and that the use of such words creates an enemy image by dehumanizing the "other."

In addition to politicians, people in the business world are fond of using ultimate terms as persuasion devices. For instance, the word *empowerment* is a modern-day charismatic term on which marketers and advertisers have capitalized. Products and services that promise to *empower* people have become unavoidable. For instance, as a former suit salesman, one of the authors was regularly asked by customers where the "power ties" could be found or what was the "power color" for ties this year. The Hotel del Coronado in Southern California offers its guests "power walks" in the morning, and one of our colleagues told us about a seminar his sister attended that teaches its clients how to take "power naps." Finally, one of the authors was recently notified that he is a *Time* magazine "Power Subscriber." He can now read the news with gusto!

Other terms that seem to have appeal these days are *extreme*, *alternative*, and *indie*. Indeed, these words are popular now as "rebel" labels for things. There is, of course, alternative music and alternative clothes (e.g., baggy pants, visible boxer shorts, tattoos, piercings). There are also extreme sports, such as snowboarding, bungee jumping, skateboarding, and mountain biking. But does placing words in front of something necessarily make it cooler, or more "edgy"? Is "alternative golf" really alternative simply because the people playing it have goatees and wear tennis shoes (instead of golf shoes)? Does throwing some bacon and Monterey cheese on a Whopper really make it an "Xtreme burger," as Burger King claims?

What is clear from this discussion is that words, when widely accepted as representing what is good or evil in a culture, have incredible persuasive potential. As we've noted, being labeled a communist in the 1950s was hazardous. In the late 1600s, being labeled a witch in Salem, Massachusetts, was deadly. In the current political climate, labeling one's opponent as a socialist or fascist seems to be popular. A little later, we explore more thoroughly the power of such labeling. But first, we examine a topic related to ultimate terms.

Aphorisms, Familiar Phrases, and Persuasion: That Rings a Bell

Aphorisms are sayings, maxims, and adages that offer advice. They may be time honored (e.g., "look before you leap") or more contemporary ("love is fleeting, herpes is forever"). They are found in economics, politics, religion, science, and everyday life. We see them on bumper stickers, political slogans, and advertising campaigns.

Aphorisms are persuasive because they are succinct, easily remembered, and appear to contain "truisms." And because they are pithy, they require far less explanation. For example, the political expression "A rising tide lifts all boats" captures the essence of "trickle-down economics," whereby economic policies that benefit the rich also benefit everyone else. Although some aphorisms may offer bad advice, Levine and Bleakley (2012) argue that aphorisms are undervalued in medicine. For example, simple adages, such as "An ounce of prevention is worth a pound of cure" and "What you don't know can hurt you," are efficient ways of explaining the value of preventive medicine. In a similar vein, Vernon (2008) highlighted the importance of aphorisms in modern politics. "In an age when the average attention span is apparently decreasing," he noted, "the sagacious soundbite could yet become the solution to—rather than a symptom of—the tendency to dumb down" (p. 50). Texting, tweeting, and other social media seem ripe for persuasion in the form of aphorisms.

When are aphorisms most persuasive? Howard (1997) conducted a study to find out when familiar phrases are influential. Using the elaboration likelihood model as a theoretical base, Howard suspected that familiar phrases would be most persuasive when people weren't able or motivated to scrutinize a message. That is, familiar phrases, Howard thought, would act as peripheral cues to persuasion. To test this idea, he had groups of students listen to radio commercials trying to persuade them to plan for retirement. The commercials contained either familiar phrases (e.g., "Don't put all your eggs in one basket") or literal phrases (e.g., "Don't risk everything on a single venture"). Half the students were able to carefully attend to the commercials, but the rest were distracted (i.e., they were asked to watch and record the nonverbal behavior of another person in the room). Results of the study indicated that the students who viewed commercials with familiar phrases were more persuaded than those who had not, but only when they were distracted. Those who were not distracted were persuaded (by strong arguments), regardless of whether familiar or literal phrases were used (Howard, 1997).

The Power of Labeling

Earlier, we stated that names such as Dweezil and Brfxxccxxmnpcccclllmmnprxvclnmckssqlbb11116 are not wrong, but we might have misled you. As arbitrary symbols, they work just fine, but pragmatically, how would you like to be saddled with such a name? Perhaps you wouldn't mind, but, whatever the case, one thing is clear: The name you use affects the way people respond to you. In fact, we know a person who changes his name every decade because he says that people respond differently to him depending on whether he's a Richard, a Jay, or a Hank. And research supports the idea that our friend is not simply a kook. For instance, according to the sources of Adler and colleagues (1995), compared to names like Percival, Elmer, Isadore, and Alfreda, common names such as John, Michael, Karen, and Wendy are rated as more likable, active, and stronger. Moreover, when such names were placed on essays and evaluated by teachers, the more common names tended to receive higher grades than the less common ones. Finally, in a small study, a graduate student at MIT put 24 photos on the website www.hotornot.com. Interestingly, with different first names attached, the same photos were judged as more "hot" or more "not" (Strasser, 2005, p. E22).

It turns out that your name doesn't just affect how others behave; it affects how you behave as well. People, it seems, respond favorably to *hearing* their names. In one study (Seiter & Weger, in press), for example, food servers who had learned their customers' names (by reading them on credit cards as customers paid their bills) addressed those customers in one of several ways. Specifically, they addressed customers (1) by using their first names (e.g., "Thank you, Babbs."); (2) by using their titles plus last names (e.g., "Thank you, Mr. Jones."); (3) by being formal yet impersonal (e.g., "Thank you, sir/ma'am."); or by using no form of address (i.e., "Thank you."). Results of the study showed that diners left significantly higher tips in the first two conditions, with younger customers preferring to be addressed by their first names and older customers (age 54 and up) preferring to be addressed by their titles plus last names.

The power of labels extends far beyond the names that people are given (see Box 12.1). To be sure, the labels we use to describe people or things reflect our attitudes about them and affect others' reactions to the people and things labeled. For example, many years ago, children with divorced parents came from "broken homes." Talk about stigmatization! Nowadays, we say children belong to "single-parent" or "blended" families.

The notion that the labels we use affect our attitudes about what we label lies at the heart of criticisms aimed at sexist language. For example, if a professor refers to all of his male students as "men" or "sirs" and to all of his female students as "girls," "broads," or "dears," it not only says something about the professor's attitudes toward men and women but it also has the power to shape attitudes. According to what is commonly known as the *Sapir-Whorf hy-*

Box 12.1

Just a Spoonful of Sugar (and a Well-Chosen Name) Makes the Medicine Go Down

In this chapter, we've shown that names affect how we react to people. As you might have suspected, they also influence our reaction to products. For example, did you know that people react more favorably to sweaters and jellybeans that are given ambiguous color names (e.g., Moody Blue, Alpine Snow, and Monster Green) than less ambiguous color names (e.g., blueberry blue) (Miller & Kahn, 2005)? Considering this, it's not surprising that a lot of attention goes into naming products. This may be especially true when naming prescription drugs.

Most of us refer to prescription drugs by their brand names. For example, we say "Prozac" rather than "fluoxetine" and "Valium" rather than "diazepam." We do this because we've been trained to by pharmaceutical manufacturers. Drug companies engage in "branding" when they air commercials and print ads urging us to "ask your doctor about _______." Is the Purple Pill right for you? Ask your doctor, but first go to the company's Website for more online propaganda to offer your doctor.

Naming a drug is extremely important to how the drug is perceived by consumers/patients and, in turn, to the drug maker's bottom line (Kirkwood, 2003). The name has to be short (no more than three syllables), unique, easy to pronounce, easy to remember, and, importantly, it must convey the essence of what the drug does. But the name cannot be false or misleading, according to the FDA. Viagra, a pill for erectile dysfunction sufferers, is a classic case of the power of naming as it applies to drugs. The name Viagra was conjured up to convey two themes: vigor, virility, or vitality and power or force, such as the raw power of Niagara Falls. Yes, the Freudian association with a torrent of powerful water is intentional. Viagra sounds more manly than sildenafil citrate, its generic name, don't you think? Celebrex, an arthritis medicine, was so named because it suggests celebrating—celebrating one's freedom to move without pain.

Companies such as the Brand Institute and Name Base/Medibrand are paid $250,0000 or more to come up with names for drugs that conjure up idealized associations. See if you can guess the positive associations pharmaceutical manufacturers are trying to create for the following drugs.

- **Alleve:** hint—it <u>allevi</u>ates something, right? (and that something happens to be minor arthritis pain).
- **Ambien:** hint—it creates a soothing <u>ambien</u>ce (to help you sleep better).
- **Claritin:** hint—it <u>clari</u>fies things, like watery eyes and a runny nose due to allergies.
- **Levitra:** hint—it <u>levi</u>tates something (need we say more?).
- **Prevacid:** hint—it <u>prev</u>ents something (and that something has to do with the last four letters of its name. Sounds better than its generic name, lansoprazole, doesn't it?).
- **Propecia:** hint—it <u>propa</u>gates something (like hair restoration).

The letters X and Z are popular in drug names because people think they sound scientific, hence names like Nexium, Paxil, Vioxx, Zanex, Zocor, and Zoloft. Now that you know how drugs are named, see if you can come up with effective names for hypothetical new drugs that would help Alzheimer's sufferers, diabetics, or kids with attention-deficit/hyperactivity disorder (ADHD).

pothesis, the language we use determines the way we understand the world (Sapir, 1949; Whorf, 1956). Thus, when women are wrongly described in ways that make them seem inferior to men, people begin to believe that women truly are inferior.

The same dynamics are at work when people use racist language, which perpetuates the illusion that one racial group is superior to another. Ethnic/cultural references carry vastly different meanings. For example, Americans with an African heritage have been identified by terms such as *African American*, *black*, *Negro*, *colored*, and more derogatory terms as well. Such derogatory terms, whether racist or sexist, have the power to shape perceptions.

Euphemisms and Doublespeak: Making the Worse Appear the Better and Vice Versa

In the fifth century B.C., a group of teachers known as Sophists created private schools in Athens, Greece. Students who wanted to learn from the Sophists were charged fees and were taught, among other subjects, oratory and persuasion. Soon, however, being a Sophist was so profitable that the occupation attracted a number of charlatans, who gave the Sophists a bad reputation (today, *sophistry* connotes deceitful or fallacious reasoning). In fact, Plato argued that the Sophists were more interested in lies than truths and more interested in dazzling audiences than in instructing them. Sophists, Plato argued, were skilled at making the "worse cause appear the better" (Corbett, 1971).

The practice of using words to make the worse appear the better (and vice versa) is still alive and well. Modern-day Sophists commonly use *doublespeak* (ambiguous or evasive language) and *euphemisms* (inoffensive terms substituted for offensive ones) to create messages with less sting. For example, in the business world, no one gets fired or laid off anymore. Instead, companies engage in "downsizing," "right-sizing," or even "bright-sizing." Mercedes doesn't sell used cars anymore; it sells "pre-owned automobiles" (try asking the Mercedes dealer, "Was this car previously used, or simply owned?"). Other companies give their employees job titles that sound more important or grandiose than they really are. A garbage collector is now a "sanitation engineer." And, in Great Britain, legislation was introduced to substitute the stigmatized word *prostitute* with the phrase *person who sells sex persistently* (Stinchfield, 2007).

The use of doublespeak and euphemisms is rampant in other places as well. For example, the military refers to civilian casualties, killing enemy soldiers, and combat operations as "collateral damage," "servicing the target," and "peacekeeping missions," respectively. The Obama administration instructed staffers to switch from the term "global war on terror" to "overseas contingency operation." Flight attendants don't talk about crashing in the ocean, only "water landings" (Murphy, 2001). In the medical field, terms such as *assisted suicide*, *transsexual surgery*, and *cancer* might instead be labeled *hastening death* (or *death with dignity*), *gender reassignment*, and *a growth*, respectively. Politicians don't raise taxes or lie, they adopt "revenue enhancing measures" and "misremember." And one of our friends is not allowed to have parties in her high school classes so, instead, has "reinforcement for desirable behavior days." In the world of undertakers and funeral directors, people "pass away" rather than die, are "interred" rather than buried, and are called "cases" or "patients" rather than corpses. Instead of saying "No," parents are fond of saying "We'll see" or "Maybe later." And finally, in the abortion controversy, the words you use probably depend on the side you take. For example, *pro-life* is more value-laden than *anti-abortion* or *anti-choice*. *Pro-choice* avoids the term *abortion* altogether and sounds much nicer than *anti-life* or *anti-anti-abortion*.

In the midst of all this word spinning, researchers (McGlone & Batchelor, 2003) have identified two possible motives people might have for using euphemisms. First, people might use euphemisms because such words are less threatening and more respectful, therefore saving the "face" of audience members. Second, people might use euphemisms in order to be regarded as tasteful and sensitive, thereby saving their own "face." To test these competing explanations, McGlone and Batchelor (2003) asked students communicating with someone via computer to describe various photographs, including two that depicted the aftermath of a urinating dog and a defecating parrot. Some students were led to believe that their identity would later be revealed to the person they were communicating with, while others were not. Results showed that the first group of students was more prone to using euphemisms, suggesting that saving their own face seemed to be their priority. It turns out, however, that when trying to create favorable impressions by spinning words, not just any euphemism will do. Indeed, a study by McGlone, Beck, and Pfeister (2006) found that because euphemisms with longer "careers" (e.g., "use the restroom," "go number two") are more familiar and draw less attention, people who use them are perceived more favorably than those who use

Box 12.2
If You Can't Say Something Nice, Spin It

If you've ever been asked to serve as a reference for someone, you know that it can be complex business. Because what you say may no longer be confidential, saying something negative can lead to all kinds of personal and legal tangles. With that in mind, Robert Thornton (2003) has created the Lexicon of Inconspicuously Ambiguous Recommendations (LIAR). Here are some examples of what to say about people, depending on their flaws:

If the person is inept: "I recommend this man with no qualifications whatsoever." (p. 33)

If the person is extremely lazy: "In my opinion, you will be very fortunate to get this person to work for you." (p. 5)

If the person is chronically absent: "A man like him is hard to find." (p. 19)

If the person is dishonest: "The man is simply an unbelievable worker." (p. 33)

If the person is a drunk: "We remember the hours he spent working with us as happy hours." (p. 20)

Although we don't actually recommend using this lexicon, we think it is an entertaining way to illustrate how tricky language can be.

newer, less familiar euphemisms (e.g., "make room for tea," "cast a pellet") (for more on doublespeak, see Box 12.2).

Language Intensity, Vividness, and Offensiveness

So far, we've examined the nature of symbols and how they relate to the notion of meaning and the process of persuasion. We now turn to a discussion of specific variables related to language and persuasion. Three of these include language intensity, vividness, and offensiveness. These three variables are closely related. For example, when studying intense language, some authors include reviews of research on profanity, which, of course, have the potential to be quite offensive. However, it is possible to use intense language without being offensive. Moreover, although some definitions imply that vividness is a component or outcome of intense language (e.g., see Hamilton & Stewart, 1993), others do not (e.g., see Bowers, 1964). Because these three topics are so closely related, we examine them together in this section. We then turn to a discussion of several theories that have been used to explain the relationship between intense language and persuasion.

##@!!!!##: Profanity and Persuasion

Even though profanity, like any symbol, is arbitrary, it clearly plays a role in the process of persuasion, mostly because such strong connotations are associated with swearing. Perhaps this is why ancient rhetoricians like Quintilian advised against using profanity (Rothwell, 1971). Because profanity is so common (Cameron, 1969), some authors have asserted that it merits more attention as a form of persuasion. For instance, J. Dan Rothwell (1971) argued:

> Despite centuries of negative criticism, verbal obscenity has become a more frequent rhetorical device. It is successful in creating attention, in discrediting an enemy, in provoking violence, in fostering identification, and in providing catharsis. Its effects are governed by a variety of circumstances which need to be understood more fully. It has precipitated a police riot, brutal beatings, and even death. Hoping it will go away will not make it so. It is time to accept verbal obscenity as a significant rhetorical device and help discover appropriate responses to its use. (p. 242)

To explore more thoroughly people's perceptions of profanity, E. Scott Baudhuin (1973) gave students "swear word" booklets and asked the students to evaluate several words according to how offensive they were. Based on the students' perceptions, he found that the words could be categorized into one of three categories: religious, excretory, and sexual. Which type of profanity did students find most offensive? The results of the study indicated that sexual words received the most negative responses. Religious profanities were perceived to be the least offensive.

If profanity is perceived to be offensive, are people who use it perceived negatively and are they less persuasive? Several studies have been conducted to test this question and most, but not all (e.g., see Rassin & Van Der Heijden, 2005), indicate that if you want to be perceived as attractive, credible, and persuasive, you should clean up your language. For example, a study by Powell and his colleagues asked students to evaluate applicants who either did or did not cuss during a job interview. The researchers found that applicants with filthy mouths, regardless of their gender, were perceived as significantly less

attractive than their counterparts (Powell et al., 1984). Similarly, Bostrom, Baseheart, and Rossiter (1973) found that, in general, using profanity damages a speaker's credibility. On the other hand, Scherer and Sagarin (2006) noted that society's stance about swearing has become more relaxed since many of these earlier studies were conducted. As such, they revisited the relationship between obscenity, credibility, and persuasion by having students listen to speeches in which a male speaker either did or did not use the word *damn*. Results showed that cussing had no effect on perceptions of the speaker's credibility, but when the speaker cussed, he was more persuasive than when he did not. Before you decide to become potty-mouthed the next time you're speaking, however, consider this: the students in this study were listening to speeches in favor of lowering tuition, a topic they presumably would be in favor of. In contrast, most of the classic studies on this topic asked participants to listen to topics they did not favor. In short, it may be that profanity is persuasive, but only under very specific conditions. Indeed, two studies found that perceptions of cussing depend on additional variables such as context and audience expectations. Specifically, and not surprisingly, Johnson and Lewis (2010) found that people who cussed in formal settings were perceived as significantly less competent than people who cussed in less formal settings. Similarly, Johnson (2012) found that when cussing violated audience expectations in a positive way (e.g., people rated themselves as positively surprised by the cussing), ratings of the speaker's competence increased.

Political Correctness

Obviously, using profanity is not the only way to be verbally offensive. Earlier we discussed the notion of political correctness, which, in many ways, is all about being nonoffensive. Indeed, political correctness refers to issues of inclusive speech and advocacy of nonracist, nonageist, and nonsexist terminology (Hoover & Howard, 1995).

Although political correctness is relevant to a wide range of contexts and topics, including issues of gender, race, ethnicity, age, socioeconomic status, and so forth, a study by Seiter, Larsen, and Skinner (1998) focused on political correctness as it related to speaking about people with disabilities. In the study, college students read one of four hypothetical scenarios, each involving a person seeking donations who portrayed people with disabilities as "normal" (e.g., "uses a wheelchair"), "heroic" (e.g., "handicapable"), "disabled" (e.g., "confined to a wheelchair"), or "pathetic" (e.g., "abnormal"). After reading the scenarios, participants rated the speakers on scales measuring credibility and persuasiveness. Results of the study showed that, compared to communicators who portrayed people with disabilities as "pathetic," communicators who portrayed such people as "normal," "heroic," and "disabled" were perceived as significantly more trustworthy and competent (Seiter et al., 1998). However, only communicators portraying people with disabilities as "heroic" and "disabled" were perceived as more persuasive than the communicator portraying such people as "pathetic." How did the authors interpret

these results? Perhaps by trying *not* to portray people with disabilities as victims, the communicator using "normal" language also did not demonstrate as urgent a need to help people with disabilities as the communicators using "disabled" and "heroic" language did (e.g., a child described as "being confined to a wheelchair," or one who is pandered to may be perceived as requiring more help than a child described as "using a wheelchair"). Whatever the case, the results of this study suggest that individuals seeking donations for people with disabilities face a dilemma: How can a person raise money to help people with disabilities while at the same time describe people with disabilities in a politically correct and dignified manner?

The Effects of Vividness: A Picture's Worth a Thousand Words

According to Nisbett and Ross (1980), vivid information captures and holds our attention and excites our imagination because it is "emotionally interesting, concrete and imagery-provoking, and proximate in a sensory, temporal, or spatial way" (p. 45). By way of example, it's more vivid to say "the glass crashed and shattered into pieces" than it is to say "the glass broke."

Although vivid words may be more effective than pallid information (bland, plain descriptors) at holding our attention (Childers & Houston, 1984), evidence that vivid information is more persuasive than pallid information is questionable (see Frey & Eagly, 1993). Although some research suggests that vivid messages are persuasive, some suggest just the opposite.

How can these apparent inconsistencies be reconciled? According to Guadagno, Rhoads and Sagarin (2011), vividness may either help or hinder the persuasiveness of a message; it all depends on what is being vivified. Specifically, these researchers suspected that when the central thesis of a message is vivified, it helps us process the message and, consequently, promotes persuasion when the message is strong. In contrast, when irrelevant features of a message are vivified, it can distract us and, as a consequence, undermine persuasion.

To test this notion, Guadagno and colleagues (2011) asked students to read the summary of a (fictitious) study, which claimed that only 3 hours of sleep, when taken in half-hour naps throughout the day and with a lot of vitamins, resulted in superior physical and mental abilities. Alongside the study's claim, one group of students read an easy-to-visualize message that was relevant to the topic (e.g., "Subjects improved their ability to snatch coins out of mid-air and became faster at solving complicated math problems while listening to the lyrics of obscene rock & roll songs."). A second group of students read vivid material that was unrelated to the topic (e.g., "An interesting subject in the study was a college student with long hair, a muscular build, and a deep tan."). A third group read pallid information about the fictional study. Results of the study confirmed the researchers' suspicions: vivid messages

"*Love it! 'People of smoke' instead of 'Smokers.'*"

that were relevant to the topic were the most persuasive. Moreover, the researchers noted that irrelevant vividness decreased persuasiveness. In short, vividness can be an effective persuasive tool; you simply need to know when and how to use it.

Language Intensity

"You are shockingly stupid" versus "You are not real smart."

"The lumber industry is raping our forests" versus "The lumber industry is cutting down a lot of trees."

In the preceding pairs of phrases, which phrase has the strongest connotative meaning? Obviously, the first phrase in each pair. The terms *shockingly* and *raping* are more intense than terms found in the other phrases. Language that is intense is emotional, metaphorical, opinionated, specific, forceful, extreme, and evaluative. For that reason, perhaps, Bowers (1964) defined *language intensity* as "the quality of language which indicates the degree to which the speaker's attitude deviates from neutrality" (p. 215). Clearly, someone who compares "cutting down trees" to "rape" is far from neutral in his or her attitudes about the lumber industry. But is a person who uses such language persuasive? The best answer to that question may be "it depends." To be sure, several variables have been found that affect the persuasiveness of intense language. With that said, let's examine four different theories that attempt to explain when and why intense language does or does not persuade.

First, *reinforcement theory* assumes that people are motivated to avoid pain and seek pleasure. Bradac, Bowers, and Courtright (1979, 1980) assumed that the same is true when people are being persuaded. If a person generally agrees with the position advocated by a source, the person will find it rewarding and evaluate the source positively. The reverse is true if the person generally disagrees with the position advocated by the source. Language intensity is believed to enhance this effect. Specifically, if the listener generally agrees with the speaker, when the speaker throws some forceful language at the listener, the listener is even more motivated to agree. However, a listener who generally disagrees will react even more negatively than he or she normally would when the speaker uses intense language (Bradac et al., 1980).

A second perspective on language intensity is found in *language expectancy theory* (see Burgoon & Siegel, 2004). This theory assumes that we have expectations about what types of language are normal to use when trying to persuade other people. For example, we may not think it is normal for a speaker to use intense words such as *rape* and *shockingly*. According to language expectancy theory, when persuaders violate our expectations concerning normal language, those violations can either help or hurt the effectiveness of the persuasive message, depending on whether the violations are perceived in a positive or negative way. How violations are perceived depends on who is using the language. For instance, Burgoon and Siegel (2004) noted that highly credible sources are granted a "wider bandwidth" of acceptable communication than those with low credibility. As such, sources with low credibility are likely to be perceived in a negative way when they use language that is aggressive and intense. This, in turn, leads them to be less persuasive. The reverse is true for highly credible sources.

Third, Hamilton and Stewart (1993) have extended *information processing theory* (McGuire, 1968, 1989) to explain the effects of intensity on persuasion. The theory argues that to be persuaded, you must first attend to and comprehend a persuasive message. If you attend to and comprehend the message, you then compare your own position on the message to the position that's being argued by the source. Ultimately, you may either accept or reject the source's position. According to Hamilton and Stewart (1993; also see Craig & Blankenship, 2011), language intensity affects this process by making a source's position on an issue seem more extreme compared to your own position. This can be good, up to a point. In general, some discrepancy between a persuader and a receiver's positions leads to increased attention and, therefore, more attitude change. Too much discrepancy may lead a receiver to reject a message or to scrutinize a message so much that he or she fails to attend to all of the message's content. In addition, intense language tends to be more specific and vivid.

Finally, *communication accommodation theory* (Giles & Wiemann, 1987; Street & Giles, 1982) argues that when we communicate with others we adjust our style of speaking to their style in order to gain approval and increase communication efficiency. For example, we may try to talk the same way others talk so that they will like us better. Aune and Kikuchi (1993) conducted a study to see if this theory would predict the effectiveness of messages that either were or were not intense. In the study, speakers delivered intense and nonintense messages to people whose language style could be categorized as either intense or nonintense. Results of the study supported communication accommodation theory. Specifically, speakers using intense language were most persuasive with people who use intense language, whereas speakers using nonintense language were most persuasive with people who use nonintense language. Speakers who "matched" the style of their audience also were perceived as more credible.

Powerless Language and Persuasion: Um's the Word

As a student, one of the authors had two speech professors who did not like the utterance *um* too much. One called *ums* social burps. The other, when listening to speeches, smacked her pencil on a desk whenever the author said *um*. It was not fun, but it beat electrical shocks. In retrospect, the author supposes he should be grateful to these professors, because *ums*, as well as a number of other utterances, prevent people who use them from being persuasive. Why? Because such utterances create the perception of *powerlessness*. In case you want to avoid using them when you talk, here is a list of such speech mannerisms with some examples in italics (also see Bradley, 1981; Erickson, Lind, Johnson, & O'Barr, 1978; Lakoff, 1973, 1975; Lowenberg, 1982; Newcombe & Arnkoff, 1979; O'Barr, 1982):

- **Hesitations** (signal uncertainty or anxiety): "*Well,* I, *uh, you know, um,* would like to borrow a dollar."
- **Hedges** (qualify the utterance in which they occur): "I *guess I sort of* like you and *kind of* want to know you."
- **Intensifiers** (fortify the utterance): "I *really* believe that and agree with you *very* much."
- **Polite forms** (indicate deference and subordination): "*Excuse me, if you wouldn't mind too much, I'd appreciate it* if you'd *please* shut the door. *Thank you.*"
- **Tag questions** (lessens the force of a declarative sentence): "This is fun, *don't you think*? Much more fun than yesterday, *isn't it*?"
- **Disclaimers** (utterances offered before a statement that anticipate doubts, signal a problem, or ask for understanding): "I know this is a *really dumb question*, but . . . ?"
- **Deictic phrases** (phrases indicating something outside the speaker's vicinity): "That man *over there* is the one who stole my wallet."

As noted previously, a considerable amount of research indicates that using these powerless forms of speech can prevent you from being persuasive (Erickson et al., 1978; Newcombe & Arnkoff, 1979), even when you are using strong arguments (Hosman & Siltanen, 2011). However, the relationship between power and speech may depend on additional factors. Two are noteworthy.

First, the type of powerless language a person uses may influence how he or she is perceived. Specifically, one problem with some research on powerless language is that it has lumped together all of the powerless forms previously discussed. However, some research indicates that this may not be the best idea, because not all of the forms may be detrimental to a speaker. For instance, in one study, Bradac and Mulac (1984) found that using polite forms actually enhanced speakers' credibility. Moreover, Durik, Britt, Reynolds, and Storey (2008) found that the use of colloquial-sounding hedges (e.g., "kind of," "sort of") undermined persuasive attempts, but the use of professional-sounding hedges (e.g., "probably," "may," "seem to") did not.

Second, the type of language that is most effective may depend on who is using it. For example, Blankenship and Craig (2007) found that when low credible sources used tag questions, the sources were less persuasive regardless of whether their messages contained strong or weak arguments. In contrast, when highly credible sources used tag questions, the sources were more persuasive, but only when their messages contained strong arguments. Why? Presumably, if you already believe a source is credible, tag questions get you to think more carefully about the message being presented. If the message is strong, you will be more persuaded by it (Blankenship & Craig, 2007).

In addition to sources' credibility, Carli (1990) found that sources' and receivers' sex affects the persuasiveness of language. Specifically, females were persuasive with men when they used powerless forms of speech but persuasive with females when using powerful speech. For male speakers, it did not matter what form of speech was used. This may mean that women, compared to men, need to be more sensitive about the style of speech they use when trying to be persuasive. Clearly, along with the topics we discussed earlier, the results of this study suggest that men have negative stereotypes about women who use powerful speaking styles.

SUMMARY

In this chapter, we examined the role of language in the process of persuasion. We began with an examination and definition of the term *symbol*. Symbols are arbitrary but have the power to shape perceptions and construct social reality. Symbols also have connotative and denotative meanings, both of which affect persuasion. For example, we examined ultimate terms, which, because of their strong connotations, have incredible persuasive power in a culture. We also examined the power of labels and how, oftentimes, through the use of euphemisms and doublespeak, persuaders attempt to lessen (or strengthen) the connotative impact of a word. Finally, we discussed several language variables that affect persuasion. By making their words more vivid, intense, offensive, and powerless/powerful, persuaders affect the way audiences respond to their messages.

REFERENCES

Adler, R. B., Rosenfeld, L. B., & Towne, N. (1995). *Interplay: The process of interpersonal communication* (6th ed.). Fort Worth, TX: Harcourt, Brace.

Aune, R. K., & Kikuchi, T. (1993). Effects of language intensity similarity on perceptions of credibility, relational attributions, and persuasion. *Journal of Language and Social Psychology*, *12*(3), 224–237.

Baudhuin, E. S. (1973). Obscene language and evaluative response: An empirical study. *Psychological Reports*, *32*, 399–402.

The best and worst of everything. (1996, December 29). *Parade Magazine*, pp. 6, 7, 10.

Blankenship, K. L., & Craig, T. Y. (2007). Language and persuasion: Tag questions as powerless speech or as interpreted in context. *Journal of Experimental Psychology*, *43*, 112–118.

Bostrom, R. N., Baseheart, J. R., & Rossiter, C. M. (1973). The effects of three types of profane language in persuasive messages. *Journal of Communication*, *23*, 461–475.

Bowers, J. W. (1964). Some correlates of language intensity. *Quarterly Journal of Speech*, *50*, 415–420.

Bradac, J., Bowers, J., & Courtright, J. (1979). Three language variables in communication research: Intensity, immediacy, and diversity. *Human Communication Research*, *5*, 257–269.

Bradac, J., Bowers, J., & Courtright, J. (1980). Lexical variations in intensity, immediacy, and diversity: An axiomatic theory and causal model. In R. W. St. Clair & H. Giles (Eds.), *The social psychological contexts of language* (pp. 193–223). Hillsdale, NJ: Erlbaum.

Bradac, J. J., & Mulac, A. (1984). A molecular view of powerful and powerless speech styles: Attributional consequences of specific language features and communicator intentions. *Communication Monographs*, *51*, 307–319.

Bradley, P. H. (1981). The folk-linguistics of women's speech: An empirical evaluation. *Communication Monographs*, *48*, 73–90.

Burgoon, M., & Siegel, J. T. (2004). Language expectancy theory: Insight to application. In J. S. Seiter & R. H. Gass (Eds.), *Readings in persuasion, social influence, and compliance gaining* (pp. 149–164). Boston: Allyn & Bacon.

Cameron, P. (1969). Frequency and kinds of words in various social settings, or what in the hell's going on? *Pacific Sociological Review*, *12*, 101–104.

Carli, L. L. (1990). Gender, language, and influence. *Journal of Personality and Social Psychology*, *59*, 941–951.

Childers, T. L., & Houston, M. J. (1984). Conditions for a picture-superiority effect on consumer memory. *Journal of Consumer Research*, *11*, 643–654.

Corbett, E. P. J. (1971). *Classical rhetoric for the modern student* (2nd ed.). New York: Oxford University Press.

Craig, T. Y., & Blankenship, K. L. (2011). Language and persuasion: Linguistic extremity influences message processing and behavioral intentions. *Journal of Language and Social Psychology*, *30*, 290–310.

Durik, A. M., Britt, M. A., Reynolds, R., & Storey, J. (2008). The effects of hedges in persuasive arguments. *Journal of Language and Social Psychology*, *27*, 217–234.

Erickson, B., Lind, E., Johnson, A., & O'Barr, W. M. (1978). Speech style and impression formation in a court setting: The effects of "powerful" and "powerless" speech. *Journal of Experimental Social Psychology, 14,* 266–279.

Foss, S. K., Foss, K. A., & Trapp, R. (1985). *Contemporary perspectives on rhetoric.* Prospect Heights, IL: Waveland Press.

Frey, K. P., & Eagly, A. H. (1993). Vividness can undermine the persuasiveness of messages. *Journal of Personality and Social Psychology, 65,* 32–44.

Giles, H., & Wiemann, J. M. (1987). Language, social comparison, and power. In C. R. Berger & S. H. Chaffee (Eds.), *The handbook of communication science* (pp. 350-384). Newbury Park, CA: Sage.

Guadagno, R. E., Rhoads, K. V. L., & Sagarin, B. J. (2011). Figural vividness and persuasion: Capturing the "elusive" vividness effect. *Personality and Psychology Bulletin, 37,* 626–638.

Hamilton, M. A., & Stewart, B. L. (1993). Extending an information processing model of language intensity effects. *Communication Quarterly, 41*(2), 231–246.

Hart, R. P. (1997). *Modern rhetorical criticism* (2nd ed.). Boston: Allyn & Bacon.

Hoover, J. D., & Howard, L. A. (1995). The political correctness controversy revisited. *American Behavioral Scientist, 38*(7), 963–975.

Hosman, L. A., & Siltanen, S. A. (2011). Hedges, tag questions, message processing, and persuasion. *Journal of Language and Social Psychology, 30,* 341–349.

Howard, D. J. (1997). Familiar phrases as peripheral persuasion cues. *Journal of Experimental Social Psychology, 33,* 231–243.

Johnson, D. I. (2012). Swearing by peers in the work setting: Expectancy violation valence, perceptions of message, and perceptions of speaker. *Communication Studies, 63,* 136–151.

Johnson, D. I., & Lewis, N. (2010). Perceptions of swearing in the work setting: An expectancy violations theory perspective. *Communication Reports, 23,* 106–118.

Kirkwood, J. (2003, September 1). "What's in a name?" *The Eagle Tribune.* Retrieved on June 5, 2005, from www.igorinternational.com/press/eagletrib-drug-names.php.

Lakoff, G. (1973). Language and woman's place. *Language in Society, 2,* 45–79.

Lakoff, G. (1975). *Language and woman's place.* New York: Harper & Row.

Lemann, N. (2000, October 16, 23). The word lab: The mad science behind what the candidates say. *The New Yorker,* pp. 100–112.

Levine, D., & Bleakley, A. (2012). Maximising medicine through aphorisms. *Medical Education, 46,* 153–162. doi:10.1111/j.1365-2923.2011.04141.x

Lowenberg, I. (1982). Labels and hedges: The metalinguistic turn. *Language and Style, 15,* 193–207.

McGlone, M. S., & Batchelor, J. A. (2003). Looking out for number one: Euphemism and face. *Journal of Communication, 53,* 251–264.

McGlone, M. S., Beck, G., & Pfiester, A. (2006). Contamination and camouflage in euphemisms. *Communication Monographs, 73,* 261–282.

McGuire, W. J. (1968). Personality and susceptibility to social influence. In E. F. Borgotta & W. W. Lambert (Eds.), *Handbook of personality theory and research* (pp. 1130–1187). Chicago: Rand McNally.

McGuire, W. J. (1989). Theoretical foundations of campaigns. In R. E. Rice & C. K. Atkin (Eds.), *Public communication campaigns* (2nd ed., pp. 43–65). Newbury Park, CA: Sage.

Merskin, D. (2004). The construction of Arabs as enemies: Post September 11 discourse of George W. Bush. *MASS Communication and Society, 7*(2), 157–175.

Miller, E. G., & Kahn, B. E. (2005). Shades of meaning: The effect of color and flavor names on consumer choice. *Journal of Consumer Research, 32,* 86–92.

Murphy, A. G. (2001). The flight attendant dilemma: An analysis of communication and sensemaking during in-flight emergencies. *Journal of Applied Communication Research, 29*(1), 30–53.

Newcombe, N., & Arnkoff, D. B. (1979). Effects of speech style and sex of speaker on person perception. *Journal of Personality and Social Psychology, 37,* 1293–1303.

Nisbett, R., & Ross, L. (1980). *Human inference: Strategies and shortcomings in social judgment.* Englewood Cliffs, NJ: Prentice Hall.

O'Barr, W. M. (1982). *Linguistic evidence: Language, power, and strategy in the courtroom.* New York: Academic Press.

Powell, L., Callahan, K., Comans, C., McDonald, L., Mansell, J., Trotter, M. D., & Williams, V. (1984). Offensive language and impressions during an interview. *Psychological Reports, 55,* 617–618.

Rassin, E., & Van Der Heijden, S. (2005). Appearing credible? Swearing helps! *Psychology, Crime & Law, 11*(2), 177–182.

Rothwell, J. D. (1971). Verbal obscenity: Time for second thoughts. *Western Speech, 35,* 231–242.

Sapir, E. (1949). *Culture, language and personality.* Berkeley: University of California Press.

Scherer, C. R., & Sagarin, B. J. (2006). Indecent influence: The positive effects of obscenity on persuasion. *Social Influence, 1,* 138–146.

Seiter, J. S., Larsen, J., & Skinner, J. (1998). "Handicapped" or "Handi-capable"?: The effects of language describing people with disabilities on perceptions of source credibility and persuasiveness. *Communication Reports, 11*(1), 1–11.

Seiter, J. S., & Weger, H. (in press). Does a customer by any other name tip the same?: The effect of forms of address and customers' age on gratuities given to food servers in the United States. *Journal of Applied Social Psychology.*

Stinchfield, K. (2007). *A synonym for streetwalker.* Retrieved on September 30, 2008, from www.time.com/time/specials/2007/top10/article/0,30583,1686204_1690170_1690508,00.html.

Strasser, T. (2005, June 2). "A big flop in the name of love." *Los Angeles Times*, p. E22.

Street, R. L., Jr., & Giles, H. (1982). Speech accommodation theory: A social cognitive approach to language and speech behavior. In M. Roloff & C. R. Berger (Eds.), *Social cognition and communication* (pp. 193–226). Beverly Hills, CA: Sage.

Thornton, R. J. (2003). *Lexicon of inconspicuously ambiguous recommendations.* Naperville, IL: Sourcebooks.

Three-year-old Hitler can't get name on cake. (2008, Dec. 17). *MSNBC.com.* Retrieved on October 25, 2012, from http://www.msnbc.msn.com/id/28269290/ns/us_news-weird_news/t/-year-old-hitler-cant-get-name-cake/#.UIl-iBjlXzl

Vernon, M. (2008, March 17). The art of the aphorism: When are the empty words of political spin profound? *New Statesman, 137*, 50.

Weaver, R. M. (1953). *The ethics of rhetoric.* Chicago: Henry Regnery.

Whorf, B. L. (1956). *Language, thought, and reality.* New York: John Wiley & Sons.

CHAPTER

13

The Group Decision-Making Process

Taken from *Human Communication: The Basic Course,* Twelfth Edition, by Joseph A. DeVito.

A great deal of your social and professional life will revolve around your participation in groups—groups for developing ideas, increasing self-awareness, learning, and solving problems. Understanding the nature and functions of small groups and learning to use these groups effectively and efficiently will help you throughout your social and professional career.

In this chapter, you'll learn about:

- the nature and types of small groups.
- the stages and formats of small groups.
- the structure and functions of idea-generation, personal growth, information-sharing, and problem-solving groups.

You'll learn to:

- use small groups to achieve a variety of personal, social, and professional goals.
- participate effectively in a variety of small groups.

Small Groups and Teams

Let's begin with some basic definitions of the small group and the team, both face-to-face and virtual. We'll then look at small group stages, formats, culture, and power.

The Small Group

A **small group** is (1) a collection of individuals who (2) are connected to one another by some common purpose, (3) are interdependent, (4) have some degree of organization among them, and (5) see themselves as a group. Each of these characteristics needs to be explained a bit further.

1. **Collection of Individuals.** A small group is a collection of individuals few enough in number so that all members may communicate with relative ease as both senders and receivers. Generally, a small group consists of approximately 3 to 12 people.
2. **Common Purpose.** The members of a group must be connected to one another through some common purpose. People on a bus normally do not constitute a group, because they're not working at some common purpose. But if the bus gets stuck in a ditch, the riders may quickly become a group and work together to get the bus back on the road. Generally there must be some similarity in the individuals' reasons for interacting.
3. **Interdependence.** In a small group, members are interdependent; the behavior of one member is significant for and has an impact on all other members. When one member attacks or supports the ideas of another member, that behavior influences the other members and the group as a whole.
4. **Organizing Rules.** Members of small groups must be connected by some organizing rules or structure. At times the structure is rigid—as in groups operating under parliamentary procedure, in which each comment must follow prescribed rules. At other times, as in a social gathering, the structure is very loose.
5. **Self-Perception as a Group.** Members of small groups feel they are, in fact, members of this larger whole. This doesn't mean that individuality is ignored or that members do not see themselves as individuals; it simply means that each member thinks, feels, and acts as a part of the group. The more members see themselves as part of the group, the greater the group cohesion (or sense of "groupness"), satisfaction, and productivity.

The Team

A **team** is a particular kind of small group. As such it possesses all of the characteristics of the small group, as well as some additional qualities. Drawing on a number of small group researchers in communication and organizational theory, we can define the team as a small group (1) constructed for a specific task, (2) whose members have clearly defined roles, (3) whose members are committed to achieving the same goal, and (4) that is content focused (Beebe & Masterson, 2009; Kelly, 2006; Hofstrand, 2006):

1. **Specific Purpose.** A team is often constructed for a specific task. After the task is completed the members may be assigned to other teams or go their separate ways. Players on a baseball team, for example, come together for practice and for the actual game, but after the game, they each go their separate ways. After the book is published, members of the book team may go on to work on different books with different team members.
2. **Clearly Defined Roles.** In a team, member's roles are rather clearly defined. A sports team is a good example. Each player has a unique

Impression Management

You've been assigned to join a team of four others to work on new accounting procedures. As the new member you want to be perceived as both likeable and competent.

What are some of your communication choices for achieving the impression you want? What would you say? What behaviors would you want to avoid?

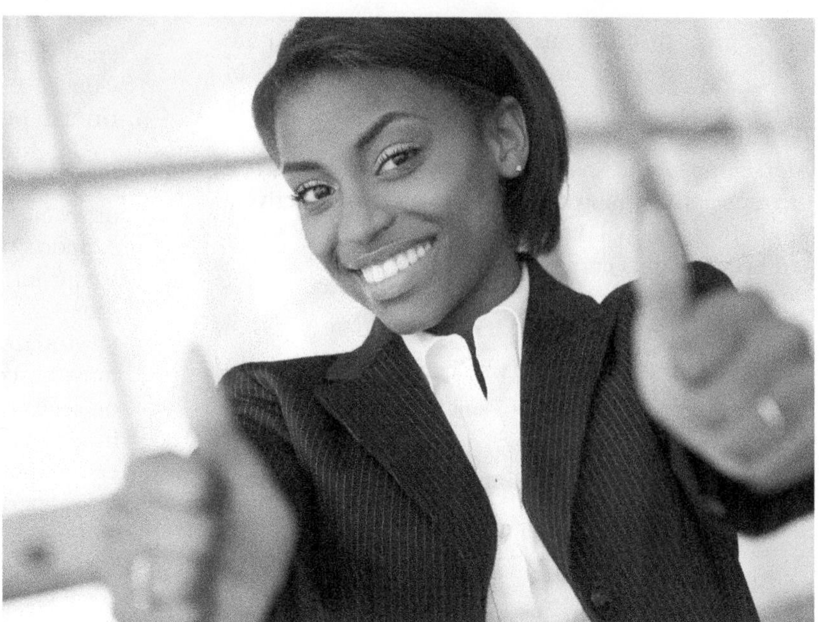

function; the short stop's functions are very different from the pitcher's or the catcher's, for example. In business, the team that is responsible for publishing a book, say, would also consist of people with clearly defined roles and might include the editor, the designer, the marketing manager, the sales manager, the photo researcher, the author, and so on. Each brings a unique perspective to the task and each is an authority in a specific area.

3. **Goal Directed.** In a team all members are committed to achieving the same, clearly identified goal. Again, a sports team is a good example; all members are committed to winning the game. In the book business example, all members of the team are committed to producing a successful book.
4. **Content Focused.** Teams are generally more content focused. In terms of the distinction between content and relationship messages, teams are generally more focused on content and their communication proceeds largely through the exchange of content messages—on winning the game or creating the book—than they are on exchanging messages about the interpersonal relationships of its members.

Virtual Groups and Teams

Small groups and teams use a wide variety of channels. Often, interactions take place face-to-face; this is the channel that probably comes to mind when you think of groups. Nowadays much small group and team interaction also takes place online, among geographically separated members who communicate as a group via computer or phone connections. These *virtual groups and teams* serve both relationship and social purposes on the one hand (these are best thought of as small groups) and business and professional purposes on the other (these are best thought of as teams).

Perhaps the best example of **virtual groups** serving relationship purposes are the social networking sites like Twitter and Facebook, where friends interact in groups but may be separated by classrooms or by oceans. And, increasingly, these social networking sites are also serving business task purposes as well. They are used for finding jobs, conducting business, solving organizational problems, and conducting just about any kind of function that a face-to-face group would serve.

The business and professional purposes of virtual groups are usually served by virtual teams. Some of these team members may be working at home, but increasingly virtual teams consist of people who are in different work spaces, perhaps in different parts of an office building, perhaps in different countries.

The same principles of effective group communication apply to all kinds of groups and teams, whether social or business, face-to-face or virtual (we'll use the most inclusive term "small group" to refer to all types of groups). Whether you're working on a team project with colleagues in different countries, communicating with new friends on Facebook, or interacting face-to-face with your extended family, the principles we discuss here will prove useful.

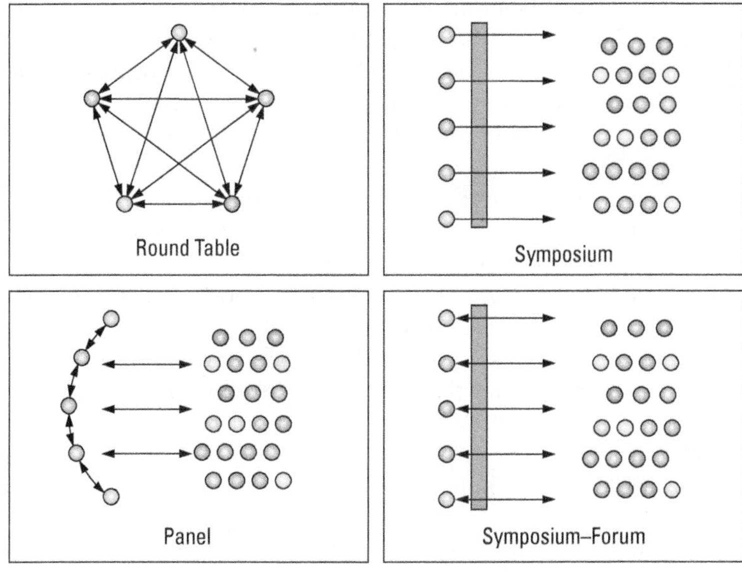

Figure 13.1
Small Group Formats
These four formats are general patterns that may describe a wide variety of groups. Within each type there will naturally be considerable variation. For example, in the symposium–forum there's no set pattern for how much time will be spent on the symposium part and how much time will be spent on the forum part. Similarly, combinations may be used. Thus, for example, group members may each present a position paper (basically a symposium) and then participate in a round table discussion.

Small Group Stages

The small group develops in much the same way that a conversation develops. As in conversation, there are five **small group stages:** (1) opening, (2) feedforward, (3) business, (4) feedback, and (5) closing.

A small group's *opening stage* is usually a getting-acquainted time in which members introduce themselves and engage in social small talk. After this preliminary get-together, there's usually *a feedforward stage* in which members attempt to identify what needs to be done, who will do it, and so on. In formal business groups, the meeting agenda (which is a perfect example of feedforward) may be reviewed and the tasks of the group identified. In informal social groups, the feedforward may consist simply of introducing a topic of conversation or talking about what the group's members should do.

The *business stage* is the actual work on the tasks—the problem solving, the sharing of information, or whatever else the group needs to do. At the *feedback stage*, the group may reflect on what it has done and perhaps on what remains to be done. Some groups may even evaluate their performance at this stage. At the *closing stage*, the group members again return to their focus on individuals and will perhaps exchange closing comments—"Good seeing you again," and the like.

These stages are rarely distinct from one another. Rather, they blend into one another. For example, the opening stage is not completely finished before the feedforward begins. Rather, as the opening comments are completed, the group begins to introduce feedforward; as the feedforward begins to end, the business starts.

Small Group Formats

Small groups serve their functions in a variety of formats. Among the most popular small group formats for relatively formal functions are the round table, the panel, the symposium, and the symposium–forum (Figure 13.1).

The Round Table

In the **round table format**, group members arrange themselves in a circular or semicircular pattern. They share the information or solve the problem without any set pattern of who speaks when. Group interaction is informal, and members contribute as they see fit. A leader or moderator may be present; he or she may, for example, try to keep the discussion on the topic or encourage more reticent members to speak up.

The Panel

In the **panel**, group members are "experts" but participate informally and without any set pattern of who speaks when, as in a round table. The difference is that there's an audience whose members may interject comments or ask questions. Many talk shows, such as *Jerry Springer* and *Oprah*, use this format.

A variation is the two-panel format, with an expert panel and a lay panel. The lay panel discusses the topic but may turn to the expert panel members when in need of technical information, additional data, or direction.

The Symposium

In the **symposium**, each member delivers a prepared presentation much like a public speech. All speeches are addressed to different aspects of a single topic. A symposium leader introduces the speakers, provides transitions from one speaker to another, and may provide periodic summaries.

The Symposium-Forum

The symposium-forum consists of two parts: a symposium, with prepared speeches, and a **forum,** with questions from the audience and responses by the speakers. The leader introduces the speakers and moderates the question-and-answer session.

Small Group Culture

Small groups, especially those of long standing, develop their own culture. Especially relevant to understanding this cultural dimension of small groups are the group norms and the high or low context with which the group operates. Let's look at each in turn.

Small Group Norms

Group norms are rules or standards of behavior identifying which behaviors are considered appropriate (for example, being willing to take on added tasks or directing conflict toward issues rather than toward people) and which are considered inappropriate (for example, coming in late or not contributing actively). Sometimes these rules for appropriate behavior are *explicit*; they're clearly stated in a company contract or policy, such as "All members must attend department meetings." Sometimes the rules are *implicit*; it is understood that members will be polite or well groomed.

Small group norms apply to individual members as well as to the group as a whole and, of course, will differ from one society to another (Axtell, 1993). For example, in the United States men and women in business are expected to interact when making business decisions as well as when socializing. In Muslim and Buddhist societies, however, religious restrictions prevent mixed-gender groups. In groups in some societies, including those of the United States, Bangladesh, Australia, Germany, Finland, and Hong Kong, punctuality for business meetings is very important. But in Morocco, Italy, Brazil, Zambia, Ireland, and Panama, time is less highly regarded; being late is no great insult and is even expected. In many Persian Gulf states the business executive is likely to conduct meetings with several different people—sometimes dealing with totally different issues—at the same time. In this situation you have to expect to share what in the United States would be "your time" with these other parties.

Norms that regulate a particular group member's behavior, called **role expectations,** identify what each person in an organization is expected to do; for example, Pat is great at formatting and editing and so should play the role of secretary.

You're more likely to accept the norms of your group's culture when you feel your group membership is important and want to continue your membership in the group. You're also more likely to accept these norms when your group is cohesive. **Cohesiveness** means that you and the other members are closely connected, are attracted to one another, and depend on one another to meet your needs. Lastly, you're more apt to accept these norms if you'd be punished by negative reactions or exclusion from the group for violating them (Napier & Gershenfeld, 1992).

REFLECTIONS ON ETHICS

Telling Secrets

In groups of close friends, among family members, or in standing workplace committees, people often exchange secrets with the explicit or only implied assumption that these secrets will not be revealed to outsiders. Revealing or not revealing such secrets often has ethical implications.

In *Secrets* (1983) ethicist Sissela Bok identifies three types of situations in which she argues it would be *unethical* to reveal the secrets of another person. These conditions aren't always easy to identify in any given instance, but they do provide excellent starting points for asking whether or not it's ethical to reveal what we know about another person. And, of course, for any situation, there may be legitimate exceptions.

- It's unethical *to reveal information that you have promised to keep secret.*
- It's unethical *to say things about another person when you know the information to be false.*
- It's unethical *to invade the privacy to which everyone has a right*—to reveal information that no one else has a right to know.

In other situations, however, you may actually have an obligation to reveal a secret. For example, Bok (1983) argues that you have an obligation to reveal a secret when keeping the information hidden will do more harm than good. For example, if a teenager confided in you that he or she intended to commit suicide, you'd have an ethical obligation to say something.

Ethical Choice Point

How would you handle the following situations? (1) An instructor who supervises your study group confides that she is a confirmed racist and proud of it. (2) A 16-year-old member of the wilderness group you're leading confides that she's having unprotected sex with her su-

pervisor at work, a married man. (3) A community religious leader confides that he's skimming a portion of the members' contributions to fund his retirement.

High- and Low-Context Cultures

A high-context culture, you'll recall, is a culture in which much of the information in communication is in the context or in the person rather than explicitly coded in the verbal messages. In a high-context culture people have lots of information in common, so it does not have to be made explicit. A low-context culture, on the other hand, is a culture in which most of the information in communication is explicitly stated in the verbal messages. In a low-context culture people do not assume they share certain information and so make all crucial details explicit.

As you might expect, group members in high-context cultures spend a lot of time getting to know one another before engaging in any important transactions. Because of this prior personal knowledge, a great deal of information is shared and therefore does not have to be explicitly stated in the group's deliberations. Members of low-context cultures, on the other hand, spend less time getting to know one another and therefore do not have that shared knowledge. As a result, everything has to be stated explicitly during the group's discussions. When this simple difference is not taken into account, misunderstandings can easily result. For example, the directness and explicitness characteristic of the low-context culture may prove insulting, insensitive, or unnecessary to members of a high-context culture.

Conversely, to members of a low-context culture, someone from a high-context culture may appear vague, underhanded, even dishonest in his or her reluctance to be explicit or to engage in communication that a low-context culture would consider open and direct.

Power in the Small Group

Power permeates all small groups and all relationships. It influences what you do, when, and with whom. It influences the employment you seek and the employment you get. It influences the friends you choose and don't choose and those who choose you and those who don't. It influences your romantic and family relationships—their success, failure, and level of satisfaction or dissatisfaction.

Power is what enables one person (the one with power) to control the behaviors of others. Thus, if A has power over B and C, then A, by virtue of this power and through the exercise of this power (or the threat of exercising it), can control the behaviors of B and C. Differences in individuals' amounts and types of power influence who makes important decisions, who will prevail in an argument, and who will control the finances.

Although all relationships involve power, they differ in the types of power that the people use and to which they respond. The self-test on page 350 will help you identify the six major types of power.

The six types of power covered in the self-test are (1) legitimate, (2) referent, (3) reward, (4) coercive, (5) expert, and (6) information or persuasion power (French & Raven, 1968; Raven, Centers, & Rodrigues, 1975). You have **legitimate power** (self-test statement 1) over another person when this person believes you have a right by virtue of your position (for example, you're the appointed group leader) to influence or control his or her behavior. Legitimate power usually comes from the leadership roles people occupy. Teachers are often seen to have legitimate power, and this is doubly true for religious teachers. Parents are seen as having legitimate power over their children. Employers, judges, managers, doctors, and police officers are others who may hold legitimate power.

You have **referent power** (statement 2) over another person when that person wishes to be like you or identified with you. Your referent power over another person increases when you're well liked and well respected, when you're seen as attractive and prestigious, when you're of the same gender, and when you have attitudes and experiences similar to those of the other person.

You have **reward power** (statement 3) over a person if you have the ability to give that person rewards—either material (money, promotions, jewelry) or social (love, friendship, respect). Reward power increases attractiveness; we like those who have the power to reward us and who do in fact give us rewards.

Conversely, you have **coercive power** (statement 4) if you have the ability to remove rewards or to administer punishments. Usually, the two kinds of power go hand in hand; if you have reward power, you also have coercive power. For example, parents may grant as well as deny privileges to their children.

You possess **expert power** (statement 5) if group members regard you as having expertise or knowledge—whether or not you truly possess such expertise. Expert power increases when you are seen as being unbiased and having nothing to gain personally from influencing others. It decreases if you are seen as biased and as having something to gain from securing the compliance of others.

You have **information power,** or persuasion power (statement 6), if you're seen as someone who can communicate logically and persuasively. Generally, persuasion power is attributed to people who are seen as having significant information and the ability to use that information in presenting a well-reasoned argument.

Now that the general nature of the small group is clear, let's look at several of the more important types of small groups you'll encounter: idea-generation groups, personal growth groups, information-sharing groups, and problem-solving groups.

TEST YOURSELF

How Powerful Are You?

For each statement, indicate which of the following descriptions is most appropriate, using the following scale: 1 = true of 20 percent or fewer of the people I know; 2 = true of about 21 to 40 percent of the people I know; 3 = true of about 41 to 60 percent of the people I know; 4 = true of about 61 to 80 percent of the people I know; and 5 = true of 81 percent or more of the people I know.

____ **1.** My position is such that I often have to tell others what to do. For example, a mother's position demands that she tell her children what to do, a manager's position demands that he or she tell employees what to do, and so on.

____ **2.** People wish to be like me or identified with me. For example, high school football players may admire the former professional football player who is now their coach and want to be like him.

____ **3.** People see me as having the ability to give them what they want. For example, employers have the ability to give their employees increased pay, longer vacations, or improved working conditions.

____ **4.** People see me as having the ability to administer punishment or to withhold things they want. For example, employers have the ability to reduce voluntary overtime, shorten vacation time, or fail to improve working conditions.

____ **5.** Other people realize that I have expertise in certain areas of knowledge. For example, a doctor has expertise in medicine and so others turn to the doctor to tell them what to do. Someone knowledgeable about computers similarly possesses expertise.

____ **6.** Other people realize that I possess the communication ability to present an argument logically and persuasively.

HOW DID YOU DO? These statements refer to the six major types of power, as described in the text. Low scores (1s and 2s) indicate your belief that you possess little of these particular types of power, and high scores (4s and 5s) indicate your belief that you possess a great deal of these particular types of power.

WHAT WILL YOU DO? How satisfied are you with your level of power? If you're not satisfied, what might you do about it? A good starting place, of course, is to learn the skills of communication—interpersonal, small group, and public speaking—discussed in this text. Consider the kinds of communication patterns that would help you communicate power and exert influence in group situations.

Idea-Generation Groups

Idea-generation groups are small groups that exist solely to generate ideas and often follow a pattern called brainstorming (Beebe & Masterson, 2006; DeVito, 1996; Osborn, 1957). **Brainstorming** is a technique for bombarding a problem and generating as many ideas as possible. This technique involves two stages. The first is the brainstorming period proper; the second is the evaluation period.

The procedures are simple. A problem is selected that is amenable to many possible solutions or ideas. Group members are informed of the problem to be brainstormed before the actual session so that they can think about the topic. When the group meets, each person contributes as many ideas as he or she can think of. All ideas are recorded either in writing or on tape.

A variation on this idea is known as *electronic brainstorming* (EBS). Often aided by special software, members of this virtual group gather at their individual computers, which may be spread out throughout the world, and respond to a question with ideas. The ideas are immediately submitted to the screens of other members anonymously. This anonymity of contributions makes it easier for members to disagree with ideas (when that time comes), but also prevents the eventual solution or grand idea from being identified with any one person; instead, the result is the property of the group.

During this idea-generating session, four general rules are followed.

- **Brainstorm Rule 1: Don't Criticize.** In a brainstorming session all ideas are recorded. They're not evaluated, nor are they even discussed. Any nega-

MEDIA LITERACY

The Third-Person Effect

The *third-person effect* concept is a theory of media influence claiming that people routinely believe they are influenced less by the media than their peers are. So, according to this theory, we tend to believe that our friends, neighbors, and coworkers are influenced more by the media than we are. We mistakenly believe ourselves to be more resistant to media influence than others. A variety of studies conducted on college students have supported this idea (Davison, 1983). Whether the topic was political advertising, rap music, or pornography, students felt they were less susceptible to media influence than were their peers (Hoffner et al., 2001). This belief, research finds, is especially strong when the media message is a negative or socially unacceptable one; for example, people think that messages of violence, racism, or sexism influence them much less than their peers. The effect is weakened but still present when the message is a more acceptable one (for example, public service announcements).

> "We mistakenly believe ourselves to be more resistant to media influence than others."

Try testing out this theory. For example, survey 10 or 20 people and ask them how influenced they feel they are by, say, media violence or racism. Then ask them if their friends and relatives are influenced by such media messages more than they are. Then conduct the same type of two-step survey with a more socially acceptable message, such as a media campaign on the value of education or the importance of proper diet. On the basis of your research, what can you add to this discussion?

tive criticism—whether verbal or nonverbal—is itself criticized by the leader or the members. This is a good general rule to follow in all creative thinking: Allow your idea time to develop before you look for problems with it. At the same time, don't praise the ideas either. All evaluations should be suspended during the brainstorming session.

- **Brainstorm Rule 2: Strive for Quantity.** Linus Pauling, Nobel Prize winner for chemistry in 1954 and for peace in 1962, once said, "The best way to have a good idea is to have lots of ideas." This second rule of brainstorming embodies this concept. If you need an idea, you're more likely to find it in a group of many than in a group of few. Thus, in brainstorming, the more ideas the better.
- **Brainstorm Rule 3: Combine and Extend Ideas.** Although you may not criticize a particular idea, you're encouraged to extend it or combine it in some way. The value of a particular idea may be the way it stimulates someone to combine or extend it. Even if your modification seems minor or obvious, say it. Don't censor yourself.
- **Brainstorm Rule 4: Develop the Wildest Ideas Possible.** The wilder the idea, the better. It's easier to tone an idea down than to build it up. A wild idea can easily be tempered, but it's not so easy to elaborate on a simple or conservative idea.

Sometimes a brainstorming session may break down, with members failing to contribute new ideas. At this point the moderator may prod the members with statements such as the following:

- Let's try to get a few more ideas before we close this session.
- Can we piggyback any other ideas or add extensions on the suggestion to . . . ?
- Here's an aspect we haven't focused on. Does this stimulate any ideas?

After all the ideas are generated—a period lasting no longer than 15 or 20 minutes—the group evaluates the entire list of ideas, using the critical thinking skills developed throughout this text. The ideas that are unworkable are thrown out; those that show promise are retained and evaluated. During this stage, negative criticism is allowed.

UNDERSTANDING THEORY AND RESEARCH

Group Power

Recall (from Chapter 2) that high-power-distance cultures are those in which power is concentrated in the hands of a few and there's a great difference between the power held by these people and the power held by the ordinary citizen; in contrast, in low-power-distance cultures power is more evenly distributed throughout the citizenry (Hofstede, 1997). Groups also may be viewed in terms of high and low power distance. In high-power-distance groups, the leader is far more powerful than the members. In low-power-distance groups, leaders and members differ much less in their power.

Of the groups in which you'll participate—as a member or as a leader—some will be high in power distance and others will be low. The skill is to recognize which is which, to follow the rules generally, and to break the rules only after you've thought through the consequences. For example, in low-power-distance groups, you're expected to confront a group leader (or friend or supervisor) assertively; acting assertively denotes a general feeling of equality (Borden, 1991). In high-power-distance groups, direct confrontation and assertiveness toward the leader (or toward any person in authority, such as a teacher or doctor) may be viewed negatively (Bochner & Hesketh, 1994; Westwood, Tang, & Kirkbride, 1992).

Working with Theories and Research

- *Visit one of the online databases to which you have access and search the communication and sociology databases for power. What types of questions engage the attention of researchers?*

Personal Growth Groups

Some **personal growth groups,** sometimes referred to as support groups, aim to help members cope with particular difficulties—such as drug addiction, not being assertive enough, having an alcoholic parent, being an ex-convict, or having a hyperactive child or a promiscuous spouse. Other groups are more clearly therapeutic and are designed to change significant aspects of an individual's personality or behavior. Still other groups are devoted to making healthy individuals function even more effectively.

Personal growth groups vary widely in their procedures, so it's not possible to provide a standard pattern that all such groups follow (as is the case with brainstorming groups, discussed above, or with problem-solving groups, discussed later in this chapter). But let's look briefly at three well-known types of personal growth groups: the encounter group, the assertiveness training group, and the consciousness-raising group.

The Encounter Group

Encounter groups, also known as "sensitivity groups" or "T [Training]-groups," for example, constitute a form of psychotherapy; these groups try to facilitate members' personal growth and foster their ability to deal effectively with other people (Hirsch, Kett, & Trefil, 2002; Rogers, 1970). One of the encounter group's assumptions is that the members will be more effective, both psychologically and interpersonally, if they get to know and like themselves better. Consequently, members are encouraged to look at themselves and their relationships honestly and in depth and to react to others in the group openly and honestly. Members are encouraged to express their inner thoughts, fears, and doubts in the encounter group, in which interactions are always characterized by total acceptance and support.

The Assertiveness Training Group

The **assertiveness training group** aims to increase the willingness of its members to stand up for their rights and to act more assertively in a wide variety of situations (Adler, 1977; Bishop, 2006). Distinctions are made between being assertive (which is good and effective); being nonassertive (which is ineffective, because your own wants and needs are unlikely to be met); and being aggressive (which also is ineffective, because it contributes to escalating the conflict and causing resentment). The group

BUILDING COMMUNICATION SKILLS

Combating Idea Killers

Think about how you can be on guard against negative criticism and how you can respond to "idea killers" or "killer messages." Some expressions, such as those listed below, aim to stop an idea from being developed—to kill it in its tracks before it can even get off the ground. As you read down the list of these commonly heard killer messages, formulate at least one response you might give if someone used one of these on you or if you yourself used it to censor your own creative thinking.

1. It'll never work.
2. No one would vote for it.
3. It's too complex.
4. It's too simple.
5. It would take too long.
6. It's too expensive.
7. It's not logical.
8. What we have is good enough.
9. It just doesn't fit us.
10. It's impossible.

Creativity needs a great deal of freedom to develop; try not to stifle it by allowing ideas to be put down before you have a chance to examine them carefully.

aims to increase the assertiveness skills of its members, who are likely to be people who feel they are not assertive enough.

The Consciousness-Raising Group

The **consciousness-raising group** aims to help people cope with the problems society confronts them with. The members of a consciousness-raising group all have one characteristic in common (for example, they may all be women, unwed mothers, gay fathers, or recently unemployed executives). It's this commonality that leads the members to join together and help one another. In the consciousness-raising group the assumption is that similar people are best equipped to assist one another's personal growth. The procedures generally followed are simple: A topic is selected, and each member speaks on the topic as it relates to the general group topic. For example, if the group consists of unwed mothers, then whatever the topic (taxes, children, school, prejudice), the members address it in the context of the group's focus on unwed motherhood. No interruptions are allowed. After each member has finished, the other group members may ask questions of clarification. The feedback from other members is to be totally supportive. After the last member has spoken, a general discussion follows. This procedure is designed to help raise members' consciousness by giving them an opportunity to formulate and verbalize their thoughts on a particular topic, hear how others feel and think about the same topic, and formulate and answer questions of clarification.

Information-Sharing Groups

The purpose of **information-sharing groups** is to enable members to acquire new information or skills through a sharing of knowledge. In most information-sharing groups, all members have something to teach and something to learn. In some, however, the interaction takes place because some members have information and some don't.

Educational or Learning Groups

In **educational or learning groups**, the members pool their knowledge to the benefit of all, as in the popular law and medical student learning groups. Members may follow a variety of discussion patterns. For example, a historical topic might be developed chronologically, with the discussion progressing from the past into the present and perhaps predicting the future. Issues in developmental psychology, such as physical maturity or language development in the child, also might be discussed chronologically. Some topics lend themselves to spatial development. For example, study of the development of the United States might take either a spatial pattern, going from east to west, or a chronological pattern, going from

BUILDING COMMUNICATION SKILLS

Listening to New Ideas

A useful skill for listening to new ideas is PIP'N, a technique that derives from Carl Rogers's (1970) emphasis on paraphrasing as a means for ensuring understanding and Edward deBono's (1976) PMI (*plus*, *minus*, and *interesting*) technique. PIP'N involves four steps:

P 5 Paraphrase. State in your own words what you think the other person is saying. This will ensure that you and the person proposing the idea are talking about the same thing. Your paraphrase also will provide the other person with the opportunity to elaborate or clarify his or her ideas.

I 5 Interesting. State something interesting that you find in the idea. Say why you think this idea might be interesting to you, to others, to the organization.

P 5 Positive. Say something positive about the idea. What is good about it? How might it solve a problem or make a situation better?

N 5 Negative. State any negatives that you think the idea might entail. Might it prove expensive? Difficult to implement? Is it directed at insignificant issues?

Try using PIP'N the next time you hear about a new idea; say, in conversation or in a small group. For practice, try PIP'N on the PIP'N technique itself: (1) Paraphrase the PIP'N technique; (2) say why the technique is interesting; (3) say something positive about it; and (4) say something negative about it.

It's often easier to analyze an idea when you follow specific steps; in this way there's less likelihood that you'll omit some crucial element in the process.

1776 to the present. Other suitable patterns, depending on the nature of the topic and the needs of the participants, might be developed in terms of causes and effects, problems and solutions, or structures and functions.

Perhaps the most popular is the topical pattern. A group might discuss the challenges of raising a hyperactive child by itemizing and discussing each of the major problems. The structure of a corporation might also be considered in terms of its major divisions. As can be appreciated, topical approaches may be further systematized; for instance, a learning group might rank the problems of hyperactivity in terms of their importance or complexity or might order the major structures of the corporation in terms of decision-making power.

Focus Groups

A different type of learning group is the **focus group,** a small group assembled for a kind of in-depth interview. The aim here is to discover what people think about an issue or product; for example, what do men between 18 and 25 think of the new aftershave lotion and its packaging? What do young executives earning more than $100,000 think about buying a foreign luxury car?

In the focus group, a leader tries to discover the beliefs, attitudes, thoughts, and feelings that members have so as to help an organization make decisions on changing the scent or redesigning the packaging of aftershave lotion, or constructing advertisements for luxury cars. It is the leader's task to prod members to analyze their thoughts and feelings on a deeper level and to use the thoughts of one member to stimulate the thoughts of others.

Generally, approximately 12 people are assembled. The leader explains the process, the time limits, and the general goal of the group—let's say, to discover why these 12 individuals requested information on the XYZ health plan but purchased a plan from another company. The idea, of course, is that these 12 people are representing a wider population. The leader, who is usually a professional focus group facilitator rather than a member of the client organization itself, asks a variety of questions such as: How did you hear about the XYZ health plan? What other health plans did you consider before making your actual purchase? What influenced you to buy the plan you eventually bought? Were any

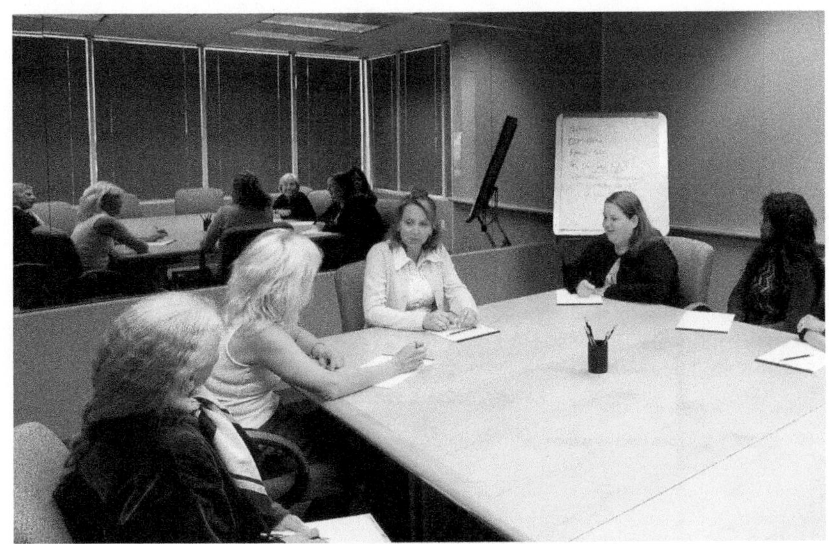

Stimulating Contributions

You're in charge of a focus group discussing what they like and dislike about the websites they visit. The problem you anticipate, based on past experience, is that a few members will do all the talking and the rest will hardly talk at all. You want to encourage all members to participate fully.

What are some of the ways you can confront this problem? What might you say?

other people influential in helping you make your decision? Through the exploration of these and similar questions, the facilitator and the relevant members of the client organization (who may be seated behind a one-way mirror, watching the discussion) may put together a more effective health plan or more effective advertising strategies.

Problem-Solving Groups

A **problem-solving group** is a collection of individuals who meet to solve a problem or to reach a decision. In one sense this is the most exacting kind of group to participate in. It requires not only a knowledge of small group communication techniques, but also a thorough knowledge of the particular problem. And it usually demands faithful adherence to a somewhat rigid set of rules. We'll look at this group first in terms of the classic and still popular problem-solving approach, whereby we identify the steps to go through in solving a problem. In the context of this sequence, we'll consider the major decision-making methods. Finally, we'll survey some types of groups that are popular in organizations today: the nominal group, the Delphi method, and quality circles.

The Problem-Solving Sequence

The approach developed by philosopher John Dewey (1910), the **problem-solving sequence,** is probably the technique used most often. The six steps of the sequence (see Figure 13.2) are designed to make problem solving more efficient and effective: (1) Define and analyze the problem, (2) establish criteria, (3) identify possible solutions, (4) evaluate solutions, (5) select the best solution(s), and (6) test the selected solution(s).

Step 1: Define and Analyze the Problem

In many instances the nature of the problem is clearly specified. For example, a group of designers might discuss how to package a new soap product. In other instances, however, the problem may be vague, and it may remain for the group to define it in concrete terms. Thus, the general problem may be that your company wants to increase profits, and the solution that needs to be found is a way to make the company more profitable. But such a broad and general topic is difficult to tackle in a single problem-solving discussion, so it may be helpful to specify the problem in more specific and limited terms. Perhaps this hypothetical problem will need to be dealt with in a series of problem-solving discussions on "How to reduce waste," "How to increase market visibility," and/or "How to improve the company website."

Define the problem as an open-ended question ("How can we improve the company website?") rather than as a statement ("The company website needs to be improved") or a yes/no question ("Does the website need improvement?"). The open-ended question allows greater freedom of exploration. Some appropriate questions for most problems revolve around the following issues:

- **Duration.** How long has the problem existed? Is it likely to continue in the future? What is the predicted course of the problem? For example, will it grow or lessen in impact?
- **Causes.** What are the major causes of the problem? How certain can we be that these are the actual causes?

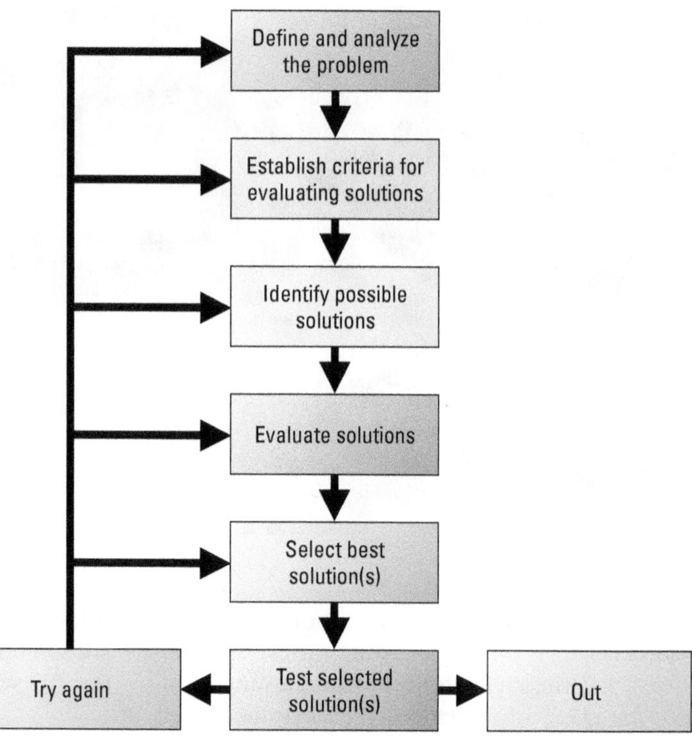

Figure 13.2
Steps in Problem-Solving Discussion
Although most small group theorists would advise you to follow the problem-solving pattern as presented here, others would alter it somewhat. For example, the pattern here advises you first to define the problem and then to establish criteria for identifying possible solutions. You would then keep these criteria in mind as you generated possible solutions (step 3). Another school of thought, however, would advise you to generate solutions first and to consider how they will be evaluated only after these solutions are proposed (Brilhart & Galanes, 1992). The advantage of this second approach is that you may generate more creative solutions if you're not restricted by standards of evaluation. The disadvantage is that you may spend a great deal of time generating impractical solutions that would never meet the standards you'll eventually propose.

- **Effects.** What are the effects of the problem? How significant are they? Who is affected by this problem? How significantly are they affected? Is this problem causing other problems? How important are these other problems?

Step 2: Establish Criteria for Evaluating Solutions

Before any solutions are proposed, the group should decide on the criteria or standards for evaluating the solution. This step will enable you to rule out unacceptable solutions and to devote your time to solutions that seem possible and workable. At this stage you identify the standards or criteria that you'll use in evaluating solutions or in selecting one solution over another. Generally, two types of criteria need to be considered:

- **Practical criteria.** For example, you might decide that solutions to the website problem must not increase the budget, must lead to a higher volume of business, must be constructed in-house, must load almost immediately, and so on.
- **Value criteria.** These are usually more difficult to identify. These might include, for example, requirements that the website reflect the culture of the company, that it represent the company's commitment to multiculturalism, or that it serve to benefit the community.

Step 3: Identify Possible Solutions

At this stage identify as many solutions as possible. Focus on quantity rather than quality. Brainstorming may be particularly useful at this point (see the earlier discussion of idea-generation groups). Solutions to the website problem might include incorporating reviews of publications by company members, reviews of restaurants in the area, recruitment guidelines, and new employment opportunities within the company.

Step 4: Evaluate Solutions

After all the solutions have been proposed, go back and evaluate each according to the criteria you have established. For example, to what extent does incorporating reviews of area restaurants meet the evaluation criteria? Will it increase the budget? Each potential solution should be matched against the criteria.

An especially insightful technique for evaluating solutions is presented in Table 13.1.

Step 5: Select the Best Solution(s)

At this stage the best solution or solutions are selected and put into operation. For instance, in the company website example, if "reviews of area restaurants" and "listings of new positions" best met the evaluation criteria, the group might then incorporate these two new items in the redesign of the website.

Table 13.3
The Six Critical Thinking Hats

This technique involves thinking with six different "hats" and, in doing so, subjecting an issue to a six-part analysis (deBono, 1987).

Hat	Focus	Possible Questions to Ask
The Fact Hat	Focuses on the data—the facts and figures that bear on the problem.	▪ What are the relevant data on the website? ▪ How much does it cost to establish and maintain a website?
The Feeling Hat	Focuses on your feelings, emotions, and intuitions concerning the problem.	▪ How do we feel about the current website? ▪ How do we feel about making changes?
The Negative Argument Hat	Focuses on the possible negative aspects of a proposed solution.	▪ Why might this proposed solution fail? ▪ What is the worst-case scenario?
The Positive Benefits Hat	Focuses on the possible positive aspects of a proposed solution.	▪ What benefits will this website provide for employees? ▪ What is the best case scenario?
The Creative New Idea Hat	Focuses on new ways of looking at a problem and can be easily combined with the techniques of brainstorming.	▪ In what other ways can we look at this problem? ▪ How can the website provide a service to the community?
The Control of Thinking Hat	Focuses on the thinking processes that are going into finding a solution.	▪ Have we adequately defined the problem? ▪ Are we focusing too much on insignificant issues?

Groups may use different decision-making methods in deciding, for example, which criteria to use or which solutions to accept. Generally, groups use one of three methods: decision by authority, majority rule, or consensus.

Decision by Authority. In decision by authority, members voice their feelings and opinions, but the leader, boss, or CEO makes the final decision. Sometimes, the authority is an expert who is called in to make the ultimate decision—as might be the case in, say, deciding what surgical procedure to use in a specific case. This is surely an efficient method; it gets things done quickly, and the amount of discussion can be limited as desired. Another advantage is that experienced and informed members (for example, those who have the most experience with these types of operations) will probably exert a greater influence on the final decision. The great disadvantage is that group members may not feel the need to contribute their insights and may become distanced from the power within the group or organization. Another disadvantage is that this method may lead members to tell the decision maker what they feel she or he wants to hear, a condition that can easily lead to groupthink.

Decision by Majority Rule. With this method the group members agree to abide by the majority decision and may vote on various issues as the group works toward solving its problem. Majority rule is efficient, as there's usually the option of calling for a vote when the majority is in agreement. One disadvantage of this method is that it can lead to fractioning, in which various minorities align against the majority. The method may also lead to limiting discussion once a majority has agreed and a vote is called.

Decision by Consensus. In small group decision-making, consensus means reaching agreement. The agreement does not have to be unanimous; it is, rather, something that the group members can live with. The members agree that they can and will do whatever the group's solution requires (Kelly, 1994).

Consensus also implies that all members of the group had their say and that their opinions were carefully considered. The best of these opinions (in the group's estimation) are then combined and synthesized into a solution that the group as a whole gives agreement and permission to follow. It does not imply that you—as an individual group member—agree with the solution but only that you agree that (at this time, for this situation, for this group) this solution should be adopted and followed.

Here are a few hints to working in a group designed to achieve its solution by consensus; members and leader should:

- understand the nature of consensus, what it is and what it isn't.
- be willing to abide by the group's decisions.
- feel free to express their opinions, openly and honestly, while listeners must be open-minded, with a willingness to change their own initial opinions.
- make an honest attempt to incorporate as many of the members' needs, thoughts, and proposals into the final solution as reasonable and possible.
- be willing to put the group's needs ahead of their individual needs.

Consensus is the most time-consuming of the decision-making methods. However, it is also the method that best secures the cooperation and participation of all members in implementing the group's decisions. If you want members of the group to be satisfied and committed to the decision, consensus seems the best way to select a solution (Beebe & Masterson, 2009).

Step 6: Test Selected Solution(s)

After solutions are put into operation, test their effectiveness. The group might, for example, poll employees about the website changes, examine the number of hits, or analyze the advertising revenue.

If the solutions you have adopted prove ineffective, you will need to go back to one of the previous stages and repeat part of the process. Often this takes the form of selecting other solutions to test. But it may also involve going further back—for example, to a reanalysis of the problem, an identification of other solutions, or a restatement of evaluation criteria.

Problem-Solving Groups at Work

The problem-solving sequence discussed here is used widely in business in a variety of different types of groups. Let's examine three group approaches popular in business that rely largely on the problem-solving techniques just discussed: the nominal group technique, the Delphi method, and quality circles.

As you read these discussions, realize that the available technology will dictate some of the ways in which these groups operate. If all the members have is a whiteboard, then much will be recorded on the board. If all members have laptops connected to the company website, then much of the record keeping will go onto the website and at the same time into each laptop.

The Nominal Group Technique

The **nominal group** technique is a method of problem solving that uses limited discussion and

Critical Thinking

You're on a team (all equal in your organizational position) charged with designing the packaging for a new cell phone, and you need to establish how a decision will be made.

What are some of your decision-making options? What are the advantages and disadvantages of each decision-making option?

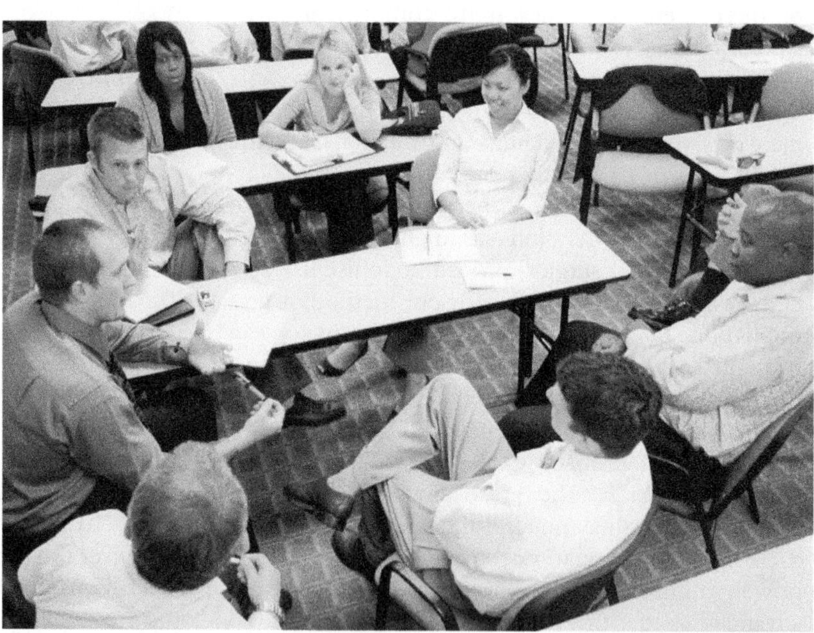

confidential voting to obtain a group decision. It's especially helpful when some members may be reluctant to voice their opinions in a regular problem-solving group or when the issue is controversial or sensitive. The nominal group approach can be divided into eight steps (Kelly, 1994):

1. The problem is defined and clarified for all members.
2. Each member writes down (without discussion or consultation with others) his or her ideas on or possible solutions to the problem.
3. Each member—in sequence—states one idea from his or her list, which is recorded on a board or flip chart so everyone can see it. This process is repeated until all suggestions are stated and recorded.
4. Each suggestion is clarified (without debate). Ideally, each suggestion is given equal time.
5. Each member rank-orders the suggestions in writing.
6. The rankings of the members are combined to get a group ranking, which is then written on the board.
7. Clarification, discussion, and possible reordering may follow.
8. The highest-ranking or several high-ranking solutions may then be put into operation and tested.

The Delphi Method

In the **Delphi method** a group of "experts" is established, but there's no interaction among them; instead, they communicate by repeatedly responding to questionnaires (Kelly, 1994; Tersine & Riggs, 1980). The Delphi method is especially useful when you want to involve people who are geographically distant from one another, when you want all members to become part of the solution and to uphold it, or when you want to minimize the effects of dominant members or even of peer pressure. The method is best explained as a series of steps (Kelly, 1994).

1. The problem is defined (for example, "We need to improve intradepartmental communication"). What each member is expected to do is specified (for example, each member should contribute five ideas on this specific question).
2. Each member then anonymously contributes five ideas in writing.
3. The ideas of all members are combined, written up, and distributed to all members.
4. Members then select the three or four best ideas from this composite list and submit these.
5. From these responses another list is produced and distributed to all members.
6. Members then select the one or two best ideas from the new list and submit these.

UNDERSTANDING THEORY AND RESEARCH

Group Polarization

Groups frequently make more extreme decisions than individuals—a tendency known as group polarization (Brauer, Judd, & Gliner, 1995; Bullock, et al., 2002; Friedkin, 1999). For example, a group will take greater risks if the individual members are already willing to take risks (a condition known as the "risky shift phenomenon"), or will become more cautious if the members are already cautious. What seems to happen is that as a group member you estimate how others in the group feel about risk taking. If you judge the group as one of high-risk takers, you're likely to become more willing to take risks than you were before the group interaction. Similarly, if you judge the group members as cautious and as low-risk takers, you'll become even more cautious than you were before the interaction. In other words—and not surprisingly—your own attitudes toward risk will be heavily influenced by the attitudes you think the group possesses, and you're likely to change your attitudes to more closely match those of the group.

Working with Theories and Research

- *Have you ever observed group polarization? What happened? What implications does this theory have for, say, gang members, professors joining a new faculty, or investment analysts?*

7. From these responses another list is produced and distributed to all members. The process may be repeated any number of times, but usually three rounds are sufficient for achieving a fair degree of agreement.
8. The "final" solutions are identified and are communicated to all members.

Quality Circles

A **quality circle** is a group of workers (usually about 6 to 12) whose task it is to investigate and make recommendations for improving the quality of some organizational function. The members are drawn from the workers whose area is being studied; for example, if the problem were how to improve advertising on the Internet, then the quality circle membership would be drawn from the advertising and technology departments. The basic assumption is that people who work on similar tasks will be best able to improve their departments or jobs by pooling their insights and working through problems they share.

Quality circle members investigate problems using any method they feel might be helpful; for example, they may form face-to-face problem-solving groups or use nominal groups or Delphi methods. The group then reports its findings and its suggestions to those who can implement the proposals.

As you can see from just this one chapter, small groups exist in a variety of forms or types—each with their own rules and goals. Knowing how these groups can be used most effectively will prove a great asset in personal life and perhaps especially in the workplace. Another essential part of small group competence is knowing how to function as both a group member and a group leader.

Summary: Small Group Communication

This chapter introduced the nature of the small group and team and discussed four major types of groups (idea-generation, personal growth, information-sharing, and problem solving) and their functions and procedures.

Small Groups and Teams

1. A small group is a collection of individuals who are connected to one another by some common purpose, are interdependent, have some degree of organization among them, and see themselves as a group.
2. Small groups make use of four major formats: the round table, the panel, the symposium, and the symposium–forum.
3. Virtual groups, such as mailing lists and chat groups, serve both relationship and professional purposes.
4. Most small groups develop norms or rules that operate much like cultural norms, identifying what is considered appropriate behavior for the group members.
5. Power operates in all groups. Six types of power may be identified: legitimate, referent, reward, coercive, expert, and information or persuasion.

Idea-Generation Groups

6. The idea-generation or brainstorming group attempts to generate as many ideas as possible.

Personal Growth Groups

7. The personal growth group helps members to deal with personal problems and to function more effectively. Popular types of personal growth groups are the encounter group, the assertiveness training group, and the consciousness-raising group.

Information-Sharing Groups

8. Information-sharing groups attempt to enable members to acquire new information or skill through a mutual sharing of knowledge or insight. In educational or learning groups, the members pool their knowledge to the benefit of all. The focus group aims to discover what people think about an issue or product through a kind of in-depth group interview.

Problem-Solving Groups

9. The problem-solving group attempts to solve a particular problem, or at least to reach a decision that may cause the problem to solve itself.
10. The six steps in the problem-solving sequence are: Define and analyze the problem; establish criteria for evaluating solutions; identify possible solutions; evaluate solutions; select best solution(s); and test solution(s).
11. The six critical thinking hats technique is especially useful in analyzing problems and evaluating solu-

tions. This technique consists of focusing on different aspects of the issue: facts, feelings, negative arguments, positive benefits, creative or new ways of viewing problems, and control of thinking processes.

12. Decision-making methods include decision by authority, decision by majority rule, and decision by consensus.
13. Small group approaches that are widely used in business today include the nominal group, the Delphi method, and quality circles.

Key Terms

assertiveness training group
brainstorming
coercive power
cohesiveness
consciousness-raising group
critical thinking hats technique
Delphi method
educational or learning groups
encounter groups
expert power
focus group
forum
group norms
idea-generation groups
information power
information-sharing groups
legitimate power
nominal group
panel
personal growth groups
power
problem-solving group
problem-solving sequence
quality circle
referent power
reward power
role expectations
round table format
small group
small group stages
symposium
team
virtual groups

Thinking Critically: About Small Group Communication

1. **Small Group Creativity.** Studies find that persons high in communication apprehension are generally less effective in idea-generation groups than those who are low in apprehension (Comadena, 1984; Cragan & Wright, 1990; Jablin, 1981). Why do you think this is so?
2. **Group Norms.** What norms govern your class in human communication? What norms govern your family? What norms govern your place of work? Do you have any difficulty with these norms?
3. **Chat Groups.** In research on chat groups, it was found that people were more likely to comment on a participant's message when that message was negative than when it was positive (Rollman, Krug, & Parente, 2000). Do you find this to be true? If so, why do you think this occurs?
4. **Developing Criteria.** What type of criteria would an advertising agency use in evaluating a campaign to sell soap? A university, in evaluating a new multicultural curriculum? Parents, in evaluating a preschool for their children?
5. **Uses and Gratifications.** One study identified seven gratifications you derive from online communication: being in a virtual community, seeking information, aesthetic experience, financial compensation, diversion, personal status, and maintaining relationships (Song, LaRose, Eastin, & Lin, 2004). How would you describe the gratifications you receive from online groups?

CHAPTER

14

Appraising Argumentation

Taken from *Argumentation and Critical Decision Making*, Eighth Edition by Richard D. Rieke, Malcolm O. Sillars and Tarla Rai Peterson.

When you interview for a job, you and the interviewer are engaged in reasoned argumentation. The position announcement should set the broad **criteria** that will be used to judge your application, and the interview will flesh them out. Here is a position announcement:

We are looking for an administrator in our downtown office. This person will support our Information Technology consulting services operations for our national clients.

- Excellent MS Office solid Excel and PowerPoint skills
- Organized and detail-oriented
- General understanding of IT terminologies and technologies
- Good writing skills
- Good phone and interpersonal relationship skills
- Good typing skills
- Good conceptual skills with an ability to crunch numbers and generate reports

In return, you can expect the following:

- Join a stable, fast growing technology company
- To be treated with respect and make a contribution to our growth and success

When you go to the interview, they could well ask, "Why should we hire you?" This is an invitation for you to present arguments on your behalf, complementing those in your application. What will be the strongest arguments you can make? At this stage, your best bet is to follow the criteria set out in the job announcement and argue this way:

ULTIMATE PURPOSE: TO BE HIRED BY THIS COMPANY

PROPOSITION: I have the ability to be an excellent employee.

CLAIM #1: I have excellent MS Office and solid Excel and PowerPoint skills, and I have a general understanding of IT terminologies and technologies.

SUPPORT: My transcript shows courses in these areas;

CLAIM #2: I am organized and a detail-oriented person, with good conceptual skills and an ability to crunch numbers and generate reports,

SUPPORT: The letter from my last employer mentions these skills;

CLAIM #3: I am effective in writing, typing, phone, and interpersonal relationships,

SUPPORT: My letters of recommendation report on these skills, and I have samples of my written work.

Figure 14.1
Arguments Based on Criteria

If you can convince the interviewers of each of these points, and if they truly are the criteria being used to make this decision, it would be reasonable for them to hire you. It would be a **critical decision**. Of course, they could interview five people, all of whom meet these criteria. It would be reasonable to hire any one of them. So, a critical decision does not mean resolution of uncertainty. It does not necessarily mean finding the one correct decision. It means selecting and applying a set of criteria designed to generate the best possible decision.

What will probably happen is this: During the interview, the employer will refine the criteria as you develop your arguments. They will try to make value judgments about the quality of your credentials compared to other applicants, and, before making a hiring decision, they will probably discuss the applicant pool with other colleagues to add their particular criteria.

Before a job offer is made, still other criteria may be applied, partly in response to arguments you make. For example, you might comment on their promise of treating you with respect and allowing you to participate in their growth and success. You might say, "I value your promise of treating me with respect, and in return I commit myself to working for the growth and success of this company."

Critical decision is one that can survive the test of a relevant set of criteria, one that can stand up to *criticism*. We also said that argumentation and critical decision making involve choice in a context of uncertainty.

In this chapter, we will talk about how people apply criteria to arguments, and how they can use such criticism to increase the quality of their decisions even in the face of uncertainty. We introduce the term **reasonable** to describe the process through which arguments are tested and finally granted adherence because they rest on reasons and reasoning that reflect the standards of the sphere within which they are being critically examined. First, we will identify some of the forces that tend to reduce the reasonableness of decisions. Then, we will give greater detail about how people make reasonable decisions.

Argumentation and Being Reasonable

Critical appraisal of argumentation applies to you in two interacting ways: (1) When you *present* an argument, the better you understand the way it will be evaluated, the stronger you can make it; (2) When you *evaluate* an argument, the better you understand the relevant criteria (tests for argument evaluation), the better (more critical) will be your decisions. These two points interact in the sense that presenters and evaluators of argumentation do their jobs best when they consciously operate within a common set of criteria.

Why People Advance Unreasonable Arguments

Unreasonable arguments cannot stand up to critical appraisal. Often, the sphere defines what counts as an unreasonable argument. For example, in hiring decisions, laws specify that the company may not use criteria based on age, gender, religion, race, national origin, marital status, and so forth, and to bring up arguments about these categories would not stand up to criticism. The laws were passed to counter the *beliefs* some people have about age, gender, religion, race, and many other discriminatory concepts that have been used to make unreasonable decisions.

Beliefs Are Not Necessarily Reasonable

The Wizard's First Rule tells us, "Given proper motivations, almost anyone will believe almost anything. . . . They will believe a lie because they want to believe it's true, or because they are afraid it might be true" (Goodkind 560). Even when no one actually believes something, if no one can disprove it, then "a lie unchallenged is very soon stronger than a truth unsupported" (Hill 238). Novelist and law professor Stephen L. Carter puts it this way: "We're reasoning creatures. . . . We're designed to breathe the truth. We need it to live. When the truth we crave is hidden away, we'll breathe the lies to keep from smothering" (436). Although your beliefs are important and meaningful to you, they may not have come from a reasonable foundation or they may be applied in a way that cannot survive critical scrutiny.

Patrick Colm Hogan reports a variety of studies showing that beliefs operating in systems are behind a good deal of our tendency to conform to political and ideological positions even when the beliefs are quite untrue or at least without clear support (58–86). People develop fundamental beliefs during childhood that continue to influence their decisions throughout life. "They distort people's perceptions and even their memories, reforming individuals' experience in their image. For many years, cognitive scientists have been aware of a broad human tendency to reinterpret experience in conformity with basic beliefs " (74).

Glenn D. Walters argues that criminal behavior can be best understood by examining the development of individuals' belief systems. He defines a **belief system** as a "group of interrelated convictions of truth or statements of perceived reality" (21). They involve, he says, not only cognitive elements but also behavioral, sensory, motivational, and affective features. Walters says that beliefs interact both with the internal elements just mentioned and with one's experience. Beliefs are, says Walters, "more than what fills a person's head. . . . [P]eople construct their own realities and then proceed to defend these realities against alternative perspectives" (21, 44).

Your beliefs function, as these authors suggest, in belief systems that we will call **worldviews**. It is from your worldviews that you experience stereotypes, prejudices, norms, folkways, language, and culture. Worldviews are neither inherently reasonable nor unreasonable. They enable you to make it through life more comfortably. Having a common language is obviously important. So is sharing common narratives, scripts, or stories of how to go about your daily life: how to dress, eat, play, worship, form relationships, educate children, and care for the elderly. What you perceive as commonsense in any occasion is determined by your worldviews. You may have noticed, however, that your commonsense is different from that of, say, your acquaintances from other parts of the world. You may feel that other people's commonsense is unreasonable; they may think the same of you.

Thinking Is Not Necessarily Reasonable

More than a half-century of psychological research supports the claim that people use a variety of biases and heuristics (shortcuts in thinking) to guide their decision making in ways that depart from what rational theory would predict (Gilovich and Griffin 4–16). For example, thinking may be guided by facts that happen to be readily available or easy to access rather than those most significant to supporting your point. For example, when you do an Internet search to prepare a research paper, you may be confronted with thousands of items. Do you evaluate all the hits and make sure you are using only the most reliable, or do you look just long enough to meet your immediate needs and then write the paper (a heuristic called *satisficing*)? No one expects you to look at all the many hits that come up, but you are expected to evaluate the quality of those you do use. Even numerical data presented in graphs can lead to less than optimal decisions when managers use their ideas of what is generally true in their experience to interpret the data. "A large body of evidence suggests that prior beliefs significantly distort perceptions of correlation, such that people overestimate relationships that are expected and underestimate relationships that are unexpected. . . . [This is] the failure of analytic thinking to overcome informal prior impressions" (Hutchinson et al. 628).

A study of juror decision making found that jurors' race, the interpretation of the presumption of innocence, and the amount of evidence they were expected to consider had the "potential to decisively alter the outcome of critical judgments" (Tamborini et al. 354). Researcher Ron Tamborini and his associates observed that people can approach decision making from two forms of cognitive processing: systematic processing (what we describe as critical decision making) or heuristic processing which they conceptualized as "a more limited mode of information processing that requires less cognitive effort and fewer cognitive resources than systematic processing" (342). For example, a juror might look at the defendant and decide on guilt or innocence simply because he or she was more or less attractive, of the same or different race as the juror, or consider the defendant's gender, dress, behavior, and so on. This would exemplify heuristic processing.

The point is that while people are capable of systematic processing, the use of heuristic processing is easier and thus quite likely to be employed when motivation is low (Gilovich & Griffin 16).

The Mind Is Not Necessarily Reasonable

Ever since Plato assumed a separation of mind and body, and Aristotle proclaimed human beings to be rational animals, scholars have operated on the assumption that our mind functions in an inherently logical way. Aristotle's rhetorical system is premised on the assumption that people are able to find truth, even when it is mixed in with a great deal of nonsense, because they have a rational capacity. To this day, some logicians, linguists, psycholinguists, and cognitive psychologists continue to claim that the human mind operates according to formal logical rules or probabilities (Braine and O'Brien; Oaksford and Chater).

[We were once told by a clerk of courts that he and his judge could tell just by looking whether the defendant was guilty or not. He thought it a special gift they had.]

Figure 14.2

In his 1637 *Discourse on Method,* René Descartes announced, "I think, therefore, I am," giving his support to the notion that the mind can be separated from the body so as to operate logically. In his 1994 book, *Descartes' Error,* Antonio R. Damasio says this about Descartes' claim: "The statement, perhaps the most famous in the history of philosophy . . . illustrates precisely the opposite of what I believe to be true about the origins of mind and about the relation between mind and body." We should say, "I am, therefore I think" (248). He claims the mind cannot be understood apart from knowledge of neuroanatomy, neurophysiology, and neurochemistry. There is considerable evidence, says Damasio, that efforts to find an inherently logical function in the mind are doomed to failure.

Gerald M. Edelman, director of the Neurosciences Institute and chair of the Department of Neurobiology at the Scripps Research Institute, agrees. He reports that people are physiological and social beings capable of thinking and feeling, but there is no evidence of a rationality of mind that can be separated from our totality as human beings.

Our minds sort sensory stimuli into meaningful units. In this way, our mind creates its own reality to serve our needs. But no matter how helpful that reality may be, Philip Regal points out that it is an "illusion organ" (69). That means sometimes your reality could get you into trouble. In the summer of 1999, John F. Kennedy, Jr., his wife, and her sister died in a plane crash off Martha's Vineyard, Massachusetts. Investigation revealed that the plane dove straight into the water at a high speed and no mechanical problems were discovered. Our friend, a retired colonel in the U.S. Marine Corps who started his flying career in World War II fighters, said what probably happened is that Kennedy's mind told him he was flying level even though the plane was on its downward course. "A pilot," our friend said, "must learn to ignore personal reality and stick totally with what the instruments say. Kennedy just didn't have enough instrument flight experience to be able to do that."

Research is now able to "observe" the mind at work through various imaging technologies, and the results are discouraging. It appears as if when you need to make a decision, you receive inputs from different parts of your brain and nervous system ranging from the most evolutionarily advanced parts such as the prefrontal cortex to the most primitive parts such as the amygdala or the limbic system, and they rarely give a consistent message. When making a decision, you are bombarded with contradictory choices, and silencing the debate through the force of the executive power of the prefrontal cortex could well cause you to make the wrong decision: a possible explanation of the Kennedy crash (Lehrer 217).

Social Influence Is Not Necessarily Reasonable

Solomon Asch reports experiments in which he asked people to judge the length of one line compared to a series of other lines. He adjusted the task until people judging alone made almost no errors. He then selected four experimenters who were instructed to announce an incorrect answer and put them with a series of naive subjects who did not know the experimenters were being intentionally incorrect. One by one, the experimenters would announce an incorrect choice, and then the naive subject was asked to respond. Imagine the social pressure this placed on the naive subjects. They had just heard four apparently honest people give answers that seemed obviously wrong. In the research, about a third of the naive subjects chose to give the same incorrect answer rather than disagree with the others.

Some subjects later said they actually saw the incorrect response as correct, whereas others said they simply went along with the group rather than oppose the majority. In this instance, social influence moved people to doubt their personal judgment, which almost certainly would have produced a correct response.

The emergence of social media has demonstrated the power and danger in social influence. The rise of movements overthrowing autocratic leaders in the Arab world in 2011, according to some observers, could be traced to the availability of more widespread interaction than had been possible earlier. People could share experiences, learn of inequities, and discover social support that gave them the courage to revolt. By the same token, it was social media and the power of some opinion leaders that led many people, including Donald Trump, to believe that U.S. President Obama was foreign born and a Muslim long after clear evidence to the contrary was available. How many times have you abandoned what you thought was right when your friends said you were wrong? How many times have you stubbornly insisted you were right in the face of unanimous opposition? Maybe you were. Maybe you weren't.

Characteristics of Reasonable Arguments

So, what makes one argument more reasonable than another? From the examples we have given, you can see that arguments derive their force either from the criteria already in people's minds, or from criteria that emerge in their minds during an argument.

When your arguments—claims and support—square directly with the criteria in the minds of the decision makers, the arguments will draw power from those criteria and thus be more influential. In contrast to past philosophical thought, arguments are not necessarily more powerful by virtue of their internal logical validity or by passing some scientific test. As we will explain later in this chapter, concepts of logical validity and scientific significance, *when they are part of the criteria decision makers apply,* will support the reasonableness of your arguments. But you cannot count on this process always happening.

If arguments are tested by criteria in the minds of decision makers, how does argumentation differ from persuasion in general? What makes argumentation different from what we see on TV, read on billboards, or hear from some fast-talking salesperson? The answer is, first, that argumentation is a relatively distinct dimension of persuasion that includes many of the strategies found in ordinary advertising or political campaigning (Willbrand and Rieke, "Reason Giving" 57).

Second, argumentation is a distinct dimension of persuasion, in that people tend to use it when they want to make wise decisions, and the strategies used in argumentation tend to be different from other forms of persuasion. Arguments employ more of the forms of criteria that we discuss later in this chapter, than do common persuasive messages, and argumentation occurs within spheres that demand such criteria. Argumentation appeals to the reasonableness of the decision makers by consciously focusing on criteria that are carefully selected, subjected to criticism, publicly accessible, and open to continual reexamination. Many commentators on critical thinking and informal logic argue that *all* persuasion should be subjected to argumentative analysis. If this were done, they say, people would be less likely to be taken in by unreasonable persuasive efforts.

Argumentation serves as the process through which people seek to enhance the positive contributions of their personal reality while holding in abeyance its unreasonable tendencies. Argumentation is the process through which people take advantage of the positive influences in their society and culture while holding in abeyance the perilous social pressures that produce unreasonable behavior. By employing messages predicated on carefully chosen and socially scrutinized criteria, argumentation becomes that form of persuasion dedicated to making the best possible decisions. This almost always means taking advantage of types of criteria and social processes that have proved helpful over the years in yielding reasonable decisions.

Why People Seek Reasonable Arguments

The ultimate purpose of argumentation is to make the *best* possible decisions, where best is defined in various ways. At a basic level, best means to be able to state a basis for decision that satisfies the expectations and demands of the appropriate decision makers. When the decision is important enough to do more than trust chance (flip of a coin) or the of undefined influences of beliefs, thinking, mind, or society, best means to do the systematic processing or analytic thinking demanded by the sphere: to be able to assure the decision makers that they can rely on your arguments at the highest level and thereby produce a decision at the highest level. Another meaning of best is a pragmatic one: decisions that work or do what the sphere seeks to have done: to fulfill the ultimate purpose of the sphere, whatever that may be. To assure, for example, a sphere of medical specialists that your arguments and the resulting decisions will be consistent and effective in terms of their ultimate purpose of health/healing. In law, people are held responsible for their acts on the assumption that they had conscious choice or free will and were not simply at the mercy of their beliefs, thinking, mind, society, or chance. Our discussion of those forces could lead one to conclude that conscious choice is almost impossible, but we do not suggest that. In this context, best means to take responsibility for your arguments and authorize others to hold you accountable for them. Eliezer J. Sternberg, writing in his book *My Brain Made Me Do It,* rejects the implication of his title and argues instead:

> Our ability to go beyond the algorithms—to achieve understanding, to appreciate meaning, to imagine, to consciously deliberate, to reason through boundless problems, and to act as free agents—is what separates us from lower animals, from computers, and from all other machines. It is what makes us human (179).

The Bases of Reason in Argumentation

Argumentation is the product of centuries of evolution in social practices aimed at resolving or creating uncertainty. We try to resolve uncertainty by making wise decisions that cannot be held absolutely, and we create uncertainty by raising doubts about ideas that may no longer deserve support (Goodnight 215). During this evolution, people have developed a number of systematic practices designed to improve the quality of argumentation and the decisions it produces. In this section, we identify some powerful concepts that provide the necessary common bonding for reasoned interaction to take place and that form a fundamental test of the strength of an argument.

Starting Points for Argumentation

Argumentation works by connecting understandings people possess with claims to which they are being asked to grant adherence. If they grant adherence to those claims, then the newly accepted claims can be used as the connectors to still other claims, leading finally to a decision. The energy or power that drives argumentation is found in people: that which they believe provides the foundation for that which they are asked to believe. In any argumentative interaction, then, some **starting points** (understandings people already possess) must be identified—those powerful concepts that will start the connecting process: language interpretation strategies, facts, presumptions, probabilities, and commonplaces.

A general focus for reasonable arguments is to examine the nature and quality of the powerful concepts invoked. If they are mistaken—either not shared by all the relevant decision makers, or controversial—then the arguments that flow from them become suspect.

Language Interpretation Strategies

The most fundamental starting point is language and shared **interpretation strategies**. English is widely spoken in India because of the many years of British rule, and English is spoken in the United States for the same reason, but such sharing of a common language does not guarantee sufficient commonality for argumentation. With the development of calling centers in India, training sessions in speaking U.S. English are being conducted in India. The interactants will need to negotiate some common strategies for interpreting their common language before critical argumentation can occur.

Language is commonly referred to as human symbolic activity. The symbols that make up language are arbitrarily assigned meaning when people interpret them as part of interaction. You have meanings in mind when you speak or write, but they are based on your prior experience and education. In the immediate context in which you are speaking, writing, or reading, the meanings of the words will depend on the context in which you find yourself at the time, and the people with whom you are interacting.

The first step in evaluating arguments is to open up interpretation strategies for examination. Disagreements may dissolve as strategies are made to coincide, but so might agreements. Before advancing or evaluating an argument, you must satisfy yourself that you understand what is being communicated.

Facts

Facts can become issues, questions around which controversy occurs. However, as starting points of argumentation, **facts** are empirical knowledge (see, taste, touch, hear, smell) derived from observation or experience over which there is no controversy.[1] The morning sun appears in the east. Caviar costs more than chopped liver. Mothers who abuse drugs during pregnancy endanger the health of their babies. These are facts that could very well be the starting points of arguments because the decision makers regard them as facts beyond question.

There are profound differences in what is accepted as fact as you move from one sphere to another. Millions of people acknowledge the "fact" that Jesus is the Messiah, and millions reject the idea totally. Even among scientists, there is significant disagreement about what to count as fact, and advances in science are often based on revisions of what is fact. In assessing the reasonableness of arguments, one place to look is at the facts used as starting points because people may accept facts that, on reflection, they should not.

Think back to that Internet search when writing a paper. The sequence in which items appear in the search has nothing to do with the quality of the facts they allege. On the contrary, they may reflect what someone is willing to pay the search engine to put first. The Internet is a sea of garbage with occasional gems of value floating here and there. Special interests will do their best to have you accept what they say as fact. Even friends can forward messages with strange claims of fact that have been passed along without fact checking. People use techniques such as stating facts without justification, using spurious examples, or graphics such as this:

> **FACT:** Eating asparagus can cure cancer.

Or they can beg the question (a fallacy that assumes as fact that which has not yet been accepted as fact):

> **DID YOU KNOW** that eating asparagus can cure cancer? It's true!

The Internet is filled with efforts to have you accept what they say as fact. When you accept their word without doing your own testing, your arguments may be rejected when others, who have done their homework, show you to be wrong.

Presumptions

Another powerful concept that serves as a starting point for arguments is presumption. A **presumption** occurs when one statement occupies the argumentative ground or position "until some sufficient reason is adduced against it" (Whately 112). Like facts, presumptions may reflect considerable experience and observation, but they usually involve a broader generalization or a point taken hypothetically for the sake of argument.

Many presumptions have been formally stated in legal decisions. Children are presumed to have less ability to look out for themselves than adults; so, society demands more care for them. U.S. criminal law presumes people to be innocent until proven guilty. As this presumption suggests, all presumptions are subject to challenge and may be overturned. In fact, people may start with a presumption they really do not believe, just to get the argumentation going. Without a presumption to work from (say, the presumption of innocence), they would not know who has to start the argument and who wins in the absence of clear superiority of one argument over another. The U.S. criminal law presumes innocence, so the state has to open with a claim of guilt: the burden of proof. The individual citizen does not have to prove innocence. If the state fails to win the argument, we choose to let the citizen go free rather than risk convicting the innocent.

Part of understanding the reasonableness of argumentation is examination of presumptions. Because presumption is more or less arbitrary, it is possible for one position in the discussion to claim presumption and use it as a tool to force others to defend their position. In a university class on argumentation, a student said, "There has never been an astronaut on the moon. It was faked by the government." The professor replied, "Can you prove that?" The student immediately came back, "Can you prove I'm wrong?" Who should have the presumption in this case? Putting an unreasonable burden of proof on one point of view can lead to an unreasonable decision (Gaskins).

Probabilities

As starting points of argument, **probabilities** consist of commonly held beliefs about what is likely to happen, what is ordinary, and what is to be expected. Such beliefs can be used as premises for arguments. After extensive observations, we hold powerful concepts of such probabilities as the times of the tides, the movements of the planets, the changing of the seasons, or the behavior of matter under various conditions. We reason from biological probabilities such as what plants will survive in certain climates, how animals will respond to loss of habitat, and how diseases disseminate. We hold concepts of how people will probably act under certain circumstances: They will look to basic needs such as food, clothing, and shelter before considering such abstract needs as self-fulfillment; they will seek pleasure and avoid pain; they will organize themselves into societies.

Like presumptions, probabilities vary from one sphere to another. Many hold the probability that human beings will seek to avoid death, but some spheres hold that death in a holy cause is desirable.

Where presumptions may be points that are taken for the sake of argument without solid proof of their validity, probabilities get arguments started because they are likely to be accepted as well established by proof while falling short of the confidence given to facts. Their susceptibility to challenge makes it necessary to present claims resting on probabilities with some statements of *qualification.*

Stephen Toulmin says that when people qualify claims, they "authorize . . . hearers to put more or less faith in the assertions . . . treat them as correspondingly more or less trustworthy" (*The Uses of Argument* 91). Because argument functions within uncertainty, there is always some degree of qualification on claims. Sometimes you use words: *likely, almost certainly, probably, maybe.* Sometimes you use numbers: 90% chance, $p < .05$, three to one odds. No matter how you express these probabilities, they communicate the force with which an argument is advanced, the degree of faith you authorize others to place on your claims.

The reasonableness of arguments, then, necessarily involves an examination of the probabilities on which they rest and the qualifications with which they are presented. A point of criticism is to ask the basis of the probability statement.

In deciding what and how much higher education you need, you may turn to statistics that indicate probabilities about what kinds of majors will be most in demand when you graduate and what value advanced degrees may produce. The U.S. Bureau of Labor Statistics projects that between 2008 and 2018, the careers most likely to increase, produce a high salary (ranging from $70,000 to $85,000), and require a bachelor's degree include biomedical engineers, network systems and data communication analysts, financial examiners, and computer software engineers. In the same time, a similar increase will occur in home health aids, personal and home care aids, skin care specialists, and dental hygienists, producing salaries between $20,000 and $66,000 but requiring only short on the job training or an associate's degree. Will the cost of an extra two or more years of college be worth it? Would you be just as happy to take one of the lower paying jobs that do not require college? What is the probability that after you complete college, no such high paying job will be available because economic conditions have changed?

Commonplaces

In argumentative practice, various ways of putting arguments together become standardized, common, widely recognized, and accepted. These **commonplaces** are lines of argument or places from which arguments can be built. Aristotle spoke of logic in the form of induction or generalization: reasoning from specific instances to a generalization; or deduction (syllogisms or enthymemes): reasoning from a generalization to a specific application. Aristotle mentioned rationales such as opposites: What goes up must come down; You are either with us or against us. He called these processes, depending on which translation you use, *topoi,* topics, lines of argument, or commonplaces (Roberts, W. Rhys 1396). Perelman and Olbrechts-Tyteca call them *loci* (83). We will call them commonplaces.

The reasonableness of arguments is measured, in part, by the commonplaces on which they are developed. For centuries, logic was considered the prime example of how to put an argument together, but today we see that logic has a limited application in actual argumentation. We have mentioned the commonplace of opposites as an example. If one argues from this commonplace, the critic must test the assumption of opposition. Up and down do not work the same in the weightlessness of space, of which Aristotle never heard, and in the war on terror, for example, countries such as Pakistan seemed to be both with us and against us.

An argument based on genealogy was also common in Aristotle's time, but it is less likely to survive critical scrutiny today. To argue, for example, that people are suitable for high office because of the high status of their parents is not well received in a democracy. However, genealogy still functions as a commonplace in certain argumentative contexts. The selection of a British monarch or a Japanese emperor rests on it. Many people point with pride to their distinguished ancestors, and we pay attention to the children of celebrities and distinguished families.

A *fortiori* (more or less) argues, for example, that if you can perform the more difficult task, you can surely perform the easier one. Or, conversely, if you can't do an easy task, you won't be able to do a more difficult one. The argument "If we can put a man on the moon, we should be able to solve the hunger problem" rests on the commonplace of a *fortiori*. So does this one: If you cannot pass the introductory course, you surely will flunk the advanced one.

Considerations of *time* work as commonplaces. Professionals charge fees based on the time spent for a client or patient. Most wages are calculated on time. Forty hours is deemed enough work for a week, and any more deserves better pay. Students argue for a better grade on the basis of how much time was spent on an assignment. We presume that a person can't be in two places at the same time; so, the accused may argue an alibi based on the time to go from point A to point B. Commonplaces vary from sphere to sphere. For example, the commonplace of cause and effect is interpreted in quite different ways within different spheres.

Language interpretation strategies, facts, presumptions, probabilities, and commonplaces are powerful concepts that work as socially generated starting points for argument. When you make an argument, you will want to think carefully about where you can start it with reasonable assurance that there is common ground between you and your decision makers. In your critical appraisal of the argumentation of others, you must scrutinize the starting points to see whether they were well selected.

On the playground, a little girl and boy are in an argument:

GIRL: "You're a liar."

BOY: "No I'm not, 'cause my pants aren't on fire."

GIRL: "Good point."

What do people mean when they say, "Good point" or "That makes sense" or "That's reasonable" or "That's logical?" In the case of the little girl, the boy invoked a familiar refrain, "liar, liar, pants on fire," which many children learn. He connected his claim with knowledge already possessed by the girl so that she perceived it as a good point. Adults smile at the exchange because they have learned more complex and effective ways of telling if someone has supported a claim. It was an argument, but not a good argument. In this chapter, we will explain some of the ways people have developed, over thousands of years, of making arguments—connecting claims with knowledge possessed by decision makers so they can grant adherence.

The Model of an Argument

We start by introducing you to a modification of a model developed by Stephen Toulmin (1963, iii) to help you understand the parts of an argument and their interrelationships. In the past half-century, Toulmin's layout of argument has become the standard pattern for examining arguments and his terminology of claim, grounds, warrant, backing, qualifier, and rebuttal/reservation has become widely adopted (Hitchcock and Verheis). The model we are using is useful to analyze an argument, but be aware that you will put an argument together for communication in a completely different format. We illustrate the model with this argument:

On May 23, 2011, *The Chronicle of Higher Education* reported new data from the U.S. Census Bureau revealing that the median income of people who graduated with a major in petroleum engineering was US $120,000, more than any other major. Students interested in maximizing their lifetime income should seriously consider majoring in petroleum engineering.

Claim

A **claim** states the idea or action for which you are seeking adherence—it is the end goal of the argument, and it is the place you begin:

(Claim) Students should major in petroleum engineering.

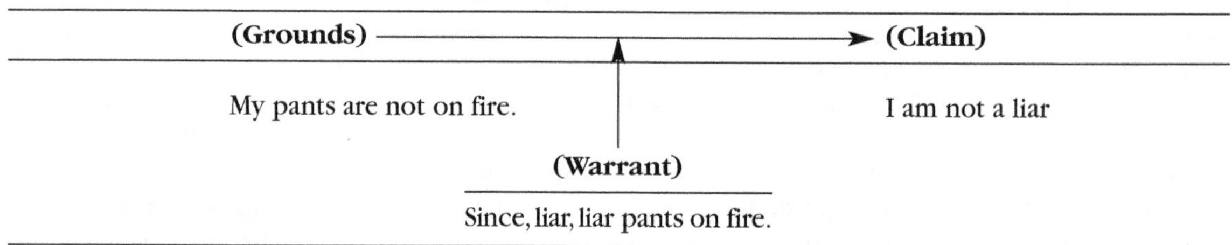

Figure 14.3

(Grounds) ———	———➤ (Claim)
People who graduate with a major in petroleum engineering earn more than those with any other major.	Major in petroleum engineering.

Figure 14.4

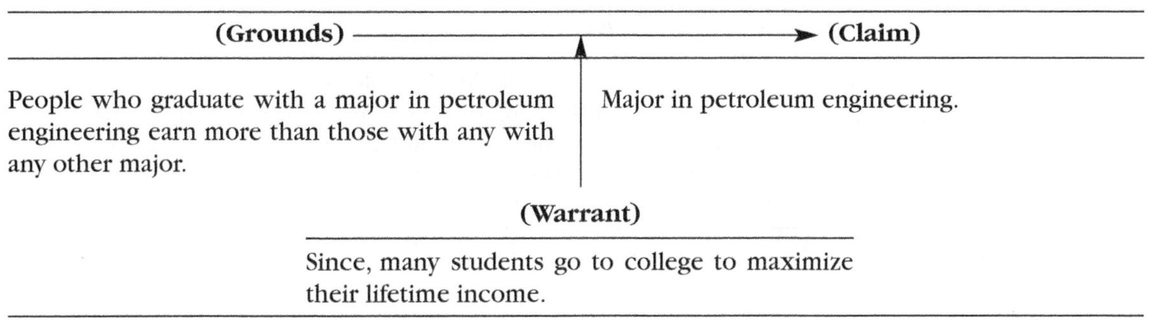
(Grounds)
(Claim)
People who graduate with a major in petroleum engineering earn more than those with any with any other major.
Major in petroleum engineering.
(Warrant)
Since, many students go to college to maximize their lifetime income.

Figure 14.5

Grounds

Grounds provide the primary source of support in answer to the question: "Why should I agree with your claim?" "What have you got to back it up?" "What facts do you use to get there?" Grounds consist mostly of evidence, as well as values and credibility.

Warrant

Rarely, do the grounds alone allow the decision maker to grant adherence to the claim. Usually, an argument includes, either stated or implied, a general statement mostly in the form of a value or a variation of a value statement in the form of a reason, law, principle, rule, maxim, rationale, custom, procedure, rule of thumb.

Backing

For some people, "claims, grounds, and **warrant**" are all an argument would need. They would accept the reasoning and find the claim acceptable. Others, however, particularly on controversial questions, would want more. They would require backing for either the grounds or the warrant. **Backing** *is any support (specific instances, statistics, testimony, values, or credibility) that provides more specific data for the grounds or warrant.* In today's communication scene, characterized by blogs, social networking, commentators, as well as the usual interactions, it is quite common for people to assert facts without saying where they came from or how others can confirm their accuracy. In other words, they need to provide backing. Notice we have had to add backing to the warrant because none was originally supplied.

Qualifier

To be reasonable, an argument must have a claim and grounds for that claim, and the link between the two must be justified by a warrant. The grounds or warrant may need backing, depending on the level of questioning by decision makers. Sometimes, you have to look very carefully at the claim to see how much is being claimed. Some claims will have a **qualifier**, *a statement that indicates the force of the argument.* Words such as *certainly, possibly, probably, for the most part, usually,* or *always* show how forceful a claim is. The qualifier in this argument is "seriously consider" which shows less force than "certainly major in petroleum engineering" would have shown. Remember, the force of an argument is an expression of the confidence in the claim the arguer is willing to express, and the extent to which the arguer is willing to be held responsible for the claim.

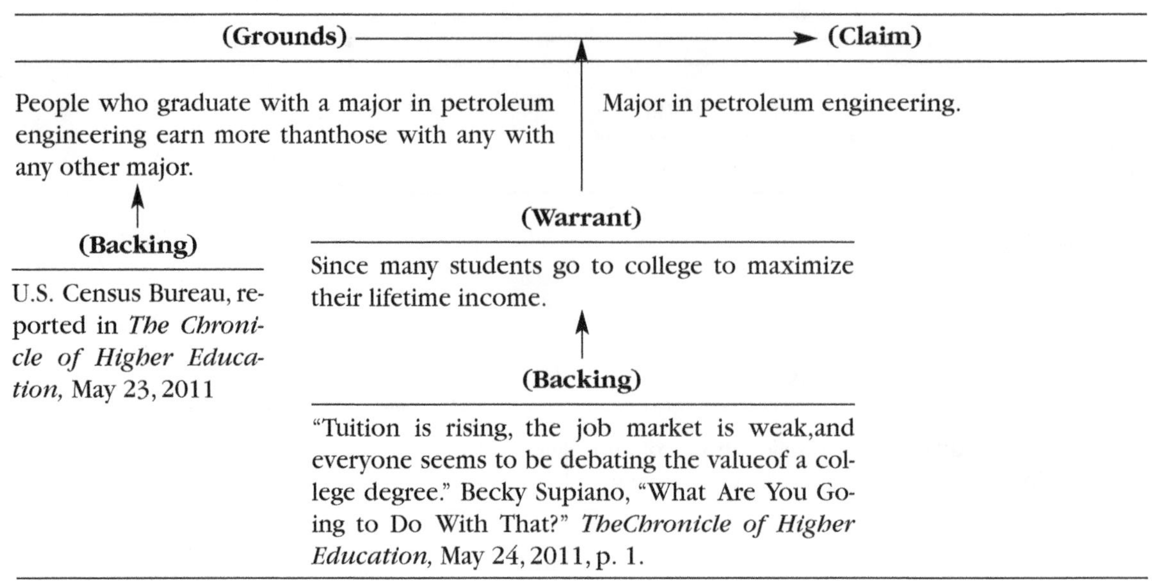

(Grounds)
(Claim)
People who graduate with a major in petroleum engineering earn more thanthose with any with any other major.
Major in petroleum engineering.
(Warrant)
Since many students go to college to maximize their lifetime income.
(Backing)
U.S. Census Bureau, reported in *The Chronicle of Higher Education,* May 23, 2011
(Backing)
"Tuition is rising, the job market is weak,and everyone seems to be debating the valueof a college degree." Becky Supiano, "What Are You Going to Do With That?" *TheChronicle of Higher Education,* May 24, 2011, p. 1.

Figure 14.6

Rebuttal/Reservation

The actual strength of this argument has to be judged as well by possible **rebuttal/reservation,** *the basis on which the claim could be questioned by decision makers and the limits the arguer puts on the claim.* The rebuttal reflects the arguments that detract from the claim, and the reservation explains the qualifier. It says "seriously consider," but with the reservation that only select students will do so. The rebuttal/reservation itself is another claim, for which you could develop an entire argument. It is possible that at a certain point, the rebuttal may become strong enough to replace the claim, at which point, the original argument would become the rebuttal. In this case, you have probably already started rehearsing rebuttals to the argument: not everyone goes to college just to make more money, you can make just about as much money in other majors, not everyone is qualified to major in engineering, petroleum engineering might not be a career you would enjoy, petroleum engineers usually have to work in places where oil is being pumped such as Saudi Arabia or Nigeria, which may not be where you want to live. You might have reservations about working in the petroleum industry because it has been charged with damaging the environment or because the importance of petroleum will decline in the future as alternative sources of energy are developed.

Not all arguments are the same. Some will be found reasonable without backing. Some parts will not be stated. Some will be carefully developed. Some claims will be subject to significant rebuttal, others to little. Some warrants will be specific, others will be vague. You will find some arguments much easier and others more difficult to diagram than this one on choosing your college major. However, the Toulmin model should help you evaluate the argument when someone asks, "Is this a good argument?" It will also be useful to you in understanding the reasoning processes.

Reasoning Processes

Earlier in this chapter, we identified the commonplaces of arguments: those principles that are used to generate starting points of argumentation. Among the commonplaces were certain **reasoning processes: logic** or **deduction, generalization, cause, sign, analogy,** and **authority**. These constitute the basis for most arguments. The purpose of this section is to look at those principles more carefully to see how they are applied in all but the most specialized situations and how they differ in the nature of their grounds, claims, and warrants.

There is no natural superiority of one type of argument over another. However, their relative usefulness will vary from sphere to sphere. Logic is still influential in technology, science, and law, but it rarely appears in other spheres. Authority is a crucial form

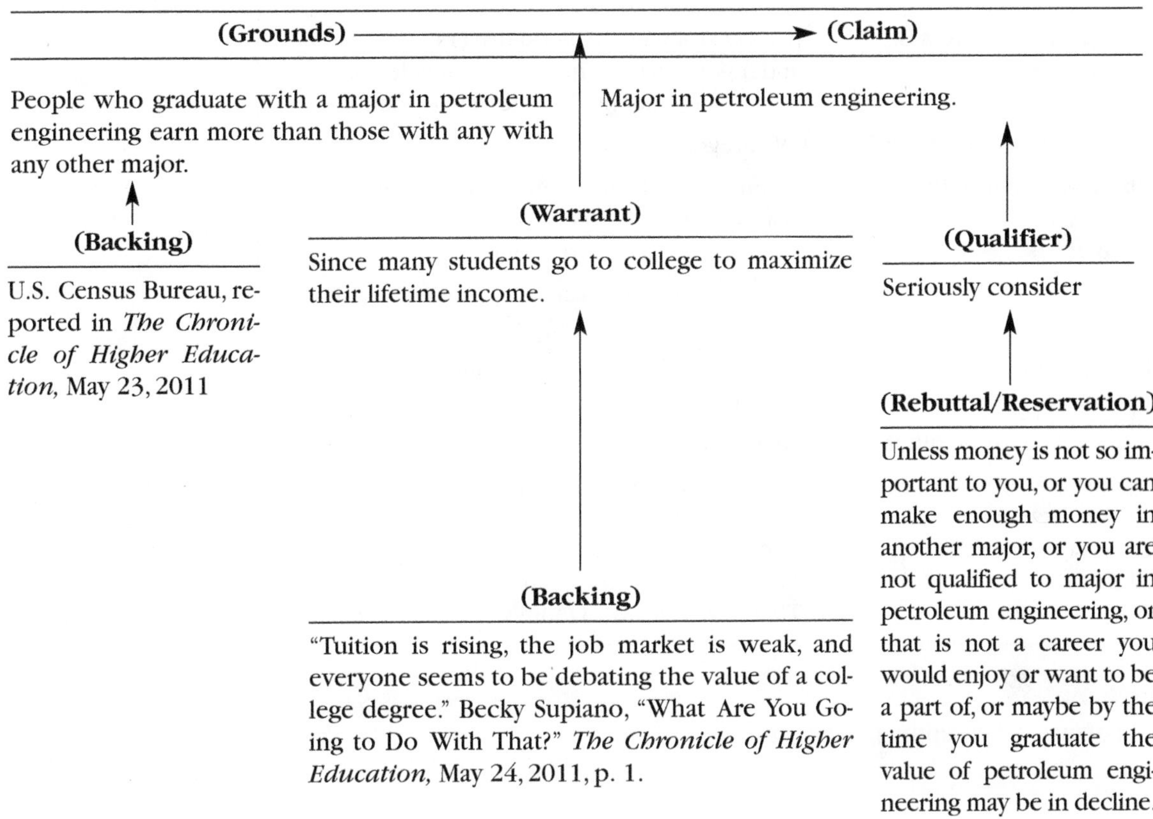
(Grounds)
(Claim)
People who graduate with a major in petroleum engineering earn more than those with any with any other major.
Major in petroleum engineering.
(Backing)
U.S. Census Bureau, reported in The Chronicle of Higher Education, May 23, 2011
(Warrant)
Since many students go to college to maximize their lifetime income.
(Qualifier)
Seriously consider
(Rebuttal/Reservation)
Unless money is not so important to you, or you can make enough money in another major, or you are not qualified to major in petroleum engineering, or that is not a career you would enjoy or want to be a part of, or maybe by the time you graduate the value of petroleum engineering may be in decline.
(Backing)
"Tuition is rising, the job market is weak, and everyone seems to be debating the value of a college degree." Becky Supiano, "What Are You Going to Do With That?" The Chronicle of Higher Education, May 24, 2011, p. 1.

Figure 14.7

of argument in religion but is less significant in science. Analogy, a strong force in legal and political argumentation, is frequently considered suspect by social scientists. Economists, epidemiologists, and weather forecasters consider sign arguments quite useful. Nonetheless, each type of argument has its use and the chances are that not a week goes by that you do not use them all.

Argument by Logic/Deduction/ Syllogism/Enthymeme

Aristotle set out a pattern of formal relations by which arguments could be tested for validity. That is to say, if you begin with true premises, this **logic** can dictate the ways in which they can be combined to yield true conclusions. The pattern is called **syllogism (deduction)** and is taught, with the modifications that have been made over the years, as formal logic. We explain below, however, that logic works only with abstract terms such as A's and B's or P's and Q's. When practical arguments in ordinary language are put into the pattern, the logic loses its certainty and becomes a rhetorical syllogism or **enthymeme**. The pattern of arguments in logical form has been set for centuries and well before the advent of the Toulmin model. We will present logic as it has traditionally been displayed.

Typical examples of the validity patterns in syllogisms are the *categorical, hypothetical,* and *disjunctive.* We will give simple examples of each.

You should see at once that when we put ordinary language in the place of abstract symbols, the arguments require grounds, backing, and qualifiers. Validity means only that there is no internal contradiction in the logic. It does not assure the conclusions can be held with confidence.

Modern formal logic texts (Smith, *An Introduction to Formal Logic*) illustrate the various valid forms of these syllogisms and show how validity can be tested symbolically in a method closely resembling mathematics. Because of different basic assumptions and requirements, this logic deals with

Categorical: If all A is B,	If good students are good drivers,
And if all C is A,	and if good drivers have fewer accidents,
Then all C is B	then, good students have fewer accidents.
(There are many other valid forms of categorical syllogisms.)	
Hypothetical: If A, then B	If you have a degree, you will earn more money.
So if A exists	You do have a degree,
Then B exists	so, you will earn more money.
(Modus ponens—one of two valid forms of hypothetical syllogisms)	
Or,	
If B does not exist,	You are not earning more money,
Then A does not exist)	so, you must have no degree.
(Modus tollens—the other valid form of the hypothetical syllogism)	
Disjunctive: Either A or B	Either the team wins or the coach is fired.
So if A exists	The team is winning,
Then B does not exist	The coach is not fired.
or, if B exists	The coach has been fired.
then A does not	The team was not winning.

Figure 14.8
Valid Forms of Syllogisms/Enthymemes

tasks such as computer programming, which fall outside the domain of argumentation. That is to say, this logic is the calculus of certainty. The search for mathematical certainty grounded in logic goes back at least to Euclid in ancient Greece. Throughout the first half of the twentieth century, mathematical philosophers attempted to organize every possible assumption and principle used in mathematics into logical patterns, complete with strict rules for moving from one step to the next. Mathematics was fundamentally changed when, in 1931, Kurt Gödel published a paper arguing that mathematics "is both incomplete and inconsistent" (Peat, 41). The search for a "new" logic continues to this day.

Martin D. S. Braine and David P. O'Brien explain in detail their theory of mental logic consisting of "a set of inference schemas. For example, when one knows that two propositions of the form *p* or *q* and *not p* are true, one can assert *q*" (3). They provide an extensive list of such schemas, although it does not claim to be exhaustive. Although we disagree with their contention that the human mind naturally employs such logic, we agree that people are quite capable of learning and using it.

During the last half of the twentieth century, there was much philosophical discussion of the viability of formal logic in argumentation (Toulmin, *The Uses of Argument;* Perelman and Olbrechts-Tyteca). At the same time, work in artificial intelligence presented computer programmers with the need for a goal-directed, knowledge-based logic (a logic of uncertainty) suited to describing how people actually go about the business of practical reasoning (Walton 1990).

The result has been what is called **informal logic** (Johnson and Blair). In many ways, its contribution is directed toward the discussion of fallacies. In its more conservative form, informal logic employs the patterns of deductive logic to criticize arguments within the realm of argumentation. Thus, the concept of validity is retained, but the force of conclusions does not reach the certainty of formal logic. Perelman and Olbrechts-Tyteca speak of *quasi-logic,* meaning the use of syllogistic forms in presenting arguments to benefit from the widespread respect given to logic by many decision makers.

Douglas Walton (1990) offers a goal-directed pattern of informal logic appropriate for both artificial intelligence and practical reasoning. Walton sees informal logic, unlike formal logic, as working with reasoning in a problem-solving context, involving some value-laden mandate (must, should), premised on known requirements and consequences, projecting into the future, assessing costs and benefits, and calling for a shift or adjustment in the collective

1. Participants must not try to silence each other to prevent the exchange of arguments and criticism.
2. If you make a claim, you must be willing to provide support if it is requested.
3. When you criticize someone's argument, you should be sure you are talking about what they really said.
4. You should defend your claims with arguments relevant to them.
5. You should not claim that others have presumed something they have not, and you should be willing to admit your own presumptions.
6. You should not try to start argumentation with a starting point others do not accept, and you should not deny a genuine starting point.
7. You should not say your claim has been established unless you have provided proper argumentative support.
8. You should stick to arguments that are logically valid or can be made valid.
9. If you fail to establish your claim, admit it; if others establish their claims, admit it.
10. Avoid unnecessary ambiguity, and try to interpret other's arguments as clearly as possible.

Figure 14.9
Pragma-Dialectical Discussion Rules

commitments of the relevant decision makers (*The New Dialectic* 83).

The argumentation scheme Walton offers is this:

A is the goal.
B is necessary to bring about A.
Therefore, B is necessary.

This is used, says Walton, to convince someone to take whatever action is entailed in B. Critical appraisal of such argumentation, according to Walton, follows these questions:

1. Are there alternatives to B?
2. Is B an acceptable (or the best) alternative?
3. Is it possible to bring about B?
4. Does B have bad side effects? (85)

Walton has described a new dialectic that returns to the dialectical writings of the ancient Greeks "as a general perspective and way of evaluating arguments in a context of dialogue." He seeks to provide "a new theoretical basis for logic which can be used to evaluate arguments that arise in everyday conversational exchanges" (*The New Dialectic* 4–36).

Frans H. van Eemeren and Rob Grootendorst have proposed a set of rules by which critical decision making can be guided. They speak of dialectical constituents of argument as the logical or reasonable foundation. They list 10 rules for critical discussion:

Argument by Generalization

Generalization, or rhetorical induction, is an argument in which individual instances are assembled to allow the assertion of a general principle. At its most basic, a generalization is formed by looking at individual elements so that a general statement can be made that fairly reflects the individual data. For example, the U.S. Federal Reserve divides the country into 12 districts. Economic activity in each district is examined regularly and a general statement on the nation's economic health is announced. Information collected on May 27, 2011 was published on June 9, 2011. According to *The New York Times* of that date, the nation's economy continued to grow but was held down by high food and energy prices and an earthquake and tsunami in Japan. Some districts performed better than others, but the generalization was faithful to the central tendency. On the basis of that information, arguments from generalization were then made about how well the economy would do in the future.

Argument by generalization is regularly made through a sampling process. If you want to make a general statement that fairly describes a large number of instances such as the entire population, you do not need to look at each person or instance. You can, instead, examine a **sample** of that population and generalize that what is so about your sample is also so about the entire population. The critical element in this is the selection of the sample, usually by a form of randomization, so that you can properly claim that all members of the total population had an equal chance of being included in the sample. When the Pew Research group said that only 32% of Americans believe that life has evolved over time, they only questioned 2,001 people (Fox, popsci.com).

Examples are also part of reasoning by generalization. Aristotle called examples rhetorical induction (40). You might advance a general claim, "The number of emergency-management programs in higher education has increased dramatically from 2001 to today." Then, you can provide grounds for the claim by citing examples: State University of New York, New Paltz, Fordham University, and Eastern Kentucky University (Foderaro A19). These three examples or individual instances (and there is rhetorical power in three as opposed to one or two) communicate support for the generalization and help the decision makers grant adherence.

Argument by Cause

Since well before Thomas Aquinas argued the existence of God by saying, "Things do not change unless some agent changes them," people have acted on the presumption that effects have causes. Only God, claimed Aquinas, could be the unmoved mover. Captain Von Trapp, in the film *The Sound of Music,* sings "Nothing comes from nothing, nothing ever could." An **argument by cause** can reason from cause to effect or from **effect to cause**.

John Stuart Mill suggested that causal arguments can be developed by using the methods of **agreement, difference, correlation, and residues** (278–291). Scientific arguments are frequently based on cause and effect. We will illustrate Mill's methods with an example from epidemiology.

During the summer of 2011, a deadly outbreak of *Escherichia coli* bacteria occurred in northern Germany. Reasoning from effect to cause, the effect was obvious: 39 people died, around 3,500 people in 12 countries were stricken with serious illness, and farmers were hurt when people stopped eating vegetables they thought might be carrying the bacteria. The question was: What actually is the cause? Using the method of agreement, authorities asked, "What is the one and only thing common to all the people who have suffered?" If they could find, for example, that all had eaten the same food, it would probably be the cause. In fact, it was quickly found that people had probably come in contact with the bacteria after eating salads, but salads contain a variety of ingredients—which one was the culprit? At first, the suspect was Spanish cucumbers, but it was found that some people had eaten salads without cucumbers and still became sick. The method of difference was used to zoom in on salads as the cause because people in the same circumstances who had not eaten salads did not get sick. So, the question was what single ingredient was in all the salads (method

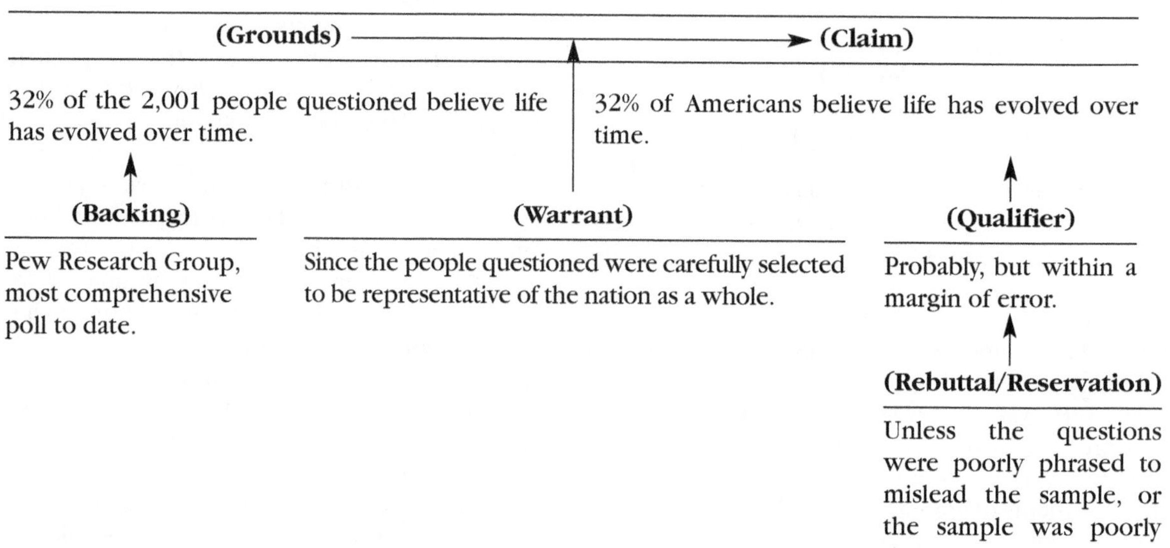

Figure 14.10

of agreement)? It was, apparently, bean sprouts from a single farm (Rohan). More than a month later, the method of agreement led to a search for a shipment of 16 tons of tainted fenugreek (a version of bean sprouts) seeds sent from an Egyptian organic farm and used to grow the sprouts in the German salads, as well as those in France, Britain, Austria, and Spain.[2]

Reasoning from cause to effect, suspicion had fallen early on organic farms because they use manure as fertilizer. This helped investigators locate the farm that produced the tainted bean sprouts through correlation: *E. coli* is often found in and around manure. Using the method of residues, the various ingredients of salads including cucumbers, tomatoes, lettuce, and bean sprouts were tested. When cucumbers, tomatoes, and lettuce were found to be untainted, suspicion fell on the (residue) remaining ingredient: bean sprouts.

Argument by Sign

Argument by sign is closely related to causal argument but is different. A sign argument is based on a warrant that most things, conditions, or ideas have characteristics that will signal their presence. The sign is closely associated, but is not necessarily the cause or effect, of the thing signaled. We have just mentioned correlation as involved in cause–effect reasoning, but it is also part of argument by sign. A correlation says that two phenomena vary together such that one may be the cause of the other or they both may be the result of an external cause. For example, auto insurance companies will typically reduce premiums for drivers under 25 years of age if they have maintained a B or better grade average. What research has told them is that good grades are significantly correlated with safe driving. That is, the good grades are a sign of safe drivers. Getting good grades does not necessarily cause safe driving, nor does safe driving cause good grades; they just seem to go together, and it is far easier and cheaper for insurance companies to get grade transcripts than it would be to come up with a measure of safe driving tendencies.

Specialists in business and finance make regular use of argument by sign. The *Composite Index of Leading Indicators* is an example. "The index is made up of 10 economic components, whose changes tend to precede changes in the overall economy" (Investopedia). The components, such as average weekly hours worked by manufacturing workers, the amount of new building permits, consumer sentiment, and the S&P 500 stock index, taken together have been shown to be reliable signs of the direction of the economy. There is no singular

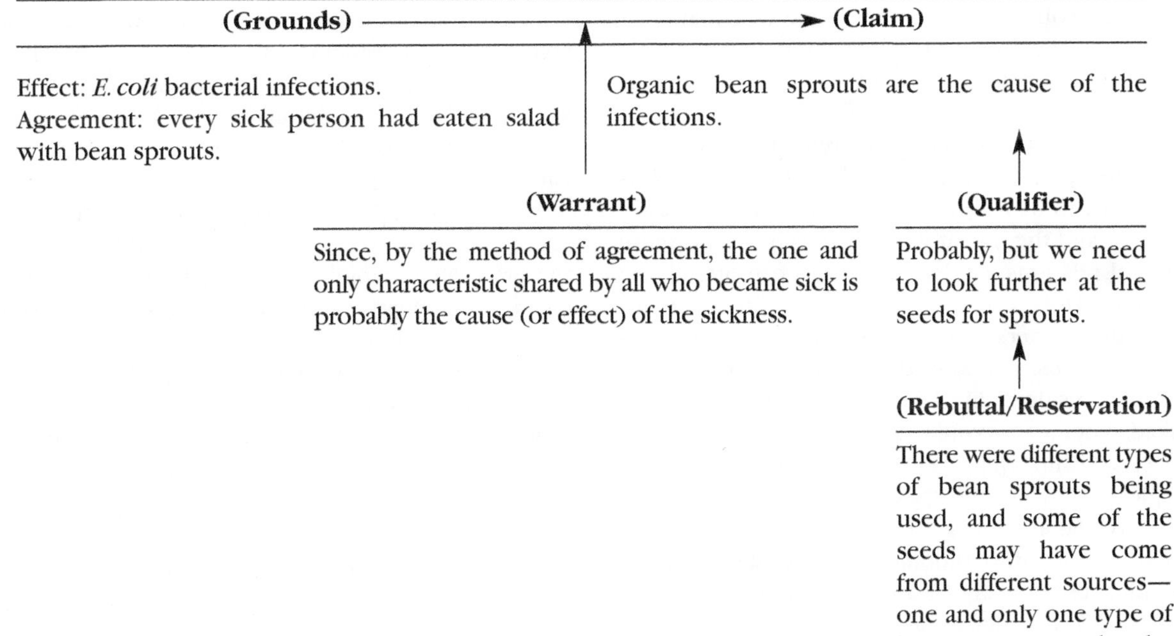

(Grounds)
(Claim)
Effect: E. coli bacterial infections.
Agreement: every sick person had eaten salad with bean sprouts.
Organic bean sprouts are the cause of the infections.
(Warrant)
Since, by the method of agreement, the one and only characteristic shared by all who became sick is probably the cause (or effect) of the sickness.
(Qualifier)
Probably, but we need to look further at the seeds for sprouts.
(Rebuttal/Reservation)
There were different types of bean sprouts being used, and some of the seeds may have come from different sources—one and only one type of bean sprout may be the cause.

Figure 14.11

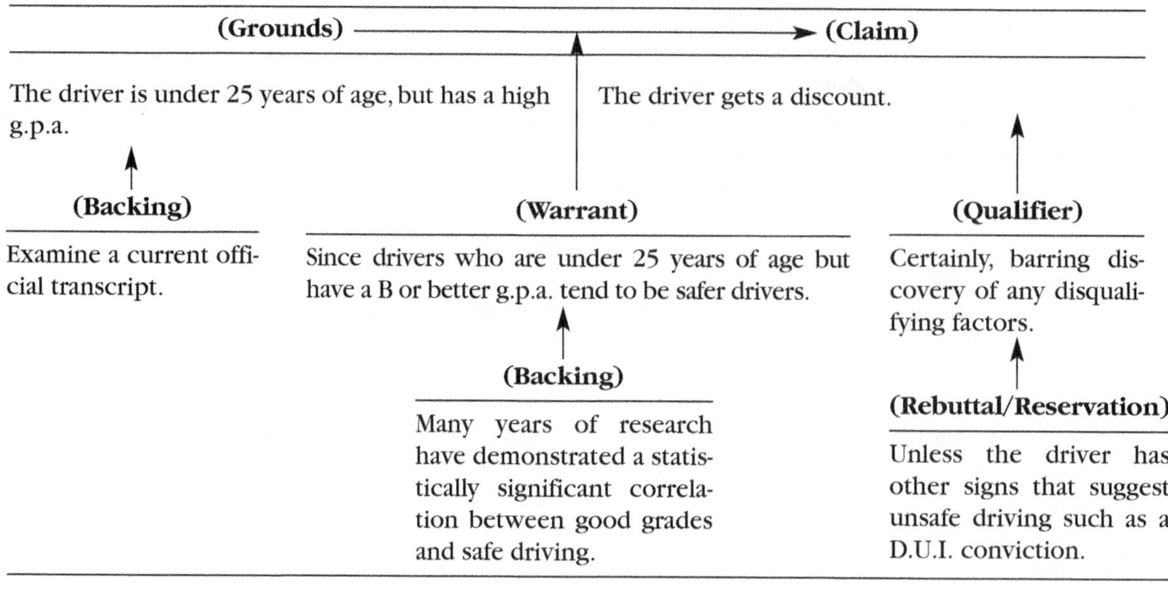

(Grounds)
(Claim)
The driver is under 25 years of age, but has a high g.p.a.
The driver gets a discount.
(Backing)
Examine a current official transcript.
(Warrant)
Since drivers who are under 25 years of age but have a B or better g.p.a. tend to be safer drivers.
(Qualifier)
Certainly, barring discovery of any disqualifying factors.
(Backing)
Many years of research have demonstrated a statistically significant correlation between good grades and safe driving.
(Rebuttal/Reservation)
Unless the driver has other signs that suggest unsafe driving such as a D.U.I. conviction.

Figure 14.12

cause–effect relationship, but the 10 components function as a good sign of the economy. Notice also that by examining 10 individual signs and then generalizing about the economy as a whole, the index argues by generalization as well.

Argument by Analogy

In **argument by analogy**, you compare two situations that you believe have the same essential characteristics and reason that a specific characteristic found in one situation also exists in the analogous situation.

It has been traditional to differentiate between literal and figurative analogies. The literal analogy is presumed to be based on factual comparisons of situations, and the figurative analogy is based on more fanciful relations. No two situations can literally be identical. However, some comparisons are more material than others. For example, when a prize winning journalist announced that he was an undocumented resident in the United States, someone asked whether it would hurt anything to give him his citizenship. One answer was: no one is hurt by a single snowflake, but get enough of them and you can have an avalanche. This would be called a figurative analogy in traditional terms because undocumented residents and snowflakes are materially different. Still, it makes a point more rhetorically compelling.

From the perspective of reasoning, materially similar comparisons are more significant because decision makers tend to take them more seriously. A claim reasons that what is so about one point of comparison is arguably so about another, or can be used to argue a point based on comparison. DC Comics has renumbered its entire DC Universe line of comics. In September of 2011, 52 series started anew, each with an issue No. 1 (Gustines C1). Collectors buy these No. 1 issues of comics by making an analogy: The legendary Action Comics No. 1, which introduced Superman, has become quite valuable today, and readers in the past have shown increased interest in buying comics when they can start with No. 1. So, the claim is this: by restarting the numbering of all their comics, DC can significantly increase sales.

Argumentation in law, reports how important reasoning by analogy is to lawyers and judges. Under the principle in which courts want regularity in law (*stare decisis*), arguments are based on comparing the present case with earlier cases that have already been decided. The argument is this: the court decided a previous case, which is analogous to our present case, in a certain way, and under *stare decisis,* the court should decide the present case in the same way.

Argument from Authority

Credibility can support the adherence decision makers give to your argument. Even persons of high credibility, however, frequently use the credibility of others to argue a claim. In **argument from author-**

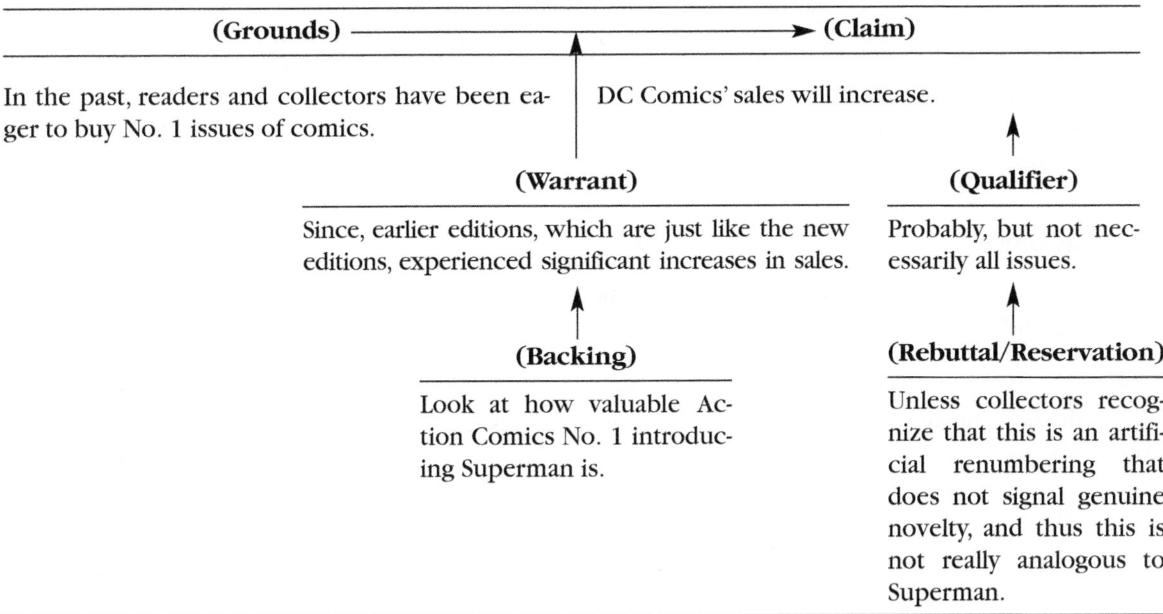

(Grounds)
(Claim)
In the past, readers and collectors have been eager to buy No. 1 issues of comics.
DC Comics' sales will increase.
(Warrant)
Since, earlier editions, which are just like the new editions, experienced significant increases in sales.
(Qualifier)
Probably, but not necessarily all issues.
(Backing)
Look at how valuable Action Comics No. 1 introducing Superman is.
(Rebuttal/Reservation)
Unless collectors recognize that this is an artificial renumbering that does not signal genuine novelty, and thus this is not really analogous to Superman.

Figure 14.13

ity, you argue that a claim is justified because it is held by a credible person, ordinarily someone other than yourself. The most common way of presenting such an argument is to cite an authority.

When U.S. Army Private Bradley E. Manning was alleged to have helped pass thousands of classified prisoner dossiers and embassy diplomatic cables to WikiLeaks' founder Julian Assange, he was jailed and subjected to much public discussion. The questions turned on whether Manning should be considered a traitor for helping make government secrets public, or a patriot who exposed information that should not have been withheld from the public. Stephen M. Kohn, executive director of the National Whistleblowers Center, writing in *The New York Times,* claimed that Manning was a whistleblower and a patriot and supported his argument with the authority of the Congress of the United States acting in 1778. Kohn told the story of 10 revolutionary sailors and marines who reported the misdeeds of their captain. When the captain retaliated against his men, Congress enacted the first whistle-blower-protection law, stating, "That it is the duty of all persons in the service of the United States to give the earliest information to Congress of any misconduct, frauds, or misdemeanors." (Kohn A21). In the United States, the U.S. Congress is recognized as the ultimate authority concerning the military, and the first Congress, sitting in 1778, consisted of the founding fathers and other patriots who are regularly cited as the ultimate authorities on what it means to be a patriot. Congress even directed Sam Adams to ensure that the lawyers who represented the sailors and marines in the case were paid for their legal services (US$1,418).

There is another kind of argument from authority that is considered more questionable. It is called *bandwagon* or *ad populum.* It says that a claim is good because people believe it. Although it is considered a fallacy by many, its acceptability depends on the sphere in which it is used. Professor S.I. Hayakawa said, "Commonsense is that which tells you the world is flat (29–30). So, commonsense cannot be invoked as authority except in the most unsophisticated contexts. However, in a democratic society, it is a powerful kind of political argument. It rests on the authority of majority opinion, a strong political value. Or it could rest on the authority of those most involved.

These five reasoning processes (logic, generalization, cause–effect, sign, analogy, and authority) constitute the arguments you are most likely to find in your own argumentation and that of most others, although there are special variations on these in some spheres. For example, ***narratives*** or stories carry a heavy burden of communicating reasoning in many instances. Legal argumentation appears in narrative form at many points in the decision making process.

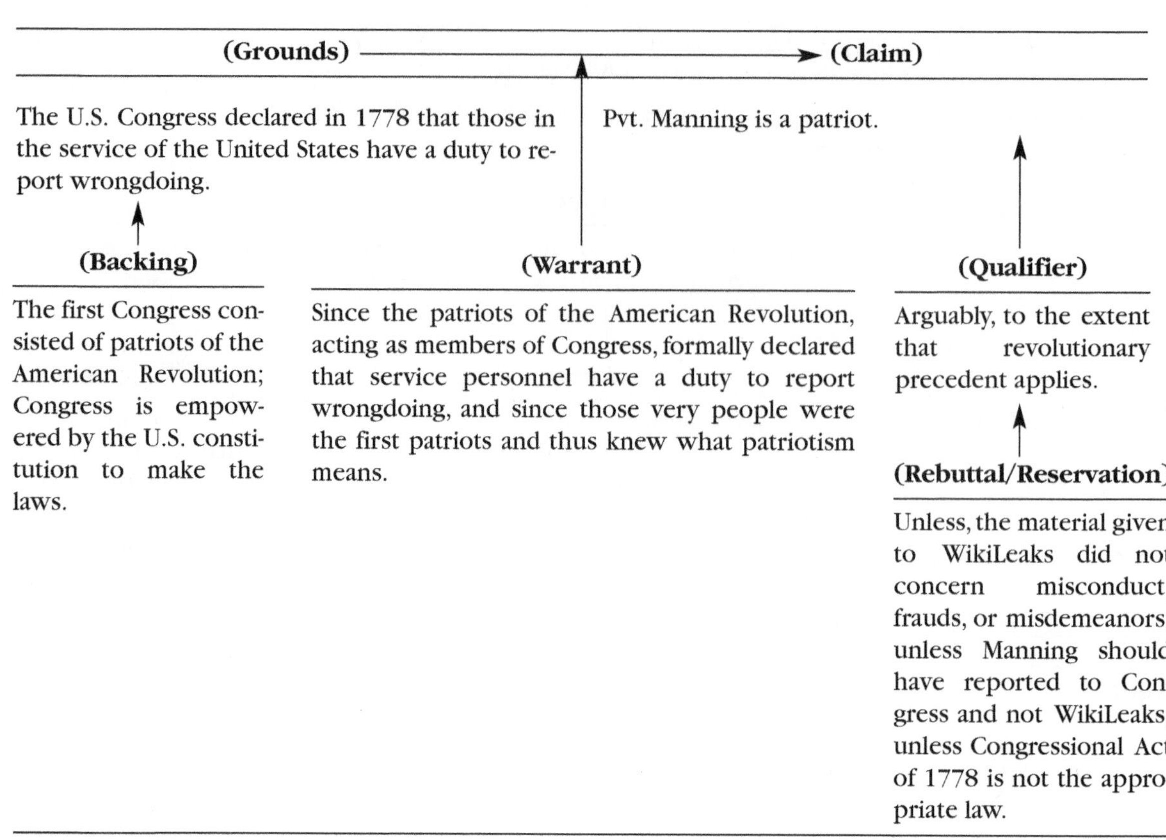

Figure 14.14

In the personal sphere, people reason with each other through narrative most of all. If you concentrate on reasoning processes, diagram them to see their parts and the reasoning that holds them together, you can better evaluate the quality of the arguments. Later in this chapter, we will look more carefully at how to analyze the arguments you encounter. First, however, you should consider an important special kind of argument: argument by definition.

Definitions as Argument

In **argument by definition**, definitions serve to identify exactly what is being argued. Even in situations of strong disagreement, disputants should try to agree on the subject of the disagreement. Definitions are claims that must be supported by effective argumentation because meanings are based on consensus. Value-laden terms such as *love, knowledge, justice,* or *God* clearly have no single precise definition. Neither do such apparently straightforward terms as *climate change, gun control, abortion,* or *economic prosperity.* When you use words, you cannot appeal to a single correct definition. You must present a convincing argument to support your interpretation. Definitions can be used as support for your arguments only if you have a common interpretation with the decision makers and hopefully with opponents as well. There are several common ways to build an argument in support of your definition, and we will discuss some of them.

Formal Definition

A formal definition involves the development of an enthymeme or a deductive logic-based argument where a term is located within a general class for which there is a high probability of a common audience interpretation, and then differentiating it from other aspects of the class. The formal definition is usually the first one given in a dictionary.

> *A democracy,* as Americans use the term, is a form of government [general class] in which the people either directly or through elected representatives exercise power [differentiation].

Climate change is long-term significant change in the weather patterns of an area [general class] influenced by the greenhouse effect [differentiation].

Fundamentalism is a movement in American Protestantism [general class] based on a belief that the Bible is a literal historical record and incontrovertible prophecy [differentiation].

Definition by Example

Just as examples can serve to support an argument and are essential to argument by generalization, they can define an unknown idea. In definition by example, you identify examples that decision makers are likely to know, and relate your concept to them.

Holocaust is mass murder of Jews (and others) by the Nazis in World War II, any wholesale destruction, especially by fire, a great slaughter, or massacre.

The *New Deal* is characterized by, for example, such programs as Social Security, the Federal Deposit Insurance Corporation, and the Securities and Exchange Commission.

Marsupials, mammals that gestate their young in a pouch or marsupium, rather than in a uterus, comprise koalas, wallabies, kangaroos, and the only one found in North America, the opossum.

Functional Definition

Sometimes a good way to make a convincing definition is to illustrate how a concept functions.

Spark plugs ignite the fuel mixture in an internal combustion engine.

Dental floss cleans the areas between your teeth.

A heuristic device gives students a guide to use for learning on their own.

Definition by Analogy

You can establish a clear meaning for a concept by using argument by analogy to show how a term is like or unlike other familiar concepts. Remember, arguments by analogy work by placing a concept under study alongside one on which there is agreement. If they can be shown to have significant similarities, the unknown concept can take on meaning from that which is already agreed on.

Definitions by analogy resemble formal definitions, but they are subtly different. In formal definitions, concepts are identified logically as part of a class. In definition by analogy, concepts are explained by their similarity to a more familiar concept.

School vouchers are like business vouchers that can be exchanged for goods and services. They differ in that they can be exchanged for private school attendance.

A *historical novel* is like a history book in that it is based on the study and interpretation of the past, but it differs in the fact that the author is free to include imagined characters, conversations, and events.

An *oboe* is like a clarinet in that it is a slender woodwind musical instrument, but it differs in that it has a double-reed mouthpiece.

Definition by Authority

Arguments based on authority are common in definition. The most obvious authority is a dictionary, which for many situations is all the authority you need. Resist being entrapped, however, by a veneration of authority leading you to believe that the dictionary is the final or only authority on word meanings. Often, it is the worst because dictionaries cannot possibly be updated fast enough to keep up with the dynamics of language. However, they will give you a general guide to three factors that will strengthen your argument in many situations.

Usage identifies how a word commonly appears in our communication, what people usually mean. Widespread use of a word for a certain meaning provides some authority for that meaning or definition.

Etymology reports the history of a word from the earliest languages. In the past, an argument for a definition that was based on what the root of a word meant, for instance in Greek or Latin, was more powerful than it is today. Today, such an argument is mostly effective with people who still believe that words possess inherent meaning.

Wordsmiths, or the people who create or modify words, can be used authoritatively to support a definition. When physicists theorized the existence of subatomic particles as the fundamental units of matter, they needed a new word for them. They turned to literature in James Joyce's *Finnegan's Wake:* "three quarks for Mr. Marks," and named their particles *quarks.* Academics, adolescents, gangs, ethnic groups, musical groups, artists, and others commonly create new words and can serve as the authorities on definitions.

Earlier, we used "democracy" to illustrate a formal definition. Now, we can point to a current political debate over whether the United States is a democracy or a republic. Richard W. Rahn, writing in *The Washington Times* for May 17, 2011, argues that Founding Fathers understood that unchecked democracy assigned what he called dangerous power to the majority of people. So, Rahn says, we actually created a republic that involved checks and balances to resist rapid changes that come from majority wishes. He bases his definition on the authority of the Founding Fathers and the U.S. Constitution.

The Analysis of Arguments

You can see from the examples we have discussed in explaining the types of arguments that people do not organize their arguments exactly according to our model or any other model. That is because arguments are aimed at decision makers who know things about the subject, share values and credibility assumptions that the arguer need not mention, and respond to language structures that change the order of the model in actual use.

Consequently, the Toulmin model is a useful analytical tool to check your own arguments and the arguments of others. In this section, we will explain some of the characteristics of arguments that make the application of the model difficult, some guidelines for using the model to help you in analyzing arguments.

Characteristics of Arguments

Arguments are difficult to analyze, but if you recognize why that is the case, it will help you to use the model more effectively. They are difficult because they usually have parts missing, the order of the parts may vary, and they may overlap with one another.

Parts Missing

Most arguments have parts left out. If the arguer believes the decision makers accept the grounds, then he or she will sometimes provide no backing. Warrants are frequently omitted because they are clearly implied by the other statements the arguer makes.

It is not the lack of a stated warrant that poses a problem for decision makers. The warrant is clearly implied. The real concern is on the level of adherence the decision makers give to the implied warrant.

Sometimes even claims are not stated. This is particularly true of argumentation that follows a strategy of telling stories. You could tell stories about people who defended themselves from assault by having a weapon in their possession without ever stating the claim that people should carry a weapon for self-protection. The claim is not stated but the decision maker knows that is the claim because the overall orientation of the argument clearly implies it.

Order in Arguments

Arguments do not necessarily follow the order: grounds, warrant, claim. Indeed, they most frequently begin with the claim. However, in scholarly arguments, it is common to start with a discussion of the issues and the prior research on them, with claims coming toward the end. In argumentation in the sciences and social sciences, grounds are always developed first and the claim then developed from those grounds. Such an approach is seen by many as objective. The arguer wants to imply that the evidence is studied before a claim is made, although it is, of course, an argumentative strategy. The arguer knew the claim all along but chose to delay revealing it to decision makers. So, you must remember that analyzing arguments is different from communicating them, and technical spheres typically prescribe the organizational structure of arguments.

Overlapping Arguments

Frequently, two or more arguments are developed in the same paragraph because the arguer sees them as linked. An argument, reported in *The New York Times,* claims that high school students use tranquilizers or prescription drugs for recreational use more than heroin and cocaine combined. It then adds another claim that in the past anti-drug laws have been able to oppose all use of drugs such as heroin and cocaine to reduce their recreational use, but that is not possible in relation to prescription drugs that also serve medicinal uses. The two arguments overlap in the same paragraph (Zuger, D1). In analyzing the argument, you need to separate the claims, grounds, and warrants, and so forth of each line of argument.

Frequently, arguments are linked to one another, their parts do not appear in any particular order, and parts are left out. Consequently, you may have trouble seeing in an article, television commercial, or speech what an argument is and what its parts are. Here is a useful sequence of guidelines for analyzing an argument:

1. Discover and state the claim or claims. What is it the arguer wants you to believe, value, or do? Claims may appear anywhere in the argument but they most likely appear at the beginning or the end.
2. Look for the subclaim of the grounds. It can best be determined if you know the claim first and then ask yourself "On what basis am I supposed to give adherence to the claim?"
3. Look for the warrant. Because it most frequently will be the part omitted, it will be the most difficult to find. But if you know the claim and the grounds you can find even an unstated warrant because it is the statement that would justify the movement from grounds to claim. If stated, it will frequently be identified by words such as *for, because,* or *since.*
4. Examine the warrant to determine the kind of argument you are analyzing. Look back over the examples we have used and you will see it is the warrant that identifies the kind of argument by identifying the commonplace (or principle) behind it. Here are a few of the warrants we have used:

   "The 12 Federal Reserve Districts are representative of the U.S. economy." [generalization (representative, comprehensive, overall)]

   "*E. coli* in bean sprouts caused illness." [cause (effect, generate, because, lead to, result in)]

   "The Index of Leading Indicators signals economic change." [sign (indication)]

   "The facts of an already decided case are just like the facts of this case." [analogy (parallel, like, alike)]

   "The patriots of the American Revolution in Congress know who is a patriot." [authority [expert (knowledgeable, trustworthy, skillful)]
5. Look for backing (evidence, values, credibility).

Figure 14.15
Guidelines for Analyzing Arguments

CONCLUSION

When you evaluate the reasonableness of argumentation, when you try to decide what arguments are acceptable, what ones are not, and what decision makes the most sense, you will necessarily make your judgments under the influence and within the limits of your genetic make-up, the environments in which you have lived, your worldviews, and the social interactions you have experienced. Sometimes these factors will help you act wisely, and sometimes they will get you into trouble.

Over many centuries, people have developed systematic argumentation practices that can increase the likelihood that you will make sensible decisions. When properly used, these will help you make critical decisions. Powerful concepts such as language interpretation strategies, facts, presumptions, probabilities, and commonplaces can serve as starting points for argumentation. They establish a foundation on which everyone can argue and provide some ready rationales on which to build claims.

Arguments appear in a wide variety of situations, and they differ in their nature from one context to another. Yet, all arguments can be diagrammed by a variation of the Toulmin model, which illustrates how a claim can be justified only by showing that there are warranted grounds for it. In addition, grounds and warrants may need backing; claims may need to be qualified and stated with a reservation to avoid rebuttal.

Although the model provides a basis for the analysis of all arguments, not all arguments are alike. Certain types of arguments (commonplaces) can be observed.

Arguments using logical forms present relationships such that conclusions are drawn validly. Argument by generalization attempts to draw a general claim from a series of instances. It is a rhetorical induction, the argument form closest to pure induction. Arguments may claim cause and effect relationships either of cause to effect or effect to cause. They may claim the existence of one condition as a sign of another. Arguments may claim that one condition is analogous to another, and they may be warranted by the credibility of an authority.

It is frequently necessary to develop an effective argument in support of a definitional claim before using it as part of the larger argumentation. Definitions can be formal or functional, by example, analogy, or authority. Definitions should be agreed to by decision makers and, if possible, by opponents.

The Toulmin model is an analytical tool. People do not organize their arguments according to the model because decision makers already know something about the subject. So, with most arguments, parts are missing, the order is different from the model, and arguments overlap. To analyze such arguments, start by stating the claim(s) and then find the grounds. Once this is complete, you should be able to find the warrant (frequently unstated) that justifies the supporting relationship between grounds and claim. This should also tell you what kind of argument is at hand.

Finally, take notice of the materials that serve as backing, qualifiers, refutation, and reservation. These pieces of information will permit you to evaluate the quality of the argument for the decision makers.

Exercises/Projects

1. Write a description of a job interview you have had. Did you understand the criteria to be used in making a hiring decision? Did you make arguments in response to the criteria? Did the job decision rest on the criteria? In all, do you think the decision was critical or uncritical, and why?
2. Identify the career choice you currently prefer, then do an Internet search of it. Keep a record of all the responses that come up, separating the unusual language usages: fact claims, presumptions, probabilities, and commonplaces (look particularly for generalizations, cause and effect claims, a fortiori, and opposites). Then write an argument supporting your career choice with material drawn from your search. Does your argument seem reasonable? Did your work change your career thinking? Where did you find unreasonable arguments?
3. Bring to class one example of each of the types of arguments. Look for these in contemporary publications such as newspapers, magazines, advertising flyers, or on Internet sites. Be prepared to explain each argument by relating its parts to the Toulmin diagram. Your instructor may assign different types of arguments to different class members.
4. Select an argument supporting a claim that you **already agree with.** Do an analysis of the argument and then build a case for how reasonable and well-meaning people could disagree with this claim. Join with a group consisting of people who started either agreeing or disagreeing with the claim, and discuss the strengths and weaknesses of each others' reasoning.

Key Terms

agreement
argument by analogy
argument by cause to effect
argument by definition
argument by effect to cause
argument by generalization
argument by sign
argument from authority
backing
belief system
claim
commonplaces
correlation
criteria
critical decision
deduction
difference
enthymeme
facts
force
grounds
informal logic
interpretation strategies
logic
narrative
pragma dialectical discussion rules
presumption
probabilities
qualifier
reasonable
reasoning processes
rebuttal
reservation
residues
sample
starting points
syllogism
warrant
wisdom of crowds
worldviews

Notes

1. We do not mean to say that these so-called facts are beyond controversy. At one time, people held as *fact* that the world was flat. We use fact here to mean a powerful concept that is widely accepted without controversy, *at the time of the argument,* to the extent it can be invoked as the starting connection for further argumentation. Today, we might be able to invoke the "fact" that the universe is constantly expanding as a starting point for the argument, only to have people a hundred years from now laugh at the idea the same way we laugh at the idea that the world is flat.
2. William Neuman, "A Search Is Under Way for Tainted Sprout Seeds," *The New York Times,* July 6, 2011, B3.

CHAPTER

15

Political Communication

Taken from *News: The Politics of Illusion*, Ninth Edition by W. Lance Bennett.

Journalists today find fault with most everything that politicians say and do. The press no longer even has much respect for public officials' private lives—even their bedroom behavior is fair game for news stories.

—Thomas Patterson

. . . People may expect too much of journalism. Not only do they expect it to be entertaining, they expect it to be true.

—Lewis Lapham

Online information sources from blogs to WikiLeaks are pumping political information into the news stream in ways that are changing the gatekeeping control and editorial policies of mainstream news organizations. Further transforming news standards are the economic pressures. One sign of the new economic reality is the trend toward delivering content to draw valued demographic audiences. When marketing research and cheap production considerations drive the news, the result is generally a decline of hard news about politics and the rise of more soft stories about celebrities, lifestyles, and political scandals. All of these factors come clearly into play in a rapidly fragmenting media sphere in which cable channels pick up spin from dubious blog and online sources and market news and commentary to the political viewpoints of increasingly partisan audiences.

For example, FOX News has found its viewers responsive to conservative slants, and to highly dramatized framing of many stories. The combined impact of poorly checked information from the blogosphere and the dramatic impact of charging the Obama administration with being "racist" led to a scandalous accusation that an administration official named Shirley Sherrod gave a racist speech at the 2010 Freedom Fund Banquet of the National Association for the Advancement of Colored People (NAACP). It later turned out that the charge was based on a short clip from the speech that was taken out of context from a much longer long speech talking about how Ms. Sherrod had overcome feelings of racial prejudice. The clip was distributed online and to FOX by a conservative blogger and political operative named Andrew Breitbart who had a history of politically slanted attacks on Democrats.[1] The clip was from the opening of a story about how Sherrod and her family had suffered from racism, and that she was initially reluctant to go out of her way to help a poor white farmer who came to her agency for help. Had anyone involved in publicizing the out of context clip listened to the whole speech, they would have heard Sherrod go on to say that she realized this was wrong, and then went out of her way to help the farmer and his family. The farmer later supported Ms. Sherrod's account.

Fueled by the prospects of a media scandal and press feeding frenzy, the following events unfolded rapidly in the hours following Breitbart's blog post on Monday morning July 19, 2010. Despite the lack of fact checking, Breitbart's intentionally scandalous accusations appeared within a few hours on FOX Nation, the social networking site of the news organization, under the headline: "Caught on Tape: Obama Official Discriminates Against White Farmer." The video clip also appeared on the FOX Web site, along with charges of racism against Sherrod, the Obama administration, and the NAACP. After learning that the episode would be taken up as a cause célèbre on FOX TV later that day, the head of the Agriculture Department asked for Ms. Sherrod's resignation.[2] Indeed, in his show taped just ahead of news of Sherrod's firing and aired a few hours later, Bill O'Reilly called for her immediate resignation, later creating the appearance that his program alone had made it happen.

Although intended to head off the news scandal, the forced resignation only made matters worse by appearing to validate the charges and touching off a major frenzy on FOX TV the next day. Anchors and commentators called for a response from the NAACP and from the U.S. Department of Agriculture. Sean Hannity referred to the speech as "just the latest in a series of racial incidents" coming from the Obama administration. And Newt Gingrich described her speech as "viciously racist."[3]

The speed at which misinformation turned into news in this case was breathtaking: Breitbart posted the misleading clip of the speech on his Web site on a Monday morning, and Bill O'Reilly used his top rated program to call for Sherrod's removal that evening (by which time she had already been fired). The only problem was that nobody bothered to look at the rest of her speech to discover that the moral of the story was overcoming racism and recognizing that poor black and white people had been at odds for generations, while failing to recognize that their mutual condition centered around poverty, not racial difference. But telling the whole story would have robbed the news of its scandal value and its political slant, and thus, would have been of little interest to FOX News (or presumably much of its audience). Although Sherrod later received an apology and an offer of a new job at the Agriculture Department, the lasting image as the scandal swept through the media was one of racism in the Obama administration and the NAACP, an image suffered by Ms. Sherrod.

Later in the same week, FOX artfully dodged its role in promoting the scandal and denied any responsibility for Ms. Sherrod's firing. Sunday news anchor Chris Wallace engaged in a heated debate with former Democratic National Committee chair Howard Dean in which Wallace blamed the government for firing Sherrod before checking the facts.[4] As for Andrew Breitbart, the blogger/operative who spun the story, he later did both FOX and CNN interviews in which he boldly claimed that the excerpt from the speech was fair because it demonstrated racism at the NAACP, which again magnified the media impact of the intended political spin from the story.[5] Breitbart implied that turnabout was fair play, admitting that his spin campaign was payback for the earlier NAACP challenge to the Tea Party to get racists out of its ranks. And so, an essentially false story raced through the new media landscape, becoming a spin vehicle for the strategic political message that the Obama administration and the NAACP are racist.[6]

How Spin Works

While the above example may take the battle between spin and facts to a new extreme, it illustrates a growing concern in the news system. The moral of the story seems to be that facts should not get in the way of good spin. It may be obvious why politicians attempt to control the news, but the journalistic response to news control is more complicated. When news management operations by officials are competent and journalists are heavily spun, the mainstream press often has trouble reporting independently on stories, with the result that the news sounds much the same no matter which mainstream outlet one consults. True, the *New York Times* may have more stories on more subjects, and contain more detail than *USA Today*, but neither strays far beyond official messages and spin. Even FOX News, with its distinctive political flair, merely samples more from one side of the official spectrum than the other. This curiously American form of journalism becomes all the more confining as shrinking news budgets restrict investigative reporting and squeeze the space for hard news in favor of more entertaining soft news and features. The spiral of managed news intensifies as newsmakers compete to get their messages into that shrinking hard-news environment. As a result, today little room is afforded either by news organizations or politicians' communication strategists for candor, complexity, dialogue, or risk in public life.

The communication offices of government and political interests may set the tone and the boundaries of hard news so effectively that spin from established sources may be reported to balance a story even when there is little evidence to support it. This can result in years of strategic political diversion of national attention from pressing issues, such as global warming and other environmental issues. The quest for balance can be so ritualized that news organizations may impose it even when investigative reporters reveal situations that seem to have the evidence clearly stacked on one side. For example, Ken Silverstein, an investigative reporter for the *Los Angeles Times*, told of his experience doing a solid piece of investigative reporting on Republican efforts to use influence in St. Louis to disqualify African American voters in the 2004 presidential election. He found that the Republican abuses in Missouri might have been significant enough to affect the outcome of the election, while alleged transgressions by the Democrats were comparatively minor. Despite this finding, his editors chose to run a more "balanced" story about the parties charging each other with dirty practices. In Silverstein's view, creating artificial balance out of political spin rather than reporting the actual independent findings was anything but balanced. He went public with his frustrations, saying: "I am completely exasperated by this approach to the news. The idea seems to be that we go out to report but when it comes time to write we turn our brains off and repeat the spin from both sides. God forbid we should . . . attempt to fairly assess what we see with our own eyes. 'Balanced' is not fair, it's just an easy way to avoid real reporting and shirking our responsibility to readers."[7]

The greatest irony of this system is that considerable competition exists among journalists for what generally amounts to a pretty homogeneous result—with the notable exception of the recent trend to market political content to partisan audiences on FOX and MSNBC. Perhaps the next greatest irony is that so much antagonism between journalists and politicians also exists, even though they frequently end up serving each other's mutual interests. Journalists often resent the canned news they end up serving to audiences, and so look for moments of spontaneity or poorly staged news events. And the drift toward sensationalism magnifies the tendency of journalists to turn against politicians at the hint of a slip, a rumor, or an accusation from an opponent. Thus, politicians may suddenly find reporters biting the hand that feeds them (recall "feeding the beast" from the last chapter) if they slip or indulge in a spontaneous moment that can be interpreted as a problem. As a result, the press is often kept at a distance from the officials they cover, particularly the president. As noted in the last chapter, even presidential news conferences have declined sharply over the past several decades. The result is that the journalists who cover the most storied political office seldom have much to distinguish their stories from one another. Former White House correspondent for CNN, Charles Bierbauer, has described the intense scramble for some nugget or nuance that makes a report different, something that leads someone else's editor to call and say "Bierbauer's got the story. Where's yours?"[8]

This strange American news pattern alternates between publicizing patent political spin and trying to trap politicians in slips and scandals. Far from enhancing public respect, the press politics game conveys an air of smug insiders often struggling over little of substance while ignoring gaping realities. When the press pack attacks, the adversarial behavior appears largely ritualistic. This "gotcha" journalism often comes across to audiences as posturing—as a game that journalists play to make themselves appear independent and adversarial.

The press also played "gotcha" with Democratic presidential candidate Al Gore during the 2000 election. Leading news organizations, such as the *Washington Post* and the *New York Times* ran incorrect and out-of-context versions of Gore's remarks on his involvement with facilitating access to the Internet and helping establish a program to clean up toxic waste sites. He soon became branded in the national press as a "serial exaggerator" (a term supplied by the Bush communication team). Late-night comedians made him a national laughingstock. Between February and June of 2000, a sample of 2,400 national news articles showed that 76 percent of the stories contained charges that Gore lied, exaggerated, or was somehow involved in scandal. The students and teachers at the New Hampshire high school where the most damaging press misquote originated tried in vain for months to fix the inaccuracy and came away discouraged. A media literacy class at the school compared their tape of the Gore visit with national coverage and issued a press release titled "Top Ten Reasons Why Many Concord High Students Feel Betrayed by Some of the Media Coverage of Al Gore's Visit to Their School."[9]

In the 2004 presidential race, the press anointed former Vermont governor Howard Dean as the early frontrunner, and then just as quickly changed the narrative in response to Democratic insiders who pronounced him unelectable. Dean suddenly became a candidate who was too angry and hotheaded for voters and who could not challenge President Bush on Iraq (even though Dean's rise to the top in the first place was based largely on his opposition to the war). Dean suffered a surprising defeat in the Iowa caucuses, and the press had new frontrunners to take to the next primary, creating new plot material for the familiar horse race story that journalists tell in every election.

In the 2008 race, it was not long after Arizona Senator John McCain appeared to have the Republican nomination sewn up that stories began to surface about his legendary anger, suggesting that many moments in which he smiled through intense debate exchanges or heated interviews with journalists were forced efforts on his part to mask his inner rage.

This chapter explores why so much journalism falls into the two broad categories of (a) reporting the official lines of the day and (b) then playing personal "gotcha" games, often with the same officials and newsmakers. This dynamic is at the core of the authority-disorder syndrome, and it contributes in various ways to the other news biases as well. Both of these reporting tendencies present serious problems for citizens and their relation to government. The tendency of the press to open the gates to officials and their carefully managed messages is hard to reconcile with the common assumption that the media are (or at least have the potential to be) objective, independent, professional, and even adversarial in their relations with news sources. The problem of a free press relying so heavily on what officials (and, more important, their handlers and their opponents' handlers) feed it is so perplexing that the reasons have been explored by a number of researchers in the fields of communication (e.g., Jay Blumler, Michael Gurevitch),[10] sociology (e.g., Herbert Gans, Gaye Tuchman),[11] and political science (e.g., Bernard Cohen, Timothy Cook).[12]

The second tendency of the press to bite the hand that feeds it is in many ways equally puzzling because the resulting adversarialism is more often personal than substantive. As Thomas Patterson has pointed out in the larger analysis from which the epigram that opens this chapter was drawn, the resulting news content is an odd mix: a narrow range of political ideas, interspersed with cranky criticisms of politicians and the games they play. Patterson describes the rising levels of journalistic negativity as follows:

> . . . negative coverage of politics has risen dramatically in recent decades. Negative coverage of presidential candidates, for example, now exceeds their positive coverage. . . . By 1990, negative coverage of Congress and its members was over 80%. Each president since 1976—Carter, Reagan, Bush, and Clinton—has received more negative coverage than his predecessor. Federal agencies have fared no better; in the 1990–1995 period, for example, not a single

cabinet-level agency received more positive than negative coverage. As portrayed by the press, America's public leadership is universally inept and self-serving.[13]

Although different researchers propose different specific reasons for why the news comes out in this odd way, all seem to agree that the general answer is a combination of four factors: (a) the economics of the news business, (b) the dependence of journalists on sources who control the information that journalists need, (c) the routine news-gathering practices of reporters and their news organizations, and (d) the professional norms and codes of conduct that grow up around those organizational routines. Because two of these factors (the political economy of the news and the information management strategies of news sources) are discussed extensively in other chapters, this chapter and the next look inside journalism itself, beginning with the organizational news-gathering routines that keep reporters and officials locked into their strange dance.

Work Routines and Professional Norms

Organizational routines are the basic rules and practices that journalism schools and news organizations train reporters and editors to follow in deciding what to cover, how to cover it, and how to present the results of their work. Journalistic routines give the news its reassuring familiarity and create a steady supply of news product in a competitive marketplace. *Professional norms* are those moral standards, codes of ethics, and guidelines about inserting one's voice and viewpoint into a story that enable journalists to make personal decisions. In addition, these codes of the profession enable news organizations to justify what they produce. Both of these factors are shaped strongly by the business pressures. The recent wave of economic change sweeping the news industry not only introduced changes into reporting practices, but also created serious strains in important journalistic norms, such as objectivity.

It is increasingly clear that the everyday work routines inside news organizations bias the news without necessarily intending to do so. Our first order of business (and the focus of this chapter) is to show how the everyday practices of journalists and their news organizations contribute to the authority-disorder bias, as well as to personalized, dramatized, and fragmented news. In addition to explaining how reporting practices bias the news, it is important to understand why these habits persist and why neither the press nor the public seems to grasp their true political significance. For example, many members of the press continue to defend their reporting habits as being largely consistent with the professional journalism norms of *independence* and *objectivity.* These standards may go by different names, such as *accurate, fair, unbiased,* or *nonpartisan,* but the point is that a surprising number of American journalists continue to espouse some notion of objectivity. The peculiar nature of objectivity is so important to understand that the next chapter is devoted primarily to its origins and its defining consequences for American news. In the discussions of professional norms and work routines in this chapter, the critical focus is on how they contribute to the news biases and to the capacity of politicians to make the news.

A word of clarification is in order about the intent of this critical discussion. In many instances, the practices and professional standards of American journalism have been commendable. In a few celebrated cases, for example, reporters and editors have even gone to jail to protect the confidentiality of sources or to defend the principle of free speech. Moreover, routine news coverage of some political issues and situations is rich and full of diverse viewpoints. For example, both reporting and entertainment media treatments of the divisive national issue of abortion have been as full of information, as rich in competing viewpoints, and as diverse in the social voices represented as we can expect a democratic communication system to be.

In other respects, however, the professional norms of independence and objectivity have backfired. In fact, American journalism may have become trapped within an unworkable set of professional standards, with the result that the more objective or fair reporters try to be, the more official bias they introduce into the news.[14] A five-nation study of political journalists by Thomas Patterson and a group of international colleagues produced a startling finding: Although the American press is arguably the most free or politically independent in the world, U.S. journalists display the least diversity in their decisions about whom to interview for different hypothetical stories and in what visuals they chose for those stories. Patterson concluded that the strong norms of political neutrality or independence among American journalists actually homogenize the political content of their reporting. By contrast, reporters in countries such as Italy, Britain, Sweden, and Germany (the other nations studied) are more likely to regard political perspectives as desirable in covering events. As a result, journalists in other nations tend to cover the same events differently—

that is, by interviewing a broader range of political sources and using different visual illustrations.[15]

Explaining Differences in the Quality of Reporting

It is important to remember that different news organizations occasionally report original investigations. These moments of independence from spin remind us of how important the press can be for engaging publics in a democracy. For example, in 2010, the *New York Times* ran a series of investigative reports on the somewhat mysterious military outsourcing firm Blackwater (which changed its name to the even more mysterious Xe, following the criminal prosecution of five employees for shooting unarmed civilians in Iraq).[16] However, most routine news most of the time looks much the same, because most news organizations direct their journalists to use similar news-gathering methods. The resulting quality of the reports (factual correctness and richness, points of view included and excluded) can vary widely depending on various factors, such as how powerful sources are spinning stories, and the economic incentives to look beyond the spin (or not).

When is high quality—more information-rich, diverse, and broadly based—news coverage likely to emerge in the U.S. system? News content is most diverse, detailed, and open to competing views when public officials are willing to debate issues openly for extended periods. This is what the indexing theory introduced in earlier chapters predicts about the quality of news. When powerful newsmakers engage in open public debate, news organizations are more likely to cover issues in depth and follow the political process through the halls and hearing rooms of government, and citizen comprehension often increases. We find such relatively open and detailed coverage in a handful of historic cases, such as Vietnam or the Watergate investigations, and more often in coverage of the moral issues that rage through American politics. Abortion, civil rights, gun control, the role of religion in public schools and other places, and other enduring moral controversies often pit politicians and parties against each other, expand the range of political viewpoints, and take the public on extended tours of government at work. In these cases, the news may show citizens how issues move from elections to legislatures, to executive offices, to courts, to regulatory agencies, and at times spill over into the streets in sustained political conflicts.

By contrast, officials are often more guarded about going public on economic issues such as business subsidies or the political influence of banks and energy companies, or on foreign policy issues such as war and covert operations. Thus, the discovery that the CIA and military had engaged in illegal activities involving torturing prisoners in the war against terror became a rather tortured story in the press.[17] As a result, many issues that are important to America's future are apt to be reported in the fragmented and officialized language that keeps people guessing about what is going on and why. Many important events receive detailed media attention only after poorly understood policies have already become facts of life.

An important case in point is the war in Iraq. Even years later, most citizens were unsure about its origins and rationale. When President Obama delivered a speech in September of 2010 announcing the end of U.S. combat operations, he received a 57 percent approval rating on handling the war—one of the few positive areas in his presidency at the time.[18] Yet the speech was no declaration of victory. Obama even remarked beforehand that his speech would be no "victory lap."[19] Indeed, the fighting was not over, the Iraqi government was in disarray, and the promises to rebuild the country seemed empty to many Iraqis. All that seemed clear to most Americans is that they wanted to get out. Yet few understood why we were there in the first place.

Among the factors contributing to public confusion and disillusionment with the war were the successful spin efforts by the Bush administration to sell the war to the public in 2002-2003.[20] The result was a stunning absence of uncritical reporting in the mainstream media, effectively making the press an important player in the sales effort. That lack of another side to the story can be attributed, in part, to the absence of organized Democratic opposition for the simple reason that the party did not want to oppose a then popular president who had stirred up a national patriotic (media) rally in support of war. (It is ironic that the depth of public support may not have been all that great. As a result, the majority of Washington elites quickly joined the national rally.

With elites lined up in favor of the war, critical voices seldom passed through the news gates. For example, in February 2003 on the eve of the invasion of Iraq, some 15 to 20 million people around the world took to the streets to protest the impending war and to urge their governments not to support it. These were the largest organized protests in human history. Although large demonstrations took place in many American cities, including hundreds of thousands who turned out in New York, relatively little attention was given to this expression of public opinion in the news. When the president was asked to comment, he said that they were entitled to their

Case Study

Top Ten Reasons the Press Took a Pass on the Iraq War

"Weapons of Mass Deception" was the headline on Jon Stewart's *The Daily Show* after the U.S. military had finished months of unproductive searching for weapons of mass destruction (WMD) in Iraq. The administration's case for the war had been built on fearful WMD scenarios, capped by Saddam Hussein seeking nuclear weapons that might be used against nations in the Middle East and even in attacks on American cities. The case for war was also built on claims that Iraq had connections to al-Qaeda and to the events of 9/11. As the Iraq invasion turned into a messy occupation, it became clear that many of the claims used to convince the public and quiet the opposition had little supporting evidence and a good deal of intelligence information that contradicted them. It even seemed likely that key players in the Bush administration promoted these fearful images to sell a war that they had sought even before 9/11 happened. Enough of this was known to the press in time to generate a healthy public debate before the invasion took place. Few news organizations, however, offered any serious challenge to administration news management efforts.

It was even clear beforehand that the administration was marketing the war as a partisan political product. In a good piece of investigative reporting (lamentably not followed up by the *Post* or other news organizations), two journalists for the *Washington Post* described a systematic media campaign that began in August 2002 with the formation of the White House Iraq Group (WHIG) aimed at rolling out communication strategy for the coming war. WHIG's "strategic communications" task force planned publicity and news events for a campaign that would start in September, after most Americans (and Congress) had returned from their summer vacations. As former White House chief of staff Andrew Card put it in an interview that the *New York Times* ran in September 2002, "From a marketing point of view, you don't introduce new products in August."[21]

The selling of the war went according to plan. The nation's talk shows on the weekend after Labor Day 2002 were filled with administration officials staying on-message and reading from a script that turned out to be more scary fiction than fact.[22] On NBC's *Meet the Press,* Vice President Cheney raised the specter that Saddam's nuclear, chemical, and biological weapons presented an immediate danger to the United States. National Security Advisor (later Secretary of State) Condoleezza Rice acknowledged on CNN's *Late Edition* that solid evidence was scarce, but that waiting only increased the risk. Her punch line was: "We don't want the smoking gun to be a mushroom cloud." Defense Secretary Donald Rumsfeld warned the audience on CBS's *Face the Nation,* "Imagine a September 11 with weapons of mass destruction. It's not 3,000, it's tens of thousands of innocent men, women, and children."[23] Like many of the emotional images in the campaign to sell the war, this one was based on little evidence beyond administration claims themselves. Why did this campaign pass through the press so easily, being reported just as it was scripted?

At least 10 factors converged in Perfect Storm fashion to push the press pack to write stories that seldom challenged administration framing even though gaps in the credibility of that framing were available to knowledgeable reporters at the time.[24] Here are the ten factors that created this perfect propaganda storm:

1. *9/11 happened.* The national public was softened by those horrific events to accept almost anything that might produce closure, leading to restrictions of civil liberties on the domestic front and the rise of empire discourse from administration officials such as Paul Wolfowitz, Richard Perle, Dick Cheney, and Donald Rumsfeld, who had long harbored fantasies of a militarist reassertion of American power. Where was the press after 9/11? Apparently too wrapped in its cultural-patriotic storytelling to find credible sources to challenge that vision. Thus, the administration was able to push a weak case for war based on fantastic assertions of an al-Qaeda–Iraq link, and the even stealthier innuendos that Saddam Hussein was somehow involved in the 9/11 attacks—a connection that 71 percent of the public attributed to the administration as late as the summer of 2003.[25]

The capacity of the administration to successfully push deceptions and misrepresentations through a docile press to an emotionally volatile public may stand as the most ruthless press control operation in history—an operation that achieved such sophistication that the next three factors involve separate forms of press management.

2. *Master scripting and directing by Karl Rove.* Often called "Bush's Brain," Karl Rove had managed Bush's rise to Governor of Texas, and then on to the White House, where he was chief communication and policy advisor until he stepped down on the heels of a scandal in his boss's second term. The Rove White House communication operation made Reagan press management under Deaver and Gergen seem modest by comparison. No news management opportunity was missed, from the Top Gun carrier landing, to edgy assertions that Iraq was a key front in the War on Terror. Even the president's deer-in-the-headlights media presence was countered, with the relentless spin that he in fact had a natural "swagger."

3. *Beyond spin: Outright intimidation.* Intimidation of journalists and news organizations began within hours of the 9/11 catastrophe. The censorship campaign involved a chorus of conservative talk and news media that shouted down any news organization that deviated from patriotic support of the administration. Key moments of punctuation were provided when administration officials called out reporters and other media personalities who dared to question the administration. This intimidation campaign continued through the aftermath of the war in Iraq. When whistleblowers came forward—from former Ambassador Wilson who investigated claims of the alleged Iraq–uranium connection, to former Treasury Secretary O'Neill and security advisor Richard Clarke who reported rapid efforts inside the administration immediately after 9/11 to

link the terrorist attacks to Iraq in an effort to set up an invasion–they were swiftly shouted down in public and intimidated with personal reprisals.[26]

4. *The press was embed(ded) with the military.* A good journalist is likely to be a vicarious adventurer who seeks to be at the scene of the action, telling a "big story." Apparently, one could not be closer to the Iraq War story than inside a tank hurtling across the desert toward Baghdad. Nearly every respected journalist (including those too old to go into action themselves) initially hailed the military embedding as a ringside ticket to great journalism, a perspective that would bring the uncensored reality of war to the American people. Only later did some journalists admit what they might have seen beforehand: that the "big story" was dictated from Washington, and the scenes from inside the tanks were little more than B-roll filler that authenticated a story told by the government. If the embedding operation was as telling about the dramaturgy of the press as about the press-control proclivities of the administration, the next factor moves us even farther into the realm of press responsibility.

5. *Telling the story that promises maximum drama and most likely plot advancement.* When journalists make story choices, they favor narrative elements that are most likely to advance a coherent, dramatic story into the future. In some cases, those choices produce stories that ignore potentially damning evidence to the contrary. Such cases typically involve looking away from sources less likely to deliver future installments and favoring (usually official) sources more prepared to deliver regular updates. Consider the reporting decisions to downplay the volume of doubt linking al-Qaeda—and, more generally, 9/11—to Iraq. Consider, too, the volume of doubt about Saddam's weapons of mass destruction. Although doubts were reported, they were pegged largely to foreign sources and domestic protesters and were dismissed insultingly by Rumsfeld and company.

At the same time, few mainstream news organizations even noted the strong al-Qaeda links to Saudi Arabia, a friend of the Bush administration. Few stories followed up a postinvasion revelation by Saudi officials that al-Qaeda operatives had continued to conduct training operations as late as July 2003 on Saudi farms. And few reports challenged the Bush administration's refusal to release an intelligence report allegedly linking al-Qaeda to prominent members of the Saudi political elite. One exception was independent journalist Seymour Hersh, who published an early investigative report in *The New Yorker* presenting evidence against the Iraq connection to al-Qaeda, while pointing something of a smoking gun at Saudi Arabia.[27] Such rare acts of investigative journalism were virtually ignored by the larger press community because standard Washington official sources would offer nothing to advance those stories. They served up, instead, daily installments on Saddam and terrorism. What would it have taken for the press to turn those potential blockbuster alternatives into serious frame challenges to the administration? Did I mention the Democrats?

6. *Where were the Democrats?* Apparently, the defeated Democrats had been advised to offend no one and to take no political risks. Although this advice might be questioned as making them seem even more defeated by looking weak and indecisive, they apparently paid enough for their professional communication counsel to follow it. Thus, the party left criticism to a few isolated representatives and to a pack of 2004 presidential candidates who criticized each other more often than they criticized the president. News organizations are so dependent on prominent official sources to advance challenges to a leading news frame that the strategic silence of the Democrats all but killed media deliberation about the war.

Why were the concerns of 2004 presidential primary candidates such as Howard Dean or Dennis Kucinich not enough to reframe the story? Because the U.S. press is taken with reporting only who and what the Washington consensus anoints with *gravitas*. Without major figures weighing in, strong antiwar sentiment among the public went largely unreported. Consider a small case in point. In January 2003, I was called by a *Newsweek* reporter who asked the stunning question (as I paraphrase it): "We in the press have become aware of a substantial antiwar movement. Why do you think we are not reporting it?" Why, indeed, did the press fail to report organized large-scale opposition? I explained that the failure to report on the antiwar movement was due to the dependence of the press on official opposition, and the Democrats largely took a pass. And so, on February 15, 2003, when between 15 and 20 million people across the globe raised their voices in what may well be the largest coordinated public demonstrations in world history, the American press allowed the president to dismiss it as the ramblings of a "focus group" to which he would not respond.

7. *The absence of credible progressive think tanks.* News stories are often advanced through reactions from experts at think tanks who promote the political policy objectives of those who fund these high-level opinion-making operations. The conservative right has enjoyed considerable media success through a combination of aggressive news management (see point 2), dense networking of radio and TV talk pundits, and rapid-response networks to create a public "echo chamber" to support policy initiatives and attack opponents (see point 3)—all supported by the timely delivery of think-tank reports and experts to journalists. Perhaps it is because of funding disparities between the Left and the Right—or simply because of the dim capacities of the Left to understand how the press works—that there was virtually no coordinated expertise to counter the Bush administration's war frames.

8. *Press construction of a spectator public.* It is some consolation that publics form their opinions only in part through cueing from the news. In their lives beyond the media, people look elsewhere for clues about what to think. Perhaps the most impressive thing about public opinion as measured by polls up to the eve of the invasion was that clear majorities favored war only if the administration could build an international coalition (one suspects that a "coalition of the willing" that included Palau and Tonga over France and Germany was not what they had in mind). However, as

(continued)

Case Study—*Continued*

the news narrative built toward inevitable war, opposition levels in the polls were reported only as footnotes for the record. It seems that polls and protests were not enough for the press to turn the public into players in the media spectacle. As often happens, journalists forgot that publics can take active roles in the news story of democracy. Yet, when the public predictably rallied their support at the outbreak of the war, it would have been easy to conclude that the public supported the rationale for the war all along. Moreover, reports of public support in the polls failed to note that the majority in favor of the war was really rather weak, as many did not really care if the war did not happen. Such weakness of the poll support was not reported in the news.

9. *Press ethnocentrism.* More than any other Western democratic press system, the U.S. press is remarkably closed to world opinion. Perhaps this reflects the press's implicit mirroring of the confusing popular cultural impulses of isolationism and patriotic intervention. The inward turn of American journalism may also reflect the unwillingness of most politicians (a.k.a. leading news sources) to risk their patriotic credentials either by questioning the values and motives behind government decisions to use force or by crediting outsiders when they do so. In any event, international reactions of outrage to the administration's "you're either with us or against us" stand on Iraq were duly noted for the news record and then easily spun away by administration news sources and journalists alike. While news features reported on boycotts of French wine and the renaming of french fries as *freedom fries*, many commentators adopted a condescending tone for discussing the din of international criticism. No national news organization was more aggressive in its patriotic support for the Iraq War—or its vitriolic condemnation of administration critics, foreign and domestic—than FOX.

10. *The FOX effect.* This is the last, and, I think, the least important factor explaining why the press faithfully reported so many administration claims that could have been challenged. Because of the levels of patriotic cant from FOX reporters, anchors, and talk-show hosts alike, many observers felt that FOX exercised a chilling effect on a competition that was worried about ratings losses among audiences allegedly swept with patriotic fervor. It is true that new standards of jingo-journalism may have been set by the FOX anchor who described antiwar protesters in Switzerland as "hundreds of knuckleheads," or by the decision to run a crawl at the bottom of the screen branding nations that refused to join the "coalition of the willing" as the "axis of weasels."[28] FOX's hyperbolic reporting notwithstanding, we should not forget the stiff competition among television news organizations during the first Gulf War to display their patriotism—long before FOX News was a gleam in the eyes of Roger Ailes and Rupert Murdoch.[29] If FOX's competition took a pass on critical journalism, I would argue that the effects of factors 1 through 9 were considerably more important than looking over their journalistic shoulders at the FOX effect.

The emerging conclusion about mass-mediated democracy is that news debates tend to be more open and informative when the government itself is already functioning ideally—that is, when government officials are openly debating and investigating public policies in front of the news cameras. On the other hand, when elites are not debating policy options in public, journalism routines close the news gates on stories that might be quite important to the public interest. The weakness in the American information system appears to be those crucial and all-too-common cases where government officials do not confront difficult issues or choices. Should information be shaped so thoroughly by what elites and elected officials are doing in public? In the remainder of this chapter we examine how the daily work routines of journalists keep them so focused on the inner circles of power.

opinion, but that he would not be swayed by a "focus group." The press continued its march to war guided by spin from the administration, reporting few perspectives from outside high official circles.[30]

The full story behind one of the most successful (and perhaps misguided) spin campaigns in history involves more than just the Democrats and indexing. Indeed, selling the Iraq War to the press and, in turn, to the American public resulted from something of a perfect storm of political factors that favored the communication strategies of the Bush White House. The case study in this chapter provides an analysis of why the press overwhelmingly reported Bush administration spin during the time when public opinion on that war mattered most.

How Routine Reporting Practices Contribute to News Bias

Much like any job, reporting the news consists largely of a set of routine, standardized activities. Despite some obvious differences involving the nature of assignments and personal writing styles, American reporters (as noted earlier) tend to cover news events in remarkably similar ways. A fascinating example of how these work routines affect news content was discovered by Timothy Cook in a study of international crisis coverage in the United States and France. In the months after the Iraqi invasion of Kuwait, crucial international diplomatic efforts attempted to prevent the looming war. When news of these efforts broke, television networks in both countries assigned their reporters to get reactions from key sources. American newscasts flipped through the "golden triangle" of Washington news beats: the White House, State Department, and Pentagon. Even though there was no official U.S. reaction to be had, the reporters were pressured to say something, and they effectively invented the kinds of vague pronouncements that one might expect from officials in sensitive political posts at the early stage of a world crisis. By contrast, French reporters (who do not operate with a U.S.-style beat system) interviewed various political party leaders and generated a comparatively broad range of political views about the meanings and implications of the diplomatic talks.[31]

The existence of standardized reporting behaviors and story formulas is not surprising when one considers the strong patterns that operate in the news environment. For example, the events staged by political actors tend to reflect the predictable political communication goals. Moreover, most mass media news organizations tend to impose fairly similar constraints on reporters in terms of acceptable story angles, deadlines, and news-gathering resources. Also, reporters are subject to the standardizing influence of working in close quarters with one another, covering the same sorts of events under the same kinds of pressures.

In short, reporters confront three separate sources of incentives to standardize their reporting habits:

- Routine cooperation with (and pressures from) news sources
- The work routines of (and pressures within) news organizations
- Daily information sharing and working relations with fellow reporters

Each of these forces contributes to the development of standardized reporting formulas that favor the incorporation of official political messages in the news, interspersed with the feeding frenzies that may undermine the officials themselves. These reporting patterns also lead reporters to write personalized, dramatized, and fragmented news stories. We will now explore each source of everyday pressure on journalists.

Reporters and Officials: Cooperation and Control

Most political events are so predictably scripted that reporters can condense them easily into formulaic plot outlines: who (which official) did what (official action), where (in what official setting), for what (officially stated) purpose, and with what (officially proclaimed) result. For example:

> President __________ met at the White House today with President __________ from __________ to discuss mutual concerns about __________. Both leaders called the talks productive and said that important matters were resolved.

It does not take a careful reading to see that such a formula is virtually devoid of substance. The pseudo-events that provide the scripts for such news stories are generally designed to create useful political images, not to transmit substantive information about real political issues. Because such events are routine political occurrences, reporters quickly develop formulas for converting them into news whenever they occur. Compounding the temptation to report official versions of political events is the fact that reporters live in a world where the "divide and conquer" mentality is ever present. Careers are advanced by receiving scoops and leaks and are damaged by being left out in the cold, excluded from official contact. Like it or not, reporters must depend on the sources they cover. When those sources are powerful officials surrounded by an entourage of eager reporters clamoring for news, it is always possible that those who report what officials want them to will be rewarded, whereas those who fail to convert key political messages into news will be punished.

In view of the patterned nature of political events combined with the press tactics of politicians, it is not surprising that the news seems to emerge from formulas that virtually write themselves.[32] Of course, knowing the formulas does not mean that reporters will always use them. However, in a workday world filled with short deadlines, demanding editors, and persuasive news sources, the formulas become the course of least resistance. Even when a formula is abandoned, there is seldom enough other information available in a typical political setting to construct another story.

In the illusory world of political news, formulas describe official actions, and the seal of official approval becomes a substitute for truth and authenticity, which in turn makes the formulas seem legitimate.[33] Robert Scholes developed these ideas a bit further when he said:

> Perhaps the credulous believe that a reporter reports facts and that newspapers print all of them that are fit to print. But actually, newspapers print all of the "facts" that fit, period—that fit the journalistic conventions of what "a

> story" is (those tired formulas) and that fit the editorial policy of the paper. . . .[34]

Anyone for changing that famous slogan to "All the News That Fits, We Print"? The formulas used to select and arrange facts in the news are produced largely through the mutual cooperation of reporters and newsmakers. These partners may not share exactly the same goals or objectives, but together they create information that satisfies each other's needs. It is all in a day's work.

The Insider Syndrome

In addition to developing work habits that favor official views, reporters are also human beings. Behind the occupational roles are people who sometimes identify with the newsmakers they cover. Because reporters have regular contact with officials under stressful conditions, it becomes easy for them to see these officials as sympathetic characters. Of course, when officials go out of their way to antagonize the press, as the Nixon administration did during the early 1970s and as the Clinton administration did for most of its first term, it is more difficult for reporters to identify with the officials. When officials court the favor and understanding of reporters, they are often paid back with sympathetic coverage that sticks close to the officials' political lines.[35] Such coverage is easily justified as an objective account of the officials' public actions.

Yet another aspect of the subtle working relations between reporters and officials is that journalists who cooperate with powerful officials often receive recognition and flattery and are taken into the confidence of those officials. In the intensely political environments in which most of our news occurs, nothing is valued as much as power. If one cannot possess power (and there always seems to be a shortage), then the next best thing is to be on the inside with the powerful—to be seen with them, to be consulted by them, to socialize with them, and perhaps even to have them as friends. As Tom Bethell puts it:

> To be on close terms with elite news sources is to be an "insider," which is what almost everyone in Washington wants to be. It is interesting to note how often this word appears on the dust jackets of memoirs by Washington journalists. But Nixon—his great weakness!—didn't like journalists and wouldn't let them be insiders. . . . Kissinger, on the other hand, was astute enough to cultivate the press, and he survived—not merely that, was lionized as "the wizard of shuttle diplomacy." (Is it not possible that the most awesome "lesson of Watergate" . . . will be a social lesson?)[36]

The perils of being a Washington insider were summarized by Tony Snow, a Detroit news columnist and former speechwriter for George H. W. Bush: "We spend a lot of time hanging out with the high and mighty. It's intoxicating. In Washington, access to people in power is important, if nothing else for social reasons, for name dropping."[37] Snow went on to become press secretary for George W. Bush. As the distinguished reporter Murray Kempton put it: "It is a fundamental fact about journalism, and might even be a rule if it had the attention it deserves, that it is next to impossible to judge any public figure with the proper detachment once you begin calling him by his first name."[38]

Ellen Hume, a journalist and scholar of the press, says that she has come to feel that journalists can be "more powerful than any elected official" and that something "urgently" needs to be done to "dynamite" the insiders out of their privileged positions.[39] Steve Goldstein, Washington correspondent for the *Philadelphia Inquirer,* suggested term limits for Washington journalists. If news organizations would agree to rotate their stars out of Washington, the power of the "unelected media elite" might be diminished. Even more important, says Goldstein, media term limits:

> . . . might counteract the potential for disconnection, whereby the correspondent suffers a loss of understanding of issues that Americans really care about. Federal policy-making and the impact on the folks at home is supplanted by the view from Washington. There is a difference between Here and There. In Sodom-on-the-Potomac the political culture is secular, while most of America is religious. Here the character issue is often framed as: Did he/she sleep with her/him/it? Out there, the issue is often one of fairness, justice, integrity. All the sleaze we print doesn't fit.[40]

In a lighter vein, Goldstein suggests the following "self-test" for Washington reporters. Offering apologies to David Letterman, he lists the "top 10 telltale signs that a journalist has been in Washington too long":

1. You cannot recall the area code of your hometown.
2. Your best sources are at other news organizations.
3. You go to Duke Ziebert's a second time [a restaurant notorious as a meeting spot and watering hole for the power elite].

4. You think a regional story refers to Upper Northwest [a district in Washington, DC].
5. The conductor of the Marine Band salutes you.
6. You reject an interview with the mayor of your hometown because it conflicts with Gridiron rehearsal [a Washington journalist's club that puts on an annual show in which press and politicians satirize each other].
7. *The Capitol Gang* [a TV pundit gathering] offers honorary membership.
8. Larry King calls you by your first name.
9. You cover the story by watching CNN.
10. You become eligible for Redskins' season tickets.[41]

However, before thinking that journalists and the officials they cover are too cozy, or that they are any cozier than in earlier eras, it is important to remember that "cozy" is hardly the way most of them would describe their relationship. Many politicians today describe their relations with the press as regrettably antagonistic and, therefore, necessarily guarded. Reporters often complain that they never get close to officials and must fight through the "spin patrol" of handlers, consultants, and flaks. It is surely the case that today's political scene is, in many ways, far less cozy and more filled with "gotcha" journalism than in the years before Vietnam and Watergate. In those bygone days of greater direct contact between reporters and officials, many prominent journalists and officials were more likely to socialize, be friends, drink and party together, and go off the record after 5 p.m. However, the greater personal distance in press-source relations today does not mean that reporting is less dependent on official spin. Far from it.

Reporters as Members of News Organizations: Pressures to Standardize

If reporters' relations with officials breathe new life into old news formulas, their own news organizations reinforce the use of those formulas. Novice journalists experience constant pressures (subtle and otherwise) from editors about how to cover stories.[42] These pressures are effective because editors hold sway over what becomes news and which reporters advance in the organization. Over time, reporters tend to adjust their styles to fit harmoniously with the expectations of their organizations.

In many cases, these organizational expectations are defended by journalists as simply preserving the "house style" of the news organization—the tone, editorial voice, and format that makes one news outlet distinguishable from another. This level of formula reporting is as unobjectionable as it is inevitable in any kind of organization that has standard operating procedures. However, there are deeper levels at which organizational preferences for story formulas do matter. To an important extent, there are industry-wide norms about story values that define what news is and that, in turn, open the news to biases. For example, one young reporter serving an apprenticeship with a major big-city newspaper talked about the somewhat mysterious process of having some stories accepted and others rejected without really knowing the basis for many of the decisions. Equally mysterious were the conversations with assignment editors in which the editor seemed to know what the story was before it had been covered. Over time, the socialization process works its effects, and young reporters learn to quickly sense what the story is and how to write it.

Beyond the style of this or that news organization, the whole media system begins to emulate particular formats, themes, and news values. Bending news genres to fit commercial values and socializing reporters to recognize how potential stories fit the familiar formulas are the roots of the news biases. In all of their variations, however, organizational pressures result in news that typically fits a formula.

Why Formulas Work

Standardized news is safe. Managers in news organizations must constantly compare their product with that of their competition and defend risky departures from the reporting norm. As Epstein observed in his classic study of television network news, even TV news assignment editors look to the conservative wire services for leads on stories and angles for reporting them.[43] The wires cover the highest portion of planned official events and stick closest to official political scripts. Following the daily lead of the wires becomes the most efficient way to fill the news hole.

Other organizational arrangements also strongly influence standardized reporting. Among the most powerful standardizing forces are daily news production routines. Newspapers and news programs require a minimum supply of news every day, whether or not anything significant happens in the world. Perhaps you have seen a television news program on a slow news day. In place of international crises, press conferences, congressional hearings, and proclamations by the mayor, the news may consist of a trip to the zoo to visit a new "baby," a canned report on acupuncture in China, a follow-up story on the survivor of an air crash, or a spoof on the opening of baseball spring training in Florida. Slow news days occur during weekends or vacation periods when governments are closed down. News organizations run fluff on slow days because their daily routines report official happenings from the news centers of government.

The News Hole

For a news organization to function, it must fill a minimum "news hole" every day. Producing a large amount of cheap, predictable news normally means assigning reporters to events and beats that are sure to produce enough acceptable stories to fill the news hole by the day's deadline. During normal business periods, the public relations (PR) machinery of government and business fills these organizational needs by producing events that are cheap, easy to report, numerous, and predictable.

With the advent of 24-hour news channels and Web sites linked to papers and broadcast organizations, the news hole has become a gorge. Pressures increase to update stories many times a day, in contrast to once or twice a day in the old era of morning and evening news. The journalistic credo of "advancing" a story has become an obsession for many organizations. Reporters learn to ask leading or challenging questions, often based on little more than trying to elicit a reaction from a newsmaker in an effort to generate new material to report. "President Obama denied rumors today . . ." becomes a familiar lead in a news age with an ever-larger news hole to fill.

Beats

Filling the daily news hole on time means that news organizations must figure out how to make the spontaneous predictable. The obvious solution to this problem is to anticipate when and where the required amount of news will happen every day. Because this task is made difficult by the size of the world and the smallness of reporting staffs, the solution is to implicitly adjust the definition of news so that things that are known to happen on a regular basis become news. Reporters can be assigned to cover those things and be assured (by definition) of gathering news every day. As a result, the backbone of the news organization is the network of beats, ranging from the police station and the city council at the local level, to Congress, the Supreme Court, and the presidency at the national level. Beats produce each day's familiar run of murders, accidents, public hearings, press conferences, and presidents entering helicopters and leaving planes.

Special Assignments

To break the daily routine, some reporters are given special assignments to cover big stories, such as elections or spontaneous events like assassinations and floods. However, the expense of special-coverage assignments dictates that even the truly spontaneous must be translated into familiar formulas. If an event is important enough to justify special coverage, then it must be represented in dramatic terms. Even assassinations, invasions, and floods quickly become scripted. For example, when it became clear that the United States was planning an invasion of Haiti in the summer of 1994, television news organizations readied large libraries of canned material on the island nation and extensively scripted their coverage well in advance.

Because special coverage is costly and must be kept going, even no news often becomes news. Frank Cesno, a former Washington Bureau chief for CNN, told of his week of special coverage when John F. Kennedy Jr.'s airplane was missing in July 1999. He personally anchored much of the coverage and spent a good bit of it announcing that there was not much news from the search-and-rescue teams. However, making the decision to go live and assigning the story the top priority for the network required being on the air and keeping the news flowing.[44]

Bureaus

In addition to beats and special-coverage assignments, many large news organizations have developed a third news-gathering unit, the geographically assigned crew. For example, television networks have news crews (a correspondent and video and sound technicians) stationed in large cities, such as Chicago, New York, Houston, Los Angeles, and Miami. The assumption is that enough news will be generated from these areas to warrant assigning personnel to them. The use of geographical assignments reflects another way in which organizational routines have shaped the definition of news into a convenient formula. Because national news cannot all come from Washington, reporters must be assigned to other locations. But what other locations? Any location chosen suddenly becomes a defining center for national news. As Epstein discovered in his study of television network news, almost all non-Washington news originates from the handful of cities where the networks station their crews.[45]

To an important extent, the reliance on bureaus has decreased in recent years due to budget cuts that eliminated many of these branch offices. As the profit imperative has been felt at both print and broadcast organizations, expensive bureaus are often the first things to be cut. Among American television news operations, only CNN has retained a substantial network of worldwide information-gathering outposts—in large part because CNN also runs an international channel that demands serious world coverage. However, all major news organizations have dropped bureaus and reporting staff. The result is that ABC, CBS, and NBC have increasingly settled for buying their raw product secondhand from a variety of world TV wholesale news suppliers. In the newspaper business, pressures to cut luxuries such as remote bureaus have been equally intense. Many big-city papers have been purchased by large conglomerates, which feed all the papers in the chain the same material from centralized bureaus. The few remaining independent big-city papers increasingly rely on secondhand suppliers, such as the Associated Press, the *New York Times,* and the *Washington Post,* which continue to maintain extensive bureaus and sell their stories to smaller organizations. The overall trend is an increasing consolidation of the information channels on which media organizations rely for their daily supply of news.

Public Relations and News

The PR industry has grown in size and technological sophistication in recent decades. The goal of many PR and communications campaigns is to place news stories that advance the images and political goals of clients. As news organizations reduce staff, shrink bureaus, and become more conscious of budgets, the supply of PR events and news releases becomes more attractive as news material. Indeed, PR wires run into most newsrooms, and PR workers (who often have experience as journalists) work up contacts with journalists and supply them with story ideas and sources. As a result, packaged pieces on personalities, movies, entertainers, and, more generally, staged events in communication campaigns become featured in the news. Good news organizations with reasonable reporting budgets avoid packaged PR fare, but small-market TV stations and low-budget papers may succumb to the temptations of using these news helpers.

Reporters as a Pack: Pressures to Agree

As a result of the increasingly routine nature of news gathering, reporters tend to move in packs. They are assigned together to the same events and the same beats. More than most workers, they share close social experiences on the job. Together they eat, sleep, travel, drink, and wait, and wait, and wait. They also share that indescribable adrenaline rush of "crashing" a story—hurtling through those precious minutes between the release of key information and the deadline for filing the story. As a result of such intimate social contact, reporters tend to develop a sense of solidarity. They learn to cope with shared pressures from news organizations and news sources. They come to accept news formulas as inevitable, even though they may cynically complain about them in between mad scrambles to meet deadlines. They respect one another as independent professionals but engage in the social courtesies of comparing notes and corroborating story angles.

In his insightful description of press coverage during the 1972 election, Timothy Crouse called the reporter's social world "pack journalism."[46] He concluded that reporters come into such close contact while under such sympathetic conditions while covering such controlled events that they do not have to collaborate formally in order to end up reporting things the same way. Once a reporter has been assigned to a routine event for which news formulas are well known, there is a strong temptation to produce a formula story. Added to this are a tight deadline and an editor who will question significant departures from the formula used by other reporters; as a result, the temptation to standardize becomes even stronger. Finally, put the reporter in a group of sympathetic human beings faced with the same temptations, and the use of formulas becomes easily rationalized and accepted with the social support of the group.

So strong are the pressures of the pack that they have been felt even by a trained sociologist who posed as a reporter in order to study news gathering from an insider's perspective. While working as a reporter for a small daily paper, Mark Fishman was assigned to the city council beat. He quickly fit into the routine of writing formula stories that mirrored the council's careful efforts to create an image of democracy in action—complete with elaborate hearings, citizen input, serious deliberations, and formal votes. In a rare case when an issue before the council got out of control and turned into a hot political argument, the reporters at the press table reacted strangely. Ignoring a bit of news that did not fit the mold took some social prompting from various members of the pack. As Fishman described it:

> The four members of the press [including Fishman] were showing increasing signs of impatience with the controversy. At first the

reporters stopped taking notes; then they began showing their disapproval to each other; finally, they were making jokes about the foolishness of the debate. No evidence could be found in their comments that they considered the controversy anything other than a stupid debate over a trivial matter unworthy of the time and energy the council put into it.[47]

Fishman noted the strength of group pressure operating against independent news judgment: "Even though at the time of the incident I was sitting at the press table [as a reporter] making derisive comments about the foolishness of the council along with other journalists, it occurred to me later how this controversy could be seen as an important event in city hall."[48]

Just as Fishman succumbed to the pressures of the pack while still recognizing them at a conscious level, most reporters are aware of group pressure but seem unable to escape it. In a study of the Washington journalism corps, the nation's reporting elite, Stephen Hess found that reporters regarded pack journalism as their most serious problem.[49] As Hess noted, however, pack journalism will persist as long as news organizations establish their routines around the predictable actions of officials.

Although the pack generally feeds on the handouts offered by spin-doctors and political handlers, it can also turn on the unprepared or vulnerable politician. Cases of the pack devouring its political prey are legendary: Lyndon Johnson fell to a feeding frenzy over the Vietnam War; Richard Nixon lost control of the press during the Watergate crisis; Jimmy Carter was himself held hostage in the Oval Office by the press for 444 days during the Iranian hostage crisis of 1979–1980; Gary Hart withdrew his presidential candidacy in 1984, when the press pack took up his challenge to prove that he was having an extramarital affair; the first George Bush plummeted from his standing as the most popular president in the history of modern polling as the press pack followed the Democrats in attacking him for an economic recession; and Bill Clinton saw the customary presidential honeymoon period curtailed prematurely by a feeding frenzy. The growing chaos and criticism surrounding the Iraq crisis provided openings for the press pack to turn on George W. Bush, but those openings were balanced against the somber fact that the country was at war. The press pack reached consensus early in the Obama administration that the president had lost control of his "narrative." Whether the members of the press pack accept their daily news handouts with equanimity or bite the hand that feeds them, the problem remains much the same: The resulting news becomes standardized and distorted.

Feeding Frenzy: When the Pack Attacks

Although the political content of the mainstream press may be remarkably uniform, it does not always follow the scripts of politicians. What is often mistaken for a critical, independent press is a phenomenon popularly known as the "feeding frenzy."[50] When politicians become caught up in personal crises, scandals, or power struggles, the news media may descend like a pack of hungry dogs to devour the political prey. Add the hint of a sex scandal or produce the proverbial smoking gun of political corruption, and the frenzy can bring down the high and mighty.

Few politicians have felt the sting of the feeding frenzy as repeatedly as Bill Clinton. The news was spiced during the 1992 election by charges of Clinton's extramarital affairs, pot smoking, draft dodging, and other personal issues. Clinton's character became a major preoccupation of the press during the campaign.[51] The resulting challenge for the Clinton communication team was to reassure voters about the character defects raised in the news and reinforced by opponents during the primaries and the general election. The fact that Clinton survived the nearly nonstop negative news and then won the election struck one Republican media consultant as something close to a miracle. He likened Clinton to the crash test dummy of American politics: "I've never seen anybody come back from being attacked in that fashion. It's like going through a car crash with no seat belts and then going through the window and hitting a wall and walking away. It's absolutely astounding."[52]

After the election, Clinton and his staff remained bitter about their treatment by the press during the campaign. When they came to Washington, it seemed as if they felt that they could govern much as they had won the election, by going over the heads of the press through electronic town halls, controlled news events, and heavy polling and image construction. The daily world of Washington politics proved different than the campaign trail, where paid advertising and controlled events stand a better chance of countering press attacks. The now-famous decision to close the corridor between the press room and the White House communication office amounted to a declaration of war on journalism's elite corps. The icy relations left the press pack surly and ready to pounce at the hint of a scandal or personal failing. Clinton's run of personal incidents continued after the inauguration, and the press pounced on such items as Clinton's expensive haircut aboard an idling Air Force One on a Los Angeles International Airport taxiway and a scandal in the management of the White House travel office that was quickly dubbed "Travelgate" in the media.

One analysis of this nonstop feeding frenzy opened with the observation that "Twelve days after President Clinton took office—with *only* 1,448 days left in his term—Sam Donaldson of ABC *News* was on a weekend talk show saying "This week we can all talk about, Is the presidency over?"[53] Another reflective piece was titled "The White House Beast" after the derisive nickname given the press corps by George Stephanopoulous, who was Clinton's early (and disastrous) communication director, and now serves as a pundit for ABC *News*. As *Washington Post* correspondent Ruth Marcus put it in that article, "The White House press corps is like this large, dysfunctional family. It's weird. It's not normal. Half the time I'm at the White House, my attitude is: No one would believe this."[54]

There are at least three reasons for the series of feeding frenzies that plagued the Clinton presidency from the start. As these factors often contribute to other feeding frenzies, they are stated here in more general terms:

- Cooperative relations between the president's communication staff and the press had broken down.
- The communication staff seemed to think it unnecessary (or beneath the dignity of the office) to follow the basic rules of news management in response to the initial outbreaks of negative coverage. They provided few packaged stories to interrupt the negative news, and they had no apparent game plan to spin the incidents that kept the feeding frenzies going.
- The charged and actual offenses involving the president resulted in numerous uncontrolled news situations.

With the exception of the stories that David Gergen was allowed to manage during his brief stay in the Clinton White House, press relations for much of the Clinton first term remained rocky. For example, influential *New York Times* correspondent (now an influential columnist) Maureen Dowd listed the numerous instances of poor press handling on the part of the press office staff during a European trip commemorating the 50-year anniversary of D-Day. She recounted a reflective moment at a British pub after a missed deadline: "Sipping champagne ordered by the *Paris Match* reporter, I fantasized about replacing the corner dartboard with the head of one of Clinton's prepubescent press-minders."[55]

Relations between press and president may have hit an even lower point in the George W. Bush administration. Traveling extensively in order to get messages directly into local news markets, relying on tightly crafted news events, and using a national conservative talk-radio echo chamber to spread its messages, the Bush communication team often bypassed the national press corps, which it seemed to hold in disdain. The feeling soon became mutual and bubbled into frequent squabbles between reporters and administration communication staff. For example, when Vice President Cheney accidentally shot a friend on a hunting trip in 2006, the press feeding frenzy lasted more than a week. When did the president know? Why did Cheney wait hours to tell the press? Why was the story given to a small Texas local paper and not the national press? The questions went on, indicating that the press is sometimes capable of sustaining a story without the cooperation of the officials at its center. It is unfortunate for the democratic role of the press that such independence seldom appears in stories of greater importance.

As President Obama lost his narrative, the opposing Republicans were ever ready to supply theirs to the press. The Republican minority managed to capture a substantial portion of the news by threatening to filibuster Obama initiatives in the Senate, and echoing the Tea Party activities in the streets. Meanwhile the administration seemed unable to generate or stay on messages of its own, preferring to continue to communicate directly with its supporters through social media networks, which worked far better to mobilize public support during the election campaign than in the governing process.

The Paradox of Organizational Routines

The problem with routine news gathering is that most of the news on most of the channels starts looking pretty much the same. The paradox is that because there are many papers, radio programs, and television broadcasts from which audiences can receive the daily news, it is hard for competing organizations to establish a competitive edge in the news market. In short, routine reporting of news may be efficient, but it limits the share of the market that any media source can capture. For example, if all the news on television is pretty much the same, each network should capture an equal share of the audience, all other things being equal. Thus, efficiency may impose an unintended ceiling on audience share, which limits the growth of profits in the news organization—and news is, after all, a business. The ways around this dilemma involve marketing strategies, budget cutting, and various other business moves—none of which improve the quality of news.

Breaking out of the news routine toward more independent, less sensational news has not been attractive to news organizations because it is not clear what the alternative would look like even if it were profitable enough to worry about. For example, television executives may point to the *News Hour* on the Public Broadcasting Service (PBS) as an example of how more in-depth reporting only drives audiences away. Some critics argue, however, that PBS news, while more detailed and more likely to broadcast hard news over soft, is otherwise very similar in content to that available on the commercial networks. Why should audiences seek a bigger dose of the same product?

Because news is largely the result of convenient conventions between politicians and journalists, it is not clear where to look for guidance in reforming the product. Any new format would surely draw criticism from politicians and other news organizations, and it might startle the public, risking the possible loss of audience share. As a result, the media do not like to think too much about tampering with the standard news-gathering routines. Instead, the competition in most news markets tends to be waged in terms of marketing strategies, brand images, and other matters of style over substance.

Should the Market Rule the News?

After receiving a survey of audience reading habits, the management of one major daily paper reportedly issued a memo to reporters calling for more "fine examples" of rapes, robberies, and auto accidents on page 1.[56] Whether the marketing strategy involves more human-interest stories or more stereotyped coverage of political heroes in action, the result is the same as far as political information goes: The news trends are toward replacing coverage of government and civic affairs with sex, personality, lifestyle, entertainment, sports, weather, and mayhem.

The contribution of the news doctors to standardized news raises a number of important questions, including the following:

- Should news be based on market considerations, or should it be based on some independent criteria of importance and newsworthiness?
- Because some people (i.e., enough to turn a profit) watch or read news about fires, murders, accidents, and political scandals, does this necessarily mean that (a) they want more of it, (b) they think these things are important, (c) they think these things belong in the news, (d) they do not want alternatives to formula news, and (e) they would not be engaged by news that actually explains more about politics and society?

Such questions are dodged by news doctors and media executives, who reply simplistically that they are only interested in making the news more relevant to people. It is doubtful that current marketing surveys really measure popular demand at all.[57] For example, most media surveys are designed with the assumption that formula news is a given. Audiences are not asked if they would prefer alternatives to news formulas; they are simply asked which news formulas they like best. Thus, the standard excuse that the news reflects what the people want might be stated more properly as "the news reflects what people prefer among those choices that we find profitable and convenient to offer them." This is not the same thing as saying that the news is responsive to popular demand.

When Journalism Works

Within the limits of business pressures and journalistic routines, there are clearly some news organizations that seem to make greater commitments to news content that displays more diversity, detail, and coherence. Journalists turn out to be among the most self-critical of professionals. Perhaps because they receive such volumes of criticism from all sides (public opinion, politicians, other journalists, and media scholars), they sometimes experiment with news formats in an effort to try to improve the quality of their product. Although these changes are often modest in their impact, they are worth noting.

Fighting the Mayhem? A Hopeful Trend in Local TV News

In Austin, Texas, the news looked pretty much the same on all the channels: more mayhem than at least some local journalists felt accurately reflected life in the increasingly cosmopolitan Texas capital. Then, ratings leader KVUE-TV broke from the pack. News executives decided that they would screen the mayhem stories for their social or political significance before making an automatic story assignment based on the "if it bleeds, it leads" principle. For example, before a crime story would be shown on KVUE, it had to meet at least one of five significant criteria:

1. Does action need to be taken?
2. Is there an immediate threat to safety?
3. Is there a threat to children?
4. Does the crime have significant community impact?
5. Does the story lend itself to a crime prevention effort?[58]

Soon after these standards were developed, they were put to a test by a Saturday night brawl in a local town that resulted in a triple shooting and murder. KVUE investigated the incident and judged that none of its significance criteria was engaged. The station held its ground and did not report the story, while its competitors gave it the prominent play generally assigned to such a good example of local mayhem. As the news director at Austin's K-EYE put it simply, "When somebody's killed, that's news."[59] Perhaps it was easier for KVUE to try a new kind of journalism in Austin because it was already the ratings leader. However, the ratings for the new format made for happy news executives. The ratings for the first full month of the experiment were the best ever for the station's 10 p.m. newscast, and over time, the station became the ratings leader for all of its evening newscasts.[60]

A more general look at national trends shows that KVUE is not alone in its efforts to improve the quality of local TV news. For example, KARE in Minneapolis features a lengthy report on an important issue of the day, and its ratings have risen. KAKE in Wichita has twice the national average in issue coverage and is also doing well in the ratings. WCTV in Tallahassee goes where others have closed operations (such as reporting on state government) and leads its market. These examples are from a larger study of 61 stations in 20 cities conducted by Columbia University's Project for Excellence in Journalism.[61]

The most interesting finding from the study is that serious news tends to be compatible with good ratings primarily when a station makes a commitment to breaking completely with the mayhem format. In other words, stations that incorporate a mix of serious issues and mayhem are not as likely to be rising in the ratings as stations that either make serious news their dominant format or that continue to go with "more mayhem most of the time." This interesting finding was summarized and interpreted this way:

> The stations least likely to be rising in the ratings were those in the middle, which were often hybrids—part tabloid and part serious. This suggests that audiences are not schizophrenic—they are segmenting. There is a group that embraces news full of revelation, scandal, and celebrity. There is another group that prefers a more sober, information-based approach.[62]

With the exception of five out of the eight stations in the high-quality group that were experiencing rating gains, the rest of the picture was decidedly mixed. Indeed, the overall profile of the 8,500 stories from the 600 broadcasts monitored on the 61 stations in the study was not an optimistic portrait of a revolution sweeping local TV:

> Despite the good news, the study found that most local newscasts are far from excellent. The general picture of local TV news is superficial and reactive—journalism on the run. Almost half (46%) of all stories were about commonplace events. Less than 10 percent originated from ideas in the newsroom. Of stories involving controversy, many (43%) gave only one side.[63]

Although this study found a somewhat more reassuring crime volume (28%) than other research (using different samples) has found, the substantive problems with local news still seemed large. The Project for Excellence team cited major failings on the local scene with "sourcing, getting both sides of the story, thinking ahead."[64]

Reforms on the National Scene

The economic crisis in journalism is producing a wave of innovation and experimentation in small online news organizations, blogs, and hybrid organizations such as the *Daily Beast* and *Huffington Post*. Yet most so-called legacy or mainstream news organizations seem incapable of much innovation, and continue to deal with the crisis through budget cuts that further undermine the quality of their product. The power of organizational routines and the inability to rethink the definition of journalism, itself, seem to hold these organizations in place even as they face their own demise.

Even when news organizations vow to improve the quality of coverage, other pressures in the information system often intrude. For example, CBS announced a policy in the 1992 presidential campaign to reverse the trend toward shrinking "sound bites" (those direct statements by candidates and politicians that are sandwiched in television news packages). According to a study by Daniel Hallin, the length of the average sound bite hit an all-time low of under 10 seconds during the 1988 campaign.[65] The CBS goal of running at least 30 seconds of direct statement from the candidate in each story was soon abandoned, however, as it became clear that the media managers who run campaigns had learned to script their candidates' performances with those ten-second political marketing jingles in mind.[66] As a result, the length of the sound bite shrank even further in 1992 to 8.4 seconds. Although it seems impossible to shrink candidate statements much farther, they weighed in at a puny 7.2 seconds in the 1996 election, according to a study conducted mid-way through the campaign by the Center for Media and Public Affairs.[67] The 2000 election held firm at 7.3 seconds, with candidates getting only 11 percent of campaign news time.[68] Election night TV coverage has reduced the role of reporters familiar with campaigns and candidates in favor of greater face time for star anchors and pundits who now talk in clipped, rapid-fire exchanges.[69]

The shrinking sound bite and rapid pace of TV talking heads are signs that it is hard to change news formats in the direction of more information-rich fare. The sound-bite trend reminds us that not all of the inhibitions to change arise from inside news organizations. Candidates hire communication consultants who are also quite comfortable shrinking ideas to fit media formats. Critics argue that the now-standard 30-second ad spots used in election and issue campaigns permit candidates to skip over the details of their proposals and aim at often volatile public emotions.[70] Yet many media consultants like former Clinton advisor Dick Morris see no such problem. According to Morris, "There is literally no such thing as an idea that cannot be expressed well and articulately to today's voters in 30 seconds."[71]

Democracy with or without Citizens?

Political communication scholar Robert Entman has argued that our mass-mediated democracy is in danger of becoming a *democracy without citizens.* This is in part because most news coverage is driven by forces that involve people more as passive consumers than active citizens.[72] For both politicians and journalists, the public has become more of a market to be tested, persuaded, and sold than an equal partner in communication and government. The reality of much opinion and participation is anchored in electronic images that move people psychologically in private worlds that may be detached from society and face-to-face politics.[73]

The irony in this is that the technology exists to communicate more information—farther, faster, from more sources, and to more people than ever before. At the same time, the political and business pressures operating behind the news may create just the opposite results. Perhaps the electronic age would not be so worrisome if politicians and the press used the potential of today's electronic technology to communicate critical ideas to people. The question is how to move politicians and journalism away from the paths of least political and economic resistance in their communication strategies.

In short, it is not hard to imagine how the news could be more citizen-oriented than it is. For example, the press could keep more citizen voices in reporting on important issues—even when public officials attempt to manage, downplay, or ignore those voices. News organizations could require their reporters and editors to run more direct statements from newsmakers and less commentary from journalists. News organizations also could minimize the writing of rapid "meta-narratives"—such as the campaign horse race or the authority-disorder plot—that can be applied to almost any generic political situation.

Above all, citizens and their activities should be covered in the news even when officials are not engaged with the issues or viewpoints in question. News organizations could include citizens in their reports and create paths from the broadcast or the news page to Web sites where audiences can learn more about what they can do to make a difference. There are signs of movement in this direction as journalists laid off from news corporations begin to explore how digital technologies may attract more active audience involvement. Recent years have seen the rise of blogs, discussion forums, instant polls, YouTube channels, social networking sites, and invitations for citizens to report stories they have documented on cell phones and digital cameras. What do you think? What kind of news would best fill the needs of a *democracy with citizens?*

NOTES

1. See his news online service: www.breitbart.com/. Accessed September 8, 2010.
2. The timeline of these events is documented by the liberal media site Media Matters: http://mediamatters.org/research/201007220004. Accessed September 9, 2010. Another interpretation of the same event is available on the conservative site: www.rightpundits.com/?p=6778. Accessed December 11, 2010. A more detailed account can be found in Wikipedia: http://en.wikipedia.org/wiki/Resignation_of_Shirley_Sherrod. Accessed December 11, 2010.
3. An account of the FOX coverage is offered by Media Matters: http://mediamatters.org/blog/201007200060. Accessed September 8, 2010. The key issue in FOX spinning the incident is the claim that Sherrod was fired before Bill O'Reilly's program aired, and that therefore FOX did not cause the firing. This begs the fact that the story had already appeared in FOX online before the firing, and in firing Sherrod the secretary of agriculture clearly anticipated the full scandal coverage from FOX, which in fact occurred. At the same time, the firing was conducted in response to the anticipated media scandal, and without consulting the facts of the situation, either. All of which suggests that media scandals take on their own realities, often independent of underlying facts.
4. Hal Boeodeker, "Shirley Sherrod: Fox News Becomes an Issue on *Fox News Sunday,*" July 25, 2010. http://blogs.orlandosentinel.com/entertainment_tv_tvblog/2010/07/shirley-sherrod-fox-news-becomes-an-issue-on-fox-news-sunday.html. Accessed September 8, 2010.
5. See Breitbart's own account on his blog: http://biggovernment.com/publius/2010/07/21/breitbart-its-not-about-shirley-sherrod-its-about-naacp-attacking-tea-party/. Accessed December 11, 2010.
6. For an account of the sequence of events, see Howard Hurtz, "Finger-pointing at Fox in Shirley Sherrod Firing," *The Washington Post, July 22, 2010.* www.washingtonpost.com/wp-dyn/content/article/2010/07/22/AR2010072201265.html. Accessed September 8, 2010.
7. Quoted in Michael Massing, "The Press: The Enemy Within," *The New York Review of Books* 52, no. 20 (December 15, 2005).
8. Remarks at the conference "Politics and the Media in the New Millennium," hosted by the Annette Strauss Institute, University of Texas, Austin (held at Belo Mansion, Dallas, Texas, February 18, 2006).
9. "Al Gore and the 'Embellishment' Issue: Press Coverage of the Gore Presidential Campaign." Kennedy School of Government Case Program, C15-02-1679.0.
10. See, for example, Jay G. Blumler and Michael Gurevitch, "Politicians and the Press: An Essay in Role Relationships," in *Handbook of Political Communication,* eds. Dan Nimmo and Keith Sanders (Newbury Park, CA: Sage, 1981), 467–493.
11. Herbert J. Gans, *Deciding What's News* (New York: Pantheon, 1979); and Gaye Tuchman, *Making News* (New York: Free Press, 1978).
12. Bernard C. Cohen, *The Press and Foreign Policy* (Princeton, NJ: Princeton University Press, 1963); and Timothy Cook, *Governing with the News* (Chicago: University of Chicago Press, 1998).
13. Thomas E. Patterson, "Doing Well and Doing Good: How Soft News and Critical Journalism Are Shrinking the News Audience and Weakening Democracy—And What News Outlets Can Do About It," Joan Shorenstein Center on the Press, Politics, and Public Policy, Harvard University, December 2000, 10.
14. See the argument in Robert W. McChesney, *The Problem of the Media: U.S. Communication Politics in the Twenty-First Century* (New York: Monthly Review Press, 2004).
15. Thomas E. Patterson, "Irony of a Free Press: Professional Journalism and News Diversity" (paper prepared for the Annual Meeting of the American Political Science Association, Chicago, September 3–6, 1992). See also Patterson's *Out of Order* (New York: Knopf, 1993).
16. An archive of these reports can be found here: http://topics.nytimes.com/top/news/business/companies/blackwater_usa/index.html. Accessed September 9, 2010.
17. See W. Lance Bennett, Regina G. Lawrence, and Steven Livingston, *When the Press Fails: Political Power and the News Media from Iraq to Katrina* (Chicago: University of Chicago Press, 2007).
18. CNN poll reported in CNN's Politicalticker: http://politicalticker.blogs.cnn.com/2010/09/03/cnn-poll-obama-approval-up-after-iraq-speech/. Accessed September 9, 2010.
19. Sam Youngman, "Obama Promises No 'Victory Lap' During Address on Iraq," *The Hill*, August 31, 2010. http://thehill.com/homenews/administration/116621-obama-promises-no-victory-lap-during-iraq-address

20. See Frank Rich, *The Greatest Story Ever Sold: The Decline and Fall of Truth in Bush's America* (New York: Penguin, 2006).

21. Barton Gellman and Walter Pincus, "Errors and Exaggerations: Prewar Depictions of Iraq's Nuclear Threat Outweighed the Evidence," *Washington Post National Weekly Edition* (August 18–24, 2003): 6.

22. "With Few Variations, Top Administration Advisors Present Their Case," *New York Times*, September 9, 2002: A8.

23. Todd S. Purdham, "Bush Officials Say Time Has Come for Action in Iraq," *New York Times,* September 9, 2002: A1.

24. See Bennett, Lawrence, and Livingston, *When the Press Fails.* Also see Robert M. Entman, *Projections of Power* (Chicago: University of Chicago Press, 2004).

25. Paul Krugman, "Bush and Blair, So Far, Face Different Fates," *International Herald Tribune*, July 30, 2003: 7.

26. See, Bennett, Lawrence, and Livingston, *When the Press Fails.*

27. See Entman, *Projections of Power* (Chicago: University of Chicago Press, 2004).

28. Ken Auletta, "Vox Fox," *New Yorker* (May 26, 2003): 64.

29. See Daniel C. Hallin and Todd Gitlin, "The Gulf War as Popular Culture and Television Drama," in *Taken by Storm: The Media, Public Opinion, and U.S. Foreign Policy in the Gulf War,* eds. W. Lance Bennett and David L. Paletz (Chicago: University of Chicago Press, 1994), 149–166.

30. For a more detailed analysis of press coverage of the Iraq War, see Bennett, Lawrence, and Livingston, *When the Press Fails: Political Power and the News Media from Iraq to Katrina.*

31. Timothy Cook, "Domesticating a Crisis: Washington Newsbeats and Network News After the Iraq Invasion of Kuwait," in *Taken by Storm: The Media, Public Opinion, and U.S. Foreign Policy in the Gulf War,* eds. W. Lance Bennett and David L. Paletz (Chicago: University of Chicago Press, 1994), 105–130.

32. See, for example, the numerous accounts of reporters, including Lou Cannon, *Reporting: An Inside View* (Sacramento: California Journal Press, 1977); Robert Darnton, "Writing News and Telling Stories," *Daedalus* 104 (Spring 1975): 175–194; and Lewis Lapham, "Gilding the News," *Harper's* (July 1981): 31–39.

33. For an excellent discussion of this syndrome, see Tuchman, *Making News.*

34. Robert Scholes, "Double Perspective on Hysteria," *Saturday Review* (August 24, 1968): 37.

35. For a detailed analysis of how this pattern occurs, see Leon Sigal, *Reporters and Officials* (Lexington, MA: Heath, 1973).

36. Tom Bethell, "The Myth of an Adversary Press," *Harper's* (January 1977): 36.

37. Ibid., 31.

38. Quoted in David Owen, "The Best Kept Secret in American Journalism Is Murray Kempton," *Esquire* (March 1982): 50.

39. Steve Goldstein, "How About Term Limits for the Unelected Elite," *Columbia Journalism Review* (May/June 1994): 35.

40. Ibid.

41. Ibid., 36.

42. See, for example, Warren Breed's classic study, "Social Control in the Newsroom," *Social Forces* 33 (May 1955): 326–335.

43. Edward Jay Epstein, *News from Nowhere* (New York: Vintage, 1973).

44. Frank Cesno, "The New News Environment," Brownbag Lunch, Joan Shorenstein Center, Kennedy School of Government, Harvard University, September 21, 1999.

45. Epstein, *News from Nowhere.*

46. See Timothy Crouse, *The Boys on the Bus* (New York: Ballantine, 1973).

47. Mark Fishman, *Manufacturing the News* (Austin: University of Texas Press, 1980), 80–81.

48. Ibid., 81.

49. Stephen Hess, *The Washington Reporters* (Washington, DC: Brookings Institution, 1981), 130.

50. See Larry Sabato, *Feeding Frenzy* (New York: Free Press, 1991).

51. See W. Lance Bennett, "The Cueless Public: Bill Clinton Meets the New American Voter in Campaign '92," in *The Clinton Presidency,* ed. Stanley Renshon (Boulder, CO: Westview Press, 1995).

52. Quoted in Maureen Dowd, "How a Battered Clinton Has Stayed Alive," *New York Times,* March 16, 1992: 1.

53. David Shaw, "Dire Judgments on Clinton Started Just Days into Term," *Los Angeles Times,* September 16, 1993: A1.

54. Jacob Weisberg, "The White House Beast," *Vanity Fair* (September 1993): 169.

55. Maureen Dowd, "Beached," *New York Times Magazine* (June 19, 1994): 18.
56. Fergus M. Bordewich, "Supermarketing the Newspaper," *Columbia Journalism Review* (September/October 1977): 27.
57. See, for example, Philip Meyer's criticism of market research and defense of more reliable social science investigations in his article, "In Defense of the Marketing Approach," *Columbia Journalism Review* (January/February 1978): 61.
58. Reported in Joe Halley, "Should the Coverage Fit the Crime? A Texas TV Station Tries to Resist the Allure of Mayhem," *Columbia Journalism Review* (May/June 1996): 27–32.
59. Ibid., 28.
60. See: www.austin360.com/television/new-keye-formats-slip-some-kvue-leads-news-712979.html. Accessed September 9, 2010.
61. Based on studies by the Project for Excellence in Journalism at Columbia University, as reported in Tom Rosenstiel, Carl Gottlieb, and Lee Ann Brady, "Local TV News: What Works, What Flops, and Why," *Columbia Journalism Review* 37, no. 5 (January/February 1999): 65–70.
62. Ibid.
63. Ibid.
64. Ibid.
65. Daniel C. Hallin, "Sound Bite News: Television Coverage of Elections, 1968–1988," Woodrow Wilson Center Paper, 1991.
66. See John Tierney, "Sound Bites Become Smaller Mouthfuls," *New York Times*, January 23, 1992: 1; and Richard L. Berke, "Mixed Results for CBS Rule on Sound Bite," *New York Times*, July 11, 1992: 7.
67. Mitchell Stephens, "On Shrinking Sound Bites," *Columbia Journalism Review* (September/October 1996): 22.
68. Center for Media & Public Affairs, September 28, 2000. www.cmpa.com/pressrel/electpr5.htm.
69. Thomas E. Patterson, "Diminishing Returns: A Comparison of 1968 and 2000 Election Night Broadcasts," Shorenstein Center on Press, Politics, & Public Policy, December 2003. www.shorensteincenter.org.
70. See, for example, Kathleen Hall Jamieson, *Dirty Politics* (New York: Oxford University Press, 1992).
71. The statement is from Morris's memoir *The New Prince,* quoted in a review by Andrew Sullivan, "As the Focus Group Goes, So Goes the Nation," *New York Times Book Review* (June 13, 1999): 8.
72. Robert M. Entman, *Democracy Without Citizens: Media and the Decay of American Politics* (New York: Oxford University Press, 1989).
73. Dan Nimmo and James E. Coombs, *Mediated Political Realities,* 2nd ed. (New York: Longman, 1989).

CHAPTER

16

Visual Communication

Taken from *Persuasion, Social Influence, and Compliance Gaining*, Fifth Edition by Robert H. Gass and John S. Seiter.

Want to capture an audience's attention? Try taking off your clothes. You wouldn't be the first to use this approach. People for the Ethical Treatment of Animals (PETA) use this strategy to protest wearing leather and fur. Their "Naked Truth" campaign features attractive models and celebrities, sans clothing, with the caption "I'd rather go naked than wear fur." Not to be outdone, Spencer Tunick, a performance artist/photographer convinced 18,000 people in Mexico City to strip naked for a photo shoot. He sees mass nudity as a form of collective defiance against social norms. Nudity, however, is not reserved for protesters and artists. When a German supermarket offered free groceries to the first 100 naked shoppers, more than 200 people showed up (Zimmerman, 2012). The promotion worked! We suspect that the male shoppers avoided the frozen food aisle.

Hang on. Before you give your next class presentation in the buff, we should warn you that while nudity may be a great attention getter, your "visual aids" may serve as a distraction during the rest of your presentation. Moreover, you may encounter a good deal of audience resentment. Lots of folks tend to react negatively to nudity (Christy & Haley, 2008). With that said, and, now that we have your attention, we'd like to examine the role of images in persuasion.

Image Is Everything

We are living in an increasingly visual society. Gurri, Denny, and Harms (2010) underscored this trend, commenting that "Many more images than ever before are available, and many more people are paying a disproportionate amount of attention to them" (p. 101). Fewer people are reading newspapers and books. More people are watching movies and TV. As Metros (2008) observed:

> politicians wage campaigns not on issues, but through their visual persona; wars are televised live through the eyes of embedded journalists; criminal trials have become 24/7 international spectator events; newspapers have had to reduce text to pack their pages with charts, graphics, and photos to compete for market-share; and even radio directs its listeners to Web sites to illustrate the spoken word. (p. 109)

In television commercials, magazine ads, and billboards, images are primary and words are secondary. Politicians worry about "bad optics," such as being on vacation when a crisis unfolds. The World Wide Web is chock full of images. Facebook, Flickr, YouTube, and other social media are saturated with images. Video mashups are increasingly popular. And it is not only mass media that rely on visual cues. Protest marches, sit-ins, demonstrations, rallies, and picketing are highly visual acts that are intended to persuade.

Oral communication relies on images, too. Public speaking has always featured visual aids. But nowadays audiences expect "wowie-zowie" presentations loaded with "eye candy." Try giving a PowerPoint presentation with text-only bullet points and you may find your audience nodding.

In this chapter, we examine some of the important ways in which images shape beliefs, attitudes, and behaviors. First, we consider the importance of visual stimuli and how images persuade. Next, we examine art as a form of persuasion, cinematic influence, images in advertising, and photojournalism as a form of persuasion.

Overlooked and Under-Appreciated

"Visual images," writes Taewon Suh (1999), "have become a predominant means of transmitting information in the twentieth century and may be even more so in the next century" (p. 3). Yet, despite the increasing importance of visual persuasion, the topic has been under-studied in the field of communication. Traditionally, the study of persuasion has focused on influence attempts that take place within the world of words. Messaris (1997) underscored this point when he noted, "although the study of persuasive communication has a history of more than two millennia, the focus of this scholarly tradition has tended overwhelmingly to be on verbal strategies. With a few notable exceptions, the systematic investigation of visual persuasion is still in its infancy" (p. vii).

The Power of Images

Images are powerful. They can move us in ways that words cannot. Their potency stems partly from their perceived "realness," or the idea that seeing is believing. As Gurri, Denny, and Harms (2010) noted, "with visual media, however, the illusion is created that we are gazing out a window at the real world" (p. 102). The power of images also arises from their emotional force. Joffe (2008) emphasized the advantages of images over words when she noted that "the most salient distinction between the relative effects of textual/verbal versus visual messages concerns their emotive impact" (p. 84). The grim photo of a Sudanese infant starving to death (see below) demonstrates this capacity. The ghoulish image won a Pulitzer Prize in 1993.

Despite the traditional emphasis on words, studies have revealed a *picture superiority effect* for images. Pictures are more easily recognized and recalled than words (Hockley, 2008; Stenberg, 2006). For example, one study compared a "words-only" ad with a "words plus picture" ad (Edell & Staelin, 1983). Recall was significantly higher in the "words plus picture" condition. One explanation for the picture superiority effect is that pictures, unlike words, are processed via two different modes and can be recalled via either mode (Paivio, 1986, 1991). Images also cross languages and cultures more easily.

How Images Persuade

What is it about images and other visual stimuli that make them so persuasive? We take up this question here. In doing so, we rely heavily on Paul Messaris's (1997) conceptualization of the role of images in persuasion. He suggests that images persuade in three basic ways: through *iconicity, indexicality,* and *syntactic indeterminacy.*

Iconicity: Bearing a Resemblance

One way images persuade is by functioning as *icons,* which simply means that they resemble the things they represent. An image can stand for an idea or sum up a concept. The stick figure on a "pedestrian crossing" sign is an icon. A caricature of a politician drawn by an editorial cartoonist also is an icon. The statue of Liberty, Uncle Sam, and the bald eagle are all icons of America. All of these are iconic because they are representations of people, events, or things. Insofar as their iconicity is concerned, it doesn't matter whether they are accurate representations or not, as long as people understand what they represent. This is, perhaps, the most important property of images: to summarize ideas and concepts. As Messaris (1997) noted, "If there is one property that most clearly distinguishes pictures from language and other modes of communication, that property is iconicity" (p. 3).

Photo: Kevin Carter 1993 Corbis Images.

A good illustration of the iconic nature of images can be found in Philip Morris' Marlboro man. The Marlboro man is immediately recognizable around the world. He is a mythical American hero. He represents the Old West. He symbolizes an idealized image of the cowboy—a rugged, self-reliant individual. He's always pictured outdoors, on the range. Without even seeing the brand-name or the slogan, most people can spot the Marlboro man in an instant. And boy can he sell cigarettes! Marlboro cigarettes are the most popular brand in the world (de Guzman, 2007). For this reason, the Marlboro man has been called "the most universally recognized, consistently profitable, and aesthetically appealing image in the advertising world" ("Selling Tobacco," 1990, p. 84). Now that's an icon!

As part of their iconic nature, images also can be selective. They can accentuate certain features while minimizing others. A photo taken at a Tea Party rally might accentuate the positive by showing a jovial fellow wearing a three-cornered hat or accentuate the negative by showing an angry man holding up a misspelled sign. At the same time that images represent reality, then, they also can highlight certain aspects of reality, subtly or to the point of extreme exaggeration.

Another iconic function of images is that they can violate the reality they represent (Messaris, 1997). An image can make something look real even though it isn't. For example, a busy mother who has her hands full doing the laundry, cooking dinner, cleaning house, and taking care of the kids could be pictured with four arms rather than two. An ad for a pain reliever might show someone suffering from a splitting headache, whose head actually appears to be splitting in two. Images can thus simulate a reality that doesn't exist.

Indexicality: Seeing Is Believing

A second way in which images persuade is through *indexicality* (Messaris, 1997). This refers to the ability of images, in particular photos and video, to document that an event happened or that something took place. For example, photos of Iraqi detainees being abused at Abu Ghraib prison, images of U.S. troops urinating on dead Afghan insurgents, and pictures of Pakistani children killed by drone missile strikes function as "proof" to many people in the Middle East that the United States does not have their interests at heart.

Indexical images often function as a form of sign reasoning or circumstantial evidence. For example, fossilized dinosaur footprints indicate that large reptiles once roamed the earth. A fingerprint lifted from a crime scene is a sign that the defendant was in fact there. A diet advertisement might show a person holding up a huge pair of his or her old pants. The pants demonstrate how obese the person was before and how much weight the person has lost since.

The documentary aspects of images, however, also can be misleading. In this regard, Messaris (1997) cautioned, "photographs, of course, can lie. The picture of a model in a fashion ad can be made more attractive through airbrushing, and voter interviews or product demonstrations can be staged" (p. xvii). Let's say we are watching the news and we see a political candidate, shirtsleeves rolled up, wearing a hardhat, while touring a factory. The image emphasizes the candidate's "plain folks" appeal. He or she identifies with ordinary workers. But would the candidate have rolled up his or her sleeves, donned a hardhat, and toured the factory in the absence of any camera crews? The cameras are recording an event that might not take place in their absence.

Perhaps you've seen news footage of angry citizens in foreign lands burning the American flag to protest U.S. foreign policies. It seems fair to ask, however, whether the cameras are there because the protesters are burning the flag or the protesters are burning the flag because the cameras are there. A critical viewer should, therefore, question the indexicality of visual records of events. Media events can be staged. The presence of cameras and film crews can alter people's behavior. Photographs and videotapes can be digitally altered to create the appearance that events occurred when, in fact, they did not, or did not occur in the way they are pictured.

Syntactic Indeterminacy: Don't Look for Logic in Images

A third way in which images persuade is through *syntactic indeterminacy.* This simply means that, unlike words, pictures cannot convey precise relationships between things. Messaris (1997) thus noted, "what visual syntax lacks, especially in comparison to verbal language, is a set of explicit devices for indicating causality, analogy, or any other relationships other than those of space or time" (pp. xvii–xviii). The problem is that images lack logical operators. That is, they can't explicitly state if-then relationships, either-or relationships, or other logical connections between people, objects, and events. As an example, a picture can show what a person's abdominal muscles looked like before using the new "Monster Ab-Cruncher." Another picture can show what the person's abdominal muscles look like afterward. However, pictures themselves can't specify a cause-effect relationship.

The fact that images can't convey logical relationships, such as "A causes B," "A is analogous to B," or "either A or B will happen," is both a blessing and a curse. The blessing is that pictures can be used to equate one thing with another, via association. Pictures can imply an association without actually saying so. This can work to a persuader's advantage. A persuader can foster subtle associations through images without making the associations explicit in words. For example, an advertiser can equate a product with being cool, being sexy, or conferring social status simply by pairing the product with cool, sexy, or classy images.

The curse is that images can never suggest the precise nature of relationships, so it is up to the observer to guess what the relationship is. A commercial might show a happy family carrying kayaks from their hybrid SUV to a river. Rather than make the consumer want a hybrid SUV, as the advertiser intends, the sequence of images may make the consumer want to go camping, or buy a kayak, or spend more time with the family instead. This is not a serious drawback, however, for two reasons. First, advertisers have decades of practice at manipulating lighting, camera angle, color, and other aspects of images to achieve the results they want. Second, advertisers use words when they want to make a point explicitly and pictures when they want to make a point implicitly. Thus, they enjoy the best of both worlds.

Now that you have a better understanding of how images persuade, we can turn our attention to some of the intriguing and important ways visual stimuli affect us. We begin by examining art as a visual form of influence.

Art as Persuasion: *Mona Lisa* Made Me Do It

The use of art to further political and religious ends dates back to ancient civilizations. In fact, works of art—sculpture, painting, pottery, and so on—were funded by the state to promote its own ends. Greek friezes and frescoes taught citizens moral lessons involving Greek gods and Greek mythology. In the Middle Ages, organized religions sponsored art to further religious ends. The Catholic Church commissioned thousands of works of art to promote Catholicism. As only one example, Michelangelo's painting of the finger of God reaching out to man that adorns the ceiling of the Sistine Chapel endorses a biblical view of creation. Many of the most famous paintings on display in museums throughout the world were funded by the church or religious benefactors to promote religious ideals.

The Paintbrush Is Mightier than the Sword

Governments, especially totalitarian governments, have used art as a form of political propaganda (Clark, 1997). Under Stalin, the Soviet Union declared all art to be subservient to the interests of the state. "Socialist Realism" became the officially recognized standard for art, and its purpose was to advance the political and social ideals of communism. All artists were required to join a government-controlled union. Only certain "themes" were deemed appropriate for artists. Not surprisingly, paintings and posters from this era featured workers—dedicated members of the proletariat—working side by side in factories and on farms. Such iconic representations idealized communism. Clark (1997) explains how such politicized art modeled behavior for the masses:

> in paintings, novels, and films, Socialist Realism created a parallel world peopled by heroes and heroines who personified political ideals. As tireless labourers, courageous Red Army soldiers, diligent schoolchildren, or dedicated Party activists, they demonstrated exemplary behaviour and the attitudes of perfect citizens. (p. 87)

Similarly, under Mao, China produced a great deal of art aimed at promoting Communist ideology. When the Communists assumed power in 1949, posters and murals contributed to the deification of Chairman Mao. Graphic arts also were used to mobilize and indoctrinate the people during the Cultural Revolution. Posters showed smiling, cherubic children, peasants, and soldiers all harvesting bumper crops together—a tribute to the agricultural achievements of the revolution.

Meanwhile, in the Western world, art was not only sponsored by governments but was directed against governments as well. Eugène Delacroix's well-known painting *Liberty Leading the People* (1830) now hangs in the Musée du Louvre in Paris. The painting shows a mythical lady liberty, rifle in one hand and French flag in the other, leading French citizens in a charge during the French Revolution. Through its iconicity, the painting both endorses and romanticizes the revolution. Diego Rivera's *History of Mexico* (1929–1935), a large mural painted on the walls of the National Palace in Mexico City, depicts the domination of Mexico's peasants first by Spanish conquistadors, then the Catholic Church, then the Mexican army, and finally by wealthy landowners. The painting reveals the struggle of the downtrodden against oppression, a struggle that culminated in the Mexican Revolution. These are but two examples of socially and politically inspired art.

This poster from the Chinese cultural revolution portrays an idealized view of agrarian life.

Reprinted by permission. Chinese Poster Collection, Centre for the Study of Democracy, University of Westminster.

Activist Art: I Must Protest

Not all art is created for art's sake. Art serves more than an aesthetic or decorative function. Contemporary artists have strong opinions on political and social issues, and they express them in and through their work. Berthold Brecht's oft-cited quip that "art is not a mirror to reflect reality, but a hammer with which to shape it" (as cited in McLaren & Leonard, 1993, p. 80) sums up this view.

A contemporary manifestation of this perspective can be found in protest art or the art of social activism. These artists use art to critique society and promote social change (Hobbs & Woodard, 1986; Lippard, 1984). Activist artists seek to engage the public in their art and increase the public's social consciousness. As Felshin (1995) notes, such artists are "attempting at the very least to 'change the conversation' to empower individuals and communities, and ultimately to stimulate social change" (p. 26). For example, a popular graffiti artist, known as Banksy, stencils images onto walls and buildings in public places at night (Pryor, 2007). One of his works depicts Dorothy and Toto, from the *Wizard of Oz.* Her basket is being searched by an officer in riot gear wearing latex gloves. The image suggests that society's paranoia over security has gone too far.

Awareness Through Interpretation

How do activist artists go about persuading? One method is by increasing *awareness through interpretation.* Activist art might consist of an exhibit that is odd, disturbing, or peculiar. The artist seeks to pique the viewer's curiosity and pull him or her in. In the process of trying to understand the work, the viewer's awareness is increased. Interpretation requires active thinking or central processing, which, as we learned earlier, is more likely to trigger lasting attitude change.

As an illustration, Suzanne Lacy created a public work titled *Three Weeks in May* (1977) to increase awareness of the crime of rape. She began with two large maps of Los Angeles that were placed on display at a local mall. Each day, she stamped the word "RAPE" on the map in large, red block letters at locations where rapes had taken place the previous day. Before long, the map was covered with stamps, many of them overlapping. The exhibit provided a graphic revelation to shoppers of the scope and severity of the problem. Her aim was to provoke a public discussion about the silent, often unreported crime of rape. Next to the map was a list of names, addresses, and phone numbers for rape counseling centers.

Awareness Through Participation

Yet another approach is to increase *awareness through participation.* Such art is collaborative or interactive. As Felshin (1995) comments, "participation is a catalyst for social change" (p. 12). By way of example, Wafaa Bilal created an interactive installation, called "Domestic Tension," in a Chicago art gallery (Bilal & Lydersen, 2008). Bilal, an Iraqi artist living in political asylum in the United States, occupied a Plexiglas room for 1 month. During this time, people went online and shot at him using a robotically controlled paintball gun. This went on 24 hours a day. They shot him in the head when he fell asleep and in the groin when he stood up. More than 60,000 shots were fired at him by strangers from more than 120 countries. Over time, some sympathetic viewers formed a "human shield" by trying to aim the gun away from Bilal. Others hacked in to the system to make the gun fire more rapidly. By the project's end, the room was drenched in paint and Bilal was suffering from posttraumatic stress disorder.

So what did viewers' participation mean? Clearly, many people had no qualms about shooting a person online. Others were confronted with their own morality in choosing to shoot, or not shoot, another human being. The project laid bare cultural, ethnic, and religious tensions between Westerners and Middle Easterners. By allowing virtual strangers to shoot him, Bilal focused attention on how desensitized modern societies are to violence. Killing has become robotic, clinical, and—like his project—carried out from afar. When innocent civilians are killed by drone missiles, they are simply labeled "collateral damage." People living comfortably in stable societies are blithely unaware of the suffering of people in conflict zones.

Another example of collaborative art is the AIDS Memorial Quilt, founded by Cleve Jones and others more than a decade ago (Jones & Dawson, 2000). The quilt, also known as the NAMES Project, is a folk art project commemorating those who have died of AIDS. It is comprised of thousands of 3' × 6' panels, each dedicated to the memory of a specific person. The AIDS Memorial Quilt was first displayed on the Washington Mall in 1987, and again in 1992 and 1996. There are now so many panels that it would be difficult, if not impossible, to assemble them all in a single location. Indeed, the AIDS Memorial Quilt has become the largest community art project in the world. Portions of the quilt are now part of traveling displays that are shown throughout the world.

The AIDS Memorial Quilt persuades in a variety of ways. We often hear statistics about AIDS, but the quilt puts a human face on these numbers. Every panel is a handmade testimonial to a specific individual's life. When people see the quilt they understand, in concrete rather than abstract terms, the toll taken by the disease. The very choice of making a quilt was a persuasive one. Cleve Jones was attracted to the idea of quilting because it is a traditional American folk art. Quilts conjure up images of home and family. AIDS, however, was thought of as a

The AIDS Memorial Quilt, also known as the Names Project, is an example of folk art, activist art, and a social movement all in one.

Alamy Images. Reprinted by permission.

promiscuous gay male disease. The quilt served as a means of countering that image. As Jones and Dawson (2000) note, "There was hope we could beat the disease by using the quilt as a symbol of solidarity, of family and community; there was hope that we could make a movement that would welcome people—men and women, gay and straight, of every age, race, faith, and background" (p. 108).

The AIDS Memorial Quilt increased the public's awareness of the disease. It also brought people together. Loved ones who didn't know how to grieve found an outlet in creating a panel. This was truly participatory art. Students who have seen the quilt reported that the experience reduced their homophobia and increased their desire to practice safe sex. This fact alone demonstrates the quilt's persuasiveness as a work of art.

Activist art is often controversial. Indeed, that is its purpose. It is precisely because art has the capacity to arouse people's interest, attention, and ire that it is influential. A primary goal of activist artists is to raise the public's consciousness on a variety of social and political issues (Felshin, 1995; Hobbs & Woodard, 1986; Lippard, 1984; Von Blum, 1976, 1994). Art can challenge the existing social order. It can make people angry. It can offend. At the same time it can heighten people's awareness. It can make people question their assumptions. It can change the way they see things. It can make them reconsider long-held beliefs. In doing, so art persuades.

Cinematic Persuasion: Sex, Drugs, and Popcorn

Upon receiving an award from the American Museum of the Moving Image, Steven Spielberg remarked that cinema "is the most powerful weapon in the world" (cited in Fuller, 1995, p. 190). There are several factors at work that lend films their power to persuade.[1] First, there is the potential for mass suggestion. Millions of people are exposed to movies in the United States and abroad. In fact, movies are one of America's leading exports. Thus, movies reach vast audiences. Second, movies are told in a *narrative* form, that is, as stories. Stories possess an aura of believability not found in other mediums for communication. When we watch a movie we engage in a "willing suspension of disbelief." In order to follow the story, we have to lose ourselves in the imaginary world of the film. In so doing, we give up some of our ability to think and reason. Third, the power of films to persuade is aided by the fact that when people sit down in a theater they don't expect to be persuaded, they expect to be entertained. Therefore, they tend to let down their guards and become more open to suggestion. We believe this is one of the reasons that *product placement*—the practice of inserting brand name items into movie scenes—is so prevalent. Lastly, films are carefully crafted works. Considerable planning and attention to detail go into the making of a film. Something as simple as a close-up or a swell in the music can enhance the intensity of emotion on the big screen. Thus motion pictures represent finely crafted messages. Few real-world persuaders, such as salespeople, attorneys, or politicians, have the luxury of lavishing so much time and attention on their persuasive messages.

Movies can persuade intentionally or unintentionally. Al Gore's documentary *An Inconvenient Truth* was clearly designed to increase awareness of global warming. Michael Moore's documentaries, or "mockumentaries" as some call them, espouse particular points of view. Other films persuade unintentionally, or accidentally. For example, the movies *Juno, Waitress,* and *Knocked Up* tacitly endorsed a pro-life point of view, when the female characters, all of whom experienced unplanned pregnancies, opted to give birth rather than seek abortions. In *Juno,* for example, Ellen Page's feisty character visits an abortion clinic. The clinic is gloomy and uninviting. The grim receptionist hands her a clip board and announces that she has to list her entire sexual history on the form. Juno flees the clinic and opts to have the baby instead.

Acting Out: How Movies Persuade

Movies persuade in multiple ways and on multiple levels. Some of the influential features are unique to particular genres of film. Docudramas, such as *JFK* or *Titanic,* for instance, may convince viewers that a subjective interpretation of events is an objective recounting of the facts (Simpson, 2008). Dramas and romantic comedies may model traditional or nontraditional gender roles. Violent movies, such as *Pulp Fiction, Kill Bill,* and *Natural Born Killers,* may desensitize people to violent or aggressive behavior. We examine some of the most important ways that films persuade here.

Exporting Values Abroad

The first of these is that movies, American movies in particular, *export Western values.* As one commentator noted, "Hollywood films are America's biggest cultural export, consumed by billions around the globe" (Hey, 2001, p. 4). People in remote areas of the world know who Sylvester Stallone is, based on the film character *Rocky.* They know who Julia Roberts is from her role in *Pretty Woman.* American films embody Western values. Rocky was the blue-collar guy who made his dream come true. Julia Roberts was the prostitute with a heart of gold.

Not everyone is happy about the values promoted by American movies. Foreign audiences often resent the infusion of Western values such as promiscuity, violence, and drug use into their own culture (many in the United States aren't too thrilled with these values either). Others resent the emphasis on materialism and conspicuous consumption. At the same time, movies can advance positive values such as freedom, human rights, and equality. The point is that movies tacitly endorse Western values that may or may not be shared by people in other cultures.

On the positive side, movies can promote prosocial values. The movie *Finding Nemo,* for example, featured those with disabilities in a favorable light. In this way, the movie normalized disabilities. *Forrest Gump* demonstrated that values such as honesty and compassion can triumph over mental and physical limitations. Fate may throw hardships in our way, but Forrest showed us that it is how we deal with adversity that determines who we are. *Dead Poets Society* promoted values such as individualism, nonconformity, and living life to the fullest as per the film's motto, *carpe diem* (seize the day).

Promoting Popular Culture

A second way in which movies persuade is by *promoting popular culture* both at home and abroad. Fashions, hairstyles, habits, lifestyles, and slang terminology are often emulated by moviegoers (Chansanchai, 2001; Unterberger, 2001). If you are old enough, or into retro fashion, you may recall the popularity of white, three-piece suits following the release of the disco film *Saturday Night Fever,* starring John Travolta. *Donnie Darko* and *The Crow* inspired "Goth" culture. After seeing the movie *300,* many guys hit the gym to work on their abs. As a function of their iconicity, movies have a way of idealizing and romanticizing trends and lifestyles. Cinema, then, is a major vehicle for the dissemination of fads, fashions, and trends.

Modeling Behavior: Social Proof

A third way movies persuade is by *modeling behaviors.* People may gauge what constitutes appropriate behavior in social situations by taking a movie character's lead. Albert Bandura's *social cognitive theory* maintains that adolescents observe behaviors that are modeled in the media and then imitate those behaviors in real life (Bandura, 1986, 1989). For example, young teens who watch movies about dating and relationships, such as *Mean Girls, American Pie,* and *10 Things I Hate About You,* may take their cue about how to deal with love and relationships based on behaviors they see in movies (Behm-Morawitz & Mastro, 2008). At a subconscious level, people may enact scripts they've learned from movies as well.

Characters in movies also model risky, unsafe, or violent behaviors. This can have the effect of legitimizing such behaviors. Movie characters rarely wear seatbelts. They often engage in unprotected sex. They frequently smoke, use drugs, get drunk, and drive recklessly. Oh, and they kill lots of people. Regardless of whether these activities are intentional, their prevalence in movies tends to glamorize them. The actions of the characters in movies may be seen as placing a stamp of approval on those behaviors. For example, there is strong evidence that adolescents who see a lot of smoking on the big screen are more likely to light up. A study by Heatherton and Sargent (2009) reported that teens with high exposure to smoking in movies were three times more likely to smoke than those with low exposure.

Cultivation Theory: It's a Mean, Scary World

Other studies have examined the effects of a steady diet of violence on TV. *Cultivation theory* maintains that the more violence people watch on TV, the more likely they are to develop an exaggerated belief in a *mean, scary world* (Gerbner, Gross, Morgan, & Signorielli, 2002). In addition to developing a jaded view of the world, viewing violence tends to increase aggression and antisocial behavior in people. "Fifty years of research on the effects of TV violence," notes John Murray (2008), "leads to the inescapable conclusion that viewing media violence is related to increases in aggressive attitudes, values, and behaviors" (p. 1212). With respect to cinema's influence on behavior, Oliver Stone, who directed *Natural Born Killers,* commented, "Film is a powerful medium. Film is a drug. It goes into your eye. It goes into your brain. It stimulates, and that's a dangerous thing" (cited in Leiby, 1995, p. G1).

Viewer Identification

A fourth way in which movies persuade is by promoting viewer identification. Moviegoers may idolize a particular actor or actress or a specific character played by that actor or actress. Perhaps you know a few Angelina Jolie or Johnny Depp "wannabes." Sometimes the story of the character overlaps with the viewer's own experience, causing the viewer to identify with the character in the film. If you've ever felt like an outcast, a nerd, the underdog, or misunderstood, you might identify with movies such as *Napoleon Dynamite, Ghost World, My Big Fat Greek Wedding, Happy Times,* or *Pretty in Pink.* In this way, movies establish a common bond with viewers.

Viewer identification can take place even if a viewer's experience doesn't directly overlap with that of a character in a movie. None of us have met an extraterrestrial (okay, *most* of us haven't), but we can still identify with a movie such as *E.T.,* because all of us have had to say good-bye to someone we love. None of us are green ogres, but we can identify with Shrek because we've all felt like outsiders from time to time.

Perpetuating Stereotypes

A final way in which cinema shapes public perceptions is by fostering and perpetuating stereotypes. Hollywood frequently typecasts minorities, women, overweight people, the elderly, and other groups into limited roles (Benshoff & Griffin, 2009). This may create the impression that these are the only roles these groups are capable of performing. Although the number of parts for minorities has increased, the parts often involve the same predictable stereotypes. Middle Easterners, for example, are frequently cast as terrorists. When they aren't terrorists, they are often cab drivers. Hispanics are often depicted as drug dealers or gangbangers. While the situation has improved, many roles for Hispanics remain tied to cultural stereotypes. Asians also tend to occupy stereotypic roles in films. If Hollywood is to be believed, every Asian is skilled in martial arts. They are often undersexed and romantically awkward (Whitty, 2001). As with other minorities, things are changing, but slowly.

In a similar vein, African Americans have been historically typecast (Entman & Rojecki, 2001). African American males fit the mold of athlete, drug dealer, or musician (Waxman, 2000). African American women tend to be relegated to stereotypic roles such as beautiful wife, beautiful girlfriend, or beautiful prostitute. African Americans also are typecast as the funny sidekick in "buddy" movies. Eddie Murphy, Martin Lawrence, Chris Rock, and Chris Tucker have all played such parts. These, too, are narrowly defined roles. The situation has improved. Halle Berry, Jamie Foxx, Denzel Washington, and Forest Whitaker have all won Oscars for best actress or actor. Their success may convince filmmakers and the movie-going public that African Americans can be taken seriously on screen.

When it comes to stereotypic roles, women fare no better. With few exceptions women have to be thin and beautiful to land starring roles (Benshoff & Griffin, 2009). Women also tend to be confined to traditional roles: mother, wife, mistress, girlfriend. This isn't particularly surprising, given that fewer than 10 percent of screenplays are written by women, and fewer than 6 percent of movies are directed by women (Maher, 2009). Admittedly, there are some women in nontraditional roles. Nevertheless, roles for women, especially older women, remain limited.

If there is a silver lining, it is that younger moviegoers tend to be more tolerant, if not completely color-blind (Welkos, 2001). This is evidenced by the box-office success of recent multiethnic, multicultural movies, such as *Kite Runner, Joy Luck Club,* and *Slum Dog Millionaire.* Because youth culture includes more African Americans, Asian Americans, and Hispanic Americans, filmmakers are producing more multiethnic movies to meet the demands of a new generation of viewers.

Images in Advertising: And Now a Word from Our Sponsors

"Advertising," write Woodward and Denton (1999), "is undoubtedly the most pervasive form of persuasion in our society" (p. 286). When we think of pure cases of persuasion, advertising immediately comes to mind. Roughly $280 billion per year is spent on advertising in the United States, whereas all other countries together spend about $241 billion (Berger, 2011). Various estimates suggest that the average person is exposed to more than 3,000 advertising messages per day (Dupont, 1999; Simons, 2001; Woodward & Denton, 1999). Some estimates are even higher. If all the money spent on advertising were divvied up, it would work out to about $800 per person in the United States and $40 per person in all other countries combined (Berger, 2011). Most of us are "armchair" experts in advertising, having watched so many commercials during our lives. Indeed, the average American spends about one hour per day watching television commercials (Salter, 2009). That works out to more than 2 years of commercial viewing over an average lifespan.

Advertisements, whether on television, in a magazine, online, or some other medium, feature images. The visual components of such ads are often key to their effectiveness. Apple's "Get a Mac" campaign relied on a visual metaphor to show that PCs, played by John Hodgman, are square, stuffy, and boring compared to Macs, played by Justin Long, which are cool, casual, and creative (Livingstone, 2011). Old Spice's ad, called "The Man Your Man Could Smell Like," became a viral video hit based on its humor and visual sleight of hand. The commercial, filmed in one, continuous take, features a buff male who maintains eye contact with the camera as his location shifts from place to place. "Anything is possible," he proclaims, "when your man smells like Old Spice and not a lady." The spots increased sales by more than 100 percent (Summers, 2012). Visually oriented ads work their magic in a variety of ways. We don't have enough space to examine all the ways here, so we focus on four of the most important ones.

Visual Extravaganzas: Now You've Got My Attention!

One challenge that advertisers face in trying to convince consumers to buy their products is *media clutter.* There are so many ads competing for consumers' attention that it is difficult for a message to stand out in the crowd. Commercials have to grab and hold viewers' attention. Thanks to CGI, it is now possible for advertisers to create and manipulate images in ways previously not possible. A plain-vanilla commercial simply won't hold up to an eye-popping extravaganza, especially when viewers have low involvement with the topic or issue.

Anti-Ads: You Can't Fool Me

Another challenge facing advertisers is that consumers are increasingly cynical about advertising. They don't trust Madison Avenue. But that skepticism is the very premise on which *anti-ads* are based. Anti-advertising, or "subvertising" as it is sometimes called, caters to consumers who distrust the media. Anti-ads mock advertising itself (Axelton, 1998; Beato, 1999). They denounce traditional advertising to gain acceptance by consumers.

Many anti-ads are spoofs on commercial advertising (see www.adbusters.org). Others are designed to sell actual products and services. POM Wonderful poked fun at itself by sponsoring Morgan Spurlock's product placement parody, *The Greatest Movie Ever Sold.* Geico spoofed insurance comparison ads by conducting a mock insurance "taste test." Consumers who sampled a glass of Geico said "mmm, yum," while consumers who taste-tested a competing brand of auto insurance said "ugh, yuck!"

An antismoking commercial also offers an example of an anti-ad. The spot shows two cowboys in a downtown setting, one playing guitar and the other singing. The singing cowboy, however, is singing through a hand-held device pressed against his neck (an electro larynx). He's had a laryngectomy. He sings, "You don't always die from tobacco, sometimes you just lose a lung. Oh, you don't always die from tobacco, sometimes they just snip out your tongue." This ad mocks the rugged cowboy mystique associated with Marlboro cigarettes.

In essence anti-ads are telling viewers, "Hey, you're on to us. You're too smart to be fooled." But of course, that strategy is itself a ploy designed to appeal to jaded consumers. Such an approach creates the perception that the advertiser respects the viewer's intelligence. Advertisers are constantly finding ways to reinvent themselves. As consumers have grown more skeptical, advertisers have found ways to adapt to, and capitalize on, their skepticism. Anti-ads or subvertising thus mark another evolutionary phase in advertising.

Image-Oriented Advertising: Materialism as Happiness

In addition to using vivid imagery and anti-advertising, advertisers also seek to create positive associations between their brands and idealized images or lifestyles. This approach is known as *image-oriented* or *image-based advertising* and it is the bread and butter of modern advertising campaigns. Image-oriented ads rely on the syntactic indeterminacy of images. Remember, images don't contain logical operators, so they can't make clear-cut claims. That turns out to be a plus, however, because by pairing a product with a favorable image, an advertiser can equate the two without actually saying so in words. Messaris (1997) underscored this feature stating that "this ability to imply something in pictures while avoiding the consequences of saying it in words has been considered an advantage of visual advertising since the first days of its development as a mass medium" (p. xix).

Let's consider some examples of this in action. Oil companies don't want you to think about tar-covered birds on an oil-stained beach when you envision petroleum products. They want you to associate oil companies with pro-environmental attitudes. Hence, Chevron's "People do" advertising campaign, which portrays Chevron as a guardian of endangered species.

Image-oriented ads portray a brand as the embodiment of an idealized lifestyle. Equating the brand with an idealized lifestyle creates identification with that brand. When we buy that brand we are buying into that lifestyle. Some brands are *luxury brands,* prestigious, yet within reach of many consumers (Ralph Lauren, Mercedes). Some are *aspirational brands;* few people can afford them, but they hope to own them one day (Armani, Rolls Royce). Still others are *authentic* or *genuine brands* (Gilmore & Pine, 2007; Rosica, 2007). These brands are unpretentious. In a marketplace filled with fake, phony products, consumers value what seems real. A smaller brand with a story to tell may be more desirable than a mass-produced commodity. Organic foods, handmade goods, and artisanal beers fall into this category. With a little practice, you should be able to watch a TV commercial or view a magazine ad and decipher the favorable image or association the advertiser is trying to manufacture. Some of the most common associations are as follows:

- *Social status and elitism:* Ads for luxury cars and expensive watches often associate owning these products with prestige and success. Ads for expensive wines, luggage, jewelry, and other upscale goods often imply that the products are symbols of taste and refinement.
- *Sex or romance:* Ads for perfume, lingerie, and hair care products often equate the products with sexiness, allure, and romance. The association established by many perfume ads is that if you wear that fragrance you'll be more sexy, or other sexy people will be attracted to you.
- *Cause-related:* Some brands have a cause to promote. Consumers aren't just buying a product or service, they are also helping to feed starving children, save rainforests, or protect endangered species (Adkins, 1999; Pringle & Thompson, 1999). TOMS shoes and (Product) Red exemplify this approach. Ben & Jerry's promotes social change as well by donating a percentage of their profits to social causes.
- *Power, speed, and strength:* Ads for tools, trucks, SUVs, computers, and nutritional supplements often equate buying a product with conferring power on the user. Dodge trucks are "Ram tough." Chevy trucks are built "Like a rock." You, too, can have rock-hard abs or buns of steel. If you've got the newest, fastest computer, you are a "power user."
- *Youth culture:* A number of products are marketed by associating products with youth culture, rebelliousness, and an alternative lifestyle. Soft drinks, clothing, fast food, skateboards, small electronics, makeup, and many other goods and services appeal to what is hip, trendy, or cool. These commercials are often shot with handheld cameras and employ rapid editing techniques to simulate the look of "reality TV."
- *Safety, security:* Ads for banking, insurance, and retirement accounts try to foster images of being safe and secure. Consumers want peace of mind and a sense of stability when it comes to their finances and retirement.
- *Sense of place, belonging:* Ads for foods, restaurants, furniture, and other household goods often strive to create a sense of hominess. The advertisers want you to get a warm, comfortable, familiar feeling when you think of their products.

These are only some of the important values and lifestyles to which advertisers attempt to link their brands. When you watch a commercial or read a print ad, you should examine the associations the advertiser is trying to establish. For decades cigarette ads fostered the association that smoking was cool. More recently, antismoking ads have associated smoking with being uncool. Both approaches rely on the underlying assumption that "being cool" is what really counts in life. Is it? When evaluating a commercial or print ad, ask yourself three important questions:

1. What image or lifestyle is being associated with the product?
2. Is that image or lifestyle actually desirable? Is that the image I'm really seeking or the lifestyle to which I truly aspire?
3. Would buying the product actually grant me the image or lifestyle equated with the product? If so, how?

Shock Ads: Edgy Images as Persuasion

Images also figure heavily into the form of advertising known as *shock ads*. Shock ads, or "shockvertising" as it has also been called, push the boundaries of taste and propriety (Lazar, 2003; McCarthy, 2000). The goal is to sell products by being edgy. Some shock ads are vulgar, some erotic, some humorous, and others nauseating. Some adopt an "in your face" style of advertising.

As part of its "Unhate" campaign, Benetton ran ads of world leaders kissing one another on the lips. The digitally altered images featured Barack Obama smooching with Hugo Chavez, Angela Merkel necking with Nicolas Sarkozy, and Pope Benedict XVI locking lips with Imam Ahmed el Tayyeb. After the Vatican threatened a lawsuit, Benetton pulled the latter ad from its website (Osborne, 2011). Ads by PETA often rely on shock to garner attention. In one commercial, "Sex Talk," parents urge their daughter to have sex. "Get out there and nail everything you can" the father advises. "My little girl's gonna get some," the mother proudly states. At the end a caption reads, "Parents shouldn't act this way. Neither should people with dogs and cats." The analogy between irresponsible parents and irresponsible pet owners was offensive to many viewers. But that was the purpose of the spot. Shock ads seek to cut through media clutter by provoking controversy and garnering attention.

Even shock ads can go too far. One such controversial TV commercial was Reebok's "I am what I am" spot, starring 50 Cent. In the ad, the gangsta rapper counts to nine, which is the number of times he's been shot. The ad, which was heavily criticized for glamorizing violence, was subsequently pulled by Reebok. In the United Kingdom, hundreds of readers complained when they found a full-page ad showing a newborn infant with a cockroach in its mouth. The ad was sponsored by Bernardo's, a children's charity group, and was designed to draw attention to the plight of children living in poverty. The ad was banned by Britain's Advertising Standards Authority.

Given their widespread use, do shock ads really work? A study by Dahl, Frankenberger, and Manchanda (2003) suggests they do. These researchers concluded that "shocking content in an advertisement significantly increases attention, benefits memory, and positively influences behavior" (p. 1). Other studies also support the effectiveness of shock ads (Scudder & Mill, 2009). But shock ads must walk a fine line. If they aren't shocking enough, they won't provoke the public dialogue and publicity they seek. If they are overly shocking, they may prompt a consumer rebellion. Furthermore, consumers may build up a tolerance to shocking images. One commentator warned that shock ads were analogous to drug addiction; a larger and larger dose is required to achieve the desired effect until consumers eventually overdose on the strategy (Black, cited in Klara, 2012).

Photojournalism as Persuasion: The Camera Does Lie

Even without any accompanying text, photographs tell their own persuasive stories. Because there are entire courses offered in photojournalism, we won't attempt to explore the whole field here. What we wish to emphasize is that still photographs can make powerful statements. They can affect people's perceptions of events. They also can reach people on an emotional level in ways that words alone cannot. As Zumwalt (2001) noted, "There is tremendous potential in a photograph to inflame emotions" (p. B12). Because photographs don't require literacy or familiarity with a particular language, they also are more universally understood than messages that rely on words. Photographic images also can distort reality, as we shall see.

Many well-known photos serve as iconic representations of events or eras in history (Hariman & Locaites, 2007). In all likelihood, you've seen Joe Rosenthal's famous 1945 photo of U.S. Marines raising the Stars and Stripes at Iwo Jima. The picture symbolizes the determination of the United States to win the war in the Pacific. You may have seen John Filo's photo of a female student at Kent State University in 1970, kneeling over the body of a fellow student who was slain by the National Guard. That picture symbolized the schism between the protest movement and the government, as well as the generation gap of the late 1960s. You may have seen the photograph taken by Nick Ute in 1972 of a naked, 9-year-old Vietnamese girl, running down the road, with napalm burns from the bombs that had just been dropped on her village. The photo epitomized the feelings of many Americans that the United States was involved in an unjust war in Vietnam.

Photos can sum up social problems or controversies. They can document events in ways that words cannot. This is where the old saying, "a picture is worth a thousand words" applies. Owing to their iconicity, photographs can cement themselves in the public's mind. They function as touchstones that capture entire events in our collective conscience. The fact that so many cellphones now have cameras

Box 16.1

On Your Guard: Remaining Vigilant against Visual Deception

Images, whether in the form of television commercials, cinema, magazine ads, photojournalism, Web pages, or other media, function as powerful tools for influence. They give us a vicarious sense of "being there." For this reason, we must remain wary of visual communication designed to persuade us. We've all seen supermarket tabloids with doctored photos claiming "Martian now on Supreme Court" or some other such nonsense. We know these images can't be trusted. But images may be manipulated by others as well. Politicians may manipulate images for propaganda purposes. Images may be manipulated by lawyers to make a defendant seem innocent or guilty ("If it doesn't fit, you must acquit."). Images may be used by the media to increase ratings ("Stay tuned, film at 11!") and by advertisers to sell goods ("Get the body you want now!"). With this in mind, we offer the following tips and advice when evaluating persuasive images.

1. Try to improve your *visual literacy,* that is, the ability to critically analyze and evaluate visual communication (Felton, 2008). As Messaris and Moriarty (2005) note, "visual literacy can . . . be seen as a potential antidote to attempted manipulation of the viewer in TV, print, and Web-based advertising; visual journalism; and other forms of pictorial entertainment, information, or persuasion" (p. 482).
2. Don't succumb to the old adage "Seeing is believing." The camera does lie (Brugioni, 1999). What you are seeing may well be a manipulated image. When you see a fashion model on a magazine cover, for example, don't assume she or he looks that good in real life. The cover photo has probably been digitally altered to remove blemishes, whiten teeth, highlight hair color, etc.
3. Be especially wary of images on the Internet. Anyone can digitally alter an image on a home computer nowadays using Photoshop. If you are unsure whether to trust an image or not, try checking out some useful Web-based resources that identify hoaxes. We like the Urban Legends Website, at www.snopes.com (check out their photo gallery link); Skeptical Enquirer, at www.csicop.org; and Hoaxbusters, at http://www.hoaxbusters.org.
4. When watching so-called reality shows on TV, remember they may bear little resemblance to reality. Reality shows are carefully engineered productions. Guests or contestants typically try out for the show and are carefully vetted. This selection process allows producers to cast contestants for maximum dramatic effect. Footage can be edited so a contestant seems braver, cleverer, more devious, more hostile, or more psycho than she/he really is. Hosts may encourage or reward certain types of behavior while discouraging others. You don't really think that every guest on the Jerry Springer show threw a chair on his or her own initiative, do you?
5. When viewing documentaries, keep in mind that they do not objectively recount events. They advocate a point of view. Documentaries often use techniques such as re-enactment (recreating scenes for which no original footage is available), substituted or modified footage (film of something similar or related, but not the same thing), time compression (cramming years or even centuries into a one-and-a-half-hour-long movie), and composite characters (combining several different people into one). While all these techniques may make the story easier to follow and the narrative more compelling, they come at the expense of impartiality. Some exemplars of this genre, such as Michael Moore's *Fahrenheit 9/11* and Morgan Spurlock's *Supersize Me,* have been dubbed "mockumentaries" or "shockumentaries" because the director's bias is so intense.
6. Beware of images in diet ads, cosmetic surgery ads, supplement ads, and infomercials. Take a typical ad for a weight loss product: Notice that the person in the "Before" photo usually has a bland expression, poor posture, pasty skin, unkempt hair, unflattering clothes, and unflattering lighting. In comparison, the person shown in the "After" picture is usually smiling, has an upright posture, stylish hair, a tan and/or makeup, and flattering lighting. Does the ad say both photos are unretouched? Does the fine print acknowledge "Results may vary" or "Results not typical?" If a diet ad claims a user lost 30 pounds in 2 weeks, but you can see the person's hair is much longer in the "After" photo, then you would know that more than 2 weeks passed between photos. Testimonials and the photos that accompany them are always subject to the "hasty generalization" fallacy.
7. The context and captioning of images can have an important impact as well. Following the aftermath of Hurricane Katrina, newspapers printed two photos of survivors wading in the flood water. One Associated Press photo showed an African American male clutching a six-pack of Pepsi with the caption "A young man walks through chest deep flood water after looting a grocery store . . ." (Ralli, 2005). Another AFP/Getty photo, showed a white couple and carried the caption, "two residents wade through chest deep water after finding bread and soda from a local grocery store . . ." The captioning implied a clear double-standard: Blacks were looting, but white folks were acting out of necessity.

has elevated the role of amateur photographers. Photos can be uploaded instantly to Facebook, Twitter, and other social media.

Playing Tricks with the Camera: Photographic Deception

An important point to keep in mind about photographic images is that they aren't objective, impartial representations of things. As iconic representations, their documentary qualities can be deceiving. Someone has to aim the camera. Photographs give us the journalist's point of view, which is simply that—one point of view. The photographer decides which events to capture on film, and which aren't worth capturing. The photographer decides on the distance, camera angle, lighting, shutter speed, and so on. The photographer decides which pictures to develop, how to edit or crop them, and which prints to offer for public consumption.

Some well-known historical and recent examples of photographic deception serve to illustrate how easily this medium can be manipulated. On June 27, 1994, *Time* magazine darkened O. J. Simpson's mug shot on one of its covers, making him appear more sinister and menacing. In the year 2000, a brochure for the University of Wisconsin-Madison was doctored by adding an African American student into a photo of fans cheering at a football game. The manipulation was done to make the campus seem more ethnically diverse. *Newsweek* cropped Martha Stewart's head onto another model's body for one of its covers in 2005. The National Press Photographers Association labeled the act a "major ethical breach." In 2003, the *Los Angeles Times* ran a front-page photo of a British soldier who appeared to be aiming a rifle at Iraqi civilians and ordering them to sit down. The newspaper fired the photographer, Brian Walski, after he admitted that he had digitally altered the image. In 2006, photojournalist Adnan Hajj was fired by Reuters for a similar offense.

Outside of photojournalism, photos also are not carbon copies of reality either. Political attack ads often show a politician at his or her worst. Fashion magazines show models at their best. When people join online dating services, they often alter their profile photographs to appear more attractive (Hancock & Toma, 2009). These examples underscore the point that seeing is not necessarily believing. Just because someone claims to have captured an image on film doesn't necessarily mean the image is genuine and unaltered. Box 16.1 offers some useful suggestions on how to avoid being duped by photos and other visual media.

SUMMARY

In this chapter, we've examined a variety of ways in which visual stimuli, including but not limited to images, facilitate persuasion. We have not touched on all the ways in which visual cues persuade. Yet the principles we've discussed about how images persuade through iconicity, indexicality, and syntactic indeterminacy apply to other forms of visual communication as well. Our society is becoming increasingly visually oriented. More people now get their news from television than from newspapers. More people now watch movies than read books. Persuaders are capitalizing on this trend by enlisting images in support of their persuasive endeavors. Based on what you've learned in this chapter, you should be able to watch a television commercial, see a movie, or read a print ad with a sharper eye toward the strategic choices made by the persuader. In short, we hope you will be a wiser consumer of visual persuasion.

REFERENCES

Adkins, S. (1999). *Cause related marketing: Who cares wins.* Oxford, UK: Reed Educational.

Axelton, K. (1998, March). Ads with attitude: Can you afford to use anti-advertising? *Entrepreneur Magazine.* Retrieved on September 5, 2005, from http://entrepreneur.com/magazine/entrepreneur/1998/march/15326.html.

Bandura, A. (1986). *Social foundations of thought and action: A social cognitive theory.* Englewood Cliffs, NJ: Prentice-Hall.

Bandura, A. (1989). Social cognitive theory. In R. Vasta (Ed.) *Annals of child development, 6. Six theories of child development* (pp. 1–60). Greenwich, CT: JAI Press.

Beato, G. (1999, May/June). Does it pay to subvertise? The critics of corporate propaganda co-opt its best weapon. *Mother Jones.* Retrieved on September 5, 2005, from www.motherjones.com/commentary/columns/1999/05/beato.html.

Behm-Morawitz, E., & Mastro, D. E. (2008). Mean girls? The influence of gender portrayals in teen movies on emerging adults' gender-based attitudes and beliefs. *Journalism & Mass Communication Quarterly, 85*(1), 131–146.

Benshoff, H. M., & Griffin, S. (2009). *America on film: Representing race, class, gender, and sexuality at the movies* (2nd ed.). Malden, MA: Blackwell Publishing.

Berger, A. A. (2011). *Ads, fads, and consumer culture (4th ed.).* Lanham, MD: Rowman and Littlefield.

Bilal, W., & Lydersen, K. (2008). *Shoot an Iraqi: Art, life, and resistance under the gun.* San Francisco: City Lights.

Brugioni, D. A. (1999). *Photo fakery: The history and techniques of photographic deception and manipulation.* Dulles, VA: Brassey's Publishers.

Chansanchai, A. (2001, August 19). "Starring in school: Teens are taking back-to-school fashion cues from five stylish celebrities." *The Baltimore Sun,* p. 5N.

Christy, T. P., & Haley, E. (2008). The influence of advertising context on perceptions of offense. *Journal of Marketing Communications, 14*(4), 271–291.

Clark, T. (1997). *Art and propaganda in the twentieth century.* New York: Harry N. Abrams.

Dahl, D. W., Frankenberger, K. D., & Manchanda, R. V. (2003). Does it pay to shock? Reactions to shocking and nonshocking advertising among university students. *Journal of Advertising Research, 43*(3), 1–13.

De Guzman, N. F. (2007, July 31). Special feature: The power of advertising; where there's smoke, there's Marlboro. *Business World.* Retrieved on June 27, 2012, from the Lexis-Nexis Academic search engine.

Dupont, L. (1999). *Images that sell: 500 ways to create great ads.* Ste-Foy, Quebec: White Rock Publishing.

Edell, J. A., & Staelin, R. (1983). The information processing of pictures in print advertisements. *Journal of Consumer Research, 10*(1), 45–61.

Entman, R. M., & Rojecki, A. (2001). *The black image in the white mind: Media and race in America.* Chicago: University of Chicago Press.

Felshin, N. (Ed.). (1995). *But is it art? The spirit of art as activism.* Seattle: Bay Press.

Felton, P. (2008, November/December). "Visual literacy." *Change,* 60–63.

Fuller, L. K. (1995). Hollywood is holding us hostage: Or, why are terrorists in the movies Middle-Easterners? In Y. R. Kamalipour (Ed.), *The U.S. media and the Middle East: Image and perception* (pp. 187–197). Westport, CT: Greenwood Press.

Gerbner, G., Gross, L., Morgan, M., & Signorielli, N. (2002). Growing up with television: The cultivation perspective. In J. Bryant & D. Zillmann (Eds.), *Media effects: Advances in theory and research* (2nd ed., 17–41). Hillsdale, NJ: Erlbaum.

Gilmore, J. H., & Pine II, B. J. (2007). *Authenticity: What consumers really want.* Boston: Harvard Business School Press.

Gurri, M., Denny, C., & Harms, A. (2010). Our visual persuasion gap. Parameters: *U.S. Army War College, 40*(1), 101–109.

Hancock, J. T., & Toma, C. L. (2009). Putting your best face forward: The accuracy of online photographs. *Journal of Communication, 59,* 367–386. doi: 10.1111/j.1460-2466.2009.01420.x

Hariman, R., & Locaites, J. L. (2007). *No caption needed: Iconic photographs, public culture, and liberal democracy.* Chicago: University of Chicago Press.

Heatherton, T. F., & Sargent, J. D. (2009). Does watching smoking in movies promote teenage smoking? *Current Directions in Psychological Science, 18*(2), 63–67.

Hey, S. (2001, November 12). "So will the Brits play the baddies?" *The London Independent,* p. 4.

Hobbs, R. H., & Woodard, F. (Eds.). (1986). *Human rights/human wrongs: Art and social change.* Iowa City: University of Iowa Museum of Art.

Hockley, W. E. (2008). The picture superiority effect in associative recognition. *Memory & Cognition, 36*(7), 1351–1359.

Joffe, H. (2008). The power of visual material: Persuasion, emotion, and identification. *Diogenes,* 217, 84–93. doi: 10.1177/0392192107087919

Jones, C., & Dawson, J. (2000). *Stitching a revolution.* San Francisco: HarperCollins.

Klara, R. (2012, February 20). Advertising's shock troops. *Adweek, 53*(7), 26–27.

Lazar, D. (2003, December). Shockvertising. *Communication Arts, 45*(7), 198–201.

Leiby, R. (1995, December 3). "Movie madness: Does screen violence trigger copy-cat crimes?" *The Washington Post,* p. G1.

Lippard, L. R. (1984). *Get the message?: A decade of art for social change.* New York: E. P. Dutton.

Livingstone, R. (2011). Better at life stuff: Consumption, identity, and class in Apple's "Get a Mac" campaign. *Journal of Communication Inquiry, 35*(3), 210–234. doi: 10.1177/0196859911413469

Maher, K. (2009, February 4). "What do women want? Surely not this; Can anything stop the inane decline of the chick flick?" *The Times* (London, U.K.), pp. T2, 14–15.

McCarthy, M. (2000, June 20). " 'Shockvertising' pushes envelope, risks backlash." *USA Today,* p. 6B.

McLaren, P., & Leonard, P. (1993). *Paulo Freire: A critical encounter.* New York: Routledge.

Messaris, P. (1997). *Visual persuasion: The role of images in advertising.* Thousand Oaks, CA: Sage.

Messaris, P., & Moriarty, S. (2005). Visual literacy theory. In K. Smith, S. Moriarty, G. Barbatsis, & K. Kenney (Eds.), *Handbook of visual communication* (pp. 481–502). Mahwah, NJ: Lawrence Erlbaum Associates.

Metros, S. E. (2008). The educator's role in preparing visually literate students. *Theory into Practice, 47,* 102–109.

Murray, J. P. (2008). Media violence: The effects are both real and strong. *American Behavioral Scientist, 51*(8), 1212–1230.

Osborne, A. (2011, December 18). After controversy over adverts that showed world leaders kissing, Alessandro Benetton insists good retailing is not about making people angry. *Sunday Telegraph,* London, U.K. Retrieved on July 4, 2012, from the Lexis-Nexis Academic database.

Paivio, A. (1986). *Mental representations: A dual coding approach.* New York: Oxford University Press.

Paivio, A. (1991). Dual coding theory: Retrospect and current status. *Canadian Journal of Psychology, 45,* 255–287.

Pringle, H., & Thompson, M. (1999). *Brand spirit: How cause-related marketing builds brands.* Chichester, UK: John Wiley & Sons.

Pryor, F. (2007, February 8). "On the trail of artist Banksy." BBC News. Retrieved on May 15, 2009, from http://news.bbc.co.uk/2/hi/entertainment/6343197.stm.

Ralli, T. (2005, September 5). "Who's a looter? In storm's aftermath, pictures kick up a different kind of tempest." *The New York Times,* p. 6.

Rosica, C. (2007). *The authentic brands: How today's top entrepreneurs connect with customers.* Paramus, NJ: Noble Press.

Salter, B. (2009, March 26). 8 hours a day spent on screens, study finds. *New York Times,* p. B-6.

Scudder, J. N., & Mill, C. B. (2009). The credibility of shock advocacy: Animal rights attack messages. *Public Relations Review, 35,* 162–164.

"Selling tobacco: Defending the rights of the Marlboro man." (1990, April 21). *The Economist, 315,* p. 84.

Simons, H. W. (2001). *Persuasion in society.* Thousand Oaks, CA: Sage.

Simpson, K. E. (2008). Classic and modern propaganda in documentary film. *Teaching of Psychology, 35*(2), 103–108.

Stenberg, G. (2006). Conceptual and perceptual factors in the picture superiority effect. *European Journal of Cognitive Psychology, 18*(6), 813–847.

Suh, T. (1999). Visual persuasion. *Communication Research Trends, 19*(3), 1–15.

Summers, N. (2012, April 2). Click on this ad already! *Newsweek,* 159, p. 58. Retrieved on July 4, 2012, from the Lexis-Nexis Academic search engine.

Unterberger, L. (2001, July 16). "Mimicking a movie star." *The Milwaukee Sentinel Journal,* p. 4E.

Von Blum, P. (1976). *The art of social conscience.* New York: Universe Books.

Von Blum, P. (1994). *Other visions, other voices: Women political artists in greater Los Angeles.* Lanham, MD: University Press of America.

Waxman, S. (2000, December 21). "1999 saw more roles for minorities in film, TV." *The Washington Post,* p. C7.

Welkos, R. W. (2001, July 2). "Multiethnic movies ringing true with youths." *Los Angeles Times,* p. A1.

Whitty, S. (2001, August 26). "Who are the Asians on screen? New stereotypes no better than old." *The San DiegoUnion Tribune,* p. F2.

Woodward, G. C., & Denton, R. E. (1999). *Persuasion and influence in American life* (3rd ed.). Prospect Heights, IL: Wadsworth.

Zimmerman, N. (2012, June 22). Supermarket offers free groceries to first 100 naked shoppers. www.gawker.com. Retrieved on July 7, 2012 from http://gawker.com/5920613/supermarket-offers-free-groceries-to-first-100-naked-shoppers.

Zumwalt, J. (2001, November 13). "How a powerful image can shape a war." *Los Angeles Times,* p. B12.

NOTE

1. Most of our comments about cinematic persuasion apply equally to television shows. Television shows, however, typically have smaller budgets and tighter production schedules. Hence, they are less polished works. Nevertheless, many TV series have altered attitudes and behavior in the same ways as films.

Index

S

T

Credits

Text Credits

Page 346: Stephen Coburn/Shutterstock; Page 355: Spencer Grant/PhotoEdit Inc.; Page 358: © CORBIS-NY. All Rights Reserved; Pages 438–440: Acceptance Speech for the Jean Hersholt Humanitarian Award by Elizabeth Taylor © Interplanet Productions, Limited. Reproduced compliments of Dame Elizabeth Taylor and Interplanet Productions, Limited; Page 442–443: "Testing Cars" by Lee Iacocca. Reprinted by permission; Page 446: By kind permission of Ripken Baseball Inc. and Cal Ripken, Jr.; Page 447: Reprinted by permission of the author. Copyright © 2007 by Nikki Giovanni.

Photo Credits

Page 3: © Tom Stewart/CORBIS; Page 14: © Charles Gupton/ Stock Boston; Page 21: © Royalty-Free/CORBIS; Page 23: © Richard Lord/PhotoEdit; Page 28: © Lara Jo Regan/Getty Images; Page 62: © Steven Begleiter/Pictor/ImageState; Page 38: Courtesy of Irene M. Pepperberg, the Alex Foundation; Page 39: Pam Gleason; Page 48: Dale G. Caldwell; Page 66: © Zefa RF/Alamy; Page 68: © Robert Mizono/Getty Images; Page 71: © Photolibrary; Page 89: © PhotoDisc/Getty Images; Page 91: © Bob Daemmrich Photography; Page 101: © Mary Kate Denny/PhotoEdit; Page 107: Used with permission from the National Communication Association, www.natcom.org; Page 107: zulufoto/Shutterstock; Page 110: Johnson, David W., *Reaching Out: Interpersonal Effectiveness and Self-Actualization,* 7th Ed., © 2000. Reprinted and Electronically reproduced by permission of Pearson Education, Inc., Upper Saddle River, New Jersey; Page 112: Michael Newman/ PhotoEdit Inc; Page 115: Ingram Publishing/Alamy Images Royalty Free; Page 116: Kellerman, K. "A Goal-Directed Approach to Gaining Compliance: Relating Differences Among Goals to Differences in Behavior." *Communication Research* 31, (2004) 397–495; Page 118 (left): © MTomicic/Fotolia; Page 118 (center): © Michael Flippo/Fotolia; Page 124: Boulton, R. *People Skills.* New York: Simon & Schuster. 1979; Page 132: Ury, W. *Getting Past No.* New York: Bantam Books. 1993; Page 132: Comstock Images/Thinkstock; Page 133: Ian Langsdon/EPA/Newscom.